CW00537536

"This updated and modern account of UFOs, ali‹ to conceal such occurrences in the modern wc by a respected researcher and chronicler. More‹ account by a master storyteller."
– Edgar Mitchell, ScD, Apollo 14.

"This book is essential reading for anyone with a serious interest in ufology. This 3 volume series is the nearest thing to an official history of the UFO phenomenon that we're ever likely to see. While this second volume is an authoritative account, this is no dry history - in this gripping account, Dolan captures the cases, the controversies and the characters, giving us the definitive position on one of the last great mysteries of our time."
– Nick Pope, UK Ministry of Defense, 1985-2006

"Historian Richard M. Dolan masterfully weaves 1973 to 1991 UFO reports with the warp and woof of global geopolitical events to reveal how Abraham Lincoln's government "of the people" suffered a secret coup d'etat as the power of insiders with need-to-know access about UFOs and ETs grew in Black Agencies with Black Budgets protected by classified executive orders that prevented Congress – the peoples' representatives – from even knowing what those Black Budgets financed."
– Linda Moulton Howe, Emmy Award-winning Investigative Journalist

"In a field of study and international concern as diverse as this one, Dolan has – for a second time – canvassed the most significant events clearly and accurately."
– Richard F. Haines, Ph.D., Chief Scientist, NARCAP.org

"There is no praise elevated enough and no commendation weighty enough to impress upon the world how important this book is. This long-anticipated book is the brilliant work of the formidable and incomparable Richard M. Dolan. It is a masterful follow-up to the previous book by Dolan that has become the very cornerstone for understanding the intricate issues surrounding the national security state and extraterrestrial contact. For many decades the government has worked to obfuscate the facts and history contained in these pages – thank you, Richard Dolan, for challenging "official truth" in such a comprehensive, clear and cogent way. This should be required reading for every sitting and former President."
– Paul Davids, Executive Producer of *Roswell*, the Showtime Original Movie

"Richard Dolan has braved an intellectual jungle too terrifying for academic historians, vigorously slashed away at the cancerous undergrowth of institutionalized deception, and emerged into the sunlight bearing a consciousness-raising chronicle of our puzzling relationship with the mysterious, non-human intellects who share our planet. Not for the intellectually timid – but indispensable for those wishing to view history with their eyes wide open."
– Terry Hansen, author, *The Missing Times: News Media Complicity in the UFO Cover-up*

"Richard Dolan accomplishes something extraordinary with the publication of this book. His meticulously documented narrative of UFO activity, awareness and concern during this highly charged period in American and world history offers readers an in-depth account of astonishing sweep and breadth. Layered with heretofore neglected political, financial and intrigue factors which bear directly on this singularly important story, it is never less than methodical, fascinating and chilling. A huge undertaking and a major accomplishment with the potential to make a real difference in the public's perception of the reality, seriousness and implications of UFOs and the intelligences behind them."
– Peter Robbins, co-author of *Left At East Gate: A First-Hand Account of the Rendlesham Forest UFO Incident, Its Cover-up and Investigation*

"This is an important exposition of extremely crucial facts and realities that have long been concealed and systematically lied about by clandestine and public agencies. It has been said that, "Ye shall know the truth and the truth shall set you free." So read on, gentle reader, and take a deep draught of documented truth to bolster and guide you on your path to freedom."
– Richard Sauder, Ph.D., author of *Underground Bases and Tunnels: What is the government trying to hide?*

"Richard Dolan's UFOs and the National Security State V2 is a fundamental work, slated to become the preeminent UFO historical reference text. With an intellectually inviting style, Dolan records the generational 1973 -1991 account of UFOs and extraterrestrial events. In doing so, he transforms our historical belief system, which in turn, transforms human consciousness toward exoconsciousness. The strength of his quantum perspective provides scientific validation of human consciousness engaging extraterrestrial phenomenon. Dolan's history hurls us beyond the bounds of 3D reality. His ufology is a strong account of who we are – where we came from, with whom we communicate, and what we are to be about as a space-faring civilization."
– Rebecca Hardcastle, Ph.D., author, *Exoconsciousness: Your 21st Century Mind*

"Once again, Dolan's perseverance and unwavering research result in an instant classic for any and all interested in the continuing UFO phenomenon. In Volume I (covering the years 1941 to 1973), Dolan gave us a hint of his penchant for historical accuracy; Volume II leaves no room for doubt. Little-known cases, many of which have been totally ignored by "ufologists" are brought to life with stunning detail. Dolan is to be commended for his critical eye and dedication to historical truth."
– Ronald Regehr, Deputy Director of Research, the Mutual UFO Network (MUFON).

"While studying the FBI UFO files and many other government documents, I realized that by learning The History you find The Truth. Richard Dolan's new book provides the history. Read it and decide for yourself what is the truth."
– Bruce S. Maccabee, Ph.D., author, *The UFO FBI Connection* and *Abduction in My Life*.

UFOs

and the

National Security State:

The Cover-Up Exposed, 1973-1991

 Keyhole Publishing Company
P.O. Box 92188
Rochester, New York 14692
USA

Library of Congress Cataloging-in-Publication Data

Dolan, Richard Michael
    UFOs and the National Security State: The Cover-Up Exposed, 1973-1991 / by Richard M. Dolan
638 p. cm.
Includes bibliography and index.
ISBN 978-0-9677995-1-3
1. Unidentified Flying Objects
2. History—United States—Armed Forces—Intelligence.
I. Dolan, Richard M. II. Title
Library of Congress Control Number: 2009906689

First published in the United States by Keyhole Publishing Company

First Printing: September 2009
Second Printing: October 2009
Third Printing: February 2010

Cover design by Mark Brabant (http://hoveringobject.com)

Back cover photo of author © 2008 by Karyn Dolan

Manufactured in the United States of America.

UFOs

and the

National Security State:

The Cover-Up Exposed, 1973-1991

Richard M. Dolan

Keyhole Publishing Company

Also by Richard M. Dolan

UFOs and the National Security State: An Unclassified History, 1941-1973. (Keyhole Publishing Company, 2000).

Republished as:
UFOs and the National Security State: Chronology of a Cover-up, 1941-1973. (Hampton Roads Publishing, 2002)

This book is dedicated to the silent millions who have experienced events that are not supposed to be real, but are real just the same.

Contents

Acknowledgments

Over the years I have worked on this book, I have been fortunate to receive encouragement, support, insights, and guidance from many people. Some provided important consultation in the preparation of this manuscript. There are others still who offered support and consultation on a confidential basis. They know who they are.

I wish to acknowledge Bernard Angelo, Ph.D., Sandra and Hans Baerwolf, Maurizio Baiata, Steven Bassett, Anthony Beckett, Michael Bird, William Birnes, Gregory Bishop, Gildas Bourdais, Bob Brown, the late Terri Brown, Rhiannon Burress, Joseph Buchman, Ph.D., Larry Bryant, Grant Cameron, Tom Carey, Kerry Cassidy, Aaron Clark, Colleen Clements, Ph.D., Jim Courant, Billy Cox, Debra Dalock, Tom Darling, Ph.D., the late Marc Davenport, Paul Davids, Lisa Davis, Robert Dean, Marina Diamond-Heart, Bill Doleman, Ph.D., Robert Durant, Robert Duvall, Don and Vicky Ecker, Joseph Firmage, Randall Fitzgerald, Stanton Friedman, Peter Gersten, J.D., Timothy Good, Stan Gordon, John Greenewald, Jr., Richard F. Haines, Ph.D., Leah Haley, Terry Hansen, Rebecca Hardcastle, Ph.D., Paola Harris, Jan Harzan, Robert Hastings, Diane and Lawrence Headrick, Michael Heiser, Ph.D., The Honorable Paul Hellyer, Budd Hopkins, Linda Moulton Howe, J. Antonio Huneeus, Philip Imbrogno, Nicole Irvine, Donald Johnson, Ph.D., C. B. Scott Jones, Ph.D., Cheryl Jones, Lynne Kitei, M.D., George Knapp, Melinda Leslie, Scott Littleton, Ph.D., Ted Loman, Rosanne Losee, Bruce Maccabee, Ph.D., Mark McCandlish, John Miller, M.D., Edgar Mitchell, Sc.D., Guy Malone, Jim Marrs, Sam and Julie Maranto, Chris O'Brien, George Noory, Joyce Palumbo, Nick Pope, Hal Puthoff, Ph.D., Scott and Suzanne Ramsey, Kevin Randle, Ph.D., Nick Redfern, Ron Regehr, Peter Robbins, Ted Roe, Alejandro Rojas, Christopher Rozzi, Bill Ryan, Gregory Salyards, Richard Sauder, Ph.D., Daniel Sheehan, J.D., Donald Schmitt, Michael Schratt, John Schuessler, Grace Schuyler, Rob Simone, Ray Stanford, Jennifer Stein, Paul Stonehill, Whitley Strieber, Cookie Stringfellow, Ingo Swann, Russell Targ, Thomas Valone, Ph.D., Victor Viggiani, Travis Walton, Free and Amy Ward, Donald Ware, Bruce Wiedemann, Robert Wood, Ph.D., Ryan Wood, Farah Yurdozu.

I also wish to acknowledge the direct support from a few individuals who loaned or bequeathed me their substantial libraries: Richard Heiden, Rev. Charles Roberts, Scott Santa, the late William Sherwood, and Vince White.

My parents, Barbara Dolan-Rice and Richard T. Dolan, have never failed to encourage and support my research. No matter how many battles one fights, nor how many years that go by, the love and support of one's parents is one of life's great blessings. And in this matter I have been truly blessed.

The members of my immediate family, however, have borne the brunt of my research demands. In the course of preparing this book, I have watched my son, Michael, develop into a young man, my daughter, Elaine, into a young woman. In return, they have spent their formative years observing their father prepare "The Book." Along the way, they have met many personal challenges and made more than a few sacrifices. Their unwavering support for me in this project, through all these years, is a precious gift that I will cherish all my life. To my wife, Karyn, I must say all this and more. Despite the many struggles and sacrifices that living with a writer such as myself have exacted, she has never faltered in her constant support of me and this project. To her I owe my loving appreciation and heartfelt thanks.

Notwithstanding the insights and guidance from a multitude of readers and researchers who have supported this endeavor, all limitations of this book are my responsibility alone.

Foreword

by Linda Moulton Howe

As an American TV producer and investigative journalist since graduating from Stanford University with a Masters Degree in Communication, I have produced many works for TV, radio, books and Internet. My beat is science and the environment, which includes earth mysteries. Of all the subjects I've covered, there is one that never goes away and never leaves the public's curiosity. That is Unidentified Aerial Craft (UACs), also known as "celestial," "interplanetary," UFOBs in government documents since the 1940s. Extraordinary aerial lights, beams and vehicles that defy human understanding of physics have been reported by pilots, policemen, military offices – even U. S. Presidents Jimmy Carter and Ronald Reagan. Associated with the mysterious aerial lights, beams and craft are worldwide animal mutilations, human abductions, crop formations and government cover-ups about those phenomena.

Beginning in the fall of 1979 as Director of Special Projects at the CBS affiliate in Denver, Colorado, I tried to get to the bottom of the large and small animal mutilation mystery – that leaves carcasses dead with similar patterns of bloodless excisions from body to body throughout the United States, Canada, and many other countries in both hemispheres. That's when law enforcement first told me *off* the record that the perpetrators were from outer space, because officers had seen orange, glowing spheres make 90-degree angle turns at their police cars, dive straight down into the ground, rise back up and split into two, orange, glowing spheres. Deputy Sheriff Bill Waugh of Elizabeth, Colorado, told me, "Whenever we see those fiery orange balls show up, we know we are going to have animal mutilations."

Veterinarians knew they could not remove a 9-inch by 11-inch heart from a cow without making an excision in the chest and cutting through the pericardium surrounding the heart. But, the facts were that in some necropsies on mutilated animals where there was no chest excision, all heart tissue and blood had been removed from inside the pericardium membrane, which was still intact without cuts or tears. Impossible for the most modern human medical technologies. No vet or sheriff wanted to say that in front of microphones and cameras. So, the official explanations to the public and media were predators, disease, and satanic cults. Thus, cover-ups about the truly strange physical evidence were perpetuated by local law enforcement as well as the CIA, FBI, DIA, NSA, NRO, NSC – and beyond.

I reported what I learned in a 2-hour TV special entitled *A Strange Harvest,* first broadcast in Denver and the surrounding region on May 28, 1980. Three years later on March 21, 1983, I was in New York City signing a contract with Home Box Office to produce a TV hour about *UFOs: The E. T. Factor.* That took me straight into the labyrinth of American counterintelligence, which wanted to keep me from producing the HBO special and succeeded. Eventually, I was sternly told, "We've tried to make it clear to you – we don't want UFOs and animal mutilations connected together in the public's mind. Now, lay off!"

But I kept going wherever physical evidence, eyewitnesses and facts took me, because I had a different philosophy than the government intimidators. I grew up in Boise, Idaho, where we pledged allegiance to the American flag each morning at school, had to memorize Lincoln's Gettysburg address, which stressed we had a government "of the people, by the people and for the people." We also had to outline the U. S. Constitution and Bill of Rights to learn what democratic American citizens were guaranteed. How naive others and I must seem to those who are paid to misinform and intimidate so that powerful insiders can maintain a policy of denial in the interest of national security about a non-human presence on Earth. But how, why, and when did powerful insiders secretly hijack our promised government "of the people, by the people and for the people," that would not perish from the Earth?

The answer to that question is woven throughout the next nine chapters that synthesize E.T.-related events from 1973 to 1991. As each year is examined by historian Richard M. Dolan, there are the ever-present threads of strange lights or solid-appearing craft in the sky, and human-piloted jets that chase unsuccessfully after those unidentified aerial vehicles moving at mind-boggling speeds while making 90-degree turns. There are also unusual craft and beams that touch the ground, along with animal mutilations, human abductions, geometric patterns in cereal crops – all happening in both hemispheres. There are other threads, of powerful insiders who try to keep the public and media from paying serious attention to all the high strangeness. And there is a third strand of threads, the various non-human entities that human eyewitnesses have encountered in daytime or night.

Richard Dolan takes all those threads and weaves them through the warp and woof of global geopolitical events. This book is Mr. Dolan's masterful explanation of how Lincoln's government of the people suffered a secret, silent coup d'etat by powerful insiders who probably thought in the beginning that their policy of denial was a superpatriotic act to protect tax-paying citizens from collapsing in the face of the unknown. But those powerful insiders did not collapse with their knowledge of the extraterrestrial biological entities and advanced technologies. Instead, their power grew in Black Agencies with Black Budgets protected by classified executive orders that prevented Congress – the peoples' representatives – from even knowing what those Black Budgets financed.

In the last pages of this prodigious work, with the braid plaited, Mr. Dolan concludes, "In all likelihood, secrecy relating to UFOs was a logical course of action initially that became an addiction the longer it continued. The longer the UFO secret was maintained, the harder it was to reveal and the greater the gap between official and black-world societies. One might therefore think that this secrecy, which continues to this day, is bound to last indefinitely. Such a conclusion would be logical and perhaps even seem to be inevitable. Yet, it would be wrong."

Richard Dolan unfolds how fear of E.T. disclosure in a republican system of government posed such a serious problem that clever minds "found a way to keep the original system alive while creating another, increasingly separate system that would be empowered to deal with the extraordinary intrusion of others' into our world." That clever but unconstitutional answer is a "breakaway civilization."

Linda Moulton Howe
Albuquerque, New Mexico
June 14, 2009

Introduction

The truth is incontrovertible. Malice may attack it, ignorance may deride it, but in the end, there it is.
— *Winston Churchill*

In a time of universal deceit, telling the truth is a revolutionary act.
— *George Orwell*

It's no wonder that truth is stranger than fiction. Fiction has to make sense.
— *Mark Twain*

The Problem

Across the Earth's skies and deep within the minds of humankind, UFOs are everywhere and nowhere. For years, decades, generations, and centuries, people have noticed unusual and occasionally impossible things in their skies. It will never be known how many sightings occurred in early times; today they are daily and worldwide. And yet, except for brief punctuations, the main instruments of power in our world continue to remain silent. The discrepancy between humanity's collective eyes and its voice is striking and unsettling.

There is scarcely a person on Earth who has not heard of UFOs; many believe in them. Few, however, can say much about them. Fewer still – even believers – can find much time to think about them. Life finds a way of keeping us occupied with other matters.

Simply put, the phenomenon is a bundle of contradictions. But if UFOs could be shown to be genuine, anomalous, and apparently the result of some intelligence other than that of our official and current civilization, then surely that would be *something*. Something so big, so shattering, that all other truths might well be humbled by it.

I argue that this is indeed the case, strange as this claim must seem to someone schooled in the standard histories of their world. The following pages are a methodical presentation of facts and analyses that show the

UFO phenomenon to be something most assuredly "not us."

It is also a reality that is actively being covered up. It is a phenomenon so significant that elements of the human power structure have made it their priority to keep information about it strictly to themselves, apparently at all cost. As to the identity of these secret-keepers, many sources culled from several decades of leaks, as well as broad geopolitical trends, make a reasonable case that they are "beyond" nations. The U.S. power structure, while still integral to the system of secrecy, may not be the final word as it once was.

The implications of a UFO reality and cover-up are profound. It means that our society has lived in an "official" reality so incomplete, so inaccurate, that we may with justice call it fictitious. It means that the history we have learned, the science we think we know, and the very core of who we think we are, need to be rediscovered.

There is also the knotty issue of who or what is behind the UFO phenomenon itself. Here, matters become even more complicated. It seems clear that some of the phenomena are the result of secret breakthroughs by all-too-human groups, some more covert than others. Six decades of classified expenditures (and other forms of secret spending) have provided ample resources to apply principles and technologies that have remained sealed off from the rest of humanity. This development alone is enough to justify the greatest secrecy.

But terrestrial breakthroughs do not appear to account for the core of the UFO phenomenon. The confrontational nature of the objects, the never-ending military encounters and attempted interceptions tell the reasonable mind that something else is going on. Added to this are the thousands of detailed descriptions, given by rational and intelligent people (who normally wish to remain anonymous), of having been taken by non-human beings to be studied and acted upon in various ways. These too tell us something is happening.

Separating "ours" from "theirs" can be difficult and – due to entrenched viewpoints – thankless. Still, it looks like both types of UFOs exist, adding to the complexity of an already formidable problem.

In a world that is moving fast toward a nightmarish dystopia relieved only by the distractions of a mass entertainment industry, investigating such matters may not seem to be an attractive option for many. Yet in all societies at all times, there are those who care, those who hunger for that quaint anachronism called Truth. I am here to tell you that there is such a thing. With effort and sacrifice, truth can be known. Once known, it may continue to exact a heavy price on those who possess it. And yet, it is more precious than the rarest of gems, easily worth knowing for those who dare to chase it. For it is truth, and only truth, that will ever set you free.

Main Themes

I have brought together several themes in preparing this study, which covers the UFO phenomenon from 1973 until 1991. First are the reports themselves, priority of which was given to those with military implications. In some cases this meant that the report came from a military or intelligence agency within the U.S., U.S.S.R., or another nation; in other cases it meant that reliable journalistic sources had reported an attempted jet interception or some other military encounter with a UFO; in others still it meant well-researched cases by a major UFO investigative group, such as the Mutual UFO Network (MUFON). Of course, not all UFO encounters in this book have direct military implications. Some are just good reports that were reliably investigated, important historically, or offered some other redeeming quality. Throughout, I sought to describe and analyze these cases succinctly, yet fully.

This book is more than a collection of UFO accounts, however. Ultimately, it tells a story, some of which concerns the attitudes of political and military agencies. We can learn these in several ways. One is through the available military and intelligence reports. While there are limits to what we can know based on reports of mid-level classification (i.e. "Confidential" as opposed to "Top Secret"), we can still see that the military considered many UFO encounters with great seriousness, even gravity. Responsible thinkers must ask why this was so, and why such an attitude has continually been countered by official silence and dismissal. When powerful groups dismiss something publicly, but take it seriously in private, we can assume something important is being withheld.

A related theme of this book concerns the evolution of the "national security state." During the period under review, the power of the U.S. military and intelligence communities expanded at the expense of ordinary citizens. Elsewhere, multinational structures also weakened citizen power. It is little appreciated how UFO secrecy has also eroded human liberty. From the 1940s onward, it required the creation of an apparatus that was independent of realistic oversight by elected representatives, with substantial funding and latitude of action. Indeed, secrecy on UFOs is arguably a key factor in the genesis of America's so-called "black budget." That, in turn, has shown itself to be among the most formidable enemies of classical republican government.

During the 1970s and 1980s, that American national security state was involved in secret programs that were connected with UFO phenomena, ranging from the (alleged) electrogravitic elements of the stealth bomber, ET aspects of the Strategic Defense Initiative (SDI), the UFO-hunting Defense Support Program (DSP), the testing of non-aerodynamic and radical craft in Nevada's Groom Lake and Southern California, the spreading of disinformation targeted against UFO researchers, and much more.

The final key theme of this book deals with the evolution of our own ideas about UFOs. Leading edge thinking on the topic was in a very different place in 1991 than it had been during the early 1970s. How researchers got from the one place to the other is a fascinating story. What had once seemed like a somewhat straightforward proposition – extraterrestrials visiting Earth in spaceships – went through many permutations. Researchers began to discuss subjects previously off-limits, such as dimensions, time travel, remote viewing, abductions, animal mutilations, black helicopters, crop circles, and the Nazi "legacy." Included in this explosion of new ideas were claims and details of the cover-up, and even discussion of whether or not there was a "human-alien deal" involving abductions and technology transfer. Much of the new thinking was based on solid foundations, such as government documents, open source research, or new developments in science. Some of it was fantastic and impossible to verify.

Through it all was a backdrop of global change, technological revolution, and finally the widespread adoption of personal computers throughout the U.S. and Europe, all of which affected the UFO scene.

The Story

During the early 1970s, the UFO topic was still suffering from the conclusions of the Air Force sponsored Condon Committee. In 1969, its report had concluded that the study of UFOs had not added to scientific knowledge, and that UFO reports were "not of probative value." UFO researchers responded by trying to bring respectability to the topic; hence the development of "scientific ufology." Studying the cover-up, a major tactic during the 1950s and 1960s, became passé while researchers focused on improving scientific and logical rigor, as well as improving investigative methodologies. Meanwhile, the 1970s brought many difficult, "high strangeness" reports that severely tested old ideas about UFOs. The phenomenon itself seemed to stimulate new ideas in research.

The absence of a political emphasis in UFO research did not last very long. Government denials remained the rule, but the political turmoil of Watergate and Vietnam led to a strengthening of the Freedom of Information Act (FOIA) in 1974 – which was further strengthened during the Jimmy Carter administration. The result was a flurry of requests by private citizens for documents pertaining to UFOs. Before long, thousands of pages of relevant documents had been released by the CIA, FBI, and many military agencies. Taken separately, none of these documents could be considered a "smoking gun" proving that UFOs were extraterrestrial, but the cumulative impact of the best ones was formidable. It became obvious that some UFO reports had been taken very seriously by responsible agencies while, at the same time, they downplayed UFOs to the public. Some of these documents described baffling and provocative violations of airspace by objects that simply should not have existed, and the futile attempts by interceptors to engage them. This was explosive stuff in the late 1970s, and many researchers understandably looked to FOIA as the best tool with which to pry open the secrets of UFOs.

Another prong in the attack on secrecy were leaks concerning the retrieval of crashed UFOs. Researchers had shunned the topic for years. Now, however, people began to talk, not just about Roswell (which quickly became the most prominent of them), but many other cases. Already by 1980, researchers had collected scores of accounts from former military personnel who claimed to have been present at the retrieval of a crashed UFO, or to have seen alien bodies at Wright-Patterson Air Force Base (AFB), or to have participated in the secret in some other way. Some researchers wondered whether they could make an air-tight case about one of these stories, and whether they could blow the lid off of the secrecy.

Alas, it was not to be. From all available evidence, it appears that the intelligence community initiated a counter-strike in the form of disinformation. Starting in the early 1980s, this effort has left a permanent mark on UFO research. Most prominent was the release of the "MJ-12" documents in the mid-1980s, which certainly looked like authentic, secret statements describing the extraterrestrial reality and cover-up. The problem was that they almost certainly were mailed by intelligence officers from Kirtland AFB, one of whom had previously shown another UFO researcher similar but decidedly different documents. Those documents contained information that did not easily reconcile with the later ones. On the other hand, the MJ-12 documents did contain information that proved fertile for followup investigation, and certain arcane tidbits that suggested they were genuine. Complicating matters were a series of statements by prominent members of the defense community which supported the existence of an organization like MJ-12 – that is, a UFO/ET "control group." The result was that what had seemed like a straightforward proposition, e.g. just getting hold of the "right" document, turned into an endless debate over document authenticity, while insider claims and leaks – inherently difficult to verify – were simply not enough to obtain a government admission that UFOs were real and, in some fundamental way, *alien*.

Yet, UFO research progressed markedly during this period. New issues came to the forefront, joining the FOIA effort and investigation into Roswell. Most prominent of these was the abduction phenomenon. True, the topic of alien abduction had been discussed to some extent during the 1960s, but primarily as a side issue. At best, it was considered to be a rare event, and very difficult for many researchers – to say nothing of the general public – to take seriously. But the phenomenon would not go away; researchers found themselves increasingly in the presence of people who had periods of missing time, or memories of being taken and examined by alien beings. Some eventually found it impossible to ignore any longer and began a systematic study of the phenomenon. The results caused yet more tremors in the field of ufology, more arguments, and more questions.

By the late 1980s, Roswell, MJ-12, and abductions all caused deep divisions in UFO research. But there was still an identifiable community of researchers who, in a sense, all spoke the same language. That is, they were a fairly close-knit bunch who knew each others' work, had studied the same cases, were members of one of the major organizations, and believed in "scientific ufology." Starting in 1987, this cultural unity was shattered. This was largely due to the existence of a new, wide-open forum: the Internet. Anyone with access to a computer and a modem could publish their thoughts instantly, for all of cyberworld to see. The UFO journals, governed by their various directors, editors, and submission policies, had for decades been the dominant venue for discussion. Suddenly, they were being bypassed by a steady stream of papers that before long turned into a flood, and then a veritable ocean.

The result was that the UFO community began to "let it all hang out." Claims of human-alien "deals," and the reverse-engineering of extraterrestrial technology began to surface. Discussions of global control groups like the Bilderbergers and Illuminati seeped into the mix. Increasingly, claims were made about the various types of extraterrestrials said to be on Earth.

The old guard found all of this distasteful, embarrassing, and wrong-headed: what happened to careful scientific evaluation of individual UFO cases and a suspension of judgment? Supporters of the new school countered that they had simply dragged the ever-conservative ufology into a region where it had needed to be all along.

Meanwhile, a new development in the phenomenon itself began to coalesce: the advent of the mass sighting. Surely, there had been instances before where large numbers of people witnessed a UFO. But during the 1980s, there were several places where the sightings continued over an extended period of time, and were seen by hundreds of people, sometimes thousands. The Hudson Valley region of lower New York State and Connecticut; Gulf Breeze, Florida; California's Antelope Valley; Nevada's Area 51; the town of Fyffe, Alabama; most of Belgium; and Mexico City all were host to ongoing waves of UFOs, with many witnesses, often armed with cameras and video.

Here, as in prior years, we see the strange juxtaposition of the unusual nature of these aerial phenomena, combined with a decided lack of interest in them by major journalistic sources. Most of the limited coverage they received was local; to the extent they were covered by the major media, such as the *New York Times*, they were typically dismissed as misidentifications of something conventional, or as hoaxes. Usually, they were simply ignored.

Why would major newspapers and media players ignore something that, presumably, would be a major story and therefore bring in more money? They might, if they had close relationships to those very groups intent on maintaining secrecy. In fact, during the 1970s and 1980s, several studies appeared showing just this. In 1988, Katherine Graham, the publisher of the *Washington Post* and long-time collaborator with the CIA, told a CIA audience that "there are some things the general public does not need to know and shouldn't. I believe democracy flourishes when the government can take legitimate steps to keep its secrets and when the press can decide whether to print what it knows." Somewhere along the way, the mainstream American media transformed itself from being a public watchdog into the mouth of Sauron.

Indeed, the world itself went through a major transformation. It was not simply a function of the Internet, although this was surely important. On a grander scale still, what was happening was *globalization*. The Soviet Union, increasingly unable to compete economically, began to fall apart. Elsewhere, multinational corporations assumed ever-greater power and influence in the geopolitical realm. By 1990, the President of the United

States had given a name to these changes: the New World Order.

What had happened was that the international power brokers who had always lurked behind the scenes had found better ways to govern their world. Whether or not one wishes to call this a conspiracy, we can state matter-of-factly that a Kingmaker such as David Rockefeller (who was a major factor in creating nearly all the Presidencies covered in this volume: Gerald Ford, Jimmy Carter, Ronald Reagan, and George Bush), was moving toward a goal he had openly desired for his entire life. It included, first, a diminution of traditional concepts of national sovereignty in favor of an array of transnational structures. These might be the old clubs like the Bilderbergers, Council on Foreign Relations, and Trilateral Commission, or other legal structures/entities such as the United Nations, World Bank, International Monetary Fund, the European Union, or the North American Free Trade Agreement (NAFTA). Regarding the management of UFO secrecy, such a development should well give one pause before assuming that the office of the U.S. President had the final word on such matters.

The second major result of globalization was (and continues to be) a transfer of authority from the public realm to the private. The evolution of UFO secrecy reflected this development. It is impossible to know the details, but the general picture has become clear enough. Control over key components of the UFO secret have drifted further and further away from (theoretically responsible) government and military officials, and increasingly toward private entities. This transfer of power is reflected in a number of statements from insiders, as well as by more generalized studies of the Pentagon's system of "Special Access Programs," the prototypical black budget programs. In effect, the world underwent a silent, transnational revolution during the late 1980s and early 1990s.

Another thing that had happened was that someone seemed to be developing and flying, if not actual flying saucers, then something very much along those lines. By the late 1980s the signs were becoming clear. Perhaps the Hudson Valley objects were not terrestrial objects, perhaps they were. By the end of the 1980s, however, sightings in California's Antelope Valley and Nevada's Area 51 were of objects that were surely made by the U.S. defense industry. In the judgment not merely of UFO-watchers but aviation and aerospace experts, it looked as if these objects were utilizing a form of field propulsion. That is, anti-gravity.

"Oh what a tangled web we weave when first we practice to deceive." We can assume that the original lie of the 1940s was intended to stall for time;

meanwhile, policymakers would frantically try to figure out what was going on. But this lie developed into immense, complex, and ultimately separate infrastructure. The longer it continued, the more entrenched the established parties became; the more removed they became from officially established truths; the less they were able to explain to the rest of the world what was actually going on. It was one thing to explain to the public that one or more extraterrestrial intelligences were freely operating on Planet Earth for purposes which they kept to themselves. It was entirely something else to explain that a massive black infrastructure had evolved, siphoning off public money, operating in total secrecy for years, developing new technologies, and making profits based on monopolistic exploitation of acquired ET technology. Another still to explain that the U.S. President, or other national leaders for that matter, were not necessarily the key decision-makers when it came to such matters.

Having said this, there is reason to believe that the President was not completely out of the loop, at least during this period. There appear to have been several times when a disclosure of the UFO reality was considered, one of which was during the Bush administration in 1991. Like the others which preceded it, it was an abortive attempt. From sources I have spoken to, people whom I consider to be in a good position to know, such discussions have tended to occur "every five years or so." The obstacles are daunting, primarily intransigence from within the classified world, but just as importantly the fear of repercussions throughout the social, financial, political, and legal structures.

There can be no question that the challenges of disclosure are intimidating. For those in the know, it is much easier to let matters continue as they have been, despite the difficulties already involved. That attitude can work – as long as the world does not change. But we in the 21st century are living through revolutionary times, and this revolution truly began during the period under review in this book. The world will never be ready for disclosure of this truth, just as most couples are not ready for their first child. It will come just the same, however. Like any new parent, we will have to learn and adjust on the fly.

Sources

In researching this book I was fortunate to have a vast array of resources that were not available to me for the first volume of this study. Due to the kindness of several individuals, most notably the late William T. Sherwood of Rochester, New York, who bequeathed me his entire, substantial ufological library, I have had a surfeit of books, journals, newspaper clippings, as well as video and audio interviews. Of greatest importance are government documents which are available to anyone via several large collections on the web. In addition, I found interesting and previously unknown documents while visiting the U.S. National Archives in College Park, Maryland and the Canadian National Archives in Ottawa.

Government documents are important; unfortunately they do not tell the whole story. In the first place, even during FOIA's "glory years" of the late 1970s, the UFO documents that were released had been of mid- to low-levels of classification. The few "Top Secret" documents were nearly entirely redacted. Generally speaking, this situation worsened in subsequent years to the point where FOIA became nearly useless for most military UFO encounters after the mid-1980s. A few accounts continue to make it through, however, so the effort remains important.

In preparation for this history, I also examined the journals of many major UFO organizations, including the *MUFON UFO Journal, The International UFO Reporter, The APRO Bulletin, The NICAP UFO Investigator, Flying Saucer Review*, and a host of other publications, newspaper clippings, and websites. Moreover, I have been fortunate in interviewing a number of researchers and insiders of all types, most of whom allow public attribution, and a few who do not. Using an anonymous source for any historical work is a tricky business, and in general I have avoided using them for direct attribution. In a few cases, however, I have deemed the information and source significant enough that I could not in good conscience leave it out.

Regarding the topic of UFOs, in which national security issues come into play, accompanied by official silence, disinformation, and outright lies, any history will always be incomplete. Until matters come out in the open, this is how it will continue to be. The best we can achieve is a balance between caution in the use of sources, and courage in the willingness to draw implications from the data. At all times, we must distinguish between *what we know* and *what things look like*. There are those who prefer to remain in the safe waters of the former, and others who live exclusively in the deeps of the latter. For my part, I have ventured through them all, from the calm to the treacherous.

Implications

Even for experienced researchers, UFOs can seem surreal, if only because they find so little support for the idea within respectable society. The same applies to witnesses. Scratch below the surface a little, and you will find many people who have seen, or at least believe they have seen, a genuine UFO. Although seeing is believing, the passage of time can still engulf an extraordinary sighting within the mundane necessities of daily life. The experience then becomes no more than an interesting anomaly, often forgotten or pushed aside because there is just no place for it, and they certainly do not have the stomach for the ridicule.

Setting aside the truth value of the UFO phenomenon, it is an interesting sociological reality that so many people are unwilling to discuss the most incredible – and at times traumatic – experience of their lives. What does it say about our society that this is so? My feeling is that, by its very nature, it represents a form of repression. If you are a reader who believes UFOs to be nonsense of some sort, I can nevertheless assure you that you have a friend or relation who has seen one. They have simply learned not to discuss it. Many people can live perfectly well within the constraints of repression and denial; they simply learn to shut off certain parts of their mind. It is sad, but it happens all the time.

But not everyone is the same. Not everyone is willing to do this, or even *can* do this. By any estimate, there are many millions of people on this planet who have had a powerful UFO experience. They cannot and will not be silenced indefinitely. We are today living in a period of such dramatic change – technologically, politically, socially, culturally – that I believe it is only a matter of time before something gives way.

And what of *them*? Those beings, intelligences – people? – who are behind the phenomenon itself? I have spoken about the silence of the human structure of power, but the beings who are traversing the skies, oceans, and space above the Earth are not landing on the proverbial White House lawn. They have an agenda, an interest, which they are not willing to share, at least not publicly. Many people claim to have had private communications with some of these beings, which run the gamut from the hellish to the divine. Regarding their nature and agenda, we enter of necessity the realm of speculation. Matters of *exopolitics*, that is the study of our relationship with "them," will always be premature under such circumstances.

Still, it is not outrageous to consider that, having mastered certain technologies that we ourselves may soon be acquiring – or even certain matters of mental or spiritual attainment – that multiple groups are interested in our beautiful blue orb and its abundance of life. The human species should be of prime interest to them, especially now. Consider the changes we have made to ourselves and the world within a mere century. From a world of horse-drawn carriages to cars, airplanes, radio, television, atomic weapons, guided missiles, integrated circuits, computers, and internet. An object weighing just a few ounces can let you speak, text, or see anyone in the world, hold thousands of songs, give you instant directions to anywhere, and connect you to the world's largest libraries. Experts in artificial intelligence believe we are just a few years away from having computers that will claim to be conscious in some manner, and will *seem* like they are, whatever the nature of that consciousness may truly be. Then there is the matter of nanotechnology and quantum computing, the results of which are expected to transform our world even more completely than the internet revolution already has.

In other words, humanity is in the process of reinventing itself. Any observing intelligence must be well aware that we are poised, knowingly or not, to leap into their world. We have probably been there all along, only asleep. Now we are about to wake up.

Chapter 1

Global Strangeness
1973-1975

To our utter amazement, it went straight up into the heavens. When I got off the plane I told Nancy all about it ... And we read up on the long history of UFOs.
— *Ronald Reagan, describing his UFO sighting, 1974*

It was faster than anything I've ever seen. I've observed enough launchings to know we have nothing that can compare to the speed of this thing.
— *Major Claude Riddle, U.S. Army, on UFO encounter while piloting a helicopter, 1975.*

The difference between what the most and the least learned people know is inexpressibly trivial in relation to that which is unknown.
— *Albert Einstein*

Inexplicable Technology

On October 25, 1973, during a wave of UFO sightings in the United States, two U.S. Navy personnel reported something incredible on the other side of the world. Lieutenant Commander "M" was driving from a restricted National Security Agency (NSA) and Naval Communications Station in North West Cape, Western Australia. At 7:15 p.m., he saw "a large black airborne object" about 5 miles away to the west, at an altitude of about 2,000 feet. In his written report, he stated that the object simply hovered, giving off no noise or exhaust. Then, "after about 20-25 seconds the craft accelerated at unbelievable speeds and disappeared to the north." Its acceleration was "beyond belief."

Another navy man, Fire Captain Bill L., saw the same thing from a different vantage point. He said the object "was completely stationary," except for a revolving or pulsating halo around the center. After he watched it for four minutes, it took off at "tremendous speed" toward the north and disappeared within seconds. He thought it was about 30 feet in diameter and hovering at 1,000 feet over the hills west of the base. The object appeared black, and did not show any lights.

Australian UFO researcher Bill Chalker investigated this case. He discovered that on this date the North West Cape NSA base was communicating a general U.S. alert to conventional and nuclear forces in the region – this was during the Yom Kippur War, involving Israel, Egypt, and Syria.[1]

This event highlights the complexity and intrigue of the modern UFO phenomenon. We have two descriptions of an extraordinary aerial phenomenon which appears to be technological. There was not in 1973, nor is there today, any craft that is supposed to be able to do this. Moreover, these witnesses were American military personnel whose base was secretly engaged in high stakes military activity with global impact.

So what exactly was going on? What was that black object? Was it spying on the Americans? If so, who controlled it? With a technology so far beyond anything we know of, it is not hard to see this as an intimate surveillance of human military activity by a non-human civilization.

Perhaps one might object that such a speculation is premature. Maybe the object was made by the U.S. military-industrial complex in deep secrecy. If so, more questions arise. Was such technology developed with the aid of reverse engineering studies done on alien craft? Or was it fully "in-house?" Or was it developed by a human group, but one so secret that it would be in effect another civilization. For those who get their news from CNN, this might be hard to swallow – *a secret civilization?* Indeed, but – to adapt a statement by Dr. Carl Sagan – extraordinary phenomena require extraordinary hypotheses.

Regardless of the object's origin, it demonstrates for the umpteenth time that unexplained and supremely advanced technology is traversing the skies of this world.

The State of Ufology

The "wave" of late 1973 is often said to have signaled a return of the UFO phenomenon, after a relative decline for several years prior. While sighting statistics bear this out, in all likelihood we will never truly know if this is so, considering the inexact nature of the UFO statistics themselves. Not that the massive amount of collected data on this subject is of no value; rather, it is simply woefully incomplete, and always has been. Of the hundreds of UFO witnesses this author has spoken to, perhaps five went so far as to report their sighting to some agency (the Air Force, the police, a UFO organization, etc.). Most never even wrote a personal account.

During the 1950s and 1960s, there had been Project Blue Book, the Air Force's "UFO Desk." J. Allen Hynek, consultant to Blue Book, suspected that it was the tip of an iceberg, that perhaps only ten percent of actual UFO sightings were ever reported. Jacques Vallee thought the percentage was even lower.[2] That was when Americans had a government agency that would take such reports. After 1969, the Air Force closed Blue Book, an event closely linked with the Air Force sponsored scientific study of UFOs conducted by the University of Colorado in the late 1960s. Known as the Condon Committee, the study dismissed UFO phenomena as "not worthy of scientific study." With Blue Book gone, only a few small, private organizations accepted UFO reports. This fact as much as anything else could explain the drop in UFO sightings during the very early 1970s. By the end of 1973, private UFO research was beginning to recover. At this point, there were four research groups in the U.S., small though they were, that could have some claim as a "national" organization.

One was the National Investigative Committee on Aerial Phenomena (NICAP), based out of Washington, D.C. For years, NICAP had challenged the Air Force position on UFOs and tried to jump-start open congressional hearings on the matter. But NICAP in the 1970s was circling the drain. Its longtime director, USMC Major Donald E. Keyhoe (Ret.), had been ousted in 1969 by Col. Joseph J. Bryan III, a man later discovered to have once headed the CIA's Psychological Warfare division. Leadership of NICAP passed to John Acuff, who had been the head of the Society of Photographic Scientists and Engineers (SPSE), a group with strong ties to military intelligence and the CIA. Acuff ended NICAP's criticism of government UFO policy. More significantly, he destroyed its investigative and reporting network. Acuff also plundered the organization personally, paying himself more than $20,000 per year for his "services." This was essentially all the money the organization had. The situation continued until he resigned the directorship in 1978.[3]

For years, NICAP's main rival was the Aerial Phenomena Research Organization (APRO), based out of Tucson, Arizona. Founded in 1952 by James and Coral Lorenzen, it had developed an impressive structure. A typical *APRO Bulletin* of the late 1960s listed some 40 or more Ph.D.s or M.D.s on the organization's consulting panels in biological sciences, medical sciences, physical sciences, and social sciences, as well as representatives from 40 to 50 nations. It was a worldwide network subsisting on memberships of less than $10 per year. Coral Lorenzen had a long history of frosty relationships with other UFO organizations. During the 1960s, she frequently criticized NICAP for politicizing the UFO issue. She argued that UFOs should be approached scientifically, without Keyhoe's conspiracy-mongering.

Thus, with Keyhoe's ouster and NICAP's willfully incompetent leadership, APRO was primed to lead American ufology. But APRO received its own unwelcome shock in 1969, when one of its regional officers, Walter Andrus, took many APRO members with him to form the

Midwest UFO Network based out of Seguin, Texas. Disillusioned NICAP members also joined. Soon renamed the Mutual UFO Network, MUFON quickly became a leading UFO research group. Coral Lorenzen seemed to have taken this personally. Although she was usually polite in public, she never developed a cooperative relationship with MUFON, and at times engaged in verbal exchanges and sniping at Andrus (who, it must be said, never reciprocated). Instead, Andrus focused on building a grass-roots UFO investigative organization.

In November 1973, another UFO organization joined the mix, when J. Allen Hynek co-founded the Center for UFO Studies (CUFOS) near Chicago with Sherman J. Larsen. Larsen's background is as obscure as Hynek's is famous. He was once described as little more than "a retired Glenview businessman."[4] In fact, Larsen seems almost certainly to have been in the U.S. Army Counter Intelligence Corps (CIC). During World War Two and its immediate aftermath, CIC was one of the elite U.S. intelligence agencies, the spy-catchers of the American military. Leonard Stringfield, who was a friend of Larsen's, mentioned in a 1977 book that Larsen had worked for CIC, and had even told him where CIC's headquarters were in the Chicago area.[5] Larsen had given a sophisticated presentation at a 1971 MUFON Symposium regarding government documents that demonstrated strong interest in UFOs. Larsen and an associate named Bill Laub had contacts at the RAND Corporation who obtained UFO documents that had been created for the Air Force. Specifically, Larsen said that he and Laub had "developed a technique to secure credible sources who have provided us with documents that have previously been unknown, priced out of the market, or while not classified were nevertheless unavailable."[6] Far from being a "naive businessman," Larsen seems very quietly to have been a sophisticated player within the U.S. intelligence community.

Hynek was the most famous name in ufology, due to his longtime connection with Blue Book. As far as Coral Lorenzen was concerned, fame did not equal quality. She never forgot that for years he was comfortably paid as an Air Force consultant. She and her husband long believed the government was spying on them, and they knew that the CIA-sponsored 1953 Robertson Panel, of which Hynek was a junior member, had recommended monitoring their organization. Nor was Coral Lorenzen the only one with a problem about Hynek: many MUFON members also distrusted him.

In early 1974, Hynek was seeking cooperative relationships with the other UFO groups. Andrus pledged MUFON's support, but Hynek only deepened Coral Lorenzen's suspicions when he visited APRO's Tucson headquarters in February. As Coral Lorenzen put it, he "made a pitch to be handed a list of APRO's Field Investigators along with their addresses and telephone numbers." Perhaps this was only an attempt at professional collaboration. Considering Coral Lorenzen's longstanding attitude, however, one might raise an eyebrow at Hynek's diplomatic confidence. She was "somewhat taken aback" when Hynek told her that fate had placed him at center stage of the UFO situation. Hynek did not get the list.[7]

Such were the four major American groups receiving UFO reports, conducting investigations, and trying to understand the mystery. Memberships were low. APRO and MUFON had no more than two or three thousand members each, CUFOS was in its infancy, and NICAP was hemorrhaging. NICAP had the most obvious connections to the world of spooks, but all of them had prominent members with past or current ties to the U.S. military or intelligence community. One might argue this was because the previous line of work of these individuals had stimulated an interest in the subject. On the other hand, given that surveillance of the UFO research community had been going on for years, suspicions like those of Coral Lorenzen seem justified to some degree.

Despite the personality clashes, all the groups promoted "scientific ufology." Hynek made it the guiding principle of CUFOS, and MUFON stressed it just as much. Its proponents argued that, in order for "ufology" to gain respectability, it needed to be conducted scientifically. MUFON was slowly developing an investigative methodology and a network of trained investigators. This was the ideal; reality often lagged behind. But there were MUFON investigators who rigorously investigated baffling UFO cases: doing the legwork, interviewing witnesses, analyzing possible landing sites, preparing thorough reports.

The goal of scientific ufology is surely laudable, and considering the state of affairs after the Condon Committee Report, understandable. It also served to de-politicize the issue to a large extent. Cover-ups and conspiracies were definitely *out*. So were such "simplistic" answers to the UFO mystery as the Extraterrestrial Hypothesis (ETH). Considering the Condon Committee's strong slap against the ETH, this too is understandable. More important, though, it was becoming obvious that there were simply too many bizarre reports which did not easily lead to a "nuts and bolts" explanation of alien creatures inside space ships coming from another planet.

Much of the influence behind this new perspective came from Jacques

Vallee and John A. Keel. Both argued that UFOs could not possibly be extraterrestrial spacecraft. Vallee later postulated "Five Arguments" against the ETH. First, there were too many UFO close encounters to explain them as a physical survey of the earth. Second, the humanoid body structure of the alleged "aliens" was unlikely to have originated elsewhere and was not biologically adapted to space travel. Third, the behavior as described in so many abduction reports contradicted the idea that advanced aliens were conducting genetic or scientific experiments. Fourth, the phenomenon seemed to have been recorded throughout human history. Fifth, the apparent ability of UFOs to manipulate space and time suggested different and richer alternatives to mere extraterrestrials.[8] Thus, not aliens in flying saucers, but intelligences from other dimensions, were interacting with humanity, according to this hypothesis. By the early 1970s, the idea was widespread among researchers, and has continued as a significant school of thought to the present day. Even the astronomer Hynek, who worked closely with Vallee during the 1970s, accepted a good portion of it.[9]

UFO research, in a word, was reinventing itself at the same time that it sought to establish itself on a firm intellectual footing. This was difficult enough, but researchers could not have foreseen just how intellectually active their field would become, nor how much more arduous the task of finding a common philosophical outlook and the scientific principles upon which to base their work.

UFO Crash in Wales

The United States generated few memorable UFO reports in 1974, but matters were different elsewhere, especially in Europe. Early in the year, "mystery helicopters" and cigar-shaped objects were reported in northern England, especially near the Pennine Mountains.[10] Enough reports accumulated that on January 15, police there announced they were on the alert for unusual helicopter movements.[11]

The following week, on January 23, 1974, a possible UFO crashed at Cader Bronwen, a 2,000 foot peak in northern Wales. Around 8:30 p.m., witnesses saw a bright object followed by a long, luminous tail and (according to one witness) a blinking blue light. The object seemed to be motionless for several minutes, during which it dimmed and then became very bright. One person described it as "an electric bulb shape, except that it seemed to have rough edges." When it crashed, police stations up to sixty miles away received calls about an earth tremor or quake. Police and a Royal Air Force (RAF) mountain rescue team both responded quickly. Two

RAF aircraft took photographs, and the RAF said nothing was found. The Royal Geological Institute said the object was a meteor.

Several odd sightings followed the event. Ninety minutes after the crash, a man watched a "luminous sphere" descend into the sea near the Dee Estuary, about 25 miles north of the crash. The next night, while the rescue team was in action, three family members saw a bright object in the sky near Cader Bronwen. Through field glasses they saw a disc-shaped object which seemed to be divided into red, green, yellow, and purple sections. Presumably this was not a flare. After ten minutes they called the police, and the object disappeared behind a cloud.

A local resident named Margaret Fry investigated the event and found a nurse who said she clearly saw the crashed UFO. The nurse had assumed an aircraft had gone down and drove out to help, accompanied by her two teenaged daughters. She told Fry that she saw the object fully intact, but was turned back by police and army personnel.

Twenty years later, British researcher Nick Redfern was able to corroborate that British Army units arrived. Redfern interviewed one soldier (pseudonym "James Prescott") who said he was ordered to the area with four others, and loaded two oblong boxes into their armored truck. They then drove the material about 150 miles southeast, into England, to the Chemical and Biological Defence Establishment at Porton Down, near Salisbury, Wiltshire. The men were under strict orders not to stop for anything. According to Prescott, "the boxes were opened by staff at the facility in our presence. We were startled to see two creatures which had been placed inside decontamination suits.... It was obvious that the creatures were not of this Earth, and, when examined, were found to have died." These were not little "greys." Prescott said the bodies were "about five to six feet tall, humanoid in shape, but so that they looked almost skeletal with a covering skin." He did not see a craft at the crash site, but "was informed that a large craft had crashed and was retrieved by other (British) military units."

Redfern speculated that a British version of Project Moon Dust was activated for this, which could also explain the reports of mysterious helicopters. As a 1961 U.S. defense document put it, Moon Dust was a program designed "to locate, recover, and deliver descended foreign space vehicles." The UFO connection to Moon Dust is certainly not out of the question. Of course, if the helicopters seen in the prior weeks were part of a Moon Dust type of operation, this implies some level of foreknowledge of a crash – unless there had been other, unknown crashes. Another piece to this case may have been added by British researcher Jenny Randles, who learned from a former British government official that a crashed UFO was kept at a military base somewhere in South Wales.

The British Ministry of Defence (MoD) has steadfastly refused to comment on the crash in Wales, although the mystery helicopter sightings in Britain largely ceased after this point.[12]

The French Minister of Defense

From January through March of 1974, French radio journalist, Jean-Claude Bourret, aired a series of 40 radio programs about UFOs. These were broadcast on French national radio (France-Inter). One of Bourret's guests was the current French Minister of Defense, Robert Galley, who dropped a true bombshell on February 21. Galley spoke of the widespread nature of the UFO phenomenon, the strong quality of evidence, and how he was "deeply convinced" that people needed to regard UFOs with a "completely open mind." It was undeniable, he said, "that there are facts that are unexplained or badly explained."

Galley confirmed that the French military had a strong interest in UFOs since 1954, a year of numerous sightings throughout France. He added that the military records contained "accounts of some baffling radar/visual incidents." Most significantly of all, Galley stated:

> I must say that if your listeners could see for themselves the mass of reports coming in from airborne gendarmerie, from the mobile gendarmerie, and from the gendarmerie charged with the job of conducting investigations, all of which reports are being forwarded by us to the CNES (National Center for Space Studies), then they would see that it is all pretty disturbing.

That a Minister of Defense of a major power in the 1970s could tell a journalist that some UFO reports were "pretty disturbing" – this is a startling revelation, to say the least. One can hardly imagine such a statement coming from an active American Defense Secretary. There does not appear to have been any major follow up on this statement within media or government circles.[13]

The Wave in Spain

Current events supported Galley's statement about the "disturbing" nature of UFO reports. The Wales UFO crash was serious enough, but a major wave of sightings also took place in Western Europe. A portion of these events involved sightings of alleged aliens. On January 7, while driving in the Belgian town of Warneton near the French border, a man's car suddenly died. He saw a landed UFO, slightly glowing and shaped like a British World War One helmet. Two humanoid beings approached him. They had pear-shaped heads, slits for mouths, round eyes, simple noses, and long arms. They wore internally lighted helmets, grey jumpsuit-type clothes, and gloves. One was about 4 feet tall, the other somewhat taller; a third being remained near the craft. The taller being came to within 12-15 feet of the motorist's vehicle, then opened and closed its mouth. The witness felt a kind of shock to the back of his head and heard a low-pitched sound. The two beings quickly returned to their craft, which now pulsated with an electric blue color, and quickly departed.[14]

An odd phenomenon was photographed in Italy, between Milan and Bologna, on January 18, 1974. A motorist named Giuseppe Cardelli saw a "strange shining ball" in the sky in the afternoon. He got out of his car and photographed it. He submitted the image to America's National Aeronautics and Space Administration (NASA), which replied with a letter dated June 18 that it had no solution to the image.

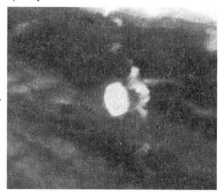

Photograph of January 18, 1974.

A NASA photographic specialist said it was "very interesting," but he had no idea what it was. A consultant wondered whether the object was a reflection in a car window (although the witness had claimed to have taken the photograph outside the car). Still, he found the "wiggly clouds to the right" interesting. No other conclusions were made regarding the photo.[15]

Several interesting aerial encounters also come from this period. On January 26, near Lisbon, Portugal, an airline crew reported seeing a V-formation of 10-15 luminous orange discs. The captain, Lars Berglund, ruled out the possibility that they could be a satellite reentry. The distances and configuration were too precise. After the formation had passed, another Portugese aircraft reported to ground control at Lisbon that they had seen the same formation. A Norwegian and British aircraft crew also reported the same observation. Visibility was good that day.[16] Another aerial case occurred in Milan, Italy, on March 9, in which a Fiat Corporation pilot chased a luminous saucer-shaped object with colored rings, an event that was tracked by Milan radar.[17]

On March 23, a very odd object was allegedly photographed in Albiosc, France, not far from Marseilles and Monaco. This was a color slide of a

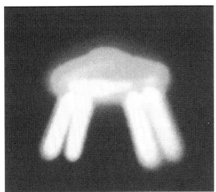

The Albiosc UFO, March 23, 1974

UFO, showing a red object resembling a domed disc and four bright beamlike extensions. UFO investigator, Jean Bedet, received this slide anonymously, along with a note stating a date of March 23. Bedet said that his wife and others had seen a UFO of this description at 11 p.m. on that very date. He showed them the slide, an   Another case, just as interesting, happened in Sweden on the same date, at probably around the same time. This was the "Anders" abduction case. A man walking along a dark road at night was surrounded by light and 'sucked up' into a UFO. A "typical" abduction experience ensued: entities, medical examination, and a probe inserted into his temple. At home, the man bled from wounds in his forehead, and his cheek burned. Extraordinary abilities appeared to follow, such as the ability to disrupt a compass needle, see vibrant auras, and telepathy. As bizarre as this sounds, the event appears to have been partially witnessed; the UFO was reported by another man a short distance away. The Swedish Home Guard assigned 50 of its personnel to work with 15 ufologists to examine the region. The group reported odd lights in the sky, but no entities.[18]

During the first half of 1974, the most intense area of reported UFO activity was in Spain. The Spanish wave is interesting for several reasons. First, the intrinsic nature of the reports themselves, which frequently involved close encounters by credible and sometimes prominent individuals, and some of which included descriptions of apparent aliens. Second, the U.S. military had some interest in this, as Defense Intelligence Agency (DIA) documents provide summary descriptions of dozens of these cases gathered from local newspaper clippings. Third, the attitude of the Spanish military toward UFOs is instructive.

The main concentration of Spanish UFO sightings was between March and June of 1974, a large portion of which occurred in a narrow longitudinal strip (5 and 6 degrees West) in the central and western portions of the country. Sightings were as far north as the Atlantic coast and as far south as Gibraltar, but in general along this narrow strip. Most of the descriptions of these sightings are truncated, as they are in the form of brief intelligence summaries by U.S. Defense Attache Office. Despite this, some are very distinctive.[19]

The entry for March 23, for instance, describes an event near Castillo de las Guardas, in the province of Seville: "Mother ship–aluminum, 150-200 meters long. Three smaller ships resembling mushrooms. Flew silently, had no windows but towers above and below." The witness was a salesman from Seville who "was pursued by one of the smaller ships, which disappeared as observer entered village." The report described another sighting from that day, fifty miles to the south at the Gulf of Cadiz. In this case, the chauffeur of the President of the Cadiz Provincial Commission was driving on the highway at 3 a.m. when he saw a "luminous, metal-like" object which "moved upward with great brilliancy." As he approached it, he felt a "strange sensation." His car then came to a near stop, "wavering back and forth like a feather."

The next day in Cordoba, two teenagers saw a "round, luminous, pink [object], not very large." The report stated the object "came with great speed at the two children, who fled behind a lamp-post. Being further pursued, they ran into a house. Object ascended and flew away."

The Defense Attache papers also describe a close encounter from the night of March 26-27 in Valdehijaderos (about 100 miles west of Madrid). A truck driver claimed to see "three silver ships on the highway with light similar to floodlight." Figures approached him, he ran, they followed. He threw himself onto the road, and they approached to within six feet. The witness saw that they were tall (two meters, or six and a half feet), had arms and legs, but he could not see their faces. They returned to their ships and left. The next day the police investigated and found a hole in the ground, which the truck driver claimed he had not made. More sightings in Cordoba were mentioned for March 27 and 28, but with little detail.

On March 30, in Hombreiro, Lugo, the Defense Attache papers describe a "blinding light from hovering object, car engine quit, lights went out. Object flew away with whistling sound, car then functioned normally." On the morning of April 4, at the northern town of Estrada, two 12-year-old girls saw a "metallic, noiseless [object], size of a bus, [with] a reflector in turret. Grey or aluminum in color." The object "stopped a few seconds about 10 or 12 meters from the ground and 100 meters from observers, then went out of sight."

Close encounters were reported from San Pedro on April 11, and Herrera de Alcantara on April 14 (involving a Professor, his wife, and a student). Then, on April 15, came an intriguing report from the Straights of Gibraltar, between the towns of Ceuta and Algeciras. Passengers on a ferry between the two cities saw a "round intense torch-like light. . . . Rose out of the water near a huge rock, traveled at low altitude, then fell into the water again. This happened twice." The same day, at the northwest coastal city of La Coruña, a newspaper photographer took four photos of a round UFO, which were published in a local newspaper. Another photograph was taken on the 21st at Hogar de Arriola (Malaga) of a triangular or conical UFO, which also appeared in a local newspaper.

Fewer sightings appeared in May, but several involved groups of people who reported objects flying over their cars. One occurred on May 10 in Alto de Cabrejas (one of the few sightings from the eastern part of the country). Another such incident was reported on May 15 in Pedroche. Then, on May 22 on the small island of Ibiza, off the Mediterranean coast, the wife of a journalist photographed an object described in the U.S.

Date	Location	Description	Witnesses	Remarks
27 Mar 74 (morning)	Córdoba	Not available.	Construction workers.	N/A
28 Mar 74 (daytime)	Córdoba	Luminous.	School children.	Appeared over Córdoba Sierra and disappeared shortly thereafter very rapidly.
31 Mar 74 (early morning)	Vigo (4221AN-0084JW)	Red.	Group of nurses.	Moving up and down over the Vigo inlet, then UFO disappeared behind mountains of the Morrazo peninsula.
2 Apr 74 (night)	La Unión (3737N-00052W)	Luminous, circular.	Ten persons on night shift at mining company.	Disappeared suddenly after having been seen several seconds.
4 Apr 74 (morning)	La Estrada (4221N-00829W)	Metallic, noiseless, size of a bus, had a reflector in turret. Gray or aluminum in color.	Two 12-year-old girls.	Stopped a few seconds about 10 or 12 meters from the ground and 100 meters from observers, then went out of sight.
11 Apr 74	San Pedro (4322N-00829W)	Oval, had no vapor trail.	Resident of San Pedro.	Was traveling at approximately 4,000 kilometers per hour, in sight for about 8 seconds.
14 Apr 74 (2 a.m.)	Herrera de Alcántara (3936N-0072AW)	Rhomboid, formed by luminous, heavy lights. In upper lefthand part there was a pink-yellowish semicircle which became a circle as UFO came near ground level. Student claims he heard a prolonged noise like that from an old alarm	Professor, his wife and a student.	Was observed at ground level from a distance of 300 meters for 5 or 6 minutes, then flew northeast.

One page of the U.S. Defense Attache files on Spain, 1974.

Defense report as "somewhat like a top. . . Remained stationary in space for some time, then rose and disappeared."

In June, more reports of tall alien figures appeared. On the 14th in Medellin, a "pot-shaped" craft hovered over a farmhouse while three tall beings with helmets were visible in a turret at the top of the vehicle. Although it was 4:30 a.m., the craft illuminated the area "like day." The defense report described an event in Caceres on the 16th in which a motorist was pursued for several miles at high speed by an object giving off "brilliant light." Three tall figures were seen standing inside the object. When the witness turned off his car lights, the object moved away. When he turned them on again, the object rapidly approached to some 70 meters over his car, following him home until he turned off his car lights again, whereupon it slowly flew away.

It is not clear what the U.S. military thought about all this. The reports were taken from newspaper clippings and forwarded to the Pentagon, "strictly for information of those parties interested." American intelligence specialists did find it "of interest" to report that in April, "teams of extra sensory perception specialists held a meeting for the purpose of scientifically studying the UFOs seen in that vicinity. Results of this meeting unknown." The U.S. military's interest in matters psychic extended beyond mere spectating, but was already moving along at high speed, as we shall see. On occasion, the "remote viewers" of the U.S. defense community even seemed to be bumping into aliens.

In addition to the cases in the official documentation from Spain are some unconfirmed ones from elsewhere in Europe, reported years later. A disturbing one concerns a British defense facility in the town of Frimley, near London. This was the Marconi facility, which dealt with classified radar-related defense projects. While at work in April 1974, a military employee learned that a break-in had occurred the night before. Initially, she knew only that the guard on duty suffered a nervous breakdown, was taken to an unnamed hospital, and not seen again. Later, she overheard a discussion in her supervisor's office and many years later repeated it "near verbatim" to Nick Redfern: "We have no way of keeping these beings out; we just don't know what to do next. If they can get in here, they can get in anywhere." She said she learned that the guard had seen an alien sifting through files and papers. A blue light emanated from its helmet, and the being quickly dematerialized before the guard's eyes.[20]

Another unconfirmed incident from April 1974 is said to have occurred at the Incirlik Air Base in Turkey, about 20 miles northeast of Ankara. This was during a period of tension between Greece and Turkey. A U.S. serviceman claimed that while on duty at 3 a.m., he saw "a white glowing UFO hover[ing] silently over the nuclear storage area . . . approximately 500 feet above the ground." The object appeared to be the size of a small car and hovered for about an hour. Then it silently accelerated towards the city of Adana. The witness was about two miles away from the object, but other security personnel were closer. The following day they told him that the only measures taken "were to set up their M-60 machines guns, and that they were not to fire on the object unless it initiated a hostile act."[21]

To be sure, April 1974 was an interesting month in the ufological history of Europe.

Analyzing the wave as a whole is challenging, if for no other reason than the inability to confirm some of these events with official government records. While the U.S. Defense reports do mean something, they are in the final analysis derived from newspaper clippings. Of course, one may ask why U.S. intelligence personnel took the time and effort to forward such reports to the Pentagon. Someone felt they were worthy of note. In addition, there is a consistency among many of these cases which transcends national borders, and the quality of at least some of these witnesses appears to have been high.

A word on the value (or lack thereof) of uncorroborated independent testimony might be in order at this point. The UFO phenomena does not usually afford researchers the luxury of restraining the observed objects for laboratory study and universally applicable protocols. Sometimes all one has to work with is a reported observation, and this often includes military reports. Different people have different thresholds of what constitutes valid data. Some people discard all testimony that lacks official, government sanction. Others discard all single-witness accounts. Others discard cases lacking physical evidence – something you could hold in your hand, for instance. Others eliminate cases that seem too strange, or simply "impossible."

But the UFO phenomenon *is* too strange by conventional wisdom, and often involves solely the claim of a reported witness. If one chooses to consider such reports worthy of study (and this author does) then the value of the report often comes down to the quality of the witness and the competence of the investigator. In the case of the alleged intrusion of the British defense installation, we have at least the benefit of an in-depth interview performed by a serious researcher. This surely is better than an anonymous posting to an Internet site, such as the alleged incident in Turkey. Both cases may be true, or neither may be. The same applies to the other cases from this wave. Yet, their credibility as *something* anomalous is enhanced by common features they share with each other, as well as with prior cases. Seen in this light, it is fair to say that something important was going on in Europe during the spring of 1974.

Such a conclusion is amplified by the statement of Spanish General Carlos Castro Cavero, divisional general commanding the air zone of the Canary Islands. In June 1976, he told journalist J. J. Benitez from *La Gaceta del Norte* that UFOs were being taken seriously at high levels. The Spanish Air Force, he said, had about twenty cases that were "thoroughly inexplicable." This included Air Force pilot encounters. He also made the statement that "the nations of the world are currently working together in the investigation of the UFO phenomenon. There is an international exchange of data." This is an astonishing admission from a general of a

NATO country, on par with Robert Galley's remarks from 1974. Cavero said that "maybe when this group of nations acquire more precise and definite information, it will be possible to release the news to the world." Of course, one might ask how many years, or decades, would be required before "more precise and definite information" would be obtained, particularly when the general had just admitted that there was a secret, international, collaborative program regarding UFOs. Presumably these intelligent people had been working together for some time by then.

Cavero offered his personal belief that "UFOs are spaceships or extraterrestrial craft." He even described a personal daylight sighting of a UFO at his ranch near Zaragoza. The event lasted for more than an hour. "It was an extremely bright object, which remained stationary there for that length of time and then shot off towards Egea de los Caballeros, covering the distance of twenty kilometers in less than two seconds. No human device is capable of such a speed."[22]

ET in the Himalayas?

Generally speaking, until the 21st century, African and Asian UFO sightings had been little more than addenda to the events reported in more developed parts of the world. Undoubtedly, this is due more to industrial development than anomalous activity, translating into better reporting systems for witnesses, although there is also good reason to hypothesize that UFO occupants are interested in human technology. Statistician Donald Johnson, Ph.D., of CUFOS, for example, conducted a study to determine whether a relationship existed between UFO sightings and nuclear facilities. He concluded it did.[23]

During the first half of 1974, there were a few interesting reports emanating from the world's two largest continents. Mostly, these were from more developed regions: a March 17 aerial encounter by a TWA airliner over Taiwan[24]; an unusual crash of a Japanese F-4E Phantom in June which appears to have been related to an encounter with a bright UFO;[25] a close encounter and possible abduction case in Rhodesia (modern Zimbabwe) in late May.[26]

But it was the June 15 sighting of a UFO by a Tibetan mountain climber in the Himalayan Mountains that could be the most interesting of the Third World at that time. While inspecting a rock formation on the upper slopes of Mount Dahjar, Keo Wha Unan emerged from a cave to see a "silvery disc hovering behind a crest of high rocks." Keo said the object was "windowless . . . shiny, silvery, spotless." It looked perfectly smooth, with no ridges or protrusions. Keo saw the object hovering about four feet off the ground, surrounded by three "humanoid" beings. They appeared to be gathering snow, ice, and rocks and putting them in their craft. He observed the activity for five minutes, when "they climbed aboard by means of a ladder-like device that descended from the center of the thing (saucer), and when they were inside, the machine started to hum." The object rose a little bit into the air and "like a flash, shot straight up and disappeared behind a variety of thick snow clouds."[27]

The story is interesting on its own merits, but also because of the history of the region. Tibetan UFO stories go back into ancient times. One of the earliest sightings of the twentieth century occurred nearby in 1926. In the 1990s and into the 21st century, reports of UFO activity in the Himalayas would increase, accompanying rumors of permanent underground alien activity.

Landed UFOs in Albuquerque

While Western Europe was undergoing *actividad extraña* in 1974, little of interest was recorded by America's four major UFO organizations. However, a significant event appears to have occurred near Albuquerque, New Mexico, on May 28, 1974, although it was barely remarked upon at the time. On that clear and sunny day, a resident of Albuquerque observed a large glowing object moving across the western face of the Sandia Mountains. It was so bright that he could not discern its structure. He opened his window and heard no sound coming from it. The object appeared to land on a nearby hill where it remained for over an hour. It then shot into the air and vanished. Some time later, an Albuquerque woman looking out her kitchen window saw an object cruising along a northerly course over the low hills near her home. She called to her husband to watch it with her; together they watched the object now flying easterly at an altitude of about two thousand feet.

NICAP, although no longer a very active investigative organization, did look into this incident. The couple told the investigator that they believed the craft was flat, "like viewing a coin on end," and perhaps 50 to 75 feet in diameter. It was greyish and did not reflect the afternoon sunlight. It appeared to be rotating around a central axis. NICAP checked with county police and learned that no reports were made.[28]

Years later, TV producer and investigative journalist Linda Moulton Howe delved further into this matter, discovering that the area had experienced a number of sightings of unusual aerial vehicles during the month of May 1974. She also interviewed several Albuquerque eyewitnesses who reported startling accounts from the date of May 28, 1974.

Three young men, each about twenty years old, were camping fairly high up on the Sandia Mountains. Around noon, through binoculars, they watched an area between Menaul and Copper, on the dirt trail side of Tramway Boulevard. There, they saw a silver-white disc resting on the ground. Next to it was a silver triangular-shaped craft that had odd rune-like symbols cut into one of the pointed ends. These men ended up in military detainment at Kirtland AFB, where they were interrogated by civilian intelligence agents wearing suits. The interrogators asked many questions about the symbols and told the young men they had seen a "Soviet incident," and were to keep their mouths shut. To back up their threat of retaliation if the men ever talked, the agents stressed that their communications would be monitored at all times, including phone calls. Only one of the three was willing to talk with Howe in 2008, thirty-four years after the Sandia event.

Howe's investigation also led her to a family which saw a large, glowing, football-shaped disc later that evening, at around 9 p.m. The object was moving from the south of Albuquerque to the northeast, slowly and steadily downward to the Sandia Mountain foothills on the eastern edge of the city. Excited, they got into their car and followed dirt roads off Menaul and Tramway Boulevard as far as they could go, until they were stopped by a state patrol officer. Beyond the officer, the family was astonished to see the glowing craft hovering low to the side of a rocky hill. It was surrounded by armed military security personnel which faced the object.[29]

Was this a recovery – or operation – of one or more UFOs?

All Quiet in the West

Other than the Albuquerque incident, very little UFO activity of any significance was recorded in the western hemisphere. One of the few interesting American cases of the year took place on February 14, about 55 miles north of Ely, Nevada. This is close to Utah, and about 150 miles from the Nevada Test Site. Two brothers were transporting their parents' furniture in a U-haul truck when, at 4:15 a.m., they noticed a round orange object that seemed at first to pace them, and then to approach. They described feeling as though they had "been hit by a blast of wind or force field." The engine and lights went out, steering was gone, and – they claimed – the truck floated momentarily, came back down and coasted to a stop. Ahead of them to the left, just over a hill, they saw a large spherical object with a domed top and sharp wings. At the same time, a huge lighted object– perhaps the original orange object – approached. It was still fairly dark, so one brother directed his flashlight at it (although shining a flashlight at a bright object makes little sense). At this point the brothers had a sensation of intense isolation from the rest of the world which lasted for perhaps twenty minutes. The disjointed nature of their account leads to the conclusion that they either concocted one hell of a story, or else had an even more bizarre experience not fully related. In any event, their truck was badly damaged, and they eventually flagged down a passing driver. When a tow truck hauled it away, the rear wheels of the damaged truck fell off. Upon examination, it needed new tires, a new rear axle, new outside housing, and gears.[30]

Elsewhere in the west, a few odd air encounters occurred, such as a March 13 event on an Argentine Airlines flight, when an airliner en route from San Juan to Argentina was flanked by two glowing objects which paced it for several minutes, then sped away.[31] Another airliner sighting occurred in July near Quebec City, Canada, when a Scandinavian Airlines reported a triangular-shaped object; the Bagotville Airport in Quebec reportedly experienced radio frequency interference.[32] On October 10, another air encounter occurred over Newfoundland, when Canadian Armed Forces pilot John Breen reported being paced by a green, pulsating, triangular object. The object did not track on radar, but it reflected in the water below.[33]

A few UFO sightings by police agencies were reported during the year. Two came from the same area within a month of each other, describing what seemed to be the same object. On July 9 in Kingston, New York, an elliptical object with body lights hovered low and moved toward a police car. When an officer turned a spotlight on the object, a brilliant white beam lit up his patrol car. On August 11 in the nearby area of Tilton and Concord, New Hampshire, two police officers saw a domed elliptical object approach their car, then veer away.[34] There is no record as to how either police force dealt with these encounters.

Back in 1967 there had been an account of a strangely mutilated horse in connection with possible UFO activity. A few similar events were occasionally reported over the next couple of years. By 1974, mutilations were receiving more media attention. An Associated Press (AP) wire service story on April 30, 1974, mentioned that some people were connecting mutilations to UFOs, although most UFO researchers remained hesitant.[35] Another interesting cattle connection – although not a mutilation case –

occurred on September 1, 1974, in Langenburg, Saskatchewan, when a man saw five dome-shaped objects either landed or hovering low over a pasture. They took off in formation and climbed into the clouds. Cattle nearby were bellowing and broke through a fence. At the landing area were five rings of depressed grass swirled in a counterclockwise fashion; there was no evidence of heat or burning. The Royal Canadian Mounted Police looked into this case, and did not believe this was a hoax. "Something was there," one officer told the press. Other circles were found in the area later that month. Researcher Jerome Clark called this a "classic case."[36]

An interesting story from the autumn of 1974 was described in a June 1989 issue of *Soviet Military Review*, in an article entitled "UFOs and Security." The article stated:

> . . . a metal disk some 100 metres (sic) across approached a South Korean anti-aircraft short battery. The commander launched a Hawk guided missile which was immediately shot down by a 'white ray' from the UFO. A second ray was directed at the battery, melting the remaining two Hawk missiles into an unrecognisable (sic) mess.[37]

The story lacks confirmation from separate sources, but it is one of many that were reported in the Soviet Union during the period of openness that preceded the collapse of that government. It is comparable to the many stories from the West (both confirmed and unconfirmed) describing hostile encounters by military aircraft with UFOs.

In November, an interesting UFO event occurred at the Yakima Indian reservation, a place with a long history of anomalous sightings. This is in central Washington, not far from Mt. Rainier where Kenneth Arnold saw flying discs in 1947. The undated November 1974 sighting took place at about 8 p.m., when some people who were getting together for a visit saw a yellowish glowing object in the distance. Not thinking much about it, they went inside. Two hours later, some of them stepped outside to notice that the light was closer now, positioned on the ground, and more intense. No one knew what to do. At 11 p.m., as the visitors were leaving and everyone stepped out on the porch, they saw a cylinder suspended in the air only ten feet away from the porch and about fifteen feet above the ground. It was about three feet long and over a foot in diameter, in a vertical orientation, and slowly rotating clockwise. Two thirds up from the bottom of the cylinder, and projecting out at a 90 degree angle, was a long, narrow beam of light about 2 inches in diameter and 3 feet long. This went on for ten minutes. Not wanting to approach the object, everyone went back inside. Thirty minutes later, the object was gone. For years Yakima continued to be the scene of anomalous lights and objects.[38]

One final case from 1974 bears mentioning. This occurred on December 18, and is recorded in a U.S. Defense memo – courtesy of a Freedom of Information Act request a few years later. The document describes what could well have been a covert military exercise or experiment. In the region bordered by Pakistan, Afghanistan, and the Soviet Union, many witnesses saw a strange light. The memo stated that "a phenomenon appeared in the sky" near Peshawar, Pakistan, for about fifteen minutes that evening. It appeared as "an immense half ball of yellowish brown smoke silhouetted against the black sky." No one could tell how distant it was, or whether it was even over Afghanistan or the Soviet Union.[39] Some speculation followed that this might have been a barium cloud experiment. Eight days after this event, the area was struck by an earthquake.[40] Interesting, but not evidence of anything truly anomalous.

Nixon, Gleason, and Alien Bodies

The UFO phenomenon provides not only an endless supply of instances in which people see things that defy all common sense, but an endless supply of intrigue, as well. During any year, almost at any time, something interesting and important concerning the topic occurs out of public view, becoming yet another part of humanity's secret history. In such a context, the question arises as to what extent Richard Nixon can be connected to the phenomenon. As all Presidents before him, he never made any controversial statements on the matter during his time in office. There is, however, one Nixon UFO story worth noting.

Nixon was in Florida in February 1973. While there, he met with Jackie Gleason at the Inverness Golf and Country Club. The two men were friends, and Gleason had a deep interest in UFOs (including a collection of 1,700 books on UFOs and related topics). Some years later, Gleason's second wife, Beverly McKittrick, wrote an unpublished manuscript in which she claimed Gleason returned home very shaken that night. He told her that the President had taken him to a heavily secured area at Homestead AFB and showed him the remains of small aliens in a secret repository.

The story was certainly dynamite, and others tried to follow up. UFO researcher Larry Bryant filed a FOIA request with Homestead, asking to see documentation on the repository and Gleason's alleged visit. He received the reply that "no such records existed." Bryant also sent an advertisement to the Homestead base newspaper seeking to contact anyone who could provide information about alien bodies or Gleason's visit. The base public affairs officer prevented the publication of the ad.

McKittrick's claim was repeated by Larry Warren, who himself had witnessed a UFO at an American military base in Britain, the 1980 Bentwaters case. Warren said that Gleason told him the Homestead story in May 1986 during a private meeting. After a few drinks, Gleason said, "I want to tell you something very amazing that will probably come out some day anyway. We've got em!" "Got what," asked Warren. "Aliens!," said Gleason. He told Warren that near midnight, following Nixon's public appearance with Gleason, Nixon showed up at his house – alone, without secret service agents. The two drove to the far end of the Homestead AFB, to a well-guarded building. The security police "just sort of moved back as we passed them and entered the structure." They passed several labs, and then entered an area where Nixon pointed out wreckage from what he said was a flying saucer, enclosed in several large cases. Gleason asked if this was a joke. Apparently not.

They entered an inner room with six or eight glass-topped freezers. Inside, said Gleason, "were the mangled remains of what I took to be children." Upon closer inspection, he saw that some of the figures looked old and as though they had been injured. Gleason could not remember if the aliens had three or four fingers on each hand, but he was certain they were not human. For three weeks after the secret visit, Gleason could not sleep or eat. He later learned that the secret service had been "going absolutely crazy trying to find out where Nixon was."

UFO researcher Grant Cameron asked, how could the most protected man in the world elude his secret service detail? According to Lewis Merletti, the Secret Service Director under President Clinton, the idea is nonsense, and only happens in the movies. However, Marty Venker, a secret service agent under Presidents Ford and Carter, believed otherwise. Venker described in his book how some Presidents were able to get some privacy. Nixon, said Venker, felt almost suffocated by his secret service, often tried to elude them, and even tried to cut his protection in 1973.[41]

Cameron, whose "Presidential UFO" website analyzes the modern American Presidency in relation to UFOs, concedes that there is no proof that Nixon and Gleason saw alien bodies at Homestead. "But everything checked out indicates it could very well have happened."[42]

The Ronald Reagan UFO Sighting

Although the event has been ignored by academic historians, Ronald Reagan had a genuine UFO sighting as Governor of California in 1974. Reagan and his pilot Bull Paynter both made statements; although neither supplied a specific date, the event probably occurred during the summer. Looking out the window of a Cessna Citation between 9 and 10 p.m., Reagan saw a bright white light zigzagging across the sky. He asked Paynter if he had ever seen anything like it. Paynter had not. "Let's follow it!," said Reagan, which they did for several minutes. Then, according to Reagan, "to our utter amazement, it went straight up into the heavens. When I got off the plane I told Nancy all about it . . . And we read up on the long history of UFOs." Indeed, a week later Reagan sat next to Norman Miller of the *Wall Street Journal* while on another flight, and told him about the sighting with great animation and enthusiasm. "Governor," Millar asked, "are you telling me that you saw a UFO?" As Miller later recalled the situation, Reagan realized that he was talking to a reporter. "This look crossed his face," said Miller, "and he said let's just say that I'm agnostic."

Bull Paynter gave more detail when he was interviewed about it. They were near Bakersfield, Paynter said, when they saw the object. "It appeared to be several hundred yards away," he said, "It was a fairly steady light until it began to accelerate, then it appeared to elongate. Then the light took off. It went up at a 45-degree angle at a high rate of speed. Everyone on the plane was surprised. Governor Reagan expressed amazement." Paynter told the others he did not know what the object was. "The UFO went from a normal cruise speed to a fantastic speed instantly. . . If you give an airplane power it will accelerate – but not like a hot rod, and that's what this was like." According to Paynter, he and Reagan discussed their UFO sighting "from time to time" in the following years, but they never filed a report "because for a long time they considered you a nut if you saw a UFO...."[43]

This story sat quietly for many years before it leaked out in 1988, as a footnote in a book dealing with Reagan's second Presidential term. The authors of that study learned of it from Norman Miller, who had never reported the conversation in the *Wall Street Journal* because he "could not figure out how to get a whole column out of it." This is an odd claim: even a brief statement from the current President on an exciting UFO encounter – one vastly more interesting than the Jimmy Carter sighting of 1969 – would merit worldwide attention. What seems more likely is that the *Wall Street Journal*, a newspaper very sympathetic to President Reagan during his eight years in the White House, simply decided that running such a story would be counterproductive. Certainly, Reagan's staff worked hard to conceal potentially embarrassing family tidbits from leaking to the public, whether it be Ronald (and daughter Maureen) Reagan's belief that a ghost inhabited the Lincoln Bedroom, Nancy Reagan's longtime reliance on astrology, or Ronald Reagan's 1974 UFO sighting.[44]

Reagan's interest in UFOs preceded his 1974 sighting. Another journalist, Bill Boyarsky of the *Los Angeles Times*, told of a conversation he had with Reagan in 1965. "We were looking up at the stars and Reagan told me he believed in flying saucers. He said he had a friend who'd actually seen one."[45]

Perhaps that "friend" was Reagan himself, for there is another story concerning a Reagan UFO sighting which allegedly took place not long after Ronald and Nancy were married in 1952. They were expected at a dinner party in Hollywood and showed up late, ashen and upset. They told the others that they had seen a UFO. In one version that was told to the author by a former friend of Reagan, they said an object landed in front of them on the road. Not much more is known of the story.[46]

When Ronald Reagan became President of the United States in 1981, he showed an unusual interest in the matter of UFOs, as well as all matters paranormal.

Political Crisis and Freedom of Information

Within the U.S., the important developments in 1974 were not ufological but political. Most important was the resignation of President Nixon on August 8, the only time an American President ever resigned from office. Nixon's resignation was a combination of Congressional authority reasserting itself against the Executive, and a probable ouster orchestrated by other elements within the American power structure.

By 1974, America had already come a long way toward replacing its traditional republican institutions with an unaccountable national security apparatus. Back in 1947, the National Security Act created an array of intelligence groups and executive bodies without active congressional oversight. This not only included the Central Intelligence Agency (CIA) and National Security Agency (NSA), but most military intelligence agencies. Several powerful intelligence agencies, such as the NSA and National Reconnaissance Office (NRO), existed for years without congressional knowledge. The war in Vietnam further weakened congressional authority. Not only were more than half a million U.S. troops fighting on the other side of the world without a legal declaration of war, but Congress had rubber stamped President Johnson's Gulf of Tonkin resolution, the *de facto* declaration of war, based upon intelligence that was deeply flawed and (in the opinion of some historians) intentionally deceptive.

When it became clear that the Vietnam War was a disaster, the backlash was strong. By the early 1970s came the release of the infamous Pentagon Papers, revelations of FBI "black bag" jobs, and ultimately the Watergate scandal, in which it became painfully obvious that the President had authorized an illegal break-in of the Democratic Party Campaign Headquarters. Watergate was in all likelihood allowed to occur, and quite possibly made to occur. Several key groups, not just Congress, benefitted from Nixon's downfall. Author Peter Dale Scott pointed out that media institutions such as the *Washington Post* and major television networks thought they were fighting for their lives and felt they had to take Nixon down. The CIA connection was also important. Nixon had never been happy with the CIA. In 1970, he unsuccessfully tried to overhaul the U.S. intelligence community, and in 1972 unceremoniously fired CIA director Richard Helms. The CIA probably infiltrated Nixon's infamous "plumbers unit" in the persons of E. Howard Hunt and James McCord. One observer remarked that the CIA was engaged in a 'coup d'etat in the making,' an elite battle at the summit of American politics.[47]

There was also a populist element in Nixon's downfall. The civil rights movement had already challenged long-established truths about how American society should be structured. Now open-government advocates added their voice in an attempt to bring "power to the people." An important result was the strengthening of the Freedom of Information Act (FOIA), as an amendment to the Privacy Act of July 4, 1974, during the death throes of the Nixon administration. Agencies were now instructed to release requested documents promptly and at reasonable cost. Each federal agency had to file an annual report on its FOIA requests to Congress, an important help for proper oversight. Citizens could also petition courts to render decisions on whether or not to release documents from agencies.[48]

FOIA soon disproved the longstanding denial of interest in UFOs by the CIA, FBI, and military agencies. Eventually, tens of thousands of UFO-related documents were released from America's national security establishment. While there would be no single confirmed document proving beyond a shadow of a doubt the existence of an alien presence on Earth – the ultimate memo from the President, for instance – there would be several that were certainly suggestive. In particular, several documents described violations of sensitive air space by unusual and extraordinary objects which, often enough, looked like flying saucers. FOIA enabled UFO researchers to demonstrate that such military encounters occurred quite a few times.

But FOIA also had limitations. Congressional oversight and agency reporting were usually superficial. Funding was poor and compliance worse. As one journalist put it, "FOIA simply doesn't work most of the time . . . . There are few news organizations and reporters who have the patience, money, and determination to work through what seems an inevitable series of appeals, requests, and other roadblocks." UFO researchers found the same problems. During the 1990s, Barry Greenwood, a researcher with extensive FOIA experience, commented that "requests now often take months or even years to fulfill. High search fees have been levied, from hundreds of dollars to as much as a quarter of a million dollars."[49] A new tradition of government intransigence tried to prevent the release of information through hundreds of court cases. Paul McMasters, a former national president of the Society of Professional Journalists, pointed out that "with few exceptions, court decisions have favored the agencies, especially in cases that involve personal privacy or national security."[50]

UFO cases come to mind, as they so frequently have involved national security. Adding to the problem were a number of obvious exemptions to FOIA, such as the NSA and North American Air Defense (NORAD).[51] Of the thousands of released UFO documents, only the smallest handful had been classified at the level of "Top Secret," such as several infamous blacked-out NSA documents. Most of the released documents were classified at lower levels, such as "Secret," "Restricted," or "Confidential." While these still had value, it became evident that the truly sensitive documents were simply not being released. Especially so since one 1949 FBI document stated that the topic of flying saucers was considered "top secret by Intelligence Officers of both the Army and the Air Forces."[52]

Thus, as UFO researchers would learn over the next few years, FOIA was no magic bullet. But such disappointment still lay in the future. In 1974, there was much to hope for.

Behind the Scenes: The Elite Organizations

Richard Nixon's resignation resulted in the ascendency of Gerald R. Ford to the White House. It was the first time a man who was not elected to either the Presidency or Vice Presidency had ever become President. Nixon had selected Ford for his Vice President when Spiro Agnew resigned amidst a corruption scandal. Ford had previously received scant public attention;

he was known primarily as a Congressman from Michigan who had been a member of the 1966 Warren Commission. That charade had been headed by former CIA Director Allen Dulles to investigate the assassination of President John F. Kennedy.

Gerald Ford was a man with the right connections, deeply connected to people and groups at the pinnacle of world power. He was a 33rd Degree Freemason, a member of the influential Council on Foreign Relations (CFR), and had attended five annual meetings of the secretive and powerful Bilderberg Group (1962, 1964, 1965, 1966, and 1970).

Gerald Ford, 38th President of the U.S.

What were these organizations? Did the Bilderbergers, CFR, and other closed societies exert an important covert influence on the American and world politics, as has often been alleged? Is the answer relevant in understanding the UFO phenomenon and cover-up? The unsettling answer to both questions appears to be 'yes,' although finding direct links to the UFO cover-up will not be easy.

The CFR, founded in 1921, is generally considered to be the most powerful private organization to influence U.S. foreign policy. Founded by Elihu Root (the attorney for J. P. Morgan), it has represented the wealthiest and most powerful interests in the U.S. Indeed, the presence of the Rockefeller family has been the most important feature of the organization's history. John D. Rockefeller, Jr. was a major benefactor. The Rockefeller Brothers Fund provided major funding for decades. David Rockefeller joined the Council as its youngest-ever director in 1949 and was chairman of the board from 1970 to 1985. The CFR's internal think tank is called The David Rockefeller Studies Program.

The CFR describes itself as "an American nonpartisan foreign policy membership organization," with the mission of "promoting understanding of foreign policy and the United States' role in the world." Journalist Joseph Kraft, a former CFR member, more accurately described it as coming "close to being an organ of what C. Wright Mills has called the Power Elite – a group of men, similar in interest and outlook, shaping events from invulnerable positions behind the scenes." CFR members have dominated every Presidential administration since the days of Franklin

Delano Roosevelt, whether Republican or Democrat.

The main thrust of all CFR policies is the promotion of a stable international order under a single governing body. Whether one calls it conspiracy or not, calling it a form of "world government" is fair enough. Prominent CFR members have often stated the matter openly. James P. Warburg, a major banker, economist, and member of FDR's administration, told a Senate Foreign Relations Committee in 1950 that "we shall have world government whether or not we like it. The only question is whether world government will be achieved by conquest or consent." A half century later, David Rockefeller was saying the same thing:

> Some even believe we are part of a secret cabal working against the best interests of the United States, characterizing my family and me as "internationalists" and of conspiring with others around the world to build a more integrated global political and economic structure – one world, if you will. If that's the charge, I stand guilty, and I am proud of it.[53]

Indeed, at least as early as 1976 if not earlier, the phrase "New World Order" was being used in connection with the goals of the Rockefeller family. Researcher Gary Allen wrote that the Rockefeller brothers themselves used this phrase to describe their global vision.[54]

The Bilderbergers are an international and more powerful version of the CFR, again dominated by David Rockefeller, but also with major influence by members of European royal families and the Rothschilde banking dynasty. Its first meeting was in 1954 at the Bilderberg Hotel in the Netherlands (hence the group's name), and was said to be founded by Prince Bernhard of the Netherlands, a man with prior connections to the Nazis and a major figure in Shell Oil. The group's true driving force was Joseph Retinger, a member of the London-based Polish government-in-exile during World War II and also – for what it is worth – a 33rd degree Mason. According to investigator Daniel Estulin, who has done extensive work on the Bilderbergers, Retinger wanted "to unite the world in peace" through the imposition of supranational, powerful organizations. Prevailing economic ideologies were irrelevant to Retinger. Multinational organizations could overcome any differences by dictating and applying economic and military policies.[55]

The Bilderberg Group is managed by a small nucleus, made up of a European Chairman, a European and American Secretary General, and a Treasurer. They invite only those with "special knowledge, personal contacts and influence in national and international circles, [who] can amplify the objectives and resources of the Bilderberg Group."[56] If by "resources" one can assume "money," then the Bilderbergers actively seek to increase their own wealth by influencing major geopolitical events and trends.

According to Estulin, "every U.S. President since 'Ike' Eisenhower has belonged to the Bilderberg Group, not that they have all attended the meetings personally, but all have sent their representatives."[57] The annual Bilderberg meetings are notorious for their absolute secrecy. Media coverage is absolutely off-limits, despite the regular attendance of important journalists (as participants). The gathering of 150 of arguably the world's most influential people is easily of equal or greater importance than a G-20 summit. Although it would be inconceivable for the G-20 to convene without any press coverage, the Bilderbergers have avoided it for more than half a century.

Returning to the Presidency of Gerald Ford, it may now seem unsurprising that he selected New York State Governor Nelson Rockefeller to be his Vice President. Perhaps in retrospect it is also less of a surprise that Gerald Ford was subject to not one but two assassination attempts during his short tenure as President. They are interesting as a study in contrasts. On September 5, 1975, Lynette "Squeaky" Fromme, a one-time member of the Charles Manson "family," approached Ford in California at Sacramento's Capitol Park, dressed in a red robe and armed with a .45 Colt automatic pistol. Although she pointed the gun at Ford with four rounds in the gun's magazine, none were in the firing chamber. She later told the press that she had deliberately ejected the cartridge before leaving home that morning; it was later found by investigators in her bathroom.

Fromme's "non-assassination attempt" became the one that the public remembered best. In fact, a real assassination attempt occurred against Gerald Ford later that month in San Francisco on September 22 by another woman, Sara Jane Moore. Moore was 40 feet away from Ford when she fired a shot at him with a .38 caliber pistol. The bullet missed Ford because a bystander pulled her to the ground. She later said she was trying to expose America's "phony system of government" by elevating Nelson Rockefeller to the Presidency. She made strange hints of a conspiracy – which somehow was not a conspiracy – during an interview with *Playboy* in June 1976.

> [There is] a part that I don't think I can talk about. I just haven't figured out a way to talk about it and protect everyone. I'm not saying that anyone helped me plan it. I'm not just saying that there are other things. . . which means there are other people, though not in terms of a conspiracy. There are areas I'm not willing to talk about for a lot of reasons.

Moore's statement was positively odd. Were there other people involved, or not? She did not say, but the Rockefeller connection must give one pause. Adding to the mystery was the action of U.S. District Judge Samuel Conti, who sealed all the evidence pertaining to the case.[58] Perhaps this was all part of the Rockefeller family's plan to get Nelson into the White House, something they are alleged to have whimsically planned for many years. Or, perhaps it was just "one of those things."

Whether or not traditional UFO researchers have seen the relevance, such "behind-the-scenes" groups as the Bilderbergers, the CFR, and the Trilateral Commission have an important influence on conventional geopolitics. If there is a UFO cover-up of any sort, one must accept the possibility that they wield an unseen hand here, too. Logically, a topic of such extraordinary and far-reaching implications as this one would be of great interest to them. One can imagine that they would also be interested in deriving as much profit from it as possible.

The Emenegger-Sandler Intrigue

1974 appears to have been the year of an abortive attempt at releasing a ufological bombshell on the public, by none other than the United States Air Force. The story goes back to the previous May (1973), when film makers Robert Emenegger and Alan Sandler were making a UFO documentary. The two were contacted by Colonel Robert Coleman, a former spokesperson for the defunct Project Blue Book, and Colonel George Weinbrenner, who had previously commanded the Air Technical Intelligence Center (ATIC) at Wright-Patterson AFB.

The colonels told the producers that the government was planning to release UFO information to the public, and that this documentary would be the first step in that process. They said they could provide extraordinary documents and images, including film footage of an alien accompanied by an Air Force officer (the alien had survived a 1949 crash and was kept at a safe house in Los Alamos until it died in 1952), a memo discussing an encounter between six CIA officers and an alien by the name of "Affa," secret photos of UFOs taken by astronauts, and more. The colonels also promised 800 feet of film showing an encounter between three aliens and officials at Holloman AFB in New Mexico. This had allegedly occurred in May 1971 (although other testimony has placed a landing there in April 1964).

The colonels then took Emenegger and Sandler – still in May 1973 – on a tour of the CIA's National Photographic Interpretation Center (NPIC), and then the producers went to Norton AFB in California. While there, they met with Paul Shartle, former head of security and chief of requirements for the audiovisual program at the base. Shartle promised them that he would get them the Holloman footage for their documentary.

But then nothing happened. Months went by, the colonels never followed up, and the film makers were left wondering what happened. Meanwhile, they continued making their film. Finally, Emenegger received a call from Coleman, who told him that "the timing was politically inappropriate, due to the Watergate scandal." Emenegger went to Wright-Patterson to talk to Weinbrenner. Inside the colonel's office, Weinbrenner walked around and loudly complained about the "damn MIG 25s." Meanwhile, he walked to his bookshelf, picked out J. Allen Hynek's *The UFO Experience*, and showed Emenegger Hynek's personal dedication to Weinbrenner on the inside cover. As Emenegger understood it, Weinbrenner did not want to be overheard in a bugged office, but was "confirming the reality of the [Holloman] film."

UFOs: Past, Present, and Future was released in 1974. Because the Holloman footage was not forthcoming, the producers used stock footage of Holloman and an "elaborate drawing of the so-called aliens." The film showed a "landing" by aliens at a hypothetical military base while narrator Rod Serling said "let us look at an incident that might happen in the future, or perhaps could have happened already."

The film became the topic of discussion among researchers. Then, on a 1988 television documentary, "UFO Cover-up: Live!", Emenegger declared, "what I saw and heard was enough to convince me that the phenomenon of UFOs is real, very real." Shartle also appeared in that documentary and described the Holloman landing footage. He said it showed "three disc-shaped craft." He continued:

> "One of the craft landed and two of them went away . . . It appeared to be in trouble because it oscillated all the way down to the ground. However, it did land on three pods. A sliding door opened, a ramp was extended, and out came three aliens . . . They were human size. They had odd grey complexions and a pronounced nose. They wore tight-fitting jump suits, thin headdresses that appeared to be communications devices, and in their hands they held a translator, I was told. The Holloman base commander and other Air Force officers went out to meet them . . . "

Another tidbit from Shartle and Emenegger was that 12 seconds of the film used in the documentary had been actual film of the Holloman landing. The film "slipped through the security net," said Shartle.

What do we make of this story? UFO researcher Grant Cameron, who looked into this extensively, believed that this was in all likelihood an abortive attempt at some form of UFO disclosure by government insiders. Since there was no public pressure on the government to do this, it was apparently all on insider initiative. He noted that several important groups were involved in covert funding for the film, such as the John MacArthur Foundation. Foundations have a long history of serving as fronts for intelligence operations to help protect identities. Cameron also pointed to a number of statements from the early- and mid-1970s claiming that there would soon be a release of UFO information: a 1974 APRO statement ("the government will release all its (UFO) information within the next three years,"); a *National Examiner* piece from late 1974 stating that " . . . the government is almost ready to release some of the [UFO] information it has reportedly withheld from the public"; and predictions by various UFO authors of "definite proof" being provided within the next year or two. The sum total of these separate facts and statements, argued Cameron, leaves the impression that there was a genuine behind-the-scenes effort by the government at UFO disclosure.

Perhaps, but it is also possible that something else was going on. Since the 1950s, the UFO field has been filled with a nearly non-stop barrage of rumors predicting an imminent government disclosure. It could be that this reflects an ongoing, start-and-stop, series of efforts to release the information, or wishful thinking combined with fantasy and disinformation, or a combination of both. There can be no question, however, that – like the claim of the apostle Paul regarding the imminent return of Christ – the claim of imminent government disclosure has become one of ufology's 'never ending stories.'[59]

On the other hand, a suggestive element about the Emenegger-Sandler film is how the drama seems to parallel some of the key events concerning Richard Nixon. Nixon and Gleason allegedly saw dead aliens at Homestead AFB in February 1973. Three months later, Emmeneger and Sandler were told that the government was planning to release UFO data. Later, during the collapse of Nixon's political power, the film makers were told that Watergate had made the incipient UFO disclosure initiative unviable at the moment. Could it be that Nixon himself gave an order to initiate the process of UFO disclosure? Could the order have come from elsewhere?

1975: An Extraordinary Year

Whereas 1974 had moments of great UFO activity as well as fairly quiet periods, 1975 was one of the most significant years in the modern history of the phenomenon. Several major themes emerge from a review of that year.

The UFO research community was busy. A new "psycho-social" school began to explain UFOs as psychologically and socially significant – but not as objectively real. Meanwhile, other researchers used the Freedom of Information Act to petition government agencies for UFO-related documents, an approach that increasingly focused on real events and real technology. Abduction research, long relegated to the peripheries, also became more prevalent. Indeed, several important abduction cases were reported during the year, including one of the most spectacular ever, the "fire in the sky" case of Travis Walton.

The phenomenon itself displayed all its variety and complexity during the year, and the United States was definitely where the action was. Many of the sightings involved U.S. military forces, including cases in which sensitive airspace was violated and attempted interceptions failed. 1975 also marked a large increase in the number of animal mutilations reported in the United States and Canada. The unusual animal deaths had been reported since the 1960s, often linked by rancher and law enforcement eyewitnesses to unidentified lights, beams, or aerial craft. But in 1975, another new development emerged that was linked to both animal deaths and UFOs: mysterious black helicopters. These were often black and unmarked, appearing at the scene where mutilations had either just occurred or were about to occur. They often flew along paths with little previous air traffic, and sometimes acted in scary ways – like hovering directly over people's homes in sparsely populated areas. No agency ever took responsibility for them, and their official status remains unknown.

The question arises whether secret military technologies could have accounted for the events of 1975. A "yes" answer would be only marginally less explosive than a "no," for it would have to explain why such extraordinary technology has remained secret for so long. It would also have to explain why such a secret operation would antagonize military forces charged with operating nuclear missiles. Finally, some funding questions would need to be answered, to wit: where would the money have come from to pay for such amazingly extravagant technology?

There is, of course, another line of speculation, that the dramatic UFO sightings of the year were caused by an entirely separate group. Presumably this would mean "alien," although – who knows? – could there be a rogue society with access to incredible wealth and technology? Or could aliens be using humans for their purposes in some capacity, perhaps breeding their own human population, perhaps enhancing them as appropriate for their specific needs?

The author concedes that above thoughts are quite candid attempts to speculate. Speculation is not a bad thing, however, as long as it proceeds from what is known. That is, from fact. With this in mind, let us tell the story of 1975.

1975: UFOs and the Spanish Military Again

Although the most remarkable UFO sightings occurred during the latter half of 1975, perplexing events happened year-round. Spain entered the new year with two UFO encounters by military personnel. The first occurred about ten miles from the town of Burgos, in the northern part of the country on the same longitude as Madrid. Four individuals who had been celebrating New Year's eve were returning to their military base academy. Although they had been enjoying themselves, none were drunk and one had taken no alcohol at all. At 6:45 a.m., the driver saw something fall from the sky, and he stopped the car. A quarter mile distant, the four men saw a luminous body "with the form of a truncated cone," which appeared to be hovering low over the ground. The object's light then went out and was replaced by four lights. The men were nervous, and the driver had trouble starting the vehicle before he drove away. Through the windows, the soldiers watched the lights, and noticed that two other vehicles behind them were near the phenomenon.

Spanish military searching for ground traces, 1/75

Almost immediately, the story reached the academy's director and his assistant, a Major Llorente. The Major met with the four men the very afternoon of January 1, and they traveled to the location. Behind a line of bushes they found a large spot of burned grass about 100 feet long and 15 feet wide. Local farmers said the burning of fields had been done several months before, but this looked recent. According to Major Llorente, the four men were "completely trustworthy soldiers." As to what they saw, "that is something neither they nor I, nor perhaps anyone, knows."[60]

One hundred miles to the east, on the night of January 2, Spanish military personnel had another UFO sighting. At 11:30 p.m., an officer and several soldiers saw two luminous, dome-shaped objects either land or hover very low on the firing range at Las Bardenas Reales near Zaragoza Airbase in Navarra, not far from the French border. The objects had orange and white body lights, and moved very close to ground at low speed. Suddenly they accelerated and climbed away. The Spanish Air Force investigation showed 'no contradictions' in the reports. The encounter is interesting also because it derives from declassified Spanish military UFO files.[61]

UFOs Over Montana Missiles

The rest of January was uneventful, but February included two unusual events from the Indian Ocean. On February 14, 1975, on the tiny French island of Reunion, about 450 miles east of Madagascar, a man named Antoine Severin claimed to see the landing of a small domed object in a field. He said that several small entities left the object and fired a white beam of light at him, knocking him out. For several days he had poor vision, impaired speech, and a medical diagnosis of shock. Police investigated the case and believed he was mentally sound and sincere. Many strongly supportive character statements on Severin were obtained by investigators. Apparently, no one involved in the case realized that the details were a perfect fit with a wave of sightings that occurred in France during the autumn of 1954, and was also reminiscent of a 1965 French case which involved claims of paralysis caused by a beam emitted by alien entities. The fact that Reunion was a French island leads one to wonder what cultural or linguistic connections were going on here. Is this an instance in which the witness knew of the prior cases and perpetrated a "copycat?" Based on the detailed investigation that took place, it would seem the answer is no, and that the experience was genuine.[62]

The case admittedly is not the strongest in the long history of UFOs. Yet, this type of craft has long been reported around the world. Just two weeks later, on February 26, on the other side of the ocean, an object similar in appearance was seen at Lake Sorell, Tasmania. A domed disc with an intense orange glow emitted a beam of light down on the lake. The witness said it sped away at "colossal speed."[63] These cases would be easier to dismiss if they were less common.

On March 2, 1975, another disc-shaped craft was reported, this time by a police officer in Phillips, Wisconsin. This was a five-minute-long event. The officer initially heard strange noises on his patrol car radio; in his words, "it went wild." He then saw a disc-shaped object with a rounded hump on its top and bottom, along with red and orange lights on its bottom edge. The officer estimated the object to be about 30 feet in diameter. When he directed his spotlight on the object, it rapidly ascended into the sky. The case was recorded by Dr. Richard Haines, a UFO researcher with expertise in interactions and apparent communication between human beings and UFOs.[64]

Throughout 1975 and well into 1976, UFOs were seen over many military bases. One such case took place on February 17, near Harlowton in central Montana. At around 9 p.m., several local officials from multiple locations saw a bright object hovering and maneuvering about 500 feet above the "Kilo One" Intercontinental Ballistic Missile (ICBM) base. One county deputy, Larry Clifford, reported that as he drove to within a mile of the object, it suddenly shot up to about 2,000 feet, stopped, and then disappeared into clouds. State game warden Gene Tierney was with Clifford during some of the observation. "I don't know what it was," he offered, "but it wasn't an aircraft." The county commissioner, Edgar Langston, observed the object through binoculars about 15 miles to the south. "It climbed at one hell of an angle, moving too fast and steeply to be an aircraft." He saw what looked like antennae at the top of the object. Deputy Herb Lynn saw the object plunge down and then shoot straight up, while another deputy, Russ Mull, was within a mile of the site and saw a bright object bobbing up and down. Base radar reported nothing, although security guards reported their own sightings.[65] If the base was truthful in stating that they tracked nothing on radar, then the object was combining astonishing performance with fully operational stealth technology. Moreover, if it was a military test, one might wonder why it was going on at an ICBM missile site.

Around this time, unusual craft were being seen in Algeria, tracked visually and on radar by the Algerian military, often with multiple witnesses. A March 7 report from the American embassy in Algiers, sent to U.S. Secretary of State Henry Kissinger, stated the "machines" were being

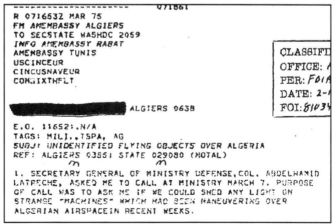

Segment of March 1975 Memo to Henry Kissinger

seen near military installations since January – that is, nearly two months. The objects were described as very bright, maneuverable, and were seen to land and take off. The Algerian military inquired about this with the U.S. embassy, which assured the Algerian military "categorically" that no objects whatsoever would be flying in Algerian air space without explicit permission of Algerian authorities. Still, the embassy checked with Kissinger to obtain a straight answer. Part of the Algerian curiosity was that the sightings coincided with the arrival of several American journalists who were covering the expected arrival of a balloon by the famous publisher and avid balloonist, Malcolm Forbes. However, the flight had been aborted at the last minute, so these sightings seemed rather puzzling. Unfortunately, no answers on this mystery have been released by the State Department.[66]

Enter the Triangles

A month later, a concentration of sightings took place in North Carolina. It was the first time that boomerang-shaped or triangular aircraft were seen in large numbers. To be sure, such shapes had been seen before. Occasional reports of triangular-shaped UFOs turned up as early as the 1950s in the records of NICAP and Project Blue Book. Victor Kean, a British researcher who initiated Project Triangle, found sightings of triangular craft from the early 1960s. Also, the reports of the National UFO Reporting Center include early sightings of triangular craft.

But the concentration in North Carolina from April 3 to April 9, 1975 was the first known "flap" of such sightings, encompassing 57 separate events. Most of these reports revealed unusual aerial characteristics, such as the ability to hover silently at low altitudes, instantly accelerate, and turn without banking. The objects were often seen at treetop level, often with a bright and maneuverable spotlight. Among the witnesses were 48 police officers.

The first report was from the town of Lumberton on April 3. At 1:45 a.m., three police officers saw a V-shaped object flying at 200 to 300 feet above the ground. It had a row of red lights on one side, a row of green lights on the other, and two spotlights. They contacted police in St. Paul's, 15 miles north, and told them to be on the alert for the object. Indeed, two officers in St. Paul's soon saw the object hovering a mere 20 feet above the ground, which they described as a blinding flash of light. One of the officers said it "just lit up the woods like a giant flashbulb." The object rose to about 300 feet and departed at an estimated speed of 200 mph. Although it was the size of a small aircraft, it made no sound. It left no traces in the fields and woods where it had been.

Later that morning, presumably the same object was reported in Hoke County, northwest of St. Paul's, near the Fort Bragg Military Reservation. Police there followed a lighted V-shaped craft as it traveled east into Cumberland County. It continued east into Sampson County to the town of Roseboro. An officer there named Jim Driver said the object passed 100 feet above him, slow and absolutely silent. When he got out of his car, a spot-

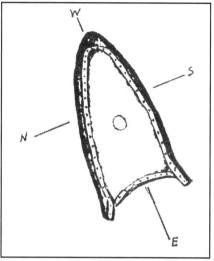

Police officer Moore's sketch

light came on and intensified. The craft then took off at high speed. The driver followed it to the town of Garland, 14 miles southeast, where he broke off the chase. The craft was next reported at Elizabethtown in Bladen County, 24 miles east of Lumberton. Another police officer confirmed the sighting there, and residents claimed the object's search lights lit the town like daylight. From there, the object moved south where it was seen in Columbus County five minutes before sunrise, at 6:55 a.m..

The next important night was Friday evening, April 4, as the dispatcher with the Robson County Sheriff's Department, Ronald Thompson, claimed he saw a flying object at 9:15 p.m. near Midway. He said the object approached from the southeast, then stopped and hovered about 300 feet away. He shut off his engine and flashed his headlights at the craft, and it flashed a searchlight back before taking off to the west behind some trees. The craft appears to have been the same as seen previously. It was silent, V-shaped, about 30 feet in diameter, illuminated from the inside, and with two searchlights. That same night at White Lake, police Chief Gary Moore reported that he was driving on a lakeside road when a lighted V-shaped object came down and lit up an area of about 500 feet on either side of the road, "like it was daylight." Moore stopped his car, got out, and studied the object through binoculars. He was dumbstruck: "I couldn't say anything for a second or two. I said if they want me, they're going to come and get me, but they didn't seem to want me." Several other drivers stopped by and watched the object through Moore's binoculars during the five minutes that the craft was hovering. Moore retrieved an airplane landing light that he carried in his patrol car, and pointed it at the object. "I blinked the light and it blinked back," he recalled. The object then moved west toward Lumberton, and Moore tried to follow it. For two miles he drove as fast as 85 mph, but the object pulled away, blinked its lights, and "went straight up and out" at about 200 mph. The encounters continued that night. At about 2 a.m. (Saturday, April 5), a state patrolman reported a slow-moving flying craft near the town of Saddletree. He got to within 300 yards of the object, and described it as having brilliant orange-red lights.

On April 6, Sunday, a daylight sighting and verified landing occurred at 5:15 p.m., although this object did not appear to be a triangle. Ray Strickland, a Pembroke State University campus policeman was driving with his wife and children just north of Pembroke, when his family saw five lights in a close circular formation, light red in color, traveling at about 50 mph and about 100 feet off the ground. It appeared to the family that the lights were about to crash into a nearby house. Instead, the lights descended into a potato field, and the Stricklands drove home to contact authorities. Dispatcher Ronald Thompson arrived from the sheriff's office with a photographer, but all that was left were five circular ash patches of a "strange blue color," each one about a foot in diameter, in a pattern similar to the formation the family had seen. Ted Phillips investigated the case for CUFOS and found other witnesses who told him they saw a chrome-like attachment between each light, so it was apparently a single object. Phillips was puzzled by several things, including what exactly could have caused such strange ash, and why no one had seen the UFO leave the site.[67]

Sightings continued throughout the week, primarily of triangular objects. Ronald Thompson said that as the county sheriff's dispatcher, he did not give any description of the UFO when notifying other units, and that he was "amazed" at the similarity of descriptions radioed back to him. There were no radar trackings

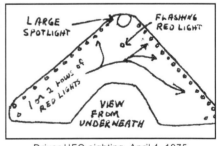

Driver UFO sighting, April 4, 1975

of unknown craft that week, according to the Fayetteville Airport. The Federal Aviation Administration (FAA) initially tried to explain the UFO sightings as a Piedmont Airlines Boeing Delta jet making test runs. Later the FAA revised the statement saying there were no airplanes in the area at the time of the sightings.

A detailed review of the North Carolina mini-wave of UFO sightings would seem to rule out naturalistic explanations such as unusual atmospheric phenomena. We appear to be talking about a craft of some sort. The question is "whose?" The top speed of the objects seen was well within the capabilities of ordinary light aircraft. But the reported shape of the object, combined with silent hovering and extremely rapid acceleration, make this difficult to explain in terms of what was then possible in aviation technology – officially, at least. More on this later.

May 3, 1975: A Forgotten Day

Although the North Carolina triangles received no major media attention, America's UFO research organizations did their best to investigate with limited resources. This was also true regarding a Mexican case from May 3, at Tequesquitengo Lake, near Mexico City. Shortly after 11:30 a.m., a young pilot named Carlos de los Santos, flying a Piper aircraft, reported being surrounded by three domed disc-shaped objects, one on each wingtip and the other beneath him (which struck the bottom of his plane leaving dents and scratches). This event was tracked by air traffic controllers who confirmed that unknown objects were near his plane. His controls failed, and the pilot felt his aircraft being pulled or lifted. The objects then departed – two of them making an incredibly sharp high-speed turn observed by the air traffic controllers. Representatives of CUFOS, MUFON, and APRO investigated the case, including J. Allen Hynek and Walter Andrus. All investigators found the young man to be credible.[68]

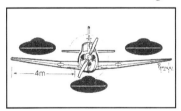

Artist's rendition of Mexican incident

On the very same day, in the same part of the world, a craft very close in description interfered with the operation of a truck. At 9:15 p.m., Alois Olenick was driving his pickup truck south of San Antonio, Texas, when a domed, disc-shaped craft approached and directed a spotlight down on him. Somehow it nearly knocked his truck off the road. When it hovered over his truck, its light became an intense red, and the truck's lights and engine died. It then passed by at enough of an angle that Olenick saw two non-human beings inside a transparent dome at the top. He stated:

> They appeared to be just as interested in me as I was in them. One of the occupants . . . had his hands on what looked like controls. He was looking up and away from me. The other occupant looked directly at me . . . and appeared to be observing me. I got a good look at both of them. They weren't human beings like we see here.

The beings were bald, seemed rather small, had slits for eyes, large noses, and greyish skin. The object left rapidly, and a strong wind rocked his truck.[69]

No one appears to have seen a connection between the two encounters of May 3, 1975, and they were quickly forgotten. Yet, it is not hard to imagine that, had they been promptly reported by American news agencies, the events could well have developed into a larger story – although the De Los Santos case did receive some press coverage in Mexico.

Incidentally, there was a strange follow-up to the De Los Santos case, one involving the legendary "men in black." Two weeks after the event, De Los Santos was scheduled to appear on a television program. As he drove on the highway to the interview, he was forced to the side of the road by two new-looking, black *Galaxie* limousines. Immediately, four large men jumped out of their cars and approached him. They wore black suits and had extremely pale skin. One of them held his hand to the door of De Los Santos's car and spoke rapidly in a "mechanical" tone. "Look boy," he said, "if you value your life and your family's too, don't talk any more about this sighting of yours." Too frightened to reply, De Los Santos turned around and went home.

He told a friend about the incident, who assured him everything would be fine, and convinced him to do another interview, which De Los Santos did. A month after the incident with the limousines, De Los Santos met with Hynek while the latter was in Mexico. Hynek then invited him for a follow-up interview in his hotel. De Los Santos got up early the next morning. On his way to the interview, he stopped at Mexicana Airlines to fill out an employment application. Then, on his way up the stairs at Hynek's hotel, he encountered one of the men who had threatened him. "You were already warned once," the man told him. "You are not to talk about your experience." This time De Los Santos spoke back. "All I did was accept an invitation. Dr. Hynek wants to know what I saw and I thought that maybe I could understand it better myself if I talked with him."

The man pushed him back several feet. "I don't want you to make problems for yourself," he said. "And why did you leave your house at six this morning? Do you work for Mexicana Airlines? Get out of here, and don't come back." De Los Santos promptly left.

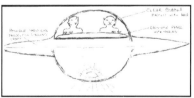

Sketch drawn from Alois Olenick's UFO encounter

Two years later, UFO researchers Jerome Clark and Richard Heiden interviewed De Los Santos and learned of his encounter with these strange men. While unable to prove his claim one way or the other, they acknowledged he seemed completely sincere. He remarked to them that the men "were very strange. They were huge, taller than Mexicans are, and they were so white." Strangest of all, said De Los Santos, is that he never saw them blink.[70]

More Military Encounters

On June 23, 1975, a British naval vessel was stationary off the west coast of Ireland in a thick fog, when a radar operator picked up an echo, presumably a surface vessel closing in on the ship. However, the object then accelerated to an "impossible" speed. The operator notified the captain, who filed a report. The case was investigated by the Ministry of Defence, later by private British UFO researchers. Temperature inversions and surface turbulence were ruled out as causes.[71]

An encounter by NATO personnel with a UFO occurred off the island of Sardinia at an unknown date in 1975, according to a report that was sent to retired Major Colman Von Keviczky from an anonymous captain in the NATO offices in Brussels. The report itself was dated November 3, 1976, and stated that soldiers of a missile battery were on duty on Sardinia when they saw a UFO hovering over the Mediterranean. Motion picture film of the object showed it to be a large domed disc, emitting light. Orders were given to fire missiles at it, but they appeared to hit "an invisible bulwark." This was surely a dynamite lead, and Von Keviczky pursued it. He contacted the Italian Ministry of Defense, which suggested that he contact Headquarters, Allied Powers Europe. There, he was informed in a letter signed by Brigadier General Fernando Buttelli that the film was not available due to the "national security policy of Italy."[72]

Another military encounter, taking place amid a spate of UFO sightings in northern California, was investigated by MUFON. On August 14 at 9:35 p.m., Major Claude Riddle was flying a helicopter at 900 feet while approaching the Stockton Metropolitan Airport. Suddenly, air traffic controller Joe Savage saw flashing lights closing in on a collision course. When he advised Riddle to take evasive action, the object turned an orange color and shot up to an altitude of 5,000 feet, where it hovered. Riddle meanwhile looked behind him and saw a light that seemed to be tailing his chopper a mile or so away. When he swung around, he saw it "shimmering like a diamond." He described it as big as a jetliner, oval shaped, and radiating a bright orange glow from the top. Two blue beams came out from the sides. Another air traffic controller, Dan Long, saw the glowing object through field glasses and said it looked "like a flying saucer."

As Riddle maneuvered his chopper to keep the object in sight, it drifted over the airport and hovered there. He said he "wasn't really interested in getting too close." After about five minutes of hovering, the object suddenly turned bright red and shot off. According to Riddle, "it was faster than anything I've ever seen. I've observed enough launchings to know we have nothing that can compare to the speed of this thing." An air controller named John Paul Ammirata watched through binoculars as the object departed. Within "five or six seconds," the object ascended to 260,000 feet and faded from view. If true, that would be nearly 30,000 mph. MUFON reported the details of the case, as did the sensationalist *National Enquirer*.[73]

1975: The State of Technology

How likely is it that some of the preceding sightings resulted from classified or experimental technology? One might assume that technologies which were experimental in 1975 would be operational and declassified by the 21st century. Not absolutely certain, of course, but a reasonable assumption for a reasonable world. Even now, there are no obvious candidates that would account for, say, the February 17, 1975 sighting over the Montana ICBM – a round object that could accelerate silently to an amazing speed from a hovering position, as well as avoid radar detection. Or the domed discs of May 3, which caused electro-magnetic disturbances and silently zoomed away.

The triangles over North Carolina during April are another story, although they too remain a challenge to explain. According to some UFO researchers and alleged insiders, triangular craft have been secretly manufactured since – depending on who makes the claims – the 1990s, 1980s, 1970s, or even 1960s. Several triangular craft have been suspected as culprits for the North Carolina sightings. One is the Aereon 26, manufactured by the Aereon Corporation in Princeton, New Jersey, which first flew in 1970. This was an experimental aircraft that combined the lifting capabilities of conventional aircraft with the lighter than air capabilities of a blimp. It was 26 feet long and powered by a piston engine which turned a propeller. Photographs of it show a lozenge-shaped fuselage with delta-shaped wings, giving a roughly triangular appearance. It did not require lighter-than-air buoyancy to take-off, although larger versions were envisaged to contain helium. The Aereon 26 did operate quietly and could fly at a slow speed, but apparently could not accelerate rapidly, as some of the reported triangles did. Frankly, its description and capabilities seem no better than a distant stretch.

Another possibility is the legendary, mythical – and possibly real – TR-3A, otherwise known as the Black Manta. It is said to be the size of a B-2 bomber, about 45 feet long and 15 feet high, with a 65-foot wingspan. British aviation writer Tim Matthews suggested that many of the triangle sightings of the later twentieth century were in all likelihood the TR-3A, or the much larger TR-3B, or some other deeply classified vehicle. Matthews argued that the TR-3B is a lighter-than-air vehicle using advanced composite materials in construction. They could be used for "covert insertion of troops, reconnaissance, moving of classified materials and other unspecified missions." The smaller version, he suggested, could be used as a stealthy, unmanned, combat aerial vehicle. While such triangles are probably capable of slow and silent maneuvering, the question of going from hovering to rapid acceleration – while remaining silent – presents a challenge even in the early 21st century. Also, it must be emphasized that although many aviation industry observers believe something like these craft do exist, their existence has never been officially acknowledged, and some analysts flat-out do not believe in them. Finally, even proponents do not claim the Black Manta or other triangular aircraft were operational as early as 1975.[74]

For now, we need not solve the riddle of the triangles; they will recur throughout this book. Let us also for the moment leave aside unverified claims of black-world breakthroughs in such exotic technologies as field propulsion (e.g. anti-gravity). This too will be explored later, particularly regarding claims of reverse-engineered alien technology at the Groom Lake facility in Nevada. For now, let us simply look at fully confirmed techno-logical research from the mid-1970s.

In the aviation field, the most interesting breakthrough was in stealth. As far back as the mid-1960s, the Northrop Corporation was looking for ways to reduce or even eliminate an aircraft's radar signature, otherwise known as Radar Cross Section or RCS. The solution was understood to come from new shapes and materials, but the devil is always in the details. Meanwhile, the Pentagon was less concerned about reducing RCS and more interested in developing aircraft that were quiet. In 1966, the Defense Advanced Research Projects Agency (DARPA), a Pentagon organization charged with pursuing advanced projects, funded a Lockheed program to develop ultra-quiet reconnaissance aircraft. Out of this came the QT-2, the Q-Star, and the YO-3A, which used silenced piston engines combined with large, low speed propellers. These aircraft proved to be very quiet on missions in Vietnam during the late 1960s and early 1970s.[75]

Stealth as we typically interpret it – the reduction or elimination of an aircraft's RCS – was still just an idea as the 1970s began. By then, however, a few aircraft designers and specialists were developing the radical idea of a "stealth fighter." As early as 1972, progress had been made in reducing RCS, and by 1974 the very word "stealth" was secret.[76] By 1975, DARPA asked General Dynamics and Northrop to propose designs for an ultra-low RCS aircraft, but Lockheed won the day with an unsolicited proposal for an aircraft design "like a cut diamond" whose unusual shape scattered radar signals. In the summer of 1976, at Groom Lake in Nevada, Lockheed made a breakthrough with the Have Blue demonstrator. This aircraft achieved the RCS of a ball bearing – an eighth of an inch in diameter. With that breakthrough, every defensive system in the world, including that of the United States, became obsolete. Within a year, Lockheed developed the basic design of the F-117 Nighthawk, the world's first stealth fighter.[77]

Stealth had not really been possible until the mid-1970s – speed and performance had always been its natural enemies. An unconventional design could reduce RCS, but it also hampered the aircraft's performance, and the trade-off never seemed worth it. Lockheed could take the path it did because advances in computing technology finally made it possible to "fly-by-wire." That is, on-board computers could make enough adjustments each second to stabilize even an aircraft with an unconventional design.[78]

What is true of the stealth fighter should also logically be true of the triangles. That is, if fly-by-wire was not possible until the mid-1970s, then realistically the triangles should not have been practical due to their inherently unstable design. The first widespread appearance of the triangles in 1975 would seem – just barely – to be within the timeframe of an operational fly-by-wire system. Still, it seems unlikely that such technology was mature enough by 1975 to have accounted for many of the UFO reports generated during the first half of that year. And the best was still yet to come. Of course, what one makes of the scattered triangle sightings of the 1960s, to say nothing of other types of UFOs such as flying saucers, is another matter entirely. Indeed, UFOs had a long history of radar invisibility going back through the 1940s and 1950s. Could secret U.S. stealth technology have accounted for that?

Stealth was not the only story in aviation circa 1975. Some of the most advanced prototypes at that time were the Northrop YF-17 (the progenitor of the Navy's F/A-18 Hornet) and the Rockwell B-1A bomber. In January 1975, the USAF announced the F-16 as the winner of its lightweight fighter technology evaluation program.[79] Each of these aircraft are triumphs of engineering and innovation, although none could be confused for UFOs. The Air Force, in fact, had at this time limited funds with which to develop new weapons systems. Money flowed much more liberally during the 1980s under President Reagan, but for now funds were relatively tight. According to an official history of the United States Air Force, new weapons systems during the 1970s were a rare event, and "older systems such as the B-52 required [the Air Force] to modify them continuously to keep them in service."[80] This is simply one more argument against the likelihood that a major breakthrough occurred in the mid-1970s which allowed for the advent of a true "flying saucer" technology.

There were a few people at this time studying more exotic means of getting objects into the air. One of these was Eric Laithwaite, Emeritus Professor of Heavy Electrical Engineering at Imperial College London, who is credited with the development of the "mag-lev" rail system in the 1960s. In 1974, Laithwaite demonstrated to the prestigious Royal Institution the apparent weight loss of a heavy gyroscope apparatus, weighing over fifty pounds. He struggled to lift it even to waist-height, but when an electric motor rotated the wheel at high speed, he was able to lift it with one hand, without any apparent effort. It appeared that his apparatus had somehow lost weight. For the first time in two hundred years, the Royal Institution refused to publish its proceedings. In the words of one writer, "in an unprecedented case of academic Stalinism, the Royal Institution simply banished the memory of Professor Laithwaite, his gyroscopes that became lighter, his lecture, even his existence."[81]

The real issue is not the small mindedness of scientists and academicians. Rather, we may wonder how likely it is that deep-black programs, far removed from the public oversight, might have pursued an interest in apparent phenomena such as this. Let us recall a statement issued on September 10, 2001 – one day before the most infamous date in American history – by U.S. Secretary of State Donald Rumsfeld. Speaking of the need to reform the Pentagon's wasteful spending, Rumsfeld made the astonishing statement that, "according to some estimates we cannot track $2.3 trillion in transactions."[82]

When one considers that the FY 2001 budget of the Department of Defense was $310 billion, the mind reels. This is approximately *seven and a half times* the amount of the official annual budget. Jim Minnery, of the

Defense Finance and Accounting Service, added, "we know it's gone. But we don't know what they spent it on."[83] Aside from the simple question of how is it even possible to lose that much money, it should be evident that such a figure cannot accrue overnight, but must be the product of a long process. In all likelihood, some of this money slipped away during the 1970s. It is surely plausible that a large sum of unvouchered money went into "deep black" scientific research and development programs, perhaps more exotic than stealth. Such a discussion brings us inevitably to the matter of the "black budget." More on this later.

As far as we can tell, aviation technology circa 1975 does not appear to explain the key UFO sightings of the time. Perhaps we should qualify this statement by changing it to "official aviation technology." Even so, the behavior of the UFOs is difficult to square with the testing of classified or experimental technology. While we acknowledge the possibility that human technology may be behind the UFO events of 1975, we are still left with (a) the lack of hard evidence supporting such a conclusion, and (b) the nagging feeling that such an explanation has gaping holes. Something more extraordinary appeared to have been at work.

The Nazi UFO Connection

There is one especially intriguing twist to the idea of man-made UFOs. This is the "Nazi connection," an idea that has lurked in the background of UFO research for many years. It is an idea that took a long time to germinate. During the 1950s and 1960s, it was still very much a *faux pas* to discuss post-war collaboration with Nazis. Project Paperclip, the American operation to bring in Nazi scientists and intelligence experts, was a potentially explosive secret. The U.S. intelligence community gave these men new identification papers and backgrounds, hiding them not just from the American public, but the U.S. State Department (which made it a felony to bring Nazis into the United States). Britain and the Soviet Union were also involved in this activity. The fact that such individuals had reprehensible political beliefs did not stop these nations from recognizing their ability to contribute to the post-war geopolitical chess game.[84]

From the beginning of the UFO phenomenon there had been specula-tion that the objects were some sort of secret project, whether American or Soviet. This was logical. The Wright brothers had flown a mere half-century before, and science fiction had given the world Buck Rogers and flights to outer space. There seemed no limit to what human ingenuity could accomplish. Flying saucers could well have been the next step.

American military analysts looked into the possibility that the Soviets, or the Americans themselves, had made a breakthrough to explain the flying discs. They also knew that the Germans had been working on certain very advanced concepts and technologies. The "V" rockets were well known, as was the excellent ME-163 rocket fighter. Less appreciated were the German developments in disc-shaped craft, for a long time dismissed as fantasy. Could flying saucers have truly been invented by the Germans during the Second World War, a secret which would have been maintained and developed by the Americans, British, and Soviets?

Beyond vague and unverifiable leaks during the 1950s, there was not much to be made of this argument until a book by the name *Intercettateli Senza Sparare* was published in Italy in 1968. It was translated and published in English under the title *Intercept – But Don't Shoot*, then republished again in 1974. Its author, Renato Vesco, made the first comprehensive argument that flying saucers should be understood as secret human technology, derived from the Nazis.[85]

Vesco made a case that the Germans had developed alternative energy in the form of the gyroscope, vortex, and other 'anti-gravity' devices. Disc-shaped and tubular craft were built and tested towards the end of the war, the 'foo fighters' being one of their experimental craft. After the war, many of these concepts made it to the Americans and Soviets and led directly to functional flying saucers.

Vesco's work focused on German technology during the war, but barely discussed the postwar transition to the U.S. and elsewhere. Later researchers argued that via Paperclip and similar other programs, these scientists came to work within deep black structures in the U.S. Some argued that German groups succeeded in escaping to South America and even Antarctica (Neu Schwabenland) where, with their advanced technologies, they established secret bases. The fundamental argument was that UFOs were top secret to all governments because they were simply too significant. As Vesco put it, "the UFOs constitute too important a trump card not to wait until the proper time to make them felt upon the course of history. History, therefore, goes on."[86] Later authors added that UFOs utilized suppressed technology and revolutionary energy sources that global elites have kept secret in order to protect current money making resources, such as oil.[87]

In the 1970s, these arguments had an extremely limited circulation. Much later, the story was re-investigated by British aviation writer Nick Cook. Cook argued that there was "a mounting body of evidence" that the Nazis had experimented "with a form of science the rest of the world had never remotely considered." They were so far ahead of everybody else that the technology was suppressed for over fifty years.[88]

What were some of the alleged Nazi achievements? The most famous claim is that a flying disc, the so-called V7, flew out of Prague on February 14, 1945. Within minutes, it was said to have climbed to an altitude of about 40,000 feet and reached a speed of 1,200 mph. It was allegedly destroyed in May 1945, although some said it was captured by the Soviets.[89] Meanwhile, German scientist Viktor Schauberger had been investigating 'free energy production' and 'levitational flight.' During the war, his work and person were taken over by the enigmatic and notorious S.S. General Hans Kammler. He appears to have developed a number of prototypes of flying discs. In early May 1945, just as the European war was about to end, Schauberger's team is said to have had major success. According to one of Cook's sources, a flying saucer prototype rose twice to the ceiling and then was wrecked. As it rose, it left a trail that glowed turquoise and silver. The manner in which it worked "was wholly unconventional" and beyond current scientific knowledge. Schauberger was immediately captured by U.S. forces, which seized everything in his laboratory, and he was held in custody by U.S. intelligence until March 1946.[90]

Cook investigated other possibilities even more fantastic, including the so-called "Bell Experiment." In the region of Lower Silesia, under the administration of Kammler, work was underway that seemed to be related to antigravity technologies. It involved using large amounts of electricity feeding into a below-ground chamber with two contra-rotating cylinders filled with mercury (said to produce terrible side effects on humans). Sixty-two scientists working on the program were allegedly shot by the S.S. a week or two before the surrender of Germany. Cook's research into this even suggested that the Bell experiments were possibly efforts related to time travel.[91]

Cook started his research with low expectations, but he learned more than he expected. Nothing amounted to a smoking gun, however. The story of the Prague flying saucer traveling at 1,200 mph strains credulity. One wonders how a pilot would have managed the feat of flying a wholly unconventional airframe at more than twice the fastest speed of any previously manned aircraft. Many aspects of "The Legend" (as the story of Nazi UFOs is often called) present serious problems of believability. Still, it has become evident that the Germans were indeed working on unconventional technologies and aviation designs, and that the Americans were deeply interested in them. Kammler, incidentally, simply disappeared at the war's end. Did he go work for the Americans? Did he escape somewhere else?

Where does all this leave the UFO phenomenon? The evidence for a man-made UFO program going back to the 1940s is stronger than most earlier researchers had suspected. By the mid-1970s, this idea was just beginning to get serious attention. But any explanation of "Nazi UFOs" has several hurdles to overcome. Why have UFOs consistently buzzed the military installations of the U.S. and other countries? Is one to believe that this was a demonstration of secret Nazi power emanating from Antarctica? No tangible evidence has ever emerged to support this thesis. Or, were all the early UFOs manufactured by the Americans and Soviets? If so, who was buzzing the American military pilots and bases with such regularity? Since there is no evidence that it was the Soviets, does this mean that a secret American flying saucer program was charged with provoking an unsuspecting American defense establishment? For more than fifty years? No proponent of the man-made UFO thesis has been able to come to terms with this issue, although one could do it by postulating the existence of a completely separate breakaway civilization. Even this, however, would not explain much of the strangeness of the UFO phenomenon, such as the many cases of alleged alien encounters.

On the other hand, it is entirely conceivable that some "flying saucers," even during the early years, were man-made. Toward this end, the contribution of Nazi science and technology programs might have been critically important – an uncomfortable fact which those in-the-know would want to keep hidden. From the 1970s onward, it became increasingly difficult to dismiss all claims of man-made UFOs. As the 1970s turned into the 1980s and beyond, the claims became stronger still.

UFO Research in 1975

By 1975, UFO research was quite active. Several organizations were trying to grow nationwide and the field explored different intellectual avenues. "Scientific ufology" was the reigning ideology. Of course, modern science is expensive, and the UFO groups never had much money. Even within financial constraints, however, progress was made. In 1975, CUFOS received a computer file of nearly 80,000 records of UFOs, called UFOCAT. This was a gift from Dr. David R. Saunders, former member of the Condon Committee, who had created it. UFOCAT provided a foundation of raw data that in the coming years would enable CUFOS to generate statistical studies of UFO reports.

Meanwhile, MUFON issued the second edition of its Field Investigator's Manual. Edited by Raymond Fowler, it listed standard investigative procedures.[92] MUFON wanted to develop an international organization of trained investigators who could research sightings as scientifically as possible. Sometimes the reality did not meet that ideal, but many MUFON investigators did rigorously investigate baffling UFO cases. MUFON's voice to the world was *Skylook*, a monthly journal about 20 pages long containing descriptions of UFO sightings, as well as commentary by researchers such as Richard Hall, Walter Andrus, Lucius Farish, Leonard Stringfield, Stanton Friedman, Ann Druffel, and others. Despite a bare bones budget, it was a quality publication under the editorial guidance of Dwight Connelly. Considering its focus was UFOs, *Skylook* was quite conservative. One senses that the writers tried to avoid any hint of sensationalism or conspiratorial thinking. *Skylook* offered almost no political analysis. The drawback of this approach is that if UFOs were real, as most contributors to *Skylook* agreed, there would surely be important and far-reaching political and social implications. But then again, such analysis went beyond a strictly scientific approach to the UFO problem. In fairness, this was quite enough of a challenge.

An important contribution toward the establishment of a proper ufology was the appearance in 1975 of a scholarly work by Temple University Professor of History, Dr. David Jacobs. *The UFO Controversy in America* was the first true history of the UFO phenomenon. Jacobs argued that the investigative efforts of Project Blue Book were a sham, described the history of important organizations such as NICAP, and the history of the UFO phenomenon from the 1940s to the early 1970s. Not having access to the many documents that later become declassified, his history reflected public sources such as newspapers and UFO journals. Still, the book remains valuable to this day, with a fine organization of the subject matter, clear writing, and an excellent bibliography.

Although writing on the conspiracy was somewhat out of favor, research efforts in this direction increased after the amended Freedom of Information Act became effective on February 19, 1975. The declassification trend had already born fruit a month earlier, when the CIA released the 1953 Robertson Panel document to Ann Druffel. Back in 1966, Dr. James McDonald had discovered the report during a trip to Wright-Patterson AFB – it had been declassified by Blue Book manager Hector Quintanilla. McDonald shared his information with others, but the CIA re-classified the report before anyone could get an official copy. The Air Force later released a sanitized version of the report which expunged all references to the CIA. In late 1974 ("on a whim") Druffel requested a declassified copy from the CIA. To her surprise, the Agency told her that she could get a 28-page declassified copy for ten cents per page.[93] It proved that the CIA had indeed organized a classified scientific panel that had set government UFO policy for decades. Seen from the perspective of the 21st century, it might seem utterly entry-level to ask whether the CIA had an interest in UFOs, but until 1975 there had been no proof that this had been the case.

FOIA thus added a new dimension to UFO research, and a new group of researchers dedicated themselves to filing Freedom of Information requests with all publicly known government agencies and departments. A new organization, Ground Saucer Watch (GSW) of Phoenix, sprang into being led by William Spaulding and W. Todd Zechel (the latter of whom was a former government employee with connection to the NSA). In the summer of 1975, GSW filed for UFO-related documents from the CIA. The Agency replied that its UFO connection began and ended with the Robertson Panel. But this fight was just beginning, and events would eventually disprove the CIA's assertion.[94]

It looked like the secrecy dam might be about to crack. Watergate and the resignation of President Nixon were still fresh events, and it seemed possible that something just might give. Another bombshell, hinting of more to come, came from Senator Barry Goldwater (R-AZ) who, in response to an inquiry about UFOs, wrote a remarkable letter on March 28, 1975:

> The subject of UFOs is one that has interested me for some time. About ten or twelve years ago I made an effort to find out what was in the building at Wright-Patterson Air Force Base where the information is stored that has been collected by the Air Force, and I was understandably denied this request. It is still classified above Top Secret. I have, however, heard that there is a plan under way to release some, if not all, of this material in the near future. I'm just as anxious to see this material as you are, and I hope we will not have to wait too much longer.[95]

Back in 1964, which was around the time he tried to learn the Air Force's UFO secrets, Goldwater was a military-friendly Republican Party candidate for President. And yet he still was denied access. The person who blocked him was his friend, USAF Chief of Staff General Curtis LeMay. Goldwater referred to the UFO subject as "above Top Secret." This accords with a statement from 1950 by Canadian government scientist Wilbert Smith, who was told by senior American scientists in Washington, D.C., that UFOs were "the most highly classified subject in the United States

Government."[96] Although conspiratorial thinking was out of fashion among ufologists, Goldwater's statement would reverberate over the years. What exactly was "above Top Secret"? And if someone of his stature was blocked from accessing UFO data, who did have access? What was the data, anyway?

Meanwhile, some students of UFOs concluded it was all, or at least mostly, in the mind. Such was the conclusion of Jerome Clark and Loren Coleman in *The Unidentified*. This work borrowed from Jungian psychology to interpret UFOs from ancient times to the modern day. They argued that UFO experiences were not the result of an alien presence, but were "primarily subjective and its content primarily symbolic" – an unconscious projection of the human mind. Not merely Jung, but Freud is detectable in their statement that "UFO visions are the psyche's attempt to escape the stranglehold that strict rationalism has on twentieth century humanity." UFO experiences were not real in an objective sense, they maintained, but were the product of unusual mental states. In time, both authors rejected their own conclusions which, as Clark later pointed out, ignored actual physical evidence of UFOs. But other proponents soon followed, resulting in what became known as the psycho-social school of ufology.[97]

Richard Hall wasted no time in criticizing this new development as "subjective, mystical, and chaotic."[98] But at least psycho-social writers held that UFOs were a legitimate topic of study. In a different category altogether was the 1974 offering by skeptic Philip J. Klass, *UFOs Explained*. Klass, an electrical engineer by training and a senior avionics editor for the trade publication *Aviation Week and Space Technology*, had been actively debunking the topic since the mid-1960s. He argued that all UFO sightings were amenable to logical, scientific explanations, provided of course that sufficient data was available. Strictly speaking, most UFO proponents would agree, but by "logical and scientific," Klass excluded extraterrestrial or other seemingly extraordinary explanations. The book used a handful of UFO cases as "remarkably accurate profiles of the whole" to demonstrate that the phenomenon was in fact easily explainable. Klass advanced what he called the Ufological Principle: that honest people, when exposed to unusual natural phenomena or an unexpected event, are often inaccurate in describing what they saw. Out of such misidentifications, he argued, grew the myth of flying saucers, the fascination of which is essentially the adult's recompense for the loss of Santa Claus. Many of the cases Klass referred to were well known, such as the cigar-shaped object described by two 1948 Eastern Air Lines pilots – a case investigated by the

U.S. Air Force and taken seriously – which Klass said was a meteor shower. He offered a similar explanation for the October 1973 sighting of a UFO by an Army Reserve helicopter crew: a fireball associated with the Orionid meteor shower. The 1964 sighting of a landed craft by a New Mexico policeman was, in Klass's estimation, probably a hoax. Readers either loved or despised Klass. In *UFOs Explained*, the prosaic explanations of a small sample of UFO cases left one either with the impression that Klass had adequately explained UFOs as something conventional, or that he simply cherry-picked his cases, offering the catch-all explanation of human fallibility or deception to account for the toughest ones. By now, Stanton Friedman had emerged as Klass's most persistent critic, and offered a rebuttal to Klass's book ("pseudoscience") in the pages of *Skylook*.[99] Friedman and Klass were developing the nasty relationship Klass previously had with James McDonald.

Another area of change was how researchers viewed the aliens themselves. The number of alleged close encounters and abductions were growing, many of which were described by witnesses who claimed to have clear recollections of figures seen near or inside UFOs. Frequently the entities were described as wearing tight fitting clothes, or some sort of silver spacesuit. Although there was still no widespread description of what would soon become known as the "greys," one type of entity consistently reported was short in stature, often with dark eyes and enlarged heads. Another type, later often designated as "Nordic," was tall and blonde, sometimes with large ears, and was often reported in Europe. Such beings usually looked "almost" human, or sometimes exactly so. The term "alien" was not yet widely used to describe these creatures. Researchers David Webb and Ted Bloecher, for instance, referred to large numbers of "humanoid" cases from the years 1973 and 1974; the term "UFO occupant" was also frequently used.[100]

Few conclusions were being offered at this time regarding these apparent non-humans. For years, many ufologists had assumed that the aliens were conducting surveillance of the planet, possibly in advance of establishing an open presence here on Earth. As the decades went by, this position became increasingly untenable. Adding to the confusion was the growing realization that what people had been calling the UFO phenomenon might be very old indeed. If so, what exactly might *they* be doing here? Surely not conducting surveillance. Other possibilities would be discussed soon enough, for in 1975 a New York City artist named Budd Hopkins carried out his first UFO investigation. Within a few years, Hopkins would express forcefully that these aliens were in fact abducting many more humans than researchers had previously thought.

Despite the infighting that has always occurred in ufology, attempts were made to foster cooperation through conferences. One of the early important ones took place in October 1975 in Fort Smith, Arkansas. Aptly, it was titled "United For Objectivity." The leaders of APRO, MUFON, CUFOS, and GSW participated, as well as members of NASA and the FAA. Philip Klass was there, too. Some attendees were persuaded that Klass was a sincere skeptic, a member of the "loyal opposition," although others thought it over-the-top that he seemed to be tape-recording nearly everything. The conference produced a joint resolution that each group would come to an agreement in the near future concerning their areas of basic emphasis for research. Predictably, this never happened, especially since each organization already had people specializing in a wide range of areas.[101]

Soon after this conference, however, Allen Hynek began to organize his own "secret" conference. He drew up a list of 138 attendees who, in his words, had "seriously investigated and reported" on UFOs "in an unprejudiced manner." No offense to those left off the list, of course. Word got out immediately, rankling many UFO researchers who were left off Hynek's secret and exclusionary list. It seemed needlessly divisive. Why the secrecy? Why prevent others from attending? Commenting on Hynek's lack of diplomacy, *Skylook* editor Dwight Connelly noted that UFO researchers were "almost paranoid in their suspicions of each other." If people thought ufology was paranoid in 1975, they hadn't seen anything yet.[102]

Remote Viewing the Aliens

Some may consider the next topic "far out" even for a book on UFOs. Remote viewing (RV) is roughly synonymous with clairvoyance or nonlocal awareness, but specifically refers to the "psychic spying" program within the U.S. intelligence community from the 1970s until the 1990s. In classified circles, teams of trained individuals used extrasensory perception to help fight the cold war, often with examples of success that defied any conventional explanation. Sometimes, these remote viewers claimed to see UFOs or alien beings.

For years, the CIA and many military units, along with their Soviet counterparts, performed experiments to harness the human mind, including ways to create a programmed killer (e.g. a Manchurian Candidate).[103] So in 1972, when the CIA approached Dr. Harold Puthoff of Stanford Research

Institute (SRI) in Menlo Park, California, to initiate a psi research program, it was simply working an old game with a new twist. If clairvoyance could really be used for espionage, one could spy on enemy installations at practically no cost. It was at least worth a try, especially since it was known the Soviets were pursuing it.

Puthoff invited New York City artist and psychic Ingo Swann to SRI to begin psi experiments. Swann's first day at Stanford University was nothing short of astounding. He was brought by Puthoff and several skeptical scientists to a building where, several floors below, was a heavily shielded device called a magnetometer. Its sole function was to measure quarks. Swann had no idea what he was going to be asked, when one of the scientists asked him if he could "perturb" the device. As Swann sat in his chair, simply trying to see the device in his mind, a scientist monitoring the magnetometer informed the group that something was wrong. The needle was moving wildly – the device was malfunctioning. This scene was repeated several more times, each time exactly when Swann was "seeing" the magnetometer. Coincidence, the skeptics argued; Puthoff was more intrigued.

Swann had many amazing successes. In an October 1972 experiment, he correctly identified a moth inside a box: "small, brown, and irregular, sort of like a leaf, or something that resembles it, except that it seems very much alive, like it's even moving."[104] In April 1973, he suggested that perhaps during weekends and free time, he try something more exciting. The Pioneer 10 space probe had been launched and would not reach Jupiter for several months. Why not RV Jupiter? Monitored by Puthoff and fellow scientist Russell Targ, Swann yielded 13 specific factors about Jupiter, none of which had been scientifically anticipated. Ultimately, 12 of these were confirmed, including the surprising existence of a planetary ring.[105]

Another RV star was Pat Price, who joined the program in 1973 and accurately remotely viewed a Soviet installation in the northern Ural Mountains.[106] In another series of experiments, Puthoff and a skeptic at SRI named Earl Jones drove to nine separate metropolitan areas, all chosen by Jones. Back at the lab, Targ monitored Price, who described seven of those places accurately. In some cases, Price did this before Jones and Puthoff had reached their target, and before Jones had even *decided* on a target. Price appeared to be moving not only through space, but through time.[107]

Price also saw aliens. He told Puthoff that there were four major underground alien bases, each within a different mountain region. Price had done this on his own and was simply giving his boss the data. The main purpose of the bases, he stated, was to "reinforce B.T.L. implants, transport of new recruits and overall monitoring function." Just what B.T.L. implants were Price did not know, nor apparently does anyone today, although the phenomenon of alien abduction certainly comes to mind. The inhabitants of the bases looked like normal human beings, said Price, although the heart, lungs, blood and eyes were different. The four sites were protected from discovery and had very advanced technology. Price also said the inhabitants of these bases used "thought transfer for motor control of us."

The first base, said Price, was at Mt. Perdido in the Pyrenees Mountains, between France and Spain. It was guarded with a two-mile perimeter of detectors, and contained several craft, apparently using an electromagnetic field propulsion system. Another was at Mount Inyangani, the highest mountain in Rhodesia (now Zimbabwe). It looked like "a maintenance and tech center." A third site was at Mount Hayes, northeast of Anchorage, Alaska. This seemed to be a weather and geological center. In the event of discovery, "personnel are deployed physically . . . to make sure of failure of that certain project. This site has also been responsible for strange activity and malfunction of U.S. and Soviet space projects." The fourth site was at Mount Ziel, in Australia's Northern Territory. This base had the most personnel, including many from the other three sites, "like a rest and recreation area." While viewing this location, Price thought he was detected, so he "left," but then returned. He noted the base was also the "homo sapiens introduction point." Price did not think aliens limited themselves to these four bases; he also sensed bases on the Moon, Mars, and under Earth's oceans.[108]

Incidentally, Puthoff later gave Price's Mount Hayes folder to Lieutenant F. Holmes ("Skip") Atwater, who tasked remote viewers for the Star Gate program, an extended remote viewing effort under the control of the U.S. Army. In 1982, Atwater asked his leading remote viewer, Joe McMoneagle, to target the area. McMoneagle perceived a mountainous region with underground tubes, tunnels, and ball shaped objects. "I've never seen anything like it," he said. "It's like walking into a place I have no familiarity with at all."[109]

Ingo Swann possibly had the most amazing ET-related experiences, the topper of which concerns his encounters with a mysterious "Mr. Axelrod." In February 1975, Swann received a phone call from a friend whom he described as "a certain highly placed functionary in Washington, D.C." The friend told him that someone under the pseudonym of "Mr. Axelrod" would soon telephone him, and that it was very important Swann did "whatever he asks, and ask no questions." Accustomed to unusual requests in his line of work, Swann agreed.

A month later, Swann received a 3 a.m. phone call from Axelrod, who asked him to be in Washington at noon that day. Swann was in New York City, but he made the trip and arrived at the appointed spot: in front of the elephant at the Smithsonian Institution. Two very similar-looking men in military demeanor, with blue eyes and blonde crewcuts, approached him from behind. Their introduction consisted of pre-written note cards, and they led him to a car. The female driver ignored him and, after a note card which apologized for the cloak-and-dagger routine, a bag was placed over Swann's head. He was put on a helicopter, flown for about a half hour, taken out and walked for a "longish distance." Then down an elevator for another long distance, taken out, walked again, and turned many times. Finally, the bag was removed.

Ingo Swann was now face to face with Axelrod, who offered him $1,000 per day for his work during the next few days. Regarding his agency, Axelrod said only "we exist without leaving a paper trail regarding our mission." There were no disclosure papers to sign, only a promise not to talk for ten years, after which "our mission will have 'disappeared' as it were."

The two became friendly. "Axel" said he knew all about Swann's remote viewing of Jupiter, and asked Swann what he knew about the Moon. Not much, said Swann. "Well," said Axelrod, "we want you to go to the Moon for us, and describe what you see." He gave Swann about ten Moon coordinates, causing Swann to wonder if Axelrod's group was looking for places to hide a Moon base, or perhaps searching for a lost, secret, spacecraft.

Swann "went" to the coordinates and saw a green haze, two rows of lights, and towers. He apologized – clearly, he was perceiving Earth, not the Moon. Axelrod seemed perturbed and asked Swann if he was sure of what he saw. Eventually it dawned on Swann: "You mean, am I to think these lights are actually on the Moon?" No answer from Axelrod. "Have the Russians built a Moonbase or something?" Still no answer. They went through the coordinates again, and Swann saw the light towers better this time, built on narrow struts. They were very tall, perhaps over 100 feet. He saw an even larger tower at the edge of a crater, as tall as a skyscraper. "Am I, then, to assume this stuff really is on the Moon?" No answer. "Am I to assume this stuff is not ours? Not made on Earth?"

Axelrod finally answered: "Quite a surprise, isn't it?"

Thus Ingo Swann remote viewed what he believed to be alien bases on the Moon. But his information did not seem to surprise Axelrod, and so Swann asked why he had been brought in. Axelrod answered cryptically that "frankly, no one has known what to do, and many mistakes have been made." Did the aliens tell us to stay away, Swann asked. Axelrod deflected that question, saying that Swann's information "might provide a kind of check point in what you surely now realize must be a mess of interpretations of the photographic and other evidence. It was my idea to find a psychic who did not know anything about the Moon, and see what might be seen there." This sounds like a test of human psychic abilities to detect an alien presence.

In other sessions, Swann saw more of the same – towers, machinery, roads, housing-like structures – and made many sketches for Axelrod. Finally, he saw what looked like humans "busy at work on something I could not figure out." Swann told Axelrod that the beings had detected his presence. "Please quickly come away from that place," said Axelrod, and Swann left.

After several days, Swann was asked to write his thoughts down on the nature of psi, three dimensionality, and communication across distances, and he gave Axelrod 15 handwritten pages. Swann was then brought home, and Axelrod indicated that he would probably contact Swann again. More on that later.[110]

Swann's story is unsupported by what any historian would consider good corroborative evidence. But to the people who know Ingo Swann, some of whom served with him in the remote viewing program, there is no question of his intelligence, rationality, and honesty. "If Ingo said it, then it happened," was the statement by one associate of Swann's, with whom the author inquired.

The small remote viewing community of the mid-1970s was of concern to certain circles within the global intelligence community – American, Soviet, and probably other nations. If one assumes the reality of an ET presence, and if one further supposes that the many accounts of alien telepathic ability have some validity, we might presume that the remote viewers were of interest to the aliens themselves. Indeed, it has been suggested to the author that Axelrod and his blonde, blue-eyed helpers were perhaps not exactly human, either, but performing their own counter-intelligence assessment of their vulnerabilities to human remote viewers.

What is beyond dispute is that by 1975, the U.S. remote viewing program was bumping into UFO-ET phenomena. Moreover, belief in an extraterrestrial presence became widespread among people involved in remote viewing. Major General Albert Stubblebine, who for years managed the Star Gate program, said "I will tell you for the record that there are structures underneath the surface of Mars . . . . I will also tell you that there are machines under the surface of Mars that you can look at."[111]

Last Hurrah of the Old Republic

The remote viewing community was very secretive, and none of the preceding information would be public for many years. UFO researchers who brought FOIA petitions knew nothing about it. But the mid-1970s did experience a temporary breakdown of decades of secrecy on a wide range of topics. Investigative reporter Seymour Hersh revealed in late 1974 that the CIA was not only destabilizing foreign governments, but was also conducting illegal intelligence operations against thousands of American citizens. On January 27, 1975, the U.S. Senate established a special body to investigate. Chaired by Senator Frank Church (D-ID), with Senator John Tower (R-TX) as vice-chairman, the committee was given nine months and 150 staffers to complete its work. They interviewed 800 individuals, and conducted 250 executive and 21 public hearings. The topics included assassination plots involving foreign leaders, secret storage of toxic agents, CIA domestic mail opening programs, activities of the National Security Agency, the FBI's "Counterintelligence Program" (Cointelpro) and warrantless electronic surveillance, improper surveillance of American citizens by the U.S. military, the Internal Revenue Service as an intelligence resource and collector, covert actions, and re-investigations of the assassinations of John F. Kennedy and Martin Luther King, Jr.[112]

In many respects, this was the only time in American history that a Senate Committee looked critically and carefully into the U.S. intelligence community. The NSA, for instance, had never before been subject to any oversight by Congress. An earlier investigation led by Vice President Nelson Rockefeller had led to discovery of the NSA's Operation Shamrock, which involved electronic monitoring of Americans. Now, facing the Church Committee questions, the NSA eventually conceded that Shamrock ended not because of legal issues, but because it simply had not produced much of value. Pushed by Church, the committee voted to make its report public, over the objections of NSA, President Ford, and its own Republican members. Church argued that there was a danger that NSA's technology "could be turned against the American people at a great cost to liberty. . .

. no American would have any privacy left. . . . There would be no place to hide."[113] The committee created the Foreign Intelligence Surveillance Act (FISA), which for the first time outlined what the NSA could and could not do. It outlawed the wholesale, warrantless acquisition of raw telegrams, such as had occurred under Shamrock.[114]

In effect, the Old Republic was giving it one last hurrah against America's true governing institution: the National Security State. Even so, resistance was strong. Although many of the committee recommendations were adopted, much was thrown out by the 1980s, to say nothing of post-911 America. Thus, the committee's conclusion that in all probability John F. Kennedy was assassinated in some sort of conspiracy remained just that – a conclusion without any legal followup or prosecution. Some of the more egregious violations of law, which included the FBI's Cointelpro, the NSA's Shamrock, or the CIA's MK-Ultra, had already been terminated, then renamed and re-established under greater secrecy.

Incidentally, when discussing any connection of then-president Gerald Ford with UFOs, attention is inevitably drawn to the fact that as a Congressman in 1966, Ford publicly discussed the topic before his colleagues, seeking to get some answers. The question arises as to what, if any, UFO information he came across in his capacity as President. In truth, there is no public information making any such connection. This is not the same, of course, as saying there was none. Many years later, UFO investigator and retired Air Force Major George Filer wrote to Ford about the existence of UFOs. Ford replied:

> During my public career in Congress, as Vice President and President, I made various requests for any information on UFOs. The official authorities always denied the UFO allegations. As a result I have no information that may be helpful to you.

Filer, an experienced researcher familiar with the ways of the military and government, concluded that "if Congress, like the President, uses its normal sources of intelligence such as CIA, DIA, NSA, NASA, they will likely get the same answer as our Presidents claim they were given." Filer suggested that U.S. government intelligence agencies "are not aware or responsive to UFO reports and a possible alien threat. We have a choice to assume they are incompetent, unaware or lying."[115]

One CIA document from 1975, obtained through FOIA, confirms that U.S. government agencies continued to collect data on UFOs. It describes a September 1975 meeting of the International Congress of Space Medicine, attended by CIA operatives. The memo stated that:

> US scientists believe that low magnetic fields, oscillating magnetic fields, and electromag-

netic fields can or do have considerable effect. There is a theory that such fields are closely associated with superconductivity at very low temperatures, such as in space. This in turn is related to the possible propulsion system of UFOs. There is a rumor that fragments of a possible UFO found in Brazil bore a relationship to superconductors and magneto-hydrodynamics.[116]

The rest of the memo is blacked out. This of course does not mean that the CIA as an organization or analysts individually thought UFOs were "real." But the tone of the memo is such that at least some members of the agency were taking this topic seriously, as though it were real. It is hard to know for sure, since nothing else of the document is available.

UFOs Elsewhere in the World

As far as UFO sightings are concerned, American reports dominated the year. As always, however, the phenomenon was global. Canada was the scene of several landing and trace cases, as well as one very interesting photographic case.

During the early afternoon of March 18, 1975, Pat McCarthy, age 19, of Hamilton, Ontario was out

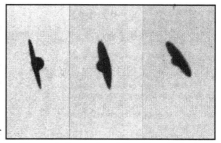

Three photographs of Hamilton, Ontario UFO, March 18, 1975

trying to photograph hawks. His camera was a German-made Praktica Nova 1, with a 135 mm lens, and was loaded with Kodak Plus X ASA 125 film. By 1:30 p.m., McCarthy had found no birds and was about to leave for home, when he saw an object resembling a frisbee. It moved too fast to be a bird, and he decided to take photos of it. Because of its speed, he had difficulty in following it with his camera, but he eventually snapped four photos, capturing the object three times. McCarthy had some knowledge of aircraft, and estimated the object to have been fairly large: twice the size of a DC-8 (which is roughly 150 feet long, with a wingspan of 140 feet).

Realizing he had photos of great potential significance, he immediately took the camera to the local newspaper, the Hamilton *Spectator*. The film was still undeveloped in his camera, and was processed there in the newspaper's own darkroom. APRO investigated the case, finding the witness credible, and also noting that the images bore a striking similarity to photographs taken in Brazil in 1959.[117]

Several apparent landing cases took place in Canada during the spring and summer of 1975. On April 26, 1975 at 2 a.m. in Chomeday, Laval, Quebec, a light was seen to descend briefly behind a school, apparently leaving behind a piece of metal and a hole in the ground. The case was investigated by Leonard Stringfield. A similar case took place on May 10 in the town of Carman, Manitoba. According to a Canadian representative of CUFOS, Dan Bjarnason, a UFO was said to have landed in a field. Employees from the Winnipeg planetarium investigated and found radioactivity four times higher than that of the surrounding land. Late in the evening two days later, in Peesane, Saskatchewan, two witnesses saw an unusual object with a green light for about ten minutes, which then moved away to the east. A perfectly round circle was found in the area, five feet in diameter, with a ring width of six inches. The Royal Canadian Mounted Police took soil samples and photographs. On July 6 at 5 p.m. in Mount Pleasant, Ontario, a man named Joe Borda saw a metallic cylinder in a field about 800 feet away. When he examined the ground later, an area fifty feet across was slightly burned, and an oily substance was found. Ted Phillips of CUFOS investigated. The same month in Sharon, Ontario, another ring was found, also investigated by CUFOS.[118]

Southern Africa experienced a rash of unusual events beginning in mid-July. One such case which elicited government attention occurred at a prison in Khami, Bulawayo, in Southwestern Rhodesia (Zimbabwe). Incidentally, this is on the other side of the country from Mount Inyangani, where Pat Price said an alien base was located. On July 15, at about 8:15 p.m., prison officials saw an orange object, almost circular with a flat bottom and rounded top, approximately one or two miles away. Thirty minutes later, another officer saw a similar object in the same place. Nothing more was reported that evening. The following night at 7:30 p.m., a bright, round, silvery object was seen hovering motionless two or three miles northeast of the prison. It then moved rapidly to the east. Late in July, a Member of Parliament asked the government to set up a committee to investigate the sightings; Rhodesian Minister of Transport and Power, Roger Hawkins, agreed that the matter deserved attention. A spokesperson for the Rhodesian Air Force, however, said that nothing showed up on radar, and added that the U.S. Air Force had found explanations for most UFO reports, a reference to the Condon Committee study of the 1960s.

On July 28, in Salisbury, Rhodesia (now Harare, Zimbabwe), two police officers drove toward an object hovering 500 feet above the ground, while three other officers watched from the roof of their station. When the two approached, the object moved away. After midnight, a motorist reported, a "big bright light" twice the apparent size of the sun, with an indentation on top, and which followed his car as he drove. The following day, in South

Africa at the southern tip of the continent in the city of Joubertina, a silvery sphere crashed to Earth, just missing a farmhouse and shattering a hard boulder. Later reports indicated that it may have been Russian space hardware.[119]   A startling case occurred on July 31 in Loxton, South Africa. At 7:30 a.m., a farmer named Danie van Graan went out to inspect his sheep herd and saw a silver, oval-shaped object resting on legs. Van Graan approached to within 15 feet. Through a large window he saw four beings, three of whom seemed to be examining some device, while the other stood near a panel of flashing lights. They were thin, pale, and seemed to be about five feet tall. They had light colored hair, slanted eyes, sharp pointed chins, and wore white coveralls with hoods. Van Graan heard a "tick" sound, and the beings became aware of his presence. A beam of light immediately hit him in the face; his nose bled and he vomited. The object made a humming sound and took off sharply. Cynthia Hind of MUFON South Africa investigated and found a circle 30 feet in diameter with four marks on the outside perimeter. Near the center was a deposit of small green granules, later determined to be carbon thaumasite, a water-retaining substance not common to the area. Nothing grew in the affected area for some time afterwards.[120] More South African sightings occurred throughout August.

Europe had its share of weirdness. On August 13, 1975, near Haderslev, Denmark, a police officer driving home at about 10:50 p.m. found himself engulfed in a bright light. His headlights and engine died, and it became hot inside the car. Shielding his eyes, he reached for a microphone and tried to call his station, but the radio was dead. He looked up and saw a beam of light from an opening at the bottom of a circular object, about 35 feet in diameter, hovering perhaps 60 feet above the ground. He took three pictures of it before it rose straight up and was gone. It had been silent the whole time. The photographs captured a "light source," and the officer turned the film over to the Danish Air Force. According to Richard Hall, no follow-up reports or images are available.[121]

Summary

Considering that 1974 and the first half of 1975 receive so little attention from UFO researchers, the two years were significant for many reasons. First were the many interesting sightings of objects supposed to be impossible, some of which were well documented and investigated. The existence of such sightings stands as a monument to the disparity between "official" and "real" truth. Something unusual was going on in Earth's skies.

Second were the political developments, the most important of which allowed for greater public access into government records, fruits of which were just beginning to be seen by 1975, proving that there was indeed a secret government interest in UFOs. Along these lines were several startling statements on UFO secrecy from leading political and military figures from France, Spain, and the U.S. Third were the strides made by researchers, particularly in America, which had by far the largest and most sophisticated civilian-based UFO investigative and reporting network in the world. American UFO research became a much more serious endeavor during this period, spurred on by the goal of 'scientific ufology.' The field developed an attractive combination of rigor and intellectual daring.

Ufology was in a crescendo that would continue through most of the 1970s. It is for this reason only that these early years have faded from memory. For the years that followed would have more of everything.

Chapter 2

Intruder Alert
1975-1976

The nations of the world are currently working together in the investigation of the UFO phenomenon. There is an international exchange of data.
— *General Carlos Castro Cavero (Spain), 1976*

... object headed for the F-4 at a very fast rate of speed. The pilot attempted to fire an AIM-9 missile at the object but at that instant his weapons control panel went off and he lost all communications.
— *Defense Intelligence Agency memo on UFO encounter over Tehran, 1976.*

Helicopters and Mutilations in the American West

Four themes dominated the second half of 1975: cattle mutilations, black helicopters, abduction cases, and violations of U.S. military air space by UFOs. There was a good deal of overlap and apparent inter-relationships among these phenomena.

Mutilations of many types of animals (not just cattle) had been noted throughout much of the U.S. and Canada since 1967, although the phenomenon spiked sharply at the end of 1974 and throughout 1975.[1] Such animals had certain typical features. Usually, an animal would be found dead, lying on its side, with no predator tracks anywhere, and no sign of struggle. An ear would be missing, along with a circle of flesh around the eye and eyeball. Much of the flesh covering the jaw would also be completely gone, leaving the bone exposed, and occasionally the teeth and jawbone itself were neatly removed. In most cases, the tongue was smoothly cut from deep within the throat, and a few necropsies confirmed the removal of the larynx and trachea. The genitals were usually cut cleanly away, leaving a flat, oval shape. In nearly all cases, rectal tissue would be removed in a hole about four inches wide and six to fourteen inches deep.

Law enforcement officers were also puzzled by the massive loss of blood, and yet no obvious place where the blood could have gone. Adding to the aura of mystery, ranchers and law enforcement officials would often see predators such as coyotes, wolves, and bears approach a mutilated animal, only to stop several feet away and circle the carcass as if an invisible barrier were present. Most dramatically, some necropsies confirmed an absence of heart tissue, and yet no evidence of cuts or tears of the clear membrane that surrounded a cow's heart. In other words, it appeared that someone was able to remove the large organ without cutting into the chest wall. Some veterinarians who studied these animals marveled, and the braver ones said that the work was done with instruments not available to them.

In her investigation of animal mutilation tissues with John Altshuler, M.D., pathologist and hematologist in Denver, Colorado, television producer and investigative journalist Linda Moulton Howe was able to confirm that excisions in several mutilated animals were cut with high heat. Further, when Altshuler examined mutilation tissues under microscopes, he found no carbon black. All Earth creatures are carbon-based life forms. If the cutting instrument were a laser or other form of electrical cautery, there would be "black pepper grain" evidence of carbon at the excisions. Altshuler told Howe, "I know we're looking at tissue exposed to heat that has cauterized, but I don't know what the cutting instrument is because lasers would leave carbon residue. Yet, there is none."[2]

A number of the mutilation cases were accompanied by reports of UFOs, strange helicopters, possible landing traces, and burned tree tops. A researcher named Tom Adams was the first to track not only the cases of mutilation, but also the mystery helicopter phenomenon. During the spring and summer of 1975, he recorded more than 200 cases of helicopters near or at mutilation sites. Not simply helicopters, however. Some individuals claimed to see stranger objects, in other words UFOs, near mutilation sites.[3]

The event that seems to have "kicked off" the new wave of mutilations occurred in December 1974, when a heifer was found inside a perfect circle of melted snow in Kimball, Minnesota. The animal's eyes, left ear, tongue, and part of its lip were removed. No footprints, tracks, or blood were found. Matters became really strange when a pilot and photographer flew over the area. A quarter mile south of the mutilation site, they saw dozens of circles in random patterns spread over several acres. The St. Paul, Minnesota *Dispatch* featured one of the photographs in an article, "UFOs Zapping Cows?"[4]

From January to May 1975, eastern Texas generated many reports of "mutes," helicopters, and UFOs. Most of these cases occurred in a corridor about 50 miles wide and 200 miles long, running between Dallas and

Austin and pointing northeast toward Arkansas.[5] A particularly interesting incident, recalling the Kimball case, came from Cochran County on March 10. There, a mutilated heifer was found in the center of a perfectly round circle 30 feet in diameter. Its head was twisted straight up in the air, the bottom of its jaw was cut back, the tongue was gone, sex organs were cut off and missing, and the naval was cut out in a circle. The animal was drained of blood and its meat was untouched. Stranger still, a mutilated steer was found in the center of another 30 foot circle only a quarter of a mile away. A team from Reese AFB came to the site to check for abnormal radioactivity, but found nothing.[6]

Texans were claiming that unmarked helicopters were flying low and harassing their livestock. One citizen asked the Federal Aviation Administration to investigate. Documents obtained through FOIA indicate that the FAA quietly contacted Fort Hood and Bergstrom AFB, the two closest military bases, both of which denied any knowledge of the helicopter flights. There is no evidence of any follow-up, either by the FAA or any other agency, although in a logical world one would assume the matter deserved an investigation.[7]

By April, unmarked helicopters were reported in Kansas and Colorado. Some of these were linked with mutilation cases, such as a May 29 incident just outside Denver.[8] Much of the activity was taking place near military installations in the central Colorado area, near the home of the U.S. Air Force Academy and NORAD headquarters. On July 6, a mutilated pregnant cow was found next to a high security NORAD entrance gate, and the sheriff's office determined that it was not caused by a predator.[9] On July 17, three girls on horseback near Colorado Springs claimed to have been chased by a helicopter. On July 23, in nearby Elbert County, Undersheriff Bill Waugh saw a silent helicopter through his binoculars. This could be significant, but there is not enough detail to know just what happened. A silent helicopter in 1975 would be very important. What we do know is that local police were concerned about these helicopters, as on the very same night, they undertook a search for a helicopter which had appeared several times in Teller County (which by then had already reported forty cattle mutilations).

The phenomenon was also being recorded in northern New Mexico, with a heavy concentration in the small town of Dulce. Gabriel Valdez, a decorated state police officer, investigated cattle mutilations as well as reports of anomalous flying lights. Neither he nor ranchers found tracks of any creature near the mutilated animals. Occasionally, they found tripod-like tracks, as well as tracks that appeared to come from small tractors. Other items and materials were also found, such as whitish powdered substances, torn and crumpled pieces of paper, and even a gas mask. Some of the cattle had marks on one hind leg, and many had broken bones, which led to the theory that they had been lifted with a rope or cable and then dropped. This would seem to point to some sort of human, covert activity connected to the mutes. Years later, this became Valdez's conclusion, after he rejected his earlier position that this was something alien.[10] Yet, Dulce remained the scene of numerous sightings of unusual nocturnal lights for years, including sightings of objects that certainly appeared to be UFOs. Such activity suggests that the mutilations may have had more than one source. By the late 1970s, rumors would develop of an underground base – possibly alien – under nearby Mount Archuleta.

As in Texas, the people of New Mexico demanded justice, not just for the mutilations, but for the harassment of the phantom helicopters. In the summer of 1975, the FAA announced it would investigate. Tom Adams tried to determine through FOIA whether this in fact happened. Instead the relevant FAA offices denied any knowledge of such an investigation, even after he provided them with a newspaper account announcing the start of the probe. As to what they may have actually found, Adams concluded "apparently, [they found] reasons not to announce their findings."[11]

A New Pattern in Abductions

In the words of Coral Lorenzen, Sergeant Charles ("Chuck") Moody was a "big, likable man" who had previously laughed off UFO stories. He was a decorated Vietnam veteran with fourteen years active duty in the Air Force, and in 1975 was stationed at Holloman AFB in Alamogordo, New Mexico. On the night of August 12/13, Moody decided to see some of the Perseid meteor shower after his shift. Shortly after 12:30 a.m., he drove about fifteen minutes out of town into the quiet night country of the American southwest. The meteor shower was not especially spectacular, but at 1:20 a.m., Moody saw something else. An object about 50 feet in diameter descended from the sky and hovered a mere 20 feet off the ground. It glowed slightly, wobbled for a short time, then became stationary and made a buzzing sound. Moody was 300 feet away from it, and through a lighted rectangular window in the craft he saw human-shaped forms moving about. Frightened, he got back into his car, but the battery was dead. When the buzzing stopped, he felt an odd sense of calm, then saw the object ascend into the sky. Thankfully, he could now start his car. The only problem was that the time on his watch read 2:45 a.m. Eighty-five minutes had passed, and Moody could not understand why. He arrived home at 3 a.m., where his wife was waiting for him. He told her about the UFO, but not about the missing time.

The next day, Moody felt lower back pain, and wondered what had happened to him. On the 14th, he bought a copy of a magazine called "Official UFO," and wrote to the editor, hoping for some help. The editor forwarded his information to the Lorenzens at APRO, who received it on August 20th. By now, Moody's back pain had worsened, and he had developed a rash on his lower body. James Lorenzen talked with Moody by phone, and then visited him in person accompanied by UFO researcher (and former military pilot) Wendelle Stevens. Coral Lorenzen also interviewed the Moodys several times. Before the Lorenzens could arrange a hypnotic regression for Moody, an old friend of his, Dr. Abraham Goldman, formerly an Air Force flight surgeon and a practicing neurosurgeon consultant, suggested a method of self-hypnosis. This appeared to work by bits and pieces. By the first week of October, Moody had some recall of the incident, which he related to the Lorenzens.

Moody remembered his captors being close to six feet tall, although the leader was less than five feet tall. They were "very much like us," he said, "except their heads were larger and hairless, their ears were very small, eyes a little larger than ours, nose small, and the mouth had very thin lips." They were also "very thin," and seemed to communicate telepathically. In fact, Moody never saw their lips move. He remembered fighting with the beings before being taken, perhaps accounting for his soreness. To disable him, they used a type of light or sound frequency. He then found himself on a table, although he did not describe any medical procedure. He felt they looked at him in a stern yet gentle manner. After a while, they let him down from the table, and he asked to see the propulsion unit, which they showed him near the underside of the craft, still from the inside. It contained three diamond or crystal like structures, and bars or rods, but Moody was unable to receive (or remember) any technical explanation. He could not understand how the various large rooms could fit into the craft. The ship was very clean, and at times smelled like a kind of burned sugar. For at least some of his time on board, Moody's breathing was labored.

There was a fair amount of communication between Moody and these beings. He learned that the ship he was on was used for "observing," while their main craft was 400 miles above the earth. They told him there were a number of races from different places who were working together. Their craft could be destroyed by nuclear weapons, and radar was a problem for them, as it acted to jam their navigation. Moody told the Lorenzens that "in the near future there will be contact made with this planet – limited contact. It is not for us as a human race to accept them, but them, for these beings, to accept us.... Possibly there will be twenty years of very limited contact and then, and only then, after deep consideration on their part, would we even be accepted."[12]

Moody's account was uncommon in 1975, but immediately following his abduction, two similar cases in the American west took place. One was on August 26 in North Dakota. A woman named Sandra Larson had left Fargo at 3:15 a.m. with her daughter Jackie, and a man named Terry who drove them west toward Bismarck on Interstate 94. She was on her way to take a real estate exam that morning. At 3:30 a.m., still not far from Fargo, they heard a noise like thunder, but "louder than any thunder imaginable." The sky lit up and eight or ten glowing objects, like orange balls, came down. Terry pulled over, but at this point memories became vague. Somehow Jackie, who had been in the front seat between Terry and her mother, was now in the back seat, although no one seemed to notice at the time. They drove on and caught up with another vehicle on the road. Sandra rolled down her window to ask, "Did you see that?" The man and woman in the other car said yes. Terry asked them to pull over, but the passenger in the other vehicle said, "We're getting the hell out of here."

The three soon realized they had about an hour of missing time. Sandra and Jackie were later put under hypnosis by APRO consultant Dr. Leo Sprinkle, Director of Counseling and Testing at the University of Wyoming in Laramie. Sandra recalled being taken aboard a UFO, stripped, and given a medical exam (including her sexual organs) by a creature "with elastic bandages for a head, or elastic bandages around its head." She remembered a sharp instrument being pushed up her nose, and claimed that her chronic sinus condition was gone after this encounter. At one point she felt as if her brain had been "taken out," had something done to it, and then placed back in her head. She also saw Terry being examined, but not Jackie. Jackie was regressed several times, and only recalled being "left stranded in a field." APRO investigator Jerome Clark investigated the case, and learned that two other witnesses had reported a UFO to the state police at the time that Sandra, Jackie, and Terry were having their experience. Allen Hynek also met with Sandra and Jackie, and although he did not become especially involved in the case, told United Press International (UPI) that Larson "seemed to live through a frightening experience (i.e.

through hypnosis). I believe she thinks she was taken aboard a UFO. I don't think she is lying, in other words." Terry, for his part, wanted no part in any investigation of the affair.

One especially interesting aspect of this case is that the regressions hinted at multiple abduction experiences for Sandra and Jackie. Sandra said the beings told her they would be back, while Jackie vaguely recalled an unsettling bedroom scenario in December, some months after the initial experience. Under hypnosis, she remembered seeing shadowy figures come to her bedroom, and many others outside her house. Clark wondered if there was a psychological explanation, but no one posited the simple proposition that mother and daughter were multiple "experiencers." In 1975, abductions were still considered peripheral to the UFO phenomenon, if they were even believed at all.[13]

The other major abduction case to take place in the western U.S. was the Travis Walton abduction, more on which later.

The FBI Backs Away

UFO sightings, unmarked helicopters, and mutilations continued on a crescendo throughout September, October, and November. Trying to make sense of these sightings is difficult, given a near-complete silence from government agencies. No group ever claimed the helicopters, yet they seemed connected to the mutilations. Researchers Lawrence Fawcett and Barry Greenwood speculated that the helicopters were a paramilitary "quick response unit" to check areas of high UFO and mutilation activity. One well-placed source told them that "some of the mutilations were UFO-related." However, the source "could not discuss the details of the cases because the information is classified." Although the authors would not reveal the source's identity, they said they knew who he was and his standing within the government.[14]

Some public figures discussed the mutilations. In August 1975, Senator Floyd Haskell of Colorado asked the FBI for help.[15] On September 4, the Governor of Colorado, Richard D. Lamm, said it was "no longer possible to blame [natural] predators for the mutilations." A special investigator for the state, Carl Whiteside, agreed.[16] Apparently, the FBI was not impressed. On September 24, the bureau announced it would not assist Colorado in investigating the mutilations, that local law enforcement was up to the job.[17]

The FBI had no motivation to investigate. Prospects for solving the mystery did not look good. It had been going on hot and heavy for most of the year, and not a single culprit had been caught. Moreover, the mutilations were already becoming associated in the public mind with UFOs, and this was a no-no for any federal agency. And what if the FBI did investigate, and concluded that the mutilations showed evidence of advanced technology, including portable lasers and covert transport of cattle? Then, it would have to *deal* with that problem. How to do that? Far better to pass this hot potato to local agencies. At least the matter had a chance of dying down and going far, far away. One could only hope.

Going Crazy in the West

Not all helicopter sightings were connected to the mutes. On September 3 in the town of Tujunga, about 15 miles from Los Angeles, three witnesses observed two helicopters following a colorful UFO. The top of the object was a vibrant blue-green, the middle portion white, and the bottom glowed red. It appeared to change its shape into a "classic saucer" and zigzagged across the sky. The event lasted from 8 p.m. until 11 p.m., and shortly before the end, the witnesses saw the lights go on at the Nike missile base in the mountains near their location. This was a very rare occurrence. Afterwards, the eyes of all three witnesses were painful and red; one of them reported the incident and was eventually led to MUFON investigator Ann Druffel. Druffel contacted every known facility involving official or private helicopters within a 300 mile radius of the area. None admitted to seeing a UFO, but the Los Angeles Police Department said one of its helicopters had been in the area that night; its pilot reported nothing unusual. Druffel also learned that the Nike missile base had been phased out the previous year and turned over to the Army Corps of Engineers. Why the lights went on at the base during the UFO sighting was never determined.[18]

Farther west, in the State of Washington, many UFOs were being reported throughout September. On the 26th, two F-106 fighters from the 318th Fighter Interceptor Squadron were scrambled from McChord AFB, near Tacoma, in search of them. In an unusual admission, an Air Force spokesman said the interceptors were sent in response to the many UFO reports over Tacoma, although neither pilot reported anything unusual. However, McChord's radar was tracking something during this period of time – the Pierce County Sheriff's Department stated that McChord had notified them that their radar was tracking an unidentified object hovering over Tacoma at 18,000 feet, although the date on this was not specified.[19]

Back in 1967, Malmstrom AFB in Montana had been the scene of an awe-inspiring display by a reddish glowing object that disabled over twenty

ICBMs at two separate sites. Now, in 1975, the region was again subjected to aerial craft with an interest in America's missiles. During mid-September, UFOs described as huge orange or red glowing discs were being seen over Minuteman missile sites at Malmstrom. Helicopters were frequently seen, as well. In Lewiston, Montana, about 100 miles southeast of Great Falls, police notified the sheriff's department that several spotlight-equipped helicopters were flying over Minuteman missile sites in that area. Authorities at Malmstrom denied these reports. According to researcher Terry Hansen, a friend later told him that during this period he had lived in Montana and owned a VHF scanning radio. With the radio, Hansen's friend heard reports that UFOs were being seen over Minuteman ICBM silos around Great Falls, "to the great distress of regional security personnel and law enforcement officials." The U.S. nuclear arsenal appeared to be a target of interest, and there was little the Air Force could do about it. The friend heard a sheriff discussing missile silos near the town of Power, Montana. He heard a statement that Great Falls radar was tracking a particular UFO, and an inquiry as to whether the Air Force's Havre radar was tracking it. Havre's reply was, sometimes yes, and sometimes no. One sheriff's deputy said over the radio, "If Havre can't see these on radar we're in big trouble."[20]

It is not clear what these objects were, but low-flying helicopters were being seen throughout the Great Falls area all through September, October, and November. Frequently they flew at night and would hover or remain in an area for an unusually long period of time. More than once they were so low that they caused homes to vibrate.[21]

Matters were becoming intense. On October 5, county sheriff officers in Colorado's Alamosa County performed a 3 a.m. chase of a helicopter that had bright search lights.[22] Around this time, in Wyoming's Uinta County, a reserve lawman engaged in a shootout with an aggressive military helicopter.[23] By mid-October, Montana was afire with mutilations, low-flying helicopters, and UFOs. A particularly disturbing mutilation case occurred near Great Falls on October 16. A cow had been in a securely locked pasture, yet its left jaw was skinned, its tongue cut out, and its right eye removed – not merely from the socket, but through the bone directly above the eye. The cow had been alive the previous evening, and no tracks were seen.[24] Then, on the night of October 18/19, Malmstrom AFB received nine UFO reports, most of which came from south of Great Falls, between 9 p.m. and 7:45 a.m. At 4:20 a.m. on October 19, the Shelby Sheriff's office reported that police had seen a fast-moving UFO which they estimated to be at an altitude of 2,000 feet. Military radar tracked this object; NORAD and Malmstrom AFB both confirmed that it was not a conventional aircraft.[25]

Unlike the mutilation mystery, which had been getting media attention, UFO sightings such as these received only sporadic local media coverage. Terry Hansen carefully studied this development, and noted that Reuters, Associated Press, and the major networks simply did not pick these stories up, essentially choking them off at the national level.

NORAD's Top Alert

According to the research of investigator Francis Ridge, NORAD appears to have gone on top alert status during late October 1975. Some years later, Ridge came into contact with a person who had witnessed a strange event that had taken place at NORAD. This was a full-scale Security Option 5 Alert, and according to information Ridge received, UFOs and investigators from the "Air Force UFO division" were part of the picture. The date unfortunately was not precisely given.

The first thing Ridge's informant told him was "We weren't drunk!" The men were all employed at NORAD's installation in Cheyenne Mountain, just outside Colorado Springs. They had been hunting all day, had a late night fire going, and were getting ready to sleep. Close to midnight, one of the men thought he saw a shooting star. Fifteen minutes later, someone else said, "Well, there's two of them!" A moment later they saw a third. The lights moved separately to various points in the sky, but eventually lined up and moved directly toward Cheyenne Mountain. Within a few minutes, they heard the buzzers indicating an alert status. The men packed their gear and headed back to their posts – although on leave, they were still on call. They drove to the mountain at top speed and entered the gate at 2:10 a.m., still in their hunting gear. They took their weapons and went to their security posts while the base stayed on alert until 6 a.m. Ridge's informant had radar duty, and later told his friends that he tracked UFOs for "a good 20 minutes." The men also learned that a significant number of jet interceptors had been scrambled.

Within a few days, some of the men started checking into records regarding the security alert. To their surprise, they found that nothing was filed, or perhaps that the key material had been pulled. Apparently their snooping caused Air Force investigators to show up; Ridge's informant referred to them as the Air Force "UFO people." These men interviewed the group one by one, and told the radar operator to file a report with them. They then told the group that what they had seen had been aircraft landing lights. Even so, the men were told to ignore the incident, go about their business, and never mention it again.

Within two months each man in the group received a written reprimand for drinking on duty – which was untrue, and in fact they had not even been on duty at the time of the sighting. Ridge's informant showed him the reprimand documents, along with a letter from a Colonel Terrence C. James, USAF, Director of Administration, stating that the information pertaining to the overflight "is properly and currently classified and is exempt from disclosure under Public Law 90-23, 5 USC 552b(1)."[26]

Up a Notch: Loring Air Force Base

The NORAD case investigated by Ridge, while appearing to be legitimate, remains officially unconfirmed by available U.S. Defense records. Not so concerning intrusions of military airspace across nearly the entire U.S. northern border. These events left a paper trail that became partially declassified a few years later. There is no reasonable argument one can make to dispute their reality. What exactly these objects were remains unknown.

The first confirmed case occurred far away from all the activity in the western U.S. – at Loring AFB in northern Maine. On the evening of October 27, 1975, the base control tower tracked a low flying craft on radar as it approached from the northeast (in Canada), but could not establish contact with it. At 7:45 p.m., Staff Sgt. Danny K. Lewis, on munitions security, saw a low flying craft moving along the northern perimeter of the base. It then penetrated the perimeter at an altitude of about 300 feet. The object had a white strobe light and what appeared to be a red navigation light. Once inside the base, it began to circle, and at one point came to within 300 yards of the nuclear weapons area, dropping its altitude to 150 feet. The Commander of the 42nd Bomb Wing, Colonel Richard E. Chapman, was notified of the situation, and brought the base to major alert status.

This object was inside the base for quite some time, as it was observed by tower patrol at 8:45 p.m. Other units of the 42nd police entered the scene. Colonel Chapman requested fighter coverage from the 21st NORAD Region at Hancock Field, New York, as well as the 22nd NORAD Region at North Bay, Ontario, Canada. In other words, jet interceptors. Interestingly, both groups denied the request. Chapman then had little recourse but to ask for help from Maine State Police. Meanwhile, he increased the base security presence and attempted to identify the craft from his resources at hand. All attempts failed. The craft, which had been in a circling pattern, began to move back toward the northeast. Radar maintained contact until it reached Grand Falls, New Brunswick, about 12 miles away. Canadian authorities were not notified, but the base sent priority messages to National Military Command Center in Washington, D.C., the USAF Chief of Staff, the USAF Forward Operations Division at Fort Ritchie in Maryland, and Strategic Air Command (SAC) Headquarters at the 8th Air Force. Loring remained in a state of high alert well into the morning hours.

The scene at Loring was repeated just twenty-four hours later. At 7:45 p.m. on October 28, three security personnel at the munitions storage area saw an object approaching from the north at an altitude of 3,000 feet. For the next thirty-five minutes, it was under constant visual and radar observation. It had a flashing white light and a solid amber light, and also seemed to have certain stealth characteristics, as it disappeared from view several times.

Once again, Commander Chapman requested air support. This time he received it from a National Guard helicopter and crew; although permission was granted only for tracking and identification, not apprehension, nor for crossing the Canadian border. Chapman must have been feeling frustrated by now, and protested. Why bother authorizing a chopper if it cannot cross the border a mere twelve miles away?* For much of its time under observation, the object kept a distance of at least three miles from the base. But somehow it penetrated security, for suddenly it appeared over the end of the runway at altitude of 150 feet.

Researchers Fawcett and Greenwood reported that a crew chief of a B-52 bomber, along with other members of his crew, saw the object when it was over the flight line. The object appeared red and orange, resembling a "stretched-out football." The crew chief said the object hovered in mid-air as everyone stared. It then turned off its lights and "disappeared." One would have to wonder how a normal object could disappear simply by putting out its lights. A low flying object, even without lights, should have been visible at night if the observer knew where to look. The object reappeared over the north end of the runway. It first moved in "jerky motions," then simply hovered. Although this was a restricted area, the crew drove toward the object anyway, getting to within 300 feet of it. They were afraid of trouble and decided not to report their sighting, but they told

---

* Helicopter border crossings were subsequently permitted, but not for this night.

the researchers that they saw the object clearly. It seemed as though it was practically on the ground, hovering "without movement or noise." It was about "four car lengths long," and described by one witness as looking "like all the colors were blending together, as if you were looking at a desert scene. You see waves of heat rising off the desert floor. . . . The object was solid and we could not hear any noise coming from it." No noise, nor did the witnesses see any doors, windows, propellers, or engines. At this time the base was on high alert, replete with the sound of sirens filling the air and police vehicles speeding around the base.

Again the lights of the object went off. When they came back on again, the object had moved close to the weapons storage area, perhaps within a quarter of a mile, still at an altitude of 150 feet. According to a Defense Department memo, this happened near 1 a.m., which would mean the encounter had been going on for more than five hours. At this time an Army National Guard helicopter attempted to "contact and identify" the intruder, but was "unsuccessful." Not much detail is offered in these Defense memos, but we learn that the object (termed an "unidentified helicopter" in the memos) remained inside the base for at least another two hours.

```
NO CONTACT. THE UNKNOWN AIRCRAFT DID NOT DISPLAY LIGHTING.
GROUND PERSONNEL WERE ABLE TO DIRECT THE AIR GUARD HELICOPTER TO
WITHIN 1000FT OF THE UNKNOWN AIRCRAFT, WITH BOTH HELICOPTERS IN
SIGHT, BUT VISUAL ACQUISITION
WAS NOT MADE. DURING THIS PERIOD A KC-135 WAS ORBITING AT 5000FT
MSL TO AID IN IDENTIFICATION AND TO ACT AS RADIO RELAY.
AT 0500Z ALL CONTACT WAS LOST.
IT IS OUR OPINION THAT THE UNKNOWN HELICOPTER HAS DEMONSTRATED
A CLEAR INTENT IN THE WEAPONS STORAGE AREA, IS SMART AND A MOST
CAPABLE AVIATOR.
LOCAL SECURITY HAS BEEN INCREASED. WE ANTICIPATE FURTHER INCIDEN
ACCORDINGLY, WE WILL REQUEST THE CONTINUED PRESENCE OF AIR GUARD
HELICOPTERS.
WE PLAN TO PURSUE INTO CANADA IF NECESSARY.
```

Segment of a memo that went to the CIA, DIA, White House, and elsewhere, regarding the intrusion at Loring AFB, 1975. The UFO was described as a "helicopter," although this was assumed – never confirmed.

At 3 a.m., it was seen over the weapons storage area, completely unlit, but its dark shape visible to ground personnel. Once again, the Army National Guard helicopter responded, but crew members were unable to see the object – a frustrating experience for ground personnel, who could plainly see both objects from their vantage point. Finally, at some point (the exact time is blacked out), "all contact was lost" with the unknown, although radar once again briefly tracked the object moving toward Grand Falls.

This event lasted no less than seven hours. Seven highly unusual hours, in which an object that invaded the air space of a U.S. base with nuclear weapons was never apprehended, nor even identified. The memo states:

> It is our opinion that the unknown helicopter has demonstrated a clear intent in the weapons storage area, is smart and a most capable aviator. Local security has been increased. We anticipate further incidents. Accordingly, we will request the continued presence of air guard helicopters. We plan to pursue into Canada if necessary. We have coordinated with Maine State Police and Royal Canadian Mounted Police and have been assured of complete cooperation of both. RCMP will respond to any landing site in Canadian territory...[27]

Another intrusion occurred at Loring on October 31. Less is known about the specifics, except that this seems more confidently to have been a helicopter.[28] The Defense Department memo stated that three security policemen reported seeing and hearing a helicopter over the base proper, although the target could not be confirmed by radar. Canadian officials were alerted to check for possible landing sites, but no request was made for a fighter launch. The memo's distribution list included the State Department, Defense Intelligence Agency, CIA, the White House, Air Defense Command, and more.[29] A letter from the base commander stated, "this incident closely parallels a similar helicopter sighting earlier this year," which was said to have occurred in January 1975. However, that claim met with a denial from the Air Force Office of Special Investigation (AFOSI), which stated their records revealed no such events from that period. Researchers Fawcett and Greenwood could find nothing else on the incident.[30]

One reason no action was taken against the objects over Loring was the fear over their proximity to the nuclear weapons. Greenwood later stated that "instructions at the time were not to put searchlights on these aircraft because they were afraid of blinding the pilot and causing him to crash into one of the buildings and creating an accident, nuclear or otherwise."[31] Some speculated about a narcotics trafficking operation, although it is not clear why a narcotics trafficking operation would provoke a military base into a major alert.

Meanwhile, the obvious question is, what flew over Loring? The dominant assumption seems to have been helicopter. The object did appear to be similar in size to a helicopter and to some extent moved like one: hovering and dropping straight down below the radar sweeps. Of course, it makes less sense considering that no sound was reported during the first two intrusions, even at low altitude. What kind of low flying helicopter cannot be easily heard on the ground? In 1975? And what of the apparent helicopter heard on the third night?[32]

While Loring was being visited by an unknown intruder, Fawcett and Greenwood learned of a possible intrusion of the Brunswick Naval Air Station, on the other side of Maine. According to Robert Kinn, he and a fellow student of Bowdoin College were near the Naval Air Station at the end of October, when they saw an object come in very low from the ocean. It was much larger than a helicopter, he said, could make ninety-degree turns, and could fly "very fast." The two witnesses thought the object might have been a vertical takeoff plane, except for the fact that the naval base "lighted up like a Christmas tree .... the excitement on the base was way out of the usual." The object remained over the base for five or ten minutes and then moved back over the Atlantic Ocean. A Brunswick spokesman denied any UFO sightings for that time. Fawcett and Greenwood found no evidence that the witnesses had known anything about the activity at Loring.[33]

Making matters even stranger was an alleged abduction experience that occurred on October 27 in central Maine at the town of Norway – less than forty miles from the Brunswick Naval Air Station, and the same date of the first intrusion at Loring. This concerned two young men named David Stephens and Glen Gray. Early in the morning, while driving on Route 26 toward the town of Oxford, an unknown force wrenched the wheel of their car, taking them at speeds up to 100 mph. They saw two bright lights in a field at the town of Poland – the lights began to rise above the trees and swerved silently in front of their car, where they made out an enormous cigar-shaped object with red, green and blue lights on the side. The men drove away, but a light struck the car and they blacked out, causing them to miss several hours of time. They woke up and continued to drive when, just before dawn, they arrived at Tripp Pond and encountered a huge UFO, possibly the same object as before, along with two other domed saucer-shaped objects above the pond. The two saucers skimmed low over the water and released a grey smoke which surrounded their car. They saw the large UFO high in the air through the smoke. Then, suddenly, all the objects disappeared, even the smoke.

The event seemed utterly unbelievable, but both men had physiological effects (swollen hands and feet, loose teeth, red rings around the neck, and chills) and took it upon themselves to speak to the local sheriff the following day. The sheriff was skeptical of their story, but over the next few months Stephens met with Dr. Herbert Hopkins, a trained hypnotherapist. He underwent eight regression sessions which revealed an abduction experience. He recalled short humanoid creatures between four and five feet tall, with large heads, slanted eyes, no hair or visible mouths, and wearing dark robes. Five or six such entities stood around a long table and had Stephens get on the table to prepare for an examination. Stephens resisted and struck one of the creatures, with no effect. He remembered a small square machine with an extension arm and probe taking samples of his skin, nails, hair, and blood. The encounter seemed to be impossible to believe, and yet offered no easy prosaic explanation. In other words, it was a fairly standard UFO abduction story.[34]

The Wurtsmith AFB Encounter

The confirmed Loring events occurred on October 27, 28, and 31. Meanwhile, on October 30, another UFO entered restricted space at Wurtsmith AFB in Michigan, a SAC base on Michigan's lower peninsula two miles west of Lake Huron. Once again, an object that resembled a helicopter – but then again not exactly – demonstrated interest in the weapons storage facilities.

Just after 10 p.m., an airman in the housing area at the southeastern portion of the base saw what looked like running lights of a low flying craft near the base perimeter south of his position. It had one light pointing down and two red lights near the back. At least part of the time this object hovered and moved up and down somewhat erratically. The witness heard no sound from this object, but did manage to hear a more distant B-52 to the north.

A few minutes later, an on-duty airman near the main gate saw several lights close to his position, near the western edge of the base. He heard no sound and watched the lights turn north and appear to lose altitude. This may or may not have been the same object. Then, three times within the space of eleven minutes, security police at the back gate reported that an unidentified helicopter with no lights entered the base itself. It was low over the ground and seen near the weapons storage area.

As in the case at Loring, no one could confidently identify this craft as a helicopter. One sergeant said he heard the sound of a "possible helicopter" coming from an area off the base toward the north. He heard this briefly, then the noise was drowned out by a military jet. When the jet passed out of range, the original noise was gone and nothing more was heard.

While these visual sightings were occurring, radar personnel reported low flying objects (plural) in the area. It happened that a KC-135 tanker with six personnel on board was then entering the area and was ordered to intercept and identify the object or objects. Vectored by the base control tower, the plane pursued what at first appeared to be a single craft for 35 miles southeast, traveling a little faster than 200 miles per hour. After some time, the crew decided they were seeing two objects. The lights on these objects flashed irregularly, making it appear that they were in communication with each other. No one could be sure, however, and radar returns could not be held for longer than ten seconds at a time. They were only about a mile behind, but every time the crew increased speed to close the distance, the object(s) simply pulled away.

31/0030E Update: Lt Col Giordano (SAC Senior Controller) updates and corrects the above information as follows: An unidentified low flying aircraft came up over the back gate of Wurtsmith and was visually sighted in the vicinity of the motor pool. RAPCON showed several aircraft at the time, one near the WSA (there was no hovering as previously reported). A tanker was dispatched and had visual and skin paint out over Lake Huron of a low flying 'rcraft (with lights on) heading SE at approximately 150 knots.

Air Force report on the Wurtsmith AFB UFO intrusion, October 1975.

At Saginaw Bay, the tanker crew lost their quarry among fishing boat lights. As they started back, it became clear that they were involved in a cat-and-mouse game. The object (apparently it was one object) began following them.

Here is an account of what happened, as told to the official base historian:

> On the way back, we picked the UFO up again at our eight o'clock position. We turned away, and it proceeded to follow us. Finally, we turned back in the direction of the UFO and it really took off back in the direction of the Bay area. I know this might sound crazy, but I would estimate that the UFO sped away from us doing approximately 1,000 knots.

That happens to be more than 1,000 mph. As the plane approached the base, lights again were seen near the weapons storage area. From available records, it is unclear how this matter resolved itself, but obviously the object left at some point. Following the mission, the crew was cautioned "not to discuss the incident."[35]

To the extent that anyone tries to explain this incident, "helicopter" is most typically offered as the culprit. But, what helicopter can travel faster than 1,000 mph?

Looking into the matter a bit further, we find that the U.S. military test-flew a very important helicopter for the very first time on September 30, 1975, shortly before all this airspace violation business began. That was the

Hughes YAH-64, a prototype of the Apache helicopter – one of the world's premier attack helicopters. Although it is ludicrous to explain the Wurtsmith case with the YAH-64/Apache, it is instructive to understand some of the capabilities of this very impressive helicopter. In the first place, during late 1975, there were only two flying models of the YAH-64. Both were in California. By January 1976, these two models had completed a total of roughly 65 flight hours. A full scale development contract did not come until later that year, and Apaches were not delivered to the U.S. Army until 1984. From its inception, the Apache was tough under combat, and reasonably quiet, although it was never silent by any means. (Major strides in helicopter noise reduction were still ten years away, when the benefits of a five-blade design were accidentally discovered.)[36] It could achieve a top speed of roughly 190 mph, with a range of about 300 miles. This range could be extended with external fuel tanks, which however would reduce the speed and general performance of the helicopter. Even the Apache of the 21st century, with its various upgrades and modifications, cannot do the things that were being reported by base personnel in 1975.[37]

What remain are reports of a silent or near-silent aircraft able to hover and maneuver like a helicopter and accelerate like a jet fighter, engaging in confrontational behavior within sensitive U.S. military installations – in 1975.

From Bad to Worse

If the military encounters with UFOs had ended at this point, they would still remain a bizarre and unexplained part of U.S. military history. But the situation worsened in November. Sightings of strange mysterious helicopters, UFOs, and animal mutilations continued.[38]

Two events were recorded at military bases on November 3. One turned out to be a completely "ordinary" security violation at Grand Forks AFB in North Dakota. According to a Department of Defense (DoD) memo, unknown persons penetrated the flight line and "at least two KC-135 aircraft were hit by small arms fire." Security forces pursued the attackers but apparently did not apprehend them. The event seemed to have no connection to the UFO intrusions, although the Air Force frequently referred to it in public statements. Not only did this deflect attention from the genuinely mysterious cases, but it led to the idea that protesters or terrorists were involved instead of actual UFOs.[39]

On the same date, an entry in the log of an Air Force Intelligence Service Alert Officer reported a UFO in Alaska. Further FOIA requests by Fawcett and Greenwood came up empty, however. According to what they were told, information on the event was not kept. "Whatever happened," they wrote, "must have been interesting!"[40]

The lack of truly comprehensive and publicly available records make it difficult to tell for sure where the densest UFO activity was at this time, but the best guess for early November 1975 is Montana. On November 2, near Fort Benton, an on-duty police officer saw a very bright UFO flying irregularly for about 30 minutes. The sheriff's department contacted Radar Approach Control (RAPCON) but was told nothing was seen on radar. On November 5, east of Great Falls, a man reported seeing six UFOs in formation at 4:10 a.m. One dropped down nearly to the level of his truck. On November 7, this time west of Great Falls, another early morning sighting took place. In this case, two women traveling on the highway at 3:38 a.m. reported being followed by a bright light, greyish in color with occasional blue lights.[41]

Malmstrom Air Force Base, Montana

Which brings us to the inexplicable events of November 7, 1975 at Malmstrom Air Force Base in Montana. At approximately 3 p.m., electronic sensors at the base detected a violation of missile site security in an area designated as K-7. An alarm was automatically triggered. Since there were no surveillance cameras in the area, a Sabotage Alert Team (SAT) was ordered to investigate. As the SAT came to within a mile of K-7, members reported by radio that they could see a brightly glowing orange disc, as large as a football field, hovering over the missile site. Presumably, the helicopter explanation can be dispensed with in this case.

As the members of the SAT watched the strange phenomenon, launch control ordered them to proceed to the site. Surprisingly, the men refused. From their safe distance, they noticed it begin to rise. When it reached an altitude of 1,000 feet, it registered on NORAD radar, and F-106 interceptors were promptly scrambled from Malmstrom.

This was clearly not an ordinary object, as it continued to rise, and rise, and rise. It eventually reached the incredible altitude of 200,000 feet (more than double the ceiling of the ultra-high-flying U-2 spy plane). At that point it disappeared from NORAD radar, and the F-106 jets arrived too late to see it. Afterwards, members of the SAT received a psychological examination which indicated that they had been through a traumatic experience. The missile at K-7 showed indications that its computer targeting system had been tampered with, and it had to be removed. It was later revealed that six other Launch Control Centers reported UFOs that day.

UFOs returned to Malmstrom the following night. NORAD radar detected unknowns heading south-southwest at 1,200 feet. Once again, two F-106s were scrambled. Sabotage Alert Teams at five areas reported seeing objects at low altitudes. Again, a pattern of cat-and-mouse emerged. Ground witnesses reported that the UFOs turned off their lights and became invisible as the intercepting jets approached, and turned their lights back on after the jets departed. At one point, teams in four different locations could see both the F-106s and the UFOs. Finally, the unknown objects rose rapidly until they were, in the words of the memo, "indistinguishable from the stars."

Throughout November, 1975, UFOs continued to enter U.S. military air space with impunity. On November 10, according to a NORAD report, a bright, silent object buzzed by Minot AFB in North Dakota at the altitude of 1,000 to 2,000 feet. Three base personnel saw it and notified the National Command Center Operations.[42] Offut Air Force Base in Nebraska also reported intrusions. A November 10 memo noted "several recent sightings of unidentified aircraft/helicopters flying/hovering over Priority A restricted areas during the hours of darkness." As in the intrusions elsewhere, however, "all attempts to identify these aircraft have met with negative results."[43]

The next day, November 11, a police captain and deputy were driving from Missoula, Montana to Great Falls when a large orange light descended, lighting up the road. The officers described the object as traveling at "incredible speed," as low as 200 feet in altitude, but silent. They reported the event to Malmstrom AFB. On the same day, an employee of the Montana Fish and Game Department saw a B-52 bomber flying over Freezeout Lake (northwest of Great Falls) being paced by an unknown object. This object briefly attached itself to the bomber, detached itself, and then climbed out of sight. Choteau County Sheriff, Pete Howard, took the report, and conducted follow-up interviews with military. Although the Air Force denied knowledge, military personnel confirmed the event and added that the plane's radar equipment went out as the object attached itself.[44]

FOIA documents also confirm a UFO intrusion on November 11 at Falconbridge, Ontario, site of a NORAD installation with nuclear weapons. Shortly after 4 p.m., civilians, police, military, and NORAD radar saw and tracked a UFO that hovered and maneuvered at high speed. According to the NORAD document, ground observers thought the object looked like a very bright star, but much closer. This was confirmed when radar picked up an object in the area at 26,000 feet. Two F-106 jets were sent from Selfridge Air National Guard Base in Michigan, but reported no contact either visually or on radar. Yet, the NORAD report states that with binoculars, "the object appeared as a 100 ft diameter sphere and appeared to have craters around the outside."[45]

This was the one instance in which NORAD personnel immediately and openly admitted they tracked a UFO. Captain Gordon Hilchie, Director of Public Affairs for Canadian NORAD Headquarters, stated "yes, we saw this so-called UFO at the same time people outside were saying they saw it, too." He added that the UFO zoomed upward from 26,000 feet to 45,000 feet, "stopped awhile, and then moved up very quickly to 72,000 feet." Lieutenant Colonel Brian Wooding, Director of the 22nd NORAD Region Control Center, agreed. Del Kindschi, spokesperson for NORAD Headquarters in Colorado Springs, added that the UFO was tracked intermittently on radar for six hours. Furthermore, the Base Commanding Officer, Major Robert Oliver, openly stated that he and five others at the base saw not one but *three* mysterious objects in the sky. "I think both the United States and Canada collect [UFO] information," he said, "and I do believe they investigate the more serious ones." When told that the U.S. government claimed it no longer investigated UFOs, he replied, "I find that strange, because in accordance with the normal procedures I classified the UFO report going to Colorado Springs as secret." Shortly afterwards, USAF General Daniel James, the Commanding General of NORAD, asked him to declassify the report. "Apparently General James wanted to provide information to people who were interested in it," said Oliver.[46]

Three years later the Canadian National Research Council announced that the UFOs seen over Ontario had been layers of crystallized ice in the atmosphere.[47] General James apparently did not think so. In his November 11 memo, he tells units throughout North America about "numerous reports of suspicious objects" at Loring, Wurtsmith, Malmstrom, Minot, and Falconbridge bases. He stated that many of these sightings were probably helicopters, but he added that "to date efforts by Air Guard helicopters, SAC helicopters and NORAD F-106s have failed to produce a positive ID." One supposes that helicopters might be more plausible than ice crystals, but skepticism is nevertheless in order considering that neither F-106 pilots, ground observers, radar operators, nor any other witnesses ever actually identified these objects as helicopters. How could so many witnesses fail to do so? The Commander expressed his concern about preventing "overreaction by the public to reports by the media that may be blown out of proportion." Presumably unknown objects over nuclear weapons facilities was not a very big deal.[48]

Meanwhile, military personnel continued to encounter UFOs. On November 12, RAPCON was contacted regarding a UFO sighting east of Fairfield, Montana, although witnesses were told nothing was being tracked on radar. On the same day at Falconbridge, two lighted objects were seen moving erratically through broken clouds, but were not tracked on radar. On the 15th at Falconbridge, a NORAD report described a bright yellow object seen visually, but not tracked on radar. On November 16, witnesses in Caribou, Maine, including police and base personnel at Loring, reported a bright light that hovered for a long while, primarily with blinking green and red lights, but often changing colors. Smoke or exhaust was also seen. On the 17th, a NORAD report described a large, stationary, orange ball in the sky near "River Court, Ontario." In fact, there is no town in Ontario named River Court, although there is an area in the city of Hamilton, Ontario, called River Court. The object had two red lights and was not picked up on radar. On the same day from Manitoulin Island, Ontario, two oval shaped objects with two yellow flashing lights were seen by witnesses; again, radar did not track them.[49]

Around November 19, another strange "helicopter" wave took place in Montana, in Cascade, Teton, Pondera, and Chouteau counties. At least two helicopters were reported over a missile site, and Malmstrom AFB verified unidentified helicopters in the area. Lieutenant Colonel Frederick Judd, Director of Public Affairs for the 24th NORAD region, conceded that "some kind of phenomenon" had been reported on six or seven occasions by SAC employees at Minuteman bases near Harlowton and Fort Benton. Incredibly, he added that these did not represent "anything that's a threat."[50]

This type of activity went on into December. At 8:47 p.m. on December 2, missile crews at Malmstrom AFB reported a low-flying helicopter near the Juliet missile site, near the town of Brady, Montana. By 9:31, Malmstrom notified Cascade County sheriff's department that two craft were being reported from different missile sites. Reports of helicopters and UFOs poured into the sheriff's office and Malmstrom. The same event recurred on December 3 with widespread helicopter sightings. At least two unknown objects were reported at the same time over a missile site, a fact verified by Malmstrom AFB.[51]

It is hard to conceive of any responsible officer not considering these to be a threat, or at least a serious problem that needed to be investigated. It is equally hard to imagine how a responsible officer would openly admit these concerns to the general public. We know these events were investigated by the Air Force and most likely by other relevant agencies, but no

BASES. SINCE 27 OCT 75, SIGHTINGS HAVE OCCURRED AT LORING AFB, WURTSMITH AFB, AND MOST RECENTLY, AT MALMSTROM AFB. ALL ATTEMPTS TO IDENTIFY THESE AIRCRAFT HAVE MET WITH NEGATIVE RESULTS.

2. WHILE AFFECTED BASES ARE NOW RETURNING TO NORMAL SECURITY POSTURE (AT THE OPTION OF THE LOCAL COMMANDER), ALL SAC SECURITY POLICE UNITS ARE REQUESTED TO MONITOR AND REPORT ALL SIGHTINGS OF UNIDENTIFIED AIRCRAFT/HELICOPTERS FLYING/HOVERING IN THE VICINITY OF WEAPONS STORAGE AREAS, AIRCRAFT ALERT AREAS AND MISSILE LAUNCH/LAUNCH CONTROL FACILITIES. AT THE DISCRETION OF LOCAL COMMANDERS, UNITS WILL IMPLEMENT AN APPROPRIATE SECURITY POSTURE UPON DETECTION OF SIMILAR CIRCUMSTANCES.

Segment of Strategic Air Command memo on the air space violations, 11/75.

conclusions are available. The National Military Command Center (NMCC) issued a memorandum on November 13 requesting a "Temperature Inversion Analysis" to determine if weather conditions could be responsible for the sightings. On the face of it, weather seems an implausible culprit, and certainly within a few years (by 1981), the Air Force stopped requiring temperature inversion analyses. Presumably they had been of little use in investigating UFOs.[52]

The real question is how a responsible news media could miss, or would ignore, the story of UFOs over military bases. The military was simply trying to do its job, and public panic would only impede its work. But Americans relied upon the news media as their "watch dog." The American news media, particularly at the national levels, failed to report these astonishing and dramatic events. One is left only with two possibilities: news media incompetence or complicity with national security groups – or some combination of both. It should be added that at no time during this wave of activity did the U.S. Senate or House of Representatives discuss the matter. Indeed, there is no evidence that either body was informed of what was going on.

The wave of air space violations was not publicly known for two years. After some documentation on these events reached the public in the late 1970s, UFO researchers inquired with Malmstrom officials, hoping to obtain more information. They were told that all documentation had been destroyed in accordance with Air Force directives.[53]

A final point to remember about these various NORAD cases is that we only have the tip of the probable iceberg, at least in terms of documentation. Judging from the serious nature of the confirmed reports, one should have expected many follow-up reports, but none are available. What we do have indicates that the U.S. and Canadian militaries had provocative UFO encounters through the remainder of the year, and well into 1976. Moreover, that the military authorities succeeded in keeping the news media, elected officials, and general public out of the loop. If not for a few dogged UFO researchers, the story would probably have never been known at all.

Some Unconfirmed Encounters

In addition to the confirmed events of late 1975, several unconfirmed reports have trickled in over the years, reported to various UFO researchers and websites.

One was a reported close encounter which occurred in Colorado in early November 1975. No precise date was given, but the encounter occurred on a Sunday, so in all likelihood either November 2 or 9. Bill and Cheryl Jackson were driving with their young child home to Sterling, just east of the Rocky Mountains. (As an aside, Bill Jackson was a reporter for the *Sterling Journal Advocate* and had written about the cattle mutilation phenomenon.) Between 8 and 9 p.m., twenty miles north of the town of Otis, a red light appeared in the overcast sky, becoming larger. Bill assumed it was an aircraft, except that it seemed unusually large. He thought the pilot was reckless, since it was coming dangerously close to the ground. He got out of the car while Cheryl watched from inside. Once outside, he realized the object was making no sound, and coming directly toward their position. It continued to approach, then passed directly over them in complete silence at a speed of less than 50 mph. It was so low that Jackson felt he could have hit it with a stone. He said it had "row after row after row of lights ... at least a dozen rows ... hundreds and hundreds of lights; red, orange, green, white, all colors.... That sucker was huge!" Cheryl described it as an enormous elongated object with many indentations across the bottom. She also said it was silent and that its altitude was less than 100 feet. The two were curious about the object, and wondered how it could have stayed in the air at such a slow speed, but as Cheryl put it, "common sense prevailed and we took off at high speed." The entire event lasted four or five minutes. UFO researcher Richard Sigismond later interviewed the couple and described them as intelligent and sincere.[54]

Three more events from this period were reported years after the fact to the website of Canadian researcher Brian Vike. The reader is reminded that these are not confirmed accounts, and the last one involves some information which is third-hand. They are offered here as provisional stories which are consistent with the confirmed events related previously.

One was said to have taken place at Warren AFB in southeastern Wyoming, just north of the Colorado border. It is reminiscent of the situation at Malmstrom AFB from November 8. The writer stated it occurred while he was on duty between June 1975 and June 1976, but since he describes snow on the ground, this would most likely be during the winter of 1975/76. He said he was a non-commissioned officer working in Keys and Codes, which issued codes for access to unmanned Minuteman missiles, and was located within Central Security Control (CSC). One night a missile launch crew reported that alarms were triggered at a Minuteman silo. Above ground from the launch center, a security police team saw "a bright white object lighting up the countryside and hovering over the silo." At this point, the team refused to respond. CSC then asked the launch crew what they thought about the situation and why the security police refused to respond. The launch crew replied that they would get back to CSC. According to the writer, "we never heard back from them during the remainder of our shift." He stated that maintenance crews reported seeing large foot prints in the snow near the silos, and that security police reported colored balls of light drifting through their sleeping quarters at the launch center sites during the night. The writer of the report received no answer as to what had happened.[55]

Another event concerned a UFO sighting over the McAlester Naval Depot in Oklahoma, said to have occurred sometime in 1975. The writer was a military policeman on patrol, driving a pickup truck. At about 7 p.m., the truck engine and radio died for no apparent reason. He saw a flashing red light, initially thought to be a tower light, but which then moved very rapidly – he estimated perhaps 500 mph or even "thousands" of miles per hour – to different locations around the base, and "then back to the start position." He wrote that several other individuals saw this. The witness added that during this period there were "reports coming in all the time," including reports of strange lights being beamed down on the bunkers.[56]

The third report to Vike stems from late 1975 or early 1976, and occurred at Clark AFB in the Philippines. The witness worked as an assistant shift leader in the base fuels distribution office, dispatching trucks. Near midnight, a truck arrived with personnel returning from a shift who were visibly shaken. They said they had been followed by a glowing orange ball about three feet in diameter. The ball had followed the truck, rising up and then dropping lower. About halfway back to the base, the object rose and disappeared. The witness later met with another individual who worked at Clark, and who related a UFO story from the same night (although one wonders how the witness knew it was the same night when we have no dates for the story). This other person received a report from a security policeman on the flight line directly in front of the control tower. The policeman had seen an orange disc directly over him, perhaps 75 or 100 feet in diameter. The disc hovered for a few seconds, "then shot straight up, disappearing almost immediately." The person receiving the report called the security police commander, who asked if he had logged the event. When he answered "no," the commander said not to bother, and "to forget that the incident ever happened."[57]

Fire in the Sky - The Travis Walton Abduction

As we have seen, amid the unexplained UFO sightings and animal mutilations that so gripped the western U.S., several interesting cases of alleged alien abduction also occurred. The one which has left the deepest impression on the public imagination is the Travis Walton abduction case.[58] The fact that it occurred within a major wave of activity concerning UFOs, black helicopters, and animal mutilations, deserves a nod of acknowledgment.

On Wednesday, November 5, 1975, in the Apache-Sitgreaves National Forest, northeast of Phoenix, Arizona, a logging crew was preparing to end their day of work. Mike Rogers, 28, was the foreman. He supervised six forestry employees, including his close friend, 22 year old Travis Walton. The other men on the crew were Ken Peterson, John Goulette, Steve Pierce, Allen Dalis and Dwayne Smith. All lived in the small town of Snowflake, Arizona.

On this day of work, however, they returned without Travis. What Rogers and the rest of the crew told the police was that they had seen a UFO and that they believed Walton had been taken by its occupants. According to their account, at about 6:15 p.m., as they were in the truck preparing to go home, all seven men saw a glowing silver object hovering 15 or 20 feet above the ground. No one actually saw the UFO move – it simply was there. "It looked like two pie pans," Rogers said. He estimated it to be about 15 feet in diameter and 8 feet high. It had markings, "too complicated to describe," and the object seemed to light up the area. It gave off a sound, described as "electrical, high and low pitch."

Walton, in the front passenger seat, got out of the truck and impulsively walked toward the object. The object began to wobble from side to side, and struck him directly on the chest with a beam of bluish white light, perhaps two feet thick. Ken Peterson said that the light beam "kind of lifted him up off the ground. His arms were outstretched and he was knocked to the ground." In panic, his companions drove off, fearing Walton was dead and that the disc was chasing them. After a few minutes, they regained enough composure to return to the scene. But neither Walton nor the object were there. The six men drove fifteen miles north to Heber and reported the experience to officer Chuck Ellison at about 7:35 p.m. Ellison later said the men were very upset and one was weeping. He did not know what to make of such a fantastic story, but said that if the witnesses were lying, "they were damned good actors." Sheriff Marlin Gillespie, along with officer Ken Coplan, soon met with the men. Rogers wanted an immediate search party organized, with tracking dogs. No dogs were available at the moment, but the officers and some of the crew went back out to look – three crew members were too upset to go.

At the scene, no physical evidence was found, and the officers wondered if Walton had been murdered. Even if Walton were alive, his jeans, tee shirt, and denim jacket would not protect him from a bitterly cold November night. That evening, Rogers and Coplan visited Snowflake to see Walton's mother, Mary Walton Kellett. Rogers told her what happened, and she asked him to repeat it. She then calmly asked whether anyone else other than the witnesses and police had heard the story. Coplan thought this was rather odd behavior. Defenders of Kellett maintained that she was a guarded person, a single mother of six children, and was trying her best not to fly apart. At 3 a.m., she phoned her second oldest child, Duane Walton, who drove to see her.

By the morning of November 6, there was still no trace of Travis, and police suspicions grew. Rogers was adamant that they continue the search. This time, helicopters, mounted police, and jeeps were used. Still no sign of Travis Walton.

The news began to spread, and UFO researchers came to see what was going on. One was Fred Sylvanus of Phoenix, who recorded interviews with Mike Rogers and Duane Walton on November 8. Some of their statements were later used by skeptics to cast suspicion on the case, Duane Walton, for instance, remarked that he and Travis were interested in UFOs (and that many years in the past Duane had seen a UFO). He also suggested that Travis would not be injured by the aliens, because "they don't harm people." William Spaulding of Ground Saucer Watch also interviewed Duane and offered the services of a doctor to examine Travis, if he ever returned. Spaulding told the press that if this case was a hoax, it was the best he had ever seen.

The weekend brought no news of Travis, and on Monday, November 10, all six crew members took polygraph examinations administered by Cy Gilson of the Arizona Department of Public Safety. Gilson asked straight-forward questions: did they cause harm to Travis (or know who had harmed him), did they know where Travis's body was buried, and did they tell the truth about seeing a UFO. The men all denied harming Travis or knowing who had harmed him. They also denied knowing where his body was, and they maintained they had seen a UFO. One man, Allen Dalis, was extremely agitated and did not complete his exam, rendering it invalid. (It was later learned that he was hiding a criminal record). For the rest, however, Gilson stated that the men's results were conclusive. "These polygraph examinations," he wrote, "prove that these five men did see some object they believed to be a UFO, and that Travis Walton was not injured or murdered by any of these men on that Wednesday." The tests apparently made a believer out of Gillespie, who seemed to accept the UFO story and said, "There's no doubt they're telling the truth."

Regarding this polygraph, one commentator, Geoff Price, wrote:

> The significance of the unanimous passing of competently administered CQT examinations by all six witnesses is considerable. Assuming independent tests, the odds of gross hoax (all participants lying about the UFO encounter) is less than one-tenth of a percent using the reasonably conservative figure of 70% for test accuracy, and on the order of one in a million using the 90% figure suggested by field tests. In short, relatively strong evidence that some kind of real event took place. [59]

Travis Walton reappeared on November 10. Close to midnight, he called his brother-in-law, Grant Neff, from a phone booth. Neff and Duane Walton drove out and found Travis, still in the phone booth, looking exhausted, confused, and with a heavy growth of beard. He was wearing the same clothing from the week before. He complained of chest pain, which he said was from tests performed on him while he was aboard a UFO. When told he had been missing for five days, he seemed stunned by the news. He said all he could remember was about two hours. After returning to his mother's home, Travis said he bathed and tried to eat, but was unable to keep from vomiting.

Surprisingly, Duane did not report Travis's return immediately. He said this was because of his brother's fragile condition, but the decision only caused more problems later, fueling suspicions that he was covering up a hoax. Duane did remember Spaulding's suggestion to keep a sample of Travis's first urination following his return, and remembered the promise of a confidential medical exam. So, on the following morning (and still not having notified authorities of Travis's return), Duane drove his brother to Phoenix to meet with Dr. Lester Steward. It turned out that Steward was not a licensed doctor at all, but a hypnotherapist. What happened at this meeting is disputed. The Waltons claimed they spent 45 minutes at his office, nearly all of which was wasted trying to determine his qualifications. Steward and Spaulding stated that the Waltons had been there for more than two hours.

After they returned to Snowflake, Spaulding phoned Duane, who told him not to contact them again. After this, Spaulding began calling the case a hoax. Coral Lorenzen of APRO also spoke with Duane, promising an examination for Travis by two medical doctors at Duane's home. Duane agreed, and the exam began later on the afternoon of November 11. The examination revealed that Travis was in good health, but with two unusual features. First, a small red spot at the crease of his right elbow that was consistent with a hypodermic injection, although the spot was not near a vein and there was no sign of drugs in his system. Second, Walton's urine revealed a lack of acetones. This was odd, since his significant weight loss suggested he had not been eating, and his body should have begun breaking down fats in order to survive, which would lead to high levels of acetone in his urine.

Another factor entered the already complex picture. The *National Enquirer* tabloid had contacted APRO, offering to finance an investigation in exchange for "cooperation and access to the Waltons." Coral and Jim Lorenzen agreed. There is no question that the money helped APRO get certain things done; no question also that the involvement of the tabloid brought harm to the case. It is true that during the mid-1970s, *The Enquirer* engaged in some legitimate journalism, including on the UFO topic. But it was still a sensationalist tabloid with very little respectability. Placing the Walton story at the supermarket check-out line was not a good sign.

Later on the 11th, Sheriff Gillespie finally learned of Travis's return and met with the Waltons. Travis told him of his encounter, which involved two kinds of beings: one type was human, the other was not. He had been examined by hairless beings in tight-fitting blue clothing in a white room. He tried to talk with them but they made no sound. When he moved to get up, they tried to hold him down, and he took a swing at one of them. The creatures simply left the room. Walton then got up and went into another room which contained a chair. He sat in it and pressed some buttons on the arms of the chair, at which point the ceiling slid back and he could see stars going by. A being wearing a helmet entered the room, smiled and silently escorted him to a large room where he saw a parked spacecraft. A device like an oxygen mask was placed on his face by people with long hair. The next thing Walton remembered was lying on the pavement near the town of Heber on the highway. A disc-shaped craft was hovering just above, then shot away. He then made his telephone call to Neff.

Travis said he would gladly take any kind of test Gillespie wanted. Gillespie said he would arrange for a polygraph, and promised to keep it secret to avoid the media circus. The two brothers then drove to Scottsdale, where they met with APRO consultant James Harder. Harder hypnotized Travis, but little more came out, and Walton believed he would "die" if the regression continued. Another APRO consultant, Dr. Gene Rosenbaum, performed "a comprehensive battery of psychiatric and medical exams." Rosenbaum's "absolute" conclusion was that "this young man is not lying, that there is no collusion involved."[60]

As promised, Gillespie arranged for a polygraph, but word quickly leaked and Duane canceled it, assuming Gillespie was responsible. Not true, countered Gillespie. The affair was already a circus – everything leaks in such a situation. As a result, *The National Enquirer* quickly arranged for a polygraph, after Duane insisted that he and Travis have the power to veto any public disclosure of the results. Harder expressed concern that Travis was too agitated to take a polygraph, but the examiner, John J. McCarthy of the Arizona Polygraph Laboratory, said this was not a problem.

Thus, on the 15th of November, McCarthy administered a polygraph examination to Travis Walton. Prior to the exam, McCarthy learned that Travis had occasionally smoked marijuana, and also that he and Rogers's younger brother had once committed check fraud some years earlier. It was Walton's only brush with the law in his life, and he was not proud of it. McCarthy then administered the test. Walton was agitated and McCarthy was hostile. He interrupted Walton 28 times during the questioning, at one point berated him when Walton was confused about dates, and actually said, "Where have you been, in a vacuum?"

McCarthy concluded Walton was engaging in "gross deception," but the conclusion was withheld publicly for many months. The Waltons, APRO and the *National Enquirer* agreed to keep the results a secret because (they maintained) they doubted McCarthy's methods and objectivity. Coral Lorenzen essentially called McCarthy biased and incompetent. She, Travis, and Duane believed that he had intentionally asked Travis embarrassing and irrelevant questions in order to create conditions more likely to produce a negative result.

In the spring of 1976, aviation writer and UFO skeptic Phillip J. Klass received a tip on the polygraph and wrote about it. This damaged Walton's standing with many UFO researchers, to say nothing of the general public. Klass launched a campaign against Walton that lasted for many years, arguing that there was a strong financial motive to the hoax. He argued that Mike Rogers knew he would fail to complete his contract with the Forest Service, and created a scheme to invoke the contract's Act of God clause. He mentioned the Walton family's alleged prior interest in UFOs, which he said brought their claims into question. He noted that NBC had aired "The UFO Incident" just a few weeks before Travis's disappearance. This made-for-television film described the famous 1961 abduction account of Betty and Barney Hill. Klass stated that Walton had probably been inspired by the program. And of course, Klass never tired of pointing out that Walton had flunked McCarthy's polygraph test.

There were counter arguments to each of these points. Travis Walton said he had not seen the television special. And Jerome Clark pointed out that Walton's account of his time on the UFO is very different from the Hill account, anyway.[61] Regarding Mike Rogers, he had completed many Forest Service contracts, and on two occasions had failed to complete them. This had not been a serious problem, and he continued to get rehired. More tellingly, Rogers never tried to invoke an Act of God clause after Walton disappeared, nor ever.

Causing more strife was the lack of cooperation and even infighting among UFO organizations regarding this case. There was a certain irony to this, considering the organizations had for some time been talking about the need for better coordinating their efforts. Yet, during the Walton affair, MUFON, APRO, NICAP, CUFOS, and GSW competed with each other and withheld information far more than they assisted one another.

With the results of the McCarthy test public, APRO quickly arranged for a follow-up examination of Walton by another polygraph administrator, George Pfeifer. Pfeifer tested Travis, Duane, and their mother, concluding that all were truthful in their accounts.

Years later, in 1993, prior to the release of the movie *Fire in the Sky*, about the Walton experience, a skeptical investigator named Jerry Black reopened the case and arranged for yet another polygraph test. Cy Gilson, the man who had performed the initial polygraph of Walton's six co-workers in 1975, was brought in again to administer tests to Travis, Mike

Rogers, and Allen Dalis (who had originally tested inconclusively). All three passed.

The Walton case, like so many other UFO and abduction cases, is like a house with many different sides, having a different appearance depending on where one is standing. For a physical scientist interested in hard proof of alien abduction, this case cannot pass the test. There was precious little that could actually count as physical evidence (Walton's puncture mark, one supposes); certainly nothing that could be analyzed and studied. The polygraph studies can be seen as helpful or not helpful, depending on how one views the McCarthy test. It does seem like a stretch to discount the testimony of Walton's crew members who all claimed that they saw a UFO issue a beam of light, striking Walton and rendering him unconscious. Although Klass did question the competence of Gilson on that very point, no polygraph expert has supported the contention that so many people could successfully lie on the same question.

If Mike Rogers and the rest of the crew were telling the truth, and they did see a UFO, it certainly would lend support to Travis Walton's own claim. The contention argued by some at the time, that there had probably been a UFO sighting but no abduction, seems rather silly in retrospect. If a UFO had shown up, where would Walton have gone? Everyone in town was looking for him, and he clearly seemed much the worse for wear upon his return. Some people noted that Walton's abduction account differs in significant ways from the "standard" abduction account of being probed by little grey aliens with big black eyes. Walton instead described beings that looked decidedly human, along with creatures that looked alien. Then again, do all aliens have to look like the Greys? Do all UFOs have to be piloted by aliens?

Regarding the presence of humans and aliens together, there are many avenues of speculation. One might concern humans that had been "bred" by non-human groups. What if "others" had arrived to Earth but could not simply walk around on the surface of the planet due to the myriad of biohazards that might exist. Would it not be convenient to have a personal supply of humans (genetically modified and perhaps enhanced artificially) at one's disposal for all types of missions? The idea admittedly has no hard evidence to support it, but within the context of the paradigm shattering reality of UFOs, it is not necessarily illogical or implausible.[62]

Summing Up 1975

In the history of UFOs, 1975 does not capture the imagination of the general public the way that 1947 does. Yet the year was nothing short of spectacular. Unlike 1947, 1952, or 1966, when UFO sightings received a great deal of coverage by the U.S. media, the events of this year – as well as 1974, for that matter – received scarcely any attention at all. In 1952 and 1966, the U.S. military made formal, public statements on UFOs. Nothing of the sort occurred in 1975, even though the situation was more grave. It is understandable that an entrenched bureaucracy would not want to make matters worse by telling the public what was going on. Whoever was behind the air space violations of 1975 – be they human or alien – had technology that the U.S. military feared, and the confidence to fly brazenly into restricted areas containing nuclear weapons, and then confidently fly away. How does one tell the public that?

The question of Human vs. Alien in this instance is clearly important. If we choose to consider that the offending aircraft were of human origin, we must ask, *which humans?* That is, an official military unit – even one that might have been deep black – conducting some sort of readiness exercise or testing new technology? There is little evidence supporting this position, and just as little logic. The objects that flew over U.S. and Canadian bases were never identified. Within an era of explosive technological growth, several decades have passed and there is yet no candidate within the U.S. military's stable of aircraft that could account for the events of 1975. If they were secret U.S. prototypes, they have never been used in any known military engagement, despite their obvious superiority to American aircraft of the day.

Could they be of human origin, but not under the strict control of the U.S. military? Such a scenario seems plausible when considering the position of some people – like retired New Mexico State Trooper Gabriel Valdez – who argued that the cattle mutilation phenomenon was entirely due to covert human action, a black-world operation essentially beyond the law. Could such a program could be run so secretly, but with such money behind it, that it would be essentially independent of formal government control? If so, why fly exotic aircraft over sensitive U.S. bases again and again? With what technology? If one sees these violations as purely human in origin, presumably the alleged cases of alien abduction that occurred in their midst would be dismissed either as fantasy, hoax, or an ultra-clandestine mind control program conducted for purposes unknown.

Then there is the alien scenario, in which the questions are surprisingly similar. If aliens were harassing these American bases, it would not be inconceivable to suppose they were interested in the nuclear weapons. One could further imagine that in their various enterprises here, from time to time they might check in on the natives. Where might such aliens be living most of the time? Perhaps, if some remote viewers were correct, under the surface of the Earth, secure from bio-hazards and frightened (dangerous? pesky?) humans. There is no lack of observational reports to conclude that *something* very bizarre has been traversing the skies and oceans of the world. If not a secret human group, then ...

Divining the response to this crisis by the U.S. military is possible only by noting the gravity of the few documents available with the utter lack of follow-up documentation. It is not credible and indeed not possible that these air space violations did not receive thorough and detailed follow-up, and yet no conclusions of any sort are available to us. The only reasonable conclusion is that the findings remain deeply hidden.

The mid-1970s were an unusual period in American history, because they represent the "high water tide" of 20th century American progressive culture, when it actually was political and before it devolved into mere "political correctness." In 1975, Americans could say with some justification (and many qualifications) that their political system "worked." They had chased a corrupt President from office, new laws promoting Freedom of Information had been passed, and it appeared that a new era of government openness might just come to pass.

But openness is relative. For even in 1975, the national security apparatus of the United States budged only a little bit, and then no more. The law on Freedom of Information had been passed, yes. But other than obtaining the CIA's report on the Robertson Panel, no one had yet forced any military or intelligence agency to give away UFO secrets. As far as the public knew in 1975, the FBI, CIA, and all the military groups were not collecting UFO data. The truth about this would be revealed soon enough, although not without major resistance and spin control.

1976: The State of UFO Research

Not all UFO researchers were talking about cover-ups, or even extraterrestrials. Jacques Vallee's *The Invisible College* continued in the vein of his "five arguments against the ETH," suggesting that "a powerful force has influenced the human race in the past and is again influencing it now. Does this force represent alien intervention, or does it originate entirely within human consciousness?" During the spring of 1976, Vallee and Hynek co-authored *The Edge of Reality*, which discussed UFOs in a similar manner. Both conveyed the feeling that the ETH could not fully explain UFOs. Although they acknowledged the phenomenon was real, its reality skirted the edges of accepted science. Some of their specifics were muddy, as when Hynek discussed "psychic projection" to resolve violations of the laws of physics. Portions of the book accused other UFO groups and researchers of amateurism and of not producing scientific papers. This was somewhat ironic, since Hynek's CUFOS had done less investigation and research to that point than any of the other groups.

Many members of MUFON were already becoming uneasy with Hynek, despite the efforts of Walter Andrus and Richard Hall to promote good relations (like it or not, said Hall, CUFOS was a rallying point for scientists who took UFOs seriously).[63] But now unease transformed into open hostility. *Skylook* editor Dwight Connolly called the attacks on MUFON and other groups "one of the more controversial, ill considered, and inaccurate sections of the book." When Hynek replied that Connelly's criticism was excessive, Connelly responded that Hynek seemed to feel he was beyond reproach. Indeed, said Connelly, Hynek happily criticized others, was uncooperative with other groups, and gained his public renown not from competent UFO investigation, but from Air Force publicity. In fact, he said, Hynek "has actually done far less with far less expertise than a great many others," and was "a walking organizational and public-relations disaster.... his own worst enemy."[64]

Two board members of MUFON even resigned early in 1976, in part because of their objection to MUFON's close association with Hynek. One of these was Deputy Director John Schuessler, who had been disheartened by the "total lack of anything worthwhile coming out of CUFOS." When Hynek initially sent out the private invitations to his conference, many leading MUFON researchers were left off, including apparently Schuessler (although Walter Andrus interceded on Schuessler's behalf). The bad blood was compounded when MUFON's Board invited Hynek to speak at their 1976 symposium. Schuessler wondered why the leadership was so accommodating not merely to Hynek, but to open debunkers as Philip Klass. Schuessler's departure was brief. He soon returned – and in later years succeeded Andrus as MUFON's Director.[65] Interestingly, Connolly resigned from *Skylook* in June 1976, for reasons which he said were personal and not related to his feud with Hynek.[66]

For all the criticisms, Hynek was trying to breathe life into CUFOS. He was active in forming the group's journal, the *International UFO Reporter*, and had arranged for CUFOS to employ full-time investigator Allen Hendry. Meanwhile, Hynek was Ufology's front man, speaking to media, hailed as the "Galileo" of ufology, and always in the hunt for funding. On April 30, 1976, the much anticipated private conference was held in Chicago. It was intended as a kind of think tank for researchers, featuring presentations on sighting waves, "exosociology," reports of aliens ("humanoids"), and more. Presenters included Ted Bloecher, Ann Druffel, Loren Gross, Richard Hall, David Jacobs, James McCampbell, David Saunders, R. Leo Sprinkle, David Webb, Ray Stanford, and others. In fact, considering all the build-up, the 1976 CUFOS Conference, as it became known, was a disappointment. The erudite Lucius Farish of MUFON called the published proceedings "utter dullsville." Lots of technical information with some value, but which made for truly boring reading. This was accurate, if a bit harsh. For better and for worse, the conference proceedings read very much like academic proceedings from any other discipline, which had obviously been Hynek's goal.[67]

The first issue of the *International UFO Reporter* appeared in November 1976, with Hynek as editor-in-chief and Allen Hendry as managing editor. Hynek wrote an "Estimate of the Situation," describing his philosophy of UFOs: he emphasized that they were *unexplained*, although noteworthy for the consistency of reports about them, and for a frequency of sightings far greater than most people realized. He chided the scientific community for ignoring the subject, but also distanced himself from the "untutored and the 'mentally tilted'" who were unfortunately associated with the subject. He wrote that the *IUR* would not allow any particular theory (such as the extraterrestrial hypothesis) to obfuscate the "open study of the phenomenon." After all, "there might be *another* answer – even several answers!"[68]

Hynek was clearly trying to put the brakes on the ETH. This position, as much as anything else, was behind his friction with other UFO researchers. Was Hynek's dissatisfaction with the ETH purely the result of detached judgment? Or were other factors involved: the ingrained conservatism of a lifelong academician, or the result of his longstanding connection with the U.S. intelligence community? The suspicions about Hynek's motives, held by different UFO researchers in the 1950s and 1960s during his Blue Book days, dogged him through the 1970s and beyond.

The main thrust of UFO research, in any case, came not from Hynek, but from FOIA researchers such as Brad Sparks, Robert Todd, William Spaulding, and W. Todd Zechel, all of whom filed requests with U.S.

government agencies regarding UFO data. Obstructionism still reigned supreme. In March 1976, the CIA told Spaulding that it had no interest in UFOs; Todd received the same answer from the NSA. Undeterred, they continued filing more requests.[69] Zechel also focused on the CIA with no initial result. In April 1976, he contacted his local congressional representative, Robert Kastenmeier, (D-Wis.). Stalling was typical, Kastenmeier said, when it came to FOIA requests – the CIA was even unresponsive with Congress in this regard. Legal action, he told Zechel, was the only real answer. Thus, Zechel began looking for financial backing to generate lawsuits against the CIA.[70]

In early 1976, another researcher began to leave his mark. Leonard Stringfield had been a UFO researcher since the 1950s, but had not written much. Now for *Skylook,* he began writing research pieces focusing on military connections to UFOs. As a former military man with an easygoing personality, he developed many inside sources of information. One of his early sources told him the military had designed a sophisticated radar system solely to detect UFOs, and that nuclear submarines were being equipped with comparable instrumentation.[71] This was just the beginning. For the next decade, Stringfield delved into the subterranean world of the military, coming back with more information than anyone could have anticipated.

Meanwhile, other people contributed in other ways. Captain Keith Wolverton, a deputy sheriff for Cascade County, Montana, co-authored a book with journalist Roberta Donovan on cattle mutilations, mystery helicopters, and UFOs. The helicopters and UFOs may or may not be related to the mutes, they argued, but either way top government officials knew what was going on.[72]

1976 Politics

UFO researchers had hope that the secrecy might end; the American political scene seemed to justify such thinking. Throughout 1976 the U.S. Senate's Church Committee inquired into secret activities of the national security apparatus. Resistance remained strong, as when Senator Frank Church (D-ID) proposed revealing the size of the black budget. This was defense and intelligence spending that, in contradiction to the Constitution, was kept secret even from Capitol Hill. The new Director of the CIA, George Bush, argued that the revelation would be a disaster and would compromise the CIA beyond repair. By a one vote margin the matter was referred to the Senate, where it never reached the floor.[73]

1976 was the year that Jimmy Carter ran for President of the United States. As early as the spring, Carter was talking openly about how he had seen a UFO with a large group of people in 1969. During a campaign stop on March 31, he was asked whether he would reveal "behind-closed-doors" information regarding UFOs. He replied that although he did not know what to make of UFOs, he would "make these kinds of data available to the public ... to help resolve the mystery about it."[74] On June 8, 1976, the *National Enquirer* ran a story on Carter entitled, "The Night I Saw a UFO," in which he was quoted as saying, "If I become President, I'll make every piece of information this country has about UFO sightings available to the public and the scientists. I am convinced that UFOs exist because I've seen one." Although such a statement from a Presidential candidate is certainly news, Carter was more cautious than some have interpreted. His position was that he would make existing information available, assuming that some UFO data was classified (a correct assumption, as FOIA was demonstrating). When asked whether he would re-establish a new UFO-investigative body, Carter answered, "I don't know yet."[75]

There was, however, one politician pushing openly for UFO disclosure. This was the Prime Minister of the tiny Caribbean nation of Granada, Sir Eric Gairy. Like Carter, Gairy had seen a UFO years before. But he was also far less constrained by political pressures than someone who was running for the U.S. Presidency. Gairy addressed the U.N. General Assembly on October 7, 1976, urging recognition of UFOs as a serious international scientific problem. "One wonders," he said "why the existence of UFOs, or 'flying saucers' as they are sometimes called, continue to remain a secret ...."[76] The U.N. took no action as a result of his statement, but this was only the beginning of Sir Eric Gairy's inquiries into UFOs at the U.N.

UFOs in the USA: 1976

Regarding the UFOs themselves, the late 1970s were generally down years compared with 1975. But "down" is not "dead." 1976 had some very interesting UFO encounters, many of which – as during the previous year – involved the military. One dates from January 21, 1976, according to a National Military Command Center report. This occurred at Cannon AFB, New Mexico, at 3:55 a.m. According to the document:

> Two UFOs are reported near the flight line at Cannon AFB, New Mexico. Security Police observing them reported the UFOs to be 25 yards in diameter, gold or silver in color with blue light on top, hole in the middle and red light on bottom. Air Force is checking with radar. Additional, checking weather inversion data

A fairly detailed description. As for checking weather data, one assumes the 'CYA' rule applies here.[77]

This event appears to have been part of a larger mini-flap of sightings. Less than 10 miles away, near the town of Clovis, New Mexico, a series of UFO sightings lasted from January 21 to January 23. More than 30 silent objects with pulsating lights were reported during night hours by civilians and police officers, and was reported on UPI wire services. On one occasion, several callers reported a group of 20 objects hovering over the Sandia Elementary School. Meanwhile, in the town of Texaco, Town Marshall Willie Ronquillo said he followed up on a report and saw a silent object hovering about 900 feet above the town. It had green, yellow, and blue lights. He gave chase when it began moving northward, and several police officers reported what appeared to be the same object. A spokesman at Reese AFB, 90 miles east of Clovis, said that nothing unusual had been picked up on base radar. A major at Cannon AFB, who was command post controller for the day, said the base had received numerous inquiries, but that "as far as the military is concerned, it is strictly no comment." A photograph taken by a reporter for the *Clovis News Journal* showed an unusual and bent streak of light, later determined by Ray Stanford a UFO researcher and photo analyst, to be an unfocused image of the planet Saturn.[78]

Perhaps the image was Saturn, but it appears something strange was going on in eastern New Mexico. Years later, Brian Vike collected several UFO reports from former servicemen who worked at Cannon AFB. All the men said they saw unknown objects over the base in January 1976. One wrote that he was in the flight tower and saw approximately a dozen UFOs through a Starlight Scope. "Flight Ops was concerned enough to scramble two F-111s to give chase." He added that there were several burned circles in a farmer's fields nearby, two of which he saw. Each was about thirty feet across and had "a dead cow in the center," typical mutilation cases. The writer claimed he spoke with an individual from Washington, D.C. about the events.[79]

The preceding report is uncon firmed, but the encounter on January 31, 1976 at Eglin AFB in Florida is well documented. According to a

U.S. Defense memorandum on UFO at Cannon AFB, 1976,

National Military Command Center report later obtained through FOIA, security policemen between 4:30 a.m. and 6 a.m. "spotted lights from what they called a UFO near an Eglin radar site." One description indicated "a row of lights with a central white light," although another report stated the lights were believed to be part of a building. Photographs were taken, but not released.[80]

Several CIA documents from 1976, also recovered through FOIA, show an interest in UFO phenomena and research. A document from January 21 entitled "International Congress of Space Medicine" deals with UFOs briefly. It is nearly entirely censored. Speaking of magnetic fields, it states, "There is a theory that such fields are closely associated with superconductivity at very low temperatures, such as in space. This in turn is related to the possible propulsion system of UFOs. There is a rumor that fragments of a possible UFO found in Brazil bore a relationship to superconductors and magnetohydrodynamics," certainly a reference to the "Ubatuba case" from 1957. Since the document was reporting on a conference, the reference to UFO "propulsion systems" was clearly a restatement of what was discussed there. Still, the matter-of-fact nature of the description, combined with the heavy redaction, give cause for wonder.[81]

Other memos from 1976 confirm CIA interest in UFOs. One heavily censored document dated April 14 references a "UFO Study" dated five days earlier, and mentions a request from a source who was seeking guidance "from CIA UFO experts as to material in his report that should remain classified."[82] An undated document from April states that the UFO study was turned over to "Dr. [redacted], who was also briefed on the developments to date." Another document from April 26 remarks:

> . . . it does not seem that the government has any formal program in progress for the identification/solution of the UFO phenomena. Dr. [redacted] feels that the efforts of independent researchers . . . are vital for further progress in this area. At the present time, there are offices and personnel within the agency who are monitoring the UFO phenomena, but again, this is not currently on an official basis. Dr. [redacted] feels that the best approach would be to keep the agency/community informed of any new developments. In particular, any information which might indicate a threat potential would be of interest, as would specific indications of foreign developments or applications of UFO related research.

This is quite interesting. The CIA had several offices studying UFOs, but "not on an official basis." A CIA analyst and apparent authority on UFOs believed that "independent researchers" were "vital" for further progress in the study of the phenomenon. Finally, the reference to "applications of UFO related research" would indicate that there were those in the CIA who assumed the UFO phenomenon had tangible value in its ability to spur scientific and technical progress.

Other CIA documents from this period have surfaced, including a memo stating that the Domestic Collections Division "has been receiving UFO related material" from Science and Technology sources "and their credentials removed them from the 'nut' variety."[83] Another document from May 27 states, "as before we are faced with the problem of having UFO related data which is deemed potentially important for the US by our [Science & Technology] sources, evaluated."[84]

Whatever kind of UFO material was arriving at the CIA's DCD, it appears that the Agency was actively researching the topic during the 1970s, and was interested in keeping its connection as unofficial as possible.

Somebody Else Is On the Moon - and Other Interesting Leaks

Meanwhile, remote viewer Ingo Swann continued his interesting adventures. During the summer of 1976, he received a plain package in the mail, lacking even a postmark (although it did have stamps). The package contained a book and nothing more: *Somebody Else is On the Moon*, by George Leonard. Leonard was a former NASA scientist and photo analyst who had obtained photographs of the Moon, several of which he published in his book, unfortunately of small size and poor resolution. But he did describe original prints, which he said were huge, and he published the identifying code numbers of the photos. Some of the images and accompanying sketches were very close to Swann's drawings for Axelrod. One photo showed a diamond shaped enclosure containing an 'L' shaped construction within. Leonard argued that NASA secretly knew of alien activity on the Moon. He also claimed that President Kennedy's initiative to put Americans on the Moon was driven by secret discoveries made from earth-based telescopes during the 1950s, virtually proving activity on the Moon. Years later, the images continued to generate opinions ranging from "crackpot interpretation" to "outstanding." Critics maintained the images show anomalies merely because of low resolution, that higher resolution images show them to be natural formations.[85]

Leonard's thesis received some support during the 1990s, when someone else claimed to have seen clear NASA photos of structures and machinery on the Moon. In 1979, Vito Saccheri, an industrial engineer, was shown a copy of Leonard's book by another engineer named Lester Howes. The two arranged to go to Houston's NASA headquarters and asked to see the photos. Since this was a first, NASA checked with Langley, Virginia (presumably the CIA). But the NASA photo archive, which housed over two million images, was legally available, and the two men were admitted to review it. "There were, however, strict rules," according to Saccheri. They had three eight-hour business days to review the material. They were not allowed any writing or recording devices of any kind, and could not be left alone with the photos.

According to Saccheri, the images were highly suggestive of anomalies, far more obvious than in Leonard's book. Some examples included:

> ... obvious machinery on the surface, showing bolted sections; three dilapidated 'bridges' crossing a chasm that reminded me of the Grand Canyon ... three surprising pyramids that prompted me later to closely study the Egyptian Giza pyramid complex; apparent pipelines criss-crossing the surface, running to and from craters; a UFO rising from the surface and photographed directly above a crater; and perhaps the most memorable, the unmistakable figure of a rectangular structure placed squarely in the biggest crater pictured – the structure looked either very old or under construction, but the crater had to be miles wide, and the camera angle gave a perfect three-dimensional view.

The best came at the end. On their last day, Saccheri was allowed by the librarian to examine a series of binders detailing NASA's scientific experiments conducted in space, as well as transcripts of the manned space flights, including the Moon landings. While browsing the transcripts, Saccheri's eyes widened:

> "Houston, we've got a bogey at two o'clock."
> "Roger that, Apollo. Switching to alpha. Roll eight degrees and begin sequence..."

Saccheri could not believe what he was reading. Looking through other mission transcripts, he found similar dialogue:

> "Mission Control, we've got Santa Claus coming over the hill..."
> "Roger, Apollo. Hold your fix. Switching bravo. Do you copy?"
> "Roger, Houston. Bravo link..."

Saccheri later learned from a Moon photo researcher named Marvin Czarnick that code words such as *alpha* and *bravo* referred to special switching stations around the country that 'switched' broadcast reception away from Houston and Mission Control to missile bases in the northwest portion of the country, as they were equipped with "secured communications equipment."

During the 1990s, UFO researcher Michael Lindemann noted that the only space mission to the Moon since the Apollo missions had been the classified, military-funded Clementine unmanned probe, which conducted hi-resolution photography of the entire lunar surface. "Almost none of those photos have been released to public view," he stated.[86]

UFOs in the Summer of 1976

Meanwhile, American UFO sightings continued throughout the summer of 1976. A memorandum described a sighting at another military base on July 30, this time Fort Ritchie, Maryland. Between 1:30 a.m. and 3:45 a.m. patrols at different locations saw objects over the base that were not supposed to be there. One crew reported "[three] oblong objects with a reddish tint." Another saw a UFO over the ammunition storage area – at the low altitude of 300 to 600 feet. From a third location, an Army police sergeant reported an aerial object estimated to be the size of a two and a half-ton truck.

It is not known what these sightings were, but we do know that the military conducted a "temperature inversion analysis," presumably to determine whether these were atmospheric phenomena. The analysis revealed two temperature inversions, one at 1,000 feet and another at 27,000 feet. An inversion is simply the trapping of a layer of cool air beneath warmer air (normally air cools at higher altitudes), and

MEMORANDUM FOR RECORD

Subject: Reports of Unidentified Flying Objects (UFOs)

1. At approximately 0345 EDT, the ANMCC called to indicate they had received several reports of UFO's in the vicinity of Fort Ritchie. The following events summarize the reports (times are approximate).

   a. 0130 – Civilians reported a UFO sighting near Mt. Airy, Md. This information was obtained via a call from the National Aeronautics Board (?) to the Fort Ritchie Military Police.

   b. 0255 – Two separate patrols from Site R reported sighting 3 oblong objects with a reddish tint, moving east to west. Personnel were located at separate locations on top of the mountain at Site R.

   c. 0300 – Desk Sgt at Site R went to the top of the Site R mountain and observed a UFO over the ammo storage area at 100-200 yards altitude.

   d. 0345 – An Army Police Sgt on the way to work at Site R reported sighting a UFO in the vicinity of Site R.

2. ANMCC was requested to have each individual write a statement on the sightings. One individual stated the object was about the size of a 2 1/2 ton truck.

NMCC memorandum on UFO seen at Fort Ritchie, MD, 7/30/76.

can cause visual or radar anomalies. It is also known that the witnesses were requested to write a statement on their sightings, but none are available.[87]

One of the most intriguing cattle mutilation cases – connected to evidence of an unknown craft – occurred on June 13 in New Mexico, and was described at length in a report by the New Mexico State Police (later declassified). The report noted the removal of body parts with "what appeared to be a sharp precise instrument ..." It stated that "a suspected aircraft of some type had landed twice, leaving three pod marks positioned in a triangular shape. The diameter of each pod was 14". The perimeter around the three pods was 16½". There were also smaller tripod impressions, which appeared to follow the cow for approximately 600 yards, and were all around the dead cow. Some of the grass around the pod marks was scorched.[88]

The most sensational UFO case of the summer took place in northern Maine. This was the abduction of four young men on a fishing trip, known ever since as the Allagash Abductions. On August 20, four art students in their early twenties left Boston for a canoe and camping trip in a wilderness area of Northern Maine along the Allagash River. Two were identical twins, Jack and Jim Weiner; they were accompanied by Charlie Foltz and Chuck Rak. On the evening of Thursday, August 26, they reached Eagle Lake, set up camp and built a blazing campfire which they expected to burn all night long. They decided to fish for trout in the canoe.

Out on the water, Charlie began to feel that the four were being watched. He turned around and saw "a large bright sphere of colored light hovering motionless and soundless" about 200 to 300 feet above the southeastern rim of the cove. All the men saw it and adjusted their eyes to the intense light. They then noticed a "gyroscopic motion" to the object, as if energy flowed horizontally and vertically, dividing it into four sections. The colors continually changed between red, green, and yellow, oscillating "like a thick sauce does as it starts to boil," in the words of investigator Raymond Fowler.

This object was no star; it was large enough that the men estimated its diameter at 80 feet, a substantial size. As it came closer to them, Foltz signaled an SOS with his flashlight. It then silently moved toward them. The men panicked and began to paddle away when light from the object engulfed them. The next thing they knew, they were standing on the bank again. Foltz pointed his flashlight toward the object, which ascended and disappeared. Only a few minutes seemed to have passed, but the campfire had nearly burned out. They did not discuss this oddity, and instead went to sleep without any discussion.

For years afterward, all four men experienced nightmares. In Jack Weiner's dreams, beings with long necks, large heads, large glowing eyes, and four-fingered hands examined his arm, while his companions sat nearby. The other three men experienced similar dreams. In 1988, Jim Weiner attended a UFO conference hosted by Raymond Fowler. Afterward, he related his encounter to Fowler, who suggested regressive hypnosis. Under separately conducted sessions, each man recalled being abducted and subjected to physical examinations, including the taking of skin and fluid samples. Their description of the aliens, the craft, and examining instruments was consistent. The men also took psychiatric examinations (all four were deemed mentally stable) and passed polygraph tests. Other than the Betty and Barney Hill incident from 14 years before, theirs was among the first well-documented, multiple abduction cases.[89]

As intriguing and well-corroborated as the Allagash abduction was, it remains in the same category as all other alleged abductions: it lacks the kind of physical proof necessary to convince a scientist used to working with physical evidence. One would hope that a competent scientist would avoid jumping to the conclusion that therefore the event did not happen; rather, that measuring and proving the event scientifically is simply not yet possible. Mundane explanations, such as hoax or shared fantasy, fall flat in this case. The obvious hurdle is accepting the reality of the UFO phenomenon as something alien. If one accepts that premise, then the conclusion that these four men were forcibly abducted by alien entities becomes the most logical.

ET over the Canary Islands?

As interesting as some of the American cases were, activity was more significant elsewhere. Several came from the Mediterranean region, including an astonishing case from the Canary Islands, while the Middle East had an "all-time classic" military encounter with a UFO.

There were also quite a few frightening aviation encounters. On March 3 near Tours, France, the pilot of a French military TE-33 saw a bright light in the distance which was rapidly approaching him. His plane was then surrounded by a green phosphorescent light that lit up his aircraft. The radar controller picked up nothing, although two other pilots saw the object. This case was later included in the 1999 Cometa Report, issued by members of the French military and defense establishment.[90] Eight days later, on March 11, an Iberian Airlines pilot saw a bright, elongated, object with "windows" which paced his aircraft near Palma de Majorca, Spain.[91] This was followed by a more dramatic incident on March 15 at Simon Bolivar Airport in Caracus, Venezuela. The newspaper *El Nacional* in Caracas reported that two UFOs were tracked on radar at the airport at 10:14 p.m. They attracted attention by their sudden appearance and extraordinary speed. Tower operators asked the unidentified craft to identify themselves, and instead they took off and "disappeared at a supersonic speed" over the Caribbean. Apparently, they crossed over the landing strips at the astounding speed of 5,000 kph (roughly 3,000 mph).[92]

Later that spring, the Canary Islands experienced a spate of UFO sightings, some of which involved the Spanish military, others civilian. Without question the most spectacular occurred on the night of June 22. Many witnesses from separate locations saw what can only be described as an enormous, transparent spherical craft containing two very tall human-like figures.

Dr. Francisco Julio Padron was being driven to the town of Galdar, on the northwest coast of Grand Canary Island, by his driver, Francisco

Estevez. As they rounded a bend in the road they saw a large spherical object hovering just above the ground, about 60 yards off the road. Estevez brought the car to a screeching halt. Padron described the object as "about the size of the 3-story building, and as perfectly round as if drawn by a compass." It was transparent enough that stars were visible through it. More amazing, he saw two human-like figures toward the center of the sphere. They were "well over" 6 feet tall, wore bright red garments, and a cloth-like helmet or some sort of turban. They seemed to be studying a control panel, and their heads appeared to glow. Estevez said that "they had two very bright, large eyes. I can swear that this was something out of this world. My nerves are shattered – I'll never forget this as long as I live."

The car radio went dead, and the two men experienced an intense feeling of cold. The sphere then began to rise and expand to an incredible size – the witnesses said it became comparable to a twenty story building. It then changed shape to that of spindle surrounded by a halo, and shot off at an amazing speed while they watched in terror.

They drove to a nearby farmhouse and learned that at least one of the residents had seen the object. A farmer said to them that he saw it as "a bright bluish sphere with two red objects inside that looked like human forms." Understandably, he dived to the floor, covered his head, and yelled to his wife to do the same. They stayed in that position until the doctor and driver arrived – just before the two arrived, the farmer's television went out.

Other witnesses saw this object. A group of friends near the town of Galdar saw something "very strange in the sky." They ran to the roof and were astonished to see a perfectly round, transparent sphere in the center of which was something they discerned to be long, bright and red. The object was stationary and seemed to expand gradually. The group watched it for 30 minutes. A tourist apparently photographed the object.

Astronomers saw it. Dr. Francisco Sanchez, director of the astrophysical observatory on Monte Izana, Canary Islands, said that several scientists at the observatory saw the object with their unaided eyes, but it was below the line of sight of their telescopes. It was very brilliant, "definitely not a planet, a bloom or smoke. I had no scientific explanation for it," said

Photograph of Canary Island UFO, 1976.

Sanchez. One of the astronomers, Dr. Fernando Bello, said the object seemed to approach the observatory until it paused for a moment, "made an abrupt 90 degree right turn and took off like a streak of light. We had it under observation for three to five minutes."

Finally, what appears to be the same object was also seen by the crew of the Spanish naval vessel, *Atrevida*, which was about several miles offshore. According to the ship's captain, they saw "an intense yellowish-bluish light" moving from the shore toward their position. The crew initially believed it was an ordinary aircraft until it stopped, turned off its light, and emitted a rotating beam of light for two minutes. It then resumed its intense halo of yellowish and bluish light, remaining in its position for 40 minutes. The light then appeared to split in half; the upper half performed a rapid spiral climb and vanished. The glow from the halo continued to light up parts of the land and the ocean. The ship's surface radar never detected an object.

This case is dramatic and difficult to deal with. Multiple witnesses, including military, seeing the same object with several witnesses describing beings inside, who looked like very tall humans. Could the sighting have been an entirely terrestrial secret program? The figures inside did look human, after all, although the technology would appear to be inexplicable – unless deep-black technology is indeed decades ahead of the "white" world, as some have claimed. Or, could this have been the sighting of a truly alien technology, but one in which humans – or genetically modified humans – were employed as "workers"? Or did the good doctor and his driver simply misinterpret, rather severely, something more mundane? If so, what could the sighting have been? James Oberg, formerly of U.S. Air Force Intelligence, and employed at NASA's Johnson Space Center on the Space Shuttle program, attributed this sighting to the launching of Poseidon ballistic missiles by the U.S. Navy within its Eastern U.S. Test Range, an enormous area covering most of the Atlantic Ocean. Oberg conceded that while the exact position of the submarines was classified, he confirmed that a missile launch did occur that day. Some have argued this proves the event was simply a missile launch.[93] Given the history of UFO sightings over U.S. missile sites, however, is it not at least as likely that the UFO appeared as a result of the missile launch?

On June 25, the Commanding General of the Canaries Air Zone designated an investigator for this and other UFO cases in the Canaries. Although the depositions were confidential, a Spanish Air Force General later gave copies to journalist J. J. Benitez (subsequently published in his book *UFOs: Official Documents of the Spanish Government*). The investigator determined there were no civilian or military aircraft that could account for what the Spanish Navy saw. The final report concluded, with a level of circumlocution impressive even for a military bureaucracy, "we would have to face seriously the hypothesis that a craft of unknown origin and driven by an energy likewise unknown is operating freely in the skies above the Canary Islands."[94]

It was at this time that the Spanish Divisional General commanding the Air Zone of the Canary Islands, General Carlos Castro Cavero, gave his interview on UFOs to *La Gaceta del Norte* (discussed in the previous chapter). Small wonder, as the sightings in the Canary Islands were inexplicable from a conventional point of view. It is curious why the interview was given at all. Perhaps the best reason was the death in 1975 of long-time dictator Francisco Franco, who had ruled the country since 1939. A major regime change often brings about sense of new possibility, new openness. After all, Spain had experienced a UFO wave in 1974, but no public statements were made at that time. Even in 1976, the Spanish military investigations were kept confidential, and not until 1992 did the Spanish Air Force begin a major declassification effort.[95]

Other UFOs were seen over the water in the eastern Atlantic and the Mediterranean at this time. For instance, in July, a British Airways Tri-Star on a return flight from Portugal was involved in an incident which led to the scrambling of fighter jets to chase four objects – two of which were round and brilliant white, two of which were cigar-shaped – 18 miles north of Faro, at the southern coast of Portugal. The captain was so alarmed by what he and the passengers had seen that he reported the sighting to air traffic controllers at Lisbon and Heathrow. According to British MoD files released many years later, fighters were immediately scrambled from Lisbon. Shortly afterwards, another Tri-Star crew on the same flight path reported a bright UFO between Fatima and Farom, while later that month two Tri-Star co-pilots and five of their cabin crew reported "passing underneath a bright white circular object."[96]

UFO reports emanated from Tunisia between August 3 and 9, during which a series of unknown objects, seen visually and often tracked on radar, were reported at various points in the country. These sightings were dramatic enough to result in a confidential memo from the U.S. Embassy stating that Tunisia's military leadership was "very concerned." None of these reports indicated necessarily unusual performance capabilities or designs, but they did perplex the Tunisian authorities to the point where they asked the U.S. Sixth Fleet, stationed in the Mediterranean, for any light it could shed. No follow-up report is available.[97]

Incident Over Tehran

On the night of September 18, 1976, the Iranian Air Force was involved in one of the most dramatic UFO events in modern history. Not only was the case itself extraordinary, but so was the documentation: namely, a four-page U.S. Defense Intelligence Agency report.[98] It was first reported in the English language *Kayhan International*, published in Tehran on September 25 and soon afterwards headlined the *APRO Bulletin*. Charles Huffer, an American in West Germany, learned about it and requested information from the U.S. Department of Defense. This was denied on July 5, 1977, but his appeal succeeded in obtaining the release of a document on August 31, 1977 via the Defense Intelligence Agency (DIA).

The strangeness began between 10:30 p.m. and 11:15 p.m. on September 18 when the control tower at Mehrabad Airport received calls about an unknown object hovering at 1,000 feet in the northern section of Teheran. The radar system was under repair and unavailable. After the fourth call, the tower supervisor, Hossain Perouzi, went out with binoculars. He saw a rectangular or cylindrical object. In his words, "the two ends were pulsating with a whitish blue color. Around the mid-section was this small red light that kept going in a circle.... I was amazed."[99]

Perouzi called the Air Force Command, which reached General Nader Yousefi, base operations commander of Shahrokhi Air Force Base, nearly 200 miles away to the southwest. He gave the order to scramble an F-4 Phantom, which took off at 1:30 a.m. on the morning of September 19. The object was intensely brilliant and "easily visible" at a distance of 70 miles. As the pilot came to within 25 nautical miles (about 29 statute miles), his aircraft "lost all instrumentation and communications." He broke off the intercept and headed back, at which point his aircraft regained all instrumentation.

The General had already authorized a second F-4. When the second pilot reached a distance of 27 NM, he obtained a substantial radar return, "comparable to that of a 707 tanker." At this point, the UFO began to move away from the F-4 at the same speed. It was extremely bright and gave off flashing strobe lights arranged in a rectangular pattern. The colors alternated blue-green, red, and orange, although the sequence was so fast that they were almost simultaneous.

The UFO then released a bright object, "estimated to be one half to one third the apparent size of the Moon." It headed straight toward the F-4 "at a very fast rate of speed." The pilot tried to fire an AIM-9 missile at it, "but at that instant his weapons control panel went off and he lost all communications." Seeking to evade, he dove and turned away, but the object followed him and turned inside his own turn. It then returned to the main object "for a perfect rejoin." The F-4 pilot then regained communications and weapons control.

At this point, another object came out of the main object and rapidly descended. The F-4 crew observed this, anticipating an explosion. Instead, the object appeared to rest gently on the Earth and cast a very bright light over an area of about 2 miles. The crew noted the object's position and then headed back.

Before landing, they circled Mehrabad Airport several times, receiving frequent interference and losing communications. A civil airliner approach-

Segment from a DIA memorandum on the UFO over Tehran, 1976

ing Mehrabad also experienced communications failure, but saw nothing. On its final approach, the F-4 crew saw a cylinder shaped object with bright steady lights on each end and a flasher in the middle. They inquired with the tower, which replied that there was no other known traffic in the area.

The next morning, the F-4 crew was taken in a helicopter to the area where the UFO was thought to have landed – a dry lake bed. They saw nothing, but picked up a beeper signal west of the area. At the point where the return was the loudest was a small house with a garden. They landed and asked the residents if they had noticed anything strange the previous night. The people mentioned a loud noise and a bright light, "like lightning."

Although the DIA memo indicated more information would be

forwarded, no follow-up military documents ever came to light. Researchers Barry Greenwood and Lawrence Fawcett stated, "reliable sources have told us the Iranian case was about one and a half inches thick, yet absolutely no admission to having this file has come from any government agency with a possible connection to the case."[100] Nevertheless, taped testimonies in later years by Iranian Air Force generals Nader Yousefi and Mahmoud Sabahat reveal that General Richard Secord, chief of the USAF mission in Iran, attended a high level briefing with Iranian authorities and the pilots. Furthermore, Lt. General Abdulah Azarbarzin of the Iranian Imperial Air Force admitted to U.S. reporters that the UFO encounter had been carefully documented and passed on to the USAF. "This was the request from the U.S. They have the procedure, if we have some information on UFOs, we're just exchanging all this information, and we did it."[101] In 2005, one of the Iranian pilots, General Parviz Jafari, confirmed the facts of the chase in an interview with Whitley Strieber and Dr. Roger Leir.[102]

U.S. intelligence analysts found the case to be spectacular. An evaluation in the DIA files stated:

> An outstanding report. This case is a classic which meets all the criteria necessary for a valid study of the UFO phenomenon: a) the object was seen by multiple witnesses from different locations ... and viewpoints. b) the credibility of many of the witnesses was high (an Air Force general, qualified air crews, and experienced radar operators). c) visual sightings were confirmed by radar. d) similar electromagnetic effects (EME) were reported by three separate aircraft. e) there were physiological effects on some crew members (i.e. loss of night vision due to the brightness of the object). f) an inordinate amount of maneuverability was displayed by the UFOs.[103]

During the 1990s, Lee Graham and Ron Regehr of Aero-Jet in California confirmed that the UFO sighting over Tehran was tracked by the U.S. military's Defense Support Program (DSP) satellite. This is a deep space platform primarily used to detect the launch of ballistic missiles. It can distinguish different aircraft by comparing their infrared signature with a comprehensive database of known aircraft. Graham and Regehr obtained print-outs showing that the DSP detected an anomalous object in Iranian air space at that time.[104]

The obvious question is, who was operating the object over Teheran? Based on the all that is known, it makes no sense to claim that this was American technology. Why would the Americans confront the Air Force of such a key ally within its own air space? Nor has there ever been any indication in subsequent years that the Soviet Union created technology responsible for this – to say nothing of the fact that for the Soviets to have engaged Iranian F-4s over Tehran in 1976 would have been even more provocative than if the U.S. had done so. Indeed, after the encounter, the Iranian government asked the governments of the USSR and the U.S. whether this had been a test of their military equipment. Neither nation claimed responsibility.[105]

The real problem is that this object so clearly outperformed American-made fighter jets. Some agency – or civilization – was responsible for it.

Henry Kissinger's UFO Memo

On the same night as the Teh-ran incident, the American em-bassy in Rabat, Morocco, for-warded a message to the U.S. State Department regarding UFOs over Morocco. Widely separated locations saw a silver, luminous, circular object in the southwest moving on a north-easterly course, leaving trails of

1976 memo from Henry Kissinger regarding UFOs over Morocco.

bright sparks and fragments. This occurred between 1 a.m. and 2 a.m., on September 19 – because of time zone differences, four hours later than the Iranian incident. The object was believed to be at about 3,000 feet altitude and made "absolutely no sound." The U.S. embassy writer stated, "I frankly do not know what to make of these sightings." It took Secretary of State Henry Kissinger a month to reply. Interestingly, he referenced the 1969 Condon Committee report, which he said demonstrated UFOs were not alien spaceships. He said he was unaware of any aircraft or satellite activity that could be responsible, but did not preclude "aircraft flights of other countries or unusual atmospheric conditions or events as a possible cause." He concluded that "one would tend to believe that the event was a meteor, and probably a spectacular one, or ... [possibly] a decaying satellite part of which there is no precise re-entry record. Kissinger." The description of the object, which included a slow speed, surely precludes that of a meteor. It has been speculated that Kissinger's reply was delayed because he received a briefing on the UFO subject. Obviously, he intended his answer as an end to the inquiry and conversation.[106]

A few unusual encounters by commercial airliners filled out the rest of 1976. The most interesting took place at Japan's Akita Airport on October 17, when the air traffic controller observed a glowing, hovering object through binoculars that looked like "two plates placed together." A pilot about to take off also noticed it. He described it as "a strange looking disc shaped object 5,000 ft. from the ground. It was something I had never seen before." The object finally flew away toward the sea.[107]

Summary

1975 was one of the most spectacular years in the history of UFOs, and many events of 1976 were equally dramatic. Researchers were fortunate in being able to obtain solid documentation on many military encounters with UFOs, some of which are the most important ever recorded. Certainly the 1975 encounters along the northern U.S. border, as well as the Iranian Air Force encounter of 1976, fall into this category. In addition, the abduction phenomenon was brought to a prominence that it had not had since the publicity of the Betty and Barney Hill case of the 1960s. But the Hill case had been considered an isolated incident. Abductions were not supposed to be all that common. During the mid-1970s, however, there were quite a few abduction cases that did not easily admit of prosaic explanations. Researchers were taking notice.

A sense of optimism prevailed. A new President was going to enter the White House, one who was not only more liberal in his attitude regarding the public's right to Freedom of Information, but who had openly admitted to being a UFO witness. Jimmy Carter had even promised to try to open government records on UFOs. Could it be that there might be a formal government 'disclosure' of the UFO reality?

Chapter 3

Great Expectations
1976-1978

[President Jimmy Carter] told me many times . . . that it was true, that there were crafts, that he believed there were occupants . . .
— *Actress Shirley MacLaine, on* The Larry King Show, *1995.*

. . . he said he's not allowed to talk about it, and that he will tell everything he knows after President Carter makes an announcement."
— *Wife of military witness of three small humanoid bodies stored at Wright-Patterson AFB, speaking to Leonard Stringfield, 1977.*

I sincerely hope that you are successful in preventing a reopening of UFO investigations.
— *Colonel Charles Senn, Chief of USAF Community Relations Division, letter to Lt. General Duward Crow of NASA, 1977.*

Jimmy Carter and the Trilateral Commission

On November 2, 1976, Jimmy Carter was elected President of the United States. He had campaigned on a liberal platform which included a friendly attitude toward Freedom of Information and government openness. One can overstate the emphasis that Carter gave to the UFO question, but that he discussed it at all was a sign of the times, even a backlash against the negativism of the Condon Committee from the prior decade.

Carter was perceived as a Washington outsider, but he had help getting to the White House. That help was named David Rockefeller, one of the richest and most powerful men in the world.[1] It was joked that, for Rockefeller, becoming U.S. President would be a demotion.[2] Rockefeller's power was such that, in 1976 when Australian President Malcolm Fraser visited the United States, Fraser met with Rockefeller before meeting President Gerald Ford.[3] In the year 1973 alone, Rockefeller met with 27 heads of state, including the leaders of the Soviet Union and Communist China.[4] He was a dedicated internationalist, a longtime Chairman of the Council on Foreign Relations, and had been a leading force of the Bilderberg Group since its inception in 1954. Both groups, however, had developed shortcomings: the Bilderberg Group lacked Asian members, while the CFR had been divided over U.S. policy in Vietnam. Rockefeller wanted a better instrument to manage the international realities of the day, and he certainly did not want it to be the highly public United Nations. For a "unified world polity," one needed free market forces that transcended national boundaries. The world had become inextricably interconnected, America's relative power was waning, and it could not by itself be the military policeman of the world.[5]

Columbia University professor Zbigniew Brzezinski had meanwhile called for a "community of developed nations," one which would include the Atlantic states (e.g. North America and Western Europe), "the more advanced European communist states," and Japan. Such a community could be an elite policy-planning group of the advanced capitalist nations.[6] Rockefeller liked this idea, and under his initiative this became the Trilateral Commission in 1973, with

Jimmy Carter, 39th U.S. President

Brzezinski as its first Chairman. Rockefeller then walked into the office of Henry Kissinger and informed him that an organization had been created to "help" the Nixon Administration take a proper course. (Rockefeller had lost patience with Nixon's economic policies of higher tariffs along with wage and price controls.) Kissinger immediately acquiesced.[7] Nixon's successor, Gerald Ford, had sought to accommodate the new reality, appointing two Trilateralists to his cabinet and selecting Nelson Rockefeller as his Vice President. David was nonetheless unsatisfied with Ford, perhaps exacerbated when Ford dropped Nelson from the 1976 election ticket. Thus he cultivated Carter, an active Trilateralist.

During his presidential campaign, Carter benefitted from Rockefeller's financial connections and support, strong media coverage, and even speeches written by Brzezinski (who became his National Security Advisor).[8] Carter stated that it was time to replace "balance-of-power politics with world order politics" and to "seek a partnership between North America, Western Europe and Japan." He appointed 26 Trilateralists to senior positions in his administration. He even offered David Rockefeller the positions of Treasury Secretary and Federal Reserve Chairman, although Rockefeller politely declined both. More than a decade before the fall of the Soviet Union, America's commitment to globalization was fully under way.[9]

While none of the above is particularly challenging history, it marked yet another step toward the obsolescence of national sovereignty. The creation of the Commission is a case study in the divestiture of public power to powerful private groups, which in turn formulate public policies to advance those very same private interests. The development is relevant to the study of UFO phenomena. If powerful private groups can so easily dominate national governments, how implausible is it that they could assume control over the UFO secret? Subsequent events indicate this almost certainly happened.

Considering Carter's previous statements on UFOs, it would not be surprising that he might inquire about them under the right circumstances. Shortly after his election victory, CIA Director George Bush telephoned Carter, offering his congratulations and tendering his resignation. Carter's reply to the latter was ambiguous. In the telephone conversation, Bush proposed they get together in order to discuss certain "exotic and very closely held items relating to sources and methods." They did so on November 19, 1976. Incidentally, this was not the first time the two had met for an intelligence briefing; Carter had already met with Bush twice before as a candidate, proving himself to be an exceptionally sophisticated and quick learner. At one point early on in the November briefing, Bush and his assistant Jennifer Fitzgerald took Carter and Vice President-Elect Walter Mondale aside to provide especially sensitive information. Just what the 'exotic' items under discussion happened to be were not explained in the CIA's official history of the meeting, except that Bush described "more than a dozen sensitive CIA programs and issues." Bush did make a play to try to maintain his position as Director of the CIA, suggesting that he might be helpful in Carter's transition to the White House, but Carter rejected the offer.[10]

Daniel Sheehan, an attorney who had worked on the cases of Daniel Ellsberg and Karen Silkwood, claims to have learned from Marcia Smith (a space policy senior analyst at the Congressional Research Service in Washington, D.C.), that Carter had asked Bush for, "the information that we have on UFOs and extraterrestrial intelligence." Carter wanted to know about this "as President." According to what Smith told Sheehan, Bush rejected this request, and said "this was information that existed on a need to know basis only. Simple curiosity on the part of the President wasn't adequate." According to Sheehan, Bush told Carter that he would consider handing over the CIA's UFO material if Carter would retain Bush as Director of Central Intelligence (DCI). Otherwise, said Bush, Carter's best strategy for UFO material would be to approach the Science and Technology Committee of the House of Representatives.[11]

Upon entering the White House, Carter immediately replaced Bush with his old friend, Admiral Stansfield Turner. It is possible that Carter hoped to get honest answers about the UFO issue. This, at least, is what he implied years later to UFO researcher Stanton Friedman when both were at Boston's Logan Airport. Friedman was briefly able to mention his difficulties in obtaining UFO data from the NSA and CIA, and Carter discussed his removal of Bush. According to Friedman, "[Carter] indicated that the reason he chose his CIA director (Stansfield Turner) was that they were Annapolis classmates and therefore he thought that he could be trusted to tell him the truth . . . [the] implication was that other DCIs had not informed their presidents fully."[12]

Freedom of Information

Trilateralist or not, Jimmy Carter came to the White House with certain beliefs. Following his inauguration on January 20, 1977, Carter spoke out against nuclear weapons and government corruption while supporting human rights and freedom of information. This spirit blew like fresh air through a musty house. During his first year as President, Carter permitted the release of documents describing illegal military and government activities.[13] The new spirit continued to influence Congress, resulting in a Senate Intelligence Oversight Committee with its own staff and files, and a House investigation on the CIA's mind control programs – indicating that mind control was still a very active pursuit in certain quarters of the Agency.[14]

But Carter distanced himself from the UFO topic. Researcher Grant Cameron studied the evolution of Carter's pledge, noting that it changed slowly until it completely disappeared. In fact, the UFO 'pledge,' while made in public and in front of the cameras, never made it to Carter's 214-page compilation of campaign pledges. Carter's science advisor, Dr. Frank Press, was blunt: "I'm not particularly interested in UFOs. I'm the President's assistant, and I'll work on anything he asks me to work on. But I can't take on every problem that comes in here."[15]

This turned out to be a lost opportunity, for in January 1977 came the release of a study on UFO sightings and beliefs of professional American astronomers by Peter Sturrock of Stanford University. Sturrock mailed out 2,611 questionnaires, with half (1,356) being completed and returned. Sixty-two respondents – nearly 5% – said they had witnessed or obtained an instrumental record of an event that they could not identify and which they thought might be related to UFOs. Moreover, 80% favored additional scientific study of UFOs.[16] In other words, a pretext was there for Carter to have used, had he tried to press the matter.

The 'pledge' generated an enormous amount of mail from citizens urging the President to follow through. An early letter came from researcher Larry W. Bryant, who worked in the Pentagon as a writer for U.S. Army publications. His request of February 6, 1977 encouraged Carter to look into the roles played by the major military and intelligence agencies in the UFO cover-up, and to make his findings public. Carter's staff were utterly unable to process the volume of mail. Ten days later, Bryant received the standard USAF letter, stating that the Air Force no longer investigated UFOs and that all Project Blue Book records could be viewed at the National Archives in Washington, D.C.[17]

Quietly, however, the White House inquired into the allegations of a UFO cover-up. Carter's Press Secretary Jody Powell and Science Advisor Frank Press seem to have done the most work on this matter. Within the first few months of the new administration, they asked the CIA and Pentagon if they were withholding documents; both agencies said no. But Press also learned that military security worked on a "need to know" basis. If military censors determined that the White House did not have a need to know, the President would not be told.[18] Powell, meanwhile, was the source of a surprising statement carried in the April *U.S. News and World Report*:

> Before the year is out, the Government - perhaps the President - is expected to make what are described as 'unsettling disclosures' about UFOs unidentified flying objects. Such revelations, based on information from the CIA, would be a reversal of official policy that in the past has downgraded UFO incidents.

Where Powell got this information is not known, but Phillip Klass immediately wrote to the magazine, offering 100 to 1 odds that there would be no "unsettling disclosures" before the year's end.

Struck by Powell's statement, Todd Zechel traveled to Washington to visit Arthur Lundahl, a former high ranking CIA official. Lundahl had reportedly briefed at least three Presidents on UFOs. Regarding the *U.S. News* story, Lundahl told Zechel that he would check with "the boys," which Zechel assumed to be former CIA Directors William Colby and Richard Helms. However, according to Zechel, Lundahl "did not pry loose much specific information of the CIA's involvement with UFOs." Ultimately, the *U.S. News* story was denied by the White House as a "misunderstanding" by Powell.[19]

All this UFO news was making for an interesting year. Researchers were requesting increasingly large numbers of UFO files from the CIA, Air Force, and other departments. Bruce Maccabee had particularly good fortune with the FBI; by the end of the year, he had received some 400 pages of UFO related documents from the Bureau, mostly generated between 1947 and 1955, with thousands more identified and requested. Several of the reports provided detailed descriptions of military encounters with UFOs.[20]

Although stonewalling remained the rule, it is interesting that the Joint Army-Navy-Air Force Publication (JANAP) 146 (E) was re-released on May 17, 1977. As in prior releases going back to the 1940s, the document mentioned "unidentified flying objects" as something that must be reported by military personnel, and distinguished UFOs from other specific types of objects (e.g. "aircraft," "missiles," "submarines," "military surface vessels," "surface vessels, submarines, or aircraft of unconventional design," or other "unexplained or unusual activity....") In other words, UFOs continued to be a legitimate target of observation and reporting by U.S. military personnel.[21]

Finally, the new 'freedom of information' extended to UFO researchers themselves, in the sense that conferences now became a regular part of their culture, and went a long way toward raising standards of professionalism. Whereas the publicity for such gatherings was always limited, the benefits of researchers meeting with each other in person cannot be underestimated.[22] By the end of 1977, at least four major UFO conferences were held – the highest total ever up to that point. It was becoming evident that conferences were now competing with each other for the time and money of attendees. Thus, MUFON's leadership actually expressed contentment in 1978 that theirs was the only major conference that year in America.[23] Before long, a mere four conferences per year would seem inconsequential.

Daniel Sheehan and the Vault

Several unverified stories add intrigue to the matter of Jimmy Carter and UFOs. Sheehan provided another through his connection with Marcia Smith. In January 1977, Sheehan, then General Counsel to the U.S. Jesuit National Headquarters in Washington D.C., was approached by Smith, who told him that Carter's people had asked the Library of Congress Research Service to study the question of whether extraterrestrial intelligence existed in the galaxy, and whether the UFO phenomenon might be related to extraterrestrial intelligence. As a result, she asked for his participation, starting with a presentation on the religious implications of extraterrestrial contact at the Jet Propulsion Laboratory in California. Sheehan agreed, but asked for access to the data to which Smith normally had access. In particular, he wanted to see "the classified sections of the Project Blue Book." Officially, there was no such thing as a classified portion of Blue Book, although rumors had always existed. Smith replied that she would try and, to her surprise, the Pentagon people she spoke to agreed.

According to public statements he made in later years, on a Saturday afternoon early in 1977, Sheehan went to the Madison Building. He was led into a basement vault area built for the Library of Congress with armed guards stationed at the entrance. The building was so new that it had not yet opened to the public. He went to a secured room, showed his identification, was told to leave his briefcase behind, and that he was not to take notes. But Sheehan kept a yellow pad tucked under his arm, which apparently went unnoticed by the guards as he entered the room alone.

The room had a reel-to-reel film machine through which Sheehan looked at films of unidentified vehicles. He eventually found a series of "unmistakable" photographs of a classic flying saucer embedded in snow and surrounded by Air Force personnel wearing parkas. The photos were so clear he could read the name tags. Some photos were of symbols on the side of the craft, which he carefully and nervously traced to his yellow legal pad. He then closed his notepad and walked out. As he came through the door, the desk officer asked to look at it and flipped through the pages. He never looked at the inside cardboard backing, which was where Sheehan had made his drawings, and returned the notepad.

Sheehan told Smith what he saw. She later drafted two reports for the House Science and Technology Committee, both of which went to President Carter. Sheehan said he saw them both: one on extraterrestrial intelligence, the other on UFOs. The report on extraterrestrial intelligence concluded there were probably between two and six intelligent civilizations in the Milky Way Galaxy more technologically developed than the human race.* The UFO report showed "drawings of different shapes of UFOs," and concluded there were many cases in which official USAF investigations could not rule out the possibility that some of these vehicles were in fact extraterrestrial.

---

*
A fascinating implication of this is that, given roughly 300 billion galaxies in the observable universe, this could easily translate to about one trillion civilizations across the universe that have surpassed the level achieved on Earth.

Sheehan retains custody of the symbols he drew. He has never published them, although he presented them at the UFO Expo in Santa Clara, California, in September 2001. According to Grant Cameron, who attended, they resembled a combination of slashes and dots. The written language that approximates this most is probably Tibetan.[24]

White House UFO Project

In 1977, Alfred Webre was a Senior Policy Analyst at the Center for the Study of Social Policy at Stanford Research Institute, where a great deal of intelligence-related research was contracted – including remote viewing work. When he arrived there in January 1977, he stated his intention to develop an "extraterrestrial communication" project with White House backing, and wasted no time in getting started. Webre assumed that, given some of Carter's public statements from the previous year, a research project sponsored by the White House (and perhaps collaborating with agencies such as the National Science Foundation or NASA), might be able to withstand challenges from elsewhere.

He planned three phases to the project. First would be the creation of a comprehensive UFO database. Next, scientific advisers would evaluate the data and construct interpretive models, including but not limited to the extraterrestrial and interdimensional model. Finally, a report and policy recommendations would be made, possibly resulting in the creation of a permanent, open, global database under independent control. Webre also envisioned a recommendation for ending the military and intelligence secrecy on the subject.

He made inquiries among White House staffers, and was eventually referred to a person whose name he has not remembered in subsequent years, referred to in a later affidavit as "Jane Doe." This person was a staff member of the White House Domestic Policy Staff (under Stuart Eisenstadt) and, according to Webre, was supportive of his proposal when he met with her that spring in Washington D.C. He returned to SRI, further developed his proposal, and received corporate approval. Before long, he flew back to Washington to meet with Jane Doe again. She told him his concept had been approved, he gave her a copy of the proposal, and they discussed the contract research process, as SRI would have to be awarded a research contract for the study. She then said she would get the proposal to her superiors. Although she did not name who these people were, Webre was unconcerned as it was still early in the discussion. Little did he know that he would not meet with his White House contact again.[25]

At this time, the White House was dealing with publicity from an article in *The Star*, a national tabloid. Its May 3 issue discussed Carter's 1969 UFO sighting and his administration's interest in the topic. This sparked another wave of mail to the White House. The White House lacked the staff to answer these letters, much less provide relevant information. Inquiries about UFOs continued to be referred to the Air Force. Few missed the irony.[26]

Things Go South

The Carter UFO initiative, such as it was, quickly approached its climax. Some individuals maintain that the President was given a UFO briefing at the White House on June 14, 1977, and afterwards was bound to secrecy. According to former USAF Captain Robert Collins, "a lone MJ-12 briefing officer" met with the President, accompanied by several independent sources. Together these sources produced a "reconstruction" of what was told to Carter, and this became known as the "Executive Briefing: Project Aquarius" document. It was later leaked to UFO researcher William Moore through a member of the Defense Intelligence Agency known only as the Falcon. Moore said that the notes he received were a typed copy of handwritten notes that had been used by the officer during the briefing. The memo itself gives the (now standard) account of multiple retrievals of alien technology.[27] Grant Cameron noted that a review of the schedule on June 14, 1977 shows that a meeting in the Cabinet room between 1:35 p.m. and 3:15 p.m., to "discuss appropriations for intelligence affairs in the 1979 Budget of the U.S." could have been a cover for another meeting which did not appear in the diary of President Carter. However, there remains no hard evidence to support the claims that a briefing took place, and no proof has shown the documents to be either legitimate or a forgery.

In this context, the author can relate an anecdote told to him privately by a well-placed source. In June 1977, a presidential aide who was "very, very close to Carter" walked into the Oval Office following a briefing that the aide knew had concerned the topic of UFOs. Carter was sobbing, with his head in his hands, nearly on his desk. Although the aide did not learn the precise reasons for Carter's emotional state, he said that a few of Carter's phrases made it clear he was deeply upset about the topic.

Probably the most dramatic UFO-related statement attributed to Jimmy Carter was made public in 1995. During a television appearance, the actor Nicholas Cage had mentioned a conversation he had with actress Shirley MacLaine. He said MacLaine had told him about various conversations she had with former President Carter, including Carter's statement to her that he had seen a crashed flying saucer and the occupants. Shortly after this, MacLaine was a guest on the Larry King television show, and a caller asked her about Cage's statement. MacLaine responded by saying:

> [Carter] didn't tell me that, but he told me many times that when I first wrote *Out On A Limb* [in 1983] that he would support me, that it was true, that there were crafts, that he believed there were occupants, [and] why should we be the only people in the universe? He wanted to shine the sunshine laws on intelligence, to expose it, to see how the people would react, but he didn't and wouldn't and couldn't as he explained to me.

The statement is interesting because it seems to indicate that Carter was telling her more than his simple belief or opinion. The statement that "it was true, that there were crafts" seems extremely specific, especially one made by a former President. Both Grant Cameron and this author have asked Ms. MacLaine for elaboration on this statement, but she has not done so officially. However, in conversation with this author, she did confirm that she was on friendly terms with the President and that he had discussed UFOs with her in very serious terms.[28]

All through the spring and summer of 1977, the UFO letters kept coming. By early July, Carter's science officials were calling the situation a "nightmare." Eventually, the Congressional Liaison Office, directed by Frank Moore, received over 9,000 letters. There is no evidence that Carter read any of them; none were answered personally, although a large pile was photographed. As Science Advisor Frank Press looked into how to answer all the mail, he observed that people interested in UFOs were being ignored, and that there was no uniform manner in which federal agencies responded to UFO inquiries.[29]

On July 21, Press wrote to Dr. Robert A. Frosch, NASA Administrator, suggesting that NASA become the "focal point for the UFO question," answering all UFO-related mail and also conducting an active research program on UFOs. Essentially, he was asking NASA to create a new Project Blue Book. "Since it has been nearly a decade since the Condon report," wrote Press, "I believe that a small panel of inquiry could be formed to see if there are any new significant findings."[30] This was an important letter coming from a man who had previously expressed no interested in the subject of UFOs. At the same time, Press's office made statements to the journal *Science* that the classification of UFO data was one of the things that "keeps alive this belief in the cover-up. Policies like these . . . need review and perhaps changing." This appeared to support what many UFO researchers had long been saying: that there was a cover-up. Philip Klass immediately took issue with this and contacted the author of the article, telling her she had been "badly misinformed" about a cover-up.[31]

By this time, Klass was affiliated with a new organization, founded the previous year by the American Humanist Association. This was the Committee for Scientific Investigation of Claims of the Paranormal (CSICOP). Stating that its goal was to combat the rise of "pseudoscience," CSICOP argued it would "not ... reject on *a priori* grounds, antecedent to inquiry, any or all (paranormal) claims, but rather to examine them openly, completely, objectively and carefully." Before long, it became evident that CSICOP engaged in very little investigation. The organization did excel at public relations, however. Members quickly published articles on behalf of CSICOP in *Smithsonian*, *Reader's Digest*, *Omni*, and elsewhere. What soon separated a CSICOP article from those submitted by academicians or scientists was typically the tone, which overtly employed standard propaganda tactics. Many offerings referred to UFO believers as "kooks" or "hoaxers," used words like "pseudoscientific" or "nonsense" in reference to UFOs, and frequently appealed to established authorities such as "scientists" or simply "authorities." All these are methods of propaganda, not of science, tools of public relations rather than detached inquiry.

Stringfield's Leaks

During 1977, no UFO researcher made a more dramatic contribution to the field than Leonard Stringfield. In May, his book *Situation Red: The UFO Siege* was released. It became one of ufology's most historically significant books. A small but important segment of the book supported the thesis that, over the years, the U.S. military had retrieved extraterrestrial hardware and possibly bodies. Not since Frank Scully's *Behind the Flying Saucers* – published in 1950 – had a UFO researcher openly supported such a claim. The book immediately prompted dozens of alleged first hand witnesses of crashed UFOs or alien bodies to contact Stringfield with their stories. Undoubtedly Stringfield's former military career helped inspire the confidence of his informants, many of whom were former military intelligence personnel. By and large, Stringfield found them credible.

Although Stringfield usually confirmed the identities of his informants, all demanded anonymity. One of his informants was a doctor ("Doctor X"), who said he had conducted tests on alien bodies at a medical facility in the eastern U.S. Stringfield eventually met with him at the medical facility where he worked. Doctor X did not answer all of Stringfield's questions, but did describe the aliens physically: they were four feet tall, forty pounds in weight, had a large head, heavy brow ridge, round eyes, no pupils, apertures rather than ears, a tiny nose, and an apparently non-functional slit-like mouth without lips or teeth. In addition, they had slender torsos, long thin arms, tan or greyish skin that was elastic and reptile-like, colorless liquid prevalent in their body, but no red blood cells. They appeared to lack reproductive organs and seemed clone-like in appearance. Doctor X thought they were possibly androids.[32]

During the summer of 1977, Stringfield gave a lecture on UFOs at the Cincinnati Chapter of the World Wings. Afterwards, a pilot told him that he had seen three alien bodies in crates at a hangar at Wright-Patterson AFB in 1953 after a UFO crash in Arizona. He had also heard rumors that a UFO was retrieved in England during the Second World War. Stringfield's check on the pilot did prove that he had an extensive military career, but little more.[32] In early August, Stringfield was contacted by a woman whose husband was in the Air Force at Wright-Patterson AFB in 1973. The husband told her he was once blindfolded and taken to a secure location where he stood guard for several high-ranking officers and scientists who were viewing three small humanoid bodies. The beings had large heads and were approximately 3 feet tall. The woman told Stringfield "he said he's not allowed to talk about it, and that he will tell everything he knows after President Carter makes an announcement."[33] In the Fall, another military informant told Stringfield of his second-hand knowledge of a 1948 retrieval of a metallic disc-shaped UFO that crashed somewhere in a desert region. The only details indicated that the craft had suffered severe damage on impact and was retrieved by military units.[34]

As intriguing as these early accounts were, much more was to come.

NASA's Troubles, and The Grenada Initiative

The UFO topic had not been a happy subject for the Carter White House. Within a mere few months, it had prompted a deluge of citizen letters, sparked futile inquiries within the national security establishment, generated unwelcome tabloid press attention, and encouraged some serious leaks.

By the fall of 1977, matters were fast approaching a climax and resolution. On September 14, Frank Press of the White House once again asked NASA administrator Robert Frosch for help with the UFO mail problem. This was unwelcome enough, but Press then compounded his *ufopaux* by repeating his suggestion from July, that maybe the time was right for another study of the UFO issue. Perhaps a panel of prominent scientists might "conduct an investigation of the validity and significance of UFO reports."[35] Frosch's shudders were enough to keep NASA out of this, but the CIA and Air Force had also been advising NASA to steer clear. Two weeks earlier, on September 1, Colonel Charles Senn, Chief of USAF Community Relations Division, wrote to Lt. General Duward Crow of NASA, "I sincerely hope that you are successful in preventing a reopening of UFO investigations."[36] Everyone knew that this had been a twenty-year public relations headache for the Air Force. NASA's hierarchy essentially agreed with the Condon Committee report. Despite the political and fiscal dangers in opposing the President, NASA's institutional instinct was to run far, and run fast. NASA did grudgingly take on additional letter-answering duties, but the Carter administration lacked the desire to push any harder for an actual investigative body on UFOs.

This is evident in the termination of Alfred Webre's proposed extraterrestrial communications project, which Webre had worked on at Stanford Research Institute through the summer of 1977, and for which he was counting on White House support. There is some disagreement as to how this actually happened, but there is no question that Webre did propose the project, and that it was terminated in September. The open question is why.

Webre maintained that he attended a meeting at SRI with his supervisor, senior administrator Peter Schwartz. In addition were two other individuals, whose names Webre could not remember in later years. One of these was another senior SRI official, which Webre indicated in an affidavit as "John Doe I." The other he said was a Pentagon liaison with SRI, indicated as "John Doe II." According to Webre, the Pentagon liaison issued a warning: if the extraterrestrial study went forward, SRI's many contracts with the Pentagon would be terminated. The reason given by the Pentagon liaison: "there are no UFOs." Webre objected, to no avail.[37] He later contended that his proposed study "was nipped in the bud by the U.S. National Security State."[38] Peter Schwartz conceded that Webre's scenario had some elements of truth, but was "substantially wrong." There was never any formal inquiry, Schwartz maintained, nor any threat to SRI to cut off funding. "There were people at SRI who were unhappy about anything controversial that might bring negative attention to the institute, but we were never threatened by DoD."[39]

Whether Webre's proposal was shut down by the Pentagon or by SRI, it is evident that the White House itself was never committed to it. The White House staffer never contacted Webre after their meeting several months before. If the White House had truly wanted this project, one assumes it would have happened.

Meanwhile, the White House had to contend with a visit from a head of state who openly intended to end UFO secrecy. Luckily for the White House, Sir Eric Gairy was only from Grenada. On September 9, Gairy met with Jimmy Carter for a 45-minute meeting. Carter's actions remain unknown, except that he gave Gairy a copy of the 1969 Condon Committee report on UFOs. It would appear that the White House attempted to erase this meeting from history; archivists at the Carter Library have found no notes pertaining to it. Indeed, the files of Carter's National Security Advisor, Zbigniew Brzezenski, who attended the meeting, are still classified more than four decades later. In a subsequent interview, Gairy avoided details of the meeting, but acknowledged that UFOs were discussed. Indeed, it is obvious what Gairy wanted. Gairy was planning a return to the United Nations to press for UFO disclosure. As the leader of a politically powerless Caribbean nation, the U.N. was his best forum, and he obviously wanted a politically friendly White House. He appears to have failed to get the support he wanted.[40]

Gairy delivered his speech on October 7, which was prepared with the help of Leonard Stringfield.[41] Gairy told the delegates that he had once seen a UFO and was "totally overwhelmed" by the experience. "One wonders," he continued:

> ... why the existence of UFOs, or flying saucers as they are sometimes called, continue to remain a secret to those whose archives repose useful information and other data. While we appreciate that some countries consider this to be in the interest of military expedience, I now urge that a different view be taken because it is my firm conviction that the world is ready, willing and ripe enough to accept these phenomena in relation to man and his existence on the earth planet and life in outer space.[42]

Gairy recommended that the U.N. establish a permanent agency to study UFOs and facilitate the exchange of data among the world's nations. A formal resolution was now needed, and this was scheduled for November 28. On the morning of the 28th, Grenada's U.N. Ambassador, Dr. Wellington Friday, received a phone call from a U.S. delegate, Coast Guard Commander John Feigle, who expressed "hopeful support," but said the U.S. position was based on the Condon Report of 1969. Friday

Grenada's Prime Minister, Eric Gairy

replied that new data had made that study "invalid." Later that day, Wellington Friday gave an hour-long speech – "a moment for history," as Stringfield called it. He suggested the U.N. study UFO sightings, alleged contacts with aliens, and work to make UFO data more accessible. He appealed to U.N. Secretary General Kurt Waldheim to convene UFO hearings.

This request was audacious, risky, even revolutionary. If accepted, it would mean virtual acknowledgment of an extraterrestrial presence by one of the world's most politically important institutions. But it bounced harmlessly off the structure of the United Nations. Waldheim assured the Grenadans that the matter would be addressed as soon as "126 global issues ranging from disarmament, to human rights and terrorism had been shelved..."[43] The U.S. delegation told the Grenadans they could not support the resolution, especially a segment that suggested governments share their UFO data. Britain agreed, and arranged for a closed-door session during which it was decided that the Grenadan proposal would be too time consuming and expensive to implement.

The rest was denouement. On December 13, the U.N. General Assembly adopted Decision 32/424, which acknowledged Gairy's resolution, forwarded it to interested member states, and shelved the matter until the next general assembly convened, which was a year later. In theory, this allowed time for member nations to evaluate their UFO data. Some, like Stringfield, hoped that by then Gairy's views might have made an impact on the world community. In reality, the decision was a failure for the Grenada delegation. Only three governments (India, Luxembourg, and Seychelles) and two specialized agencies (International Civil Aviation Organization and UNESCO) even bothered to respond, essentially with no comments. Even so, Gairy did not intend to give up.[44]

Meanwhile, NASA had already decided that it was not going to investigate UFOs. In late October, NASA scientist Herbert Rowe wrote to MUFON that "at the present time" NASA lacked the resources. "Should we arrive at the point where outside assistance is desired," Rowe stated, "we will be in touch with you."[45] Two months later, on December 21, 1977, Robert Frosch told White House advisor Frank Press that, based on a check with the CIA, it knew of no evidence of UFO reality. He emphasized the problem of devising a "sound scientific procedure" to investigate what could clearly be an elusive phenomenon. While NASA would continue to respond to UFO-related mail, it would not conduct any research into the matter until hard evidence were to arise from a credible source. Frosch closed by stressing that NASA as an institution had not come to a conclusion about UFOs ("we retain an open mind") but that the problem was one of devising appropriate scientific protocols.[46]

Dr. Dave Williamson, NASA Assistant for Special Projects, put the matter this way:

> ... we're not anxious to do it because we're not sure what we can do. It's my personal opinion that it's not wise to do research on something that is not a measurable phenomena. Spending public money for such research is questionable. There is no measurable UFO evidence such as a piece of metal, flash or cloth. We don't even have any radio signals. A photograph is not a measurement .... give me one little green man – not a theory or memory of one – and we can have a multimillion dollar program....[47]

Considering the evasiveness and difficulties presented by the UFO phenomenon, there is merit in this position. Yet, Stringfield's research was beginning to hint that actual alien craft and bodies were available for study in deeply classified "need to know" circles, although certainly not public institutions such as NASA. The claim, too, that "a photograph is not a measurement" is pithy, memorable, and wrong. Precisely because photographs do provide accurate, measurable data is why photographic analysis commands resources and respect from intelligence agencies and scientific organizations around the world.

A White House press release on December 27 made it official, stating that it accepted NASA's evaluation of the situation and would not pursue the matter any further. As 1977 came to a close, the Carter UFO initiative was dead, and the various efforts to create an institutional foundation for UFO research had all failed.

Movies and the Media

Not only were political initiatives for disclosure stirring the pot; UFOs were also receiving attention in the media. Dominating the news was Steven Spielberg's movie, *Close Encounters of the Third Kind*, released in December 1977, which dealt with the UFO phenomenon in a manner that reflected some genuine research. Even the title was derived from Allen Hynek's typology of UFO sightings. Spielberg had sought cooperation from NASA; the agency sent him a 20-page letter hoping to talk him out of the project. That was when he "found [his] faith" – if NASA was so opposed to his movie, he assumed he was onto something. This was no 1950s "alien invasion" flick. Spielberg portrayed the aliens as benign and even with smiles. Well before its release, the movie received quite a few bad reviews, with several pundits predicting "flop." But it succeeded wildly, ultimately receiving many positive reviews, albeit as a work of drama rather than something based on reality. The movie unquestionably struck a resonant chord with a worldwide public.

UFOs were also receiving media attention of a different sort, in this case the tabloid publication, *The National Enquirer*. For some time, the paper had been mixing its standard tabloid fare with UFO stories that reflected genuine investigation. On October 31, the *Enquirer* sent a series of questions to the Air Force about the intrusion of alleged unidentified "helicopters" over Loring AFB from late 1975.[48] Why not the *New York Times, Washington Post*, CBS, or other mainstream news agencies? Why the *Enquirer*?

Years later, journalist Terry Hansen interviewed Bob Pratt, the *Enquirer*'s reporter on the story. Pratt acknowledged that the tipoff appeared to have been an anonymous phone caller, possibly "with the intention of discrediting the information." After searching his notes, Pratt found a type-written statement with the name of UFO researcher Brad Sparks on the bottom, stating that on May 17, 1977, an anonymous caller had contacted the *Enquirer* about the overflights. Pratt had no recollection of this, nor of having worked with Sparks.

What makes this more interesting is that the *Enquirer* publisher, Gene Pope, had been a CIA agent during the early 1950s. What he did there remains classified, except that he was involved in the Agency's Psychological Warfare Unit. Hansen's research suggested that the CIA helped to fund the *Enquirer* when Pope took it over, most likely to provide sensationalistic coverage to certain stories as needed – a kind of 'inoculation,' just as a doctor gives a touch of disease to the patient to stimulate a reaction from the immune system. Even soberly researched UFO stories would be discredited within the confines of a tabloid dedicated to horoscopes and celebrity gossip.[49]

In fact, Pratt's article, "UFOs Spotted at Nuclear Bases and Missile Sites," which appeared on December 13, 1977, was well researched. He listed names and dates that could be used for a FOIA request, which Barry Greenwood promptly filed. While the inside tip may have been an attempt to create a stillborn, it is conceivable that this was a genuine lead from someone in the intelligence community, using a reliable CIA conduit such as Pope. The intelligence establishment is not monolithic; factions and conflicting agendas have always proliferated within it.[50]

The *Enquirer* was helpful in this case. Yet, its continued association with the UFO topic poisoned the field. UFO articles appeared in other "unrespectable" publications as well, such as men's magazines like *Playboy* and *Oui* (which featured an interview with Allen Hynek by Jerome Clark). Such a setting ensured continued disdain and ridicule from academic and scientific circles. Some UFO researchers were aware of the problem, Richard Hall being the most vocal. Others, such as Walter Andrus and Coral Lorenzen, seemed to abide by the adage that there was no such thing as bad publicity. The virtues of taking the high road on such matters may seem obvious, but it can be difficult to avoid temptation when all other avenues are shut off, year after year.[51]

Government Policies Elsewhere

While 1977 was a year when the U.S. President apparently failed to break through the secrecy surrounding UFOs, Britain maintained its status quo with less fuss, largely thanks to a law that kept government documents secret for 30 years. In 1977, this effectively ruled out the entire modern era of UFOs. Over the next few years, when British researchers applied for UFO documents created prior to 1950, they were told the reports had been re-filed with all reports for 1955 – essentially, "come back in 1985." This game continued into the early 1980s, when researchers learned that now there were no files prior to 1960.[52]

Other nations had different policies. In May 1977, France established the *Groupe d'Etude des Phenomenes Aerospatiaux Non-Identifies* (GEPAN) specifically for the study of UFOs. Under the direction of Dr. Claude Poher, the group was part of the French National Space Agency. French President Valery Giscard d'Estaing expressed interest in the project. The organization was soon investigating current cases, alerted by teletype from the French National Police Force. In 1978, from 11 case studies, GEPAN concluded that in 9 of them, the origin, propulsion, and method of operation were beyond human knowledge. Even so, GEPAN appeared to be as much public relations as actual study, and many researchers believed that the high strangeness cases went to other agencies. By the 1980s, GEPAN's activities and status had become uncertain, even among French researchers.[53]

Two additional statements from 1977, both from Japan, bear mention. The first was by Japanese Major General Hideki Komura, advisor to the Cabinet Research Office (equivalent to the CIA), who stated that there had been high level official Japanese UFO investigations during the 1950s and 1960s. This study had been based on the American Project Blue Book and cooperated closely with the United States. However, the study collapsed, he said. This was because there were too many non-credible cases being received alongside the more credible data. One might wonder why an intelligence operation would close down simply because not all the data it received was valid. Such is a universal problem in intelligence collection.[54] In September 1977, another Japanese General made a dramatically different statement regarding UFOs. Lieutenant General Akira Hirano, Chief of Staff of the Japan Air Self-Defense Force, stated "we frequently see unidentified objects in the skies. We are quietly investigating them." This statement was quickly countered by his staff, which denied that he mentioned any official investigation.[55]

1977: A Year of Aerial Encounters

UFO statistics, never complete even today, were woefully inadequate during most of the twentieth century. During the 1970s, entire regions of the world still lacked a reliable infrastructure for reports. The Soviet Union, Eastern Europe, China, Middle East, Africa, and much of the Pacific region remained ufologically 'dark.' Even so, based on the reports that have come to light, it is clear that 1977 was a very active year in terms of UFO sightings.

While the year was rich in sightings of all types, many cases involved UFOs provocatively buzzing commercial and military aircraft. This happened with such consistency and frequency in all regions of the world that an objective analyst is hard pressed to find any explanation other than that some agency was operating extremely advanced aerial technology in a direct attempt to get the attention of the world's military authorities.

One such case took place in Colombian air space on January 21. *Avianca* Flight 132 had just taken off from El Dorado Airport, Bogota, and had climbed to its cruise altitude of 20,000 feet when Captain Gustavo Ferreira and his four crew members noticed a bright light approaching them. Ferreira discussed this with his first officer, then called air traffic control at Bogota. Hoping to get the attention of the oncoming object, he turned on his plane's landing lights. When he did so, the UFO appeared to respond by changing color from white to red. Startled, Ferreira decided to turn off all of his airplane's lights, leaving it in total darkness, and then turned them back on. Again, the object seemed to respond: it flashed green lights, changed its direction, and was soon gone. As it disappeared visually, the radar operator stated, "I've lost it!" The object had performed a ninety degree turn at "fantastic speed" and left his scope.[56]

Similar events occurred in Europe. In February, a UFO followed an Italian F-104 for 23 minutes, according to a report that was later declassified by the Italian Defense Ministry. The pilot stated that the object was brighter than the Moon, and remained a mere 800 or 900 yards from his aircraft. "I alerted the nearest base," he said, "and was authorised to intercept it. When I began to show my intentions, climbing to 12,000 feet, the object kept its distance unchanged, then disappeared."[57] On March 7, 1977, a French Mirage IV bomber aircraft was approached by a UFO, an event seen visually, tracked on radar, and included in the COMETA report years later. Flying near Dijon at 31,500 feet just under the speed of sound, the pilot and navigator saw a bright light rapidly approach. Despite their evasive maneuvers, it tailed them at a distance of less than a mile, then sped away at supersonic speed. Less than a minute later, the scenario repeated. At no point was the object tracked on radar.[58]

Three days later, on the other side of the world, another UFO buzzed by an Indonesian offshore Arjuna oil field. On March 10, at 7:40 p.m., crews from two tanker vessels saw a large dark object with a red light approach from the west beneath the clouds, circle the oil field twice, emit beams of light, then fly away to the east. An Indonesian Air Force officer reported the case to CUFOS.[59]

On June 17, the Portuguese Air Force engaged UFOs. Sergeant Jose Rodriguez was flying a Dornier aircraft over Castelo de Bodedam when he saw a dark object approach. He notified ground control, which reported no other nearby traffic. As the object closed in, he estimated its diameter to be between 40 and 50 feet, and saw that its upper section was black, while the lower section had some sort of paneling. After it vanished at high speed, Rodriguez's directional electric gyroscope rotated wildly, and his plane started to dive out of control. He regained control at treetop level, and was so disturbed that he had difficulty speaking afterward. While independent

Sgt. Jose Rodriguez

ground witnesses could not confirm the UFO, they did confirm the dramatic dive of the aircraft and the apparent power surge when he regained control of the aircraft. The Portuguese Air Force offered no explanation for the event.[60]

One of the most intriguing stories of 1977 occurred on July 1, at NATO's Aviano Air Base, located northeast of Venice, and operated by the USAF under the control of the Italian Defense Ministry. The case was described by Timothy Good in the 1980s, and received extensive followup by USAF Lt. Colonel Jerry Rowles.

Good reported that an American soldier named James Blake saw a large, bright light hovering at low altitude in an alert zone where two military aircraft were being kept. Many soldiers saw the object, which appeared to be domed, spinning, changing colors, 150 feet in diameter, and making a noise like "a swarm of bees." According to this account, the event lasted for a full hour and caused a massive black out on the base. A few seconds after the object left, the base lights went back on. The official explanation was that the event "must be attributed to a reflection of the Moon on some low clouds."[61]

During the 1990s, Rowles re-investigated the event, corroborating and correcting Good's account. He obtained information from a new witness, a decorated base sergeant named Robert A. Furry, who said that at 3 a.m. in clear weather, base sensors detected an object which triggered several alarms. Part of the facility lost power, and backup systems engaged. A security policeman noticed a light (or lights) beyond the northwest perimeter fence. Furry notified the command post that a security response team had been dispatched to apprehend possible intruders. He then went outside to look, and saw a very bright, circular light that appeared to be about 30 feet above the ground, some 200 meters beyond the fence. The light was so intense, said Furry, "especially around the rim," that details were difficult to see. Yet he discerned a physical structure behind it, and heard a sound like "bees buzzing, or a humming sound." According to Furry, the object did not hover directly over the base (which was what Good had reported). U.S. Air Force security and a unit from the Italian National Police were dispatched to determine the nature of the object, but it left before the units arrived. "It just gradually inclined and took off towards the corner of the mountains," said Furry.

In Furry's judgment, the craft had simply been watching the base. "We certainly took no hostile actions toward it," he said. "Those of us who observed it were in a standoff mode." No one contacted Furry about the matter, he signed no security oaths, and the incident received no publicity. For a while, there was speculation around the base about the UFO, "but the talk just kind of dried away and the incident was more or less ignored." For his part, Furry favored an extraterrestrial answer. He did not believe any classified, experimental craft would have "floated in unannounced and then hover" next to an active alert facility.

Rowles also spoke to a base historian who found no references to the incident. Yet, Rowles pointed out, administrators have little flexibility in preparing unit histories. Since no intrusion or hostile actions were made, Rowles found it "logical and consistent with administrative procedures" that the event would not make it into the unit history.[62]

Shortly after Rowles published his analysis of the Aviano event, a geophysicist named John Derr offered that it "was clearly an electrical phenomenon, most likely an intense plasma similar to ball lightning, but generated by strain release in the earth." Derr pointed out that this period of time coincided with a series of earthquakes in the area from the year before, and that aftershocks were still occurring in 1977.[63] Furry rejected this explanation, countering that he saw a structured craft, not simply lights.[64]

Even accounting for the variations in the story as told by different witnesses, it is clear that something important happened at Aviano, important enough to create a phenomenon (or object) that gave off intensely bright light for an extended period of time, disable the air base's electrical power system, trigger a major security alert, appear to move intelligently, and evade identification. Until a geophysicist can show how the earth can generate "an intense plasma" that can do all these things, the case remains inexplicable by any conventional standards.

Later that month, another UFO event was recorded at a European military base. While the event has official confirmation, the precise date is vague. RAF Boulmer is in the north of England, facing the North Sea, not far from Scotland. In July 1977, a flight lieutenant named A.M. Wood reported seeing two luminous, round objects, four to five times the size of a helicopter, three miles out to sea, hovering at around 5,000 feet altitude. Two other base personnel, a Corporal Torrington and a Sergeant Graham, watched the objects with Wood for almost two hours, which were also tracked by base radar and another radar facility at RAF Staxton Wold. According to a report that was released in 2005, "the objects separated. Then one went west of the other, as it maneuvered it changed shape to become body-shaped with projections like arms and legs." This event was considered so sensitive to the national interest that the MoD delayed its release for an extra three years beyond its normal declassification schedule. But under the British Freedom of Information Act, which came into force on January 1, 2005, the file was finally declassified.[65]

These European reports showed a pattern of unknown objects behaving in extraordinary and provocative ways that stopped short of belligerent. Elsewhere, they had become deadly.

UFOs that Kill

China's long history of isolation from the West, rigidly imposed by its leaders over many centuries, ended during the 1970s. In 1972, U.S. President Richard Nixon initiated diplomatic relations. Four years later, Communist Party Chairman Mao Zedong died. In July 1977, the Party rehabilitated Deng Xiaoping, who had advocated greater economic openness. Now the leader himself, Deng saw links with the U.S. as a vital means of acquiring technical aid and helping the economy to modernize. Meanwhile, Chinese ufology thrived, and Chinese UFO reports became frequent. Many of these were recorded by researcher Paul Dong, including several dozen for the summer of 1977.

A spectacular case occurred on July 7, seen by many witnesses in the Zhang Po County of Fujian Province. This is in the south, across the water from Taiwan. At about 8:30 p.m., nearly 3,000 people were watching an outdoor screening of a movie, when the crowd saw two orange luminous objects, a mere ten feet apart from each other, descend toward them. These objects passed so low that they were "almost scraping the ground." Although perfectly silent, they emitted an intensely bright light and gave off heat as they passed over the crowd. The objects then ascended rapidly and disappeared within ten seconds. The sighting caused panic and a stampede: two children died and 200 others were injured. Although authorities initially suspected an optical illusion somehow connected to the film, they determined this was not so. No explanation was ever given.[66]

Dong reported another UFO encounter from an unspecified date that year, involving what appears to be the same type of object in the same region, this time directly involving the Chinese military. On the country's southeastern shore, people saw a luminous globe approach silently from the direction of Taiwan, fly over the mainland, and come down to rest on a hill. A nearby garrison was alerted, and a company of 150 soldiers surrounded the hill. The captain assumed the object was a secret American weapon. As the troops approached, it became extremely bright and gave off a "fearful noise." The captain ordered his men to fire, but bullets had no effect. The object rose off the ground, "lighting up the whole vicinity." Within twenty seconds, it was gone.[67]

Many of these Chinese sightings were reported in local newspapers and ended up in CIA files.[68] As reporting and collection methods improved in the next few years, their numbers continued to increase.

In August, in South America, Brazil began experiencing a dramatic spate of sightings, including many close encounters which extended into 1978. Reports came from at least 30 villages at the mouth of the Amazon River, near the Atlantic coast. Years later, UFO researchers Bob Pratt and Cynthia Luce investigated these. One of their contacts, a retired Brazilian Air Force Lieutenant Colonel named Uyrange Hollanda, told them an extraordinary story. At about 7 p.m. one evening in late 1977, a large disc-shaped object simply appeared directly above him and his men at an altitude of about 150 feet. There had been no warning whatsoever. He and his men were terrified. The object had a pulsating yellow glow and sounded "like an air conditioner." At its center were small yellow and orange lights; these eventually became light blue, and then dimmed. The object then disappeared toward the sea "with incredible speed."

Hollanda went to the commander of the base in Belem for instructions on what to do. He was given a team of technicians, photographers and other specialists to assist him in a classified investigation. They spent four months in Colares, Baia do Sol, and other villages north of Belem, interviewing nearly 300 people who had claimed to have had close encounters. In dozens of cases, people had been burned by UFOs, with at least two fatalities being reported. The team itself saw strange lights "almost every night" during the investigation. They took many photographs, none of which turned out well. "I had no proof of the flying saucers," Hollanda told Pratt and Luce, "only my visual information." He described several types of UFOs: domed, discs (with windows), triangular, rectangular, pyramid-like, jetliner-like, and a huge mother-ship craft. Some of the objects were seen leaving the water. Hollanda stated that some people reported seeing occupants in the objects, usually four to five feet tall, although on two occasions the beings were taller and looked ordinary.

Hollanda turned in his reports and never saw them again. Nobody ever followed up with him, although after one of his queries he was told the reports were being kept indefinitely and he was ordered to "keep quiet." For several months after his official investigation ended, he continued to look into the matter privately. Hollanda said the U.S. Air Force was "interested" in the sightings, and several times he quietly met with American military attachés over drinks to discuss his investigation.

Although Pratt and Luce could not confirm the full scope of Hollanda's story, Pratt did speak to an area doctor who confirmed UFO-related fatalities from 1977. In 2004, documents from the Brazilian Air Force's secret service revealed some of the records of the 1977 investigation. The report, called Operation Saucer, was partially released to the public, although the public portion did not offer any conclusions regarding the events of 1977. It is noteworthy that a story so amazing has found at least some corroboration via officially released documents. More research remains to confirm the details fully.[69]

The Return and Departure of Mr. Axelrod

Within the United States, the first half of 1977 was something of a "slow season" for UFOs. The most striking event, moreover, was not even an official report, but the final chapter in the saga of remote viewer Ingo Swann and the mysterious Mr. Axelrod.

Swann spent much of that summer at the Stanford Research Institute (SRI) in Menlo Park, California, where Hal Puthoff and Russell Targ managed the remote viewing program, and where Alfred Webre was trying to establish his extraterrestrial communications proposal. One Friday in July, Axelrod was somehow able to enter the secured facility. To say the least, this was not an easy thing to do. He thereupon found Swann and convinced him to leave with him. They took a Lear jet from the San Jose Airport, accompanied by "the twins" – as Swann described Alexrod's two blond-haired, blue-eyed, military-looking assistants. The four flew up the west coast to where Swann believed was in the Alaskan wilderness, although Axelrod would not say ("it's better that you not know.") They found a landing area deep in the forest, seemingly for their own use, got out and trekked for a long time, finally settling in to camp for the night. The twins wore special goggles over their eyes, while Axelrod instructed Swann simply to observe. They came to a small lake, and Axelrod said that as dawn approached, Swann would be able to see "it" through the pines. "We now wait and hope we are lucky. Say nothing, do *not* make any noise.... they detect heat, noise, motion like mad."

Dawn arrived, and Swann saw a fog developing over the lake. This went on for five minutes, until the fog developed a luminous neon-blue color. Then, according to Swann, the color changed to an "angry purple." Axelrod and one of the twins each placed a hand firmly on Swann's shoulders while "a network of purple, red, and yellow lightning bolts shot in all crazy directions through the 'cloud'." Swann said he would have jumped if the two had not held him down. He saw an object, almost transparent at first, but then "solidly visible over the lake." It was triangular or diamond-shaped, growing in size. Swann, in terror and amazement, heard a strong wind moving past, rustling the pine trees so much that some cones and branches fell on them. The object then began to shoot out "ruby red laser-like beams" as it continued to grow even more in size while maintaining its position over the lake. Very quietly, one of the twins said, "Shit! They're enveloping the area. They're going to spot us."

As Swann later recalled the event, some of the red laser beams from the object were "blasting" pine trees, and he could hear low frequency pulsations. Axelrod whispered to Swann that the beams were probably honing in on deer or other forest creatures, as they sense biological body heat. "They're sure to hone in on us," he told Swann. Just then, one of the twins literally lifted and dragged Swann away, but not before Swann noticed the water of the lake surging upward, "like a waterfall going upward, as if being sucked into the 'machine.'" The four ran quickly and at great length, sustaining minor cuts and bruises. Eventually they stopped, breathing hard, and waited for more than thirty minutes, until one of the twins said all was clear.

Axelrod then asked Swann whether he could 'sense' anything from the craft. Swann burst out laughing. "You're completely nuts, Axel! I have to be calm, cool, collected, and in good shape to sense anything." But Swann offered the insight that the craft was "a drone of some kind, unmanned, controlled from somewhere else." Axelrod asked him what it was doing there, to which Swann replied "Well, for chrissakes! It was thirsty! Taking on water, obviously. Someone, somewhere needs water ... so I suppose they just come and get it. You don't need to be a psychic to see that." Essentially, said Swann, "they" treated Earth as the neighborhood supermarket.

Before taking Swann back, Axelrod said, "I shouldn't tell you, but our mission will be disbanded shortly and the work picked up by others, because of strategic security reasons involved ..." "Others," said Swann, "who will not mix in with psychics, I take it." "You got it," Axelrod replied. Swann last saw Axelrod at the San Jose Airport, and never heard from him again.[70]

For years, Swann told no one of his encounters with Axelrod. He had signed no secrecy agreement; Axelrod had simply asked him to keep silence for at least ten years. During the 1990s, Swann recounted his experiences in the self-published book, *Penetration*. Although it will be impossible to prove the veracity of his extraordinary claims, the reader should be mindful of Swann's record of service, the documented accuracy of his predictions about Jupiter, the respect he earned from those who knew him, and the fact that none of his colleagues ever expressed doubt over the truth of his story.

A Global Aerial Crescendo

As 1977 progressed, Britain, Italy, the Soviet Union, and the United States generated the most and best UFO cases. On the night of August 3-4, three control tower employees at Naples Airport saw a circular UFO giving off intense white light. The report was declassified two years later by the Italian government.[71] On August 28, shortly after midnight, a large object with lights was seen near Windermere, Cumbria. For more than twenty minutes, British police and citizens observed it, which resembled "the shape of a stingray fish," apparently triangular in shape. It flew slowly at about 1,500 feet altitude, hovering at times. All witnesses described it as silent, except one person who heard a "quiet hum."[72] In the early fall, an anonymous British police officer in Sussex saw a UFO on a bright day while off duty and waiting for a bus. The object looked like a domed saucer, had the look of polished metal, was green-greyish in color, and had a blue-green light on top. She saw a thick black circular section on the bottom of the craft, and heard no sound. She waved to the object, which then came closer. Her memory seemed unclear after this, but when the bus arrived, she felt numb and uncoordinated. The object was gone, and she had unaccountably lost twenty minutes of time.[73] During the evening of September 30, a large and silent triangular craft was seen in Britain by a witness near Newington, who described "two very bright white beams, like headlights, [which] emanated from the object."[74]

Quiet during most of 1977, the U.S. suddenly experienced a flurry of strange aviation encounters, primarily in the American West. One case occurred near Billings, Montana on September 4, when a commercial pilot reported seeing a glowing oval object. Two more unusual incidents were reported on September 22. One was over El Paso, Texas, when a pilot saw an object overtake his airliner, make a 90-degree turn, and soar away straight up. The other occurred in Omaha, Nebraska, when four radar controllers tracked a large, extremely fast formation of large objects. "We kept watching these things," a controller said, "and they were gone from our scope in less than a minute." He calculated their speed to be an astonishing 17,000 mph.[75]

Behind the dreaded 'iron curtain,' Soviet citizens were seeing UFOs throughout the year. Some of these cases were reported in the West by Jacques Vallee and later by Paul Stonehill, occasionally lacking specific dates or other desirable details. The most important Soviet case of 1977 took place near the Finnish border on September 20. Military personnel at Petrozavodsk saw a large object glowing in the sky at 4 a.m. For fifteen minutes it showered down beams of light, giving the effect of a downpour of rain. It then moved west toward Finland. At least 170 people saw this phenomenon, including police, navy personnel, pilots, and scientists. Troops and police found that their radio frequencies were jammed and their telephones did not work. The phenomenon was observed for 10-12 minutes. Somehow, typical Soviet censorship broke down, and *Izvestia* described the event in detail.

Because of the inexplicable and dramatic nature of the encounter, as well as the nationwide publicity it received, it was impossible to ignore. In October, representatives of the Soviet Academy of Sciences met with Kremlin officials. A meeting was held in the Kremlin, the result of which was to organize a study program of "paranormal phenomena" with participation of the Soviet military. By 1978 this would evolve into two parallel UFO research programs: Setka-MO, run by the Ministry of Defense, and Setka-AN, run by the Academy of Sciences.

It was later pointed out that the Petrozavodsk event coincided with the firing of a Kosmos 955 satellite and its carrier rocket, Vostok, launched from the Plesetsk Cosmodrome. That might appear to explain it. Yet, as so often happens with UFOs, matters were not that simple. Unusual and bright objects were seen over a vast area in the northwestern Soviet Union. Several hours before the launch, for instance, a disc-shaped UFO was reported by pilots of an airplane bound for Riga, who had to maneuver their aircraft to avoid a collision. In another instance that night a spherical object about 65 feet in diameter was seen to land on a hill along the Petrozavodsk-Leningrad highway, and then vanish from view. At the western edge of Lake Lagoda, near Leningrad, a witness saw a UFO that emitted a bright sphere which landed in the forest and gave off a bright glow. Another witness, employed as a scientist and writer, saw several UFOs through a telescope that night, one of which hovered, turned around, then disappeared. At 3:30 a.m. (thirty minutes before the launch), two very large, glowing spherical objects were seen maneuvering in the sky over the town of Primorsk. This is about 700 miles southwest of Petrozavodsk. The objects moved toward Onezhsky Lake, hovered, then vanished at great speed. Soviet UFO researcher Felix Zigel compiled data from the many sightings of that night and early morning, and determined that the Petrozavodsk sighting was only one of many which occurred within a huge region between Denmark and Mongolia. Zigel concluded that neither natural phenomena nor human technology were responsible for most of these sightings.[76]

Still, not everyone believed there was a mystery here. In a jointly authored paper, two former Soviet government officials involved in the Setka programs argued that "a number of additional effects accompanying this phenomenon [were] connected with the failure in launching a ballistic rocket. The launching of the rocket took place in the same region and almost at the same time" as the strange phenomena. Unfortunately, no further detail was offered in their explanation. It would seem odd that a rocket launch could jam radios and interfere with telephones.[77]

One other Soviet account from 1977, officially unconfirmed, remains suggestive after many years, and was said to have involved a submarine repair ship. On October 7, the *Volga* was at sea when nine disc-shaped objects circled around it for nearly 20 minutes. During this time, all electronic equipment on the ship went "berserk." The Captain, named Tarantin, told his men, "I want you to observe this carefully and to remember it. I want you to take pictures and draw it, so that when we return to the Soviet Union no one will be able to say that your captain was drunk or crazy." According to Jacques Vallee, who wrote about the event, the report was either classified or never made public.[78]

Italian and American cases dominated the final months of the year. On October 27, an air traffic controller at Cagliari-Elmas airport in Sardinia, stated that he saw a UFO that flew at the speed of a jet, "at some 926 kph." The object was behind a helicopter that was participating in military maneuvers. According to an Italian military report, the sighting caused a feverish exchange of messages among personnel at Elmas, the NATO base in Decimomannu, the US aircraft carrier *Saratoga*, and several military planes in flight. Some fighter planes also saw the UFO at the very low altitude of 500 meters for several minutes.[79]

In late October or early November, Italian Air Corps helicopter pilot Major Francesco Zoppi and his co-pilot were on a training mission when they encountered a bright orange circle ahead of them, matching their speed. Other helicopters in the squadron saw the object, although it was not detected on radar. It then vanished at "a speed impossible for any aircraft of this world to equal." The story leaked to the press, although many details were not provided.[80]

Meanwhile, in the United States more aerial close encounters were being reported. Flying through Texas on October 26 between Abilene and Dallas at 19,000 feet, the pilot and passenger of a small aircraft saw a bright, red, stationary sphere straight ahead of them. As they closed on the object, the plane's navigation instruments become erratic and the radio stopped working. The sphere then changed its color from red to white, performed a high speed vertical climb, and vanished into space. According to the pilot, "as soon as the sphere left we got all of our radio gear back. Our navigation came back, and we were off course." A two-man crew of an Air Force T-38 flying in the same area also saw the object. According to that pilot, "the bright red glowing object ... appeared to be closing very rapidly." They considered an evasive maneuver, but the closing ceased. One Air Force crew member experienced considerable static over his headset at the time.[81]

Over the next month or two, similar occurrences were reported in the central and western U.S. On November 18, the pilot of a small aircraft flying at night between Vichy and Troy, Missouri noticed a bright white light quickly move alongside him, pace his aircraft for three minutes, then rapidly move away. One of his transponders stopped working during those minutes, then resumed normal operation.[82]

On December 8, two UFO sightings occurred near Oxnard, California. At 8 p.m., air traffic controllers tracked four unidentified objects about three to five miles north of Laguna Peak. "We watched the targets on the scope for nearly three hours," said one controller. The speed and maneuverability of the objects caused one controller to remark, "I've never seen anything like this in all the twenty years that I have worked as an air traffic controller." At around 9 p.m., while the controllers were still tracking the UFOs, a Golden West commuter aircraft was flying from Oxnard to Los Angeles International Airport when two large, bright lights maneuvered around it for 15 minutes. The speed and maneuverability of these objects was described as extraordinary. "Like you would just snap your fingers and it was there," said the commercial pilot. "It got so close it scared the hell out of me."[83]

On December 17, at 3:34 a.m., radar facilities in Colorado and South Dakota tracked two UFOs that gave "strong" and "unmistakable" returns, moving at the fighter-jet speed of over 1,000 mph. The objects were tracked for the next 30 minutes, during which time one of the objects made a close head-on pass at an aircraft in the area. A third radar station was unable to function while the unknowns were in the area, and one of the two operational facilities was put out of service when the main shaft holding the radar antenna was severely bent by an unexplained force.[84]

The last interesting American UFO encounter of 1977 took place on December 27, a radar-visual case involving a police helicopter in Charlotte,

North Carolina. At 10:54 p.m., a crew of two police officers on a routine helicopter patrol were flying over Charlotte at 1,800 feet above sea level when they noticed two lights approaching from the northwest. The officers assumed these to be landing lights of some aircraft or helicopter. But the lights continued to close on their position, and two minutes later shocked the officers by passing just 200 feet over them. The helicopter's pilot, Ron Garey, asked the FAA control tower whether they were painting any radar targets in the area. FAA operators confirmed two unknowns. The police officers assumed they had just encountered military helicopters heading for Fort Bragg.

Moments later, the officers again saw two lighted objects approaching them. As if to make a point, one of them shot upward at a 45 degree angle to an estimated 4,000 feet within three seconds (roughly 450 mph). The other light continued to approach at 1,800 feet altitude. Garey executed a "pedal turn" to the left as the object passed by. This is a pivot maneuver made in a stationary hover, and allowed for a closer inspection of the object as it passed by. Incredibly, as he did this, the object made a radial turn around the helicopter, and the two men lost sight of it. Garey then turned the helicopter to the right, and both officers saw that the object was right behind them. Again, Garey turned the helicopter to get a better view, and again the object outmaneuvered him.

The officers realized they were encountering something very unusual. As they observed the object more carefully, it appeared to be a globular white light with a surrounding glow. Sparks were falling away from it, and the officers also noticed a silver parachute-like object attached to the light source, with some sort of transparent section in-between. The object began to move away to the east, and the officers briefly gave chase, although it quickly outdistanced them and disappeared. At 11:02 p.m., FAA tower controller Ray Bader advised the crew that the second unknown was over the downtown area. A minute later, the pilots saw the object visually, but almost immediately it vanished – visually and on the radar scope. Thus ended the extremely bizarre aerial encounter.

MUFON investigators George D. Fawcett, P. Wayne Laporte, Henry H. Morton Jr., and David M. Oldham studied this case in detail. There was an initial claim by local students that the objects were candle-lit balloons they had launched, and that the unusual movements were due to the wind currents caused by the helicopter rotors. The winds also caused the candle lights to blow out, claimed the students, which would explain why one of the objects seemed to disappear. To test this theory, the investigators launched the same type of balloon and conferred with individuals who had experience in military radar, balloon launchings, helicopters, and jet interception. The student explanation fell short for many reasons. First, it was determined that balloons would not have been whipped around by the helicopter rotors, but sucked in. Second, the balloon had no metal in its construction and could not have shown up on radar. Third, the horizontal speeds (over 200 mph) and altitude changes (even greater) of the unknown objects vastly exceeded the capabilities of a hot-air balloon. The investigators concluded the police officers had encountered a genuine UFO.[85]

As 1977 turned into 1978, aerial encounters showed no sign of abating. 1978 started off with a clear sighting on New Year's Day by a reliable witness. Floyd Hallstrom, an experienced airplane and helicopter pilot, was flying a Cessna 178 from Oxnard, California to San Diego. He was following a friend, Jim Victor, and the two maintained radio contact. Visibility was excellent as he approached Santa Monica, when he saw an object above the airport in Los Angeles. He thought this was Victor, until the object rapidly approached him. Seeing no wings on it, he wondered if it was a helicopter, but its speed was too fast (he later estimated it at 650 mph). When it passed below him and to his left, he saw it clearly as "the complete form of a saucer shape or round object." There were 16 to 20 equally spaced windows around its circumference. For all its speed, the object was very steady, showing no sign of rotation or oscillation. It was highly polished and the sun reflected brightly off it. He immediately radioed Victor, then FAA authorities. The case reached the attention of various UFO groups, and was investigated by Lt. Colonel Robert F. Bowker USAF (Ret). It was never made clear whether the object was seen on radar.[86]

Citizens Against UFO Secrecy

The year 1978 opened with a salvo intended to crack the wall of UFO secrecy: the formation of Citizens Against UFO Secrecy (CAUS). Led by W. Todd Zechel, the group focused on using FOIA lawsuits to obtain UFO documents. The group published an official newsletter, *Just Cause*. CAUS was essentially a three-man show: Zechel, Brad Sparks, and attorney Peter Gersten, who had met Zechel when they worked for Ground Saucer Watch. The three were optimistic. "We had served the government notice," Zechel later recalled. "We weren't going to take their stonewalling anymore, and if necessary, we would haul them into court."[87] During January and February, CAUS filed requests with the State Department for classified

UFO documents, receiving the reply that nothing could be found. Eventually, after repeatedly providing highly specific information regarding the desired documents, CAUS received several. Barry Greenwood, who later joined CAUS, said that "it seemed that the only way to get documents released was to have them in the first place so that one could mail them back to the agency as proof that they existed."[88]

Other researchers petitioned the U.S. government for documents. Greenwood was independently requesting from many agencies. Early in 1978, he received FOIA request replies from the FBI and the Department of Defense. The FBI told him that it did not investigate UFOs other than during a limited time in the 1940s, while the DoD told him that the Joint Chiefs of Staff had identified 24 UFO-related documents which complied with his request. Upon his receipt of these documents, he noticed that several of them included the CIA on their distribution list. The only problem was that the Agency was still insisting that its involvement with UFOs ended with the Robertson Panel in 1953.[89] Bruce Maccabee had better luck with the FBI. By 1978, he had already netted several hundred pages of UFO related data from the bureau, and would eventually receive about 1,000. Although the documents did not prove the existence of aliens, they indicated strong FBI interest in many sightings, and also proved that the FBI had lied to the public about this interest.[90]

In early June, Peter Gersten, on behalf of Ground Saucer Watch, filed a discovery motion requesting UFO information from CIA files. His motion consisted of 635 interrogatory questions, almost 300 requests for documents, and included 60 CIA documents attached as exhibits. These questions were specific enough, it was assumed, that the CIA would either have to produce the documents being requested or acknowledge that their UFO information was classified. There was no reason to expect the CIA simply to roll over – the Agency had been contesting such motions for months already.[91] Thus, it was somewhat of a surprise when the CIA announced in August that it had found "1,000 pages of additional material related to UFOs" which would be available for release. Soon after this, the Agency indicated it had found more than 10,000 UFO related documents in its files. Zechel immediately filed another suit with the CIA, Air Force, and other agencies. There was a hope that enough evidence could be brought forth to force a disclosure of the reality of UFOs. Perhaps military officers and government officials could be compelled to testify under oath about their knowledge of UFOs. Perhaps these might even lead to admissions about the recovery of an extraterrestrial vehicle and beings. In

1978, it all seemed possible, and that one disclosure could lead to others.[92]

In November, the CIA inadvertently leaked the existence of NSA-related UFO documents, when it referred 15 documents (soon three more) to that agency for declassification review.[93] On December 22, Gersten filed a FOIA request on behalf of CAUS for 18 NSA documents. The NSA replied that it was exempt from FOIA. Undeterred, several months later CAUS expanded its request to include all NSA documents "relating to or pertaining to unidentified flying objects and the UFO phenomena." This began the David and Goliath saga, CAUS vs. the NSA, which would be played out over several years.[94]

The Crash Retrieval Syndrome

Along with researchers making FOIA requests, Leonard Stringfield continued to be a key driver of UFO research in 1978, while Stanton Friedman made a discovery that had a major impact on ufology.

In January, while lecturing in Baton Rouge, Louisiana, Friedman met the manager of a local television station who recommended that he meet a man who had handled one of those "flying saucers way back then." Friedman looked the man up in the phone book – this was retired colonel Jesse Marcel, Sr. During their first meeting, Marcel described to Friedman what has since become known as the Roswell Incident. As an intelligence officer at the 509th Bomber Unit at Roswell Army Air Field, Marcel was dispatched to retrieve wreckage from a flying disc. While he did not see any bodies, he was astounded by the debris, which included foil-like material of incredible toughness, equally strong I-beams that looked flimsy but could not be bent or broken, and which had strange hieroglyphic-like writing on them. The fragments were transported to Roswell Army Air Field, then to Fort Worth, Texas, then to Wright Field in Dayton, Ohio, for analysis. While at Fort Worth, said Marcel, he had to lie to the press and "told them we were recovering a downed weather balloon." He was "certain" the object was not a balloon, nor any type of aircraft or rocket.

Friedman was skeptical of the story until UFO researcher William Moore found the July 1947 press release which said the Air Force had recovered a flying disc, as well as a press release from three hours later claiming the object had been an ordinary weather balloon. Friedman and Moore were intrigued. Before long, they interviewed almost 100 people who knew something about the event. Most of them had not discussed the case in years.[95]

So began the Roswell story. It would be a few years before it became the dominant issue in UFO research, and then a world icon and symbol for the UFO cover-up. In 1978, hardly anyone outside of Friedman, Moore, and Stringfield knew about it. For the moment, the greatest strides in research were still being made by Stringfield, who continued to develop new sources regarding *other* UFO crash retrievals.

In April, Stringfield was led to a former sergeant of the 97th Bomber Wing. This man had learned about crashed UFOs and occupants from an Air Force general who happened to be the father of an old girlfriend. The general had related first-hand knowledge to the sergeant of a UFO crash retrieval in the American southwest in 1957. With great difficulty, four burned and damaged humanoid bodies were recovered, along with the craft, and brought to Wright-Patterson AFB. The general saw the bodies in a deep freeze. The bodies were about five feet tall and the heads were large, although badly disfigured. The general also showed the sergeant a Top Secret memo concerning an incident at Nellis AFB in 1968. The sergeant told Stringfield that the memo described how for three days a large UFO hovered over the base. Three small craft then came out, one of which landed. A colonel and security detachment came to meet it. In a scene reminiscent of the movie *The Day the Earth Stood Still*, a humanoid being came out of the craft, described in the memo as "short and stocky." Then things went very wrong: a beam of light paralyzed the colonel, the security team tried to shoot, but their weapons jammed. The being re-entered the UFO, which then joined the large craft and departed. The colonel was hospitalized and could later only recall the event in terms of mathematics, as though an attempt of communication was conducted in this manner. Stringfield did manage to confirm the existence of the general. He even obtained "additional corroborative" information about the Nellis incident, but did not say what that was. Like most of his collected material, the accounts remained suggestive but unproven.[96]

In July, he met with yet another witness to alien bodies at Wright-Patterson AFB, a lead he obtained from his son-in-law. While working in military intelligence, the man had seen nine dead aliens, four feet tall and preserved in deep freeze conditions. He had been told that the base held a total of 30 alien bodies along with an alien craft. Furthermore, he told Stringfield that certain military bases contained mobile units ready to retrieve downed or crashed UFOs anywhere in the United States. Information about all military encounters with UFOs was stored on a computer within Wright-Patterson, and duplicate files were secretly stored elsewhere. "Get the complete file dump," he told Stringfield, "both the master and the support backup files, and you've got all the hidden UFO data."[97]

Leonard Stringfield

Thus far, Stringfield had not publicized his information. Mindful of how explosive this material was, he wanted to be confident in his sources. Far from popular media portrayals as 'eccentric believers,' most UFO researchers during the 1970s were fairly conservative. A 1978 survey of MUFON members by aerospace engineer Walt Greenawald gave a good sense of the typical UFO researcher: a well-educated, upper-middle class, politically conservative, 40-something professional who had personally witnessed a UFO. Most believed that extraterrestrials were at the heart of the UFO phenomenon, and that the U.S. government was still studying UFOs, despite official denials.[98]

Still, there are many gradations of such a belief. Some researchers argued that the U.S. military never really figured out what the phenomenon was all about, or else was guilty of incompetence – essentially, a "foul up," as Allen Hynek often claimed. Others believed there was a genuine cover-up in which certain officials *believed* there was something significant to UFOs, perhaps even that aliens were responsible, but held back the information for fear of upsetting the public. But something as radical as UFO crash retrievals was typically dismissed out of hand. It is true that quiet rumors had circulated for years. Richard Hall remarked that NICAP had received ten to fifteen leads about crashed UFOs during the 1950s and 1960s, but the organization never followed up.[99] It took Stringfield's research to stretch the boundaries of the belief in a cover-up into the far more radical position that crafts and bodies had been recovered and were being secretly studied. The implications were dramatic. It would mean the existence of a *very* deep, *very* secret cover-up, and the attempted exploitation of the acquired technology.

Stringfield finally dropped the bombshell of his research at the MUFON International Symposium at the end of July. Significantly, the symposium was held that year in Dayton, Ohio, home to Wright-Patterson AFB. Stringfield announced that he had more than fifty sources with "information relative to the subject of retrievals or storage of alien craft, and/or deceased alien humanoids recovered from the craft." He presented seventeen witness testimonies to an astonished audience, which suggested perhaps nine or ten retrievals of crashed or downed UFOs.

He well understood the implications of his research. "We must now take an honest look at the old rumors," Stringfield said. "We must also take a new look," he continued,

> ... at the possibility of a grand official cover-up and why. If any one of the retrieval incidents is true, or if only one of my informants is telling the truth, then humankind is in for a shock.... if it is true that alien humanoids have been retrieved and are held in a preserved state at one or more military installations, then our government ... will have to explain their policy of prolonged secrecy. We may then rightly ask, what else is hidden about the UFO of a more frightening nature?[100]

Some criticized Stringfield as being overly gullible, others were suspicious of his unwillingness to name his informants. To be fair, confirming every lead was not within Stringfield's means; he mainly sought to collect and disseminate the information. He conceded that some of his sources could have been hoaxing him, but he believed most were legitimate. Some of his leads, he pointed out, came to him via initial research performed by other researchers. Eventually, some flaws were found in Stringfield's sources, although none that caused serious damage to the basic structure of his research. "Wherever there's smoke there's fire," he said at the symposium, "and from my position I certainly can see a hell of a lot of smoke." Not surprisingly, Air Force representatives at Wright-Patterson denied knowledge of any of Stringfield's allegations.[101]

Moving Toward a Breakout?

It seemed as though the wall of UFO secrecy could well come down. Popular belief in the phenomenon was on the rise. A Canadian-based Gallup poll in February indicated that 57% of adult Americans believed UFOs were "real," while 46% of Canadians felt the same way. (Interestingly, back in 1966, only 46% of Americans had believed UFOs were "real"). The highest levels of belief came from those with a college education and people under 30. Ten percent of the Canadian respondents, and nine percent of the Americans, believed that they had seen a UFO.[102] Several American public figures were also willing to state their beliefs in public, such as Mercury Astronaut Gordon Cooper. In April, Cooper appeared on the Merv Griffin television show, discussing what he believed to be credible UFO stories from government insiders. Griffin asked him about rumors of "occupant" stories, and whether "our government was able to keep one alive..." Cooper thought that was credible, and added that from what he had learned, they looked "no different" from ordinary humans. He did not say he had been formally briefed on the matter, rather that "there's a good possibility that this thing exists .... it makes you wonder." Not all of Cooper's colleagues were supportive: astronauts Tom Stafford, Michael Collins, and Donald Slayton all denied hearing such stories.[103]

Another step in the direction of open government came on June 28, 1978, with the signing of Executive Order 12065 by President Carter pertaining to the Freedom of Information Act. In part, this was to promote the democratic principle of a public right-to-know, but Carter also felt that over-classification worked against genuine national security. Excessive classification of documents (a process known as "classification escalation") had made government less efficient to the point where routine paperwork was becoming classified. Carter's Executive Order not only sought to eliminate this problem, but also to shorten the wait for declassification review to twenty years. The order contained a provision requiring that the public's need to know be an acknowledged part of the declassification process. Courts reviewing documents for release under FOIA, in other words, had to consider the public's interest. Finally, the burden of proof fell to the government agencies to demonstrate that releasing requested information would be "clearly harmful." These were new developments, and ultimately assisted in the release of many UFO-related documents.

There was one loophole: a restriction which pertained to "protection of legitimate national security secrets." Information that had "defense implications that possibly should be safe-guarded against immediate and full disclosure" would not be released. This had clear implications regarding UFO data, much of which affected national security in some fashion.[104]

The situation still looked very good, however, when on December 15 approximately 900 pages of CIA documents pertaining to UFOs were released under the provisions of FOIA, due to the suit by CAUS and GSW. These were documents which the CIA had previously denied, but which attested to a thirty-year interest in UFOs. Amid the cache, however, Peter Gersten noticed that, based on references in the released documents, the CIA failed to disclose the existence of 200 or more documents. It appeared that there were many thousands of classified pages of documents still within the CIA. The challenge was finding a way to pry them out.[105]

Not only FOIA, but also the United Nations continued to offer a potential avenue for a "breakout." On November 27, 1978, the U.N. Special Political Committee held meetings on UFOs. Following on the initiative by Grenada Prime Minister Eric Gairy, the idea was to create a public, worldwide program to collect and analyze data on UFOs, then to determine the best response. Some of the people who provided statements were Allen Hynek, Jacques Vallee, Stanton Friedman, Lt. Colonel Lawrence Coyne, and astronaut Gordon Cooper. Cooper described his 1951 encounter over Germany with "groups of metallic, saucer-shaped vehicles at great altitudes." His group had tried to get close to the objects, but they "were able to change direction faster than our fighters." Cooper said he believed UFOs exist, "and the truly unexplained ones are from some other technically advanced civilization." He also said that most astronauts were reluctant to discuss UFOs, but stated that several did believe in them, and that some had even seen them.

The meetings concluded on December 8, resulting in U.N. Decision 33/426 relating to the "establishment of an agency or a department of the United Nations for undertaking, coordinating and disseminating the results of research into unidentified flying objects and related phenomena." It asked members to develop scientific research and investigation programs into extraterrestrial life, including UFOs, and to report back to the U.N. This was a challenge to the U.N. as well as the Carter White House, but nothing tangible came from it. Then, rather abruptly, the whole initiative went dead in the water. On March 13, 1979, while Gairy was at the U.N. yet again to talk about UFOs, he was ousted in a coup d'etat by Maurice Bishop. That was the end of the Grenada UFO initiative.[106]

But at the end of 1978, there was even a hint of a congressional attempt to look into the UFO matter. Congressman Samuel S. Stratton (D-NY), Chairman of the Armed Services Investigations Subcommittee, had read about the 1975 UFO intrusions. On December 28, 1978, he expressed concern about "the alleged ability of unknown aircraft to penetrate airspace and hover over SAC bases, their weapons storage areas, missile sites, and launch control facilities, and the inability of Air Force equipment and personnel to intercept and identify such aircraft." The subcommittee requested all reports relating to these and "any similar incidents." A letter was sent to several Air Force groups. The Air Force Legislative Liaison replied on February 9, 1979 informing the Congressman that UFO reports were "of transitory interest to the Air Force and permanent files are not maintained." Stratton's interest in this matter was purely regarding national defense, certainly not to play the UFO card. He was the only member of Congress who ever inquired into the UFO flyovers from 1975, and he never followed up on his inquiry.[107]

The Fort Dix - McGuire AFB Incident

What follows is one of the most intriguing of all UFO/ET cases. Considering the claim, it is not surprising that it remains disputed after many decades. What is more surprising is how strong the case continues to look. The claim is that an alien being was shot and killed by U.S. military forces.

The main witness, Jeffrey Morse (pseudonym), was a security policeman at McGuire AFB in New Jersey on January 18, 1978. At 3 a.m., he was notified about UFO activity over the Fort Dix army base, which adjoined McGuire AFB. He learned that a non-human entity had been shot. A Fort Dix military policeman had been pursuing a low flying UFO which had hovered over his car. A small being with a large head and slender body then appeared in front of his car, causing the MP to panic and shoot the alien several times with a .45 automatic pistol.

The being was able to get as far as a deserted runway at McGuire, where it died. Morse and a companion found the body, then cordoned off the area in accordance with standard procedure. "Blue Beret" forces arrived to take over. Later that day, a team from Wright-Patterson AFB arrived in a C-141 cargo aircraft and took the body. Two days later, Morse was summoned to Wright-Patterson AFB and interrogated about the event. He was warned to keep quiet and shortly thereafter was transferred to Okinawa, Japan. Other colleagues of Morse who witnessed the event in some fashion were also transferred.

Morse contacted Leonard Stringfield in 1980, who interviewed him in person and by phone, as did Richard Hall. Both found him credible – in Hall's words, "completely credible." As the two men put it, "skepticism about crash/retrieval reports may be fully justified and entirely understandable on the part of UFO 'believers' and 'disbelievers' alike – unless they have met Jeff Morse ...." Morse said he was harassed and threatened by officials for having discussed the matter. In 1987 he met again with Hall and Stringfield, as well as members of the Fund for UFO Research (FUFOR), an organization established to provide funding for UFO research and investigations. Other FUFOR members attending were Bruce Maccabee, William H. Hall (brother of Richard), and Dr. John B. Carlson. All were impressed by Morse's straightforwardness and lack of embellishment.[108]

USAF Major George Filer, who worked at McGuire AFB at the time, corroborated Morse's claims. Filer was Deputy Director of Intelligence for the 21st Air Force, which included about 300 aircraft that were used for military troop carrying missions, a portion of which flew the President and other dignitaries.

On the day of the incident, Filer arrived at the base at 4:00 a.m. As he drove through the main gate at McGuire, he noticed red lights on the runway and assumed something was going on, but gave the matter little attention until he arrived at the 21st Air Force Command Post. The Head of the Command Post told him it had been a very exciting evening, with UFOs flying over McGuire "all night." One had apparently landed or crashed at Fort Dix. A military policeman came upon an alien and shot it, the officer said. When Filer heard the word "alien," he replied, "a foreigner? That kind of alien?" "No," came the reply, "an alien from outer space."

According to the officer, the creature had run away after being wounded, climbed (or went under) the fence between the two bases, and headed for McGuire, where it died on the runway. Security police secured the body and were guarding it, and a C-141 from Wright-Patterson AFB was en route to acquire the body. Filer recalled being surprised that Wright-Patterson had C-141s, and even more surprised to learn that he was to give a standup briefing on the incident to the Base Commander later that morning. "You want me to tell General Tom Sadler and everybody in the command post that we captured an alien?" he asked incredulously. Yes, came the answer.

Filer contacted the 38th Military Airlift Wing Command Post to see whether they received the same story. Yes, they had: an alien was found on the base, they told Filer. He spoke to different colonels in the command post and intelligence service who told him they had heard the same story. Like him, they had not seen the alien, but believed the story to be true. He also received a call that morning from "this sergeant who allegedly was there." In fact, this was Jeffrey Morse. The sergeant said he was "pretty sure" it was an alien – "a small person, not of this Earth." The head was disproportionately large compared to a human head. Morse sounded very frightened to Filer.

Filer readied himself to brief the General, but later that morning learned it was not to be. No one ever said anything to him other than, "Don't brief the General." Later that morning, however, while he was at the General's office, he noticed extra activity taking place, including security police personnel who were looking very disheveled. This was highly unusual, as the General was a stickler for proper military attire. Filer assumed the commotion had something to do with the incident from that morning.[109]

During the 1980s, an incident report appeared which briefly described the event. It is unclear how it surfaced, but it was dated January 18, 1978 and mentioned "reports of UFO sightings over the base and an incident in progress on the Fort Dix installation." Furthermore, the document stated that "one body of unknown origin released to the care of OSI District Commander and Special Recovery team from Wright-Pat AFB."

The National Institute for Discovery Science (NIDS) examined the story, searching for corroborating witnesses and documentation. The organization confirmed that Morse had worked as an E-4 (sergeant) at McGuire AFB, but could not find him. They interviewed General Sadler, the security police commander on duty that night, the AFOSI detachment commander, the 21st Air-Force commander, and the individual said to have interrogated Morse. All denied any knowledge of the incident. NIDS also consulted a retired senior member of the 438th security police squadron regarding the Incident Report. He said there were seven distinct discrepancies, which led him to believe the form "was probably a forgery."

NIDS's "working hypothesis" was therefore that the event did not happen, and may in fact have been a hoax. The organization conceded that

From an alleged Incident Report describing the shooting of
an "unidentified being" at Fort Dix, NJ, 1978.

being unable to locate Morse was a "major deficiency" in the investigation, and it avoided a final conclusion on the case, pending further revelations. NIDS disbanded a few years later. What is astonishing is that the organization did not bother to interview Filer, whose statements on the event were well known.

NIDS's conclusion, provisional though it may have been, was premature and naive, based on the fact that military personnel who had taken secrecy oaths (according to Morse and Filer) would not admit to the shooting of an alien being. Questions about the legitimacy of the document are valid, but the opinion of one (U.S. military) expert cannot possibly be expected to be the final word. Despite some fine work on other investigations, NIDS bungled this one.[110]

Spring Sightings

Many UFO sightings were occurring in the north central U.S. During February and March 1978, unknown objects were seen in Detroit. Several sightings occurred very low, inside airport fence lines, mostly at night. One witness, Dr. Harry Willnus, believed these UFOs were using the airport as a "hiding place," camouflaged by the many lights typically seen at busy airports at night.[111] In Minnesota, in addition to visual sightings of disc-shaped objects,[112] an interesting radar case took place on February 19. At 1:20 p.m. (the exact location was not provided), radar operators on two separate systems tracked a large UFO. When one operator obtained "a good solid signal," he put the radar on manual in order to focus on the target. As he did so, "the thing started going up rapidly." He followed it with his radar, and the object stopped, then descended. In his words, the object "appeared to be taking evasive action." He stated the object traveled 5,000 feet (about a mile) in less than one second, and moved in a vertical direction "instantaneously."[113]

Another case took place that spring which, like the Fort Dix-McGuire AFB incident, hinted at serious conflict between UFOs and U.S. military forces. What is known is that on March 27, 1978, within a nine hour period (1) an F-14 Tomcat fighter plane went out of control and crashed into the Pacific Ocean 50 miles west of San Diego; and (2) a nearby S-3A anti-submarine aircraft exploded and crashed into the sea. The next day, a college instructor and shipping company owner were talking on the phone when their line was interrupted by another conversation. Both heard what appeared to be a briefing given to a General, although they could only hear the one party, who said:

> ... same footprints as before ... one spotting, Palm Springs, eight in three months ... they dug 8 feet down, everything in the area was dead ... they had it on radar for less than 2 seconds to touchdown ... they don't know who they are or where they're from ... they told the news media that it was a meteor ... Miramar lost three planes. Everything in the planes went haywire in the same part of the stratosphere ... General Kelley is on his way out tomorrow.

The UFO Report Center of Orange County followed up, found both men credible, and obtained nothing from any government agency about this event. CAUS located one of the downed pilots, who said the accident was being attributed to "a malfunction unique to the Skyhawk."[114]

There are two General Kelleys to which the conversation might have referred. Lt. General Robert E. Kelley at the time was vice commander, U.S. Air Force Tactical Air Warfare Center, Eglin Air Force Base, in Florida. Shortly after this incident, he became commander of Tactical Training at Davis-Monthan Air Force Base, then took command of the U.S. Air Force Tactical Fighter Weapons Center at Nellis Air Force Base. Another possibility is Lt. General John R. Kelly, Jr. Near retirement in 1978, he was assigned to the Pentagon as assistant deputy chief of staff, systems and logistics. One an expert in fighter tactics, the other assigned to the Pentagon, both had a plausible reason for overseeing the aftermath of the event.

Thus, in early 1978, there appeared to be a distinct possibility that the U.S. military and UFO operators were not getting along especially well.

The Bell Island Explosion

The bizarre explosion at Bell Island, Newfoundland, on Sunday morning, April 2 must be added to the list of mysterious events for 1978, although not necessarily UFO-related. The explosion damaged several houses and electrical wires, scorched trees, and even caused television sets to explode. It was heard 60 miles away. Witnesses said they saw balls of fire in the sky descending over the island, along with "streaks of super bright silvery-white light." Two cup-shaped holes about two feet deep and three feet wide marked the major impact. Initial suggestions by the U.S. military and others included ball lightning, sonic boom, meteorite, or even "the volatility of the air itself," but a U.S. Defense Memo gave these little credence. Nor were "atomic explosions" or "flying saucers" the answer, the memo stated, although "high performance aircraft" were indicated as a possibility. Six weeks earlier, there had also been an unexplained boom over Nova Scotia. Attempts to correlate the events with the Concorde supersonic aircraft were "not conclusive," according to the DIA memo.

The Bell Island flash was so intense that it was captured by an American Vela satellite, which registered it as a "potential nuclear blast," and two representatives from a weapons laboratory at Los Alamos arrived to investigate. Despite this, Canadian authorities suggested that lightning had struck a transformer and that the energy followed the wires to neighboring houses. In later years, researchers suggested secret electromagnetic pulse weapons, either Soviet or American, as the answer to the mystery. These would involve high energy beams focused into the ionosphere, perhaps along the lines of the High Altitude Auroral Research Program (HAARP), although HAARP did not officially begin until the 1990s. There has never been a satisfactory explanation for the Bell Island explosion.[115]

U.S. Military UFO Sightings in 1978

A more obviously UFO-related incident occurred on May 14, 1978. At 10 p.m., a resident near Ocala, Florida, telephoned the Pinecastle Electronic Warfare Range Tracking Station in Jackson, asking whether they were shooting flares. The duty officer, Robert Clark, said they were not, nor were there any Navy aircraft out. Soon after, Clark took another call about a UFO. This one was being seen by multiple witnesses, described as an elongated flying object about fifty feet in diameter, "almost the color of the Moon" and with an intensely bright flashing light at its center.

It was now 11 p.m. "So we got out the binoculars and went up on the tower," Clark said. To the north about three miles away they saw a stationary cluster of glowing lights at roughly 1,500 feet altitude. They appeared to be attached to a single object. It took twenty minutes to warm up the track radar. At 11:20 p.m., radar locked on to the target. Then, after fifteen minutes, it abruptly vanished from both sight and radar. "We locked in on it," said Clark, "and then all of a sudden it was gone." Navy radar technician, Timothy Collins, said, "I've never seen anything like it. And I don't want to see anything like it again." Five minutes after the object disappeared, at 11:40 p.m., the same or a similar object appeared 15 degrees to the north. After a short while it disappeared suddenly. Then, near midnight, another object appeared, demonstrating incredible acceleration, deceleration, and hairpin turns. These events were seen visually, but this time radar could not track the objects. "The computer wouldn't handle it," said Lt. Commander John Sullivan, Commander of the Range.

All in all, about a dozen Navy personnel had seen some or all of this activity, much of which was described in the *International Herald Tribune*. According to Stonor, the Navy investigated, but came to no conclusions, at least nothing public. Allen Hendry of CUFOS also investigated, calling it a case of "high merit." CSICOP members Philip Klass and Robert Sheaffer each wrote pieces debunking the sighting. Klass argued that the radar tracking was "ambiguous"; Sheaffer argued that the planets Venus and Jupiter, and then later the star Capella, caused the mistaken visuals. Hendry replied that the radar tracking was "an unambiguous ... confirmation" of the visual sighting, and that Venus and Jupiter were in the wrong position in the sky.[116]

A month later, on June 11, another Navy UFO incident occurred, this time in New Shrewsbury, New Jersey at the U.S. Naval Ammunition Depot, Naval Weapons Station Earle. At 11:28 p.m., Gunnery Sergeant Brininger and Private First Class Johnson were on duty outside an 80 foot tall tower, when they saw a "distinctly-outlined illuminated white ball with a short conical tail behind it." They saw it initially near the horizon to the south, but within five seconds it moved west of their position, and elevated its position to 30 degrees above the horizon. Brininger later said he thought the object was only 300 feet away and about 200 feet off the ground. He turned on a Navy spotlight nearby and swung it toward the object. When he did so, the object "abruptly changed course" from its rapid horizontal flight, and instead turned away from them and flew due west, climbing away. At this point, its center seemed darker with only its rim brighter. One researcher raised the possibility of meteor, but conceded this seemed unlikely. The event is unexplained. Certainly on the face of it, it appears that a sophisticated device took evasive action after conducting some sort of surveillance or covert activity near a U.S. military installation.[117]

Yet another military case, perhaps the most extraordinary of the summer, occurred on July 23 above Lake Michigan. Between 3:53 a.m. and 7:30 a.m., personnel from four U.S. Coast Guard Stations, as well as civilians, saw and tracked a cigar-shaped object with colored lights and traveling at astonishing speeds.

At 3:53 a.m., the Two Rivers Coast Guard Station (CGS) in Wisconsin, received a call from the CGS Ludington in Michigan, requesting that they search for a UFO traveling in their direction. Ludington observers said it had red, white, orange, and green flashing lights, and was moving very fast. Within minutes, personnel at Two Rivers did see it, just as described. The object headed west toward Two Rivers until it disappeared. One minute later, at 4 a.m., personnel at CGS Sturgeon Bay in Wisconsin saw a UFO at an undetermined distance to the south. At 4:01 a.m., they saw a UFO rapidly heading west, described as having red lights and an erratically flashing strobe-type light. At 4:04 a.m., personnel at CGS Two Rivers saw an object of that description approaching. It soon passed by them. At 4:25 a.m., a light house in Green Bay reported the same object, and at 4:45 a.m., CGS Two Rivers reported a white light in the southern sky moving toward the station and blinking irregularly, which then changed direction toward the northeast, and vanished going straight up. Other civilian sightings in the area were consistent with what the Coast Guard personnel were seeing. Indeed, at 4:55 a.m., a civilian reported to CGS Ludington that a UFO had been hovering over U.S. Route 31, and then moved rapidly to the west.

The object had flashing white lights and an occasional red flash. Ludington personnel looked over the lake and saw the object, and personnel at CGS St. Joseph in Michigan took photographs of it.

According to the NORAD Command Directors Log for the month of July 1978, the object under observation at one point traveled 200 miles in three minutes, or 4,000 mph, easily faster than the top speed of what was supposed to be the world's fastest aircraft, the SR-71 Blackbird. Moreover, this speed was attained at the relatively low altitude of 6,000 feet, which should have made an ear-splitting sound, although nothing of the sort was reported. UFO researcher Robert Todd requested the photographs through FOIA in 1980, but was told by the U.S. Coast Guard that the negatives had been lost in the mail in 1978. Barry Greenwood then inquired with the Coast Guard. He was initially advised that "ten 35 mm photographs" were lost in the mail, then informed that the images were sold to the *National Enquirer* by the coast guard personnel who took them. He was also told that the "lost in the mail" explanation had been mistaken, and referred to an unrelated incident. In any case, the *Enquirer* never published the photos it supposedly had.[118]

What is remarkable about this case is the consistency with which all witnesses described this object, as well as its extraordinary capabilities. The speed alone begs an explanation, but when combined with other features, such as its exceptional maneuverability and lack of reported sound, we are once again left to ponder: was this a covert U.S. technology program, or something else?

Another U.S. military UFO encounter, lacking many details, was reported in the *MUFON UFO Journal*, and was said to have taken place on November 15, 1978 in eastern Washington State. It describes an interceptor pursuing "a green object." Four aircraft were in the air when an unknown object was detected at 13,000 feet, some 40 miles away. One of the jets at a higher altitude was ordered to approach the object. The pilot had visual contact with it as well as a radar signal, although he could not lock on. The object seemed to be stationary, and the interceptor came to within eight miles of it, then was forced to turn away due to low fuel. It seems like an odd encounter, but no other details are available.[119]

These accounts do not exhaust the alleged U.S. military encounters with UFOs for 1978. They are scattered among numerous sources, not all confirmed, nor even much investigated, often turning up years after the fact when someone finally decides to talk. Such is the nature of UFO reports, in particular those with military connections. What seems clear, based even on these few accounts, is that an unknown agency with access to extraordinary technology was having its way very easily within U.S. airspace. Against this agency, the U.S. military appears to have been helpless.

UFOs in the World, 1978

UFO statistics are perennially unreliable, based on whim and circumstance of the witnesses, the strengths and (usually) limitations of local UFO reporting systems, the incomplete nature of most investigations, and the willingness of government agencies to release any of their own data. As such, claims of UFO "waves" and "flaps" should be accepted with caution. Still, having taken all this into account, it appears that 1978 was an important year of UFO activity worldwide. In particular, parts of Europe, the Middle East, and Far East reported unusual and dramatic events during the second half of the year. Some of the Middle Eastern sightings appeared directly related to oil fields. Attempted jet interceptions occurred, and several UFOs crashed in different parts of the world. In nearly all cases, news coverage, when it existed at all, was local, so that the impact of the wave of sightings went unnoticed by the mass media.

Some people suggested that the increased UFO sightings were due largely to heightened awareness of the subject following the release of *Close Encounters of the Third Kind*. The movie was certainly a great success and made its mark on popular culture. Moreover, one of the factors of UFO reporting must be public awareness of the phenomena. It can be argued that pop culture generated visions of flying saucers and aliens among the public, who then interpreted interesting but mundane phenomena into something more exotic. The other side of that argument is that people are less likely to see things they are not looking for, and more likely once they become aware of them. When it came to seeing strange lights in the night sky, it seems plausible that *Close Encounters* could have turned these into alien spaceships in the minds of some witnesses. But in 1978 as in all years, the most interesting reports are the most detailed. Laying the bulk of these at the doorstep of Steven Spielberg is merely to take the lazy, and probably wrong, path.[120]

1978 also stands out as a year of unprecedented sightings of "humanoids" around the world. One researcher compiled over 300 cases in which witnesses claimed to have close encounters with alien beings.[121] The vast majority of these were consciously recalled experiences (i.e., not via hypnosis), and many were multiple witness scenarios. There were a great variety of reports from throughout the United States, Europe (with Italy leading the way), South America, Australia, and New Zealand. Reports also leaked out from behind the Iron Curtain, especially the Soviet Union and Poland. This was true "high strangeness." Their appearances fell within several distinct categories. Some were described as completely human looking and often "beautiful." Others were described as the typical "greys," i.e. short, large head, liquid black eyes, slit-like mouth, and so on. Not surprisingly, other variations occurred. Several cases of "clones" were reported, in which multiple beings looked identical to each other. Some were described as robot-like, other reports included alleged telepathic communication.

Three major geographic areas did not generate many "humanoid" reports: Africa, China, and the Middle East. But even China and the Middle East had some spectacular "conventional" UFO reports during the year. It was a busy year for UFOs.

Crashes and Dogfights in South America

Much strangeness came from South America, including several cases of alien-looking creatures, some suggesting abductions.[122] But the two most important cases of the year were of the more traditional sort: the crash of a UFO in Bolivia in May, and the December UFO encounters by the Chilean Air Force.

The Bolivian crash took place on May 6. At about 4:15 p.m., something slammed into a mountain near El Taire on the Bermejo River, very close to the border with Argentina. It caused a supersonic bang that was heard up to 150 miles away and cracked windows within a radius of thirty miles. Argentinian border police searched for wreckage that might have fallen in their territory. This was a difficult, mountainous region, so reporters went to the town of Aguas Blancas to await further developments and interview witnesses. The object was typically described as oval or cylindrical in shape and metallic-looking. Most witnesses, including those in the military, believed it was a UFO. Corporal Natalio Farfan Ruiz, who led an Argentinian border police unit, said the object "made the earth tremble" as it passed over. "Just imagine what would have happened," he said, "if the UFO had fallen on the houses!"

The Bolivian Air Force dispatched three airplanes and discovered the crash site on its side of the border, the southern slope of the El Taire Mountain. On May 14, it was reported that the object had been found. The police chief of the Bolivian city of Tarija said "our men have discovered the object and inspected it, but have received no instructions for further action. It is a dull metallic cylinder twelve feet long with a few dents. No one knows what is inside it, and we are awaiting the arrival of various technical commissions. A NASA expert is also expected to arrive tomorrow morning." No one from NASA arrived, but two USAF officers, Colonel Robert Simmons and Major John Heise, did. According to one newspaper account, they were officially on leave, but were instructed to take the object to the U.S. in a Hercules C-130 aircraft, waiting for them at La Paz.

```
@ 1519392 MAY 79
FM SECSTATE WASHDC
TO AMEMBASSY LA PAZ IMMEDIATE
S E C R E T STATE 126725
P.O. 11552: GDS
CAGS:   TSPA. BL
SUBJECT: REPORT OF FALLEN SPACE OBJECT
QFF; LA PAZ 3824
. PRELIMINARY INFORMATION PROVIDED IN REFERENCED CABLE
AND FBIS CABLES PANAMA 1423572 AND PARAGUAY 1619317 HAS
BEEN CHECKED WITH APPROPRIATE GOVERNMENT AGENCIES. NO
DIRECT CORRELATION WITH KNOWN SPACE OBJECTS THAT MAY HAVE
REENTERED THE EARTH'S ATMOSPHERE NEAR MAY 6 DAY BE MADE.
HOWEVER WE ARE CONTINUING TO EXAMINE ANY POSSIBILITIES.
```

U.S. State Department memorandum regarding a crashed UFO in Bolivia, 1978.

When journalists tried to confirm this information with the American Embassy in Bolivia, they received a denial. In fact, according to U.S. State Department records, Simmons and Heise were assigned to the military attaché of the U.S. Embassy in La Paz, and did fly to Tarija with an officer of the Bolivian Air Force. This was in connection with Project Moon Dust, an American program set up in 1961 to engage in rapid recovery of space vehicles of all types, including unidentified flying objects. A telex sent by the U.S. Ambassador in Bolivia, Paul H. Boeker, to the State Department, asked the agency to inquire with "relevant agencies whether they could explain what this object could be." He mentioned that "more and more UFO reports" were being generated. In a secret telex on May 18, U.S. Secretary of State Cyrus Vance replied that "appropriate government agencies" had been consulted, but that "no direct correlation with known space objects that may have reentered the earth's atmosphere near May 6 can be made." He referred Boeker to the classified State aerogram A-6343 of July 26, 1973, "which provides background information and guidance for dealing with space objects. In particular any information pertaining to the pre-impact observations, direction of trajectory, number of objects observed, time of impact and detailed description, including any markings would be helpful."

Another document obtained through later FOIA requests was a classified "Moon Dust Message" from the U.S. military attaché at La Paz. Project Moon Dust had existed since the early 1960s as a special operation designed to retrieve space debris, including UFOs. This document was dated May 24 and addressed to the Foreign Technologies Division at the Wright-Patterson AFB and USAF Headquarters. The attaché said his office "had taken pains to verify the press reports" and had met with the Bolivian Air Force and Army. The Army declared its troops had "found nothing," and that there may or may not have been an object. The attaché added that he would send two officials to Tarija, presumably Simmons and Heise.

Nothing more is known of what Simmons and Heise learned in their investigation, but the activation of Moon Dust indicates that U.S. officials did not believe the object was a meteorite; nor did anyone else seem to think so. The comprehensive data bank by the Smithsonian Institution, which has carefully tracked every volcanic eruption, earthquake, and meteorite collision since 1973, contains no reference to a meteorite at the Bolivian-Argentinian border at this time. If the object was not a meteorite, and not (in the words of Cyrus Vance) a "known space object," what else could have caused a supersonic explosion and flurry of classified memos?[123]

Once again, we are left to ponder the likelihood of an "unknown" space object. If so, it seems improbable that it was either Soviet or American, as this was clearly an object of significant mass, and not some mere piece of forgotten space junk.

A few years after this event, researchers Barry Greenwood and Lawrence Fawcett recounted "reliable information" they had obtained from a source. This person told them that one of the participants of the search team, a young Bolivian astronomer, had made several passes over the site with a Bolivian Air Force pilot, and saw a rockslide that he believed was caused by the impact of the object. Following this, a second expedition consisting of three BAF officers and a guide set out on horseback on May 23, reaching the rockslide on foot two days later. The officers told the informant that the rockslide looked recent, that parallel to it was a 100-meter long trench, three to four meters wide at the top. Some of the large rocks at the site appeared to have been burned, and the grass around the sides and top of the slide area was brown and withered, while grass further away was green.[124]

Shades of Roswell.

The aerial encounters in Chile at the end of the year remain South America's other fascinating UFO event of 1978. Antonio Huneeus investigated many of Chile's UFO encounters during 1978 and 1979, several of which were confirmed by the Chilean military.[125] The most significant of these occurred on December 16, 1978, although for years, the event was described in partial or vague terms, without doing justice to the totality of the experience. It appears, however, that the Chilean Air Force had two distinct encounters with an immense UFO in northern Chile, an event that remains as mystifying today as it was at the time.

At noon, two Chilean F-5 aircraft, piloted by captains Hernan Gabrieti Rojas and Danilo Catalan, were on a training mission near the town of Mejillones. According to a later interview with Rojas, both pilots saw an object which gave a radar return equal to 10 or more aircraft carriers, except that this object was in the air, not floating on the water. Rojas assumed his radar had failed until Catalan told him his radar had similarly "failed." Ground radar at the Cerro Moreno Airport in Antofagasta picked up the object and confirmed its huge size. The pilots continued to fly south at an altitude between 30,000 and 35,000 feet. At a distance of twenty miles, according to Rojas, the object looked "like a plantain banana ... swathed in smoke." The pilots had no missiles or weapons with which to defend themselves. "As you can imagine," Rojas said, "the fright was more or less considerable." The pilots approached the object cautiously with their gun cameras. The UFO had been motionless, but as the F-5s approached, it disappeared at an "unimaginable" speed to the west, heading towards Easter Island. All at once, it vanished from all three radar screens. The incident had lasted five minutes.

At 8 p.m. that day, a second encounter occurred in the Antofagasta-Calama region when radar detected a UFO at 10,000 feet. Three F-5Es were sent to intercept. It was a clear evening sky, and the object was seen visually by two of the pilots. The Commander described it as very bright, somehow "between round and triangular" in shape, and about 50 times larger than an F-5E.

The Chilean Air Force acknowledged the events of this day the following spring, but did not (or could not) explain what had happened.[126] After he had retired with the rank of General, Rojas also described them. While he had not been on the second mission, he believed the UFO was different from what he had encountered, mainly because of its triangular shape. He offered an insight into the workings of military secrecy regarding UFOs: "It's not that there's an unwillingness to talk, but since it is an almost intangible piece of information it cannot be handled, it cannot be processed. The base commander is informed and then the page is turned and normal activity resumes."[127]

European Encounters

Europe, too, had its mixture of 'conventional' and bizarre UFO reports, including claims of encounters with humanoid creatures. The most interesting cases were in Britain and Italy. The year was also noteworthy in that two European government sources released confirmed UFO data. In March, the Italian Ministry of Defense published six unclassified reports of military encounters with UFOs from the previous year.[128] More important was the report issued in June by GEPAN, the French government's UFO study group. This was a 500-page study distributed on a limited basis to French government officials, analyzing reports from the Gendarmerie from 1974 through 1978. The report focused primarily on 11 cases with "high strangeness" but also high credibility in terms of the caliber of witnesses, physical evidence, and other circumstances. Each case had been investigated by a four-person team which included a psychologist. In ten of those cases, the report concluded that the witness had seen a material phenomenon which could not be explained as natural phenomenon or human technology. The report's main conclusion:

> ... there generally can be said to be a material phenomenon behind the observations. In 60% of the cases reported here, the description of this phenomenon is apparently one of a flying machine whose origin, modes of lifting and/or propulsion are totally outside our knowledge.

GEPAN recommended that a "deep study" be undertaken with a "high degree of priority."[129]

By contrast, the British Ministry of Defence continued to remain close mouthed about UFOs, despite the fact that it received 750 reports and spent 11 million pounds during the year to investigate them.[130] Many of the MoD reports, released in later years, described close encounters. One was a January sighting by three British police officers of a silent, slow, and glowing UFO that appeared to land in the woods near Skipton, Yorkshire. It looked like a classic "Adamski" UFO from the 1950s, with spheres beneath spaced equidistantly around a hollow center.[131] Another landing case was reported later that month from near Frodsham in Cheshire. Four men on the banks of the River Weaver saw a silver balloon-shaped object land in a nearby meadow. According to their story, entities emerged and paralyzed a cow, placing it in a cage. The men noticed a blue-green glow around the area, panicked and ran. One of the men developed sunburn-like marks on his leg.[132] Strange stories like these were reported all year in

Britain.

Meanwhile, European pilots and airports were encountering UFOs. On March 9, 1978, several pilots between Milan and Venice reported a UFO. One of them told Milan air traffic control that it looked "something like a green rocket ... very luminous and a mile off.... I have the impression that they just made a pass over us and then made a counter thrust. I didn't say anything before because I didn't want anyone to think I was crazy." Milan replied, "No, no, the news is corroborated now. Other planes . . . are reporting a green flash, some beneath them, others report it 15 miles away from them." "Ours was very close," replied the pilot. "A little too close."[133]

Another Italian case occurred on July 4, a close encounter near Mount Etna by two Italian Air Force Sergeants, an Italian Navy officer, and another military man. All were off duty at 10:30 p.m., when they observed a triangular pattern of bright red lights in the sky. One of the lights then detached from the group and disappeared down a slope just 1,000 feet from the witnesses. They drove over to investigate, and saw a light behind a dip near the side of road. Looking over the edge, they saw a saucer-shaped object resting on a rocky precipice, estimated to be about 40 feet in diameter, with a brightly lit yellow dome. But there was more than a craft. The witnesses saw five or six very tall (human) beings with blond hair wearing black, tight-fitting suits. Two of the beings then began to climb toward the witnesses, who were immobilized. The beings came to within 15 feet of the witnesses and smiled at them. One of them then nodded toward their craft, and they both returned. The craft glowed with multicolored tiny points of light, darkened when a car drove by, then brightened again. Before long, the witnesses regained mobility and left before the craft departed.[134]

A UFO was reported to be over Gatwick Airport on August 16, an event discussed in the *Daily Mirror* and investigated by Timothy Good. Little is known about the details, except that an airport spokesman said that "the controllers definitely saw something, but they have clammed up over exactly what it was."[135] Another sighting may have occurred over Heathrow Airport in September. Although a spokesperson for the Civil Aviation Authority denied tracking a UFO on radar, he added, "It's in the interest of national security that not too much fuss is made about this sort of thing."[136]

Other cases occurred in which UFOs were seen to land, alien creatures were spotted, or in which physical effects were reported on automobiles. On September 17, near the town of Torrita di Siena in north central Italy, a woman and her son were driving when both saw a red ball descend and illuminate the area. Area houselights went out. Soon after, another motorist experienced electrical failure while a bright object descended ahead of him. According to the witness, it was a reddish domed disc, about ten feet wide, with three light beams extending to the road. A panel opened and two humanoid creatures about 4 feet tall "floated" out. They wore green coverall-type garments and had helmets with antennae. Still floating, they circled his car, then re-entered their craft, which took off "in a flash of light and explosive sound." Three scorched circles about 20 inches in diameter were found on the road surface.[137]

Reports like these became a weekly, and at times daily, occurrence in Italy as the year wore on, and to a lesser extent in Germany and France.[138]

Flurry in the Middle East

The Middle East, in particular Iran and Kuwait, also produced baffling UFO reports. In April, while flying near Tehran at 24,000 feet, an Iranian pilot and co-pilot saw an enormous glowing object. The case was described in the Iranian press and included in U.S. Defense Intelligence Agency files. A Mehrabad radar control official said an object 20 times the size of a jumbo jet had been detected several times – remarkably similar to the Chilean case later that year. In the Iranian case, the pilot was able to photograph the object, but "the security division of the civil aviation authorities" prevented him from releasing the photo. A civil aviation organization official called for an investigation, but whether any was made is not known.[139]

A month later, on May 13, an Iranian teenager took a very good photograph of a UFO. Sixteen year old Jamshid Saiadipour was studying late for exams when at 4 a.m. he looked through the window of his Shiraz/Tehran home. Outside was a glowing, hat-shaped UFO, hovering motionless in the night sky. He took a picture of it, which was published on May 18, 1978 by *Tehran Magazine*. The article and photograph were included in U.S. DIA files, and released in 1980 via FOIA. The claim has occasionally been made that the object was of interest to U.S. officials because it resembled the classified aircraft known as Tacit Blue. There is a superficial resemblance, except for the fact that Tacit Blue did not hover, did not glow, was tested in Nevada – not Iran – and was in all likelihood not yet flying in 1978. In other words, there is no reason why Tacit Blue should account for the interest in the Shiraz UFO – the object had quite enough interest on its own merits. The real questions are, who manufactured it, and how was it able to fly as it did.[140]

On July 17, another UFO was seen in Iran, also reported in local newspapers and filed with the U.S. DIA. In northern Tehran on a Sunday night, the hot weather prompted many people to sleep on the terraces of their houses. This was how so many of them saw a "strange glowing object" float by. One witness, alone on his balcony, saw the object emerge in the sky and hover directly above him. "I was so upset that I wanted to scream, but could not do so," he said. Phone calls were quickly made to the control tower at Mehrabad Airport as well as the national radio network. The control tower confirmed the existence of the object but gave no further details. A Lufthansa pilot also reported the object.[141]

On October 8, 1978, yet another Iranian teenager took a photograph of a UFO. This was a daytime photo by Franklin Youri, from outside his home near Lake Urmia in western Iran. In the photograph, the object appears behind his house, just above the line of the roof. Although it is obviously distant, its shape is discernable as identical to the May 13 photograph. The case became known three years later due to a FOIA request.[142]

It may never be known why Iran experienced this relative outbreak of UFO sightings in 1978. But it is true that the nation experienced a year-long political crisis. In November, 1978, the Shah declared martial law in response to massive rioting and a wholesale rejection of Western values. Schools and universities closed down, newspapers stopped publishing, and the oil industry was paralyzed.

Within such a context let us consider the final flurry of UFO sightings from the Middle East, which took place in Kuwait. Some details are sketchy, although the U.S. and Kuwaiti governments confirmed the basic facts. On November 9, one of Kuwait's northern oil fields, known as Gathering Centre No. 24, experienced a failure of its oil pumping station and an interruption in its communications system. While specialists tried to determine why, technicians outside saw a domed disc-like object sitting on the ground. A senior Kuwait Oil Company (KOC) official told U.S. officials that when the object vanished, the system started itself up again. This is strange, as the equipment was designed to be restarted by manual means only.

This was the first of a series of UFO sightings in Kuwait. Eight events were reported between November 9 and December 14, many of which occurred over oil fields. These sightings received the attention of the American Embassy in Kuwait City, as well as the Kuwait Institute for

Scientific Research (KISR), which produced a classified report on January 20, 1979. What is so interesting is that the Institute rejected the idea that these were "espionage devices," but remained open to the idea that they were extraterrestrial. In fact, the committee stated explicitly that it could *not* reject the idea that the objects were spaceships. KISR also said that Kuwait's air defense system "did not react in any way to the 'events' in the KOC north." Parts of the study were reported in the media, although researchers were not allowed to read the full report.

In January 1979, the American Embassy in Kuwait City wrote to the State Department about the sightings. The memo discussed the failure of the pumping station in connection to the UFO sighting of November 9, and stated further that the KISR study had not addressed this problem. The embassy stated that "even those who are not inclined to believe in visitors from outer space do tend to think something strange has been going on in Kuwaiti airspace." The embassy repeated some speculation that helicopters or hovercraft were bringing refugees or money out of Iran, but offered no explanation that was actually plausible.[143]

Soviet UFO Programs

As a result of the Petrozavodsk sighting from September 1977, the Soviet Academy of Sciences created a research program for "anomalous atmospheric phenomena," named Setka-AN. At the same time, the Soviet Ministry of Defense embarked on a similar program, dubbed Setka-MO. It is unclear how much these two programs interacted with each other. According to former Soviet ufologist Vladimir Rubtsov, they worked from different sets of data: one from the military branches, the other from scientific institutes and periodicals. The Academy of Sciences program was said to be interested in the physical nature of UFOs while the military program more pragmatically wanted to determine "their influence of the operation of military technical equipment and personnel" – vague wording pointing toward interest in national security issues.[144] More interesting still was the admission from skeptical authors Yuri Platov and Boris Sokolov – both members of the Setka programs – that the Soviet Ministry of Defense was interested in radar invisibility and "high maneuverability" of UFOs.[145] This begs the question of just what Soviet authorities assumed was causing the genuine UFO reports. If they believed they could learn something of technological value, did they really think that these UFOs originated from secret American technology that had simultaneously mastered stealth and achieved the performance of flying saucers?

The Setka programs lasted for at least 13 years and, according to accounts of former participants, it appears that the military component generated some 3,000 official reports of UFO sightings. Rubtsov said the number of unknowns was "some 300," while Platov and Sokolov wrote that "more than 400 events were registered and identified as extraordinary or paranormal" (although the latter two also stated that rocket launches and balloons alone accounted for "more than 90%" of the reports – a glaring inconsistency). Either way, the percentage of unknowns was in line with numbers derived from official programs of other nations, including Blue Book, GEPAN, or the Condon Committee. The Soviet unknowns were especially important, wrote Rubtsov, as the reports "were reliable, informative, and detailed ... filtered on the site by experienced officers." This statement is amplified by the fact that reporting UFOs was a no-win scenario: the Soviet bureaucracy demanded reports from soldiers but continued officially not to recognize UFOs. To put the matter mildly, filing a report was not seen as a good career move. Rubtsov even talked of fears by Soviet military personnel of "being sent to a hospital for a long and unpleasant examination" if they made such a report.[146]

Paul Stonehill, another authority on Soviet and Russian UFOs, suggested that Setka-AN served as a cover to distract from the workings of the more serious Setka-MO.[147] Not everyone agrees with this, but the conclusion of the Setka programs as stated by Platov and Sokolov – that all Soviet UFOs were amenable to conventional explanations – is inconsistent with the official data. In any UFO research program, what matters is not so much what caused the 90 percent of "knowns" as the five, ten or fifteen percent of unknowns. One critic of Platov and Sokolov put it well: "it is beyond reason to consider the Soviet military as complete idiots who for 13 years were persistently pursuing gas-dust trails of their own rockets." Moreover, there is no evidence to indicate that anyone in the Soviet Setka programs attempted to analyze the unknowns themselves. If this was so, then calling their endeavors "scientific" would therefore stretch the definition of the word beyond meaning.[148]

Russian UFO researcher Vladimir Azhazha, a physicist and Professor of Mathematics at Moscow University and a leading Soviet ufologist, said that the Setka-MO program generated "too many incidents that could not be denied." His statements lend support to the claim there was indeed a secret element to Setka-MO. Soviet submarines, he said, were encountering underwater objects that would follow them. These objects were initially thought to be American devices, but one incident laid that theory to rest.

A Soviet icebreaker was at work in the Arctic Ocean when, according to Azhazha, "a brilliant spherical craft suddenly broke through the ice and flew up vertically, showering the vessel with fragments of ice." Looking up, the sailors and officers on deck saw the object; looking down they saw the hole in the ice. "You don't shoot a missile that way. You have to break the ice first. Furthermore, the object was a bright sphere. We knew what nuclear missiles looked like!" As a result of encounters like these, said Azhazha, the Soviets drew up rules of engagement for UFOs: how to observe them and what to do in a confrontation. "They treated us the way we would treat a fish, or a rabbit," said Azhazha. "It is naive to assume they have any goodwill toward us, or any need to interact. They simply seem to go about their business. They coexist with us."[149]

Ultimately, much needs to be learned about the nature of official Soviet ufology. It is also well to keep in mind that Soviet science, while capable of producing thinkers of genius, was also deeply integrated into the apparatus of the State and Party. This was, after all, a system that a mere generation before had sponsored and promoted the fraudulent Trofim Lysenko, whose rejection of Mendelian genetics was official policy in the USSR until 1964. Although bureaucratized science everywhere serves the needs of the State, this tendency was brought to extreme levels in the Soviet Union. Official conclusions must therefore be viewed with caution at best, if not outright skepticism.

Although the Setka programs eventually improved reporting of UFOs, the Soviet cases of 1978 remain sketchy. One humorous incident reportedly occurred in May (no precise date) at Lake Pyrogovskoye in Russia. Anatoly Malishev, a Soviet officer, was confronted by two entities wearing dark suits who communicated with him via telepathy. He was given a salty tasting drink of some sort, and eventually suggested that his new acquaintances perform a toast with a real (e.g. alcoholic) drink. Apparently they did not imbibe, and Malishev asked them why an advanced civilization such as theirs did not drink alcohol. They replied, "Perhaps if we did, we would not be such an advanced civilization." Malishev reported his encounter to the authorities, who were unconvinced and threatened court-martial. He was subjected to hypnosis and passed a lie-detector test, and was not court-martialed. So goes the story, at any rate.[150]

More solid were the sightings by Soviet cosmonauts. On August 15, Vladimir Kovalyonok in the Salut-6 space station saw a strange object approach and distance itself repeatedly. On October 2, he saw a strange shadow hovering above the clouds, changing its appearance inexplicably.

Other cosmonauts saw UFOs not while in space, but down on Earth. Pavel Popovich, a Hero of the Soviet Union who attained the rank of Major-General, saw two. While in an airplane over Cuba, he was approached by a white triangular-shaped object. He alerted other passengers and crew members, who also saw it. The object soon passed by their own aircraft and was gone. During the same year in Soviet air space while flying in a Yak-40 aircraft, Popovich and his crew saw a bright sphere slowly approach, then fly directly at them. At the last moment it veered upward and away.[151]

China and Australia

China also had many sightings of unusual aerial phenomena. From 1978 until 1981, Paul Dong, editor of the *Chinese Journal of UFO Research*, collected hundreds of cases, some of which dated back to the first half of the twentieth century. The reports from 1978 included several interesting encounters, but the most significant was on October 23 at the Lintiao Air Base in China's northwestern Gansu Province. At 10:04 p.m., several hundred military personnel were watching an outdoor movie when a large westerly-moving object passed over their heads. Witnesses agreed that the object was elongated, with two searchlights and a glowing tail; no one recognized it. Chinese Air Force pilot Zhou Qingtong said the object was large and close to the ground. It was visible for two to three minutes, and was "clearly not a meteor, nor a swarm of locusts or birds, nor an airplane. As we are all fighter pilots we could say this with some certainty." According to a report in the CIA files, the object "covered half the sky, causing extreme astonishment." This would appear to be the effect of an enormous object flying at very low altitude, although the CIA report oddly estimated the object's altitude to be 20,000 feet – much higher than what witnesses described.[152] The Chinese government ended its long silence on UFOs on November 13, 1978, with an article in *The People's Daily* entitled "UFO: An Unknown World Puzzle." After this, an avalanche of public interest began.[153]

The rest of Asia and the Pacific reported little UFO activity during the first half of 1978. Matters were different in the second half. On October 21, 1978, two days before the dramatic Chinese sighting, occurred one of the most striking and tragic UFO-related events in history. This was the disappearance of the Delta Sierra Juliet, a Cessna 182 aircraft piloted by Frederick Valentich, a young man flying from Moorabin, Victoria, to King Island, Tasmania. This was a short trip of about 130 miles, but Valentich had to fly over the Bass Strait, the channel between Australia and Tasmania.

The strait has a history of missing aircraft and has sometimes been compared to the Bermuda Triangle.

Valentich took off at 6:19 p.m. The weather was clear with a trace of stratocumulus cloud at 5,000 to 7,000 feet. Winds were light and visibility was excellent. At 7:06 p.m., he saw an unknown object and reported to the Melbourne Flight Service Unit Coordinator. The transcript is vivid, dramatic, and tragic.

Valentich: Melbourne, this is Delta Sierra Juliet. Is there any known traffic below five thousand?

Melbourne: No known traffic.

Valentich: I am seems (to) be a large aircraft below five thousand.

Melbourne: What type of aircraft is it?

Valentich: I cannot affirm, it is four bright, it seems to me like landing lights.... The aircraft has just passed over me at least a thousand feet above.

Melbourne: Roger and it is a large aircraft confirm.

Valentich: Unknown due to the speed it's traveling. Is there any air force aircraft in the vicinity?

Melbourne: No known aircraft in the vicinity.

Valentich: Melbourne, it's approaching now from due east towards me. It seems to me that he's playing some sort of game. He's flying over me two to three times at speeds I could not identify.

Melbourne: Roger. What is your actual level?

Valentich: My level is four and a half thousand, four five zero zero.

Melbourne: Confirm that you cannot identify the aircraft.

Valentich: Affirmative.

Melbourne: Roger. Standby.

Valentich: Melbourne, Delta Sierra Juliet. It's not an aircraft, it is // open microphone for two seconds //

Melbourne: Can you describe the, er, aircraft?

Valentich: As it's flying past, it's a long shape // open microphone for three seconds // (cannot) identify more than (that it has such speed) // open microphone for three seconds // before me right now, Melbourne.

Melbourne: Roger, and how large would the, er, object be?

Valentich: Melbourne, it seems like it's chasing me. What I'm doing now is orbiting and the thing is just orbiting on top of me, also. It's got a green light and sort of metallic (like). It's all shiny (on) the outside // open microphone for five seconds // It's just vanished. Melbourne, would you know what kind of aircraft I've got? Is it (a type) military aircraft?

Melbourne: Confirm the, er, aircraft just vanished.

Valentich: Say again.

Melbourne: Is the aircraft still with you?

Valentich: (unclear) // open microphone for two seconds // (now) approaching from the southwest. The engine is rough idling. I've got it set at twenty three twenty four and the thing is (coughing).

Melbourne: Roger. What are your intentions?

Valentich: My intentions are, ah, to go to King Island. Ah, Melbourne, that strange aircraft is hovering on top of me again. // two seconds open microphone // It is hovering and it's not an aircraft.[154]

The time was 7:12 p.m. After Valentich uttered these final words, Australian traffic control heard a sound "like tin cans rolling around in the bottom of an empty oil drum." These were the words of Richard Haines, who had a recording of the transmission, and described the sound to researcher Linda Moulton Howe.

Valentich was never seen again. A search and rescue operation was undertaken immediately, to no avail.

During his six minute conversation with the Melbourne Flight Service Unit, Valentich mentioned several distinctive features about the object that was harassing him. It was elongated, shiny, metallic-looking, with bright lights and a green light. It had the ability to fly very fast, since it flew past Valentich's airplane several times. It could also hover or pace his aircraft. Twice Valentich stated that the object was "not an aircraft." It appeared that the object was deliberately engaging Valentich's Cessna, and interfered with its ability to fly.

Australian MUFON researchers Keith Basterfield and Bill Chalker investigated the case. Valentich, they learned, "lived for flying." It seemed unlikely that he would have done anything to have damaged his chances to improve his flying status.[155] Some years later, former NASA scientist Richard Haines reported that three witnesses testified seeing Valentich's aircraft descend at a steep angle while a much larger object, illuminated with green lights, flew just above it. Haines argued that Valentich's airplane probably crashed into the sea southeast of Cape Marengo between three and twelve miles offshore. "The nature of the large green-lighted object that accompanied the airplane during its steep descent remains to be identified."[156]

It was also later discovered that just twenty minutes before Valentich disappeared, another witness, Roy Manifold, had taken odd photographs showing a large, black anomaly low over the sea, apparently swirling up the water. Eastman Kodak examined the pictures and ruled out the possibility of film or processing defects. The Australian Royal Air Force said the pictures showed a cumulus cloud. Bill Chalker replied that for the cloud to have moved into view with the time sequence of the photographs stated, it would have been moving at about 200 mph.[157] Timothy Good also pointed out a little known fact: there were at least 15 other high quality Australian UFO sightings on the day Valentich was lost.[158]

More than a thousand miles to the east of Australia is New Zealand, a place about as remote to the rest of the world as one could be, particularly during the pre-Internet era of 1978. And yet, New Zealand ended the year with some extraordinary UFO reports. On October 24, the U.S. military recorded the impact of a space fragment, known locally as a "space ball," that landed on the property of a farmer named John Lovett on New Zealand's South Island. It was analyzed by the National Radiation Laboratory in Christchurch for a radioactive check (negative finding), then by the New Zealand Department of Scientific and Industrial Research (DSIR). What was truly odd, however, is that a second "space ball" landed on the property of a farmer in the same area on November 5 (whose name was also Lovett, apparently a brother to the first). The second fragment landed approximately 240 meters from the first, and in an adjoining field. This object was also turned over to New Zealand authorities.

Four similar balls had been found in the same general region six years before, believed to be from the Soviet Cosmos 482 satellite. It is easy to assume this was from the same flight, simply found after the fact, except that the analysis conducted by New Zealand scientific personnel was that at least one of the balls was too clean to have been lying about even for several months, let alone six years. Yet, it seems simplest to conclude that someone in the lab made a mistake, and that all six balls were from the Soviet satellite.[159]

The most interesting sightings occurred late in December. Near midnight on December 21-22, an Argosy freight aircraft piloted by Captain John Randle left from Blenheim heading south toward Christchurch, a path that would take it out to sea off the eastern shore of South Island. The plane was still over land moving toward the coast when the first UFO appeared. In Randle's words, the object gave off "an intense white light" that illuminated the ground as it passed over. Still, he and his first officer did not bother to report the object. Soon after, senior radar controller John Cordy at nearby Wellington Airport was advised of the sighting of five lights near the Clarence River on South Island. He and a colleague picked up the objects on radar, as did radar controllers at Christchurch Airport. The targets traveled off the coast and moved toward Wellington. At 3 a.m., Cordy picked up a large echo about 30 miles southeast of the city, which appeared to hover there for some time. Then, it abruptly moved at 120 knots to a position 50 miles southeast of the city, where it remained for at least 30 minutes.

At 3:30 a.m., a second Argosy plane took off from Blenheim headed for Christchurch, flying roughly the same course as the first. Cordy radioed to Captain Vern Powell that he was tracking a target 12-13 miles starboard of Powell's position. Powell said that he and his crew saw nothing. Within seconds, however, Cordy's radar showed that the object was on the opposite side. When Cordy asked Powell to look on the other side, Powell replied he and his crew could see a bright white light with a reddish tint. Whether through bravery, foolhardiness, or natural curiosity, they flew toward it, but it kept its distance and sometimes disappeared into the clouds. One might think this was an atmospheric or astronomical phenomenon, but Cordy said the radar target was at least as large and solid as the Argosy plane. The crew pursued the light for about ten minutes, then returned to their flight path, after which Cordy lost the target. However, as the Argosy reached Christchurch, its weather radar detected an object streaking across its path. Powell saw it: a bright flashing white light which shot past at high speed. He said it covered 24 kilometers in five seconds, making a speed of 17,000 kph or about 10,000 mph. It even made a sharp right turn before disappearing.

The event created a local stir. On December 30, an Australian news crew flew over the area in an Argosy freighter. The strangeness started almost immediately. Near the town of Kaikoura, the crew saw a row of five bright, pulsating lights which seemed to change from pinpoint size to that of a large balloon. At the same time, Wellington air traffic control told them that an unknown object was following them. The pilot made a complete turn, but no one saw it. Then, Wellington informed the Argosy that the target had "increased in size." At this point, the crew and passengers saw a light flashing white and green.

The plane landed at Christchurch at about 1:00 a.m. and took off again at about 2:15 a.m. Soon, two bright lights were in sight as the plane flew northeast from Christchurch. Wellington radar tracked neither of these, although airborne radar did track the brightest light (at about 10 miles distance), and this was a large target. Cameraman, David Crockett, observing one of the UFOs through his camera, described it as a spinning sphere with lateral lines around it, although the camera was out of focus and did not accurately represent the light or object itself. The crew members were deeply impressed by what they saw; they did not believe they were seeing ordinary aircraft or natural phenomena.

The film taken by the Australian film crew totaled six minutes and was shown worldwide. It mainly shows a single light, on which the cameraman zooms in and out. Skeptics provided many explanations. One astronomer said the UFOs were almost certainly the planet Venus; another said meteors. An atmospheric physicist said the radar echoes were a natural feature of the ionosphere during the summer, and that the lights could have been caused by refraction in the predawn sky. Still others said the objects were either balloons or unscheduled aircraft.

When Bruce Maccabee saw the film a week later, he said it took him "almost four microseconds" to realize it was not Venus, "or mating mutton birds, or light reflected from a cabbage patch." Maccabee showed the film to skeptic Robert Sheaffer, who agreed that whatever it was, it was not astronomical. Maccabee analyzed the film and interviewed the witnesses. He found it authentic and rejected the debunking hypotheses. "As yet," he stated, "no explanation in terms of known phenomena has been proposed that satisfactorily explains the film." He did determine that the appearance of rings in the film were a result of aberrations in the airplane window glass combined with the out-of-focus condition of the telephoto lens (which had not been mounted properly just before that portion of the sighting).*

The Royal New Zealand Air Force (RZNAF) put its planes on full alert and conducted a joint investigation with the police and the Carter Observatory in Wellington. Their report concluded that the Kaikoura UFOs were caused either by the planet Venus, reflections of light from a squid boat offshore, or by a train or passing car. Regarding the radar targets, these were caused by faulty equipment and novel propagation affects. The report was then stamped Top Secret and archived in the Wellington National Archives.

Many years later, a researcher named Peter Hassall convinced the New Zealand Ministry of Defence to lift the Top Secret rating and allow him to reprint the original reports. That was when he realized how terrible the investigation had been. Venus had not even risen over the horizon when most of the sightings were made. He called the investigation "a lesson in debunking." Perhaps there was a natural explanation for the sightings, he wrote, but we will never know because of the incompetency of the official investigation, which "made a complete shambles of the whole affair."[160]

Summary

Thus ended 1978, a year of important developments in all facets of UFO history. The nature of the sightings themselves, in particular the many military encounters with extraordinary (and at times enormous) craft, force us to dismiss the hypothesis that the wave was caused by Steven Spielberg. What does appear to be the case, however, is that serious conflict was

---

* This is still the only UFO sighting which has been discussed in the refereed scientific literature. See *Applied Optics*, August 1979, December 1979 and June 1980 at http://www.brumac.8k.com/NEW_ZEALAND/NZSB.html.

occurring, very secretly, between the world's military forces and something far more advanced.

If there was one cause for optimism, it was that private researchers were officially in the hunt for the truth. 1977 and 1978 had been great years in the fight against UFO secrecy. Despite government foot-dragging and obstruction, many fascinating documents were coming to light, with realistic hopes that there was yet much more to come. There seemed a chance that FOIA could be the tool that would end UFO secrecy. Aside from the search for government records was the growing number of insider leaks that were coming to researchers concerned with some of the deeper aspects of the secrecy. If just one of these cases could be proven to have merit, it would mean that the UFO cover-up had been deeper and more substantial than anyone had ever considered.

But if this were so, it would mean that certain private researchers threatened to expose a longstanding cold war between various human and non-human groups. One might well expect resistance from those quarters in which secrecy was still considered paramount.

Chapter 4

The Empire Strikes Back
1979-1980

What I do know is that it was nothing mundane. There are no words that can adequately describe the wonder of what we saw.
— *U.S. Airman First Class John Burroughs, describing his experience in the Rendlesham Forest in 1980.*

It sort of danced about in the sky and it sent down beams of light. . . . The people in the weapons storage area and several other places on the base also reported the lights. . . .[The beam was] adversely affecting the ordinance.
— *Statements by USAF Lt. Col. Charles Halt regarding events in the Rendlesham Forest in 1980.*

The events to which you refer were of no defence significance.
— *British Secretary of State for Defence Michael Heseltine regarding the events in the Rendlesham Forest.*

My source [a former CIA employee] can't talk about UFOs. He refused to answer any of my questions on the photos or the live retrievals. . . . He's had his knuckles spanked.
— *Anonymous source, speaking to Leonard Stringfield, 1980*

The 1979 Drop Off

Few years in recent history can match 1979 as a year of political upheaval. The Iranian revolution in January forced out the Shah and brought in the Ayatollah Khomeini, who quickly became 'leader for life.' The Islamic revolution transformed global politics: the U.S. lost a crucial ally, the Soviets looked with alarm at Islamic fundamentalism, and oil prices spiked. Meanwhile, Vietnam had invaded Cambodia in late 1978; China responded by invading Vietnam. By mid-year in 1979, the leftist Sandinistas took control of Nicaragua. In November, the U.S. embassy in Iran was overrun by Iranian students who took 66 Americans as hostages while Khomeini demanded extradition of the ailing Shah. In December, the Soviet Union invaded Afghanistan. President Carter, besieged by a string of foreign policy failures, abandoned SALT II nuclear weapons talks and announced major defense spending hikes.

Considering how widespread and vivid UFO sightings had been during the final months of 1978, the drop-off in 1979 was very abrupt. The tumultuous state of world affairs that began in late 1978 and continued through 1979 leads to the question as to whether there was some sort of a relationship to the UFO phenomenon. Without speaking to the UFO occupants themselves, we can have no certainty. But the flurry of sightings from 1978, particularly in the Middle East, might lead us to consider that a monitoring process was under way, one which would imply that those intelligences managing the UFOs had some level of prescience or predictive ability regarding human politics.

Despite the drop-off in sightings, one thing was becoming very clear: somebody was flying triangular craft in the United States. A case from January 5 speaks to this very clearly. In Auburn, Massachusetts, a woman driving her car in the early evening noticed three red, glowing, triangular objects flying over nearby woods. As she rounded the corner, she saw them hovering over the road directly in front of her. Her radio went dead, the car slowed to a stop (although her engine continued to run), and she was completely paralyzed. The closest object was only 30 feet away from her. She felt heat on her face, and noticed an unpleasant odor. When another car approached from behind, the three objects shot straight up, one at a time, and everything returned to normal. When she arrived home, she noticed her face was flushed as though it were sunburned. She developed a rash and some peeling skin the following day. Her car was fine. One might speculate that some triangular craft sightings from the 1970s and 1980s were tests of a stealth aircraft, but presumably three glowing, red triangles do not fit the bill. At that time, testing of stealth aircraft was being carried out at Nellis Test Site, on the other side of the country. Some of these were done at low altitudes, although hovering was out of the question.[1]

China also continued to generate some interesting reports, although most of these were not known in the west for some years. In late January, according to Chinese press accounts collected by the CIA, several witnesses saw a low flying UFO in the Fujian Province, which hovered over a road just before dawn, shining a powerful beam of light to the ground. It frightened several women on their way to the marketplace. CIA files also record a February instance in which a bright object darted across an airfield in Shanxi 'lighting up half the sky'. Similar reports came from elsewhere in the country.[2]

A few cases early in the year from Down Under bear mentioning. On February 5, in Lawitta, Tasmania, a vehicle encounter with a brilliant UFO took place, involving illumination of the car, electromagnetic effects on the vehicle, and physical-psychological effects on the driver. The case is similar to many others, but is noteworthy because of its nearness to the Valentich case, which had occurred a few months before.[3] On the night of February 8, at Liverpool Creek in Queensland, a farmer driving on the Bruce

Highway saw a dimly lit UFO sitting on the edge of the road. As he approached, it rose vertically a few feet off the ground. When he came to within 35 feet of the object, it gave off a blinding flash of light at the same time his car engine died. A little later, the engine was fine, but the man felt as though he had just awoken from a nightmare.[4]

Growing Paranoia

On the heels of obtaining the release of thousands of pages of UFO documents, researchers in 1979 began to take a hard look at themselves, in particular the relationship of at least some of them with the U.S. intelligence community. Most important was an article by Todd Zechel, entitled "NI-CIA-AP or NICAP?" Zechel had researched a number of the people involved in NICAP which, it turned out, was replete with CIA and former CIA officials. Most significant was Colonel Joseph Bryan, the man who had ousted longtime director Donald E. Keyhoe in 1969. Researcher Brad Sparks discovered that Bryan had founded the CIA's psychological warfare staff in the 1950s, a fact which Bryan confirmed to Zechel. Other NICAP members who were either CIA employees or closely associated with the agency included Karl Pflock, Stuart Nixon, and Jack Acuff. Acuff's case was especially galling, as he had personally bled the organization dry: his salary accounted for more than 80% of its total expenditures in 1979. The CIA leadership of NICAP had wrecked the group's ability to function. It certainly looked as though NICAP, the organization that had done more in the 1950s and 1960s than any other to fight against UFO secrecy, had been targeted by the CIA for destruction.[5]

Jacques Vallee added to the growing sense of suspicion with his book, *Messengers of Deception*, released in March 1979. For some years, Vallee had argued that UFOs were probably not the result of extraterrestrial activity. But now he went further, describing them as "machines of mass manipulation" seeking to alter the minds of those who experienced them, "to change our belief systems" and transform – or destroy – our present civilization. As far as *who* was behind the UFOs – whether ETs, time travelers, interdimensional beings, human covert groups – Vallee did not say. On one hand, he argued that the UFO phenomenon was ancient and that the message had changed with the times – thus, today they come in the form of highly detailed spaceships. On the other, he hinted that deeply covert human groups were somehow responsible for much of the phenomenon. He theorized that the concept of flying discs originated in Germany in the 1930s, and that an unknown private group (not necessarily the U.S.

government) gained control over them after World War Two. Human intelligence operatives, he said, pervaded the field. Contactees – people who claimed to have received messages from extraterrestrials – were being unwittingly manipulated by human programmers. Moreover, intelligence groups had penetrated much of the UFO research community, including CUFOS, a statement that surely displeased his longtime friend Hynek. Vallee's book polarized UFO researchers. Some applauded his courage and originality; others felt he had taken his anti-ET approach to an extreme point; yet others said he engaged in unprovable conspiracy-mongering.[6]

Such revelations – or allegations – were amplified in statements by former CIA agent, Victor Marchetti. UFOs, said Marchetti, were seldom discussed within the CIA, not because the topic was silly, but because it fell within the area of "very sensitive activities." He discussed rumors he had heard within "high levels" regarding the crash and recovery of UFOs and the bodies of little people. While he had not seen conclusive proof of UFO reality at the Agency, he said that CIA attempts to dismiss the topic had all the classic hallmarks of a cover-up. He suspected that the conspiracy was international in scope, the purpose of which was to "maintain a workable stability among the nations of the world and for them, in turn, to retain institutional control over their respective populations." For governments to admit the reality of UFOs, he concluded, could erode human society's power structure, as the average person would become aware of mentalities and capabilities that would be superior to ours. It could even lead to a collapse into anarchy.[7]

Perhaps the power structure was defending itself when Grenada Prime Minister Eric Gairy was deposed in a Marxist, military coup led by Maurice Bishop in March 1979. Gairy had not left the UFO issue alone. At the time of the coup, he was once again in New York City, at the United Nations to discuss a forthcoming plan of action on the UFO issue. Had Gairy been able to have the U.N. pass his UFO draft, it would have institutionalized the study of UFOs within the U.N., a situation that U.S. intelligence wished to avoid. One might well wonder if Gairy's efforts on UFOs had anything to do with the coup. Although the U.S. obviously would not have desired a Marxist government in Grenada, it is also true that Grenada was a tiny, powerless nation. More to the point, the U.S. military had no problem removing Bishop just a few years later.[8]

The House of Lords Debates UFOs

The 1978 wave of UFO sightings continued to reverberate, especially in

Britain, where the BBC had reported the recent New Zealand sightings. Within this context occurred a historic debate on UFOs in the House of Lords, which took place on January 18, 1979. It was the first time the UFO topic had ever been broached there. The person who enabled it was Brinsley Le Poer Trench, co-founder of *Flying Saucer Review*. In 1976, he became the 8th Earl of Clancarty, and soon began to press the UFO issue in the House of Lords. For some months prior, Patrick Stevens, who ran the MoD's UFO office known as S4, advised his Defence colleagues to prepare a rebuttal. Otherwise, he warned, there was "a risk that the Government will be persuaded to conduct a study of UFOs, or at least to examine the mass of evidence that Lord Clancarty and his fellow UFOlogists have assembled in the last 30 years." Privately, Stevens told Defence Minister Fred Mulley "there is nothing to indicate that UFOlogy is anything but claptrap."

The debate was one of the best attended ever held in the Lords, with sixty peers and hundreds of onlookers. Clancarty called attention "to the increasing number of sightings and landings on a worldwide scale of UFOs, and to the need for a government study of UFOs. He asked the Government to reveal publicly what it knew. Others shared his opinion. Lord Rankeillour stated, "many men have seen them and have not been mistaken. Who are we to doubt their word? ... Why should these men of law enforcement and defense lie?" The Government's position was taken by Lord Strabolgi, who had met with Stevens in preparation. He conceded that "there really are strange phenomena in the sky ... but there is a wide range of natural explanations to account for such phenomena." There was no government conspiracy on UFOs, he said, and certainly "no need to introduce the highly questionable hypothesis of alien space craft," especially when considering the vast distances in space that would make visits from extraterrestrials so unlikely.

Clancarty's motion for a government investigation of UFOs was defeated. Still, a UFO All-Party Study Group was soon founded within the House of Lords. Among its 30 members were Lord Hill-Norton (Admiral of the Fleet and Chief of the British Defence Staff from 1971-1973) and Ralph Noyes (former secretary to Sir Ralph Cochrane, Vice-Chief of the Air Staff from 1950-1952). The group lasted into the mid-1980s. The debate itself generated a tremendous amount of public interest. It filled 70 pages of *Hansard*, the House of Lords proceedings, copies of which were sold out in record time.[9]

It so happened that the British Ministry of Defence received 550 UFO sightings for 1979.[10] Some appear to have been misidentifications of space junk falling out of orbit. Other cases were not amenable to that explanation, such as the sighting by two teenaged British girls on February 22, 1979 in the town of Meanwood, a suburb of Leeds. They saw a grey, egg-shaped object, the size of a small car, with fins on the sides. This object descended near them while making a whining noise. It rested on the ground for three minutes, then began to hum and ascend. It came as close as 80 feet from them and landed again; then it began to wobble and take off. British researchers visited the site three days later, finding strange indentations in the snow in two places. The story made the press, and the girls were visited by an "official from the government." During separate interviews, they drew identical sketches of the object they saw. The official advised the girls not to discuss the matter further, but told one of the fathers, "I assure you they have seen something. That is definite, because the questions I asked them they would not be able to answer unless it happened."[11]

Mutilation Controversy

In the United States, the controversy on animal mutilations was becoming intense and political. The FBI was not investigating the matter, but in February 1979, New Mexico state police officer Gabriel Valdez told the Bureau that animals were being shot with a paralyzing agent, injected with an anti-coagulant, and drained of blood. Sometimes the cattle's legs were broken and unmarked helicopters were seen near mutilation sites. According to an FBI document at the time, Valdez believed the mutilations were a clandestine operation by the CIA or the Department of Energy connected with biological warfare research.[12] However, later that year when Linda Moulton Howe interviewed Valdez, he told her off the record that he thought the animal mutilation perpetrators were from outer space. This was in line with what other law enforcement officials told her, whether on or off the record.[13]

Throughout the year there were several American UFO reports in which objects maneuvered very low over the ground, skimmed treetops, hovered over highways, and swept areas with intensely bright light.[14] Some of these in the west seem to have been connected to cattle mutilations. Dulce, New Mexico, which at the time was a hotbed of bizarre activity, had such a case on April 9. Police officers saw a round, silent craft hovering 50 feet above the ground, with a searchlight aimed downward. This was an area close to where mutilated animals were found soon afterwards. What were these craft, and were they "ours" or "theirs"?

Further complicating matters were the events occurring at the ranch of Manuel Gomez, where a great deal of the Dulce activity was centered. From 1975 until the early 1980s, the Gomez family lost more than 50 cattle to mutilations, the highest total any family ever recorded. State police officer Gabe Valdez and Gomez discovered that animals were being marked prior to their mutilation. Using a black light, they found a glittery substance on the right side of the neck, right ear and right leg of a particular breed of cattle – the breed which happened to be the main target of the mutilations. They sent samples of the affected hides, along with control samples, to Dr. Robert Schonfeld in Albuquerque. Schonfeld said the affected hides showed significant and "highly suspicious" deposits of potassium and magnesium. He did not believe it occurred on the animals naturally. Apparently, something was quietly flying at night using an ultraviolet beam to locate marked animals.[15]

Mutilations had become enough of an issue that on April 20, 1979, New Mexico Senator (former astronaut and twelfth man to walk on the Moon) Harrison Schmitt and U.S. Attorney for New Mexico R. E. Thompson convened a public hearing on the subject in Albuquerque. Although the hearing was informal, with no power to enact decisions, the goal was to show that the mutilations were a criminal activity involving many states, and which therefore warranted federal action. Indeed, some had occurred on Indian reservations, hence federal land. About 200 people attended and offered a full range of opinions. Jim Marrs, then a journalist covering the hearing for the *Fort Worth Star-Telegram*, attended. He observed that authorities seemed to be pitted against ranchers, citizens, and researchers, especially when Thompson urged law enforcement officials in attendance "not to bring out any evidential material which might be used at a later trial." This effectively muzzled people like Gabriel Valdez.

Still, someone was listening, because on April 25 the State of New Mexico hired soon-to-be retired FBI agent Kenneth Rommel to investigate the matter. Rommel jokingly told the media that if aliens were at fault, he would bring them in by their little green ears. Such statements caused some to wonder if his investigation would be a dog-and-pony show designed to silence the matter with an official seal of approval, much as the Condon Committee had done a decade earlier regarding UFOs.[16] Later in the fall, Rommel met with journalist Linda Moulton Howe, who was also investigating the matter and was producing a documentary about it. During their interview, Rommel told Howe he was "going to prove" that animal mutilations were the result of predators. Howe, for her part, was already in possession of photographic and lab evidence to the contrary, but Rommel had made up his mind – a year before his official report was printed. It was evident that the "official" investigation of mutilations was following patterns recently described by Marchetti.[17]

1979: Mid-Year UFOs

On May 1, a UFO was seen at the government-owned oil fields of Vizcacheras, Argentina. This was a remote area, open only to employees. At 4 a.m., animal noises woke several engineers. Outside, they saw a UFO hovering silently about 200 feet from their site and 65 feet above the ground. For some reason, the men decided to wave their lantern at it. The object seemed to respond by blinking a light, and then landed nearby. More light signals were exchanged, and the UFO took off and disappeared toward the Andes Mountains at 4:35 a.m. The men inspected the landing site, and found a large circle with petrified or hardened sand. The animals refused to approach the area.[18]

A remarkable case took place in northwestern Minnesota on August 27 – in the opinion of Jerome Clark, one of the most evidential UFO cases ever recorded. The Red River Valley is about 45 miles south of the Canadian border and close to North Dakota. It was here, at 1:40 a.m., that a deputy sheriff saw a very bright UFO while driving. He lost consciousness and woke up with his head on the steering wheel. The car had skidded on the highway and was now facing the opposite direction. He radioed headquarters at 2:19 a.m., reporting that something had hit his car. One headlight had been blown out but he did not know why. The clock in his car and his wristwatch were now 14 minutes behind. Under medical examination, he showed an extreme sensitivity to light. The case was investigated by CUFOS. Although Phillip Klass tried to debunk the case, the cause of the sighting remains unknown.[19]

There were a few interesting Chinese reports during the second half of 1979, particularly of low flying objects behaving in extraordinary or odd ways. September was the most active month. On the 12th, a UFO sighting coincided with a complete power failure in the cities of Xuginglong and Huaihua in the Hunan Province. At 9 p.m., fifteen minutes after the power failure began, several people saw a silent, bright object fly overhead, emitting a vertical stream of white rays. This object then flew up and vanished, leaving behind two luminous clouds. The report led to rumors of other power blackouts associated with UFOs, although the Chinese government remained silent on the matter.[20] Nine days later, the Beijing newspaper, *Guang Ming Daily*, published an article "Do flying saucers exist?" Around the same time a physics student of Wuhan University in Hubei Province wrote to *Aerospace Knowledge* magazine, requesting his countrymen to launch a study of UFOs. Many readers responded, and soon a "China UFO Research Organization" was formed as a private initiative with apparently some modest independence from the central government.[21]

Fighting America's Goliath: the NSA

Throughout the year, Peter Gersten, Todd Zechel, and Brad Sparks of CAUS continued to press government agencies for UFO-related documents. Despite NSA stonewalling, the large release of documents from the prior December allowed for some optimism. Important documents continued to be released in 1979, the most significant of which was probably the 1961 Moon Dust document, obtained by Robert Todd. It described Moon Dust as operating on a "quick reaction basis to recover or perform field exploitation of unidentified flying objects, or Soviet/Bloc aerospace vehicles, weapons systems, and/or residual components of such equipment." Thus, UFOs were explicitly distinguished from Soviet craft. According to the document, recovered technology was to be sent to the Foreign Technology Division at Wright-Patterson AFB. Certainly this supported the growing number of allegations that recovered UFOs (and alien bodies) were being stored at Wright-Pat.[22]

With such forward momentum, one might think the future looked rosy for CAUS. In fact, the organization was 'deactivated' in September 1979. According to Larry Bryant, the problem was lack of money and public support, not pressure by government or other agencies. Search fees had become prohibitive. This may not have constituted "pressure," but high fees were becoming a key method used to discourage FOIA requests on UFOs. In response to a CAUS request for data on UFO radar trackings, for instance, the North American Aerospace Defense Command (NORAD) informed the organization that "it would require 18,383 hours and would cost $294,157."[23]

Despite the end of CAUS, the court cases against the CIA and NSA did not go away. On September 19, Peter Gersten on behalf of the UFO organization Ground Saucer Watch (GSW) met with CIA attorneys and Judge John H. Pratt at the U.S. District Court. The CIA had recently moved for a summary judgment to the case, asserting that the GSW requests constituted an "undue burden" and that the papers released so far were of little importance. Gersten replied that the released documents did indicate strong interest in UFOs by the CIA, and were most likely the tip of the iceberg. Judge Pratt gave GSW 60 days to provide a written response to the CIA motion for summary judgment.[24]

At this point the CIA and NSA were known to be withholding 57 and 18 UFO documents respectively. The CIA also refused to acknowledge another 200 UFO documents in its possession, while NSA refused to acknowledge any at all. The Air Force was also withholding all information relating to "unknown tracks," its latest synonym for UFOs. Frustrated with the stonewalling, Gersten held a press conference in late October, hoping that media pressure might be useful. It had no effect.[25] On October 29, 1979, a federal appeals court ruled that the records of the NSA were so sensitive to national security that they were afforded "special dispensation" from the scrutiny of any adversary action pursued under the terms of FOIA. Not only did this ruling effectively exempt the NSA from FOIA, it also opened a loophole for other federal agencies. What would stop CIA officials, for example, from transferring their most sensitive UFO documents to NSA?[26] Of course, a better solution, one that had probably already been implemented, would be to hand off sensitive documents and materials to trusted private contractors, making them "proprietary" and hence impervious to any form of public inquiry.

NSA's ability to exempt itself from FOIA emphasized how powerful it was. In addition to its hundreds of listening posts around the world, the NSA had its own army, navy, and air force, and massive bugs deep in space. But more than simply collecting data, it may have surpassed the CIA at this point in intelligence analysis, an area that was supposed to be the CIA's forte. CIA Director Stansfield Turner complained that some of the intelligence NSA released to other American intelligence agencies was so sanitized that it was almost useless. He believed that the NSA was deliberately withholding raw information from "the true analytic agencies" and was almost beyond control.[27]

Closing with a Bang and Invasion

As the year came to a close, other bizarre encounters occurred, a few of which were, thankfully, reasonably well documented. The most dramatic was a near air collision between a UFO and a Spanish Super Caravelle airliner flying from Austria to Tenerife on the night of November 10. At 11 p.m., two bright red lights approached the plane at "staggering" speed. The pilot, Captain Francisco Lerdo de Tejada, believed it was a single object about the size of a jumbo jet. After it took up a position half a mile away, it maneuvered around his plane, he said, in movements that were "quite impossible for any conventional machine to execute." He ordered his passengers to fasten their seat belts; one elderly man collapsed when he saw the object approach at a zigzag. Lerdo decided to make an emergency landing at Valencia. Doubtless feeling some panic, he descended as rapidly as possible. Still, the object followed him, and was visible to the airport director, air traffic controller, and ground personnel. Meanwhile, the Spanish Air Force Defense Command Center in Madrid obtained radar echoes that seemed to correspond with the UFO, and two Mirage jets attempted to intercept. They established visual contact, and one of the fighters was subjected to several sudden close approaches. Although Spain's Transport Minister ordered an investigation and stated, "it is clear that UFOs exist," no official report was released about the event. The case was reported by United Press International and included an interview with the pilot.[28]

Another interesting case occurred on November 27 in France. Known as the "Christelle" case, it involved a sighting of a landed UFO in connection with distinctive landing traces left after the object departed. Grass was flattened for several days after the observation, and samples were taken to the University of Toulouse for analysis. According to the report later issued by GEPAN, the analysis "did not give unequivocal evidence of chemical or biological disturbance of the samples ... relative to the controls." This was believed to be because the UFO was on the ground for only a short while. In following years, GEPAN would investigate stronger cases in which it appeared that landed UFOs were having definite effects on nearby plant life.[29]

The two final UFO related events of significance concerned the two major Communist nations in the world: the Soviet Union and China. Neither can be definitively nailed down, although both were reported by reputable researchers. One concerns an event said to have occurred in November over the Kaspustin Yar testing range, during secret tests of Soviet rockets. A Colonel-General Sapkov and other officers were astonished to see a bright green elliptical object, occasionally changing hues, hovering over the range for thirty minutes. As an aside, Sapkov saw the same thing there seven years later, and was assured by officers that this was a common occurrence.[30]

For several years, China had been generating interesting UFO reports, but few or none about alleged alien beings. That changed on December 13,

1979, according to a report received by Paul Dong. That evening, two truck drivers drove as a team in separate vehicles on the Xin'anjing Highway in the Zhejang province. This is very close to the eastern coast, somewhat north of Taiwan. Both men saw a bright beam of light ahead of their position. When the lead driver saw two "unusual human beings" standing on the highway, he stopped his vehicle. The beings were short, perhaps 4 ½ feet tall, and wore what looked like "space apparel." The driver behind also stopped his vehicle, but did not see the beings. The apparition vanished, and the two drivers discussed the event. They decided to switch vehicles. A few miles down the road, the new lead driver saw apparently the same beings, and the men again stopped their trucks. The drivers turned their lights off and on – the beings remained there. Only when one of the drivers came out with a crowbar did the beings disappear.[31]

On December 25, 1979, Soviet paratroopers landed in Afghanistan. Americans generally perceived the Soviet invasion as another move in their chess game for world domination, particularly as a ploy for control over Mideast oil. Actually, the Kremlin was divided over the invasion. For some years, Afghanistan had been a cold war battleground. In April 1978, Soviet-trained Afghan officers led a pro-Soviet coup. From Iran, Khomeini responded by supporting the *Mujahedeen* against the Afghan government, while the CIA supported Pakistan in training Islamic rebels (later to include Osama bin Laden). Thus, the U.S. and Iran were unspoken allies in Afghanistan, fighting against the same government. In March 1979, the Afghan government appealed to the Soviets for help. This was initially declined. Finally, in December 1979, the Soviets did enter in force, becoming sucked into a ruinous war that hastened the downfall of their own regime.

Incidentally, according to UFO researcher Paul Stonehill, 1979 was the year that the Soviet Union may have acquired two disc-shaped UFOs. One of these was said to be in the area of Zhigansk, in central Siberia, the other in the northern Urals. The Zhigansk disc was reportedly transported to the secret Soviet nuclear facility, Tomsk-7, although the Soviet authorities denied everything.[32]

1980: A Year of Intrigue

1979 was a quiet year for ufology; 1980 was not. Not so much because of the caliber of UFO sightings themselves as for the developments within the field itself. The available evidence points to the likelihood that the recent release of information, whether through official government documents or insider allegations, prompted a counter attack by the U.S. intelligence community.

Leonard Stringfield continued being the most important conduit of leaks. In January he published *The UFO Crash Retrieval Syndrome*, his first monograph to describe what he had learned, although he had presented some of this material at the 1978 MUFON symposium. His varied sources pointed to the possibility that there was not merely a single case of a crashed UFO, but many. One of his noteworthy discoveries were four separate military sources claiming to have seen a movie film depicting a crashed saucer and small alien bodies – fifteen years before the infamous Santilli film. Many researchers were impressed. The ever cautious Richard Hall stated that he was "shaken" by it.[33]

Meanwhile, the Roswell story began to reach the general public, courtesy of the *National Enquirer*. A February 26, 1980 edition of the tabloid described the story a full six months before the release of *The Roswell Incident* by William Moore and Charles Berlitz. Considering how difficult it is to obtain major media attention – even from a supermarket tabloid – one might wonder how Moore and Berlitz did it. One answer could be that the *Enquirer* had covered UFOs for years and simply recognized a good story. It is also true, however, that its publisher, Gene Pope, had long-time connections to the CIA. Co-author Charles Berlitz himself had a long history in military intelligence, and Moore would soon be eyeball deep in that world. Indeed, Moore was fluent in Russian – perhaps his choice of that language was purely an intellectual avocation, but perhaps not. What these (possible) connections to the intelligence community might mean is not always easy to answer. Could Moore and Berlitz have been supported somehow by the CIA, or another agency, that wanted the Roswell story out? And if so, could this have been to promote the story because it was known to be true (i.e. a friendly inside leak), or because it was known to be false (spreading disinformation to muddy the ufological waters)?[34]

There were few significant UFO sightings early in the year. One occurred at Burlington International Airport, in Vermont, on March 22, 1980, when airport radar tracked three small objects as they joined with a larger object and then separated. Speeds of up to 1,500 mph were recorded, and the objects quickly disappeared to the east. Observers saw them as very bright lights – "unlike anything I had ever seen before," in the words of the air traffic controller.[35]

This case was recorded by MUFON, which was one of just two American UFO groups doing any significant work – the other being

APRO. NICAP finally disbanded in 1980, its files eventually acquired by CUFOS through the efforts of Sherman Larsen.[36] CUFOS itself was in troubled times. Its publication, the *International UFO Reporter*, was on hiatus for 1980 and 1981. The plan was to publish the journal through a new science magazine, *Probe*. After this magazine failed, CUFOS attempted working with another independent publisher, *Second Look*. CUFOS during this period had little more than the name of its founder, J. Allen Hynek, and the efforts of its single full-time investigator, Allen Hendry.

As the weather heated up in the northern hemisphere, so did UFO activity and intrigue. Stringfield continued to make public appearances and cultivate new contacts. On March 22, he met with two new sources in Erie, Pennsylvania, one of whom was directly connected in some way with the covert world. There Stringfield was shown three 8" x 10" black-and-white photos depicting a frozen, mangled alien body encased in glass. He was told the location was Wright-Patterson AFB. The print quality was poor (the photos appeared to have been reproduced several times), and Stringfield thought the most striking print appeared to be retouched. He was suspicious, and decided to show the prints to a few of his sources. One of these was a scientist "working in a high level and secret capacity in New Mexico." This scientist in turn showed the images to another person who was in a "position to know." He then reported back to Stringfield, stating that the body in the glass case was genuine.

The plot thickened on May 6, when Stringfield was presented with a copy of a new pulp magazine called *UFO Sightings*. This featured an article by David McCarthy entitled "Quest for Teleportation," and featured a full-page picture of an alien body lying face up in a glass case. Its caption read: "A prototype cryogenic freeze chamber. The person inside is actually a mannequin encased in a special protective mylar foil." While not identical, the photo was strikingly similar to one of the photos Stringfield had been shown. Disturbed, he called his intermediary, who said the photos were reliable, that there were others which also showed mangled and burned humanoid forms. He suggested that the concept of the mannequin was phony, but admitted to being confused by this development. "My source is good and reliable," he said. "The photos were from intelligence files." He promised more. Sure enough, on June 2, Stringfield received eight 4" x 5" prints, seven showing different views of an alien body encased under glass, as well as various pieces of scientific equipment. One photo showed a hand with four fingers and clawlike nails. Stringfield's contact said the photo was obtained somehow from a secret study that had been conducted at the

University of Pennsylvania. The photo was striking, and Stringfield could not help but wonder that this one might have been "the key photo, the real one," and that the other photos might be "diffuser" types – to be used to discredit the real one, if necessary.[37] At the MUFON symposium of June 7 and 8, 1980, he showed the photos to a few researchers. Most were impressed by the key photo, but reserved judgment and agreed that he should look for more substantiation.[38]

Spring Sightings

Although a number of UFO researchers maintained that the animal mutilation mystery was not related to UFOs, cases continued to come along suggesting a link. Tom Adams investigated such a case from April 1980. A farmer in central Texas was walking through his pasture to check on a cow that was about to give birth; instead, he saw two nonhuman creatures carrying a calf between them, each holding one of its limbs. The farmer described them as about four feet high and of a light yellow-green color. He ran in fear, and did not return for two days, when he saw the carcass of the calf. It looked as though it had been turned inside out, and only the head, feet, and hide remained. This farmer, in the opinion of Adams, was extremely reluctant to discuss the incident any further.[39]

Throughout the southeastern U.S., unusual objects were being reported. On April 10, in the western part of North Carolina near the town of Lincolnton, witnesses saw a red, disc-shaped object shining a light towards the ground. It took off with an intense humming sound, leaving an exhaust trail. On May 7, about 25 miles to the northwest, a motorist in the town of Valdese experienced interference on his car radio and saw a domed disc directly ahead.[40] Another case of electromagnetic effects occurred on May 14, in central Mississippi. A husband and wife driving on US Route 49 at about 3:30 a.m. saw a glowing disc high in the sky. A beam of light came from it, which they drove through. As they did so, the car lights flickered about seven or eight times. They drove on without further incident.[41]

MUFON investigated several multiple witness reports from the San Francisco Bay area. In San Mateo on April 20 at 5:30 a.m., a man and his son saw five Saturn-shaped objects flying above a reservoir. They were in formation at low altitude and moving very fast.[42] During mid-morning on May 2, two county employees in the Diablo Range saw a bright, shiny, spherical object moving south. Through binoculars, they saw a blue-green band in the center and orange at the bottom. It stopped and spun over an observatory for ten seconds, then went south. The MUFON investigator checked for balloon and aircraft traffic; none matched the sighting.[43]

A dramatic U.S. military encounter with a UFO seems to have occurred in May, 1980. The account was obtained by a personal interview conducted by the author. The primary witness, a person of significant public stature, requested anonymity. In the town of Manlius, New York (a suburb of Syracuse), while driving with a friend down a quiet stretch of road during the late afternoon, the witness caught a glimpse of something in the sky to the right. "Do you see that thing?" he asked his passenger. "I'm glad you mentioned this," she said, "because I didn't know what I was going to say about that." Outside, hovering over a patch of trees, was an object described as "right out of a Steven Spielberg movie." The witness stopped the car and stepped outside; the passenger may have remained inside. The object was disc shaped and "as large as a football field." The only movement he detected was yellow, red, and green lights rotating rapidly around the perimeter. Incredulous and astonished, he simply stared at the object. He reasoned that if he and his friend were watching this object, other people also had to be seeing it. Sure enough, he said, a light commercial aircraft was visible, and he surmised its pilot had to see this object. He also saw an 'eye in the sky' news traffic helicopter. Certain that the sighting of an enormous flying saucer outside a major city would be newsworthy, he assumed that the helicopter crew was capturing the event on video. After a minute or two of observation, the witnesses became nervous. The object was still not moving, and had not made a sound. Then, two jet fighters – scrambled presumably from Griffiss Air Force Base – flew directly toward the object. At that point, the UFO took off "like a bullet" and rapidly disappeared. It was a good thing, he said, "as I was about to dive into my car." That evening, he stayed up late to watch the local news, expecting the UFO sighting to receive major coverage. Not only was the event not mentioned, he said, but the news announcer actually stated it had been "another boring day in Syracuse."

Sometime later, the author spoke to another person who may have seen the same event. The witness was in his mid-teens, living in Syracuse, when in the spring of 1980, his sister called the family outside to observe a UFO. The object was in the direction of Manlius, and was an unusual hovering object, although he could not make out significant detail. After a short while, the object departed rapidly, but he could not recall whether jets approached it.

The Myrna Hansen Abduction

Amid these cases occurred one with important consequences for ufology. This was the Myrna Hansen abduction, which took place in northeastern New Mexico on the evening of May 5. Hansen was driving with her eight-year-old son when they saw two huge, silent objects hovering over a mountain meadow. One was as large as two Goodyear blimps, the other was slightly smaller and triangular. The next thing either could remember was arriving home four hours late with no explanation. The next day, Hansen phoned the New Mexico State Police office in Cimarron. She talked about incredibly bright lights, herds of cattle, and strange people. She was frightened and asked for help. The officer referred her to Gabriel Valdez in Dulce, who was well known by then for investigating strange events. Valdez in turn phoned Paul Bennewitz, whom he knew from the town meeting on cattle mutilations sponsored by Senator Harrison Schmitt the previous year.

Bennewitz was a private scientist and proprietor of Thunder Scientific Corporation, and did contract work for the U.S. Department of Defense. He was also a member of APRO with an active interest in UFOs. He told Valdez that he could get someone qualified for Hansen to talk to. On May 7, just two days after her sighting, Hansen and her son were sitting in Bennewitz's Albuquerque home. Bennewitz had spoken to APRO's head, Jim Lorenzen, who recommended Dr. Leo Sprinkle to conduct regressive hypnosis.

Sprinkle arrived on May 11, finding Hansen and Bennewitz agitated and insisting that the regression be done inside Bennewitz's car with the windows sealed with aluminum foil. Author Gregory Bishop, who researched this matter, concluded that Bennewitz had probably been planting ideas in Hansen's mind. Under hypnosis, Hansen recalled an intensely bright light approaching her. She stopped her car and saw a second bright object. Her son wanted to leave but she was curious. An object landed, cattle were bellowing loudly, and she remembered an orange light. She also remembered being taken somehow into the craft – just before she entered, she saw a struggling cow being lifted by a kind of tractor beam into the object. She then recalled being undressed and undergoing a physical examination. In further sessions with Sprinkle, she described being taken to an underground base, seeing human body parts floating in vats, receiving an explanation from her captors as to what they were doing with her and why they were on Earth, and felt some sort of device being implanted in her body so that the aliens could monitor and control her thoughts. Sprinkle also questioned her son, who recalled the actual sighting and the panic of the cows, but little else. Sprinkle wanted to continue further with the hypnotic regression, but Bennewitz was convinced Sprinkle was a CIA agent and ordered him to leave.

How much, if any of this, was due to Bennewitz's prior influence can only be conjecture, but many years later another witness corroborated the UFOs, bellowing cattle, and something horrible happening to one of the animals. This was the wife of a Cimarron police officer who wanted to avoid publicity because of her husband's job. Only seven years later did the officer confide the event to Valdez. So Hansen's memories could not have been completely from Bennewitz.[44]

Especially interesting was Hansen's reference to being taken to an underground base. Underground bases were not a topic of discussion anywhere among the general public in 1980. It so happens that Kirtland Air Force Base has extensive underground facilities, most notably at its Manzano Weapons Storage Area.[45] It is also believed to have been the largest nuclear weapons storage site in the world. Sometime later, Air Force Special Agent Richard Doty said that, while she was under hypnosis with an Air Force psychologist, Hansen described and drew one of the facilities at Manzano in great detail. "She even knew what the elevator looked like."[46] Ultimately, the case deepened the already prominent interest Paul Bennewitz had in UFOs over the Manzano facility (which was visible from his home), and his growing conviction that there was an underground alien base in Dulce, New Mexico. More on that later.

Close Aviation Encounters

Elsewhere in the world, UFO activity was picking up, including several dramatic air encounters. On May 7, 1980, a Dutch KLM airliner was flying just over 30,000 feet above the Dachstein Mountains in Austria. At 3:50 p.m., the pilot saw a grey spherical object flying overhead. He reported this to the air control center in Vienna, which in turn contacted military headquarters of the Austrian Air Force. The Officer in Command, Major Carl Schwarz, ordered three Saab-Draken 105s to intercept. When the fighters made visual contact, two attempted to intercept, while a third took as much film footage as possible. Despite the fact that the Saab Draken 105 can achieve a top flight speed of Mach 2, the fighters were unable to maintain chase – not only was the UFO going too fast, but it made very challenging maneuvers. Soon, it was out of sight. At about 5:30 p.m., the pilot of a German Lufthansa aircraft saw a similar object. Again, Schwarz ordered jets to intercept. One of the pilots said "we were operating at a height of 12,000 meters. The 'thing' was flying very fast and then very slow. It seemed to be playing with us. The UFO was flying 3,000 meters over us, and although we tried all possible maneuvers, we couldn't catch it." When asked about the film record of the first intercept attempt, a Major Wolfgang Brauner said "the films are useless." He said he believed the object was a balloon. Few additional details about this case are known.[47]

Right after this were two even more spectacular cases. These involved the Peruvian Air Force on May 9 and 10, 1980. On the morning of May 9, a group of officers at the Mariano Melgar Air Base in southern Peru were standing in formation when they saw a round object hovering near the airfield. According to documents of the U.S. Defense Intelligence Agency (DIA), the base commander authorized an SU-22 to intercept and identify the object. The SU-22 is a top fighter-bomber that can also reach Mach 2, but apparently was no match for this object. The pilot fired upon it at close range without causing any apparent damage. When he tried to make a second pass on the vehicle, the UFO accelerated out of sight. On the following evening, a UFO returned to the same area. Again, an SU-22 was scrambled, and once again the object outdistanced the aircraft. An interesting sidelight to the story was learned by researcher Antonio Huneeus, who later spoke with the base commander. Huneeus was told that the second SU-22 was ordered not to fire on the object because the attempt from the day before had failed, and each missile was rather expensive. The object and its origins remained unknown in the DIA report. The departure speed was not indicated in the document, but the astounding thing from a technological point of view is the fact that the object had been first seen hovering. To accelerate from hovering to a speed that easily surpasses an SU-22 is something that, nearly three decades later, is not believed to be possible. Therein lies one of the key mysteries of this particular encounter.[48]

Another close aircraft encounter with a UFO occurred near Venice, Italy on June 11. Not much is known about it, except that it appeared in the records of Britain's Civil Aviation Authority (CAA), which were obtained by Nick Redfern. The report simply noted that a "UFO passed close to subject aircraft. Object appeared to be like a fighter aircraft drop tank." In other words, cylinder or cigar-shaped.[49]

On June 14, 1980 many Moscow residents reported seeing a huge reddish-orange horseshoe shaped object accompanied by swirling luminous gases. During the same evening, 250 miles to the west, a Soviet colonel named V. Karyakin heard a low frequency booming noise in his ears, and then saw a bright object in the sky less than 500 feet away from him. He ran toward it, felt some resistance but continued to push on and stopped at a distance of 150 feet. It gave off a high pitched sound and briefly emitted three white rays, then ascended rapidly, hovered for two seconds, then moved northwesterly, then vanished. Karyakin could not tell if it had moved at amazing speed, or if someone had "turned it off." Soon afterwards, over some treetops, he saw another object. This was a large, elongated, and reddish UFO. Moving to a fifth floor window, he saw another bright object accompanying the red UFO, flying horizontally and leaving a fiery trail. As many as 30 eyewitnesses saw the event, which was investigated by Soviet military and scientific personnel. They concluded that what had been seen by these witnesses were the launches of two Soviet communications satellites, a Gorizont and Kosmos 1188. Researcher Paul Stonehill remarked, "some of what was observed can definitely be explained by the launches, but what about the rest?"[50]

On June 20, a UFO was seen in Kuwait. At 9 p.m., a senior Kuwait Airways pilot was descending at 15,000 feet when he and his crew saw a "huge ball of bright light shaped like a hemisphere (half a Moon shape)." He estimated its diameter to be an astonishing ten miles, "with the flat base of the sphere approximately the same level as the aircraft." The object, or whatever it was, was northwest of Kuwait City, moving east at a slightly slower speed than his own speed of 320 knots. The object was visible until he descended below the haze and approached the runway. The crew of another flight 90 miles away reported the same thing, which was not picked up on any radar. The event was investigated by the Kuwait Ministry of the Interior and noted in a U.S. Embassy report to the State Department, Secretary of Defense, and various embassies.[51]

An interesting, though undated, 1980 photograph was taken of an apparent UFO in France. The witness was taking landscape photographs when a luminous object suddenly appeared. A wide beam emanated from the hovering object. The photograph is from the UFO files of the Gendarmerie Nationale, which offered no additional information about the picture.

1980 photograph of UFO; from the Gendarmerie Nationale

A Strange Harvest

At the behest of the State of New Mexico, former FBI agent Kenneth Rommel had investigated cattle mutilation phenomenon for about a year – from 1979 to mid-1980. Just as his investigation ended (and he was preparing his conclusion that the animal deaths were caused by predators), Linda Moulton Howe aired her documentary on the mutilation phenomenon for KMGH-TV (CBS) in Denver, Colorado on May 28, 1980, as a 2-hour special. *A Strange Harvest* provided striking visuals of the phenomenon.

One segment featured a visit by Howe to laser surgeon Arlen Meyers, M.D., at Rose Medical Center in Denver. She wanted to see how long it took to excise tissue with a laser, and how laser excisions compared with mutilation cases. Meyers demonstrated on poultry the difference between trying to cut a circle with a traditional scalpel, an electrical cauterizer, and a laser. After several minutes of applying a laser, he was able to burn a circle of flesh that was only three inches in diameter, which moreover was charred with carbon. This was nothing like the excisions from mutilation cases, some of which were twenty-four inches long and perfectly carbon-free. Further, Meyers pointed out the daunting task of transporting a 400 pound device, along with its power supply, from one mutilation site to another without attracting attention, a task made more difficult when one could not leave tracks behind, as was typically the case.

Howe also interviewed Lou Girodo, Chief Investigator for the District Attorney's Office in Trinidad, Colorado. Girodo had been assigned to investigate mysterious, bloodless, trackless animal deaths in southern Colorado and told her on camera that he and other investigators had concluded the perpetrators were "creatures not from this planet." Howe then traveled to Fort Carson, south of Denver near Colorado Springs, home of the quiet Cobra helicopter in order to determine how much noise it made at a distance of one mile. She found it to be fairly noisy; their landings and takeoffs were like "local hurricanes," she said. The documentary also featured a hypnotic regression session conducted by Leo Sprinkle with Janet Doraty, who said she witnessed a mutilation outside Houston, Texas, during the spring of 1973. Under hypnosis, Doraty described seeing a calf drawn up in a pale yellow beam of light into a UFO. She saw grey beings inside a round room with the calf, and in close detail she described how the tongue glistened as a surgical instrument cut it. She also recalled seeing the non-human entities scraping tissue from her teenage daughter's mouth.

While there had been some published research on matter of mutilations, Howe's television documentary easily reached the largest number of people, and was awarded a Regional Emmy. *A Strange Harvest* quickly became instrumental in focusing the debate among researchers as to whether or not there was a connection between UFOs and mu-

Linda Moulton Howe, filming *A Strange Harvest*, spring 1980

tilations. Three years later, Home Box Office (HBO) would contract with her to produce an hour-long documentary for its network, a story that developed its own interesting saga.[52]

Mutilation cases were frequent during the summer of 1980, most especially in Dulce, where dead and mutilated animals were being found almost weekly by Gabriel Valdez. Residents were becoming accustomed to seeing strange lights in the area, specifically near Mount Archuleta, a fact that took on additional meaning when some recalled having heard what sounded like construction activity near the mountain during the early 1970s.[53] Paul Bennewitz increasingly became convinced that an alien base was beneath the area, one which was slowly replacing Washington, D.C. as the main location of governmental and military control of the planet.[54]

Stringfield and The Photos

Meanwhile, Leonard Stringfield continued to collect accounts of alleged crash retrievals. During the summer of 1980, he obtained some corroboration of the photo of the alien under glass. This came from one of his key sources, a physician who had performed an autopsy on an alien in the 1950s, who told him the photo showed similar features to the alien he had autopsied in the 1950s. Some of Stringfield's other sources were also telling him about live aliens in military custody.

In August, another set of photos alleging to show part of an alien body recovered from the wreckage of a UFO was released through the auspices of a UFO researcher named Willard McIntyre. To the best of anyone's knowledge, McIntyre received these through an anonymous Navy source. William Spalding of Ground Saucer Watch analyzed them and suggested that the creature was a monkey used in early military rocket tests. Stringfield wondered if the photos were being used to discredit him. They were released by Charles Wilhelm and Dennis Pilichis, members of an organization called the Coalition of Concerned Ufologists, who spent much of their time attacking Stringfield's research and credibility. Wilhelm lived in Ohio, very close to Stringfield. Was it mere coincidence that Wilhelm also obtained alleged photos of an alien cadaver – photos which were shown to be hoaxes?[55]

Manzano

Elsewhere, the plot was thickening. In late July 1980, APRO received a letter with no return address from an anonymous writer claiming to be an airman assigned to Kirtland AFB. The writer described the alleged experience of an 18-year-old member of the Civil Air Patrol named Craig Weitzel. The incident took place 20 miles east of the Santa Fe National Forest, near the town of Pecos, on July 16, 1980. During a morning training mission, Weitzel and ten other people saw a UFO land in a nearby clearing. An individual dressed in a metallic suit came out of the craft and walked a short distance, and within minutes returned to the craft. The writer said Weitzel took pictures and the group was debriefed at Kirtland. The following day, Weitzel was visited by a man in a dark suit and sunglasses, claiming to be from Sandia Labs. The man demanded the pictures and warned Weitzel not to talk about the incident. Weitzel replied that he had already given them to Kirtland AFB. According to the letter, Weitzel reported the man to a "Mr. Dody," a Kirtland AFB security officer.

The writer of the letter mentioned "serious rumors" concerning crashed UFOs being kept at Kirtland's Manzano storage area. Scientists from Sandia National Laboratory had examined several UFOs during the past 20 years, including "parts of one that crashed near Roswell, NM…. That is still being stored in Manzano." Finally, claimed the writer, the Air Force Office of Special Investigations (AFOSI) had taken over UFO investigations when Project Blue Book was closed, and a secret detachment also investigated the cattle mutilation mystery.

Jim Lorenzen of APRO thought the letter was probably nonsense, but it did have dates and places that could be checked. He eventually sent the letter to William Moore, who found Weitzel and spoke to him. Weitzel confirmed he had seen a strange, silvery object in the skies, but denied taking pictures or receiving a visit from a man in black. Moreover, he claimed, the incident occurred not in New Mexico, but the southeastern U.S. The conclusion by researcher Gregory Bishop seems reasonable: the letter was "a load of manure with a rhinestone thrown in," and was concocted as a "feeler" by AFOSI to see who could be used as an insider asset. That asset was beginning to look like William Moore. Indeed, much later on, Richard Doty told Moore that he had composed the letter as "bait."[56]

But how much of the letter was manure? The Manzano Weapons Storage Area was the scene of genuine UFO activity. Shortly before midnight on the night of August 8-9, 1980, three security policemen on the eastern side of Manzano saw a "very bright light in the sky" about three miles north-northeast of their position. Initially, they thought it might have been a helicopter, but they assumed otherwise when it traveled south extremely fast and then stopped suddenly over Coyote Canyon. The light then descended and appeared to land in the Coyote Canyon area, somewhat east of the Manzano complex. The guards contacted Central Security Control (CSC) inside Manzano, which in turn contacted Sandia Security.

At about 12:20 a.m., a Sandia guard on routine patrol noticed an intense bright light hovering motionless near the ground. It was behind a building of the facility. Thinking this might be a helicopter with bright lights, he approached, shotgun in hand. When he tried to use his radio, he found it had stopped working. He then realized the light was actually a disc shaped object. It shot straight up and was gone. The other security policemen, who had originally seen the bright object, were several miles away. They also saw it shoot up at high speed and disappear.

There were other UFO landings at or near Kirtland that month. During the prior week, in fact, another Sandia guard had seen an unknown object land near an alarmed structure, but he did not report it for a month "for fear of harassment." On the night of August 10, a New Mexico State Patrolman reported a landing of an unknown craft between Belen and Albuquerque. On August 22, three security policemen (different from the ones from August 8-9) observed an object land once again in Coyote Canyon.

A report of these incidents was prepared by AFOSI Special Agent Richard Doty at Kirtland. The document was leaked to William Moore in January 1982 and was obtained in a subsequent FOIA request by Barry Greenwood. Moore and Bruce Maccabee separately investigated this case, obtaining essentially the same information. Both interviewed Doty, who stated he personally investigated the incident and that there were "most likely" other documents pertaining to it. Moore in particular interviewed other personnel who corroborated that something had happened that night at Manzano.

In 1984, Doty even told Maccabee that he had written a longer follow-up report, and advised Maccabee to write to AFOSI Headquarters to obtain all releasable information. However, when Maccabee did so, the officer there, Noah Lawrence, told him there were no other documents on file. Lawrence even phoned Doty, who now appeared to reverse direction, claiming that there was no such documentation. Lawrence told Maccabee there was a "discrepancy" in what Doty told the two of them. According to what Maccabee learned, Doty's commanding officer interviewed Doty and evidently reported back to Lawrence that Doty denied the existence of any other document. As far as Lawrence was concerned, that ended the matter.

Maccabee investigated further. He sought the permission of Russ Curtis, one of the names mentioned in Doty's document, to obtain an escort inside the restricted area of Manzano. He met Curtis and showed him Doty's report. Curtis's reply surprised him: the event never happened, the whole thing was untrue. Maccabee did not know at the time that this contradicted Curtis's statement to Moore in 1982. Maccabee left, feeling Curtis was hiding something important. He continued to attempt to obtain follow-up documents on the incident, in vain, but came away convinced the event was real. The Air Force has never disputed the authenticity of Doty's report, it has simply never admitted the existence of any followup documents.[57]

Could Manzano actually have been a location for the storage of a crashed UFO, as Doty's letter to APRO claimed? If so, could UFO testing have been going on there? Were the UFOs at Manzano extraterrestrial or 'made in the U.S.A.'?

Philip Klass: A Covert Attack

Since the 1960s, Philip Klass had been the world's most prominent UFO debunker, and certainly the most effective at influencing public discourse. As is often the case for people who live public lives, Klass's success was all in the attitude. He had outstanding connections in the academic, aviation, defense, and journalistic communities. Exuding confidence at all times, he understood that actually explaining UFO sightings was less important than making them – and their proponents – appear to be ridiculous. Among his arsenal of weapons were character assassination and overt intimidation, which he used effectively in the 1960s against the physicist Dr. James McDonald, who at the time was the most important UFO researcher in the world.

In 1980, Klass turned his sights on Stanton Friedman. Friedman had just married a Canadian citizen and was in the process of moving to New

Brunswick. Recognizing an opportunity, Klass sent a letter on August 15, 1980 to Dr. A. G. McNamara of the Herzberg Institute of Astrophysics in Ottawa.[58] This institute worked for the Canadian National Research Council (NRC) as a repository for Canadian UFO reports. Essentially, the NRC served as Canada's "Project Blue Book," accepting reports from citizens regarding alleged UFOs. Like America's Blue Book of the 1950s and 1960s, the NRC did little more than file the thousands of earnest and detailed letters from mystified citizens without ever reading them. Canadian UFO reports were something of a bastard child. No one wanted them, but the astronomers at the Herzberg Institute of Astrophysics were stuck with the job of receiving them.

Klass's letter to the NRC was a straightforward smear of Friedman. According to Klass, Friedman was a "full-time UFO lecturer (of the 'snake-oil salesman' variety)," and was moving to Canada "to become its chief UFO Guru." He was "quite a showman," wrote Klass, whose lectures were "so filled with half-truths and falsehoods that it would take me several hours to offer a rebuttal. And like wrestling with an octopus, when you manage to pin down one leg, the other seven are still thrashing about." Klass disparaged Friedman's professional credentials as a nuclear physicist, twice referred to his "mountainous ego," and called him "something of an outcast" within the UFO "movement." Klass also enclosed a "White Paper" he prepared on Friedman "that illustrates the man's modus-operandi and his distortion of facts."*

Klass's stated motive in sending the letter was to warn the scientists at NRC that Friedman would now be focusing on them. "I can assure you," he wrote, "that you and your associates will be publicly accused of a UFO Cover-up (or 'Cosmic Cover-up,' as he is prone to say)...." Klass painted Friedman as a dangerous man who must be dealt with "cautiously," as he was "inclined to distort the facts and exploit any ambiguity" in their statements. Klass made sure to request that the recipients "treat this letter in confidence, sharing it with appropriate associates as you see fit." In other words, to tell as many people as they could, but behind Friedman's back.

It was ironic that Klass twice mentioned Friedman's "mountainous ego." Klass evidently felt he had no such ego problems, despite the presumption of such unsolicited character assassination. While he and Friedman had frequently debated publicly, their relations for years were professional and cordial.

---

* This White Paper was not included in the material found by the author in the Canadian National Archives.

Obviously, the letter was not a well-meaning warning as Klass portrayed it. Rather, it was an attempt to intimidate scientists who were already uncomfortable with receiving UFO reports. Judging by the internal memos his letter generated, Klass achieved his intended effect. Ten days later, a note from one

Klass (L) with Friedman (R) at Trinity University in San Antonio, Texas, during the late 1970s.

of the scientists at NRC mentioned the letter and worried that "we can ill afford the publicity [Friedman] will generate for us." The next statement speaks volumes about how these men thought of UFOs: "Since there is no science in the subject of UFO's perhaps we should think again about the possibility of turning the so-called 'UFO file' over to some body with no responsibility for the conduct of scientific research." One cannot help but think of the thousands of Canadian citizens whose hard work authoring detailed reports of UFO sightings and encounters, was wasted when men such as these at the NRC simply cast them into the proverbial circular file unread and most likely unopened.

Although the NRC was unable fully to unload its UFO responsibilities, it did remove most of its UFO files. Apparently as a result of Klass's letter, the decision was made that as of January 1, 1981, any UFO file more than a year old would be turned over to the Public Archives of Canada.*

What Klass did was impressive. He created a bogeyman for a group of easily frightened scientists and enabled them to divest themselves of a large portion of their "UFO connection." Seen in the broader context of his career, this was his typical modus operandi.[59]

Another such "Klassic" incident occurred regarding a UFO conference that took place at the University of Nebraska on November 11 and 12, 1983. This was organized by the MUFON State Director for Nebraska, Ray Boeche. Klass learned about the event three months in advance, and immediately placed telephone calls to the Conference Coordinator, Russ Free and the Director of Conferences at the University, Robert Mortensen. Klass wanted to know why a prestigious university would sponsor such a conference. Apparently, he was so unpleasant that the University's Assistant to the Chancellor, Dr. John K. Yost, initiated an investigation. One reason

---

* Incidentally, the author was a bit startled to see the name "R. W. Dolan" at the top of the relevant document, and does not know who this person was.

was that Klass claimed there was a political agenda to the conference. In the words of Mortensen,

> Mr. Klass has a personal feeling that the nature of this conference seriously questions the integrity of the United States government. He feels that there is no scientific evidence to support the claims of the and indicated that these organizations, by publicly questioning the government, lend support to the Communist movement.

Thus Klass revealed one of his key motivations at UFO debunking to be an explicit support of the U.S. government and national security community. At any event, the conference took place as scheduled.[60]

Klass's actual analyses of the UFO phenomenon were consistently shallow and politically motivated. His true legacy lies in his efforts – sometimes quiet, sometimes public – to persuade and frighten appropriate targets away from the study of UFOs. Whether or not he did this on behalf of the U.S. intelligence community has (as of this writing) not been proven publicly. However, the ducks certainly appear to be lining up.

More Triangles

In terms of UFO activity, one of the most important developments in the U.S. was the continuing appearances of triangular aircraft. Several reports during the fall of 1980 indicate that this unusual shape was being seen in a variety of places. On September 13, people camping in Hamilton, Texas, woke up when their tent was lit up with a yellow glow. Outside was a loud humming sound; above them at no more than 125 feet was a triangular object. The underside was a greenish or greyish, and two lights appeared at each tip in a combination of yellow-white, red-green, and blue-white. The object was moving north very slowly but stopped for about ten seconds and began to pulsate, almost sounding as though it would stall. It started up again, headed north and was soon gone. Thirty minutes later, the group heard a loud explosion, and some members saw sparks from above the top of the hill. The case was investigated by MUFON, which could find no conventional explanation.[61]

An undated case of a black triangle, also investigated by MUFON, comes from the fall of 1980 and was witnessed by two women near Middletown, New York. They described it as about 60 feet long, with a bluish white light and a white spotlight. Like the Texas triangle, this object made a humming noise.[62] Yet another triangular or boomerang-shaped object was reported on October 23, 1980, seen over a copper smelting site in the town of Morenci, Arizona. This object shone a bright light downward, accelerated rapidly, and made non-inertial, non-aerodynamic maneuvers.[63]

The Roswell Incident and the Spooks

In the fall of 1980, *The Roswell Incident*, by William Moore and Charles Berlitz, was published. Stanton Friedman, who had done substantial research for the book, was supposed to get equal billing as an author, but Berlitz – a published author with substantial connections in the book industry – at the last moment changed the plan. Other than the brief passages in Stringfield's *Situation Red*, this was the first book since Frank Scully's *Behind the Flying Saucers* (1950) to argue that a UFO had crashed and been retrieved by U.S. military personnel. This time, however, the argument gained traction. Friedman and Moore, even at this early stage, had interviewed dozens of people connected to the case, and put together a reasonably strong argument that something truly exotic – not just a weather balloon – had crashed near Roswell in July 1947. To be sure, not all UFO researchers believed this. But many did, or at least felt the case warranted further investigation. Just a few years earlier, talk of crash retrievals among UFO researchers was simply *not done*. Stringfield's research had gone a long way toward changing that, but *The Roswell Incident* solidified ufology's transformation. Roswell was an idea whose time had come.

That September, William Moore did a promotional tour for the book. While at a radio station in Omaha, Nebraska, he received a phone call from someone who identified himself as a colonel from nearby Offutt AFB. The man said "we think you're the only one we've heard that seems to know what he's talking about." Moore was unable to meet him, but took his phone number. After an interview in Albuquerque, another caller told Moore exactly the same thing. Moore met with this caller, who had an Eastern European accent and said he represented a group of U.S. intelligence agents who wanted to end UFO secrecy. Their goal was to release more accurate information to the public, and they wanted to do this through a reputable researcher. But Moore would have to provide them with information, as well. The man, whose code name was "Falcon," gave no details on this yet, but Moore agreed nevertheless. There has been some discussion over the identity of the person, much of which has centered on Richard Doty. But Moore always maintained it was somebody else. According to Gregory Bishop, "Moore believed he could get his hands dirty just enough to lead those directing the process into believing that he was doing exactly what they wanted him to do. All the while he would continue to burrow his way into the defense and intelligence matrix to learn who was directing it and why."[64]

"A Mysterious Silence"

In late September, Stringfield was contacted by "Jeffrey Morse," the military policeman at McGuire AFB connected with the shooting of an alien entity in 1978, an event certainly as dramatic as the Roswell incident. In October, another first-hand informant told Stringfield of a retrieval operation in Yucca Valley, California, from 1947. By now, Stringfield had 20 first-hand reports, ten more since the publication of his monograph in January, 1980. But it was also at this time, during the fall of 1980, that he began to encounter a "mysterious silence" from all of his sources. On October 21, one of them told him, "my source [a former CIA employee] can't talk about UFOs. He refused to answer any of my questions on the photos or the live retrievals.... He's had his knuckles spanked." Stringfield's key medical source also became silent. While this person had previously been open and helpful, he now told Stringfield, "I can't comment on anything." Other sources also dried up, all at once. In late November, one of his contacts, who had been in hiding, wrote that "it seems you have struck a nerve in the spinal cord of the jokers who know what is happening." This person had been under heavy surveillance, he said, since Stringfield had spoken in June at the MUFON symposium.[65]

The Strange Signals of Paul Bennewitz

Throughout the summer and fall of 1980, Paul Bennewitz kept a close eye on the Manzano Weapons Storage Area. Bennewitz was a trained scientist who had done contract work for the Defense Department. He had an array of equipment that was picking up low-frequency electromagnetic pulses and recording aerial displays. During the fall of 1980, he called Kirtland AFB about this. He believed that the displays were genuine UFOs and the pulses were alien signals of various sorts. Some were alien messages directed to the implants of abductees (although why he believed this is not clear).* Other signals seemed to be about an alien base. Many of Bennewitz's notes are gone or unavailable, but some exist – and make for strange reading. The following are 'messages' he received with what he described as "analog recording equipment" in October 1980.

> Den under Archuleta Peak. West of peak, snow gone. Go west 1 km. Enter ram bad judgement. Attach cable. Drag ramp away. Drown good until Ant Widow beg for life. Death eats hate. Fox kill dead. Go down a railed entry. Strike fast. Enemy very tough at death. When at each turn test air. Key to effective fight, fear – ejection. Arbitrated peace

---

* Of course the impact of his encounter the year before with Myrna Hansen – an early case dealing with alleged alien implants – was clearly powerful.

no heed and deny or death take you. Do cut jugular. Go no further to arrange deal. State day they leave Earth. Near Lyra orbit. A gentle act does cause material good. Take fact first. Take until a black auto hit has seen chase. No let catch or upset you. Have Den racked. Aim well. A brave death has man.

He wrote a series of separate interpretations of these statements, and believed they were instructions on how to attack and destroy the alien base under Dulce's Archuleta Peak.[66]

Bennewitz was worried. All this seemed very wrong. His communications with Kirtland AFB resulted in a personal meeting with AFOSI Special Agent Richard Doty. Doty's office had jurisdiction over all criminal and security investigations at Kirtland and Manzano. Accompanied by Air Force physicist Lew Miles, Doty went to Bennewitz's home on October 26. They saw Bennewitz's impressive array of equipment, various photographs, and heard recordings of many of his signals – including, we might assume, the cryptic message regarding Archuleta Peak. At the request of the NSA, which had a major presence at Kirtland, Doty secretly photographed everything he saw.[67]

Bennewitz was invited to Kirtland AFB on November 10 to present his findings to a small group of officers and scientists. In attendance was commander Brigadier General William Brooksher, four colonels, two AFOSI men, and several scientists from Phillips Laboratories. Doty does not appear to have attended. Bennewitz described the Manzano UFOs, his work with Myrna Hansen, and his thoughts on ET. When he asked for financial support to continue his investigation, he was advised to apply for an Air Force grant. It is possible that Bennewitz received a grant from the NSA, which appeared to be most interested in his work, particularly the discovery of the signals emanating from Kirkland.[68]

A week later, on November 17, Doty told Bennewitz that AFOSI had decided against further consideration of the matter. This was not true. In reality, Bennewitz's story had created great concern within sectors of the military-intelligence community. Somewhere within AFOSI, DIA, or the NSA, the decision was made that Bennewitz would be allowed to continue his work, so that it could be learned how he obtained his information.[69] To do this, Doty befriended Bennewitz and expressed enthusiasm about his research. Years later, when Doty discussed this on the radio show *Coast to Coast* with Art Bell, he argued that AFOSI's interest in Bennewitz had nothing to do with UFOs or aliens.[*] Rather, it was to protect the technolo-

---

[*] Although he expressed personal belief in the reality of UFOs and extraterrestrials based on briefings he had while in the military.

gies and activities at Kirtland. What followed was a program on Bennewitz that involved monitoring and misinformation, most of it passive. When, for example, Bennewitz asked Doty to let him know if he "tapped into something" that was going on at Kirtland, Doty merely nodded and said Bennewitz had found "something unknown." Doty did not so much tell stories of aliens as allow Bennewitz's belief system to take over.[70]

Here we reach the core issue. What exactly did Paul Bennewitz uncover? Were the things he observed and recorded secret military projects that required counter measures for reasons of national security? Or were they more exotic still, in other words related to UFOs?

Let us look at Dulce first. In the margins of his transcription of the message about the "Den under Archuleta Peak," Bennewitz wrote "from this, we found the first base by helicopter." Evidently, the notes referred to something real. Bennewitz was a private pilot and flew his airplane over Dulce throughout the 1980s, finding and photographing what he believed was evidence of an alien presence on the mountain. On several occasions he flew with other people from Kirtland, including Doty and Colonel Ernest Edwards, chief of security at the Manzano facility. While many thought Bennewitz's photos were unremarkable, there is reason to believe that there were artifacts on the mountain. According to Doty, Archuleta Peak was used as a special operations training area during the 1970s until 1983. Military hardware was on the ground, as was a helicopter landing zone with landing lights. Without saying anything explicitly, he and his team nudged Bennewitz along in his belief that these were signs of an alien presence. In Doty's view, this was not part of an active counterintelligence operation against Bennewitz. "Paul made up his own mind as to what he saw."[71]

It is also true, however, that other people have trekked to the area where Paul Bennewitz is said to have gone, and found absolutely nothing. One such researcher was Richard Sauder. Armed with notes of Bennewitz's that gave detailed locations to the various artifacts to be found as well as openings to underground facilities, Sauder searched diligently, but did not find a thing. Admittedly, his search took place in the early 1990s, a full decade after Bennewitz's direct involvement with Dulce, but nevertheless not a trace was found. It was Sauder's opinion that this was because there was in fact nothing to find. However, his own extensive research into underground bases and tunnels did lead him to speculate that a "Dulce" base might have been real, but in a location other than Dulce, New Mexico, possibly closer to Los Alamos.[72]

So perhaps military hardware was the answer to Dulce, or perhaps the answer is that there was nothing there all along. But some of Bennewitz's encounters while flying around Dulce were truly bizarre. One story comes from Ron Regehr, a MUFON research specialist who was employed by the company Aerojet to build the Defense Support Program (DSP) spy satellite. During the 1980s, Regehr and Bennewitz became friends, frequently discussing Bennewitz's research. Around 1985, Bennewitz told Regehr that he flew several times around Dulce in a helicopter with Colonel Edwards. On one occasion over Dulce, said Bennewitz, a silver spherical object approached them at a tremendous speed and came to within just a few feet away. Airborne radar had even tracked it as it approached. Regehr thereupon surprised the Colonel with a visit at his office, mentioning that Bennewitz had told him some "interesting stories" about their helicopter flight over Dulce. According to Regehr, Edwards immediately repeated the exact story that Bennewitz had told him. Years later, Regehr laughed when he recalled asking the Colonel whether he thought the object was "intelligently controlled." The Colonel merely looked at him as though he lacked all common sense. In Colonel Edwards's opinion, it was clear that the object was "not one of ours."[73]

Then there is the matter of the strange signals and 'messages' Bennewitz received that suggested an alien base was under Archuleta Peak. These were coming in as early as 1980, before Bennewitz was in the crosshairs of the national security establishment. How did he get these recordings, how was he getting them in English, and where were they coming from? The author discussed this matter with Regehr, who had received many of Bennewitz's notes, photographs, and drawings. Even after reviewing all the available data, Regehr was unsure how Bennewitz got the messages. It makes no sense that Bennewitz could translate an alien code into English. Regehr speculated that Bennewitz might have received a compressed English-language audio signal, then used his equipment to uncompress it.[74] That Bennewitz was using an analog computer could have been helpful, said Regehr, allowing him to process the data with more precision, albeit more slowly. If these were English-language messages, this would not necessarily rule out an alien origin (feasibly aliens could transmit English if they wanted), but of course it could well mean that Bennewitz had intercepted a deep black message that was not meant for his ears.

So much for the Dulce connection. What of the lights and 'things' seen over Kirtland and Manzano? To be sure, there was a great deal of classified activity there. Beneath Manzano was one of the world's largest repositories of nuclear weapons, stored within a labyrinthian system of tunnels and underground facilities. There was also an interesting piece of technology known as the Starfire Optical Range. This was an extremely advanced system used to resolve overhead satellites, presumably Soviet. It had the incredible ability to read serial numbers on satellites at a distance of 100 miles traveling at 20,000 mph, and possibly to disable them.[75] Another interesting piece of technology at Kirtland was a large electromagnetic platform used to test aircraft vulnerability to electromagnetic pulses, similar to what would be encountered in a nuclear blast. It is feasible that some of the things Bennewitz saw had to do with these technologies. Yet, other people were seeing aerial displays that appeared to go far beyond these. Perhaps Bennewitz, too, was seeing and detecting something more exotic, be it homegrown flying saucers developed in the deep black, or technology belonging to other beings altogether who came by now and then to observe all the commotion.

Adding to the intrigue are rumors that a "Project Sigma," allegedly an NSA program to communicate with non-humans, was based at least in part out of Kirtland AFB since the 1960s, or even earlier. In a communication with the author, Linda Moulton Howe stated that she personally had been shown from a distance an NSA structure at Kirtland that was said to house Project Sigma. According to her source, Sigma operated by sending out various Hertz signals identified as operational with Grey, Nordic, or other craft. If Sigma was in fact real, this could easily explain Bennewitz's sightings, which would be alien craft attracted by the signals being generated. And if Bennewitz did stumble onto Project Sigma, surely this would have been more than sufficient cause for MJ-12 to order an immediate end to the threat this posed.[76]

Bennewitz was convinced he had stumbled onto a grave matter. Toward the end of the decade, he become so tightly wound that he suffered an emotional and mental collapse. In 1980, however, there is no evidence that he was unhinged, nor that he could concoct such a detailed fantasy, regardless of his personal beliefs. His notes of this period are sophisticated, clear, and precise. His scientific skills were well appreciated by those who knew him, including the many military personnel and officers he dealt with. It is entirely possible that Paul Bennewitz obtained genuine English language transmissions and saw genuine UFOs over Kirtland and Manzano. Unfortunately, the full truth of the matter may never be known outside the classified world, if it is known anywhere.

Moore Slides Deeper

During the late fall of 1980, while Bennewitz was getting the attention of the NSA and AFOSI, William Moore met again with his mysterious connection, "Falcon," in an Albuquerque restaurant. This time he was introduced to none other than Richard Doty. Moore was annoyed because he had been given bogus leads by his contact when they had met the previous month. He wanted to know what was going on. Falcon told him he had "passed the test." Moore now learned his job would be to track selected UFO researchers and report their opinions. Falcon repeated that he represented an elite group that was unhappy with UFO secrecy. He told Moore that Doty would be his main contact.

On November 17, the same day that Doty met with Bennewitz, Moore also met with Doty at Kirtland AFB. Doty brought Moore to a video screen which displayed classified communications before they were printed on a teletype. According to what Moore later remembered, the documents originated from AFOSI headquarters at Bolling AFB in Washington, D.C. The text described a detailed analysis of Bennewitz's photos and film. It also stated that the NSA was monitoring Bennewitz, and that a "Project Aquarius" was classified Top Secret with access limited to a group called MJ-12. Just what was Project Aquarius? Or, for that matter, MJ-12?[77]

There are two basic positions one can take as to what was going on here. One is that, as Falcon told Moore, there was a faction within the intelligence community that wanted to end UFO secrecy, but had to do it safely. Selected bits and pieces of information would be released to Moore. Accordingly, the release of the occasional misinformation – perhaps better described simply as variations of specific documents – would be to track the actual progress and destinations of the leaked information.

The other position is that Moore was being used to confuse the UFO research field, and was simply being fed lies. Indeed, Moore would soon be giving a tampered version of the Aquarius document to Bennewitz. If we consider this second scenario, we must ask what was being protected? Was it the thoroughly terrestrial programs that were being compromised by Bennewitz? Or did it include the objects that were being seen over Kirtland and Manzano, as well as the transmissions Bennewitz was recording? People were, after all, seeing strange, inexplicable objects over the area.

It is well to remember that interference with Bennewitz seemed to fit with a pattern emerging elsewhere against other UFO researchers, like Leonard Stringfield. It could be that the recent revelations obtained through FOIA, the leaks that passed through Stringfield, Howe's documentary linking animal mutilations to extraterrestrials, the interest in the crash at Roswell, and now Bennewitz's obsession with alien implants and messages, were becoming real threats to UFO secrecy, threats that needed to be disabled.

Toward this end, the infiltration of APRO by the intelligence community is worth noting. In 1980, Moore was APRO's most prominent member. The Lorenzens were aware that he had connections to the world of intelligence, and had known for a long time that their group was being watched. Without getting into specifics, Moore had told them several times about his connections. They urged him to continue "but keep APRO out of it." Doty claimed that APRO was "full of people" on the Air Force payroll, and Moore also said that "two or three" other APRO researchers had arrangements with the Air Force similar to his own. None of these other individuals ever came forward, even if some – such as researcher Kevin Randle – were known to be members of APRO at the same time as being members of the U.S. Air Force.[78]

Cases at the End of 1980

The relative lull of UFOs that started in 1979 continued through most of 1980. However, a flurry of encounters began in October. Paul Dong recorded 33 UFO reports from China during the last three months of the year. In northern China, people in Tianjin saw several objects over a major power plant and oil field. At 3 a.m. on October 5, five off-duty metalworkers at the Dagang oilfield saw a cone-shaped, red, glowing object. It lit the area below, and workers felt a scorching heat as it flew by and disappeared over the Bohai Sea.[79] On October 16, during the approach of an aircraft at the Tianjin airport, radar picked up a second target. It gave a strong, distinct echo, seemed to cause strong radio interference as the airplane touched down, but was not seen visually.[80] By November, the official China news agency announced that a government association was being set up to study UFOs throughout the country.[81] For China, a land so isolated for centuries, there was no longer any turning back.

Also interesting was a flap of sightings occurring in Britain, several of which involved the Royal Air Force. One undated event from November concerned RAF Neatishead, Norfolk, when ground-based radar tracked an object executing aerial maneuvers that "defied all convention." The object was seen by an RAF Phantom pilot, who described it as very bright and directly in front of him. Senior RAF personnel questioned witnesses and confiscated the radar tapes. Another event occurred on November 25, when a glowing orange ball maneuvered around an oil platform in the North Sea at 6:40 a.m. The RAF dispatched a Nimrod aircraft to the area, but no conclusions were ever officially reached.[82]

One of the oddest UFO events of the period was a series of aerial encounters over Spain that took place exactly one year to the day after a previous aerial encounter in that country. In this case, not one but *seven* commercial aircraft encountered an inexplicable green sphere that moved intelligently and with incredible capabilities. This took place in the northeastern portion of the Iberian Peninsula on November 11, 1980. The aircraft involved were an Iberia 727 flying from the province of Asturias to Barcelona; another Iberia 727 en route from Barcelona to Athens; two Iberia 727s flying shuttle services between Madrid and Barcelona; a British airliner en route from England to Alicante; an air-taxi from Palma de Mallorca bound for Marseilles; and a Transeuropa aircraft en route from the Balearic Islands to Bordeaux. Spanish journalist Juan J. Benitez investigated the cases, determining that either seven identical UFOs were involved, or a single object was responsible, one that was capable of traveling hundreds of miles within minutes. Captain Ramos of the Asturias-Barcelona flight told Benitez that at 6:40 p.m., a green light appeared from his 10 o'clock position, moving at a near collision course toward the airliner. Ramos, along with his co-pilot and two flight mechanics, watched in apprehension as the bright green light approached, appearing like a sphere or "soap bubble." He dove his aircraft 300 or 400 feet, as the sphere crossed in front of him and moved south. Other lights became visible, in particular a second, smaller, "ball." Barcelona flight control informed Ramos that the only other traffic in the area was an English aircraft bound for Alicante. Shortly after this encounter, the captain of the Transeuropa reported "green traffic" on his route.

According to Benitez, the curious thing was that this same fast-flying bright green sphere was seen at the same time from five other aircraft, each at different points in the northeastern part of Spain. In one case, while one aircraft was approaching the Barcelona Airport, the sphere came right down and buzzed the runway. It then shot straight up into the sky. The event left Benitez to conclude that the objects were "machines crewed by beings that have nothing whatsoever to do with our world." Perhaps – but perhaps also by beings that had a great deal to do with this world, but who were not openly recognized by the human power structure of 1980.[83]

Encounters in Rendlesham Forest

The Rendlesham Forest incident remains, decades after it occurred, among the most important and controversial UFO cases ever. Important because it involved a landing of an unknown craft near two Air Bases in Britain,* was witnessed by many U.S. military personnel, and is supported by military documentation. In addition, the area held a large stock of nuclear weapons, a fact that was denied by authorities for years, then admitted to be true. Yet the case remains controversial because proponents have not agreed on certain key details, and other critics have claimed it has wholly prosaic explanations. Not only this, but additional confusion has plagued the case in matters so simple as the exact dates when it occurred. A large part of this stems from the primary military document associated with the case, prepared by Deputy Base Commander Lt. Colonel Charles Halt. This was written from memory several weeks later, left a great deal out, and ascribed the wrong dates to the major events. In addition, the witnesses that did come forward did not all do so at the same time (sometimes doing so under pseudonyms), and only slowly offered key details of their experience. Nevertheless, the incredible detail provided by so many witnesses, much of which is well corroborated, makes it clear that something extraordinary happened.[84]

Rendlesham – The First Encounter

On the night of December 25/26, 1980,** while a Christmas party was in progress at one of the air bases, Airman First Class John Burroughs and Staff Sergeant Budd Steffens (although one account substitutes Steffens with Dule) were stationed at RAF Woodbridge's back gate, known as the East Gate. Burroughs noticed strange lights above the Rendlesham Forest, near the base, so they drove out for a better look. The lights were closer than they initially realized, and flickered in red, yellow, and green. As they continued to drive, a large white light appeared to come from the main object and move along the forest boundary parallel to them. It seemed very close. Feeling nervous, they returned to the East Gate and called for backup.[85]

Staff Sergeant James Penniston and Airman First Class Edward Cabansag soon arrived at the East Gate. Burroughs and Steffens explained the

---

* The Woodbridge and Bentwaters sister Air Force bases. Bentwaters was north of the forest; Woodbridge was south.

** Some accounts have this as the night of December 26/27.

situation, and Penniston assumed that a plane had crashed. "It didn't crash," replied Steffens, "it landed." Steffens stayed behind while Penniston, Burroughs, and Cabansag drove off. At a certain point while going into the forest, the road became too rough, so Burroughs and Penniston got out and walked. Cabansag stayed behind to act as a relay for radio communication.

As the two men approached the lights, animals seemed unusually active, things seemed odd. They received a radio transmission stating that an unknown object had been tracked over their base and disappeared on radar a short while earlier. Deep in the forest and approaching the strange lights, Penniston realized that he smelled no burning fuel, nor found any sign of a plane crash. A field of static electricity seemed to envelop them, making their hair stand on end. Then they lost radio contact. By now they noticed a small, shiny object with a bank of blue lights, motionless in a clearing. "It was unbelievable," said Burroughs. Although he never got close enough to see it as a solid object, Burroughs said that the light configuration gave the image of a craft. He thought it may have been a machine under intelligent control or a bizarre natural phenomenon. "What I do know," he said, "is that it was nothing mundane. There are no words that can adequately describe the wonder of what we saw."[86]

Burroughs and Penniston moved closer (although only Penniston consciously remembered details, while Burroughs later concluded that his memory was blocked.) Penniston remembered coming to within ten feet of it and paused. It was definitely a craft of some sort, about ten feet (three meters) long and seven feet high. In dead silence, he observed the object, then walked around it. It looked like "smooth, opaque, black glass." Bluish lights were visible, as was strange writing or symbols. He had brought a notebook, so he decided to write:

> Triangular in shape. The top portion is producing mainly white light, which encompasses most of the upper section of the craft. A small amount of white light peers out the bottom. At the left side center is a bluish light, and on the other side, red. The lights seem to be molded as part of the exterior of the structure, smooth, slowly fading into the rest of the outside of the structure, gradually molding into the fabric of the craft.[87]

According to one of Penniston's statements, he took out his camera and began "snapping photo after photo." Before long, all 36 exposures had been taken.[*] He became bolder and touched the object. The symbols felt inscribed or engraved, "like a diamond cut on glass." When he did this, the white light on the object grew intensely bright. Penniston jumped back, as

---

[*] There is no clear statement as to what happened to the photos.

did Burroughs who was still nearby. They threw themselves to the ground. The craft lifted silently and then slowly worked its way around the trees. Then it rose above the trees and was gone in the "blink of an eye."

Everything became normal again. The static electricity was gone, radios functioned normally, and the lighthouse beacon was clearly visible in the distance. Both Penniston and Burroughs thought they saw more lights, and walked for another 300 yards towards them before deciding they had been out too long. On the way back, Burroughs noticed three indentations in the forest floor, right where the object was first seen. Then they found Cabansag, who from a much greater distance had apparently seen what they saw, although with much less detail.

At the base, their shift commander advised them to keep quiet about their experience. Still, since radar had confirmed *something* to be out there, he suggested they look for proof of what happened. The next morning, Burroughs and Penniston inspected the site (Burroughs hoped to find nothing in order to dismiss the whole affair). Several trees had broken tops and three holes were found in the frozen soil in a triangular formation, an inch and a half deep and seven inches in diameter, matching the location of the legs seen beneath the UFO. Penniston even made plaster casts of the indentations. Ground traces with radioactive readings were also found. Skeptics later challenged the significance of the radiation. Nick Pope, however, who ran the "UFO Desk" in the British Ministry of Defence during the 1990s, said the radiation levels were ten times higher than expected. In addition to these ground readings, an A-10 aircraft flew over the site the following morning and detected infra-red radiation.

At 10:30 a.m., RAF Bentwaters called the Suffolk Constabulary, who met with Penniston and Burroughs. According to Penniston, the police officer refused to write any information relating to a UFO incident, only that there were "strange lights" that could have been from the nearby lighthouse and that the landing marks looked like "rabbit scratchings." Penniston tried to explain that he had seen an actual craft, and that the three indentations were identical and equidistant. The officer would not listen.

Incidentally, John Burroughs has never been able fully to recover his memory about what happened to him as he approached the strange object that night. In 2008, he communicated with Linda Moulton Howe, who arranged for him to work with a professional hypnotherapist. Through a hypnotic regression session, Burroughs recovered more details about his experience. This time he remembered that he, like Penniston, had approached the craft very closely, and even thought the lights of the craft might be "alive."

Rendlesham – The Second Encounter

Then, on the night of December 27-28, security personnel saw strange lights floating in the sky above the forest. Lt. Col. Charles Halt, Deputy Base Commander at USAF Woodbridge, led a team to the area. He had heard the rumors about Penniston's and Burroughs's encounter, and "was determined to put an end to this nonsense." He brought a Geiger counter, gas powered arc lights, and a microcassette recorder. In the woods, the Orford Ness Lighthouse and the Shipwash lightship were both easily visible. Something seemed to be interfering with their equipment. The light-alls failed even after different ones were brought back from the base. The radios were problematic, as well, according to Halt: all the frequencies were intermittent, and none worked properly.[88]

At 1:48 a.m., a group of men, including John Burroughs and Sergeant Adrian Bustinza, saw a glowing light resting on a pillar of yellowish mist. Before long, Halt saw it. It has been claimed that the Orford Ness Lighthouse, which is six miles away from Rendlesham Forest, was the source of the pulsing light. Halt disagreed, stating that they could see the lighthouse distinctly, off to the side of the main light by about 30 degrees. "This object was no lighthouse," he said. "It was dancing about in the forest, woods and all."[89]

Halt's cassette recording (which ran for 20 minutes and covered a span of over three hours) conveyed the excitement as well as the data. "Okay," Halt spoke into the tape,

> ... we're looking at the thing, we're probably about two or three hundred yards. It looks like an eye winking at you. It's still moving from side to side and when you put the star scope [a night vision device] on it, it's like this thing has a hollow center, a dark center.[90]

The object flashed so brightly through the star scope, Halt said, that it almost burned his eyes. There was a noticeable field of static electricity as well. The object then maneuvered out of the forest to the middle of a farmer's field, and Halt's group pursued it. It was yellow and red, and seemed to be throwing off sparks -- Halt later likened it to "molten metal." According to Sergeant Monroe Nevilles, "it looked like a large brick" through night vision goggles. "The heat was coming off it. Every once in a while it would flash, throwing off sparks."[91]

What happened next is disputed. According to Adrian Bustinza, who had left for Woodbridge and then returned, Halt was with 20 to 30 other men near this object. They had managed to get very close to it and had apparently surrounded it – something plausible if the object had been in the field long enough. Halt denied this, simply claiming that the group watched the pulsating object move through the trees to the farmer's field, then silently explode with a bright flash. At that point, it separated into three to five white lights, all but one of which quickly disappeared. One hovered motionless and began to shine laser-like beams of light down all over the forest and RAF Woodbridge. According to Halt:

> It sort of danced about in the sky and it sent down beams of light.... falling different places on the base.... The people in the Weapons storage area and several other places on the base also reported the lights.... [The beam] stayed on for about 5-10 seconds and just as abruptly as it came, it disappeared...

Other objects became visible, making high-speed angular movements. Witness Sergeant Bobby Ball later recalled that the objects appeared to be searching for something, as if they were performing a grid search.[92] Halt called on his radio to learn if radar had picked up anything. He heard voices on the other end saying that beams were coming down on the base. Halt had no idea what these beams were, and he was concerned. For years, there were claims that the beams penetrated the Weapons Storage Area at Woodbridge, and even that the beams disabled some or all of the nuclear weapons stored there. Given the history of UFOs and their proximity to nuclear weapons, it is certainly plausible. Indeed, according to the statement of Rendlesham researcher Peter Robbins, this is exactly what happened. In February 1993, Robbins and Larry Warren interviewed Charles Halt. According to Robbins, Halt admitted to them that the beams of light from the UFO somehow penetrated the alternating layers of steel, earth, and concrete of the hardened bunkers. Ultimately they reached the secured areas where the weapons were stored, "adversely affecting the ordinance," in the words of Halt. Although Halt has never confirmed this statement, Robbins stands by it "absolutely."[93]

The men stayed out until after 4 a.m. Incidentally, photos taken that night of the landing site came out fogged, according to the base's photography lab, although Halt suspected that the photos were simply switched out.

Halt wrote a memo of the incident dated January 13, 1981. The document is of great significance in that it clearly describes how on two separate occasions a UFO was seen by base military personnel. However, Halt suggested that there was much he left out of that report, and the biggest part appears to have been the story of Larry Warren.

Rendlesham – The Third Encounter

Larry Warren was a member of the USAF Security Police who had been posted to RAF Bentwaters in early December 1980. Indeed, it was his account in 1983 that first made the story public. Obtaining certainty about which night Warren had his encounter, however, is difficult. For some time he believed it took place on the night of December 29/30, although he later corrected it to 28/29. There is even the possibility that his encounter took place the same night as Halt's, which would mean that there were two nights of UFO activity over the base, not three.[94]

Warren was on security duty ("guard mount") at a Bentwaters Perimeter Post 18, apparently on the night of December 28/29. Having just returned from leave, he was unaware of the recent strangeness near the base. Shortly before midnight, he heard radio transmissions about "some funny looking lights bobbing up and down" over the forest near RAF Woodbridge. He saw nothing unusual, but soon heard the hooves of panic-stricken deer running past him. Five minutes later, a security vehicle arrived at his post. Sergeant Adrian Bustinza was driving with a Second Lieutenant Englund and two other security officers. Warren was relieved of his post, got into the truck, and drove to the Bentwaters motor pool with the group. On the way, he heard radio communications from Woodbridge requesting that the Wing Commander, Colonel Gordon Williams, be contacted. More vehicles were at Bentwaters' main gate, and Warren's group joined them in a convoy toward Woodbridge.

RAF Woodbridge teemed with activity. Warren's convoy turned left at the East Gate and continued down the dirt road track which eventually led to a large clearing named Capel Green. Other vehicles and personnel were already there, and one group was walking down a narrow trail into the woods. Other officers came to the group, and the men were given weapons and ordered to maintain silence. They were then directed into the woods "to investigate a disturbance." Warren checked his watch; it was 12:30 a.m.

They walked deep into a densely wooded area, experiencing an increasing static electricity charge in the air as they advanced. They soon came to a large field where about forty or so military personnel had gathered. The men were ordered to surround what appeared to be a bright fog or mist. When his group entered the field, Warren saw it was a glowing, yellow-green circular object, not more than a foot in height. At times it almost seemed transparent. Two officers walked around it with Geiger counters, someone took photographs, others operated movie cameras. Radios were active, and he heard what sounded like a pilot stating, "Here it comes. Here it comes. Here it comes." In the distance, over the North Sea, Warren saw a small red light. This light approached his group far too fast and silently to be any aircraft he knew. Warren checked his watch again; it was 1:30 a.m.

The red light cleared the trees bordering the field and made a downward arc until it was directly over the illuminated object. It hovered at twenty feet above the ground, roughly the size of a basketball, and of an unusual shade of red. It then exploded in a blinding flash which gave off no heat. Now, instantly, less than 25 feet away from Warren, was a large, pyramid-shaped object, topped by a glowing red light. He described the main body as 'pearl white, with a rainbow-color effect.' Somehow, its appearance was distorted, and it was easiest to see by peripheral vision. At the base was a bank of intensely bright blue lights. Warren thought he saw landing gear. Covering the entire surface were what looked like boxes and pipes, but no identifying markings, windows, or doors. It looked solid and heavy.

Cameras continued to film, and the men were ordered to maintain a tight cordon around the area. An officer ordered Bustinza and Warren, who was now feeling nauseous, to follow him as he approached the object. Carrying their Geiger counters, they came to within ten or fifteen feet of the object, and Warren's eyes watered profusely. Before long they were ordered back to their positions. Warren saw military personnel confiscate the camera of a British police officer who had taken pictures, and heard the argument that ensued.

Suddenly a staff car arrived, carrying Colonel Gordon Williams and his staff. Most were in civilian clothing, including Williams. Now, from behind the object, came a bright bluish ball of light. It moved slowly and deliberately just off the ground, then stopped. That was when, according to Warren, he and Bustinza noticed something inside the glowing ball – what looked initially like children. However, Warren could tell by their large heads and "catlike" dark eyes that these were not human beings. He could not make out any other facial features, but noticed their bright silvery clothing.

Warren observed Colonel Williams slowly approach these beings. Just five feet apart, they stared at each other. No conversation could be heard, but Warren believed they were communicating, though not in any conventional sense. Another officer handed Williams something. Soon after, men began to leave the field, and Warren's group was told to return to the trucks. As Warren walked back into the woods, he turned around one last time to see the object and entities. Warren arrived back at Central

Security Control at 4:30 a.m. His eyes hurt, he had a bad taste in his mouth, and heard a ringing sound in his ears. Looking in a mirror, he noticed a shock of gray hair. He was relieved from duty, went to his room, and collapsed.

Warren also stated that the next morning he and other witnesses were soon ordered to appear at the Bentwaters law-enforcement desk at 11:00 a.m. Once there, Major Malcolm Zickler told the men they were going to be debriefed concerning what they had experienced the night before. A long counter held numerous documents arranged in stacks. Warren and the others were told to sign them, though not given time to read them fully. It was clear they were agreeing that what they had seen were unusual lights in the forest and nothing else. One airman protested, but was told to sign them and go into the office. Two rows of folding chairs had been set up and a movie screen stood at the front of the room. A projector sat on a desk toward the rear of the room already loaded with a reel of film.

Three men stood in a corner of the room. A uniformed Commander from the Office of Naval Intelligence (ONI) introduced himself, then introduced two men in suits from the Air Force Security Service (USAFSS). The Navy commander told Warren and other men that, among other things, what they had seen in the forest "represented technology far advanced to our own." Numerous civilizations, he said, visit this planet, and some have a "permanent presence here." The debriefing concluded with the screening of films composed of wing camera footage from World War II and Korea, on the ground in Vietnam, and allegedly on the Moon, all of which included UFOs. Prior to the film it had been made clear to the men that keeping the secret would help their careers, but it would be no problem if anyone talked, since "bullets are cheap." Everyone laughed, but the threat was real.

There was a final part to Warren's involvement with this affair. He received a phone call in his barracks dormitory instructing him to be outside in twenty minutes to get into a car. Warren did as ordered, and also saw Adrian Bustinza there. Two men wearing civilian clothing got out of the car, and Warren and Bustinza entered. The interior was unusually bright, with a greenish glow. As Warren got into the car, "everything went black." He was in a semi-conscious state, feeling as though he had been anesthetized. The next thing he remembered was the engine of an A-10 taking off, and that he was on the Bentwaters flightline. He was then led out of the car and walked somewhere, then descended somewhere as if in an elevator. He felt a pressure change to his ears and lost consciousness again. When he awoke, he was in a small cafeteria-style dining area; other airmen were there, too, looking lost. Warren still felt heavily sedated. He walked along a hallway, clearly remembering rooms with high-tech machines and computers with technicians dressed in orange and blue uniforms. Two men in black SWAT-type uniforms led the small group of airmen through a large door which quietly opened. They entered a large, dimly lit room. The wall to Warren's left had a large glass or plexiglass window with glass sides for peripheral vision. The opening was about four feet wide, allowing only a few people at a time to enter. Warren stepped into the confined area and looked into a gigantic, dark, cavernous space – it strangely reminded him of the interior of the Houston Astrodome. Far below, he saw movement on a "liquid black floor," possibly people, and something very similar to the object he saw in the forest, resting in a far corner of the facility. He also saw other strange objects flying across his line of sight. To his right were curved tiled walls that looked wet, and three bands of light. One of his escorts said it was a tunnel that led to the North Sea.

Warren and presumably his companions were directed down a hallway to a small room with rows of cushioned chairs. He sat in the first row, next to Bustinza. Before them was a large translucent screen, and the men were somehow frozen into place. Behind the screen, Warren discerned the silhouette of a small, motionless figure. However, he felt a communication from it – it addressed him by his first name and demonstrated an intimate knowledge of his personal life. In his mind, Warren asked the being who it was, and it said it was from a place he would never understand, from a different reality. It said that he was in a facility far below the air bases, and there were apparently many such places with beings of its kind, accompanied by human support personnel. This particular facility had been there since the 1940s, and expanded during the 1960s. Their crafts entered and exited through an extensive tunnel system. Many civilizations from off-world were living here, and they had been intimate with the governments of the U.S., U.S.S.R, U.K., and Japan since World War Two. Its race had blended into human society at many levels. The being added that religion was created for the human race (a statement that disturbed Warren and which he refused to believe), that wars were fought for "human entertainment" (presumably as a way to keep human energies occupied),[95] that the Cold War was phoney, and that future battles would be fought in the Third

World.* The facility where Warren happened to be was one of many processing zones throughout the world. He and the other witnesses were "selected" because the beings "knew" them. The being mentioned something about politics and corporations and that Warren would not remember most of his experience, mainly for his own protection. It then said, "Larry, in your life, strive to remember."

Warren fell into blackness. When he regained consciousness, he was walking through a door and facing bright sunlight. He was disoriented, taken to a bus and brought to the dorm area. He strove to remember everything while at the same time trying to kill the memory. It was New Year's Eve, December 31, 1980.

Warren's claims of many military personnel at the scene, the extremely close encounter with the craft, the threats to keep silent, and his underground encounter were not mentioned in Halt's memo, and not surprisingly have been challenged by skeptics. Of course, it would not be surprising that Halt's memo left out some of the more striking details – something that, years later, Halt acknowledged. Finally, there is the possibility that Warren and others who were debriefed were subjected to some form of mind altering processes.

That Warren's account differs from the other witnesses may not be a major problem. Nick Pope pointed out that police agencies have long understood that witnesses do not always see events in the same way.** After Warren's book, *Left at East Gate,* was published, Pope spent a great deal of time with him and co-author Peter Robbins, and the three frequently discussed the case. Pope was "personally convinced" that Warren was there, and "witness to some quite extraordinary activity." It was equally clear to Pope that what Warren witnessed was not referred to in Halt's memo.[96]

Rendlesham – "No Defence Significance"

Warren's account made the press in October 1983. In 1984, a poor copy of Halt's tape came into the hands of researchers. The audio quality was poor, but a better copy eventually became available and was transcribed for Georgina Bruni's *You Can't Tell the People*, published in 2000. Over the years, the case gained a great deal of attention. Lord Hill-Norton, former

---

* This would mean, of course, that the human species had been controlled and manipulated for eons by non-human intelligences – with an agenda, moreover, that most humans would undoubtedly see as harmful to humanity's best interests.

** Indeed, in this case, there is the distinct possibility that not all of these airmen even experienced the same events, even though they were in exactly the same geographic location.

Chief of the Defense Staff and Admiral-of-the-Fleet, inquired with Secretary of State for Defence Michael Heseltine about it. Heseltine released the statement to Hill-Norton that "the events to which you refer were of no defence significance." Hill-Norton replied that "there would seem to be some defence significance either in an unknown object's entering and possibly landing on British territory or, alternatively, a deputy base commander of an RAF/USAF base filing a ludicrous and make-believe report." In November 1983, Heseltine wrote to British M.P. Merlyn Rees: "... that there is not a grain of truth in the allegation that there has been a 'cover up' about alleged UFO sightings... nor was any unidentified object seen on radar." Researching this contention, Nick Redfern received proof that Heseltine's statement was completely wrong. Squadron Leader (for Officer Commanding) E. E. Webster confirmed to Redfern in an official RAF correspondence dated October 25, 1988, that their log book showed that a UFO was reported by RAF Bentwaters at 0325 GMT on 28 December 1980.[97]

Detractors of the case, most notably science writer Ian Ridpath, argued that the nearby Orford Ness Lighthouse can create the impression of a light hovering just above the ground, especially so during the misty weather of the nights in question. If a UFO had been present, he suggested, the men should have reported two sources of light, e.g. the lighthouse and the actual UFO. He further argued that on the Halt tape, one can hear an airman call out "there it is again...there it is," with the same frequency at which the lighthouse flashes. The radiation readings, argued Ridpath were also questionable, as the equipment used by Halt's team was not intended to measure background radiation; therefore the readings at the low end of the measurement scale were meaningless.[98] Further claims were made that the so-called landing marks were simply rabbit diggings. Moreover, Dr. John Mason, who collected reports of meteor sightings for the British Astronomical Association, said that a meteor "almost as bright as the full Moon" flew over southern England at exactly the time of the initial reports of a bright object landing in the forest. UFO researcher Steuart Campbell suggested that the meteorite, which was actually hundreds of miles away over the North Sea, was mistakenly interpreted by guards to be an aircraft crashing in the forest. Campbell also suggested that the object later seen by Halt and his men was the Shipwash lightship, and the unusual lights in the sky were bright planets. Other explanations for the incident have included a downed Soviet spy satellite or a nuclear incident.

Hoax theories have always been prominent in relation to the case. In

2005, the BBC reported that a former U.S. security policeman, Kevin Conde, claimed responsibility for creating strange lights in the forest by driving around in a police vehicle whose lights he had modified. Later, however, Conde said he believed his prank took place at another time, and was "not the source of this specific incident."[99]

While acknowledging multiple possible explanations for a UFO event can be a virtue, the skeptical case hinges entirely on assuming the incompetence of large numbers of military personnel, including a Deputy Base Commander, during multiple sightings. The amount of detail offered by the witnesses, including the transcript of Halt's recorded narrative, force the skeptical arguments to rely on numerous unrelated events that, frankly, do not match the explanatory power of multiple detailed and consistent first-hand accounts from the people who were there. As the years go by, the incident at Rendlesham Forest has continued to grow, not diminish, in its power as a bona fide UFO encounter.

The Cash-Landrum Incident

From opposite sides of the Atlantic Ocean, two important UFO events closed 1980, nearly simultaneously. The December 29 incident near Huffman, Texas, a few miles northeast of Houston, was important not merely for the sighting of the craft itself, but because of the military helicopters that followed it, the physical effects on the witnesses, and the obstinate stonewalling about it by the U.S. government.

While, across the ocean, the Rendlesham Forest was the scene of dramatic UFO activity, Betty Cash, Vickie Landrum, and Vickie's grandson Colby Landrum were driving in the State of Texas, on the Cleveland-Huffman Road on the way to the town of Dayton. At about 9 p.m., a bright, diamond-shaped object descended over the road ahead of them, a mere 25 feet from the ground. It made a beeping noise of some sort, and the three immediately felt tremendous heat coming from it. It was so bright that it lit up the night landscape and hurt their eyes. A row of blue lights ran across its center, and flames occasionally shot out from beneath it.

Betty stopped the car, and all three got out to look at the amazing object. Several helicopters were visible in the distance. Colby, who was just seven years old, was quickly frightened and returned to the car with his grandmother. Betty stayed outside and approached it in fascination. It gave off such intense heat that she returned to the car after only a few seconds. Despite it being mid-winter, she burned her hand on the door handle when she returned to the car. Inside the car, it was so hot that they turned on the air conditioning. The object continued to hover, bobbing slightly. When it rose and moved off to the southwest, Betty began to drive again. They saw it again soon enough, this time accompanied by more than 20 military helicopters, making a tremendous noise. Most of these were double-rotor helicopters, believed to be CH-47 Chinooks. A few smaller, single rotor helicopters were also there. Betty kept driving, and the three were able to watch the object and choppers for at least another ten minutes. She dropped Vickie and Colby off at their home, and arrived at her own home at 9:50 p.m.

Other people saw this spectacle. An oil worker in Dayton saw the object, describing it as diamond-shaped and "shooting brilliant blue flames out the back." An off-duty Dayton police officer and his wife saw the helicopters shortly after Betty, Vickie, and Colby had their experience.

The three main witnesses immediately exhibited symptoms consistent with radiation poisoning. Betty, who had the most exposure to the object, had the worst reactions. She suffered from severe headaches, nausea, diarrhea, swelling of the neck, and red blotches on her face and head. Some days later, her eyes swelled shut and the blotches became blisters. She was hospitalized for two weeks as a burn victim, losing patches of skin from her face and much of her hair. Vickie and Colby had similar symptoms that did not require hospitalization.

In February 1981, Betty asked NASA if the agency had flown an unusual craft that night. Not surprisingly, the answer was no, but a NASA representative referred her to John Schuessler as a private party who might be able to help her. In addition to being MUFON's Deputy Director, Schuessler was a Project Manager for Space Shuttle Flight Operations with McDonnell Douglas Corporation. He took a very active role in investigating the case, receiving some help from aerospace scientist Alan Holt. It was obvious that an extremely unusual high performance vehicle had been in the area, an object that moved like a helicopter but did so without propellers, or indeed any known means of propulsion. This object was highly radioactive, and presumably was nuclear powered.

Betty later developed breast cancer which required a mastectomy. Eventually, she, Vickie, and Colby hired Peter Gersten to sue the U.S. government for damages. The problem was that no government agency took responsibility for the helicopters, to say nothing of the UFO itself. The Air Force stated in 1983 that "our investigation has revealed no evidence of involvement by any military personnel, equipment, or aircraft in this alleged incident." Schuessler described stonewalling by the military that was simply outrageous, especially to such trusting, patriotic citizens as Betty Cash and Vickie Landrum. The case never went to trial because the judge simply refused to hear it.[100]

A case can be made that this was an experimental military vehicle gone awry. While it is not unusual for witnesses to experience real physical effects from UFOs, this was obvious radiation poisoning. Several sources claimed that the craft was one of "ours." Richard Doty and William Moore claimed the machine was a nuclear powered antigravity craft on a test mission that developed engine problems.[101] Researcher Tom Adams met a military source who claimed to have been one of the helicopter pilots during the event. He had been stationed at Fort Hood, and told Adams about a special alert that occurred in late December 1980. He and other pilots were vectored to a location where they would see an "unusual aircraft flying below radar," where they would have to "go visual." As he understood the mission, it was to "force the object to land or keep it at a low altitude." Within the large group were four contact teams responsible for securing the area if the craft came down. At the targeted area, he said he saw "the biggest damn diamond I have ever seen in my life! I have no idea what the object was." The helicopters followed it for seven to ten miles at a very low altitude. Then the object stopped producing sparks, became stationary in the air, and began to glow. The pilots received orders to abort the mission and return to their various bases. After returning to Fort Hood, he was told the craft was an experimental aircraft which had experienced problems and gone astray.[102]

Schuessler's opinion evolved from an initial hunch that it was a secret military project to the belief that it was extraterrestrial. "I imagine some UFOs are part of classified military operations," he stated later. But he saw no evidence that the U.S. military was developing diamond-shaped objects remotely like the Huffman, Texas object. "The best way to evaluate this situation is to consider that we are not flying disc shaped aircraft. The only ones ever built didn't exceed 200 mph. We do not fly cigar-shaped vehicles, other than rockets and missiles. We do not fly half mile wide triangular craft that can hover and then shoot away at lightspeed. We do not fly spherical aircraft, other than balloons that can move only with the wind, not against it."

Whatever the provenance of the object, the Cash-Landrum case is significant. The object which injured Betty Cash, Vickie Landrum, and Colby Landrum was able to fly using principles and technology beyond what officially existed in 1980. That by itself warrants attention. In addition, the stonewalling and obstruction by the U.S. government gives reason to believe that somebody, somewhere in a position of power knew more than they were telling.

Summary

Since its inception during the early cold war years, UFO research had undergone constant change. Still, the late 1970s had been transformative. The release of thousands of pages of government UFO documents, particularly in the aftermath of Watergate, made it clear that the only way to get truth from the government was by dedicated arm twisting. The results were energizing: the longstanding claims of a "cover-up" were shown to have merit. Some of the released documents indicated grave concern by responsible authorities about intrusions of sensitive airspace by UFOs. These documents described the objects just as thousands of civilian reports had done: as mechanical, technological objects far beyond what the science of the day seemed capable of producing. The "nuts and bolts" school of ufology was back in force.

Just as important were the leaks. While information from anonymous military insiders lacked the virtue of official confirmation, their collective value was obvious – as was their danger to the status quo. The various accounts coming to researchers like Leonard Stringfield, William Moore, Stanton Friedman, and others had a compelling consistency, and it seemed inevitable that one of these leaks could eventually enable a breakthrough of sorts, something that would lead to confirmation. By the end of 1980, some people believed that the Roswell case just might be The One. Then there was the investigation conducted by Paul Bennewitz, which was turning out to be a very high stakes affair.

But something else happened. Stringfield's sources suddenly began to dry up. Someone or some group was pressuring them into silence. At the same time, the intelligence community began cultivating Moore, offering the promise of inside information in return for reports on other UFO researchers. Moore hoped that he could navigate his way through the murky world of spooks and gather a few morsels of truth along the way. Perhaps the people he worked with were genuinely interested in helping him end UFO secrecy. Perhaps, too, they would provide him with disinformation that would muddy the ufological waters for years to come.

Air Force intelligence and the NSA also began to take notice of Paul Bennewitz, and indeed William Moore soon became one of the means by which they would spy on him. Bennewitz's case is perplexing. He was clearly photographing, seeing, and recording strange phenomena over a sensitive U.S. military installation. Somehow, he was 'translating' audio signals that suggested the existence of an alien base beneath Dulce's Archuleta Peak. Whether or not Bennewitz was accurately doing this, there is no evidence that these early signals were part of an intelligence disinformation campaign. That may well have come later, but it was these 1980 signals that placed Bennewitz in the crosshairs of the spooks.

Thus, the ufological victories of the late 1970s appear to have led to a program of surveillance and infiltration of UFO research by the intelligence community – a 'counter attack' of sorts.

Behind all of this were worldwide sightings of objects behaving in extraordinary and impossible ways. The global nature of these encounters was not yet fully appreciated by most western researchers: the Chinese and Soviet information in particular was still locked behind barriers of language and politics. Peaks of astonishing activity occurred in the spring of 1976 and again during the latter half of 1978. Explaining these as experimental or secret U.S. technology makes no sense, at least not in any conventional way of looking at the matter.

Is it possible that breakthroughs, in anti-gravity for instance, had been made within secret American installations? The leaked information available to researchers in 1980 did not provide much testimony to conclude in the affirmative. As the following chapters will demonstrate, however, testimony later arose that pointed to such programs, nearly all of which connected them to alien reverse-engineering efforts. But even if a breakthrough was made, say, in the early 1970s (as would be later claimed), could this account for the Spanish cases of 1976? Or the Valentich case? Or the encounters by so many national air forces, such as Chile, Peru, France, Britain, Italy, Austria, China, Iran, Kuwait, the Soviet Union, and the United States?

Perhaps the most suggestive new development in UFO sightings were the triangles. Although there was not, within the context of known 1970s technology, the capability to fly these objects in the manner witnesses reported, it is reasonable to conjecture that such devices were possible, given a secret development project. It is also suggestive that nearly all the reported triangle sightings during the 1970s occurred within the United States.

Still, it must be acknowledged that any of the difficult UFO sightings, including most of the triangles, involved capabilities that, quite simply, were not supposed to exist. Whether these events were human, alien, or both, the implications are clear: something very, very big was happening, and the official institutions of power and learning around the world were simply not talking about it.

Ronald Reagan was elected America's 40th President in November 1980, signifying a national political sea change. Even well before the end of the Carter administration, the great hope of Freedom of Information had been showing signs of sputtering out. Now, the advent of an administration far more friendly to the military establishment, while making a number of Americans happy for a variety of reasons, promised to put UFO research on the defensive. And yet, the 1980s were no dark age of UFOs. In a world in which the only constant was change itself, new opportunities would arise to take on the secret keepers.

Chapter 5

Cloak and Dagger
1981-1983

Something impossible according to the laws of physics.
— *Cosmonaut Vladimir Kovalyonok, on seeing a UFO while in Earth orbit in 1981*

I have long ago given up acquiring access to the so-called blue room at Wright-Patterson
. . . . this thing has gotten so highly classified . . . it is just impossible to get anything on it.
— *Senator Barry Goldwater (R-AZ), 1981*

Certain materials reported to have come from flying saucer crashes were extremely light and very tough. I am sure our laboratories analyzed them very carefully.
— *Retired defense scientist Dr. Robert Sarbacher, 1983.*

Trans en Provence

While Rendlesham is widely understood to be Britain's most important UFO case, another major case took place in France less than two weeks later. It involved a close encounter by a reliable witness, physical trace evidence, and extensive investigation by qualified scientists. Although less dramatic than Rendlesham, the physical evidence it left behind makes it the most important case in French ufology.

At his home near Nice during the afternoon of January 8, 1981, 55 year-old Renato Niccolai heard a whistling sound outside and went to investigate. On the edge of his property, just above the trees about 250 feet away, he saw an object that looked like two saucers, one upside down against the other. It was dull grey and about four or five feet high. The object landed in his field of wild alfalfa, but stayed on the ground only briefly. He soon heard the whistling sound again, louder this time. The object rose to treetop height and shot off to the northeast. Before it left, he noticed additional details, including landing feet and trap doors.

Niccolai told his wife and the police, who arrived within 24 hours. They in turn notified France's official UFO investigative body, GEPAN, part of the Centre National d"Etudes Spatiales (CNES). They found a circle on the ground about seven feet in diameter; nearby plants looked diseased or damaged. Several laboratories studied plant and soil samples, showing consistent and bizarre results. The leaves in the affected area had lost 30% to 50% of their chlorophyll pigment. Scientists could not duplicate this effect, even with radiation. Speculation centered on "some type of electric energy field" causing the damage. Niccolai was interviewed many times, with no indications of mental issues, dishonesty, or even exaggeration. Forty days after the event, traces of the craft's impact were still perceptible.

GEPAN produced a 66-page report, concluding that "a significant physical phenomenon had indeed interacted with the environment at the site, producing abrasions, thermal impact and unexplained effects on plants." A few years later, Jacques Vallee conducted a follow-up investigation. He interviewed the witness and his wife, studied the landing site, and brought original soil samples from the earlier investigation to an American laboratory. These results were consistent with the original analysis, and added that there was no residue that could have come from tractors or other farming equipment, such as cement powder, oil, or chemical contaminants. The event remained unexplained.[1]

Thus, it appears that a small disc-shaped craft had landed in southeastern France, and its pilot did not want to interact with, or be seen by, the locals. It traveled by an unknown, but extremely efficient, means of propulsion. It was also apparently dangerous, judging by the dramatic effect it had on plant life after only a brief landing. Perhaps this helps to explain the pilot's skittishness.

The Reagan Administration

Ronald Reagan was elected president in November 1980, and took office on January 20, 1981. In many respects, Reagan's views were a throwback to the 1950s. Courting Christian evangelicals, he argued that the liberalism of the 1960s and 1970s was a mistake, and that the nation needed to return to 'family values.' Reagan the candidate was also the quintessential anti-elitist – as much as a former Governor of California could be. He had attacked Jimmy Carter's many connections to the Trilateral Commission and Council on Foreign Relations, the two most obvious "insider" organizations. In similar manner, he attacked competitor George Bush (who had belonged to both the Trilateral Commission and CFR until 1979). Reagan even promised that Bush would never receive a position in his government.[2]

Rhetoric was one thing; reality another. Reagan may have believed some of that rhetoric, but even during his California governor days in the 1960s, he had surrounded himself with Rockefeller men.[3] Early on in his journey to the White House, Reagan replaced his campaign manager with longtime CFR member William Casey. During the summer of 1980, he shocked his supporters by choosing Bush as his running-mate. In September 1980, Reagan gave a "Prelude to Victory" party at which the ultimate power player, David Rockefeller, sat to Reagan's immediate right.[4] Following his election, his 59-member transition team consisted of 28 CFR members, at least 10 Trilateralists, and 10 Bilderbergers. His most important cabinet appointees were all CFR members: Alexander Haig (State), Casper Weinberger (Defense), Donald Regan (Treasury), and William Casey (CIA). Reagan selected James A. Baker III to be his chief of staff; Baker had not only been the campaign manager for George Bush, but was from a family long associated with Rockefeller oil interests.[5] Reagan may have campaigned against the elite, but checkmating him proved easy enough.

On March 30, 1981, just two months after taking office, Ronald Reagan was struck and almost killed by an assassin's bullet, an event that would have put George Bush into the Oval Office. The would-be assassin, John W. Hinckley, Jr., was portrayed as a lunatic who was obsessed with the actress Jodie Foster. Hinckley's ties to the Bush family were hardly mentioned in news reports. His father was a Texas oilman and longtime friend of George Bush. His brother Scott was scheduled to have dinner with Bush's son Neil on the evening of March 30. When a journalist asked Vice President Bush of the connections between the two families, and whether Bush might have known the younger Hinckley, Bush blandly replied, "it's certainly conceivable that I met him or might have been introduced to him."[6]

Even more strange is that the elder Hinckley ran a "World Vision" mission in Denver, Colorado. This was a CIA-connected evangelical church group that seems to have been involved in mind control – some of the people connected to it were cult leader Jim Jones and Mark David Chapman, the murderer of John Lennon. The late conspiracy investigator Jim Keith believed Hinckley Jr. was a prime candidate for mind control assassination programming. He had been receiving mood altering drugs from his psychiatrist, and was on Valium when he shot Reagan. Keith also argued that Hinckley had a "double," a man named Richardson, who followed Hinckley in Colorado and wrote the love letters to Jody Foster that Hinckley allegedly wrote. Richardson was a follower of Carl McIntyre, leader of the International Council of Christian Churches – which in turn was part of World Vision. When one considers the many connections between George Bush and the CIA, to say nothing of the other elite fraternities,* the overt lack of follow-up by the major media was as suspicious as Bush himself.[7]

Reagan may have survived the attempt, but George Bush gained greater ascendancy, anyway. At 70 years of age, Reagan was the oldest man ever inaugurated as President. His mind was already deteriorating, and the assassination attempt accelerated this process. Over the next few years, Bush chaired a "Special Situation Group." Contained within this bland title was a powerful network of organizations: the Standing Crisis Pre-Planning Group, the Crisis Management Center, the Terrorist

Ronald Reagan and George Bush: the front man, and the man behind the scenes.

Incident Working Group, the Taskforce on Combating Terrorism, and the Operations Sub-Group. Bush brought on his former CIA associate, Donald Gregg, as his main advisor on national security. Gregg in turn brought with him a CIA assassination manager, Felix Rodriquez, whom Bush had known during the 1961 Bay of Pigs invasion. During the 1960s, Gregg and Rodriquez had organized assassinations and drug-running in Southeast Asia with CIA officer Theodore Shackley. Now working for Bush, these men – and others such as Lt. Colonel Oliver North – would soon orchestrate the illegal drugs and weapons operation known as Iran-Contra.[8]

Reagan's survival was an unexpected boon for the elite. Out of his depth in dealing with the true power players, told only what Baker and his other handlers decided he needed to know, effectively barred from speaking spontaneously to the media, and requiring daily afternoon naps, Reagan provided cover for Bush, Casey, and the rest of the 'team' to run their sundry national security and financial operations. With conviction in his heart, Reagan could describe the Soviet Union as an Evil Empire plotting world domination, call for a "crusade of freedom," and even promote Henry Kissinger's idea of a winnable nuclear war. 'The Great Communica-

---

*
Indeed, the day before the assassination attempt, Bush had addressed a Trilateral Commission meeting in Washington. The afternoon of the 30th was to have been the occasion of a meeting of Trilateral officials with Reagan in the Oval Office. See Rowland Evans and Robert Novak, "Bush and the Trilateral Commission," *St. Petersburg Times*, 4/12/81.

tor' – who was after all a former Hollywood actor – became the ultimate pitch-man for the global power elite.

An interesting sidelight to this is that the 1981 Bilderberg meeting, which took place in Burgenstock, Switzerland, discussed among other things "changes in the Soviet Union," Soviet intentions, and what Western policy toward the Soviets should be. Clearly, whatever the conclusions of these discussions were, the Bilderberg Group saw major changes ahead. Within a few years, major change would indeed come.[9]

Reagan's Soviet policy meant heady times for the U.S. military and intelligence community. During his first four years in office, military spending grew by nearly 50 percent, surpassing $300 billion annually. In addition, $75 billion went toward strategic modernization, and $75 billion more for research and development.[10] Special forces and covert operations were big winners. One of Reagan's earliest executive orders (#12333) allowed the CIA to conduct 'special activities' within the U.S., as long as these did not influence the domestic politics, media, or public opinion – as if the CIA had ever refrained.[11]

More important was the deregulation of many American industries, of which the savings and loan industry was one example. As a matter of principle, deregulation can have great merit. In practice one has to watch out for the wolves. By the end of the 1980s, the once-tightly regulated industry was a mess: over 1,000 S&Ls had failed, costing the nation an estimated $150 billion and contributing to the 1990-1991 economic recession. Later investigation showed that many of the failed S&Ls had been owned by people with ties to the CIA, and many of these had made large unsecured loans to others linked to the CIA and organized crime. The debacle, called "the largest and costliest venture in public misfeasance, malfeasance and larceny of all time," was in part the work of the intelligence community and organized crime, which had systematically looted America's S&L institutions.[12]

In a study of UFOs and associated cover-up, such information is useful to remember when considering how it might be possible to fund the (presumably) deeply covert programs connected with the topic, especially when no such funding officially exists in any part of the U.S. government's enormous annual budget. In all likelihood, we will never know what happened to all the stolen S&L money, but the point is that when secrecy of a program is absolutely paramount, then secrecy of funding is equally important. In such a context, there is nothing more attractive than an enormous supply of unvouched and untraceable money, for which one need not answer to public institutions or oversight.

Finally, in attempting to discern UFO-relevant policy during these years, it is crucial to recognize where the true power lay: not with Ronald Reagan himself, despite his known obsession with UFOs.[13] Regarding such matters as UFO secrecy, the Strategic Defense Initiative (SDI), or other covert actions taken regarding the UFO matter, we must assume that the initiative came from elsewhere – perhaps Bush, but certainly some reliable representative of the elite interests that dominated Reagan's Presidency. This includes several developments during the 1980s that hinted at attempts at some form of UFO disclosure.

The State of Ufology, 1981

Unlike during the election of Jimmy Carter four years previously, UFO researchers expected little support from the Reagan White House. They seemed to understand they were on their own. Considering the state of organized ufology at the time, the circumstance was not auspicious.

NICAP, for instance, had ceased to operate. Its director during the 1970s had been John Acuff, former head of the CIA-connected Society of Photographic Scientists and Engineers (SPSE). Acuff had personally orchestrated NICAP's emasculation until he was fired by its Board of Governors in 1978. Claiming that NICAP owed him $20,000 for "contractor" services, he held the organization's thousands of case files in his personal possession, essentially as ransom. According to Todd Zechel, Acuff was still working covertly for the FBI.[14]

CUFOS was going through a major downsizing. The organization had always struggled financially – for the past year it had not even published its own journal. By March 1981, its Evanston, Illinois office was closed and the files transferred to the home of Allen Hynek. Even worse, it not only eliminated its office secretary from the payroll, but also chief investigator Alan Hendry. Although CUFOS eventually rebounded, matters were bleak enough in 1981 that the end looked near.[15]

APRO was in trouble. The basic problem was that James and Coral Lorenzen were getting older, and were not delegating responsibilities or training new leaders. There was still an active member base, but the publication of the *APRO Bulletin* was becoming sporadic. Cooperation with MUFON and CUFOS was essentially zero. Moreover, APRO, which had been watched by the intelligence community since the 1950s, was now part of an Air Force intelligence disinformation campaign through the graces of William Moore, Richard Doty, and the good people at AFOSI.

That left MUFON as the sole active American UFO organization. Its members did what they could to get the word out. In February 1981, MUFON members Richard Hall, Bruce Maccabee, and Don Berliner appeared for three hours on the Larry King radio show, reaching millions of listeners.[16] Later that month, Trinity University in San Antonio held a debate on UFOs between MUFON's Stanton Friedman and Philip Klass of CSICOP. No winner was decided, but three times as many people assembled around Friedman afterwards as around Klass, according to Walter Andrus.[17] The general public maintained a taste for ufology. The problem was reaching that public. MUFON's membership and resources, while greater than the other three groups, remained insignificant in the real world. Occasional forays into the public realm were helpful, but not really enough to make a lasting impact.

Meanwhile, there seems to have been a concerted effort against the credibility of Leonard Stringfield. A group calling itself the Coalition of Concerned Ufologists issued statements questioning his information and sources. Like Stringfield, its members – primarily Willard McIntyre and Dennis Pilichis – were based in Ohio. Early in 1981, the coalition sent out a booklet with its own 'alien' photographs. Researchers were baffled by this development, which certainly made it harder to analyze all this new (and now conflicting) crash retrieval information. Several researchers wondered whether the 'Coalition' was an intelligence operation.[18] Indeed, Willard McIntyre had a longstanding connection to the Society of Photographic Scientists and Engineers (SPSE), an organization closely connected to the CIA. Could this have been part of an orchestrated plan against ufology, one prong in a general attack which also included the compromising of William Moore?

The deepening of the Paul Bennewitz saga during the spring of 1981 might support this theory. AFOSI and NSA were both paying close attention to Bennewitz by now, and he was receiving all sorts of visits, with and without his knowledge. Richard Doty and Dr. Robert Fugate stopped by during the spring. Fugate ran the Air Force's Star Fire Optical Range at Manzano, which contained some of the technologies Bennewitz may have been seeing. To their surprise, they learned that Bennewitz had invented a machine to detect magnetic fields surrounding the UFOs he was watching. Fugate studied the device closely; after returning, his technicians built an improved version. Gregory Bishop, commenting on this, said "how the Air Force eventually employed this device remains a mystery."

One obvious answer would be: to detect UFOs. In any event, strange things were happening at Bennewitz's home. William Moore was another frequent visitor during the early 1980s. On one occasion, Moore noticed a bright orange-yellow ball of light, hovering in a corner, with a pale blue halo. He asked Bennewitz about it, who was also mystified but said "they keep showing up." The orb then winked out suddenly. Doty and two NSA operatives also saw this phenomenon when they broke into Bennewitz's home on one occasion. All three men were perplexed. Something was happening at the home of Paul Bennewitz, and it is not clear who or what was behind it.

It has been claimed that Air Force intelligence and NSA were attempting to steer Bennewitz away from the real technologies at the Kirtland-Manzano complex in favor of a phony alien base beneath Dulce. Richard Doty, for instance, claimed that AFOSI created the illusion of an underground base beneath Dulce for the sole purpose of fooling Bennewitz. This claim went very far, indeed: that AFOSI improved old, out-of-the-way dirt roads, airlifted mothballed equipment to the area, and placed fake air vents on Mount Archuleta – all for Bennewitz. Calling this "over the top" would be a mild statement. State police officer Gabriel Valdez also saw the vents, and vehemently disagreed that they were fake. Like so much else in the cloak-and-dagger world of UFOs, this matter remains unresolved.[19]

One thing is known: as a result of everything he had been seeing and recording, Bennewitz began writing to New Mexico Senators Pete Domenici and Harrison Schmitt, describing his observations and giving his opinion that aliens were taking over the base beneath Dulce.[20]

World Sightings through May

After Trans-en-Provence, UFO sightings slowed down. A British CAA report described an interesting radar target near Lyons, France, on February 13. Although it was not seen visually, it was "a sizeable oval shaped target" that moved toward an aircraft "at very high speed."[21] After this, the next important sighting did not occur until May, and that happened to be in Earth's orbit.

This was aboard the Soviet Salyut-6 space station on May 5, 1981. Oddly (or not), the United States had recently launched its first reusable manned space vehicle, the Space Shuttle *Columbia*. Its first mission, known as STS-1, lasted from April 12 to 14, 1981. Three weeks later, the Salyut-6 was in orbit over Southern Africa, and cosmonaut Vladimir Kovalyonok had just finished exercising when he looked through a porthole. Astonished, he saw a rotating, elliptical object, flying along with the space station.

Lacking all reference points in space, he could not determine either its distance or its size. He called his partner Viktor Savinykh to observe, who was about to photograph it when the object exploded in "golden light." This was followed immediately by a second explosion, leaving behind two "golden and very beautiful" spheres and a residue of white smoke. The space station soon entered the Earth's shadow, and the spheres vanished into blackness. As cautiously as possible, the men reported their sighting to mission control.

Later, Kovalyonok learned that Soviet scientists had registered an unusual radiation emission the day of their sighting. The Soviet press covered the event, generally excluding extraterrestrial answers. In 1993, by then a major general, Kovalyonok publicly described the event, calling it "something impossible according to the laws of physics." He said "it was probably a UFO, but it was definitely not mysticism; two people watched it at the same time.... I do not believe it when astronauts say they have never seen anything extraordinary in space."[22]

More strange still is a sighting by Kovalyonok and Savinykh that reportedly occurred between May 14 and 18, following the docking of the Soyuz T-4 with the Salyut-6. The event was first described during the days of *glasnost* and later by Paul Stonehill. According to the account, the two cosmonauts saw an unidentified, spherical ship, about 30 feet in diameter. This object approached their position, occasionally moving erratically, even vanishing, then reappearing. It looked metallic, had many windows and was well lit inside. When it approached to the incredibly close distance of 100 feet, the cosmonauts looked inside with binoculars. They saw three brown-colored beings with slanted bright blue eyes, straight noses, and bushy eyebrows. The beings expressed no emotion and appeared to resemble robots. Soviet mission control would not permit direct contact, so the two crews tried to communicate through other means: display of various mathematical equations, maps, and Morse code (apparently the equations and maps elicited some sort of response from the aliens, and the Morse code did not). At one point, the aliens left their spaceship without apparent protective suits.

It was claimed that the cosmonauts filmed the incident and that after they returned to Earth, Lt. General Georgy Beregovoy, who led training programs for Soviet cosmonauts, led a meeting of 200 party leaders and scientists in Moscow to show the film. According to Stonehill, those who tried to see the film were warned off.[23]

Incredibly enough, there was another incident from this month, also unconfirmed, that rivals the Soviet sighting for sheer drama. According to Merle Shane McDow, who was attached to the U.S. Navy Atlantic Command, a UFO was tracked on at least five radar scopes moving at high speed up and down the Atlantic coast. "We knew that it wasn't the Soviets," said McDow, who related this event years later to Steven Greer and the "Disclosure Project." The Command Center was put on Zebra Alert, the Navy's highest level of alert, and Admiral Harry Trane gave the order to force the object down and recover it. For more than an hour, U.S. jet fighters chased the mysterious object, sometimes seeing it visually. The UFO easily evaded them. McDow discussed the threats, intimidation, and confiscation of log books that occurred after the event.[24]

Setbacks in the Fight Against Secrecy

Throughout the late 1970s, the Freedom of Information Act had been the bright hope of UFO researchers, the wedge that might pry open the door of UFO secrecy. But that wedge was wearing away. The lawsuit against the NSA received a setback on November 18, 1980. Following an *in camera* affidavit by the NSA, Judge Gerhard Gesell dismissed the suit, stressing "the sensitive nature of the materials and the obvious effects on national security their release may well entail." Not only the NSA documents, but the affidavit itself was itself classified Top Secret. NSA's argument was that the documents would reveal how NSA acquired its information – its methods and sources.[25] The CIA lawsuit was still in appeals, and the newly formed Fund for UFO Research (FUFOR) awarded a $2,500 grant to underwrite litigation to obtain copies of 200 known CIA documents relating to UFOs.[26]

By the summer of 1981, citizen-based lawsuits against the CIA, NSA, DIA, and FAA had all been decided in favor of the defendants. The organization Citizens Against UFO Secrecy, riding on financial fumes, could only afford to appeal two of the rulings, and so the CIA and NSA were selected. No one expected either to succeed. To make matters worse, the NSA was pressing for dispensation from FOIA – that is, to be exempt altogether – on the grounds that its mission and modus operandi were too sensitive for public viewing. "The foot in the door," wrote Larry Bryant, "is getting numb from the tight fit."[27]

Meanwhile, Leonard Stringfield continued to encounter obstacles in his research into the subterranean matters of UFO conspiracy. On the one hand, his sources were drying up – several explicitly said they could no longer speak to him. On the other, he was experiencing a personal assault from a so-called "Hoax and Fraud Committee." On July 1, 1981, its chairman, Charles Wilhelm, gave a public ultimatum. Stringfield had 60 days to answer questions regarding his photographs and sources, or else be 'exposed' as a fraud. A definite piling on effect was taking place: *FATE Magazine* writers Jerome Clark and George Early also questioned Stringfield's credibility. Stringfield, meanwhile, insisted he was doing the best he could do, under the circumstances. He reminded researchers, as he had done many times before, that his informants needed confidentiality. He also began to wonder aloud whether he was the victim of an orchestrated attack.

Stringfield retained many supporters, however. Richard Hall, for instance, pointed out that crash retrieval stories had circulated for a long time. During the 1950s and 1960s, he said, NICAP received perhaps a dozen crashed UFO leads, but performed minimal follow up because the stories seemed too outrageous. "Since then," wrote Hall, "some of the stories have been traced to the source."[28]

The attacks on Stringfield seemed suspicious, but Paul Bennewitz was a more obvious victim of underhanded actions. For some time now, Bennewitz had been photographing apparent UFOs and picking up strange signals from near the Manzano Weapons Storage Area. As a result, he had been the target of military surveillance since the end of 1980. Now, during the summer of 1981, more active disinformation began when William Moore gave Bennewitz an altered version of the Project Aquarius document. Moore had seen the original in November 1980, and had his own copy since February 1981. He gave Bennewitz this document on behalf of Air Force Intelligence, knowing it had been altered. He felt guilty about it, but did it in order to retain his access to inside information.

The memo marked the first time that the alleged UFO control group known as MJ-12 made its appearance in a public document. It stated that "the results of Project Aquarius are still classified Top Secret with no dissemination outside official intelligence channels and with restricted access to 'MJ Twelve.'" According to Moore, the original memo stated that the NSA had analyzed Bennewitz's photographs, and incidentally found them to be authentic. In the altered memo, NSA became NASA.

Regarding the existence of Project Aquarius, it turns out that there have been several classified projects by that name. In 1985, researcher Chris Lambright requested a response via FOIA from the NSA regarding three project names. Two were dismissed in the reply, but NSA said the third one – Aquarius – would require a $15,000 search fee with no promise of results.

After further inquiry, the agency wrote "even the release of the project name could reasonably be expected to cause grave damage to the national security." Further research uncovered a Project Aquarius operated by the Defense Advanced Research Projects Agency (DARPA) around 1970 to "demonstrate the feasibility of detecting both submarine launched ballistic missiles and low-flying aircraft ...." Thus, rather than being a complete hoax, the Project Aquarius document is probably a tangle of fact and lie. How else could a deeply classified NSA project by that very name have crept into it?[29]

There may be several reasons Bennewitz was given an altered Aquarius document. First, to be able to track the distribution of the document (easily done by the "NASA" marker it contained). Assuming Bennewitz's research threatened security interests at Kirtland and Manzano, it would be helpful to learn the extent of his personal network. It cannot be known if another motive was to confuse UFO research by introducing this tainted document. However, this was by far the most lasting effect. If Bennewitz was in fact obtaining UFO data and photos, then giving him a tampered Aquarius document could have been an attempt to discredit him.

One of the pleasant respites from the depressing fight against the spooks and The Establishment was the conference circuit. The MUFON Symposium that summer offered a breadth of topics: Peter Gersten on FOIA struggles and successes, Allen Hynek on scientific ufology, Budd Hopkins on abductions ("an invisible epidemic"), and Stanton Friedman and William Moore on the newly emerging Roswell case, which they described as a kind of "cosmic watergate." Moore's dealings with the intelligence community would not be known for many years; meanwhile he was riding high as ufology's newest star.[30]

CUFOS, operating in downsized mode, nevertheless continued to publish a small bulletin, and even organized its own conference that fall – its first since 1976. The conference was limited in attendance, serious in tone. Hynek, Hopkins, Bruce Maccabee, and Mark Rodeghier presented, among others. Claims of recovered alien debris and bodies were studiously avoided, although Stringfield, who attended, spoke privately about it.[31]

The discussions at such conferences were essentially internal dialogues; the rest of the world hardly noticed. Yet, the value of these gatherings was becoming evident: researchers were talking to each other, strengthening relationships, and getting fresh ideas. Five major conferences took place in 1981, a large number at the time, although small by later standards.

Abduction Debate

By the early 1980s, it was not merely the debate about Roswell or other possible UFO crash retrievals that was transforming ufology. The matter of alien abductions had arrived.

Starting in the 1950s, ufology had developed a substantial literature on the theme of human-ET contact. Some writers, notably the 'contactees' of the 1950s, described voluntary and positive encounters with human-looking aliens who warned of the threats posed by reckless misuse of human technology. In time, a darker trend emerged: people who claimed to have been forcibly taken and examined by beings, some of whom looked decidedly non-human and appeared to lack human emotions.

The Travis Walton case of 1975 had triggered a stronger interest by researchers in abductions. In 1977, Coral and James Lorenzen had written a book on abductions, compiling two decades worth of cases. Most of the aliens they described were small, with large heads and eyes, no hair, and communicated by telepathy. The Lorenzens suggested that abductions were the latest logical step in a kind of alien information-gathering process. Each abductee, they believed, had specific information of value to the aliens.[32]

In 1979, Raymond Fowler had published the *Andreasson Affair*, detailing the experience of Betty Andreasson. Her hypnotic sessions produced a detailed story of interaction with creatures with grey skin, large heads, cat-like eyes, tiny mouths, three-fingered hands, and dark blue uniforms. They moved by gliding and communicated telepathically. One night in January 1967, several of these beings entered her Massachusetts home through a solid door. They "switched off" all of the family members except for Betty and her daughter Becky. They then took Betty alone into their ship, leaving Becky behind but "frozen."

Betty was physically examined. A needle was inserted up her nose and into her head, but without any sensation of physical pain. Somehow, she was transported to an alien realm, whether physically or by means of mind-control. She went through tunnels, saw a red and then green atmosphere, strange creatures and plants, and pyramid-like structures. With a message focusing on love and nature, the aliens explained that humans were destroying the Earth. Because of great love, said Betty, "they cannot let man go in the footsteps he is going..." A better understanding of nature and humanity's place within it were essential.

The culminating event was when she witnessed a giant phoenix-like bird burn up and then reappear from the ashes as a giant worm. A presence she understood to be God told her that she had been chosen. The event symbolized the rebirth of mankind after going through a terrible tribulation. The aliens indicated that they shared Betty's belief in the sacredness of Jesus Christ and affirmed that he was "coming soon."

Betty's Christianity was a distinct feature of this case, and some researchers wondered if this biased her recollection in some way. Yet, Fowler conducted his investigation thoroughly and sincerely, and his book made a strong impact. Over the decades, he continued to follow Betty's case, reporting his findings in subsequent books.[33]

Abduction literature was becoming more detailed and bold. The publication in 1981 of Budd Hopkins's *Missing Time* brought abductions to center stage in UFO research. Hopkins was a successful artist, with works in the permanent collections of many major museums. Through the 1970s his interest in UFOs and abductions became increasingly active, and in *Missing Time* he documented several studies of apparent alien abductions, looking for consistencies and patterns.[34]

Missing Time was a pioneering work that introduced two new ideas. First, that a period of unexplained missing time was a typical aspect of the abduction experience. Second, that abductions seemed to be far more common than previously thought, and their significance far greater. "We have no idea how many such kidnappings may already have taken place," Hopkins wrote, "but I believe there are vastly more than the mere 200 or so incidents which have been investigated."

There seemed to be an ulterior purpose, "as if these quite similar abductions constitute some kind of systematic research program, with the human species as the subject." This program involved abducting people, performing procedures, then erasing their memories through some sort of post-hypnotic suggestion. Hopkins conceded the possibility that there was a psychic element to abductions, but emphasized that these were real and physical events. Witnesses described their ordeals, and even the equipment used by the aliens, with astonishing consistency. Many of them had scars, 'scoop' marks, and incisions that inexplicably appeared on their bodies. As to the 'why,' Hopkins briefly touched on the idea of alien-human hybridization, a theme he expanded on in later books.

The information in *Missing Time* came primarily through hypnotic regression, although Hopkins did not conduct any of the sessions. Instead he secured the aid of licensed psychologist Aphrodite Clamar, Ph.D. Clamar also conducted psychological tests on the abductees (finding them to be normal, albeit stressed and perplexed by their experience). The hypnosis was necessary, said Hopkins, to break the barrier of silence often built around the minds of abductees.

Not surprisingly, not everyone saw things this way. Two early critics were D. Scott Rogo and Hilary Evans. Both argued that abductions appeared to be a feature of the human mind. UFO abductors, said Rogo, communicate through absurdities, space-time incongruities, and symbols. It could not be mere coincidence that this was the language of dreams. Somehow, he maintained, these so-called aliens were linked to our minds.[35] Similarly, Evans argued that abduction reports suggested ancient archetypal encounters with fairies, angels, and demons. He believed there was something to the phenomenon, but that it was probably based in a reality vastly different from the ordinary human experience.[36]

Such criticisms were mild compared with allegations that Hopkins was acting irresponsibly, that hypnosis was just as likely to produce fantasy as accurate recollection. The 1980 study, *Memory*, by psychologist Elizabeth Loftus, provided an intellectual foundation for this position. She argued that human memory is a frail thing "continually being altered, transformed, and distorted." Hypnosis does not reliably retrieve buried memories, she concluded, and can even make things worse when people confidently 'recall' events that never happened.[37] Hopkins and his supporters countered that his subjects were never asked leading questions, and were often asked questions specifically designed to screen out hoaxing or confabulation.

Given the nature of the abduction phenomenon, it is inevitable that the argument would come down to human memory. Even physical elements such as scars and scoop marks could be explained away by skeptics as ordinary events of which the person was simply unaware. Yet, as the testimony and literature on alien abduction continued to grow, so did the number of converts to the idea that something serious was going on.

In a few brief years, the UFOs phenomenon had gone from being a mystery about lights in the sky to one of retrieved alien technology, and now to intimate interactions between the aliens and humans, a phenomenon believed to be so widespread that it could affect one's very family.

Sightings: June through December 1981

In Britain, another new phenomenon had arrived. For the past few years, mysterious circular depressions and combinations of circles had been discovered on the farmland and fields of southwestern England. During the summer of 1981, British researcher Pat Delgado publicized the "crop circles." A bevy of explanations soon arose, ranging from weather to magnetic fields to hoaxers to extraterrestrials. Inevitably, the phenomenon began to be felt among UFO researchers, especially when the circles became more complex at the end of the decade. For now, however, they remained a curiosity.

After the spectacular Trans-en-Provence case in January, 1981, the rest of the year produced relatively few UFO reports. Even so, a few cases were noteworthy. The strength of a case always comes down to two factors: the level of strangeness and nature of the evidence. Judging them cannot be done with mathematical precision, but must be handled within the messy domain of human judgment.

One example is the sighting of a luminous object by students in China's X'ian University in the Shanxi Province on June 5, 1981. At 10 p.m., witnesses saw an object which split into two parts, then three, then four. The various parts separated and converged, and another object appeared and merged with it. This object then split again, diminished in size, and vanished at 10:20 p.m. Any object that can separate into multiple pieces and converge before astonished witnesses would appear to be indicative of extraordinary technology, begging the question of 'whose.' The strength of this case comes down to the reliability of the witnesses; enough for some investigators and not enough for others.[38]

Several interesting vehicle encounter cases occurred that summer and fall, including a few involving apparent alien beings and even abductions. Such may have been the case in Shewsbury, Britain, when three women driving in the early hours of a July morning saw an object with red and white lights in a field. They remembered their car losing, then regaining, power. Discovering they were missing twenty minutes of time, they went to the police. The three later underwent hypnosis and described various entities. Although diverging in some details, their accounts were basically congruent.[39]

Close encounters were reported in places as divergent as Temuka, New Zealand (July 12), Lieksa, Finland (July 31), eastern Zimbabwe (August 15), and several in California during August and September. All involved explicit sightings of an unusual object with high performance characteristics. The New Zealand case involved a brightly lit dome-shaped object with 'windows' approaching a car then shooting away.[40] In Finland, a black sphere with lights approached a motorboat, surrounded it with a fog, and induced witness paralysis, missing time, and other physiological effects.[41] In California UFOs, some of which were triangular, were reported buzzing vehicles, often near freeways.[42] The Zimbabwe case occurred at a large private estate known as La Rochelle, in the Imbeza Valley near the

Mozambique border. In the early evening, a man named Clifford Muchena saw a ball of light maneuver around various buildings, and soon afterward saw three beings wearing silver coveralls. An intense light blinded him and he fell to his knees. Later he said "there was a power coming from them." Other witnesses also reported seeing the ball of light and the entities. How the beings or light departed was not indicated.[43]

A noteworthy case took place in Britain on September 11, 1981. A woman named Denise Bishop saw a large, dark grey object hovering over her house, shining several beams of light from beneath. Frightened, she tried to enter her house, but a beam of green light hit her hand for about thirty seconds, paralyzing her. For several days, her hand was burned, and a mark was still visible ten months later when Timothy Good visited her. He described Bishop as sensible and sincere, with no prior interest in UFOs. The Ministry of Defense apparently did not investigate.[44]

In most of these cases, UFOs and their occupants interacted closely with human witnesses. A few airliner and military encounters took place that summer. One was a jumbo jet encounter on July 4 with a silvery disc-shaped object over Lake Michigan.[45] More dramatic was an unofficial account given by an informant to Nick Redfern. This was said to have occurred at the island of Cyprus on August 16, 1981. Presumably it involved one of Britain's two Sovereign Base Areas (SBAs) on the island, Akrotiri and Dhekelia. An object described as "vast" approached the island, tracked at 30,000 feet and 900 mph. Initially, it was believed to be a conventional aircraft, until it came to a sudden stop and hovered over the base for forty five minutes. Many photos were taken, and witnesses described the object as a bright white triangle over 700 feet long. Oddly, according to the informant, prior to the sighting the Ministry of Defence in London had sent an encrypted message to the base. This ordered "a complete stand-down of aircraft in the event that any strange 'aerial phenomena' was sighted in the vicinity of the base airfield." The following day, a man and woman arrived at the base, stayed for six hours, then left with all evidence. Redfern's informant stated that shortly afterwards, American AFOSI and British personnel met at RAF Lakenheath to discuss the case. They were "really bothered about it."

Did prior knowledge by British military authorities imply this UFO was actually an experimental aircraft? Redfern's informant did not believe so. "Whatever we saw, it was not man-made.... this thing was really alien." Perhaps the MoD had already detected the UFO and then simply warned other bases to leave it alone. The case is almost typical in that it is both spectacular and unconfirmed – one of many.[46]

Equally intriguing as the Cyprus case, but quite definite, is a UFO photograph taken on Vancouver Island in British Columbia on October 8, 1981. Hannah McRoberts was on vacation with her family. At 11 a.m., they were at a rest-area on the east coast of the island, thirty miles north of Kelsey Bay, when Hannah photographed one of the mountain peaks. No one saw the object that appeared so clearly after the picture was developed. The photograph shows an object to the right of and above the peak, a perfectly clear and classic daylight disc.

For nearly a year, they showed the image only to friends and relatives. Then, in the summer of 1982, they visited the Vancouver Planetarium and were persuaded to lend their negative for analysis. Eventually, Richard F. Haines of the *Journal of Scientific Exploration* obtained it and conducted detailed analyses using micro-densitometry and various computer enhancements. He found no evidence of a hoax, atmospheric disturbance, or photographic defects. He also conducted a site survey and interviewed the McRoberts family – "middle-class, hard-working people," he said, who were genuinely puzzled by the photograph. Haines concluded that the disc was an unidentified "three dimensional object."[47]

The Hannah McRoberts 1981 photo, enlargement of object shown in inset (left).

Assuming Haines' analysis was correct, the photograph provides clear evidence that some agency was flying perfect disc-shaped objects. Another interesting aspect of this case is that the disc was apparently able to camouflage itself from unaided human eyes, although not from a camera. To some researchers, 1981 may not seem particularly early in the game. After all, good UFO sightings and photographs had been reported for a long time by then. But 1981 is also not yesterday. Whether this was secret human-derived technology, or something wholly alien, that is a long time to keep something secret.

There were several interesting aerial events in the fall of 1981, one an alleged Soviet Air Force encounter in October, taken from the files of the Russian UFO Center. A MiG pilot encountered a glowing sphere which accompanied his plane for a short while, jamming his radio and shutting his engine down. When the sphere moved toward the tail, it apparently caused an explosion that damaged the fin. After it vanished, the engine restarted and the pilot landed. Soviet investigators concluded that a glowing plasma ball was the culprit.[48]

The most important UFO-related development in late 1981 was the onset of the "Hessdalen Phenomenon." Starting in November 1981, the thinly populated valley of Hessdalen in central Norway began to experience sightings of anomalous lights which lasted through the 1980s and even beyond. They usually came in between mountains, stopped and hovered for as long as an hour or more, then quickly ascended or accelerated horizontally. Hundreds of such sightings were made over the next few years, usually luminous objects seen at night, but sometimes also metallic cigar-shaped objects seen during the day. Objects were observed singly or in groups, moving sometimes slowly, sometimes at great speed, sometimes in a simple path, other times in highly complex maneuvers. Even after several good photographs were taken, they continued to resist conventional pigeonholing. Radar equipment was brought in and tracked the objects at a speed of more than five miles per second, or more than 18,000 mph. Throughout the duration of the phenomenon, no sounds were ever heard, a noteworthy fact considering that this was an area so isolated that residents could hear cars and tractors several miles away. Essentially, the phenomenon resisted any interpretation, being far too complex for any naturalistic explanation such as "earth lights" or the result of the Earth's magnetism. In 1981, this phenomenon was just beginning.[49]

Correspondence on UFO Secrecy

By late 1981, the new American President was receiving letters from citizens about UFOs and extraterrestrials. One of these was dated September 28 from Major (Ret.) Colman VonKeviczky, formerly of the Royal Hungarian Army and now Director of the "Intercontinental UFO Galactic Spacecraft Research and Analytic Network" (ICUFON). VonKeviczky claimed UFOs were an intergalactic task force that would destroy earth unless world leaders collaborated. Perhaps surprisingly, he received a reply on November 21 from the Chief Military Advisor of the White House, Major General Robert Schweitzer, who wrote, "The President is well aware of the threat you document so clearly and is doing all in his power to restore the national defense margin of safety as quickly and prudently as possible."

VonKeviczky went public, believing he had a direct acknowledgment of

UFOs by the Reagan administration. An embarrassed Schweitzer had to tell the Associated Press that he thought VonKeviczky was talking about the Soviets, that his reply was a mistake. Considering that VonKeviczky's five page letter mentioned UFOs 49 times (not even counting the 17 pages of attached documents), the denial lacked a certain credibility. Grant Cameron put it clearly: "it is absolutely impossible that the VonKeviczky letter could be mistaken for a Soviet threat." Schweitzer's salvation was that his reply did not mention UFOs. Still, it did not prevent him from being fired immediately afterward by National Security advisor Richard Allen.[50]

The VonKeviczky correspondence is suggestive of UFO secrecy. But the letter from Senator Barry Goldwater from October 19, 1981 makes the matter as clear as day. Goldwater was a five-term Senator, a former Republican Party nominee for U.S. President, and an Air Force reservist with the rank of Major General. He had been close friends with legendary Air Force General and former Chief of Staff Curtis LeMay. In 1982, Goldwater was inducted into the National Aviation Hall of Fame. If any American politician could lay claim to being a military-friendly insider, it was Barry Goldwater. Thus, a letter from him to a constituent on the matter of UFOs must be taken seriously. Responding to a constituent query regarding the rumors of bodies and technology held at Wright-Patterson AFB, Goldwater wrote:

> I have long ago given up acquiring access to the so-called blue room at Wright-Patterson .... this thing has gotten so highly classified, even though I will admit there is a lot of it that has been released, it is just impossible to get anything on it.[51]

Goldwater had written letters in a similar vein in 1975 and 1979. In these letters, it has become clear that a person of Goldwater's stature was still unable to penetrate the secrecy and classification system of UFOs.

By the end of 1981, researchers were noticing that the new administration was not especially friendly regarding FOIA requests. In October, researcher Robert Todd learned that North American Air Defense (NORAD) would no longer waive search and duplication fees, even when no responsive records were located.[52] Then, in early November, a federal court reinforced its earlier decision to withhold NSA documents pertaining to UFOs.[53]

1982: Pennsylvania UFOs

Like the previous year, 1982 was another quiet year in terms of UFO activity. For the first half of 1982, the most interesting UFO reports came from the state of Pennsylvania. An important reason for this was the diligence of UFO researcher Stan Gordon, MUFON's State Director of Pennsylvania, who ran a UFO reporting desk and actively investigated leads. The Pennsylvania flap was a reflection of genuine UFO activity which was recorded by a motivated and competent researcher.

Gordon received information on the sighting of a triangle near the town of Scottdale, in the western part of the state, at around 9 p.m. on March 22, 1982. The object was described as very large and silent as it hovered near a man's car and followed him for a short while. Another UFO was reported in western Pennsylvania on March 23, this time by an off-duty police officer on Route 65 who saw a bright, round object in the late afternoon above the roof of his house. He notified another officer, who also saw the object when he arrived. It then followed the patrol car down Route 65, at times from behind and at times directly above. Another officer was called to the scene, this one with a camera, but the object was too far off and almost out of sight by the time he arrived. On the 29th, yet another UFO was seen in the western Pennsylvania borough of Oakmont. At 3:30 a.m. on that day, a witness reported a bright, silver, metallic disc-shaped object hovering over the area. Gordon investigated and thought the object was not likely to be a balloon, but was otherwise unknown.

Amid this sharp upsurge in sightings, another triangle was reported on April 1 in the town of Petrolia, not far from Pittsburgh. At 7:15 p.m., three men were re-pairing a jeep when one of them noticed an unusually bright object just above the trees with a flashing red light. A few minutes later they noticed the object had doubled its altitude. As it was getting dark, the men turned on the headlights of their vehicle to continue working on it. Almost immediately, the bright object moved toward them. Wondering what would happen,

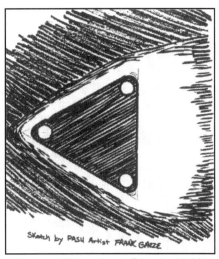

Drawing of Pennsylvania Triangle, 4/1/82.

they turned the jeep lights off, and the object backed away. They turned the lights on again, and it approached, this time passing almost directly over their heads at no more than 250 feet altitude. As the object passed over them, the bright light went out and its triangular shape became clear. This object was very large, a dull gun-metal color, and was surrounded by a luminescent mist. At each point was a light: a red light in front, with a white and amber light at the other corners. While watching this display, the awestruck men saw two bright lights shoot away from the triangle, one going north and one south. No sound was heard throughout any of this. A jet plane approached from the east, and the object seemed to stop completely and become very bright. Then it rose straight up until it was out of sight.

Gordon investigated this case, as well. Two of the witnesses told him that while observing the object, they had the feeling that "their skin was crawling off their body." For several days, they had severe headaches, and one had diarrhea. Other residents from the local area reported similar observations.

Sightings continued in western Pennsylvania. On April 14, 1982, in West Sunbury, sky observers watching the planets through their telescope saw a large disc-shaped object move across the sky. The witnesses said they had observed many types of aircraft previously, but that the shape and movement in this instance were unlike conventional aircraft. On April 21, in the town of Derry, residents reported two bright orange balls hovering over trees. After several minutes, one of the lights disappeared toward the south, while the other light ascended straight up and was gone. At 8 p.m. on May 5, at Youngstown Ridge in Latrobe, a witness saw a top-shaped object with a small dome on top. Within the dome was a red pulsating light. It appeared to be the size of a small aircraft and moved slowly at an altitude of about 1,000 feet. This object was first seen to move east, then to hover, and finally to move west and disappear.

Later that night, another triangular UFO was seen near Pittsburgh. At 11:17 p.m., police radio networks were filled with reports of a bright nocturnal light. One witness, a pilot who heard the reports over his scanner, ran outside to see if there really was anything unusual. He saw no light source, but something even stranger. Moving in a southeastern direction was a triangular object about the size of a Lear jet and approximately 1,000 feet altitude. The strange thing about the object was that only the front section appeared to have a solid outline. The rest seemed transparent, as the brighter stars could be seen through the middle structure. For about twenty seconds, he watched the object glide quickly and silently across the sky.

Gordon recorded another UFO case from the town of Jeannette (not far from Pittsburgh) on May 19, 1982. Shortly after 9 p.m., as a thunderstorm was moving into the area, a man noticed what he thought was a helicopter about to crash on the far side of a hill. A search by state police, fire departments, and civil air patrol units failed to locate anything. Neither Westmoreland control tower or the FAA flight service office indicated any unknown aircraft in the area at the time. Gordon interviewed the witness, who said the object was dark, solid-looking, and had three distinct brightly lit windows. Gordon found other witnesses who reported a similar object in the South Hills area of Pittsburgh two hours later.[54]

Elsewhere within the U.S., probably the most interesting UFO report was a police officer's encounter with a diamond-shaped object in East Texas, not far from where the infamous Cash-Landrum case occurred in 1980. John McDonald was a deputy sheriff for Liberty County, on patrol during the night of May 22, 1982. Just before 11 p.m., he noticed two bright lights above tall pine trees. Thinking he was seeing a low flying airplane, he pointed his spotlight toward them as the lights sank out of sight. But then the lights reappeared and passed over his head at a low altitude, perhaps 1,000 feet. McDonald shone his spotlight again, and "could plainly see ... it was in a diamond shape," albeit with four rounded corners. The object was greyish in color and large – he estimated ten cars could fit inside it. Despite the quiet night, he heard no sound at all from it as it moved away to the southwest. Seconds later he heard a high-pitched whine as the object quickly departed. Unlike the witnesses of the Cash-Landrum incident, McDonald suffered no physical side effects. He prepared an official "offense report," a copy of which John Schuessler obtained.[55]

World Sightings, early 1982

Unusual atomospheric activity occurred near the Finnish-Soviet border, tracked by the U.S. military. A U.S. Defense Informational Report discussed "lighted objects in the sky to the east of Finland" seen on February 16 and 19. Although much was redacted, the memo indicated that the light on February 16 was visible for five minutes and made two large counter clockwise circles while moving toward the northeast. It was accompanied by "a bright star like object that appeared to be exuding gas" moving to the north. On the 19th, a bright ball was seen traveling northeast "on a slow, flat trajectory," and then disappeared. Two lights were then seen following each other, but most of the memo is blacked out after this.[56]

Meanwhile, Norway was the scene of unexplained lights. Researchers from the group UFO-Norge arrived in the Hessdalen area in late March, and a town meeting was held nearby on March 26, attended by 130 local residents. Since the previous December, when the "Hessdalen phenomenon" started, about thirty sightings had been reported. Most had been of a round, yellowish light; others were cigar shaped; others had red or yellow lights attached to them. A few cases even included physical effects, animal reactions, or radio or TV interference. Two officers from Trondheim's Vaernes Air Force Base also arrived on the scene. They saw no UFOs, they told the media, but did see lots of shooting stars, satellites, and aircraft. "Not the least," they told reporters, "we saw a lot of UFO hunters in the area."[57]

Sporadic and unofficial reports were the rule for most of the year. This is not to say that they were of no interest. A June 1 incident at the Soviet cosmodrome was reported in *Flying Saucer Review*. According to the account, two UFOs hovered over for 14 seconds and allegedly "sucked out" the bolts and rivets of the support towers at the launch pad and caused damage to nearby houses. The cosmodrome was reportedly shut down for repairs for two weeks.[58]

A British CAA report described a "Large translucent object 500 feet long at 41000 feet" over Dinkelsbuhl, Germany, on June 12, 1982. According to the report, the object, seen "by all on board," was described as having the form "of a double rectangle surmounted by a globe (egg shaped) crowned by a silver one."[59]

A great deal of activity was being recorded in northern China during June 1982, reaching a peak on the 18th between 9 p.m. and 11 p.m. One of these was reported by five Chinese Air Force pilots flying on patrol over the northern military frontier, an event called by Paul Dong "one of the most intriguing military cases." At 10:06 p.m., a large object appeared in the clear sky over northern China. It was yellowish-green and initially the apparent size of a full Moon. However, it soon grew, and black spots became visible near its center. In an all-too-common pattern, five fighter aircraft lost their communication and navigational systems and were forced to return to their base. Their feeling was that the object released strong electric currents of some kind. One pilot told the Chinese *Journal of UFO Research:*

> ... when I first saw the object, it flew toward me at a high rate of speed, whirling fast. While it was whirling, it created rings of lights. In the center of the light ring was fire. After 10 seconds, the center of the ring exploded like a hand grenade. Then the body of the object enlarged rapidly.

The other four pilots also gave statements to the journal, which published an account of the incident in its first issue in 1983.[60]

Three days later, at the heel of Italy by the Adriatic Sea, a British CAA report recorded another aerial encounter. According to the report, the pilots saw an object pass down along their left side, roughly two miles away. It was described as a "black shiny doughnut shape about the size of a car. Object was tumbling and judged to be stationary." If this were falling space debris, why would it look stationary?[61]

The Lid Stays On

Regarding UFO research, 1982 started out with a new *International UFO Reporter* by CUFOS. From this point onward, CUFOS published the *IUR* on a regular schedule, mainly on the efforts of Jerome Clark, Nancy Clark, and Mark Rodeghier.

In January, Australian researcher Bill Chalker made the first visit to the Royal Australian Air Force (RAAF) archives in search of UFO documentation. He found "a residue of provocative reports that survives the gauntlet of both official and civilian investigation." Rather than conspiracy, he leaned toward institutional confusion as the key response to UFOs by the Australian military. To him, the RAAF was probably "as confused and uncertain as many civilian research groups on what to do about provocative UFO sightings."[62]

The "cloak and dagger" activity of recent years continued in 1982. In early February, William Moore received a plain envelope from one of the intermediaries of 'Falcon.' Inside were Air Force documents signed by Richard Doty regarding unexplained lights over Kirtland AFB and Manzano during August and September 1980. Moore, and later Bruce Maccabee, examined the documents and conducted a detailed on-site investigation. They found extensive corroboration and no contradictions.[63]

In March and April 1982, the *National Enquirer* published a series of provably false articles on UFOs. To many, this would not seem like an important or unusual development, and indeed the *Enquirer* had done this kind of thing before. What complicated matters is that in recent years it had also been publishing UFO-related articles that were well-researched and accurate, most notably those by Bob Pratt. The articles from the spring of 1982, however, were analyzed by Swedish UFO researcher Anders Liljegren. They included "Soviet Ships Buzzed by UFOs from Under the Sea" (3/30/82), "Space Alien Blasts Forest Rangers With a Bizarre Ray" (4/6/82), and "Space Aliens Blast Holes in Windows" (4/13/82). He fact-checked all three, finding errors indicative of intentional disinformation.

The first article referred to 190 sightings of UFOs diving into the sea by Soviet ships. One included a "9,000 ton freighter, Vladimir Vorobyev," the crew of which supposedly had an encounter in the Sea of Japan in August 1980. Liljegren determined that there was such a ship with that name, but was a small research/fishing vessel, built in West Germany. Considering the *Enquirer's* CIA connections via its publisher, Gene Pope, such disinformation seemed designed to sow confusion, impede genuine research, and cast doubt over the legitimate reports.[64]

Through the spring and summer the lawsuit against the NSA by CAUS continued to muddle on. Early in 1982, Peter Gersten filed a petition for the Supreme Court to hear the case of CAUS v. the NSA. He argued that the NSA did not clearly justify its reasons for withholding the requested UFO documents. He questioned the actions of the court in not reviewing the documents first-hand, and its decision to rely upon a Top Secret summary prepared by the defendant of what the files contained. His petition was denied by the Supreme Court on March 8, which ruled that releasing the NSA's files "could seriously jeopardize the work of the agency and the security of the United States." Thus, the NSA's 135 UFO documents remained classified, unseen by even a single judge. Still, the battle continued. On April 27, Gersten on behalf of CAUS filed a request with the NSA for all legal documents, memos, records, affidavits, and notes used to prepare and argue the Civil Action case as well as the appeal. He also requested all or any part of the 21-page top secret affidavit.

Oddly, the NSA partially declassified the 21-page NSA affidavit on May 18. Although nearly all reports of UFOs were censored out, it became known that a total of 239 UFO documents had been discovered by the NSA in its files, with 79 originating from other government agencies. That means 160, not 135, documents originated from within NSA. One reference in the material even described the NSA's ability to deal with "unusual phenomena." Lawrence Fawcett and Barry Greenwood puzzled that the affidavit was released so quickly (albeit censored) following a simple letter from private citizens, after it had been completely withheld throughout three legal actions.[65]

Any victory attained by the limited release of the NSA documents was snuffed out by an executive order signed by President Reagan on April 2, 1982. This was Executive Order #12356, which eliminated response time limits to FOIA requests. Almost immediately, searches for UFO documents were significantly delayed. Henceforth, it would not be uncommon for a search to last two years or more. Search fees rose accordingly, sometimes substantially – as high in one instance as $250,000. This was clearly unattainable for private citizens and nearly all organizations.[66] The Executive Order served notice that the glory era of the Freedom of Information Act had ended. The Act continued to be useful to researchers of all types, but the UFO data slowed to a trickle compared with earlier years.

Although Reagan's order hindered the public's ability to investigate the UFO cover-up, he himself retained a strong interest in the topic. His several public statements about the topic are well known. On June 27, 1982, Reagan hosted Steven Spielberg at the White House for a private screening of the latter's soon-to-be-released movie *ET: The Extraterrestrial*. The movie concerned a stranded extraterrestrial who was trying to return to his world, while U.S. government agents tried to capture him. Along with the Reagans and Spielberg, thirty five others attended the special screening, including Supreme Court Justice Sandra Day O'Connor. The movie deeply affected the Reagans, and the President said quietly to Spielberg, "you know, there aren't six people in this room who know how true this really is." Apparently, the surrounding crowd made further conversation impractical. The story came from Hollywood television producer Jamie Shandera, who said that Spielberg had told him this personally shortly after the incident occurred, while Shandera was involved in making a documentary on Spielberg. (Shandera would also soon play a major role in the MJ-12 document controversy). Several attempts to follow up on this story failed. During the mid-1980s, Linda Moulton Howe, who was working on a script for a new documentary, spoke with Spielberg's appointment secretary about arranging a phone interview with him to discuss the Reagan statement. She was told that no interview was possible, as Spielberg was then on the other side of the world directing a feature film. In 1988 Grant Cameron inquired with Spielberg about it, receiving the reply from Spielberg's publicity coordinator that Spielberg was away and "unable to personally answer your question." Billy Cox, reporter for *Florida Today*, also tried reaching Spielberg. Cox was told by Spielberg's publicist, Marvin Levy, that "Mr. Spielberg does not wish to discuss any private conversation held with the President."[67]

What makes this story more interesting is that the following morning, Reagan was briefed on the U.S. Space Program. Initially meeting in the highly secure White House Situation Room with Chief of Staff James Baker, Attorney General Edwin Meese, and Deputy Chief of Staff Michael Deaver, the four then met with six members of the National Security

Council (NSC) – but no one from NASA. Grant Cameron noted NASA's absence from this kind of meeting as "unheard of." It would seem that NASA had become irrelevant to the true U.S. space program.[68]

On a related matter, the author can disclose a discussion he had with one "insider" who was well-placed in the intelligence community during the Reagan years. When asked the question "how much do the Presidents know" about UFOs, this person stated that "some knew more than others." While hinting that he did not believe Presidents Clinton or George W. Bush had been briefed significantly on the topic, it was his knowledge that President Reagan had been briefed (and his near certainty that Presidents Carter and George Bush Sr. also had).

Intrigue thickened in early July during a MUFON Symposium in Toronto. According to William Moore, at some point during the proceedings he went out privately with Allen Hynek for a drink. On the way, he stopped at a store to drop off some film to be developed. The two then went to a bar, and Moore began to discuss the Bennewitz case. After a few beers, Hynek made a shocking statement. Each year, he said, the Air Force gave him a certain amount of money to do consulting work, just as he had received during the days of Project Blue Book. During the previous summer – that is, 1981 – Hynek was tasked with delivering a new computer and program to Bennewitz. However, he did not tell Bennewitz that this was done at the request of the U.S. Air Force. In other words, Hynek was working for the U.S. military-intelligence community, presumably in an attempt to spy on and influence Paul Bennewitz. Moore did not know what to make of this claim by Hynek, but received supporting information from Bennewitz himself, who later told him that his program to monitor alien communications had "been modified by the aliens themselves," in order to facilitate better communication with him.

Moore's story continued. The following day, his hotel telephone rang. It was Falcon. "How did the pictures turn out?" he asked. Apparently Moore was not as alone with Hynek as he had thought. Falcon told Moore he was being watched. Of course, it was possible that Hynek was informing Falcon of Moore's activities. Nothing could be sure. Gregory Bishop even speculated that perhaps Hynek had been told to tell the computer story to Moore in order to gauge his reaction. None of Hynek's former associates has supported this story, although Bishop, who received it directly from Moore, trusts and believes his source.[69]

The Smith-Sarbacher Connection: Uncovered

The Hynek story may have some truth to it, but corroboration is unlikely and so it remains only an allegation. Meanwhile, traditional research methods were making significant strides toward getting under the real cover-up. Canadian researcher Arthur Bray uncovered a very important lead in 1982. While going through the papers of the late Wilbert Smith, Bray discovered handwritten notes relating to a conversation Smith had about UFOs in September 1950 with a key American scientist. It had previously been learned that Smith wrote a secret memo that year to his government on this topic, indicating that UFOs were "the most highly classified subject in the United States Government." But the memo had given no names. In his handwritten notes, however, Smith revealed that his main source was Dr. Robert Sarbacher, a brilliant scientist who was very prominent within the Pentagon, and whose laboratory had been near the Canadian Embassy in Washington. Most interesting was that, in 1982, Robert Sarbacher was still alive.

Several researchers quickly followed up, most notably Stanton Friedman and William Steinman. To the amazement not only of UFO researchers but elite members within the aerospace community, Sarbacher confirmed Smith's account and more. He said, for instance, that prior to his conversation with Smith, he was invited to Wright-Patterson AFB for a briefing on the recovery of a flying saucer in the western United States. In late 1983, he wrote a two-page typed letter to Steinman saying that while he was not directly involved in retrievals of downed flying saucers, "John von Neumann was definitely involved. Dr. Vannevar Bush was definitely involved, and I think Dr. Robert Oppenheimer also." He added

> ... certain materials reported to have come from flying saucer crashes were extremely light and very tough. I am sure our laboratories analyzed them very carefully.... I remember in talking with some of the people at the office that I got the impression these 'aliens' were constructed like certain insects ....[70]

Later, Sarbacher told Steinman that a certain Dr. Eric Walker was involved. Walker was another prominent scientist and former President of Penn State University. Sarbacher told Steinman that Walker ("for sure") attended UFO meetings at Wright-Patterson AFB in the early 1950s. Walker, too, was still alive. Steinman found Walker and spoke to him, receiving the startlingly candid reply, "yes, I attended meetings concerning that subject matter..." Walker said he had known of MJ-12 since 1947, but told Steinman he was "delving into an area that you can do absolutely nothing about," and advised him to "leave it alone."[71]

Bray's discovery of the Wilbert Smith notes was the most important research discovery of 1982, but Leonard Stringfield continued to develop interesting sources and leads. One was a Lieutenant Colonel who claimed that a secret underground military base existed in Texas, beneath the Fort Hood Army Military Reservation. He claimed to have intimate knowledge of the installation and told Stringfield about squadrons of unmarked helicopters with sophisticated instrumentation to monitor UFOs, or airlift them out of the area in the event of a crash.[72]

Incidentally, Charles Wilhelm, of the "Coalition of Concerned Ufologists," who had been attacking Stringfield so stridently for some time, published a booklet on the alleged alien body photos, concluding that Willard McIntyre contrived the whole affair and that he had been taken in as a pawn. This leaves the question of, who was Willard McIntyre, and why did he create a campaign to smear Leonard Stringfield?[73] The answer is not difficult to envision, since McIntyre was previously associated with the CIA-connected Society of Photographic Scientists and Engineers (SPSE), and in any case the U.S. intelligence community appears to have been busy monitoring all areas of the UFO front.

On June 2, 1982, a new organization, the Society for Scientific Exploration (SSE), met for the first time at the University of Maryland. Led by Peter Sturrock of Stanford University, it included over 100 professors from North American universities from a range of disciplines. The society's goal was to provide a forum discussion and analysis of anomalous phenomena, including but not limited to UFOs. Its tone was decidedly scientific and non-conspiratorial.[74] Two months later, the group held its first meeting in Europe (Munich), and was the subject of a classified DIA report. Obviously, somebody was interested.[75]

Slowly but surely, researchers were making some strides in studying the UFO phenomenon and even uncovering elements of the cover-up. Still, skeptics scored a public relations victory on October 12, 1982, when PBS television aired a strongly debunking piece on UFOs that was produced by BBC/NOVA. Entitled *The Case of the UFOs*, it was advertised as a "rigorous, scientific investigation of the fact, fiction and hoax of unidentified flying objects." It gave extensive coverage to Philip Klass, James Oberg, and Michael Persinger, the last of whom argued that UFO sightings and experiences were triggered by electrical phenomena produced by stress along geological fault lines. Persinger suggested the Travis Walton case was caused by an "electrically induced confabulation." Brief appearances were made by Bruce Maccabee and Alan Hendry, both of which were edited to look as though they agreed with the debunkers. Allen Hynek was interviewed at length but did not appear. Liberal use of terms like "buff" and "believer" were scattered throughout. The tenor of the show was not surprising, considering that Kendrick Fraser, editor of CSICOP's *Skeptical Inquirer*, provided the list of participants to the producers. Kenneth Arnold, America's 'original' flying saucer witness, now getting on in years, wrote to BBC producer John Groom, calling the program a "stupid, ignorant distortion of facts that I know were available to you."[76]

As Noam Chomsky frequently pointed out, the relative openness of Western societies required a more sophisticated form of propaganda to manage public opinion than was needed in more authoritarian societies.[77] Not surprisingly, control over public opinion on UFOs was more heavy handed in the Soviet Union. There, according to Russian ufologist Valerie Sanarov, many UFO publications were simply confiscated by postal authorities "as prohibited items."[78]

America: First Among Equals

One of the difficulties in understanding the nature of the UFO cover-up comes from its obvious international nature. UFOs are seen everywhere, not just in the United States. Why, then, would not some other nation go its own way and acknowledge the reality? Could the U.S. really control all other nations on this matter – or within the context of the Cold War, at least all allied nations?

One way to look at this question is to observe the relationships between the U.S. intelligence community with sister intelligence communities. For instance, in April 1982, war in the Falklands Islands broke out between Argentina and Great Britain. During the fighting, the British government came to realize that it was entirely dependent on America's NSA for signals intelligence – as much as 98 percent of Britain's intelligence on Argentina's naval and military movements came from the NSA. While cooperation was generally good, one British official said "there may be targets they [the Americans] don't want to cover." Britain simply could not afford the kind of satellite coverage that the Americans were able to produce.[79]

In other words, American dominance in matters of national security – even *other nations'* national security – was frequently a given. It is not hard to see how America could exercise its military, intelligence, and economic might to influence other nations regarding UFO policy. It is also helpful to remember that the dominance of national structures by private individuals and groups was an old story by 1982, and firmly entrenched in the U.S.

and elsewhere. Nationalism may have been going strong within the many world cultures, but was fast becoming irrelevant in the realm of power politics and control of global resources.[80]

As with Europe, so with Latin America, where the United States continued its long history of propping up and destabilizing regimes as it saw fit. Indeed, shortly after the end of the Falklands war, the CIA recruited a motley assortment of drug dealers and gun runners to train the so-called Nicaraguan Contras,* and then deftly rigged elections in El Salvador.[81] Meanwhile, a drug dealer named Barry Seal, allegedly connected with the CIA, began smuggling drugs through an airstrip at Mena, Arkansas. Seal was convicted of drug trafficking in 1984. In exchange for leniency, he agreed to work undercover for Oliver North's contra network. The smuggling operation continued.[82]

Big Brother Grows Up

Meanwhile, an especially unsavory chapter in the secret history of the U.S. was unfolding. In 1982, the U.S. Justice Department granted the contracting firm Inslaw $10 million to adapt a certain computer program to the needs of U.S. attorneys in tracking criminal cases from office to office. The program, called Prosecutors Management Information System (PROMIS), had the vital capability of interfacing with other databases. PROMIS soon became an astonishingly powerful program which certain insiders at the Department of Justice (and beyond) realized could provide applications for a wide range of other uses, a number of which were clearly illegal, but immensely profitable.[83]

Shortly thereafter, PROMIS developer William Hamilton learned to his surprise that he had lost his contract with the Justice Department. A sympathetic insider eventually told him why: his software had been pirated and was being resold with astonishing modifications. Thus began an extended legal battle of the Hamiltons against the Department of Justice, which ultimately involved the NSA, organized crime, and much more. It eventually resulted in the murder of journalist Danny Casolaro – but not in justice for the Hamiltons.

According to Ari Ben-Menasche, a former Israeli Mossad agent, PROMIS was used to tap into the computers of telephone companies, water utilities, credit card companies, and other public organizations to search for specific information. It allegedly had a "backdoor" which allowed

---

* Soon dubbed "freedom fighters" by President Reagan.

entry into the files of any foreign intelligence service using the system. Some considered this backdoor capability to be pure fantasy, although the secret may not have been with the software but rather the hardware. Such was the information that came to PROMIS developer, Bill Hamilton, who was told that "extra chips" were able to broadcast the data inside PROMIS to satellites owned by the NSA. This scenario neatly bypassed objections that physical access was required for a backdoor to work.[84]

One of the modifications to PROMIS apparently included artificial intelligence, a feature developed by computer engineer Barry Kusnick. This ostensibly allowed PROMIS to deduce from personality characteristics the potential action of a person being traced. Kusnick had previously done communications and intelligence work for Northrop and the U.S. military. He went missing during the early 1990s, presumably killed.[85]

It also appears that PROMIS was useful to the military regime in Guatemala, where it tracked leftist insurgents. According to Ben-Menasch, even if a dissident traveled under a false name, characteristics such as height, hair color, age, were searched through the database, while a local army commander could learn that a dissident matching that description had been in his area several days before, took a train, then a bus, stayed at a friend's house, and was now on the road under a different name. "That's how frightening the system was."[86]

Most important of all, PROMIS was used for money laundering. According to information leaked to the Hamiltons, the software was installed throughout the BCCI banking empire to track wire transfers of money, all being monitored by the NSA. [87]

Journalist Gordon Thomas later published an authorized history of the Israeli Mossad intelligence agency which included admissions about the theft and re-sale of PROMIS. His research showed that Israeli intelligence collaborated with the U.S. Justice Department to steal the software in the first place. The FBI and CIA were then among the U.S. agencies that adapted PROMIS to track the intelligence information they produce. Elements in U.S. intelligence also adapted it to track financial transactions in the banking sector. Furthermore, U.S. and Israeli intelligence created a Trojan horse version of PROMIS which they then sold to foreign intelligence agencies (for approximately $500 million), and promptly used it to spy on them.[88]

Although the PROMIS saga displayed government corruption at its most banal, its known relationship to the UFO phenomenon and cover-up was at best indirect. Yet it is important here as a key moment in the expansion of the national security state. The matter of obtaining government 'disclosure' on UFOs takes on a different meaning when the very nature of one's government is being transformed.

Sightings in Late 1982

With a few notable exceptions, the latter half of 1982 was a quiet period of UFO activity. On September 17, 1982, the crew and captain of the Romanian cargo ship "Bosca" saw a UFO off the coast of Brazil, near the equator. The event was spectacular, though sketchy on the details. The ship was 200 miles off the coast, just outside of Brazilian territorial waters. Shortly after 9 p.m., captain Stefan Freitag and his crew saw an object that looked like a full Moon, accompanied by a smaller, star-like object. This smaller object grew and became brighter, eventually equaling its companion. Both objects then disappeared, leaving behind a shiny cloud. But the scene had not ended. Another moon-like object appeared, during which a silent explosion occurred, and an orange light radiated from the object. By now, Freitag and fourteen of his men were watching and photographing this display. A fourth "Moon" then appeared; either this or the other object rapidly approached the ship, causing the crew to panic and the ship's dog to howl. Then a fifth phenomenon appeared. Although it is not clear how this series of events ended, it appears to have faded out, leaving a glow that lasted for 30 minutes. Freitag communicated with the Brazilian coast guard, but received no answer. No heat was felt by any of the crew, although radiation levels were higher than normal.

James Oberg expressed regret that the case was even recorded and suggested that researchers should have investigated "some of the more obvious" terrestrial stimuli before rushing into print with such a report. Although he offered no theories, it is conceivable that some sort of aerial test was underway.[89]

Even more dramatic was an incident from October 4, 1982, in which a UFO sighting allegedly almost caused a nuclear war. This case comes from the famed "KGB files" on UFOs, and was examined by ABC news correspondent David Ensor in 1995. At a Soviet military base in Byelo-koroviche, Ukraine, an object of astonishing size – reportedly 2,900 feet in diameter – hovered over a nuclear missile site. Many witnesses confirmed the sighting to Ensor, including missile engineer, Lt. Colonel Vladimir Plantonev, who described the UFO as silent, disc-shaped, with no portholes and a completely even surface. The missile silo at the base contained a fully functional warhead pointed at the United States. Plantonev was in a bunker while the object hovered overhead; on the control panels, signal lights suddenly turned on briefly, indicating that the missiles were preparing for launch. However, no orders had come from Moscow, nor had anyone at the base pushed any buttons. For fifteen seconds, the base had lost control of its nuclear weapons. Was this a malicious joke played by an alien prankster?[90]

Less dramatic but more interesting from a scientific point of view was the "Amarante" case that occurred at Nancy, France, on October 21, 1982. The witness, a biologist, reported that an oval-shaped object descended into his garden, hovering just one meter above the ground. He watched the object for twenty minutes, when it then lifted straight into the sky. There was no sound during the encounter, the witness felt no heat, nor were there any traces on the ground afterward. One oddity, however, was that just before the object left, the grass blades stood straight up. Later investigation by GEPAN/SEPRA succeeded in duplicating this phenomenon in the laboratory by using intense electric fields. The investigators also noticed that the plants near the object had become desiccated while similar plants further away were in normal health. The fruit of plants near the landing site looked as though they had been cooked.[91]

An interesting military encounter occurred on November 2, in the Estremadura province of Portugal. A Portuguese lieutenant was flying a DHC-1 trainer from the OTA Air Base at 10:50 a.m. during clear skies. Below the plane near the ground, the pilot saw a small shiny object and reported the sighting to his base. Ten minutes later, the pilot and passenger of another trainer saw probably the same object as it gave off flashes of red and green light. The object circled for about ten minutes, at one point flying between the two aircraft, enabling a reasonable estimate of its size – roughly six or seven feet in diameter. Finally it made a pass at the first plane and sped off out of sight.[92]

By the end of the year, a far more interesting and lasting development was occurring in the northeastern U.S. These were the triangle and "boomerang" sightings, investigated by a number of investigators, most notably a local science teacher named Philip Imbrogno, who described the phenomenon in the book *Night Siege*. Most of these sightings were in lower New York State or Connecticut, an area known as the Hudson Valley. They typically involved low flying, silent, objects hovering over highways, shining bright lights to the ground, and gliding away, sometimes slowly, sometimes rapidly. By the mid-1980s, witnesses numbered in the thousands and covered the full sociological spectrum.

One of the early compelling sightings occurred on New Year's Eve, December 31, 1982. A retired New York City police officer, outside his home in the town of Kent, just a few miles from the Connecticut border, was cleaning some debris from a New Year's champagne christening of his new home. The time was near midnight. Overhead, red, green, and white lights moved slowly across the sky. They appeared to be connected in a boomerang or V-shape. A faint, deep hum came from it, which the witness said sounded "like a factory with a lot of machines running in the distance." He called his wife, who came out with a video camera. They videotaped the object while it passed directly over their house just 500 feet above. As it passed over, the retired officer felt a deep vibration in his chest.

The strangeness did not end there. The multi-colored lights then vanished and three bright white lights appeared in a triangular shape. The white lights then went out, and about fifteen multi-colored lights came on. It passed slowly out of sight towards Interstate 84, at the state border. "This was not any type of aircraft that I know of," the witness said. Unfortunately, the video came out poorly; the bright white lights were discernable, as were some other colored lights, but no structure could be seen.

Philip Imbrogno found other witnesses to this sighting. One was a man driving home on Interstate 84 who saw many cars pulled off the road and a bright light in the sky, making slow, tight circles in the air and scanning the ground with a searchlight. Initially, he assumed it was a helicopter, but could not see the structure. Then the object descended toward his car, turned off its searchlight, and hovered about 300 feet off the road. The witness told Imbrogno it was "shaped like a boomerang with lights running up and down its wings.... so huge it filled up the entire sky." From fear and nervous reflex, he blew his horn. When the object shot another beam of white light onto the highway, he shielded his eyes. As the beam became closer, his nervousness became panic, and he pleaded from within his car for the object to leave. He felt a kind of communication with whatever intelligence was connected to the object, and said he heard a "voice" that told him not to be afraid. Suddenly the object turned away and the beam of light vanished. He hurried home and told no one of his experience for quite some time.[93]

Sightings like this were only the beginning. The Hudson Valley was about to experience the most startling wave of UFO activity in modern history. Explanations essentially came down to a few candidates: genuine UFOs (that is, alien vehicles), experimental or classified aircraft, or ultralight aircraft flying illegally in close-knit formations at night. Close examination of most of the cases over the next few years ruled out the ultralight explanation, as those aircraft lacked hovering ability, were considerably louder than what witnesses described, could not legally fly at night, were not safe in close formations, and could not carry powerful search lights. In addition, it was illegal and extremely dangerous for any aircraft flying at night to shut off its lights for any extended period, as these objects repeatedly did.

The experimental aircraft solution is a better candidate, but also problematic. For instance, the first deployment of the F-117 "Nighthawk" stealth fighter took place in 1982, and its existence remained classified for another six years. It is conceivable that another classified project began to deploy at this time, although problems of explanation remain: what principles of flight could account for its extraordinary characteristics? What would be the mission of such boomerangs? Why fly them so close to densely populated areas?

Indeed, such questions apply regardless of whomever, or whatever, lay behind these mysterious craft.

Star Wars, the Soviets, and ET?

By 1983, the Cold War had taken a decided turn in favor of the United States. Longtime Soviet leader Leonid Brezhnev had died in 1982, the CIA-supported war in Afghanistan continued to bleed the resources of the USSR, and the military spending of the Reagan administration surely worried Brezhnev's successor, Yuri Andropov. In January 1983, Andropov proposed a new East-West summit to create "nuclear free zones" in parts of Europe and the Mediterranean, ban the sale of weapons to the developing world, and reduce the number of Soviet SS-20 missiles in Eastern Europe. He also proposed a non-aggression undertaking in which NATO

and Warsaw Pact members would agree not to use force against each other, nor against members of their own bloc (a move that obviously mattered more to the Warsaw Pact members than to NATO). It was a clear break with the past.

Reagan was of no mind to compromise. In March 1983, he issued several confrontational public statements and

President Reagan giving his famous "Star Wars" speech, March 23, 1983.

private directives. On March 8, he referred to the Soviet Union as an "evil empire," and Soviet leaders as "the focus of evil in the modern world."[94] On March 23, the same day that flight testing resumed on the B-1 bomber at Edwards AFB, the President gave his famous "Star Wars" speech.[95] Like Andropov, Reagan too broke with the past, but in the opposite direction of his Soviet counterpart. Rejecting the age-old idea of Mutual Assured Destruction (MAD) – that a preponderance of missiles by both sides would deter either from initiating a nuclear war – Reagan promoted a "Strategic Defense Initiative" (SDI). This was an ambitious project to construct an anti-missile system in space. Using ground-based and space-based weapon systems, SDI was to act as a defensive shield to intercept and destroy incoming hostile projectiles. Thus, not weapons reduction, but escalation, was Reagan's answer to Andropov.

Much of SDI's science was developed at Lawrence Livermore National Laboratory in a program headed by physicist Lowell Wood, a protégé of Edward Teller – the "father of the hydrogen bomb." Indeed, Teller himself told Reagan of the program's capabilities in early 1983. SDI used such technologies as lasers, x-ray weapons, and even an exotic "Kinetic Energy Weapon" which could fire a seven-gram projectile from a light gas gun at a velocity of more than 23,000 feet per second (over 15,000 mph).

Yet, it seemed too exotic to work for the 1980s, and quickly drew criticisms. Nobel physicist Hans Bethe, a man who had worked with Teller on the atomic and hydrogen bombs, argued that a laser defense shield was too costly, too hard to build, too easy to destroy, and liable to be over-whelmed by decoys. Diplomacy was the only way to end the threat of nuclear war, he maintained. SDI could even worsen matters, causing the Soviets to view it as a positive threat. Europeans were also alarmed that the "shield" apparently covered only America – leaving them as the main target.* Nor had Reagan provided any analysis of the technological problems or likely cost of this futuristic program. Andropov, for his part, rejected SDI as futile.[96] An unsympathetic media dubbed the program "Star Wars," initially as a pejorative to indicate that the whole idea was no better than fantasy, although Reagan soon embraced the term.

Seen conventionally, SDI was a dubious bulwark of national security. From the beginning, however, conjecture arose that the program was connected to the UFO situation, a speculation amplified by Reagan's

---

* Even Margaret Thatcher, Reagan's closest international ally, tried to persuade him to modify the plan to include NATO allies.

several "alien invasion" remarks from later years.* Yet, interpreting SDI in connection to UFOs is tricky. If such an array of space-based weapons could not be expected to stop Soviet missiles, how could it deal with an alien menace? One obvious possibility is that SDI was not meant as a final answer, but as a starting point. Presumably, the anti-missile, anti-Soviet, component of SDI could serve as cover for the more exotic aspects and covert missions.

There are reasons to suppose there was more to Star Wars than met the eye. In the first place, several insiders and alleged insiders have spoken about a secret space program and of covert interactions with ET. This author spoke at length to a former USAF Telecommunications Specialist named Simone Mendez (and reviewed her military records). During the early 1980s, Mendez had a Top Secret Clearance while working at Nellis AFB with the 2069th Communication Squadron. In October 1981, a friend gave her a Top Secret message stating that NORAD had detected deep space objects entering Earth's atmosphere. Mendez subsequently underwent intensive interrogation by the Air Force which sparked depression and psychological problems for years.

Another individual known to the author, Ronald S. Regehr, has provided substantiation of claims that "fastwalkers" (e.g. UFOs in space) are constantly being tracked. Regehr is a leading expert on the Defense Satellite Program (DSP), for which his employer Aero-Jet was a contractor. During the 1990s, Regehr accidentally, but legally, came into possession of many pages of the DSP's "Individual Target Event Data Base" (nicknamed "Ittybitty"). This database was a list of fastwalkers tracked by the DSP satellites, which Regehr argues are ideally designed for detecting UFOs. The database certainly supports this belief: during the period under review for this book (the years 1973 to 1991), the database recorded 283 space-based UFOs, an average of more than one per month. In 1982, DSP sensors had tracked 15 UFOs; in 1983 the total was 17. These were not primarily "deep space" UFOs, but it is indicative that the U.S. space program encountered UFOs with regularity.[97]

One of the most amazing fastwalker encounters by the DSP system occurred on May 5, 1984, when a UFO entered Earth's atmosphere from

---

*   Indeed, the author had a bizarre experience while standing in the Newark, New Jersey airport in July 1983. Having just seen on the airport television a news story about SDI, a man in a business suit approached him and said, "you realize what that program is really about?" "What do you mean?" replied the author. "That's about UFOs and aliens," stated the man. After a brief and uncomfortable silence, the man walked away. The author promptly forgot about the meeting for the next 15 years, only recalling it while writing the first volume of this historical study.

deep space, slowed, turned, and returned to deep space. The observation lasted for 9 minutes, and the object came to within a mere 3 kilometers of the satellite. A detailed investigation failed to explain what caused the sensor reading, other than a real object of some type. As if this were not enough, another deep space platform, with whom Regehr's group cross-tracked the sightings data, also detected this object optically.[98]

Other researchers have obtained similar information regarding the frequency of fastwalker encounters. *New York Times* journalist Howard Blum, in his 1990 book, *Out There*, said that NORAD deep-space radars regularly tracked many UFOs. Also, according to UFO researcher and activist, Dr. Steven Greer, NORAD sources told him that the Air Force tracked about 500 fastwalkers entering Earth's atmosphere each year – more than one per day. Other sources told Greer that rogue units within unacknowledged Special Access Programs – the prototypical black budget operations within the Department of Defense – secretly developed SDI weapons to shoot down UFOs.[99]

Attorney Stephen Lovekin, who had worked for the Army Signal Corps during the Eisenhower and Kennedy years, also stated his opinion that SDI was to be used against extraterrestrials. In 2005, Lovekin spoke with filmmaker Peter Janney about the extraterrestrial presence on Earth and its associated cover-up. In 1995, he said, he attended a conference on SDI in Monterrey, Mexico, that included high level American and Russian participants. "Star Wars," Lovekin said to Janney, "was not meant to keep us from a Russian attack, but it was there to put a curtain, if you will, over Russian territory as well as our territory. We were there to try to protect the Russians. The Russians knew it." Lovekin added, somewhat unclearly, that he had seen Russian films of "UFOs trying to get away .... It was brought down ... exactly what Star Wars was supposed to do."[100]

Certainly, a large number of anomalous events are recorded by NASA, as well as by the European Space Agency, the Russians, and the Chinese.[101] Their abundance suggests at the very least a motivation to develop secret components to a space program – after all, if there are strange things going on in space, one would presumably want to investigate them. In a few instances, it looks as though actual space-based weapons were used against alien objects.

A strange object was recorded visually in space just a year and a half after Reagan's Star Wars speech. This was during NASA's STS-51 mission by the Space Shuttle *Discovery*. In November 1984, as the shuttle approached the Westar VI satellite (built by the Hughes' Space and Communications

Group), its video camera recorded a sphere that seemed to materialize from a distance near the top center of the frame and then move with slight undulations across the right side of the frame in a curved path. The Earth is visible in the background. Despite the video's extraordinary implications, it has received no significant public analysis.

In correspondence with the author, Navy optical physicist Bruce Maccabee confirmed that the STS-51 video was real and not a hoax. He added his personal opinion that NASA was probably hiding secrets on UFOs in space. Maccabee was unsure, however, whether the STS-51 video showed an alien craft. The object, he said, might have been "a reflection of something in a window or a small nearby particle." He simply did not know what it was.[102]

The object was captured on video for two seconds. It was clearly three dimensional, and did not look like recognizable debris – such as ice crystals – that might have been ejected by the shuttle. More to the point, the object's apparent diameter can be seen to grow during the first second it appears, when it is still above the horizon of the Earth. The effect is noticeable, and gives the distinct impression that the ob-

Still frame from the November 1984 STS-51 mission. The unknown object appears as a slightly flattened sphere just above the curve of the Earth.

ject was moving toward the camera. Shuttle debris must be ruled out, as debris would move *away* from the shuttle, not toward it. Perhaps, as Maccabee speculated, the image was a reflection of something, although the video shows no evidence of reflection at any point. Considering all the factors involved, the possibility of a genuine space anomaly must be considered. Indeed, it appears to be the strongest hypothesis until a detailed scientific analysis is undertaken.

Undoubtedly the most famous space video of a UFO was taken during the Space Shuttle Columbia's STS-48 mission in September 1991. This showed what appeared to be the firing of a weapon at an object entering Earth's orbit. While there are no easy answers for this video, it must be said that the official explanation (booster rocket firing which thereby moved ice particles and debris in various directions) has been energetically argued to be impossible. More on this case later.[103]

It also appears that the Soviets had a specific concern about Star Wars, and not the one conventionally described in history textbooks – that Star Wars threatened to make their missile system obsolete. In the words of a June 1989 issue of *Soviet Military Review*:

> This ballistic missile defense is designed to control outer space and destroy near-earth, air and space targets. Any system can be effective only if it is managed by super-quick computer systems. It is most important here to correctly identify targets. So, corresponding computer cells must 'know' what signal characteristics of the object it is tracking [that] can make it a potential target. We believe that the lack of information on the characteristics and influence of UFOs increase the threat of incorrect information. Then, mass transition of UFOs along trajectories close to those of combat missiles could be regarded by computers as an attack.[104]

In other words, the USSR was concerned that UFOs could be misidentified by SDI as attacking Soviet missiles. This exactly mirrored the fears expressed by the American UFO research organization NICAP during the 1950s and 1960s. It was imperative, argued NICAP Director Donald Keyhoe and former CIA Director Roscoe Hillenkoetter (who was on the NICAP Board) that UFOs be taken seriously by the military so as not to confuse UFOs with Soviet missiles. Of course, the reality back then was that, contrary to public statements by the military, UFOs were being taken very seriously. For that matter, it is just as likely that the problem was understood equally well during the 1980s.

Runaway Government

During early 1983, the Reagan Presidency undertook measures to tighten control over government secrets. On March 11th, President Reagan authorized National Security Decision Directive (NSDD) 84, which substantially increased government control over federal employees, particularly their relationships with the media. Various government agencies, such as the CIA, had long been using secrecy contracts and lifetime censorship to prevent employees from revealing sensitive or embarrassing information. Congress with some success had blocked the spread of this trend, enabling federal employees to become "whistle blowers" on waste, fraud, and abuse within the federal government. Reagan's directive effectively overturned such Congressional attempts, and applied to all executive branch agencies – including more than 100,000 government employees. The directive mandated that all employees who had access to sensitive information were now subject to lifetime censorship of their writings and speeches on those topics.

Researcher Terry Hansen pointed out that this directive would enable the president to lie about foreign policy matters, "and senators and representatives who knew he was lying could not contradict him using information that was classified." Despite arguments that the directive undermined the underlying purpose of the First Amendment – which was to preclude such restraints on speech, especially on behalf of the public good – the directive has gone through its inevitable expansion. As legal theorist and writer Frederick W. Whatley put it: "Governments invariably favor prior restraint. A free society should not." The slippery slope toward an American police state had just become steeper.[105]

The directive came at an inconvenient time – or convenient, depending on how one looks at it. For instance, it might have been inconvenient had Vice President George Bush's relationship with Panamanian dictator Manuel Noriega been fully known at that time. Bush had personally intervened to keep Noriega funded by the CIA, despite his known role as a smuggler of cocaine into the United States. Indeed, the two conspired to create a CIA-backed army of "contra" mercenaries that directed terrorist attacks against the Nicaraguan government and people.[106] Yet, Noriega was becoming a problem for U.S. policy makers. He was playing both sides of the game, including sending guns to leftists in Latin America and high-technology to the Soviet Union.[107]

The Contras were an interesting problem, as they seemed to be more interested in making money in narco-trafficking than in toppling Nicaragua's Sandinista government. This was during President Reagan's "War Against Drugs," punctuated by the slogan "Just Say No." The obvious question arises, how much did U.S. intelligence know about the drug trafficking, and how guilty were they in allowing it to happen? The question was made public in 1996, when journalist Gary Webb published a three-part exposé entitled "Dark Alliance," squarely laying much complicity on the CIA. Immediately, the hounds were unleashed upon Gary Webb – in the form of the *New York Times*, *Washington Post*, and *Los Angeles Times*. He lost his job within a year, and ten years later died of two "self-inflicted" gunshot wounds to the head. In short, it appears that Gary Webb was "suicided."[108]

1983 was noteworthy for many such subterranean developments. During the year, the stolen "Big Brother" software known as PROMIS was probably installed in the World Bank and International Monetary Fund (IMF). At least, this is what two computer experts from the World Bank later told the owners of the software, Bill and Nancy Hamilton. The experts added that while the "hardest evidence" pointed to those two institutions, the program was almost certainly being "much more widely used."[109]

The issue of secrecy becomes more complicated when one considers how government functions increasingly became privatized. This trend was moving at a brisk pace during the 1980s. 1983, for instance, saw the founding of the National Endowment for Democracy (NED), an "establishment-oriented" organization managed by individuals such as Henry Kissinger, Sally Shelton-Colby (William Colby's wife), Barbara Haig (Alexander Haig's daughter), and similar luminaries of the elite. Although it was furnished with $80 million in financing from Congress, its private status kept it safe from FOIA requests and government audits. It soon became a kind of private CIA. Among its hundreds of programs were: destabilizing Ferdinand Marcos in the Philippines and Manuel Noriega in Panama, supporting the Nazi PAN party in Mexico, channeling money to the Contras, and supporting operatives of the Medellin drug cartel. In other words, this "foundation" was – and remains – a private intelligence network with a definite agenda; some observers have claimed its operations are more extensive and more effective than those of the CIA.[110]

One dimension of secrecy concerns the ability to develop secret bases. To what extent are significant underground bases feasible? To what extent do they exist? The expansion of secrecy within the United States government makes a definitive answer to the second of these questions difficult, although the first can be answered more confidently. In June 1983, the Los Alamos National Laboratory (LANL) proposed the creation of an underground science facility to be constructed deep beneath the nuclear test site in southern Nevada. The proposed facility was planned to be an astonishing 3,500 feet underground, although the study left open the possibility of extending it down to 6,000 feet – more than a mile underground. It is unknown whether such a facility was actually built. Still, one can assume that those who made the proposal recognized the technical feasibility of a mile-deep underground installation.[111]

The Hudson Valley Objects

Meanwhile, the UFO phenomenon escalated in the northeastern United States, particularly New York State's Hudson Valley. Quite a few of the 1983 sightings were dramatic, often involving low flying objects and astonished motorists.

One such case took place on February 26 near the town of Kent, New York. Close to 8 p.m., a mother and her teenaged daughter were driving home when the car radio began to hiss. Outside their window, they saw as many as 50 intensely bright lights moving slowly across a clear night sky.

They pulled the car off the road, and realized the lights were part of one object which had stopped over a pond. Despite her daughter's screams of terror, the mother went out to get a better look. She saw that the pond ice reflected the object's red and blue lights, which flashed "like crazy," and she also noticed a large central amber light. The entire object appeared to be quite large, perhaps 200 to 300 feet long.

What followed next was an apparent mental communication between the woman and the UFO. For three or four minutes, the object simply hovered over the frozen pond; then it began to move away. She then issued a thought to the object: *"please don't go. I want to look at you some more."* At that moment, the object stopped, made a complete turn, and moved slowly toward her. This frightened her, and she quickly moved toward her car. In apparent response, the object stopped and moved away. After returning to the car, she regained some courage and decided to follow. She blew her horn to get the attention of others, and eventually some other cars stopped. Soon a small group of people were observing the object glide across the sky, convinced that no one else would believe what they were seeing.

Moments later a few miles away, a teacher and two friends (both air traffic controllers) were exiting Interstate 84 at Danbury, Connecticut, when they noticed odd colored lights in the pattern of a boomerang. They stopped their car and got out. Once again, the object approached them – this time hovering directly above them. It was low enough – about 1,000 feet in the air – that they could see the lights were part of a solid object, and they discerned a black underside. Even so, they heard no sound from it. The object drifted off to the northeast and disappeared, leaving the witnesses utterly baffled. They agreed not to talk about what they saw, but changed their minds when others reported the same thing. When local investigator Philip Imbrogno contacted the Danbury police about this incident, he was simply told that "stable people do not report UFOs."[112]

February 26, 1983 had been a busy night, but the sightings were only beginning in the Hudson Valley.

The sightings of March 17 were more dramatic still. For an incredible 30-minute period, many people within a ten-mile radius in the Hudson Valley reported seeing a large boomerang-shaped object. At 8:40 p.m., a Brewster woman named Linda Nicoletti looked out of her house window to see a large V-shaped object hovering over Interstate 84. It had rows of multi-colored lights along the sides and a bright light in the center. She watched in amazement as it made a right angle turn, and she also noticed her neighbor, Dennis Sant, watching the object from outside his house.

The object moved over his house and bathed the area in bright light. The object then stopped and hovered directly over him. Concerned for her neighbor and herself, Nicoletti phoned the sheriff's office in Brewster. The dispatcher told her that there had been quite a few UFO calls that night, and that several police officers had reported a UFO. What she was seeing, the dispatcher told her, was a type of experimental vehicle from Stewart Air Force Base (a statement the sheriff's office later denied making). As she hung up the phone, the lights moved slowly away to the north. Others also saw this object, one of them a pilot who was "sure" that it was not any type of aircraft he was familiar with.

Sant, who was a deputy clerk for Putnam County, confirmed the event to UFO investigators. "It seemed about the width of a football field and was a dark, very grey metal," he said. "It was so close you could hit it with a baseball." He said the object had been quiet, but not silent. He heard "a low engine sound, very finely tuned."[113]

The sightings continued. Exactly one week later, on March 24, 1983, people reported the same craft behaving just as it had done before. Throughout the Hudson Valley, between 7:30 p.m. and 9:30 p.m. that night, switchboards were jammed with reports of a large UFO. Judging from the reports, it appears that two objects of slightly differing sizes were patrolling the area, as witnesses fifteen miles apart simultaneously saw a low-flying object with red, blue, and green lights arranged in a boomerang pattern. At least one of these objects was silently moving back and forth across the Taconic Parkway; motorists left their vehicles to observe. Several witnesses reported a bright beam of white light coming from the bottom of the object, shining down on the cars.

There are many detailed accounts from this night. A doctor and his family saw a white beam of light descend from the object; a small red object then traveled halfway down the beam and shot off across the horizon. A couple driving in a car described an object at least six stories high, which shot across the horizon and came back to a hovering position near them again, all within a split second. A woman driving alone saw a distant object which then moved rapidly and directly over her car. An executive saw a light "jump" from one part of the object to another. A police officer saw an object that turned 180 degrees around, as if on a wheel, then slowly drift away. An aircraft designer described a UFO "as at least twice the size of a large jet with brilliant white lights in the shape of a V." He tried to convince himself it was a plane. "But it didn't act like one." Another witness was a chief meteorologist for the National Weather Corporation.

He, too, was unable to identify the object, even though it was a mere 1,000 feet above him. It was "as large as an aircraft carrier" and totally silent. All at once its string of lights came on and it hovered for a few seconds. Still another witness described the object that night as "a flying city."[114]

Perhaps the most amazing account from that evening came from Gene Mallon, a New York State corrections officer, described as a "level-headed family man" by investigators Chris Clark and Philip Imbrogno. The experience upset Mallon deeply. He had been driving two teenagers, a brother and sister, to their home in his Jeep, when he noticed very low lights in the sky. Much brighter than car headlights, they quickly changed to multiple colors. He stopped his Jeep, got out, and watched the lights approach him. Soon they were hovering directly above him.

From a distance, the lights had appeared in a V-shaped formation, but it was now evident to Mallon that they were part of an object, and that the object was circular in shape – a very large circle, perhaps 200 feet in diameter. It was either silent or else humming slightly. Soon, the teenaged boy got out of the car while his sister remained inside, hysterical. Mallon simply continued to watch the object. He counted as many as 30 lights outlining the object, making the edges look bright and the center dark. He stayed beneath this object for a very long period of time – he claimed a total of ten minutes, although quite possibly not that long.

He eventually responded to the crying of the girl in his car and drove to a nearby restaurant. From there he called his father-in-law, who was nearby. The father-in-law immediately saw the object, which to him looked like an enormous silent boomerang. Soon, it began to move away. Mallon tried to follow it, but it disappeared sometime after 9:15 p.m., going west over Interstate 84.

It had been an amazing evening. Indeed, the local UFO hotline eventually received about 300 calls regarding that night.[115]

So it was in the Hudson Valley for the rest of the spring, the rest of the year, and the next several years. The UFO sightings received a good deal of local publicity. On March 26, the *Westchester-Rockland Daily Item* ran the headline, "Hundreds see UFOs!" It was at this point that the 'pranksters-flying-ultralight-aircraft-in-formation' theory was used to explain the sightings. The theory was ludicrous from the outset, but necessary to help minimize panic. An ultralight – essentially a hang glider equipped with a seat and a small engine – could in no conceivable way have been responsible for the sightings in question. One witness to the March 24 sightings, a police officer, made this very clear. "I saw the thing," he told investigators, "it hovered directly over my head for five minutes, and airplanes don't hover."

The military aircraft theory was another early offering. Police in the towns of Brewster and Carmel reported that they were told that the UFO was actually a formation of military planes being transferred from nearby Stewart AFB to a new location in New Jersey (Linda Nicoletti had been told a variation of this, when she called the police on March 17). The base had been inactive from 1970 until 1983, when the 105th Airlift Wing of the New York Air National Guard took up quarters. These pilots were said to be unfamiliar with night flying, so they followed the Taconic parkway. This might sound reasonable, except that the Taconic Parkway was a completely unlighted road, the "pilots" wandered in all directions (including north), and they never even reached their destination, since the UFO reports ended at the southern part of Westchester County.

Several UFO researchers investigated the sightings: Philip Imbrogno, Bob Pratt, Fred Dennis, Sheila Sabo, Chris Clark, and George Lesnick. Even J. Allen Hynek flew in from Evanston, Illinois. Working with limited time and resources, they contacted area police stations and airports, interviewed witnesses, and diligently investigated leads.

They saw that something important was going on that defied an easy explanation. The ultralight theory was an obvious red herring, but the possibility of military flights was more serious. A spokesperson at Stewart AFB told them that the police claim (that the base had said their aircraft were responsible) was false: there had been no flights to or from the base during the busy night of March 24. On the other hand, he said, the base did receive phone calls from citizens that night regarding low-flying formations of aircraft and helicopters – not UFOs – buzzing their homes. These aircraft were circling at low altitude, as if they were looking for something. Perhaps, the investigators wondered, some government agency was monitoring the UFOs.

Inquiries with the Westchester and Dutchess County airports had similar results. The Westchester County Airport received calls about UFOs on the night of the 24th, but nothing showed up on its radar (which could not track below 1,000 feet). After receiving so many phone calls about an object, air traffic controllers tried to make radio contact with it, but with no success. At the Dutchess County Airport, controllers saw a formation of multicolored lights at 9:10 p.m., but could not track them on radar. They assumed they were seeing small aircraft flying in illegal formation, but still could not understand how the planes could keep such a tight formation, or hover, or remain virtually silent.[116]

It became evident that aircraft explanations of any sort were problematic. No agency came forward to claim any of the Hudson Valley objects. While it was always conceded that classified or experimental aircraft were possible culprits, there remain no obvious candidates even decades later. The F-117A stealth fighter, sometimes argued to be the cause of occasional UFO sightings, was angular enough that it bore a superficial resemblance to a boomerang. Yet, it was based on the other side of the country, in Nevada's Tonopah Test Range, and did not become operational until October 1983. Nor were the stealth fighter's capabilities even remotely comparable to the object described by these witnesses. If the UFO was man-made, it would have to have been from a project more deeply classified than this, one that has remained classified for several additional decades. It is worth asking, too, how such a large craft could move so silently and slowly – and why it was tested over such a densely populated area?

As the sightings of boomerangs continued, so too did sightings of mysterious squadrons of helicopters and what became known as "mystery planes." These were unmistakably conventional aircraft, yet unidentified. Eventually, *real* ultralights flown by hoaxers further muddied the waters.[117] The appearance of such obviously conventional aircraft enabled police agencies to explain all sightings in this manner. The Federal Aviation Administration (FAA), forced into making public statements, said that as long as the lights avoided restricted airspace and commercial flight paths, they would probably do nothing. On the face of it, this was an odd position to take, since if conventional aircraft were responsible, many of the flights would have been illegal.

The FAA had an institutional aversion to truth on this matter. Any public investigation held out a likelihood that a culprit would not be found. Worse, it would open public discussion on the matter, and the true strangeness of the object would be plainly evident. Denial would no longer be tenable, public positions would become unstable, and public panic would be a real possibility. Bureaucracies, by their very nature, are designed to stifle initiative or individual responsibility; no bureaucratic institution would want to admit that there was an unknown, incredibly advanced, piece of technology traversing the skies of lower New York State.

Behind everything, of course, was the obvious question, the inescapable issue haunting the valley. Were the boomerangs genuine UFOs – that is, alien? If so, they were unlike all previous UFOs. In the first place, the boomerang shape was something quite new. Moreover, they flew again and again over a densely populated region during ideal evening viewing hours, where they were seen by thousands of witnesses. This too was something new.

Many witnesses were not prepared to accept that these were actual UFOs. This was the case during an all-too-typical, all-too-extraordinary family highway encounter on the night of March 26, 1983. The family saw a V-formation of lights low in the sky which approached their car to within 300 feet. The father, a high school physics teacher, said it was "much more silent than any engine I ever heard." The family clearly saw that a single object was connected to the lights, more than 75 feet long from tip to tip. Everyone in the car screamed wildly, including the father, although he later told investigators he believed it was a hoax. "I mean, it has to be a hoax," he said. "These things [UFOs] don't exist, that's what I feel." He believed the police ultralight theory, and that the craft "must have had extensions on its wings to make it look bigger, and the lighting was lightweight." Investigators pointed out that adding any extension to an ultralight would increase its uplift ratio and make it nearly impossible to control. "You're right," he said. "But that's the only explanation I can come up with to explain the object."[118]

Other witnesses were similarly disinclined to accept their encounter, including those that suggested an abduction experience. From the beginning, there were several Hudson Valley cases that had a possible abduction connection. In one instance, three witnesses who had been together during their sighting afterward all had vivid UFO-related dreams. One of them underwent hypnosis and recalled an alien abduction ("don't worry, we won't hurt you"), although he himself remained skeptical of the event, insisting it was just a dream.[119]

Generally, the investigators who took the time to review the reports believed that something alien was staging a dramatic display in the sky.

Linda Moulton Howe meets Richard Doty

While the Hudson Valley experienced a wave of UFO sightings and President Reagan was busy promoting SDI, America's intelligence community was making further inroads into the UFO research field.

On January 10, 1983, Richard Doty of AFOSI met with three individuals in an Albuquerque restaurant to discuss extraterrestrials and UFOs: UFO researchers Peter Gersten and William Moore, and a San Francisco television producer named Ron Lakis. Among their topics of discussion was the August 9, 1980 incident at Manzano. Athough Doty was short on details, he gave the impression that he knew a great deal about UFO investigations. The following day, Doty and Gersten met alone. Doty said that his involvement with UFOs began at Ellsworth AFB in 1977, when a craft landed. A document associated with this incident (alleged to be a hoax) stated that a beam of light had been fired at a security guard, disintegrating his gun and burning his hand. The two also discussed a group called MJ-12, which Doty said stood for "Majority 12." The government knows that UFOs are extraterrestrial, said Doty, and that they come from fifty light-years away. At least three UFO crashes have occurred, and bodies have been recovered. There had been an arranged meeting between aliens and U.S. military on April 30, 1964. The NSA was communicating electronically with ETs through project Aquarius. Spooks were collecting information and spreading disinformation within the UFO community. The most sensitive cover-up documents were going to be impossible to retrieve. The U.S. government had made an agreement with extraterrestrials in which the ETs could conduct animal mutilations and land at certain bases. In exchange, the U.S. government obtained advanced alien technology. Indeed, said Doty, the Cash-Landrum UFO of 1980 had been an attempt by the military to exploit such technology. Finally, the media establishment was preparing the public to accept the reality of visitation by beings from other worlds.

Judging the veracity of these statements, especially when coming from a U.S. intelligence officer, is not particularly easy. Doty even asked Gersten, "how do you know that I'm not here to either give you misinformation, or to give you information which is part of the programming, knowing you're going to go out and spread it around?"[120] Gersten did spread it around. He phoned Barry Greenwood about it, and in early April, 1983, he met with Linda Moulton Howe in New York City. Gersten said that Doty might be able to give her information concerning the Ellsworth incident. As Howe was then working on a documentary for HBO dealing with extraterrestrials entitled *E.T.s: The UFO Factor*, the information seemed propitious.[121] Howe was soon in Albuquerque developing her script. Indeed, it was to include a study of the claims of Paul Bennewitz and report on the strange activities at Kirtland AFB and the Manzano Weapons Storage Area.

She met Doty on April 9, although he was not at the airport to meet her as they had agreed. Howe had to phone Gerald Miller, Director of Weapons Testing Evaluation at Kirtland AFB – the same Miller mentioned in the NSA Project Aquarius document, and with whom she had already known through prior communications. Miller drove her to his home, and from there was able to reach Doty, who came to pick up Howe. Doty never offered a logical reason for why he had not been at the airport. He drove directly to Kirtland AFB's Office of Special Investigations (AFOSI). On the way, Howe mentioned the alleged Holloman UFO landing by saying, "Bob Emenegger told me the date was May 1972." To Howe's surprise, Doty acknowledged that it happened, and said with irritation, "That's bullshit! The date was April 25, 1964." Doty seemed unusually certain about this, Howe thought. The Socorro, New Mexico, sighting by policeman Lonnie Zamora, which had occurred the late afternoon before, had been a "mistake," Doty told her. Zamora had seen an alien craft at 6 p.m., Doty explained, but the arrangement had been for 6 a.m. the next day. "We, or they . . . someone blew the time and coordinates," said Doty. "What Zamora saw was an advance military scout ship. We got it corrected and the Ebens came back to where they were supposed to be, at the Trinity site in White Sands the next morning at 6 a.m., April 25, 1964."

The two drove toward the Kirtland AFB entrance gate. On the right Howe could see Bennewitz's Thunder Scientific Corporation. Through the gate, they drove to a small building that had an AFOSI identification sign. Doty said that he had permission to use his boss's office. As they walked into a large office, Doty said to Linda Moulton Howe, "You broadsided the U. S. government with that documentary." This of course was a reference to her television film, *A Strange Harvest*. "It came too close to something we don't want the public to know about." Why were extraterrestrials mutilating animals? Howe asked. Doty replied that the subject was classified beyond his need to know.

Then, Doty sat down behind a large desk that had someone else's name plate. They talked about Ellsworth AFB, and Doty showed Howe a document that described the encounter. There had been a UFO intrusion, Doty said, but what amazed AFOSI in this case was that the "inner zone alert" went off, indicating that something had entered the underground chamber. Yet, the entrance hatches were untouched.

Doty then took out a Manila envelope. "My superiors have asked me to show this to you," he said. "You can read these and you can ask me questions, but you can't take any notes. And I want you to move from the desk to that chair." He pointed at a large, green, leather chair in the middle of the office. Howe was confused by what was happening, but was so stunned to read the top page of what Doty handed her that she followed his instructions. A few years later, she was told by a source that she was audiotaped and videotaped during that meeting to learn her reaction to what she read. The top page of the documents was in all capital letters and entitled, BRIEFING PAPER FOR THE PRESIDENT OF THE UNITED STATES OF AMERICA ABOUT THE SUBJECT OF UNIDENTIFIED AERIAL CRAFT (UACs). The opening pages contained summaries of government efforts such as Project Sign and the Robertson Panel concerning extraterrestrials, the 1948 crash of USAF pilot Thomas Mantell after a disc encounter, and a list of several UFO crashes and retrievals. Howe recalled that the earliest on the list was 1946, but other dates included 1947, 1949 and the early 1950s. These occurred in Roswell (1947 and 1949); Aztec, New Mexico; Kingman, Arizona; and northern Mexico south of Laredo, Texas.

According to the document, radar interfered with the aliens' guidance system. Bodies and craft had been taken to secure government facilities such as Los Alamos National Laboratories (LANL) and Wright Field, Ohio. The word "extraterrestrials" was used in the document Howe read. These creatures were described as grey in color, three to four and a half feet tall, with long arms, four fingers on each hand, and no thumbs. They had webbing between their fingers and claw-like nails. Small holes existed where one would expect noses and ears. Howe noted this description differed from the large beaklike nose described by Robert Emmeneger of the beings at Holloman AFB.

The briefing paper also described a live extraterrestrial recovered from a 1949 crash near Roswell that was transported to LANL. This creature died of "unknown causes on June 18, 1952." During those three years, "EBE" – an acronym for "extraterrestrial biological entity" – communicated telepathically and verbally about his civilization. Ebe's civilization came from the binary star system, Zeta Reticuli 1 and 2, about 38 light-years from Earth. His species had been coming to Earth for at least 25,000 years. The government has been trying to learn about the ETs, stated the document, and there were four projects mentioned on the last page. Project Garnet dealt with questions and mysteries about human evolution. According to the document, "All questions and mysteries about the evolution of Homo sapiens on this planet have been answered and this project is closed." Project Sigma was designed to communicate with extraterrestrials by using various electronic frequencies, one-way or two-way, and had been running since 1964. Project Snowbird provided research and development of alien technology, including efforts to fly one or more of the ET craft. Project Aquarius was a general project to gather all information about the aliens. Howe read that some of the data collected in this program had been used to advance the U.S. space program. The "presidential briefing paper" also related how, at various intervals in Earth's history, the extraterrestrials had come "to manipulate DNA in already-evolving primates to create Homo sapiens." She recalled that 25,000, 15,000, 5,000 and 2,500 years ago were given as time intervals when E.T. manipulation of primate DNA occurred. Another bombshell statement in the briefing paper was that "two thousand years ago extraterrestrials created a being" to teach mankind about love and nonviolence. When Howe read this she looked at Doty and said, "we're talking about Jesus Christ, here?" Doty nodded silently.

Howe saw a reference to another alien type, referred to as "the Talls." She mentioned that there were two types of ETs often described in mutilation cases: the smaller greys, and taller beings sometimes called Nordics, "and maybe you call the Talls. Who are they?" Howe wrote that Doty's face turned red. She later realized that he must have been tape recording the conversation and she must have interfered with this when she approached him with her question. He explained that there was friction between the greys and the tall ones, but that "they tolerate each other." In fact, Howe recalled cases in her research where there seemed to be collaboration between greys and Nordics.

"Why are you showing this to me?," she asked him. "Why not the *New York Times* or the *Washington Post* or *60 Minutes?*" Those institutions were problematic, he replied. Independent people are easier to manipulate, control, or discredit if the need arose. But there was more, Doty said. He was showing all this to Howe because his superiors intended to release several thousand feet of film including images of crashed discs, alien bodies, the live ET known as "Ebe," the truth about Lonnie Zamora's UFO encounter, and the Holloman landing. Howe was going to be permitted to use this for her HBO documentary, and she was going to receive support by official government confirmation. Doty would call her and use the code name Falcon.

Howe felt "as if fragile pieces of ancient scrolls" were being put in her hand. Yet why was Doty telling her so much? And wasn't it dangerous for Doty to tell her of all this? His answer startled her: "I have been told to tell you. We want you to do the film."

Doty had to leave, but the two met later for dinner in a noisy restaurant where overhearing quiet conversation would be difficult. He told her the planet of the "Ebens" is a hot desert, and they live in houses carved out of rock and soil, something like Pueblo Indians. This was known, he said, because some human research scientists had been studying their planet, just as the Ebens are studying Earth. Doty added that the aliens can control gravity, and manipulate DNA "like a child can build with blocks." There were spiritual truths, as well. Ebe had said souls recycle, and that reincarnation is real. "It's the machinery of the universe."

Alone in her hotel room, Howe was struck by the enormity of what Doty had told her. Feverishly writing down everything she remembered, she did not think it would have been possible for Doty to have made this all up to manipulate her for some secret agenda. She phoned her producer at HBO. She told her about the meeting and the potential historic film release. The two agreed to say nothing until Howe actually got something. They also agreed that HBO should get something in writing from the government "affirming its intention to release film" for inclusion in the HBO documentary.[122]

Through April and May 1983, Howe and Doty spoke by phone several times about getting an official letter of cooperation to HBO that would confirm the government's intention to release sensitive film. Howe needed that letter delivered before her next meeting with HBO in New York City, scheduled for May 18, 1983. But no government communication had reached HBO by the time she arrived. Bridgett Potter, second in charge to HBO head, Michael Fuchs, made the surprising statement that she would not authorize production funds without the government's UFO films delivered to HBO – along with the firm backing of "the President, Vice President, Secretary of Defense, Secretary of State and the Joint Chiefs of Staff." From New York, Howe called Doty at Kirtland AFB about her frustration. He replied that his superiors did not work for HBO; they had their own timetable. Also, the release of the film to her had been delayed for "political reasons." However, he had good news for her: she would be allowed to interview the colonel who had spent a great deal of time with Ebe during the early 1950s. Appointments were repeatedly set and then cancelled.[123]

In June 1983, Doty told Howe there were more delays and that he was leaving the project. Others would contact her. He gave her the name of someone in Washington, D.C., who called her home office three times when she was out (that name was written on phone message pads on three different dates variously by her husband and their housekeeper). By October 1983, HBO had withdrawn its funding and dropped her documentary. Then, in the spring of 1984, Howe received another call to tell her there was still government interest in having her produce a film –

not for HBO but perhaps the Corporation for Public Broadcasting – although nothing could be done until after the November 1984 election. In fact, nothing was ever released to her.[124]

For more than three years, Howe told no one of her experience with Doty, other than a few close associates. Then, in June 1987, MJ-12 documents were first made public, showing an obvious relationship to the documents she had seen during her 1983 meeting. In October 1987, at the request of *Just Cause* publisher Larry Fawcett, Howe described her saga with Doty and the subsequent developments. She concluded that in all probability "MJ-12 did not want the same filmmaker who did *A Strange Harvest* to focus on the UFO phenomena for a national TV audience."[125]

Doty quickly denied most of Howe's main points. In a letter to Larry Bryant, he stated that the meeting was "a simple matter" between himself and Howe. He conceded that they did meet at Kirtland (covertly monitored by two supervisors), but all this was from her initiative. She wanted to know about the 1980 Kirtland incident and implied she had information about it, he said. They discussed that and the Ellsworth AFB incident, and then Howe mentioned her HBO film project. Regarding the last, Doty said, he had no information for her, certainly no historic film footage. He claimed she insisted on discussing MJ-12, extraterrestrial beings, and Project Aquarius, but maintained he had "no knowledge of any of those subjects." He also denied showing Howe a "Presidential Briefing Paper" or a "so-called Project Aquarius" document. Indeed, he claimed to Bryant, government investigation indicated that there was no project known as Aquarius.[126]

The contradiction in accounts could not be more stark, but no one seems to have believed Doty. The amount of detail offered by Howe, and subsequent correspondence she published, was simply overwhelming. Doty clearly was lying.

As the years went by, Doty told another version of this story. In a 2008 correspondence with the author, he hinted that Howe was targeted because it was believed she had cultivated inside government sources during the making of *A Strange Harvest*. This concerned the intelligence community, which wanted to learn who these sources were. Ultimately, Doty said, none were found, at least none who had contributed to her documentary. While "the Linda Howe operation" was a failure, he added that many others relating to UFOs, still withheld from the public, were successful. Indeed, Doty claimed that there were other intelligence operations on Howe going on at the time. HBO's cancellation of her documentary was not a result of

AFOSI's actions, but of "other entities" within the U.S. government.[127]

Howe's encounter with Doty was the first significant entry of MJ-12 into UFO research. True, Moore had already introduced it in 1981 by passing off an altered version of the Aquarius Document. This was far more substantial, however. Twenty months later, in December 1984, the situation became more complex still when the well-known MJ-12 documents were mailed to researchers Jaime Shandera and (through him) Bill Moore. These were sent from Albuquerque, almost certainly from Doty or others he worked with. The two sets of documents had certain similarities, as well as key differences. Most notably, the MJ-12 documents made no mention of a UFO crash at Aztec, nor of live aliens. Indeed, they explicitly stated that the aliens recovered by U.S. personnel were all dead. Why was Linda Moulton Howe told of a UFO crash at Aztec and of live aliens having been recovered, when the same source (Doty and AFOSI) propagated different information via Moore?

In his correspondence with the author, Doty said the papers he showed Howe (presumably the Presidential Briefing Papers) were a "scripted document." This meant they were "part truth and part disinformation" with the intention of convincing her it was all legitimate. This is a classic disinformation ploy, particularly in conjunction with the "look but don't touch" technique. It was used by the British Army's psy-ops unit in Belfast during the 1970s. Journalists were taken into back rooms and showed "secret documents" – some were forgeries, but others were genuine – which they could read but not copy, then hopefully write about in their newspapers. The reason is that falsehoods, properly packaged, can tarnish any truth.[128]

It seems reasonable to consider the documents shown to Linda Moulton Howe, as well as the MJ-12 documents, to be some form of disinformation. But this is very different from labeling them as hoaxes, which is a much more simplistic argument and implies that they were complete fiction. After all, the "Aquarius" document Moore gave to Bennewitz was also disinformation, but as far as anyone knows, only a small part of that document was altered. If the MJ-12 documents were completely fake, it would have meant that a section within Air Force Intelligence (or the CIA) created a detailed ufological history from whole cloth. This seems unlikely. The true pattern of disinformation is to take something that is true and alter it, thereby more easily discrediting it.

It is more logical that Howe (and Bennewitz) were targeted because they were delving into exactly what they thought they were delving into: topics relating to extraterrestrials that were of extreme importance to national security. Howe put it clearly enough: intelligence insiders were concerned that a credible television producer was filming law enforcement officers and ranchers who spoke openly about "silent, shape-shifting helicopters over pastures where mutilated animals were found."[129] That Doty's role was to create confusion cannot be doubted. That it was solely to hide purely terrestrial Air Force programs, as argued by some, is doubtful.[130]

As breathtaking as Doty's information for Howe was, she did not discuss the meeting for several years. But she did suspect that something very important was behind Doty's meetings with her, and that there was probably some truth in what he told her. The problem was, as it remains to this day, in sorting out just what that truth is.

Taking ET Into Custody?

In the early 1980s, the Roswell event was still new to researchers, and there were only the barest hints – to a few researchers like Stringfield – that anything more spectacular had occurred. Yet vague rumors had existed for some time of a landing at Holloman AFB by an extraterrestrial craft, and another rumor about a program to accommodate alien "guests" of the U.S. government. In 2005, retired Air Force Captain Robert Collins wrote *Exempt from Disclosure*, an insider's account of the UFO cover-up, with extensive consultation from Richard Doty. The book was controversial for several reasons, not the least of which was Doty's obvious authorship of several substantial sections, although he quickly disavowed the book. Of particular note are appendices containing photocopies of three alleged CIA and Majestic 12 documents. These concern aspects of Majestic's attempts to manage the existence of an alien "guest," known as EBE-2.

This author spoke to a source with senior-level CIA experience, who offered his judgment that although he had no opinion about some of the other documents listed in the book's appendix, he believed these three were genuine. Obviously, leaked documents like these can almost never be definitely proven to be authentic. Until the CIA comes forth to claim them, they will remain orphans without a home.

The earliest of these documents was dated May 14, 1980. Its text reads:

> The Texas incident will present a problem for us. Must determine more info in order to develop dis-info plan. Why do these things always happen when MJ12 is gone. Luck is never on our side. Let R-3 know something is up and that we will need their support to get through this one. Don't make anymore phone calls on KY [unclear: 3 or 8] until the new code is changed. Too many of the wrong people might be listening. I don't trust R-2A. Could be leak there. One more thing, EBE-2 has expressed a desire to visit ocean. I

don't know what the hell to do on that one. If we don't let him, he'll just disappear. Can't allow that to happen again. MJ6 is working on that. TREAD open/or will be. MJ9.[131]

The second of the "EBE-2" memos was dated June 24, 1982. Of the three, this one received the strongest endorsement from the author's intelligence source as being "almost certainly authentic." Its text reads:

Yesterday R2 requested briefing on Project "A". In particular, he wanted updated info from EBE-2. MJ3 advised that that info was not available to R2. Apparently, White House requested info because of large volume of FOIA requests. Can't seem to make those fools realize EBE-2 info is not available for any dissemination, per EO 01156, regardless of who requests info. Contact T-2R and see if he can assume custody of the matter. Don't allow AF to evaluate IDENT info. They may open up a little too much. KEND-3 can assist to some extent. MJ5.[132]

Like the others, the document was stamped "Top Secret" and "Handle on Strict Need-To-Know Basis."

The third alleged leaked memo is dated December 28, 1982. It reads:

TR-3 related both phases of OP-KIWI compromised by leak. Terminate phase I and re-direct energy to dis-info. EBE-2 can't be located at this time. R4 has placed him in safehouse somewhere near Edwards. I don't even know the exact location. No transfer will be approved until Phase I in DD23. CAP-3 not ready to receive EBE-2. Don't even know if they have facilities available for holding. CLASS YY-II only available at Kirtland or Los Alamos. Must make decision before Jan 15. No other options open. NORAD not cooperating with MJ4 on D-SITE studies. We may have to contact KERW-302 personnel and have them conduct study. NORAD still operating on old system. The big problem is only a few of NORAD's personnel are clear for SONG-DANCE info. PETE-23 open class II. REPEAT BLOCK NOT USED. DON'T NEGLECT MAKING CHANGES TO BOTH BLOCKS. CODES EXPIRE ON 31 DEC. MJ5.[133]

These documents have exactly the right tone, language, acronyms, abbreviations, and other details for what they purport to be. If they are forgeries, we can assume they came from someone (or some group) with a sophisticated background in U.S. intelligence. They have persuaded several people of distinguished backgrounds that they are legitimate. If true, they support the contention that there was indeed at least one alien "guest" of the U.S. government. The documents seem to indicate that the UFO control group (MJ) possessed authority above and beyond that of NORAD and the President of the U.S. in matters related to the topic of extraterrestrials.

Exempt from Disclosure also contained statements by Richard Doty concerning his alleged viewing of alien bodies at Wright-Patterson AFB in 1982.[134] More spectacularly, he claimed that on March 5, 1983, he was permitted to witness an interview with EBE-2 in a highly secure facility at Los Alamos National Laboratory. After a table and recording equipment were set up, a short "non-human looking creature" entered the room, wearing a tight fitting cream-colored suit. The being sat in a chair across the table from two civilians and an Air Force Colonel. According to Doty, EBE-2 said in perfect (albeit machine-generated) English that its world orbited the star Zeta 1, was warm, dry, and had long periods of sunshine. The being gave great detail on weather patterns and climate. Its society was highly regulated, and each member had a specific job. Doty said he did not actually hear any questions asked by the three humans. Either the questions had already been given, or the humans were thinking the questions and EBE-2 was responding to them. The interview ended after an hour, upon which EBE-2 left the room.[135]

Whether the above documents and stories are authentic, disinformation, or outright lies will undoubtedly be a matter of debate until and unless relevant authorities open the books and stand by them in a credible manner, or provide incontrovertible evidence to the contrary. The wait might be a long one.

Ufology in Retreat

Amid the developments at ufology's leading edge, a more conservative element remained influential, arguing that the claims of crash retrieval and abduction, while interesting and possibly fruitful, still lacked sufficient scientific evidence to be taken seriously. Hynek and Richard Hall were most prominent in this regard. In Hall's opinion, these were ufology's "extremes," not its norm. Yes, he acknowledged, they should be investigated, but the "core of the mystery" lay in the CE-II cases, that is, close encounters of UFOs by reliable witnesses. Like Hynek, he championed "scientific ufology."[136]

Hynek, meanwhile, was going down a curious path. By the early 1980s, he was, like Vallee, becoming more skeptical of actual, physical extraterrestrials. Vallee had presented five arguments against the ETH; Hynek now offered seven. (1) Sophisticated surveillance systems failed to detect incoming or outgoing UFOs. (2) So-called extraterrestrials had no difficulty dealing with Earth's atmosphere or gravity. (3) Sheer statistics indicated a truly intense amount of traffic, rather like launching an Apollo space probe every half hour. (4) UFOs and their alleged occupants behaved in an elusive and absurd manner. (5) People often reported an "Oz-like" experience near UFOs, in apparent space-time isolation. (6) Most UFOs appeared to be "space unworthy," with cramped conditions and no room for supplies and equipment that would presumably be needed to last for years – although on this point he acknowledged the possibility of mother ships. (7) Finally, the great astronomical distances between the stars. "There is nothing in our present or foreseeable technology," he stated, "that gives us any clue as to how these distances can be traversed in any reasonable time."

Hynek conceded that the UFO phenomenon was real. He just did not believe they were the product of beings from outer space. Unfortunately, his points amounted to little more than objections against how UFOs defied common sense. They possessed no scientific rigor, some were frankly absurd. This was a sad state of affairs for a man considered the Dean of Ufology. Point #1, for instance, was downright silly, blithely ignoring the possibility of anything like a cover-up. One wonders what the actual objection to Point #2 even was, other than that the aliens would possess better technology than humans. And so on. None of Hynek's objections negated the possibility that UFOs were alien; in fact, most of them would have been better used to argue why UFOs were in fact extraterrestrial. All of them could have been explained by reference to advanced technology, the psychological differences of a variety of intelligent species, or a combination thereof. That UFOs defied common sense was nothing new.[137]

The most scientific work in ufology was regarding the Hessdalen phenomenon. By mid-1983, members of UFO groups in Norway, Sweden, Finland, and the "Society of Psycho Bio Physics" formed Project Hessdalen under the direction of Leif Havik, Odd-Gunnar Roed, and Jan Fjellander. Through several universities, the group was able to obtain radar equipment, a seismograph, a fluxgate magnetometer, a spectrum analyzer, Geiger counters, infrared viewers, and various cameras. Thus armed, they began sentry duty in the bleak Norwegian landscape. Whether from the laughter of the gods or the whim of the UFO operators, the Hessdalen phenomenon nearly ceased for much of the year. Yet, the planning and persistence of the investigators would pay off by early winter.[138]

Still, Richard Hall felt that ufology was in a period of "retreat." Few well-attested sightings, effective debunking, excessive pop-culture emphasis, and insufficient inroads into the wider public were the main factors he cited. That summer, Hall resigned as editor of the *MUFON UFO Journal*, and was replaced by Bob Pratt. Pratt had been the main UFO writer for the *National Enquirer* for some time. As recently as June, the *Enquirer* had published an article on UFO sightings in 1980 in Peru and Kuwait, as well as the 1980 Kirtland-Manzano report. There is no question that Pratt had done legitimate journalism, also none that the *Enquirer* had key connections to the CIA. One of Hall's complaints about ufology was the lack of attention it received in serious journals. Emphasis in tabloids like the *Enquirer*, no matter how accurate some of its pieces may have been, hurt the reputation of ufology.[139]

A glimmer of optimism remained. By the summer of 1983, there were rumors about a major new book soon to come out that would incorporate many of the recent FOIA reports, and was poised to serve as a kind of sledgehammer at the wall of secrecy. This was *Clear Intent*, co-authored by Barry Greenwood and Lawrence Fawcett, and scheduled for release by Prentice-Hall for the spring of 1984. Hynek had written the Foreword, and Walter Andrus predicted it would be "the vehicle that will force the Pentagon and our government intelligence agencies to reveal why they have conducted a 'cosmic watergate' or cover-up with respect to their involvement with UFOs."[140]

At the same time, frustrations at the never-ending ufological wheel-spinning resulted in another attempt at creating organizational unity. In the summer of 1983, Richard Haines founded the North American UFO Federation, enlisting support from the major people in most of the UFO organizations – the notable exception being APRO, which remained aloof. Haines hoped for a collaborative effort to resolve the UFO phenomenon, but lack of sufficient funding doomed the effort to failure.[141]

Matters were difficult for American UFO researchers, but such was the case everywhere. In France, GEPAN seemed to be little more than a public relations endeavor at this point, with no political incentive to promote actual investigations. Its chief noted that "we are collecting UFO reports, but we don't know what to do with them. Once a case has been investigated, we publish a note on it, and that is that. We have no scientific structure behind GEPAN." Elsewhere, political repression was more straightforward: in the Soviet Union, for instance, postal interception of UFO-related publications was a regular occurrence.[142]

Philip Klass: One Man Disinfo Band

During the summer of 1983, skeptic and CSICOP member Philip Klass published *UFOs: The Public Deceived*. Not only did the book deny the reality of UFOs as extraterrestrial, but it ruled out UFOs as advanced military technology. Klass argued that there was no government cover-up on the matter. If UFOs were extraterrestrial, he reasoned, there would be more CIA documents to examine. All the significant data was available, he said, and all actions taken by the CIA were in good faith.

Much was ignored in this study. The possibility that the topic might be handled in deeper secrecy *if* UFOs were extraterrestrial was one example. So was the determination of the CIA to conceal its control of the 1953 Robertson Panel – a fact that was only learned through the determined effort of outside researchers. Classic UFO cases and events were typically misrepresented and distorted such as the 1950 Montana movie film, the 1952 Tremonton film, and the 1973 Ohio helicopter case. The last of these, for instance, was alleged by Klass to have been caused by a fireball, despite the detailed descriptions by multiple witnesses, despite no fireballs having been reported that night, and despite the fact that the UFO had been visible for several minutes, ruling out a fireball. Klass's argument was simply contrary to all reason. Regarding another dramatic case, the Cash-Landrum incident of 1980, Klass implied that it was probably a hoax. Many UFO researchers were attacked by name: Allen Hynek, Bruce Maccabee, Richard Hall, and others.

Serious UFO researchers saw the book as little more than a public relations ploy or government propaganda. Klass, after all, was not just a "professional" skeptic, but a senior editor for *Aviation Week and Space Technology*, a publication with close ties to the U.S. intelligence community. However, the book was well-written and – to those not well-versed in UFO research – had the ability to persuade.

Klass was busy all year debunking UFOs. As mentioned in the previous chapter, he worked hard, albeit in vain, to derail a UFO conference which was held at the University of Nebraska on November 11 and 12, 1983. Klass was at it again on December 8, during a television appearance with Larry Bryant on Philadelphia's KYW-TV. Constantly interrupting, correcting, and criticizing Bryant, he tried to turn the tables on UFO researchers, including himself as a UFO researcher, claiming that "we" were the ones involved in a cover-up – not the government. This ignored the 4,000 government documents that had so far been released under FOIA.[143]

Encounters 1983

While 1983 was most significant for UFOs in the Hudson Valley and intrigue from the world of intelligence, there were other events of interest in the U.S. and around the world. A UFO encounter by the RAF and USAF appears to have taken place on March 15 in Oxfordshire, Britain. An American air traffic controller tracked the object between 5 p.m. and 9:15 p.m. Civilian witnesses saw it as a slow, brilliant white light. Inquiries with British authorities were met with silence and obstruction.[144]

Another air traffic incident occurred later that month in Gorky, USSR.

On March 27, controllers that evening saw a grey cigar-shaped object flying toward them, and they tracked it on radar for 40 minutes. Attempts to establish radio contact failed. The object was the size of a conventional aircraft, but had no wings, tail or fin. It moved at a normal speed and altitude but behaved erratically, making many turns. It vanished about 25 miles north of the city, and was said to receive serious attention by the Soviet authorities.[145]

There were other events and alleged events, most notably the landing or crash of the so-called Ordzenikidze Object in the Soviet Union in early May, generally believed to be fake, but the origins of which remain unknown. The object was photographed as somewhat similar in structure to the lunar modules of the Apollo program; except that this was 250 feet high, more than half the height of the Great Pyramid at Giza. Speculation centered on the object being a prop from an abortive Hollywood movie shot between 1985-1987 (apparently the photos did not turn up until later).[146]

The Hudson Valley provided the best confirmed UFO cases of the year, indeed of the early 1980s. Sightings continued frequently through the spring and summer of 1983, the most intriguing of which took place near the town of Danbury, Connecticut on the evening of July 12. At 9:30 p.m., a police officer answered a call at a location southeast of Danbury, where he saw several people standing outside looking at a circular pattern of lights in the sky. The lights, which flashed red, blue, and green, appeared to be attached to a silent object, as no stars could be seen inside the ring of lights. The most startling part of it was that the object appeared to be less than 500 feet in altitude and the enormous size of 300 feet in diameter. The officer decided to shine a powerful spotlight on the object. When he did so, the object projected a brilliant flash of white light downward, covering everyone there. It then moved quickly toward the north and was lost behind trees.[147]

The same type of object and behavior was seen just a few hours later, at 10:55 p.m., by four people in a small fishing boat. Police Chief Nelson Macedo, his brother in law Charles Yacuzzi, Yacuzzi's 15-year-old son Michael, and retired police officer Jim Lucksky were in the boat. As they talked, they noticed a grey, circular object, fairly high in the sky. It was motionless, silent, and very large. They discerned twenty to thirty bright lights on it – blue, red, orange, and green – moving in a circular pattern. The men turned off their boat lights, and the object shut off its own lights. For several minutes all was quiet. Charles Yacuzzi then turned the boat lights on and off, whereupon the object switched on very bright lights and moved behind the mountains. Michael, the teenager, was so frightened that he nearly jumped overboard.[148]

Thus, not all the Hudson Valley objects were of a definite boomerang pattern. As the flap continued, however, towns such as Brewster, Ossining, Croton Falls, Yorktown, Mahopac, Poughkeepsie, Hyde Park, Fishkill, Rhinebeck, and others reported triangular or boomerang formations of lights, typically brilliant white but also red and green. Bright spotlights emanating from a large object over the Hudson River were also reported that summer.[149]

Three hundred miles to the southwest, in western Pennsylvania, researcher Stan Gordon collected similar reports of low-hovering objects. One of these was a July 25 sighting from the town of Latrobe. A man named Tom Jackson was getting ready for work at 5:15 a.m. when he saw a bright light outside his bathroom window. Upon opening the window, he saw a huge object hovering over a group of pine trees about 250 yards away. The object was a metallic grey color, elongated in shape but with the front and back ends dropping down. The object was flat on top and bottom, with two rows of evenly spaced windows. Jackson described the object as possibly 300 feet in length. The bright light was attached to the front of the object, and could swivel. Jackson ran outside and observed the object. It was completely motionless and silent. After five more minutes, it began to move toward the town's sewage plant. Gordon also received reports of other residents in the area reporting a brilliant orange light over the sewage plant. Still other residents, unaware of these sightings, were awakened by a loud, high-pitched sound so intense that it caused several headaches and disturbed neighborhood dogs. This was typical of the reports Gordon received throughout the year: large, extremely quiet objects that maneuvered at very low altitudes, often hanging motionless above the road.[150]

The Cold War Escalates

The Cold War, already moving along with renewed impetus, received a high-octane jolt on August 31, 1983 from the infamous KAL 007 incident. A Korean airliner carrying 269 persons, flying from New York to Seoul via Anchorage, was shot down by a Russian Su-15 fighter. It had strayed 365 miles off course and was inside Soviet airspace, well into a particularly sensitive security zone. The Soviet fighter pilot followed all the international protocols for warning a civilian airliner that it was off course. As a final warning, he fired multiple bursts from his cannon. The pilot had no tracers, so these shots could not have been seen by the KAL 007 crew. Soviet military authorities were nonetheless astonished that none of their pilot's actions elicited a response from the airliner. They concluded that it was a U.S. military reconnaissance plane on a spying mission, undoubtedly equipped with electronic espionage equipment. They ordered the shoot-down as the airliner was leaving Soviet airspace. U.S. intelligence officers quickly produced edited tape extracts as evidence of Soviet treachery. Reagan referred to the incident as the "Korean airline massacre," a "crime against humanity [that] must never be forgotten" and an "act of barbarism ... [and] inhuman brutality." In fact, it is not farfetched to consider the possibility that the U.S. did indeed equip the Korean airliner with instrumentation to spy on the Soviet base, and had thus essentially used the commercial aircraft as cover for a covert operation – and the civilian passengers as hostages.[151]

The U.S. went on the offensive immediately, announcing the deployment of the formidable Pershing II missiles in Europe (which began in January 1984). Then, on October 25, 1983, America unleashed Operation Urgent Fury, better known as the invasion of Grenada. It took a few hours for a 7,000 strong U.S. invasion force to overcome a 600 man Grenadan army. Several factors were cited by the Americans for the action: the illegal execution of Grenadan Prime Minister Maurice Bishop and resultant political instability, the presence of Cuban advisors on the island which (in Reagan's words) had turned the British Commonwealth member into a "Soviet-Cuban colony," the construction of a new airport that was going to be used for long-range Soviet supply aircraft, and the presence of American medical students at St. George's University on Grenada. There was in fact a small number of Cuban advisors on the island nation, although Cuba condemned the execution as much as anybody, and insisted that it would not defend the nation from an American attack. The airport was being built by a British company for tourism. Indeed, Grenada was a member of the British Commonwealth, and British Prime Minister Thatcher told Reagan she was "deeply disturbed" by the U.S. invasion. But it was popular in America, and most Americans accepted Reagan's line that Grenada was "being readied as a major military bastion to export terror and undermine democracy." More realistically, the invasion was a tune-up for the U.S. military, being its first major military action in nearly a decade. According to an official history of the U.S. Air Force, "the greatest outcome of the operation ... was the realization that ten years after Vietnam, command and control functions still had kinks that needed to be worked out."[152]

A ten-day series of NATO exercises immediately followed on the invasion, designed to practice high-level command coordination during a nuclear attack. The Soviet leadership was concerned that this could in fact be a ruse for an actual nuclear strike by the U.S., and moved to high alert. Although the event is generally forgotten, it was possibly the most dangerous nuclear threat since the 1962 Cuban missile crisis. When Reagan learned that the Soviets actually thought he might initiate a nuclear strike, he was "seriously disturbed." Thus, according to some historians, began a feeling in Reagan that a face to face meeting with the Soviet leaders was necessary.[153]

Stealthy UFOs

Through the fall and winter, UFO activity was comparatively slow. Within the U.S., the best reports were confined to the northeast, primarily New York, Pennsylvania, and North Carolina. Typically, they involved night-time, low-flying objects which came alarmingly close to motorists.

Such was the case with an October 15 report from Altoona, Pennsylvania, when a motorist named Catherine Burk saw a large, bright, silvery disc pass over her car shortly after 8:30 p.m. The force of the object somehow lifted the right side of her car briefly off the road, caused her car lights to blink out, and the engine to stall. She suffered hearing loss in her right ear, had severe headaches, and also developed problems with her shoulder, chest, and spine. The event was investigated by the local police, which noted that she was "visibly shaking." Her case was reported in the *MUFON UFO Jour-*

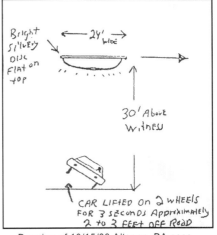

Drawing of 10/15/83 Altoona, PA case.

nal and the local Altoona newspaper. Burk, a sincere and religious person who did not believe in aliens, believed it was something the government built. "I always said the government was trying out stuff. But I never want to see nothing like that again." Unfortunately, there were no other witnesses to the event.[154]

Another close-range motor vehicle case was reported on October 26 in

West-Central North Carolina. At 9 p.m., David Keener reported to the Catawba County Sheriff's Department that he saw a diamond shaped UFO above his car on Highway 321, northeast of the town of Hickory. The object was bright green in the back and red in the front; it hovered and then moved to a higher elevation. He watched the object for about five minutes. It was silent throughout his encounter.[155]

Another interesting Hudson Valley case occurred in New York's Putnam County on October 28, involving a biomedical engineer named Jim Cooke. At 2:15 a.m., while driving by the Croton Falls Reservoir on his way home to Mahopac, Cooke saw what looked like aircraft lights approaching and dropping very fast. Then, oddly, they seemed to hover for a while – then go out. Cooke got out of his car, walked toward the shore line, and saw an object hovering less than 15 feet above the water. It was extremely non-reflective, but he could make out a triangular shape. Cooke had done airplane repair work while in the military, but he had never seen anything like this. It was only 200 feet away from him, yet he heard no sound. After a few minutes, nine red lights came on from its sides. Then, a red beam of light from the underside appeared to probe the water. The object moved to four locations over the reservoir, each time shining the red light on the water, all the while remaining steady at 15 feet above. Each time a car drove by, its lights went out. Cooke estimated the object was at least 100 feet long at the base and 30 feet at the apex. After it finished whatever it was doing, it "just lifted and silently drifted upward the way it came. It went up at about a 30 degree angle until it was lost in the sky." Cooke's total observation time was 10 to 15 minutes. Thus it would appear that whatever was operating the Hudson Valley UFOs was interested in quietly searching bodies of water, of which that area has an abundance.[156]

One of the last interesting American UFO sightings of 1983 took place in Winston-Salem, North Carolina, on November 28. It was another night-time sighting. At 8:40 p.m., a woman noticed a ball of light approaching. It was unusual enough that she entered her house to get her boyfriend and two children. The four people watched the light approach to within 400 feet, where it hovered at treetop level. It appeared to be about half the size of a house. Three smaller objects came from behind the object and traveled southeast; they seemed to land in a swampy area near a manufacturing facility. While the woman and her children ran through a field toward the large object, her boyfriend jumped into his car to pursue it. At one point he saw the object hovering near a small lake less than 200 feet away from him. Within seconds, however, the object vanished, like turning off a light.

In the aftermath of the event, all four witnesses experienced eye irritation, and the man said his face and hands turned red and felt sore.[157]

From elsewhere in the world came scattered reports. One from the Soviet Union emerged from Colonel Boris Sokolov, in a statement he made to American UFO researchers ten years later. The event, he said, took place on October 5, 1983 at an ICBM base in Ukraine. Sokolov said he received an order to leave immediately for the base since, as reported by the base commander to the Chief of the General Staff, a UFO had been observed near the base from 4 p.m. until 8 p.m. During that time, the launch codes for the ICBMs had mysteriously been enabled. "They received an order to prepare the launch of the ICBMs," said Sokolov.[158]

In late October, a craft of some sort reportedly hovered for twenty minutes over the town of Hollesley, not far from the Rendlesham Forest in Great Britain. The size of craft was not indicated, but it projected three powerful white lights down to the ground. Witness Ron Macro said the lights formed a triangular shape and remained perfectly still. The object then flew over Macro and other witnesses. There was at least one report of car trouble related to the sighting, and local residents demanded a meeting with RAF Woodbridge. Captain Kathleen McCollom, the base public information officer, would only comment "nothing was seen on radar. I cannot say more than that."[159]

Finally, the Chinese Air Force had an interesting UFO encounter on November 2. A bomber aircraft reportedly encountered an unknown object at about 40,000 feet. The aircraft immediately lost its guidance systems and the plane began to shake violently from side to side and lose speed. With great difficulty, the crew members landed the plane. Upon landing, they learned that a portion of the tail was missing. This encounter was reported on the radio in Beijing and Shanghai and relayed by Paul Dong.[160]

Whereas the Soviet and Chinese stories cannot be easily confirmed, and the British case was reported in Britain's oldest tabloid, they were all investigated by responsible researchers and appear to have occurred. The American cases seem to be quite reliable, competently scrutinized, several of which involved multiple witnesses.

Two Important Stories Break

UFO activity in 1983, even the dramatic Hudson Valley cases, received little more than local publicity. None of the cases reached the general public. Toward the end of the year, however, two important UFO stories broke. The first was on the December 1980 Rendlesham Forest case by

News of the World on October 2, 1983. Other publications, even more sensationalist, picked it up, getting many of the basic facts wrong. Some researchers wondered whether this was an intelligence operation, a kind of damage or spin control, since the story was in the process of breaking throughout 1983.[161]

The *London Times* quickly debunked it, but neglected to interview any of the witnesses or investigators that originally broke the case. Instead, *The Times* interviewed a young government worker in the forestry office who suggested that the marks on the ground were scratchings made by rabbits. This was obvious nonsense but, supported by *The Times,* the notion became widespread. When investigator Jenny Randles spoke to this "expert," he told her that his theory "just seemed like a good idea at the time."[162]

At the BBC, there were those who were genuinely interested in the case. Randles knew one producer who wanted to make a serious documentary, something even-handed and not stridently debunking. He tried repeatedly to persuade his supervisors to let him do so, but was refused each time. Instead, skeptic Ian Ridpath was asked to produce an exposé. According to Randles, Ridpath did not consult with anyone who had previously investigated the case. Instead, he took a crew to the forest and filmed the lighthouse, which he made look strange by using a zoom lens and some creative editing. Ridpath stated that there had been a meteor on December 26, 1980 which probably sparked the UFO sighting itself. The conclusion, as aired on BBC: "another UFO case bites the dust." Other major media outlets also debunked the case, even though the British MoD still considered it unexplained. Randles herself was refused several times by mainstream publications to present a counter-argument.[163]

The other important breakthrough was not reported in the news, but soon made the rounds of UFO researchers and interested parties. This was a two-paged, single spaced, typed letter from retired scientist Dr. Robert Sarbacher to researcher William Steinman concerning UFO crash retrievals. Sarbacher had been an important physicist, missile expert, and consultant to the Defense Department's Research and Development Board, and Steinman was following a lead.

As mentioned previously, it had previously been known that the late Canadian government official, Wilbert Smith, had met with unnamed American officials in 1950 to discuss the matter of flying saucers. From that meeting, he wrote a memo to the Canadian government stating that, based on the information he obtained in that meeting, that flying saucers did exist, and were "the most highly classified subject in the U.S. government, ranking even higher than the H-bomb." But it was not known with whom Smith had met until Canadian researcher Arthur Bray discovered in Smith's papers that Sarbacher was at least one of Smith's contacts. What made all this especially interesting was that Sarbacher was still alive. Although Bray did not try to contact him, Stanton Friedman was able to phone him and then visit him. Sarbacher immediately admitted the truth of the Smith connection to Friedman, who then passed the information on to William Moore. Moore, in turn, told William Steinman, who then wrote to Sarbacher.

Sarbacher replied on November 23, 1983. He confirmed he was "invited to participate in several discussions associated with the reported recoveries" of UFOs, although he was unable to attend the meetings. Some famous individuals were "definitely involved" in the program, such as Vannevar Bush, John von Neuman, and probably Robert Oppenheimer. American laboratories analyzed the material that came from UFO crashes, and the hardware was "extremely light and very tough." Sarbacher described the beings that controlled the UFOs: "I remember in talking with some of the people at the office that I got the impression these 'aliens' were constructed like certain insects we have on Earth."[164]

Friedman asked Sarbacher whether he could recall anyone who attended the meetings at Wright-Patterson AFB. Sarbacher could not, but gave enough clues that when Steinman reviewed the conversation in 1987, he believed all clues pointed to Dr. Eric A. Walker, who had been the Executive Secretary of the Research and Development Board. As we shall see, Sarbacher's and Walker's testimonies would strongly confirm each other, and the existence of MJ-12.[165] These statements would also be confirmed independently by Canadian researchers Grant Cameron and T. Scott Crain.[166]

Summary

The UFO phenomenon went through changes during the early 1980s. The quantity of sightings appeared to dip, although strangeness remained high enough. A truly spectacular photograph was taken in Vancouver, British Columbia, in 1981. Triangular and boomerang craft were being seen more frequently, particularly in the lower Hudson Valley. Commercial and military aircraft continued to have close calls in the air with UFOs, a concern that unsurprisingly received no public attention. And very soon, the strange phenomenon in Hessdalen would become utterly mystifying.

Ufology moved ahead slowly but surely. With the publication of *Missing Time* by Budd Hopkins, abductions became a key topic of discussion, and was now frequently paired with Linda Moulton Howe's research on animal mutilations at conferences, adding a darker and more ominous tone to the UFO phenomenon than had existed previously. In addition, analysis of the conspiratorial aspects of the phenomenon received a boost with the 1983 letter by Robert Sarbacher. Yet there were definite setbacks. The court battles to release contested UFO documents from government agencies did not go well. To some seasoned observers, ufology appeared to be in a state of retreat, with a drop in sightings, no sign of imminent government 'disclosure,' little to no interest from science and academia, and a public connection with such tabloids as the *National Enquirer*. There seemed to be a definite interest shown in the field of UFO research by the intelligence community. Bill Moore was getting his hands dirty through an association with Air Force Intelligence. Paul Bennewitz – convinced that he was seeing UFOs over an Air Force base and obtaining alien signals – was certainly getting attention from the same groups.

The encounter by Linda Moulton Howe with AFOSI Special Agent Richard Doty underscored interest from the spook world. By Doty's own admission in later years, several agencies monitored Howe, attempted to learn her sources, and succeeded in preventing her from producing a UFO documentary for Home Box Office. The documents Doty showed Howe (but did not permit her to copy) were clearly related to the infamous MJ-12 documents released 20 months later. Yet they were different enough to make one wonder what was going on. Whether she was shown some version of something genuine, or an earlier version of what became the MJ-12 documents, they seem to have been used for purposes of disinformation that specifically targeted the UFO field. Considering the areas that Howe, Bennewitz, and others were looking into at the time, it makes the most sense that this disinformation targeted the UFO field, and was not simply designed to protect conventional technologies from the Soviets.

A number of the difficulties encountered by UFO researchers can be traced to policies of the Reagan administration. The Executive Order of April 1982 relating to FOIA requests stands out as an obvious example, and the intransigence of the federal agencies during the legal battles is closely related to this. More generally, what was happening was a substantial assertion of federal power, much of which was of dubious constitutionality or even clearly illegal (as in the shenanigans relating to the theft of PROMIS software). The Big Brother State expanded during these years, as

America began to reassert her military establishment through massive spending increases, military tuneups such as the invasion of Grenada, and the introduction of a space-based weapons platform.

Indeed, conventional historians have failed to grasp the full significance of SDI. Fixated on the Cold War, they have ignored the evidence relating to U.S. military interest in UFOs that might have affected the decision to implement the program. One need not refer to the strong personal interest that President Reagan had in UFOs, nor even the fact that he was a witness to one. Rather, the inexplicable encounters with UFOs in Earth orbit by U.S. and Soviet astronauts, as well as the confirmed tracking of UFOs by Defense Support Program (DSP) satellites, supply reason enough that "Star Wars" could well have had an ET-component. Something was going on in space, and only the grossest negligence would permit America's national security apparatus to ignore it. At the same time, only the most reckless indiscretion would allow anyone to talk about it.

Chapter 6

Calm Before the Storm
1984-1986

We had it on camera for 15 minutes.... Whatever it was, it was larger than a C-5A, which is the largest aircraft in the world.... This was much larger. It seemed very brazen. It acted like it didn't care who saw it.
— *Security Officer at Indian Point Nuclear Facility, New York, 1984.*

We have things out there that are literally out of this world. . . . Better than Star Trek. *Groom Lake non-commissioned officer, 1985.*

This was no ordinary UFO. Scores of people saw it. It was no illusion, no deception, no imagination.
— *Air Marshall of Zimbabwe, Azim Daudpota, 1985*

At least 20 unidentified objects were observed by several aircrews and on radar.
— *U.S. Defense Intelligence Agency memo, on UFO sightings in Brazil, 1986*

State of Ufology: 1984

UFO sightings continued in the Hudson Valley during 1984, and indeed activity seems to have picked up elsewhere. Still, many researchers thought they were in something of a lull.[1] Partly, this was because many of sightings were beyond the reach of American researchers, in places such as the Soviet Union. Even the Hudson Valley sightings needed time before their full impact was recognized.

Ufologists at this time were doing some good work, but there was also concern over the state of their research. John Schuessler mentioned several obvious problems: the lack of solid data available to researchers or the public, trashy news coverage, and personal attacks by zealous skeptics that could intimidate witnesses and researchers alike. Each of the major organizations had declining memberships. CUFOS was elitist, out of touch, and needed a management overhaul. At APRO, the Lorenzens were in poor health, notoriously uncooperative with other organizations, and not cultivating new leadership. MUFON, too, while fairly grassroots and diverse, nevertheless suffered from an authoritarian structure, although Schuessler did not get into specifics.[2]

Allen Hynek, meanwhile, was frustrated by timid mainstream scientists who felt UFOs were too strange to study, leaving the field to amateurs.[3] This was a bigger problem than the alleged cover-up, which he called overblown. In Hynek's opinion, the military attitude toward UFOs was best characterized by apathy, although he acknowledged a kind of "cover-up of ignorance." In other words, the military was embarrassed to admit that it could not control certain objects within U.S. airspace. Of course, this important point supported the contention that there *was* a cover-up. Hynek amplified this by conceding that he had seen deliberate attempts by the military to withhold good UFO reports from the media and invent false explanations for difficult cases.[4]

Hynek's attitude, while frustrating to experienced researchers, meant that he could more easily speak to the mainstream and his fellow scientists. During the spring of 1984, he presented 400 UFO cases at the annual meeting of the American Association for the Advancement of Science. He told the overwhelmingly skeptical audience that responsible witnesses around the world had seen UFOs, "some of whom were independent of each other but observed the same event (and sometimes in daylight) which defied both common sense and common physical sense." Because such sightings appeared to be outside the current scientific paradigm, most scientists simply dismissed the phenomenon. Hynek cautioned that "in the light of the history of science, this may not be an entirely wise step." Perhaps these remarks resonated privately with some scientists; publically, nothing changed.[5]

Simply put, scientists were not researching UFO-related topics. As always, the best work was being done by private individuals. Such was the case regarding abduction research, in which the Fund for UFO Research provided financial support to Ted Bloecher, Budd Hopkins, and Dr. Aphrodite Clamar. The three conducted an experiment to have an accredited psychologist administer standard tests (Rorschach, TAT, Wechsler Adult Intelligence Scale, Minnesota Multiphasic Tests) to people with alleged alien abduction experiences. The twist was that the psychologist had no knowledge of this fact, and was told only that the persons were being tested for emotional and psychic stability. The important conclusion of the study was that all persons tested out as normal, meaning that people who claimed to have had alien abduction experiences were not psychologically aberrant.[6]

The most important contribution to ufology in 1984 was the publication of *Clear Intent* by Barry Greenwood and Lawrence Fawcett. This was the first collection of FOIA-released government documents relating to UFOs. Most of these documents had been known to researchers, but none had been published in a book. The most dramatic documents dealt with the airspace violations of 1975 over Loring, Wurtsmith, and Malstrom air force bases. The reproduction of so many confirmed documents seemed to make it undeniable, even to the staunchest skeptic, that something serious and unexplained was going on.[7]

Skeptics did criticize the book, however. One argued that the authors were guilty of "the craft fallacy" – automatically assuming that lights in the sky were solid objects, and ignoring recent studies suggesting such lights often formed along areas of geologic stress. This was not a reasonable criticism. In the first place, the documents themselves frequently described the phenomenon as "objects" or "craft," often unambiguously so. Moreover, none of the 1975 cases occurred over geological fault lines.[8] More on target were criticisms about the book's haphazard organization and occasional lack of in-depth commentary.[9] Such quibbles aside, *Clear Intent* was something of a culmination of the recent FOIA bounty. Moreover, while few researchers were foolhardy enough to expect government disclosure about UFOs, the book did revive hopes that, perhaps with enough solid documentation soberly presented to an impartial public, the tide might turn against the secret keepers.

Interest in *Clear Intent* was strong, and publisher Prentice-Hall received an unprecedented number of inquiries for it. Even so, the publishers cut back on the book's original publicity schedule and severely underprinted it. The book immediately sold out and was unavailable all summer. A second printing in late August also sold out immediately. Presumably, the stop-and-start printing schedule did not help sales, but a harder blow was the establishment news media's refusal to review it.[10]

MUFON and the *National Enquirer*

Clear Intent prompted fresh thinking at MUFON. In the first place, Andrus and other MUFON leaders decided to "de-Klassify" the *MUFON UFO Journal* – that is, remove the skeptics.[11] They also reconsidered MUFON's relationship to the *National Enquirer*. For years, it had been obvious that the *Enquirer* was a poor choice for getting the word out. Indeed, it seems astonishing that an organization seeking to promote "scientific ufology" had wished to cultivate such a relationship. But MUFON's leadership – most prominently Andrus himself – had been seduced by the tabloid's circulation in the hopes that memberships, and thereby revenues, would increase. It is also true that amid the tabloid's weekly serving of trash were some legitimate UFO pieces, mostly written by Bob Pratt. Indeed, Pratt within his own person linked the tabloid and researchers: in 1984, he was editor of the *MUFON UFO Journal.*

All of this might seem innocuous, until one considers the history of the

Enquirer's publisher, Generoso (Gene) Pope. Pope came from a Mafia background and had been a CIA intelligence officer during the 1950s; the *Enquirer* itself appears to have started with CIA slush money. Ever after, Pope remained tied to the national security world. A friend once asked him how he knew so many top-level American political figures. Pope answered enigmatically, "one hand washes the other." Former Nixon Defense Secretary Melvin Laird even gave the eulogy at Pope's funeral in 1988.[12]

Seen in this light, the *Enquirer* looks like a publication designed, among other things, to manage the UFO phenomenon within popular culture along the lines recommended in the 1953 Robertson Panel. Since it was impossible to block completely the flow of UFO reports, the *Enquirer* would disable those that slipped through. Consider: (1) the U.S. military and intelligence establishment were publicly hostile to the idea of UFOs; (2) Pope was their loyal friend; (3) his laughingstock tabloid regularly reported on UFOs, sometimes accurately, sometimes deceptively. (If all UFO stories in the *Enquirer* were true, somebody might catch on; hence the sporadic false stories). Good UFO reports making it into the *Enquirer* – such as the 1975 airspace violations – died a quick death. Mainstream journalists, academicians, and scientists never followed up.

So what was going on with MUFON and the *Enquirer*? Were the players witting agents of the intelligence community, or just being manipulated? By all appearances, Bob Pratt was serious and legitimate. Unfortunately, MUFON's connection to the world of intelligence has never been fully explored. This author has spoken to several prominent MUFON members and officers who expressed suspicions that intelligence operatives existed high within the structure of the organization. No one was willing to go on record, however.

It has to be considered, at the least, that MUFON's relationship to the intelligence community was similar to that described by Francis Stonor Saunders in her work *The Cultural Cold War*. Saunders studied CIA penetration of ostensibly independent cultural organizations during the 1960s, most notably the Congress for Cultural Freedom. Such organizations ran the gamut from liberal to conservative, and their loyal members had no idea that CIA operatives were working behind-the-scenes. Short of a high-level confession or smoking gun evidence in the form of government documentation, there is no firm proof that MUFON, CUFOS, or other UFO organizations were infiltrated. Nevertheless, the collected pieces of evidence add up to a reasonable case that the intelligence community penetrated and manipulated America's major UFO organizations at this time.

Governmental Policies

Several governments took actions regarding UFO reports in 1984. Each year the British Ministry of Defence received hundreds of UFO reports from the public, police, airport authorities, and military. On March 4, 1984, for the first time ever, the MoD released some of these cases to the public. Sixteen reports, albeit mostly blacked out and missing key data, were sent to the British UFO Research Association (BUFORA). The MoD's public position was that UFOs as such were of no concern to them, except for those with possible defense implications. When asked about possible landing cases, such as the 1980 Rendlesham incident, Defense Under Secretary for Procurement John Lee replied that these were not separately identified from other reports. In any event, he said, "none of these reports was of any defense significance," and therefore no records were kept. Thus began the British MoD tradition, to which it has steadfastly adhered over the years, of pretending to provide good-faith disclosures of its UFO data.[13]

Two months later, the Australian Ministry of Defense echoed the British position. Stating that since nearly all of the UFO reports filed by the public were of no defense significance, and only three or four percent were unexplained, they would henceforth only investigate "unusual aerial sightings which suggest a defense or national security implication." Of course, presenting misleading information about UFOs is an old game, and Australian researcher Bill Chalker used the RAAF's own statistics proving that the true figure of unexplained sightings was closer to eight percent. Writing for CUFOS's *IUR*, he suggested it was "unwise – or at least premature" for Australia's military to dismiss UFO sightings as having no national security significance nor any scientific relevance." This criticism certainly was valid, but also naive – much like CUFOS in general – in assuming that the Australian military was not actively dealing with UFOs on a more covert level.[14]

The United States also took UFO-related measures in 1984 when it began procedures to seize 89,000 acres of public land surrounding the Groom Lake Facility (Area 51), in Nevada. The land was finally taken in 1988, although the Air Force overlooked 3,900 acres which continued to afford a good view of activities going on there. Glen Campbell, a private citizen who investigated happenings at the Groom Lake Facility during the

1980s and 1990s, would soon dub this area "Freedom Ridge."[15]

In the Soviet Union, the government took a different approach to managing its UFO problem. For years the Soviet Academy of Sciences had discouraged reports from the general population. Now, the government encouraged them by creating "anomalous phenomena commissions." These were said to be independent groups that would take UFO reports from the citizens without ridicule, but were in fact a cover to assist the Soviet government to collect UFO data.[16] A possible reason for this new policy, as we shall see, was the occurrence of several disturbing Soviet military UFO encounters that year.

Late in the year, the British Ministry of Defense was reorganized, making the group Sec (AS) 2a as its main focal point for receiving public UFO reports. Its mission was "to determine whether or not UFOs present a threat to the security and defence of the United Kingdom." This appeared to be very much along the lines of the U.S. Air Force's old Project Blue Book, right down to the fact that the group's actual investigatory role was minor. It had no specific UFO budget other than minor staff costs, and (according to Nick Pope), its records were "unclassified in nature." On the other hand, Timothy Good uncovered evidence to show that Britain's Provost and Security Services (P&SS) at RAF Rudloe Manor were conducting more serious and secret investigations of UFO activity. Finally, in 1995, an MoD letter to a UFO researcher confirmed that "in the past, Rudloe Manor was indeed the RAF co-ordination point for reports of "unexplained" aerial sightings," a fact that had been denied by the MoD for years.[17]

Hessdalen

In the realm of conventional history, 1984 is a year memorable for many reasons: the landslide re-election of U.S. President Ronald Reagan, the boycott by the Soviet Union of the 1984 Olympics, the year of the first Apple Macintosh, the great famine of Ethiopia, the entry of crack cocaine into the U.S., and, perhaps most of all, for its service as the title of George Orwell's classic dystopian novel. And yet, there is something else that occurred during that year, something of equal significance: the occurrence of UFO sighting waves over two distinct regions in the world. First, the area in Norway around the remote village of Hessdalen, where a most unusual phenomena was being recorded by dedicated observers. Second – for a much longer and more intense period – the area north of New York City known as the Hudson Valley, where, week after week, distinctive and unusual craft were being seen by hundreds of amazed residents. Rounding out this were sightings and encounters elsewhere in the world that made the year surprisingly significant in terms of UFO activity.

From January 21 through February 26, 1984, the area around the small town of Hessdalen in central Norway was a perfect scene of UFO activity. Night after night, bizarre light phenomena were observed and recorded by a team armed with cameras, radar, Geiger counter, seismograph, and infra-red viewers. During that month, members recorded 188 specific observations. Of these, 53 were of sufficient quality (level of detail, witness caliber, and strangeness) to be considered valid "Hessdalen Phenomena."[18] But while something was obviously going on in the remote valley, whatever it was remained elusive.

Typical reports were of strangely maneuvering lights that had no reasonable explanation. On January 27, 1984, for instance, an elongated light was observed at 5:32 p.m. It was red and white in color, and blinked unevenly while traveling north, eventually disappearing over the horizon. The team tracked it on radar but failed to photograph it. The following afternoon, the team picked up a fast-moving, strong radar signal to the west. It divided into two parts and went in different directions. The team shot fourteen frames of film in the direction of the echo, but nothing showed up.

The phenomenon was fascinating, tantalizing, frustrating. On January 29th, the team again tracked something on radar, close to their position and moving north. They saw nothing. The same thing happened on the 31st, and again on February 1. The latter date marked the second time within a few days that an event was recorded at 3:49 p.m. There were also several sightings at 2:05 p.m. Leif Havik, one of the project leaders, speculated that such exact replication "would seem to be beyond a natural phenomenon, or would it be?"[19]

Photo taken by Roar Wister, Hessdalen, Norway, February 18, 1984

On the night of February 2 the team had a "first class" observation.

Unfortunately, it was the only evening during the month that they were not monitoring the radar. One of the members was on the phone when a neighbor barged in at 8 p.m. and announced "it's coming." Havik ran outside with a camera and 400mm telephoto lens. He saw a bright, oblong yellow light with red in the front, traveling north in a wavelike motion. Nine people from three locations saw it. The photographs came out poorly, indicating just how hard it can be to photograph UFO phenomenon, even in an active hotspot with dedicated people.

Eventually, the perseverance paid off. On February 18, team member Roar Wister saw a light in the east-northeast direction, moving eastward for two minutes, constantly changing intensity from weak to strong. He took several photographs, five of which captured the light very well. He did even better three days later, at 7:23 p.m., capturing an oscillating light moving across the sky.[20]

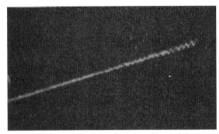

Photo taken by Roar Wister, Hessdalen, Norway, February 21, 1984.

This would not be the last time the phenomenon would be photographed. Indeed, researchers have continued studying it to the present day, amassing an impressive collection of video and photographic evidence, as well as data derived from instrumentation. Over time, they have categorized the phenomenon into three general types: (1) a white (or blue-white) flashing light, normally high in the air and lasting a short while; (2) a yellow light, with a red light on the top, sometimes flashing; (3) most commonly, a slow-moving, roundish yellow or white light able to maneuver, stop for an hour or more, and continue maneuvering.[21] After many decades, there is still no single theory that has covered the full spectrum of the observed phenomenon. The provisional conclusion from the 1984 study still holds today: "We have not found out what this phenomenon is. That could hardly be expected either. But we know that the phenomenon, whatever it is, can be measured." Interestingly, the team was able to obtain measurements with radar, lasers, and cameras, but not with seismographs, Geiger counters, or infrared viewers. This would suggest that an actual object has been observed, but that geological activity or radioactivity were not involved. The objects have appeared at times not merely to be intelligent, but mischievous. "Many times during the project period," noted the project's final report for 1984, "the cameras failed. This happened mostly when we needed them most."

The Hessdalen phenomenon is particularly odd considering the remoteness of the location, the difficulty of the terrain, the lack of anything of obvious significance there. One would think this is some sort of natural phenomenon, except for times when the lights seemed intelligently controlled – or intelligent. Could it be a natural phenomenon? Is there a connection to a military program? An alien intelligence? Now observed for decades, the Hessdalen phenomenon continues to elude identification. Moreover, as baffling as the lights are, and despite the attention they have deserved from the media and scholarly community, the phenomenon has received next to none.

Triangles and Balls of Light

Although, as we shall see, triangular and boomerang-shaped objects continued to dominate New York's lower Hudson Valley in 1984, similar objects were being reported elsewhere in the U.S. The area northwest of Detroit, Michigan, was such a scene of activity on February 22 and 23. For two nights near the town of Flushing, objects with triangular lighting patterns shone beams of light to the ground. The lights approached the car of one witness who said they were part of a cigar-shaped craft 100 feet off the ground. A jogger reported a light from above so intense that it hurt his eyes. Another person said a craft with triangular shaped lighting hovered less than 200 feet above the ground, illuminating the area behind her house and panicking her outdoor cats. Two more craft passed over her house. She called the police, although the officer could hardly explain the event. MUFON investigator Shirley Coyne learned of twelve people who saw the lights during these two nights, but only three would give her a report. Most avoided getting involved, and only spoke to her because she knew them.[22]

Western Pennsylvania had similar sightings, mostly recorded and investigated by Stan Gordon. One took place near Mechanicsburg on February 29. A woman observed a dark, diamond-shaped object approaching at no more than 50 feet off the ground. White lights were at the front and back, blinking red lights were at the sides, and smaller lights were between each of the four points. She described it as being "as long as a tractor trailer and wide as two tractor trailers." Wobbling slightly, it passed over trees and disappeared to the southeast.[23]

More boomerangs were reported in the southeastern Georgia town of Claxton on March 21 by a mother and daughter who were driving south along Perry Road. The mother held an executive position with a prominent firm, and approached the media only on condition of anonymity. At around 8 p.m., they noticed an unusual light through the trees off the road. As they topped a hill, they slowed the car to a near stop when they noticed three boomerang-shaped objects hovering above a field: a large one and two smaller ones. Each object had two large lights in the center as well as a row of small, multi-colored lights that blinked in rapid sequence. Initially curious at seeing such a spectacle, the two soon became terrified once one of the objects began to move. The mother, physically shaking, drove while her daughter cautioned her not to crash. The large object flew over their car in perfect silence. As it did so, the two witnesses looked directly at its underside – it was of dark metal and the mother estimated its wing span to be at least 40 feet. "It just floated over the car," she said. "There was no sound at all. I didn't notice any heat." The witnesses never saw the other two objects approach them, and the mother kept driving. While she believed that she and her daughter saw something "from another world," she added, "if the United States has something like that, and that's what we saw, then I'm proud for our country because we're so far ahead of everyone else, we don't have anything to worry about."[24]

In California, too, triangles were reported. Near Napa on April 25, three people driving at night on the American Canyon Road saw a huge triangular object "at least the size of a football field," hovering a mere 100 feet off the road. They passed beneath it, and the object soon moved out of sight.[25]

As Hessdalen showed clearly enough, not all UFOs are objects. A certain number of them are strange, seemingly intelligent, light phenomena. Two such cases were reported near the Pacific coast early in 1984. In late February at 3:30 a.m., a driver in Everett, Washington, saw a silvery green, egg-shaped object moving toward his car from a wooded area. It was between a softball and soccer ball in size, and within a few seconds it bounced from one side of the road to the other, passing over his car's front fender. A nearly identical event was reported the following month from Santa Monica, California. On March 25 at 8:55 p.m., a driver reported that a bright red ball of light, about 10 inches in diameter, maneuvered around her car with a bouncing motion. It approached to within a foot of her car, lighting up the hood and windows. Her sighting lasted for nearly a minute.[26]

The Barbados Incident

There is at least one UFO sighting from the spring of 1984 of undeniable defense significance, as it was described as "a serious defense and security alert" in an Incident Report from the U.S. Embassy in Barbados.[27] At 2:10 a.m. on April 12, air traffic control radar at Grantley Adams International Airport tracked a large number of UFOs. These were 30 miles southeast of the island in four "loose but distinct formations," approaching at around 100 mph. Local authorities immediately notified Prime Minister Tom Adams, as well as the Barbados Defense Force (BDF) and the police commissioner. Within minutes, the entire BDF, in full battle uniform and with loaded weapons, was placed on Red Alert. Adams, a political friend of Ronald Reagan and key ally during the Grenada invasion, roused the U.S. Embassy to get answers. By 2:20 a.m., the formation was 14 miles off the coast. Two of the targets then veered off to the island's west side, two others moved toward the east, while the remainder continued moving north. By 3 a.m., the U.S. Defense Attaché arrived at the BDF situation room, where he was briefed and remained for three hours. Police were deployed to the beaches to guard against a seaborne landing. The Barbados government asked Martinique if they had an exercise in progress; the answer was "no." At 3:30 a.m. the BDF launched a patrol boat and scrambled a Cessna – neither party found anything. Airport radar was still tracking nine objects at 4 a.m., which by then were over the northern part of the island. Since Barbados is scarcely more than 20 miles long, they must have slowed down considerably or else loitered about. By 4:10 a.m., the objects disappeared to the west toward Martinique.

Atmospheric conditions and technical malfunction were both considered. According to the U.S. State Department document, there appeared to be a "weather inversion" over Barbados early that morning. Adams, however, did not accept this as the cause of the incident, nor did the BDF Chief of Staff. The Soviets, on naval exercises in the Caribbean, were of special concern to the Barbadians. The only problem was that they were more than 1,500 miles away, near the Yucatan Peninsula. Nor does the U.S. military appear to have been responsible, as the U.S. Embassy informed Adams after checking with Washington.

This is all that is known of the incident. Weather remains a possible cause. And while the Soviet explanation seems unlikely, that cannot be ruled out either, as the region had a history of silent Cold War confrontation (including an incident near Barbados from 1977, mentioned in the document). What cannot be denied is that the invasion of national airspace is always a serious matter for defense forces. The Barbados incident is known to us because a single document was obtained through FOIA; the event described within it, as well as its serious tone, is consistent with many other such documents. These reports are not obtained in any kind of comprehensive, systematic manner, but only through the perseverance and luck of dedicated citizens. The number of similar incidents that have escaped the scrutiny of researchers will always remain an interesting matter for speculation.

Giant UFOs Over the Hudson Valley

Like the valley near Norway's Hessadalen, New York's Hudson Valley was the scene of unexplained lights and objects traversing the skies, low to the ground, silent, unlike anything people had seen before. Yet this was a place as different from Hessdalen as can be imagined: a densely populated region just north of New York City.

1983 had been the Hudson Valley's "breakout year," but 1984 had more of everything. After a winter lull, sightings picked up in the spring. A March 11 incident in Wolcott, Connecticut, just after midnight, involved a mother and her daughter seeing a large cylindrical object through the window of their home, just a few feet away. For seven long minutes, it hovered low over the ground. Then it moved away, never once making a sound.[28] On March 21 at 8 p.m., a trucker driving south on NYS Route 87 saw a massive boomerang-shaped object with red, white, and green lights along the side. The object was incredibly low in the air: the driver estimated it to be about 100 feet off the ground. As a result, he could see the enormous, dark structure that unified the lights. He said it was "at least the size of a 747" and made no sound, even after he rolled down his truck window. He assumed it was an experimental vehicle. Then it vanished.[29]

New York State's Taconic Parkway meanders along on a picturesque north-south course, roughly 15 miles from the Connecticut border. On the night of March 25, 1984, near the town of Peekskill, hundreds of people saw low-flying lights over this road. Drivers stopped their cars, stepped outside, and watched in amazement. Descriptions were consistent: a slow-moving, boomerang-shaped object with six intensely bright lights and a green light in the center. The lights moved like one object, even when making a sharp turn. Many people had to shield their eyes, but at least one witness, a professional photographer, discerned a dark structure connecting the lights. He estimated it to be at least 300 feet long and flying at 30 mph. It moved over the water when, "all of a sudden, the lights were out and the thing was gone." He videotaped the event, but his tape came back blank.

Local police were overwhelmed with phone calls that night, although researchers, receiving only stonewalling, were for a long time unaware of this fact. Eventually, they learned that the official policy in most towns was to discourage police from talking about the sightings. Some were dismissive or even insulting to witnesses that night. In Danbury, Connecticut, one officer told a resident that "it can't be UFOs because they don't exist." Another advised a caller to "sleep it off and the pink UFO will go away." Presumably statements like these were in the days before the adoption of "community policing" principles.[30]

The incident of March 25 repeated itself six days later, on the 31st. Once again, motorists on the Taconic Parkway saw V-shaped lights moving slowly overhead, sometimes stopping and hovering. Hundreds of people got out of their cars. Most astonished witnesses could hear no sound except for a very quiet hum.[31]

April was quiet – until the night of the 25th, when the Taconic Parkway was again visited by a huge, hovering object. It had brilliant white lights in a half circle, along with smaller red lights, and some witnesses discerned a football-field-sized dark structure, silent and motionless. Drivers swerved in their vehicles as they saw this object. One witness phoned the New York State Police, which informed her she "probably saw those hang gliders from Stormville Airport."[32] Events like this continued all through the spring and summer, overshadowing all other UFO activity anywhere else in the world. Local researchers such as Philip Imbrogno and Peter Gersten interviewed witness after witness, collecting more than 90 reports of a large V-shaped formation in just one month, from late May through June 1984.[33]

Considering all that was happening, the paucity of news coverage was striking. Local newspapers continued to cover the sightings, but the wire services and major media stayed away. The official word was simply that there was no phenomenon happening, other than some stunt flyers playing pranks. The discrepancy between witnesses and authorities was vast even when the witnesses *were* authorities. On June 11, a New Castle police lieutenant named Peterson called the Westchester Airport about an object he and others had seen. His concern was simple. "If this thing can come in here and do whatever it wants," he said, "I want to know where the hell are our government's defenses." The airport representative told him what he saw was probably airplanes in formation. When Peterson adamantly disagreed, the representative replied, "just tell the people they saw planes.... It's planes, at least that's what I was told." Researchers contacted the FAA the next day, and were told the conversation had never taken place.[34]

Matters became more serious when a triangular object entered the premises of the Indian Point Nuclear Facility, in Westchester County, on

June 14, 1984. This turned out to be the first of two air space violations over the facility that summer. At 10:15 p.m., several plant employees saw an immense ("football-field sized") boomerang-shaped object enter their airspace. It had intensely bright lights along its sides and moved very smoothly, despite the high winds that evening – certainly no weather for ultra-light flyers. For twenty minutes, the object alternately hovered and moved, finally departing slowly. It did not bank when it turned, but moved as if on a horizontal plane. Witnesses were adamant that there was a dark mass visible behind the lights.[35] Either this or a similar object was seen elsewhere that night, even videotaped, although the video showed only lights. One witness insisted that the center of the object was hollow.[36]

And so it continued. A large V-shaped object was seen flying low over Hyde Park on June 21.[37] The same night, 50 miles to the south, unidentified lights were seen over the Wanaque Reservoir in New Jersey. Four anonymous calls were made to the local police between 9:44 p.m. and 12:17 a.m. about "lights" over the reservoir. Police saw nothing, but local press interviewed a witness who claimed to have seen an egg-shaped object "moving too fast for a blimp."[38] On the 22nd, a three-minute video of a close light formation was recorded and brought to a scientifically trained, experienced pilot. His only certain conclusion was that these were not conventional aircraft (if indeed the lights were separate objects) and that private pilots were not at the controls. He doubted that even special military aircraft would use such a dangerous formation. Investigators contacted FAA to learn whether anyone had clearance for formation flying in the area. The answer was negative. (The FAA spokesperson added "it is the policy of the FAA that UFOs do not exist, so we do not collect any reports of such.")[39] On June 24, witnesses observed a "big, giant thing in the shape of a V," flying over the road.[40] On the 25th, near Bethel, Connecticut, a slow moving, huge object with many lights was seen for twenty minutes. While people saw normal aircraft elsewhere in the sky, this object looked like an enormous Ferris Wheel on its side.[41]

A major event took place July 12, about 20 miles east of the Taconic Parkway, just over the Connecticut border. Police in the towns of Danbury, Ridgefield, Bethel, New Fairfield, and New Milford received report after report of a low flying, slow moving object "as large as a football field." Its lights were incredibly bright, and intense beams of light were directed to the ground. It also gave off heat to those beneath it. Yet, its light pattern was not a boomerang, but circular. Many formerly skeptical members of the Danbury police saw the object. After this, they were believers.

Local publicity for this event was strong, and newspapers listed the telephone numbers of some of the local UFO investigators. They were immediately flooded with calls, and investigators later estimated that 5,000 witnesses saw the object that night. A police officer from Bethel told them that not only had many officers seen the object that night, but they had been asked by the FAA to stonewall both press and investigators. If pressed, they were to explain the lights as caused by stunt fliers, primarily to prevent panic.[42]

More sightings occurred in the coming weeks, but the major event of the summer occurred on July 24. This time, video was recorded in Brewster that was good enough for professional analysis. The same night, the Indian Point Nuclear Facility was once again the scene of an overflight by an enormous object.

The video was recorded by Bob Pozzuoli, a New York City electronics executive. At 10 p.m., he videotaped a large object with a string of six bright lights around it. He briefly lost it to view behind a pine tree; it emerged with a string of rotating multicolored lights in the shape of a disc, and a flashing red

Frame from the Pozzuoli video

light at the rear. It then vanished behind some houses. Pozzuoli's video also captured airplanes flying overhead in formation, very useful for analysis. The impressive video was studied by many groups, including ABC television and the Jet Propulsion Laboratory in Pasadena, California. All agreed it was authentic, and none could explain the object.[43]

Just a few miles away was the Indian Point Nuclear Facility, in Peekskill. It was there that the most extraordinary UFO event of the year occurred – indeed, an argument can be made that it was the most extraordinary event anywhere on Earth during 1984.

On the night of July 24, 1984, at least a dozen plant workers and security guards at the facility watched a boomerang pattern of lights approach. Seen from below, the object resembled an ice cream cone – triangular but with a curved string of lights in the back. They could plainly see that these were not disconnected lights, but a solid body of enormous size, "about the size of three football fields," as one guard later put it. Despite winds that gusted at 30 mph, the huge object moved with cool purpose toward Reactor #3, the sole operational reactor at the plant. The guards stood, awestruck, as the object hovered directly above it. "That's what got our supervisor worried," one of them said. "This thing got to within thirty feet of the reactor."

Even more extraordinary, as the object approached the reactor, the plant's security and communications systems were rendered inactive. The computer controlling them simply shut down.

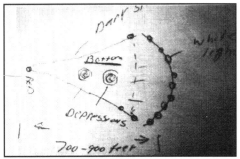

Sketch of triangular UFO made for Philip Imbrogno by a security officer from Indian Point Nuclear Facility.

It need hardly be mentioned that this was a serious matter. No aircraft of any kind was allowed to fly over the reactors without proper clearance. Video cameras at the facility filmed the object, and the officer in charge of filming later spoke to researchers. The object, he said, had eight bright lights in a wide V-formation. "It was one solid structure and very large. We had it on camera for 15 minutes.... Whatever it was, it was larger than a C-5A, which is the largest aircraft in the world.... This was much larger. It seemed very brazen. It acted like it didn't care who saw it."

The shift commander contacted nearby Camp Smith, a New York National Guard base, requesting identification of the object. As the base had no answer to give him, he asked for an armed helicopter to shoot it down. He then ordered his men to prepare to fire on the object. "We had shotguns and were waiting for the final word to fire on it," said one guard – an incredible statement that was confirmed by other personnel.

All seemed ready for a hopeless armed confrontation. But before the command was given to launch the helicopter, the object glided away. The next day, the commander of the security guards informed his staff that "nothing happened." They were told to forget the event.

Researchers had already known that Peekskill police had received many phone calls that night from area residents describing the same object. The encounter at Indian Point, however, was not known by them until early September. At that time, a plant employee contacted Philip Imbrogno and wanted to tell the story. Somehow, clearance was initially granted for a few researchers to meet witnesses and visit the reactor on September 5. Then, without any reason given, the visit was cancelled and the employees forbidden to talk. At this point, an angry Imbrogno threatened to go public. That was when management relented. The guards were once again allowed to meet with the researchers, but not at the facility, and only with a security supervisor present. Two meetings subsequently took place.

In the days after the July 24 incident, officials of the U.S. Nuclear Regulatory Commission visited the plant, and, according to Imbrogno, the entire security system underwent a shakeup. One journalist received an acknowledgment from the plant that sightings *had* occurred, and that New York State police had arrested four Cessna pilots in connection with it! This was simply too absurd, and the UFO researchers checked state police records which showed that no pilots had been arrested. Plant authorities had simply lied. FOIA requests were filed with New York Power Authority, U.S. Department of Energy, and the U.S. Nuclear Regulatory Commission. Each of these agencies replied that they knew nothing about an incident from July 24. Authorities also denied the existence of any video tape that may have recorded the incident. Researchers attempted to obtain copies of radio communications that night, but none reportedly existed. Imbrogno summed up the matter well: such obstruction was tantamount to proof that UFO reports, when they involve national security, were exempt from FOIA.[44]

Years later, Imbrogno privately added a few important – and astonishing – details regarding Indian Point. He indicated that he had sworn testimony from several plant security personnel that in fact there had been a crack in the wall of Reactor #3, and that they had not only seen an enormous UFO hovering above, but some had seen non-humans walking through the containment wall of the reactor. Apparently, the beings had saved the plant from a nuclear disaster.[45]

The Hudson Valley UFO Conference

After the July 24 sightings, researchers began receiving phone calls from a man who said he was a specialist in satellite intelligence for the National Security Agency. Despite this weighty connection, he claimed to be contacting Imbrogno for personal, not professional, reasons. He wanted to know about Imbrogno's research, was very interested in learning Allen Hynek's opinion on the matter, and especially wanted to see a copy of the Pozzuoli video tape. As they spoke, Imbrogno noticed a clicking sound every fifteen seconds or so. The two agreed to meet when the caller was in the area. Somehow, Imbrogno checked into this man's background and learned that he actually was an agent for the NSA.[46]

All through August, this man phoned Imbrogno and other researchers. He often gave the impression that he was monitoring their other phone calls, as he would sometimes refer indirectly to other conversations they had. In one instance, a mere five minutes after one of them had ended a telephone call with Hynek, the NSA caller phoned. Had they learned anything new from Hynek, he asked? Another odd development was that the FAA began making counter-statements on new sightings before the researchers had even publicized them. This caused Imbrogno, Gersten, and their colleagues to suspect a direct link between their NSA connection and the FAA. They borrowed equipment to detect telephone taps, and the result was a probable yes, although proving an NSA tap was no enviable task.

The investigators met their mysterious NSA man in mid-August. He read their reports and transcripts with interest. They discussed whether or not the CIA was flying special aircraft in the area in order to confuse the issue. The researchers had a good source that the CIA was using nearby Stewart Airport for some type of operation, and another source who had seen small planes taking off in formation from the airport at night. The NSA man acknowledged that counterintelligence was a CIA specialty, and that such an operation was within its capability. The most unsettling moment of the meeting was when he asked for the Pozzuoli tape. With no guarantee of full exchange of information, with no trust, this would have amounted to a blank check. The researchers said no. He replied, "you know, Phil, the government has done away with people for a lot less."[47]

Imbrogno and Gersten had meanwhile been organizing a conference, which they planned for August 25. Gersten did an excellent job at promotion and organization. When it convened at a middle school in Brewster, 1,500 people showed up – triple the seating capacity. Allen Hynek was there, as were several major media organizations, the mysterious contact from the NSA, various people from the FBI, and senior officers from Pease AFB. For twelve hours, attendees listened to presentations, discussed the lack of government action, and mainly (since most were actual UFO witnesses) shared stories. An incredible 900 people filled out UFO sighting reports. The impressive Pozzuoli tape was shown; ABC technicians who analyzed it could only say that the lights were not airplanes.[48]

The media coverage was mostly skeptical. First local newspapers, then the *New York Times*, for instance, emphasized a police sergeant's claims that the affair was caused by a group of close formation aircraft with black undersides and bright lights that could change color. The reporter did not challenge this bizarre claim, nor did he ask the reasonable question of why had authorities not identified or apprehended the perpetrators of such illegal activities? Journalist Terry Hansen argued that the *New York Times* covered the event only because it had to – the sightings were in its own backyard, as it were, and were now receiving significant coverage elsewhere. What distinguished the *Times* coverage, wrote Hansen, was "a noteworthy lack of commitment and curiosity." Such an attitude was entirely consistent with that newspaper's history of UFO coverage.[49]

While sightings of the "Hudson Valley Object" continued through August and beyond, people also saw more and more obvious formations of low-flying light aircraft and helicopters. Many of these occurred in Brewster and Putnam Lake townships, over land that researchers learned was owned by the NSA. Imbrogno and other researchers concluded that the U.S. government owned and operated the planes, either to confuse the UFO issue, or else to conduct its own surveillance over the area. In fact, a local television news story quoted an FAA spokesperson who said the government *was* carrying out surveillance, although the FAA soon denied this.[50]

Within a few months the Hudson Valley mystery had exploded onto the world. There is ample evidence showing covert interest by the U.S. intelligence community, an overwhelming desire by authorities to keep this matter from getting out of hand, and cooperation with authorities from the major media. The phenomenon had also unsettled UFO researchers. What was happening there had no precedent. For decades, UFOs had come in a few basic shapes, mostly disc-variants, although some triangular shapes were reported in earlier years.[51] There had been low-flying UFOs in the past, there had been large UFOs, and there had been quite a few reports from densely populated areas. There had also been a few extended sighting waves from specific geographic regions. But there had never been anything in ufology that combined all of these features, and certainly no specific wave that had lasted this long. Plus, the boomerang-shape appeared to be something completely new.

Something new was happening here. The newness raises a simple question: why?

Was this a demonstration of a new but still secret terrestrial technology? If so, it might not necessarily mean a breakthrough in physics. One hypothesis is that the Hudson Valley Object was a type of lighter-than-air technology (LTA) – in other words, some form of rigid dirigible. The LTA hypothesis has been used to explain the sightings of large triangular craft ("Big Black Deltas") during the 1990s, although it is not universally accepted. One anonymous author of a 2002 paper submitted to the

National Institute for Discovery Science (NIDS) theorized that LTA vehicles powered by "electrokinetic" drive have been operated by the U.S. military since the early to mid-1980s.[52] An electrokinetic LTA craft would not need propellers or jets, but instead would use aerostatic lift gas. Since its energy could be fed remotely by a ground based power system using microwaves, it would not need a power supply. According to the paper, the maximum transmission distance would be about 62 miles. The craft would have an outstanding thrust to mass ratio, enabling it to accelerate very quickly, including up. One problem is that such a beamed microwave system would require a line of sight that is dangerous to anything that gets in its path, such as birds. There are no known reports of dead birds accompanying sightings of the Hudson Valley boomerang, or for that matter of later sightings of BBDs. Another difficulty of linking the LTA hypothesis with the Hudson Valley sightings is the very shape of the object in question: whereas LTA vehicles appear designed solely for a blimp or delta shape, none are known to be designed for a boomerang-shape. This is not to say such a design is impossible: it may be that a terrestrial design team succeeded beyond their wildest dreams in creating a boomerang-shaped LTA for covert testing or missions over the Hudson Valley in the early 1980s. If so, or if this is some other terrestrial breakthrough, it is a breakthrough that has remained secret for 25 years as of this writing.

But perhaps other possibilities exist. If the Hudson Valley object was a "true UFO," it was still different enough from previous UFOs to give pause. It could indicate that the "others" operating UFOs were using different technologies and tactics to interact with the people on Earth. Of course, the object could also have signified the presence of a different group altogether. The presence of helicopters in the area during the fall of 1984 might indicate that a covert group was looking into that possibility.

Dangerous Soviet UFOs

From what we can tell of Soviet UFO history, 1984 was an interesting year. There appears to have been a UFO crash in the mountains of Azerbaijan on July 20, although next to nothing is known about the details.[53] A case with more information, albeit no date, is said to have occurred near Astrakhan, on the northern shore of the Caspian Sea. An anti-aircraft unit was alerted to a spherical object flying along the coast at about 6,000 feet. Requests for identification were ignored. Two fighters were scrambled and tried to shoot it down, but the object descended close to the ground, preventing the fighters from firing any further. Photographs apparently were taken. When, near Krasnovodsk, a helicopter attempted to shoot it down, the object climbed above it and hovered. After the helicopter landed, the UFO disappeared over the sea.[54]

The most dramatic Soviet UFO encounter of 1984 took place during the early morning hours of September 7. A Tu-134A passenger plane was flying north to the Estonian city of Tallinn. While near Minsk at 4:10 a.m., the pilots saw what looked like a large, bright, elongated star, directing a thin ray of light toward the ground. Before long, the ray opened up to become a cone of light. Another cone quickly followed, then a third. The pilots decided that the light source was 80 miles away, and the co-pilot drew a sketch of what he saw. The light turned a blinding ray directly at them. It then appeared to explode, being replaced by a greenish cloud. Next, it displayed maneuverability far beyond anything in the known inventory of the world's air forces: this "object" approached them rapidly, stopped dead, descended, ascended vertically, then moved left and right. Finally, it stopped in front of the Tu-134A, apparently pacing them close to their position. The crew now saw multicolored lights within the green cloud which flared and died away. The cloud changed shape, developed a tail which then ascended, leaving the cloud in a rectangular shape. Co-pilot Lazurin shouted that the object was teasing them. It certainly seemed to be doing just that.

A second Tu-134 was 60 miles away and was ordered to approach their position. Although the giant cloud should have been easily visible from such a distance, the commander of the other plane saw nothing – until at eight miles distant he saw the UFO in great detail. Such a development might suggest the object had an ability to cloak itself for all but very close distances. It then turned around and directed a light at the new aircraft, then downward to trace out a rectangular shape. The UFO made zigzag movements and illuminated the rectangle below. Then it descended and stayed below the aircraft. Ground control informed the second Tu-134A that Soviet cosmonauts had seen the object from their orbital station. At 5 a.m., the crew saw running multicolored lights along the object's side. It is not clear how the object departed, but the encounter had tragic results. Within a year, the captain of the second Tu-134A, a V. Goridze, had died of electromagnetic radiation; the pilot had developed heart disease and lost his job; and a stewardess developed a complex skin disease. All had been hit by the object's ray during the encounter. The Tallinn crew suffered one casualty, a steward, who developed similar ailments.

There were many ground witnesses to this UFO. One of these, retired

Colonel A. Kovalchuk, described it as a cigar shaped object about 330 feet long surrounded by a greenish halo. He described two powerful lights on it, and a bluish light that came straight to the ground. He said the object at times moved as slowly as 40 miles per hour. He was aware of no Soviet aircraft like it.

Russian ufologists could not agree on what this object was. They established that a rocket was launched from the Cosmodrome at Plesetsk, many hundreds of miles to the northeast, and that this is what caused the greenish cloud and other light effects. Other details of the case pose greater problems. One speculation is that this was a military experiment involving the creation of an artificial cloud for some purpose. Another is that this was a genuine UFO coincident with the rocket launch. As in so many of these baffling reports, the origin and control of the UFO is itself secondary to the reality of its very existence. The encounter was so dramatic, seen by so many people, that even Soviet censorship was not able to stop it, and it appeared in *Tass* in January 1985.[55]

One more Soviet sighting of note for 1984 was a landing case in the eastern Urals, northwest of Chelyabinsk, in late September or early October. A local militia captain and patrolman were driving at 9 p.m. when they noticed odd-colored lights to their right, about 25 meters away in a field. They saw a large triangle outlined by multi-colored, sequentially flashing lights, either resting on the ground or perhaps just above it. The captain later sketched the object with 11 lights on the left and right sides, and another 13 going up the center. The men stopped their car and stared. At some point, the object simply became dark and impossible to see. The next day, the captain returned to the area and found three round depressions in the soil about 10 inches deep and 36 inches in diameter. They were at the corners of an equilateral triangle with sides of about 25 feet.[56]

Meanwhile, the limited Western coverage of the Soviet scene was marked by glib explanations that Soviet UFO reports were government disinformation to cover up serious experiments and activities, even illegal strategic weapon testing. NASA employee James Oberg in particular argued that some sightings were experiments of the Fractional Orbital Bombardment System (FOBS), which the Soviets had secretly built in violation of the 1963 Outer Space Treaty. This treaty forbade the stationing of weapons of mass destruction in orbit.[*] Because the launches of rockets and the fiery returns to earth of dummy warheads could not be concealed, the govern-

---

[*] Although it did not ban systems that were capable of placing weapons in orbit, and the Soviets only conducted tests without live warheads.

ment decided to present them as a UFO mystery, argued Oberg.[57] Undoubtedly there were tests of Cosmos satellites, or perhaps of laser beam weapons as some speculated, that were mistaken by Soviet citizens for UFOs. The western media grabbed hold of this idea – that "flying saucers became part of the KGB's arsenal of deception." It was a thesis not only with some logic, but it was easy to grasp. In reality, the UFOs always managed to leach out beyond such tidy explanations.[58]

Media Damage Control

The Hudson Valley sightings continued through the remainder of the year. Finally, on October 5, two of the investigators, Phil Imbrogno and Fred Dennis, saw the object while driving. It had a large array of six lights that seemed to be connected by a structure. They watched it flip over on its side and rotate like a Ferris Wheel. They tried to follow it, but lost it after they turned a corner. It had vanished.[59]

In the November issue of *Discover* magazine came a dismissive article by Glenn Garelik on the sightings, attributing them to private aircraft secretly flying in formation. Repeating the August absurdities of the *New York Times*, Garelik suggested these amazing aircraft could fly as close as six inches from each other and turn off their navigation lights while in flight. No evidence was offered, no identification of the offending pilots, no aircraft descriptions. Two debunking sidebars accompanied the article, one claiming that UFOs existed only to fill a psychological need, the other informing the public that UFOs had been investigated by the Condon committee and shown to be without substance.

To a casual reader, the article seemed like a disinterested analysis, but several interesting features hinted otherwise. First, the non-existent logic, to say nothing of science, evident in the article itself. Second, the long history of *Discover*'s parent company, Time, Inc., as a CIA-friendly publication. Third, Garelik's own background in Soviet studies, his fluency in Russian, and his expertise on the Soviet space program. He completed assignments in the Soviet Union for *Discover,* and wrote about the post-Soviet KGB for the *New York Times.* This was an American journalist with obvious connections to the world of power and the intelligence community. Was his purpose purely detached, or was he serving a deeper agenda?[60]

If this was an instance of collaboration between American media and government, it would simply fit the longstanding pattern of American media compliance with the interests of national security. For example, in December 1984, the launch of a U.S. military satellite was voluntarily censored by the Associated Press after Secretary of Defense Casper Weinberger asked them not to report it; NBC followed suit. During this time, also, AP choked stories about cocaine trafficking by the infamous Nicaraguan Contras, and *New York Times* correspondent Raymond Bonner was pulled from Central America for investigating the El Salvadorian death squads.[61]

Towards a New Era

Three events, none of which were major news at the time, ended the year. Each of them signified a major break with the past. Each pointed the way toward the future.

In December 1984, Bob Gribble, who operated the National UFO Reporting Center in Seattle, discontinued sending UFO reports to MUFON. He now began sending them to a computer network called Compufon, administered by Michael Hart. The World Wide Web would not be in place for another ten years, but the beginnings of the Internet were there, mainly through the bulletin board system known as Usenet. Gribble's UFO telephone hotline number had extensive coverage throughout the United States, particularly with police agencies and airports. Moving to the Internet, undeveloped though it was, was a signal of things to come.[62]

On the grand stage of geopolitics, too, the world was about to change. In December 1984, Mikhail Gorbachev, not yet Secretary General of the Soviet Communist Party, visited British Prime Minister Margaret Thatcher. She was duly impressed. "I like Mr. Gorbachev," she said. "We can do business together." That month, Gorbachev took his stand firmly with the forces of reform within his country, delivering a major speech introducing two new concepts to the Party: glasnost and perestroika. Openness and restructuring.

Finally, a matter that would forever change ufology. On December 11, 1984, a manila envelope arrived at the home of television producer Jaime Shandera in Burbank, California. Shandera was a close research partner of William Moore. The envelope, which had no return address, had an Albuquerque postmark and was dated December 8. Two more envelopes were inside, then a roll of undeveloped 35 mm film.

When developed and printed, there were seven pages included. The first was a cover sheet stamped "Top Secret/Majic Eyes Only" entitled "Briefing Document: Operation Majestic 12 Prepared for President-Elect Dwight Eisenhower: (Eyes Only)." It was dated November 18, 1952, although the date format was shown as 18 November, 1952 (a format style that would later become a major issue of contention among researchers).

The second page gave a brief description of "Operation Majestic-12." Admiral Roscoe H. Hillenkoetter (designated as MJ-1), was listed as the briefing officer. Majestic 12 was described as a "Top Secret Research and Development/Intelligence operation responsible directly and only to the President of the United States," and "was established by special classified executive order of President Truman on 24 September, 1947, upon recommendation by Dr. Vannevar Bush and Secretary James Forrestal." The page then listed the 12 original members. In the order and manner of listing, they were: Adm. Roscoe H. Hillenkoetter, Dr. Vannevar Bush, Secy. James V. Forrestal, Gen. Nathan F. Twining, Gen. Hoyt S. Vandenberg, Dr. Detlev Bronk, Dr. Jerome Hunsaker, Mr. Sidney W. Souers, Mr. Gordon Gray, Dr. Donald Menzel, Gen. Robert M. Montague, and Dr. Lloyd V. Berkner. A note at the bottom of the page stated that upon Forrestal's death in 1949, his spot remained vacant until filled by Gen. Walter B. Smith the following year.

Pages three, four, and five provided a nine-paragraph summary of the extraterrestrial presence. They mentioned how the Kenneth Arnold sighting of June 1947 had kicked off the wave of flying saucer sightings, then how "a local rancher reported that one had crashed in a remote region of New Mexico," 75 miles northwest of Roswell Army Air Base. The document stated that secret recovery operations were begun on July 7, 1947 and that "aerial reconnaissance discovered that four small, human-like beings had apparently ejected from the craft at some point before it exploded." All were dead and badly decomposed. Strange writing was found in the wreckage, and could not be deciphered. Nor had the ship's method of propulsion been identified. Bodies and wreckage were all carefully removed and sent to various locations. Study of the bodies, led by Dr. Detlev Bronk, indicated that they were not human, although they had many human features. They were designated as "Extra-terrestrial Biological Entities," or EBEs. While some speculated that these beings possibly came from another planet in the solar system, others such as Dr. Menzel believed they were from another solar system.

The document also mentioned a second UFO crash which occurred on December 6, 1950 in the El Indio-Guerrero area of the Texas-Mexican border. This object was nearly completely incinerated, but was transported to the Atomic Energy Commission's facility in Sandia, New Mexico.

The origin and intentions of these visitors remained unknown, according to the document, and concern was high throughout 1952 that "new developments" might be imminent. The need to avoid public panic was paramount, as was the necessity to understand this exotic technology. The Majestic-12 Group had decided unanimously that the strictest security precautions be continued into the next (Eisenhower) Presidential administration.

Page six of the document listed eight additional attachments (various Status Reports and Analytical Reports) which were not included. Page seven was a memorandum dated September 24, 1947 and signed by President Harry Truman. Addressed to Secretary of Defense James Forrestal, it authorized him "to proceed with all due speed and caution upon your undertaking. Hereafter this matter shall be referred to only as Operation Majestic Twelve."

In summary, these were the MJ-12 documents. Upon initial review, they certainly looked as though they might be legitimate. Moore and Shandera were now faced with a daunting task: to determine whether or not they were. One thing that struck them both immediately had to do with the list of MJ-12 members, which contained one shocker: Dr. Donald Menzel. Before Philip Klass, Menzel had been the world's most prominent UFO debunker. His inclusion in the list appeared to be a joke.

In general, the MJ-12 documents were similar to the documents that AFOSI Agent Richard Doty had shown Linda Moulton Howe in the spring of 1983. However, there were also discrepancies, the most significant being that while the MJ-12 documents stated that two UFOs had crashed, one near Roswell in 1947 and the other at the Mexican border in 1950, there was no mention of numerous other crashes which were discussed in the papers Howe had seen, including one said to have occurred at Aztec, New Mexico.

Who sent the undeveloped film to Shandera? Although the envelope had no return address, it had been postmarked from Albuquerque, which is of course where Richard Doty worked. Doty was also handling Moore throughout the 1980s. It seems obvious that Doty was the source, although decades later, he continued to deny that this was so. The only question is, how authentic were any of the documents he was connected with? Were the documents that Doty showed Howe in 1983 all true, partially true, or not true at all? If partially true, which parts? The same questions apply to the Eisenhower Briefing Document, and would later apply as well to the many "Majestic" documents leaked during the 1990s, which did not appear to have any connection with Doty at all.

In the ensuing years, every UFO researcher developed an opinion. A distinct majority came down on the side of hoax or disinformation, a persistent minority argued that the documents were valid. Extensive document analysis revealed one thing beyond question. The documents, if hoaxes, were not cheap or simple. That goes not only for the original documents leaked in 1984, but many others leaked during the 1990s. Indeed, when stacked, the documents are more than an inch thick, of great variety and sophistication, covering a broad range of technical disciplines, historical data, writing styles, perspectives, and jargon. The amount of planning and coordination going into the making of them would have been substantial – well beyond the capability of any one person. In other words, if hoaxes or disinformation, the documents would most likely be the result of an intelligence operation. But if this is so, would not such an operation add credibility to the reality of UFOs? Why go through the difficulty of creating so many sophisticated fake documents if UFOs were silly nonsense? The most likely disinformation scenario would be that there is indeed reality to UFOs, and that the documents were created in order to lead researchers into dead ends. As Barry Greenwood later put it, "MJ-12 did immense damage to document research. Now I look at anything written about UFOs and I say, is that for real?"[63] Perhaps this was the intention.

Such debates and uncertainties, however, lay in the future. For the next few years following receipt of the MJ-12 documents in December 1984, Shandera, Moore, and (very soon) Stanton Friedman kept their existence a closely guarded secret. Meanwhile, they tried to determine how exactly one could authenticate them.

Leaks and Lore, 1985

In the modern history of UFOs, certain years are sometimes listed as "down" years when subsequent research indicates otherwise. 1985, however, *was* a slow year. For whatever reasons, sightings dropped around the world. Even the Hudson Valley experienced a significant decline in sightings. The global geopolitical scene was more interesting, as were some very intriguing leaks from the covert world.

By the mid-1980s, America's national security establishment was riding high. Four years of the Reagan Presidency had brought a renewed confidence to the military and intelligence community – a confidence buttressed by many billions of dollars. Government secrecy was in the ascendant. General William Odom, a man who equated journalism with espionage, became the new director of the NSA. "Quite simply," said Odom to a group of colleagues, "there is no comprehensive 'right to know' included, either explicitly or implicitly, within the first Amendment." Such was the prevailing attitude.[64]

The stealth fighter was operational and still secret. The stealth bomber was being test-flown in the mid-west, occasionally causing UFO reports.[65] And the first hint of a mysterious new aircraft appeared in a U.S. Defense budgetary request for Fiscal Year 1987. Within a section entitled "Strategic Reconnaissance" was a reference to a project known as "Aurora." No one knew of it, and fewer cared to discuss it. Some $455 million were requested for the program – for production, not research. In all likelihood, the Aurora aircraft – believed to be a high altitude, high speed reconnaissance platform that succeeded the SR-71 Blackbird – was flying at this time.[66]

Interest in space weapons and systems was strong. This was the year that the SDI programs began making notable progress, including the Mid-Infrared Advanced Chemical Laser (MIRACL), which successfully destroyed a Titan missile booster during a simulation, and the High Precision Tracking Experiment (HPTE), designed for Earth to Orbit laser tracking. General Odom pushed for a satellite program that would be survivable in the event of a Soviet attack. According to journalist James Bamford, most senior officials at NSA thought the idea "loony," though one may wonder whether additional motives were at work – if rumors of ET-connections to the Strategic Defense Program are to be believed.[67] Other programs operated on the principal that the best space defense is a good space offense. During 1985, an anti-satellite missile (launched from an F-15) successfully hit a target 290 miles above the Earth, moving at 17,500 mph.[68]

It is interesting that the annual Bilderberg meeting discussed SDI that year. The conference strongly supported further development of SDI. According to Bilderberg Group watcher Daniel Estulin, members did so "on the premise that it would grant unlimited riches to the Masters of the Universe." Such riches, if nothing else, would come in the form of defense contracts, but most likely the assumption was that domination of space was a prerequisite for domination of the battlefield in future wars – something that America's satellite program would prove decisively during the 1991 Gulf War. In any event, several strong SDI proponents were known Bilderberg attendees, including Richard Perle, who attended a 1983 meeting, and Paul Nitze, who attended many meetings going back to the 1950s. Whether an extraterrestrial connection was quietly made by some

Bilderberg members can only be guessed at. Clearly, even in a group such as the Bilderbergers, knowledge of the UFO reality and extraterrestrial presence must have been on a "need to know."[69]

Another secret program at the time, purely at the research stage, later became the High Frequency Active Aural Research Program (HAARP). In 1985, Bernard J. Eastlund, a physicist for ARCO Power Technologies, applied for the patent "Method and Apparatus for Altering a Region in the Earth's Atmosphere, Ionosphere and/or Magnetosphere." The idea was to use high-frequency radio waves to beam unprecedented amounts of power into the ionosphere, more than 100 miles above the planet's surface. The beam would energize and heat the ionosphere, disabling incoming missiles and knocking out enemy satellite communications. Well into the 1990s, ARCO scientists expanded Eastlund's ideas to develop new weapons capabilities. In the midst of the Alaskan wilderness, a large clearing was made to create the HAARP Array.

The anti-missile aspect of Eastlund's work may have been discarded later, but HAARP of the 1990s and beyond contained definite military applications. It could disrupt satellites and communication systems. It could also use Earth-penetrating tomography to search for natural gas or petroleum deposits, or even artificial structures like underground military bases. HAARP has been accused of being able to change weather patterns (perhaps in concert with the notorious chemtrails), and even disrupt human mental processes. The Official HAARP Homepage denies these claims while acknowledging that the array can generate Extra Low Frequencies (ELF). While ELFs can affect biological systems, HAARP's defenders argue the signals are negligible and have no effect on humans or other biological systems.[70]

That HAARP can be used to "see" below the Earth's surface is a fact of the greatest importance. One HAARP project manager stated that the program could, in fact, be used to locate underground bases, presumably those belonging to military adversaries. By the mid-1980s, the technology was in place to create hardened underground facilities under virtually all conditions. The only constraint was money. Such was the conclusion of a 1985 report by the U.S. Army Corps of Engineers. Underground base researcher Richard Sauder pointed out that, given the substantial buildup in military budgets under the Reagan administration, money may not have been a drawback at all. A 1986 report from Los Alamos National Laboratories called for using a fission powered, nuclear subselene to provide the heat to "melt rock and form a self-supporting, glass lined tunnel suitable for

Maglev or other high speed transport modes." This report was not even directed toward Earthly purposes, but rather at NASA plans for tunneling on the Moon. Such devices would be automatic and remotely operated. The following year, Lloyd A. Duscha, Deputy Director of Engineering and Construction for the U.S. Army Corps of Engineers, mentioned in a speech that several of the Corps' "most interesting" underground facilities were classified, and that there were projects – which he would not identify – with "multiple chambers up to 50 feet wide and 100 feet high." In other words, enormous secret underground facilities were very much in existence by this time.[71]

Indeed, claims of secret underground bases were beginning to leak from the covert world. Several, replete with connections to UFOs and reverse engineering, pointed to Fort Hood in Texas.* Researcher Richard Sauder communicated with a former member of the Army who claimed that to reach his work station beneath Fort Hood, he had to travel through two miles of tunnel. There was evidently much more beyond that. When Sauder asked him whether his work underground was UFO-related, the man remained sphinx-like, but intimated yes. Another military source told Sauder of an underground base at Fort Hood dating back to the 1950s, if not earlier. More recently, Sauder expressed his firm conviction that there are multiple, massive facilities beneath Fort Hood, perhaps even a labyrinth of tunnels and bases.[72] Yet another person, writing anonymously to the UFO news repository, *Filer's Files*, claimed to have interviewed during the 1980s several individuals connected with Fort Hood. He concluded there was a secret base below, containing either captured or man-made UFOs. Some of his sources claimed to have seen UFOs taking off or landing in a restricted part of Fort Hood.[73]

This was still several years before the claims of Robert Lazar regarding the reverse engineering of an alien saucer at the Groom Lake facility south of Area 51 in Nevada. But even by the mid-1980s, aviation writer James Goodall was interviewing people who worked there. Goodall wrote many articles on aviation and black technology for *Jane's Defense, Aviation Week and Space Technology*, and *Interavia*. One of his sources had worked at Groom for twelve years. When asked whether he believed in UFOs, the man replied: "Absolutely, positively, they do exist." "Can you expand on that?" asked an intrigued Goodall. "No, I can't," came the reply. A few years later the same man told Goodall, "we have things in the Nevada

---

* Indeed, one of Leonard Stringfield's sources suggested that Fort Hood was a source of the UFO that severely burned three people in 1980 – the infamous Cash-Landrum case.

desert that would make George Lucas envious." Another source, a Chief Master Sergeant with three tours at Groom Lake, told Goodall around 1985: "We have things out there that are literally out of this world.... Better than Star Trek or anything you can see in the movies." Goodall asked him to expand on this statement; he refused.

Based on his many first-person interviews in the 1980s and early 1990s, Goodall concluded there were at least eight black programs flying out of Groom Lake, entirely separate from the known stealth programs. At least two of these were of very high speed aircraft; another was of a high-altitude, slow, and quiet stealth aircraft. Another was of a silent flying triangle. "Unconventional" technologies were in use, said Goodall.[74]

Even more incredible information was coming to Linda Moulton Howe, who had cultivated military sources describing exotic programs and more. Studying alien technology was the least of it. Howe was given a veritable mountain of information (or disinformation, depending on one's analysis) about the extraterrestrial presence on planet Earth. For one, there was an active program to communicate with extraterrestrial biological entities, called "Ebens." She learned of a "Yellow Book" – a device brought by the Ebens on April 25, 1964 – which provided holographic images of many things, including Earth's history and alleged images of Christ.

There was also a "Red Book," written by humans based on the information gathered about the extraterrestrials. Some of the information contained within it was nothing short of astounding. Alien-made tunnels were common beneath the Earth. The Ebens knew the past and future, and wanted to change the catastrophes awaiting mankind. However, they preferred to convince humanity to change its ways, rather than directly interfere.

One of Howe's contacts believed there may have been a war 6,000 years ago between two extraterrestrial races, the Ebens and Nordics, over territorial rights to a certain planet, which may not have been Earth. These extraterrestrials – masters at manipulating DNA – have designed and enhanced creatures from many worlds. The extraterrestrials also have an interest in our souls, possibly in a predatory way, possibly not. One of Howe's sources once asked an elderly member of MJ-12 about souls and why the Ebens "made" humanity. The reply he received was "you don't want to know that."[75]

By the mid-1980s, the information leaking out of the black world was far more detailed and bizarre than anything that had previously escaped. The 1980s were truly "The Decade of Leaks."

Conservative Ufology

There was no question that a popular demand existed for ufology, if only someone knew how to tap it. In January 1985, Oprah Winfrey, hosting the television show *AM Chicago*, did an hour-long segment on UFOs. The same month, CNN produced a special documentary on the Rendlesham Forest Incident, obtaining cooperation from researcher Lawrence Fawcett.[76] But despite the obvious popular appeal, proponents of scientific ufology steered clear. Most of these researchers also refused to give credence to the leaks that had been seeping from the covert world.

At CUFOS, Allen Hynek's deteriorating health meant that the organization was inexorably devolving into other hands. In the spring of 1985, he resigned as President and designated Mark Rodeghier his successor. The editorship of the *International UFO Reporter* passed to Jerome Clark. The new lights at CUFOS sought to continue Hynek's tradition of providing a scientific voice to ufology, although for the most part the group had to be dragged forcibly into doing any true research. In fairness, membership was limited and funds less so. Yet, the entrenched conservatism of the organization meant that it often played catch-up to everyone else. Clark, for instance, acknowledged that there was something serious about UFOs. "Beyond that," he said, "we hold forth for no particular interpretation." He considered all the talk of reverse engineering, underground bases, to say nothing of Ebens and Nordics, as a plague of "mystery mongering," "credulity" and "loose thinking." Ufology was sinking into a morass of pop culture, said Clark, and needed a good housecleaning.[77]

Some CUFOS members, it is true, were unhappy with the organization's stubborn intransigence regarding these new developments. Clark was even unimpressed by the Hudson Valley sightings, calling the case a "scam" in the debunking journal *Saucer Smear*. At this point, Hynek took exception to Clark's position. Though ailing, he had recently visited the area, and came away impressed by the researchers and their data.[78]

When the *IUR* did try to confront ufology's leading issues, like the crashed saucer thesis, the results were tepid, such as in a 1985 debate between David Jacobs ("absolutely no") and Richard Hall (a definite "maybe"). For Jacobs, the concept was so outlandish, the alleged cover-up so immense, that nothing less than actual alien hardware would suffice as proof. He argued that nothing in the released FOIA documents indicated that the U.S. government systematically investigated UFOs, much less retrieved crashed UFOs. The only evidence presented for UFO crash retrievals was anecdotal, he said, mostly anonymous, and none from actual scientists. Following up on such so-called leaks, said Jacobs, promised to be a waste of resources; he dismissed such testimony as too fantastic to be considered. Case closed. Hall, for his part, conceded the "historical ridiculousness" of the idea that UFOs had crashed, but acknowledged "a small but growing body of credible reports" that were suggestive of exactly this. He pointed out that Dr. Robert Sarbacher, a man who certainly qualified as a leading scientist, made several statements about UFO crash retrieval programs. Hall counseled his skeptical colleagues to use more caution before condemning the idea that crashed UFOs may have been retrieved.[79]

Absent from the debate was a recognition of just how revolutionary the crash retrieval concept was to ufology. Accepting its reality would transform the entire concept of secrecy. It would mean that the government was not merely hiding the existence of the reality of UFOs from the rest of the world, but also its possession of exotic technology, the probability of hiding a great deal of money for secret research and development, and the likelihood that private groups would have gotten in on the "gravy train" to benefit from such secrets.

Whereas American ufology could be recalcitrant enough regarding evidence of a grand conspiracy, British ufology had practically tossed out the ETH altogether. Across the Atlantic, paranormal and psychological theories were explaining UFOs; conspiracies were right out. British researcher Jenny Randles speculated that one reason might have been the difficulty in obtaining UFO data from the British government. In the U.K., the Official Secrets Act provided for prison sentences relating even to the release of minor data. Without obtaining any evidence of actual government data on the subject, conspiracies were a tougher nut to crack.[80]

Meanwhile, after a long and productive existence, the Aerial Phenomena Research Organization (APRO) was beginning to shut down. The July 1985 *APRO Bulletin* announced that health problems in the Lorenzen family would cause the publication to be suspended indefinitely. APRO did not have to go this route. With better cultivation of new leaders, this organization had the capability of sustaining itself and growing through the years. But it was not to be. Soon, Jim and Coral Lorenzen would be dead, and APRO gone forever.[81]

Hynek's health, too, was in decline. In the latter half of 1985, he underwent extensive cancer treatment and moved to Scottsdale, Arizona. He had already been stepping back from management of CUFOS. By the end of 1985, Sherman Larsen was the organization's chief executive officer,

Mark Rodeghier its deputy scientific director, and Jerome Clark the editor of the *IUR* (for which Larsen was also the Production Manager).[82] One of the odd features of Hynek's move to Arizona was his connection to a woman named Tina Choate. Little is known about her, except that she appears to be a member of the prestigious Choate family, one of the early families of New England. Choate, and her partner Brian Myers, lured Hynek to come to Arizona with promises of research money. These were never fulfilled, and Hynek soon broke off relations with the two in disillusionment. Choate and Myers would take on a more significant and darker role in ufology a few years later, after the death of the Lorenzens.[83]

1985: A Quiet Year

In terms of actual UFO activity, 1985 was as quiet as any year in modern times. There appears to have been a glimmer of activity in the Soviet Union, where – coincidentally or not – major political changes were beginning. On March 11, 1985, following the death of Communist Party Secretary General Konstantin Chernenko, Mikhail Gorbachev was unanimously selected to lead the country. Gorbachev electrified the Soviet Union; yet he did not seek to overthrow the system. He sought radical reforms, not revolution; greater freedoms, but the retention of communism. Within a few years, however, his reforms had spun out of control, leading to the unthinkable: the dissolution of the Soviet Union.

One of the Soviet encounters from the year involved a radar station in the Krasnovodsk region, in Turkmenistan, near the eastern shore of the Caspian Sea. A Captain L. Valuev registered an unknown object at an altitude above 60,000 feet. Its size was enormous: one kilometer long. The object was stationary, but eventually a small object with a diameter of 15-20 feet flew out of it and landed at the Krasnovodsk port. Patrol-boats pursued it, but it took off and flew away for about a kilometer. The patrol boats continued to approach it; once again it flew away from them. According to the KGB's "Blue Folder," this situation occurred five times. Finally the object ascended with tremendous speed. Its radar target joined that of the mother ship, and the large object went up and away.[84]

There is another KGB file regarding an incident on May 23, 1985, in the Khaborovsk region, the country's extreme east, not far from China. A bomber regiment carrying out a scheduled mission spotted an oval, orange unknown at 10:35 p.m. Radar did not track it, but observers estimated it was traveling close to 350 mph, and they saw a light halo surrounding it. The sighting lasted for 13 minutes, during which the object occasionally descended and remained motionless. Two hours later, a similar object was seen for ten minutes, emitting beams of light. According to the official report, "the object traveled at a high altitude and with a great speed."[85]

A July report from the northeastern part of the Soviet Union was more strange, involving a luminescent sphere that flew in front of a train traveling from Petrozavodsk to Suoyrvi. The driver was unable to break at the next station; instead, the train gained speed as if the sphere were pulling it forward. The UFO then vanished. It later reappeared, apparently forcing the train to slow down considerably.[86]

A KGB file recorded an incident from November 3, 1985 in the waters near Vladivostok. At 8:30 p.m., two men of a small vessel noticed a high flying object in the north, looking a bit larger than a star, rapidly moving toward them. At some point it sent a beam of light to the Earth at a sharp angle, although the beam did not reach the ground. As the UFO approached the boat, the boat's engine stopped. The captain restarted the engine, but it died again when the object was overhead. As it moved off toward the city, the object disappeared. The boat's engine still did not start, and the men used oars to return to shore.[87]

Elsewhere in the world, sightings were sporadic. The Hudson Valley wave dropped off considerably, although several of the main investigators had their own sighting on March 21, 1985. While walking to their car after giving a local radio interview, Philip Imbrogno, Sheila Sabo, and George Lesnick saw something that was so astounding they initially thought it was a hoax. In the sky were seven intensely bright lights in an elliptical pattern. They jumped into the car and tried to follow. As they drove, they could see a dark structure connecting the lights. The object glided "effortlessly" across the sky. The investigators checked with the FAA and learned that other witnesses had also reported this. They became suspicious when the FAA told them that the sighting was actually of pilots flying their aircraft in illegal formation; incredulous when told that state police had arrested the culprits. After checking into this story, they learned that this was totally untrue. No arrests had been made at all.[88]

Several near collisions were reported from around the world. One case took place on June 11 over China, when a Boeing 747 airliner flying from Beijing to Paris encountered an object at 33,000 feet. This object crossed in front of the airliner's path at a very fast speed. It appeared to be elliptical, bright, and extremely large. The pilots claimed to see three horizontal rows of bluish-white lights, and the sighting lasted for two minutes. No passengers reported seeing the object. The incident was reported twice in

The People's Daily, which stated the estimated size of the object was an incredible six miles.[89]

Another near-collision occurred a month later in the United States. This was an incident reported many years after the fact, and not investigated independently. Yet, claimed the pilot, as he was flying his two-seater aircraft under blue skies toward the Columbus, Ohio airport, he was given permission to investigate what appeared to be a "second sun" about two-thirds the size of a football field, a few miles northwest of the airport. As he approached the light source, he could see it was a huge bright sphere. Even though airport radar tracked his own aircraft, the unknown object never registered. The pilot, a former Navyman trained in radar, believed this was impossible. "Anything that huge ... that bright ... and that close to the radar," he wrote, "should have 'blipped' like the Graf Zeppelin blimp with a full metal jacket." Frightened but curious – and prepared to eject with his parachute if the need arose – he continued to approach the UFO. At that point, the bright light from the object instantly "switched off," revealing a huge grey sphere. The truly bizarre thing was that this was not a single object, but "millions" of clearly visible, pentagon-shaped crystals, apparently partially translucent. The pilot estimated them to be six inches in diameter, all spaced identically about one foot apart. They were most definitely not moving. The pilot decided to penetrate the mass of crystals with his left wing, hoping he could knock some to the ground. As his wing sliced through, he heard what sounded like a hale storm on a tin roof, and he saw hundreds of crystals breaking at his wing's edge. To his surprise, his aircraft's turbulence did not affect these small objects. They never moved. However, their impact on his left wing nearly destabilized him. Later, he examined the ground for evidence of the impact, but found nothing; nor did he find fragments of the crystals embedded in his wing.[90]

The aforementioned encounters are interesting, but lack documentation that would make them stand up to skeptical inquiry. The situation is different, however, regarding an incident that took place on July 22, 1985, when two jets of the Zimbabwe Air Force tried to intercept a UFO. The object was first seen over the border between South Africa and Zimbabwe, then at various locations in western Zimbabwe, and finally at Bulawayo Airport by control tower and ground personnel. Two fighter jets were scrambled from Thornhill AFB at 5:45 p.m., piloted by C. Cordy-Hedge and T. R. Van Rooyen. Both men saw the bright orange object, apparently hovering 15 miles southeast of the airport at 4,500 feet. As they approached, it shot up very quickly to an altitude to 80,000 feet. Commercial traffic at the airport was delayed for several hours while the jets investigated. The object eventually accelerated at a high speed and was gone. The Air Force sighting lasted nearly an hour.

Some wondered if the object was a high altitude balloon. Such an object conceivably could appear lower from a distance, and then seem to rise as the jets approached. South African UFO researcher Cynthia Hind spoke to airport witnesses who thought the object might have been a balloon coated with a reflecting material. One of her Johannesburg contacts also told her that high-altitude balloons had been released from South Africa all month. Still, she could not understand how a balloon would move against the northeastern winds, nor why it would have hovered in one place for so long.

UFO skeptic James Oberg was unconvinced the sighting was anything anomalous. Zimbabwe, he said, "is sort of on the edge of the civilized world in terms of tracking things that might cause this kind of UFO report – like Russian and South African reconnaissance planes that, I'm sure, are flying over that airspace." Undoubtedly, Zimbabwean military personnel would have disagreed with this assessment. In any case, they were impressed by the sighting. The Air Force stated it had tracked the object on radar and was satisfied it was not a balloon. Zimbabwean Air Force Commodore David Thorne told Hind that he felt this was a genuine UFO. Later, in a letter to Timothy Good, he stated off the record that his Air Staff was "concerned" about the event, and that they believed some unexplained UFOs were "from some civilization beyond our planet." The nation's Air Marshall, Azim Daudpota commented that "this was no ordinary UFO. Scores of people saw it. It was no illusion, no deception, no imagination."[91]

Just what exactly were these objects doing in the sky? Whatever UFOs were, wherever they were from, defense implications were always obvious to militaries encountering them. In the case of Iran, which was then at war with the nation of Iraq, UFOs were probably enemy weapons. On Monday, August 5, 1985, Iranian antiaircraft fired on a shining object that flew over Tehran toward the east at 8:15 p.m. A spokesman from the Iranian Joint Chiefs of Staff said the object had not been identified, but that the unit believed it to be an Iraqi warplane; other reports speculated the object was a satellite. No other information has come to light.[92]

A baffling encounter occurred throughout central Chile on August 17, 1985. For several hours in the afternoon, many people saw distinct, luminous spots in the sky – sometimes motionless, sometimes moving slowly. Television stations filmed the objects, astronomers in Santiago photographed them, and the Comodoro Benitez International Airport in Santiago tracked them on radar. Early explanations, including by the Chilean Air Force, centered on weather balloons or research balloons. At least one of the objects remained difficult to explain, however, and a Chilean Civil Aeronautics report stated that the sightings remained "an enigma to be added to the archive of unexplained phenomena."[93]

Little else was reported for the rest of the year, except for a few triangle reports in Wisconsin during November,[94] and one more interesting sighting in the Hudson Valley on November 21. On this occasion, in the towns of Peekskill, Port Chester, and Greenwich, a large circular object with colored lights was seen by no less than 400 witnesses. Once gain, the FAA performed damage control, telling local media that these were helicopters, although no one knew where they were based. Philip Imbrogno and other researchers interviewed 25 witnesses, none of whom had heard a sound from the object.[95]

Reagan's (First) Alien Invasion Speech

Despite the scarce number of good UFO reports, and the near absence of media coverage, the issue was still seen as a serious matter by none other than Ronald Reagan, who had a longstanding interest in the matter. On November 19 and 20, 1985, at a summit in Geneva, he met for the first time with Soviet leader Mikhail Gorbachev. To their mutual surprise, the two leaders connected on a personal level. While making a toast, Reagan surprised everyone by discussing the idea of an alien invasion. As he recounted a few weeks later, Reagan told Gorbachev and the Soviet delegation how much easier their tasks might be "if suddenly there was a threat to this world from another species from another planet outside in the universe." The statement received a great deal of publicity through several major newspapers, and researcher Grant Cameron located a State Department "Memorandum of Conversation" that recorded Reagan's comment.[96]

Reagan was a former UFO witness with a possible close encounter, and so had an obvious attraction to this topic. Cameron, upon review of the files from the December 4 speech at Fallston High School in Maryland, found that the "alien invasion" reference was not in the drafts or the speech copy – Reagan had simply added it on his own. His handlers did not like these references, and such occasional public statements were certainly not a policy emanating from the national security community.[97] Yet, it would seem to matter that a U.S. President would show such a persistent interest in this subject. According to the private statement he made to a journalist years before, Reagan had read a great deal about UFOs, and there is no indication this interest ever wavered. If it is reasonable to assume that Ronald Reagan was a UFO believer, might we assume he believed in the possibility of alien visitation? And if this was so, would this belief have translated into specific attitudes and policies relating to the cold war? What makes this even more interesting is the claim, according to one of the author's sources, that Reagan was formally briefed on the matter of UFOs and extraterrestrials. If that was so, his various statements on the matter of ET would have reflected more than just a private obsession, but perhaps hinted at defying national security secrecy protocols.

Pennsylvania Triangles

In terms of UFO history, 1986 was another slow year, similar to 1985. Triangle sightings continued, especially in the Northeastern U.S., where objects continued to be reported in the Hudson Valley and Pennsylvania. One key difference in 1986 from the previous year, however, was the occurrence of a few truly historic cases that stood out from the rest.

Early in 1986, something was happening in western Pennsylvania. On January 7, an object was seen hovering above the town of Butler, emitting six beams of light toward ground. Twenty minutes later in nearby Pittsburgh, a silver grey disc with body lights was seen hovering. Mist formed around it, the object tilted, and then moved out of sight.[98] Meanwhile, UFOs and unmarked helicopters (with searchlights) were being reported with some frequency in nearby Westmoreland County. One particular area, a 60-acre swampy area on private property, was scene to many of the events, which were reported by local property owners and travelers. Researcher Stan Gordon also investigated a possible military UFO encounter from near the town of Slickville from January 23. Several people saw a large, silent, triangular object with amber-colored lights maneuvering around the countryside. After ten minutes, three military jets came in from the east, pursuing the object in the direction of Pittsburgh.[99]

Meanwhile, on January 9, in the Connecticut region of the Hudson Valley, a building inspector for the town of Torrington saw what he described as a "cigar with square windows" near the Bradley International Airport. She told the media that "this thing of it being aircraft flying in formation is a lot of crap." The FAA said the object was a blimp, although investigators found that no blimps flew in that area during the month.[100]

Such reports continued throughout the spring, including claims of low-flying objects shining down bright lights. This was reported in New Castle,

Pennsylvania, on February 28[101] and then on March 26 in Kingston, New York – another Hudson Valley UFO. The latter case involved at least 500 witnesses who described an object that looked like a "giant Ferris wheel" the size of a football field. It made a humming sound and had intensely bright lights, mostly white but also red, yellow, green, and blue. A dark mass, visible behind the lights, blocked out the entire sky. Suddenly, the object flipped over on its side before going away. One of the witnesses, a police officer, said, "up to this point, I heard about the sightings and was convinced that it was nothing more than a bunch of guys flying in planes perpetrating a hoax, but now I know this is not so."[102]

Strange objects continued to be seen in Pennsylvania and the Hudson Valley through the spring and summer, including a huge triangular object seen in late May near Harrisburg and Carlisle. According to Stan Gordon, many witnesses described it as being immense, silent, with non-blinking reddish lights at the corners, and moving steadily at 1,000 feet altitude.[103] A large, silent, low-flying, triangle was reported a month later on June 27 in the Hudson Valley, causing several minor accidents in the town of Newburgh.[104]

The Challenger and Ellison Onizuka

On January 28, 1986, one of the great tragedies of the U.S. space program occurred when the Space Shuttle Challenger exploded 73 seconds after liftoff, at 11:39 a.m. All seven astronauts aboard were killed. The event essentially grounded America's space program for two years.

An interesting prologue to the tragedy concerns a story told to NASA employee Clark C. McClelland, a long-time mission control specialist at the Kennedy Space Center in Florida. McClelland later wrote that in the days prior to the fatal launch of the shuttle, he ran into astronaut Lt. Col. Ellison Onizuka, one of the members of that ill-fated mission. The two were acquainted, and Onizuka knew of McClelland's interest in UFOs. He asked McClelland about his beliefs in extraterrestrials, and then whether his name had any connection with McClellan AFB in California (it did not). Onizuka then related a surprising experience. Many years before, during 1970 or 1971, he was on specialized military training duty at McClellan AFB, when he and his group were directed to report to a viewing room. Without any official introduction, which would have been standard, Onizuka and his fellow officers were shown a very realistic looking film of a medical room with small bodies lying on slabs. Several of the officers with Onizuka let out excited comments. The small creatures were humanoid but not human. They had large heads, large eyes, and small torsos. They did not appear to be of earthly origin. Onizuka told McClelland, "Clark, my God, these highly trained officers and I were shocked by what we saw. We were not made privy to what we would see until it happened. We were all caught off guard. Perhaps it was a test of our psyche to determine our overall reaction. Well, we were all caught by surprise." This type of scenario had been reported several times in years past to Stringfield; apparently it had happened many times. Indeed, Air Force Major George Filer stated that several Air Force officers told him they were also shown such a movie. No explanation is ever known to have been offered.

Onizuka's explanation seems logical: a test of the psyche. But why aliens? Why something so realistic? In all instances this story has been related, the film appeared to be real. Therefore, if it was a hoax created by the U.S. military, it was exceptionally well done. This begs the dual questions: why and how?

Why show something as outlandish as an autopsy of extraterrestrials to military personnel? Could it be more than just a test of the psyche, and actually a test of one's reaction to extraterrestrials themselves? According to the various leaks that have occurred, the "autopsy movie" would have been shown to military personnel for two decades at the least. This is a long time. Why make such a well-made fake ET autopsy film if there are no ETs? Why promote such an outlandish belief – unless the ET presence on Earth were real, and it was necessary to gauge the reaction of various personnel whose career paths might bring them into contact at some point with "the program." It would be important to find out in advance whether such personnel could be trusted psychologically, whether they would constitute a security risk.[105]

Dalnegorsk: The Soviet Roswell?

Less than a day after the Challenger tragedy, an unknown object crashed into the area of Dalnegorsk, a mining town in the eastern Soviet Union. The local time was 7:55 p.m. on January 29, 1986, but time zone differences meant that it occurred less than 18 hours after the Challenger explosion. Local people saw a reddish-orange sphere flying southwest at low altitude, perhaps 2,000 to 2,500 feet, moving in a level flight path and absolutely silent. This was a very slow moving object. The object was tracked by a chronometer at the very slow speed of 15 meters per second, or a little more than 30 miles per hour. The object approached a low mountain near the town and apparently slowed down. Some witnesses said the object rose and lowered itself six times. Each time it rose, the light became brighter; each time it descended, the light weakened. The object then dived at a sharp angle, dropping like a stone, and burned at the edge of a cliff for an hour.

A scientific team arrived on February 3. It was led by Valeri Dvuzhilny, head of the Far Eastern Commission for Anomalous Phenomena. Although the entire area was blanketed by heavy snow, there was no snow at the site. The team found a number of physical traces, including lead and iron balls, pieces of glass, a fine mesh or netting, traces of high temperature activity, magnetic anomalies and damage to nearby trees and stumps. Laboratories from several universities and research institutes studied the remains, and the Soviet newspaper *Socialist Industry* published some of the details of laboratory results. The so-called lead balls, for instance, were only roughly fifty percent lead, but also contained substantial amounts of silicon, aluminum, and iron. In addition, many elements were found in much smaller amounts: zinc, titanium, magnesium, silver, copper, lanthanum, praseodymium, calcium, sodium, vanadium, cerium, chrome, cobalt, nickel, and molybdenum. There were a number of other surprises about the materials recovered, as well as the crash site itself. Members of the "Council of Scientific and Engineering Societies' Commission on Paranormal Events," A. Petukhov and T. Faminskaya, wrote that "vivid interest was ... evoked by the mesh, a carbon-based composite of unknown origin." They wrote that the specimen contained quartz filaments 17 microns thick, and golden wires inside each filament. On-site researchers also showed biological effects, according to Petukhov and Faminskaya, specifically a reduced count of leucocytes and platelets within their blood, as well as changes in the structure of erythrocytes. For several years afterward, the crash scene was something of an "anomalous zone." Many UFOs were reported there, insects avoided it, and local residents appeared to have health problems.

Some investigators concluded the object was an extraterrestrial space probe of some sort. V. Vysotsky, a doctor of chemistry, stated his belief that the Dalnegorsk object was "a high-technology product and not a thing of natural or terrestrial origin." Dvuzhilny agreed that the object was "an automatic scout probe" of alien origin. Others argued the object was a "natural plasmoid." Yuri Rylkin, a physicist with the Tomsk Polytechnical Institute, presented a paper for a UFO conference in Frankfurt, Germany, in 1989, arguing that the object was of an electromagnetic nature, perhaps caused by anomalous stresses near faultlines ("geological breaking") and passing parallel to high-voltage transmission line. The "plasmoid" may have selectively absorbed some chemical elements in the process. Still others, such as noted Soviet UFO skeptic Yuri Platov, suggested the object "was connected with the conduct of a technical experiment." While this is certainly possible, there were no known rocket launches that evening, and no civilian or military traffic in the area. A Russian ufologist, Gennady Belimov, presented information in 1993 that the object was a Soviet military probe, and V. Psalomschikov, an aviation crash expert, also said the crash was of a Soviet manufactured probe. He even claimed to have ultrathin filaments, similar to those found at the site, in his possession.

Clearly, whatever crashed at Dalnegorsk was not a natural phenomenon, but something manufactured. If Soviet, it seems odd that the fragments would have gone to so many institutions for analysis; presumably this would have included classified technology. Why send it to scientific institutions for analysis if it was home-made? Why, also, did it take so long for a team to arrive on the scene, and not even a military team? This too seems confusing if the object were a Soviet manufactured object. The Dalnagorsk crash is a prime example of the blurring of the lines between what is supposed to be "alien" and "human." An answer to what crashed there may be very long in coming.

One important point of note, however, remains. On February 6, 1986, just eight days after the crash, two yellow globes were seen to approach the crash site at 8:30 p.m. They circled overhead four times, then turned back and flew away.[106]

Geopolitics and Chernobyl in 1986

The rise of Mikhail Gorbachev made international politics very interesting. In January 1986, he offered to eliminate all nuclear weapons by the Year 2000, and proposed a bilateral agreement to remove all intermediate range nuclear missiles from Europe. Many in the West regarded this as "lacking seriousness." Others saw it as simply another Moscow propaganda trick: without missiles, the Soviets would have an overwhelming conventional force in Europe. Meanwhile, Afghanistan had become a horrible mess for the Soviet Union, its greatest disaster. While Reagan continued to support the Islamic fundamentalist Mujahideen (the "freedom fighters") both publicly and covertly, Gorbachev wanted nothing more than to pull all Soviet forces out as soon as possible. He offered the U.S. a timetable for withdrawal in exchange for American support of an Afghani coalition of Communist and Mujahideen participants. America's answer was "no."

America's military was feeling its oats, so to speak. On April 15, an extraordinary air strike was made against Libya, involving 18 F-111 fighter aircraft flying from RAF Lakenheath without any European support. The strike was against Libyan leader Colonel Muammar Gaddafi. It failed to kill him, though a bomb exploded near him, his house was destroyed, at least 15 civilians died, along with with an unknown number of Libyan military personnel. An interesting sidelight of this attack is that the F-117 stealth fighter was not used, even though it was fully operational. The existence of the aircraft was still secret at this time, and it was considered so important that the risk of its disclosure outweighed its obvious tactical advantages. Considering the likelihood of reverse-engineering programs related to UFOs, one is reminded that the more exotic the technology, the more rarified its use might be. Something as radically advanced as a 'home made flying saucer' might well be reserved for missions having nothing to do with ordinary politics.

The Libyan raid and the rise of Gorbachev were both overshadowed by the worst nuclear disaster in history. On April 26, 1986, the Chernobyl nuclear power station in the Ukraine was scene to a series of operator errors and reactor design deficiencies that produced a devastating steam explosion and fuel-core meltdown in Unit 4. Deadly radioactivity streamed across Europe, causing contamination, disease, mutations, and death. Considering the substantial covert footprint left by the UFO phenomenon on world history, it should not be surprising that there have been claims that a UFO was at Chernobyl.

While the explosion was enormous, it was a thermal blast – not a nuclear explosion. As one commentator put it, had the blast been nuclear, "half of Europe would not currently be depicted on any maps." According to certain claims, technicians arriving at the scene shortly after 4 a.m. saw a fiery sphere floating near the reactor. For several minutes, two red rays extended from it toward the reactor; the rays then vanished and the object drifted away. The technicians said the UFO appeared to affect the radiation level, which dropped from 3,000 to 800 milliroentgens per hour. Others are said to have also observed an object over Chernobyl; several witnesses said it was there for six hours and that hundreds of people saw it. Some drew sketches of what they saw. For years afterward, stories persisted in the Ukraine that "the world was saved by UFOs" – that the object lowered the radiation levels enough to prevent a nuclear explosion. Of course, there is no official acknowledgment of any UFO connection to the Chernobyl disaster.[107]

Research: The Old and the New

One day after Chernobyl, Allen Hynek died in Scottsdale, Arizona, at the age of 75. For the past several years, he had been increasingly revered, often being referred to as the "Dean of Ufology" – even once as the "Galileo of Ufology." Of course, his relationship with many other researchers had long been strained, but by the end, the dominant assessment of Hynek emphasized the courage of his gradual transformation from skeptic to believer. For sure, Hynek had been in a difficult position as a professional scientist and academician. For many years, he was virtually alone among scientists in devoting so much time to UFOs. And without providing compelling physical evidence, he had to be circumspect in his presentation of the topic, else become an outcast among his colleagues. No one's life, certainly not Hynek's, can fit into a neat category. His contribution to ufology was undoubtedly substantial, in particular his emphasis on "scientific ufology," which elevated the level of discourse among researchers. During the early 1970s, after UFO research had been rebuked by the Air Force's "scientific study" of UFOs, the Condon Committee, this was very important.

Regarding any approach to the matter of UFOs, there will be strengths and limitations. The limitation of a strictly scientific approach was in its failure, or unwillingness, to investigate the political ramifications of UFO secrecy – that is, the cover-up. Such was the dominant thread of UFO research throughout much of the 1970s. When that began to change, Hynek's unwillingness to consider that a genuine cover-up was underway became seen as an archaism at best, or complicity at worst. Still, as long as the wide range of researchers are able to recognize the value in alternate approaches, each perspective can provide valuable insights. Certainly, this is true of scientific ufology.[108]

A few months after Hynek passed away, James Lorenzen died. His wife, Coral, was now the sole leader of APRO, but was herself in declining health and essentially no longer able to run the far flung organization. The result was that APRO was dead in the water.

Contemporary UFO research was not becoming unscientific per se, but simply moving into areas of high controversy not easily amenable to controlled scientific study. The secret of MJ-12 was beginning to leak to other UFO researchers. Among them were Robert Hastings and Lee Graham. In March 1986, Graham gave Hastings copies of some of the alleged documents that mentioned MJ-12, including the Project Snowbird paper and the Project Aquarius telex. When Hastings asked Graham who gave these to him, Graham said only that the person worked for the government as an intelligence operative or information conduit. This would be William Moore. Around this time, Hastings also met with Paul Bennewitz at the latter's home in Albuquerque. During their conversation, Bennewitz used the phrase "extraterrestrial biological entities" to describe the aliens. This matched the phrase in the MJ-12 briefing papers, and was a full year before the public release of these documents. Clearly, Bennewitz would not have known of this phrase without having been told by someone, presumably Doty or Moore, unless he was getting them from the signals he was receiving from Kirtland.[109]

Meanwhile, FOIA requests regarding Project Aquarius (the alleged document which contained reference to MJ-12) was stalled. The NSA stated in April 1986 that such information "has been found to be currently and properly classified" and that its disclosure "could reasonably be expected to cause exceptionally grave damage to the national security." In a 1987 correspondence to Senator John Glenn, the NSA stated that their Project Aquarius did not deal with UFOs, but that "apparently there is or was an Air Force project by that name which dealt with UFOs."[110] And thus the mystery continued.

Another deepening area of controversy concerned alien abductions. By this time, Budd Hopkins had concluded that thousands of people had probably been abducted, most had multiple experiences, and the phenomenon itself had been going on for at least 50 years. This is a long, long way from where research had been just a few years before. He added that genetic experimentation of some sort was one apparent motive. Entire families seemed to be the objects of study which spanned several generations – thus the selection of candidates for abduction was not random. By the end of the year, the author Whitley Strieber described his "experiences with the visitors," and revealed that his encounters were still continuing. Strieber's arrival to UFO research was a key moment that would soon contribute to the field essentially exploding.[111]

May 1986 - The Brazilian Air Force

One of the most important UFO sightings of 1986 took place in southeastern Brazil. On May 19, six military jet interceptors from the Brazilian Air Force were scrambled to attempt an interception of a UFO which was tracked on radar and seen visually. According to a U.S. Defense Intelligence Agency report, "at least 20 unidentified objects were observed by several aircrews and on radar."

At 6:30 p.m., control tower personnel at the São José dos Campos airport, noticed two very bright lights about ten miles away that did not correspond to any known aircraft. Thirty minutes later, personnel in São Paulo and Brazilia confirmed to São José that they had three unidentified targets on their screens. At 8 p.m., CINDACTA (Brazil's air traffic control system, similar to that of the U.S. FAA) detected up to eight targets. By 8:30, another object was seen through binoculars at the São José tower to approach the tower and then retreat; it had well-defined edges and was red-orange in color.

All of this coy behavior was strange enough. Then, at 9 p.m., an executive jet carrying the head of the state oil company *Petrobras*, Colonel Ozires Silva, was coming in to land at São José, when Silva and the pilot, Commander Alcir Pereira, saw in their path several colored lights resembling ping pong balls; these were also detected on their aircraft radar. The jet attempted to follow the lights for 10 minutes, then came in for a landing. At this moment, a new, large, luminous object headed toward the aircraft. The São Paulo tower confirmed two echoes: the Xingu and an unknown. Within minutes, the Air Control Center in Brasilia (ACC-BR) informed Brazilian Air Defense Command of the situation. By 9:25 p.m., the unknown radar target was gone, and the executive jet attempted another landing. However, the São Paulo tower reported yet another object, which was seen by Commander Pereira. He briefly attempted to follow the object, but at 9:30 p.m. was at 10,000 feet altitude and about to attempt a third landing. At this point ACC-BR reported yet more objects. Silva and Pereira both saw three luminous objects flying low over the Petrobrás refineries and moving towards Serra do Mar. Finally, the men landed in São José dos Campos. Sporadic sightings of luminous objects were reported from São José dos Campos, including one surrounded by smaller lights at 9:50 p.m.

Finally, at 10:23 p.m., an F-5E jet fighter was scrambled from nearby Santa Cruz AFB, and another at 10:45 p.m. A Mirage F-103, armed with Sidewinder and Matra missiles, was also scrambled from Anápolis AFB. By 10:55 p.m., Anápolis detected the unknown objects on radar. The Mirage pilot, flying at 850 mph, could not see any UFO, but did detect a target on his onboard radar. He came to within 6 miles of his target, which was zigzagging on his radar scope. Suddenly, it disappeared. A second and third Mirage F-103 were soon scrambled from Anápolis.

At 11:15, Lt. Kleber, who was piloting one of the F-5Es, made visual contact with a ball of light, confirmed by ground-based radar, and chased it at about 850 mph. He got to within 12 miles of it. This object also zigzagged from left to right, then began to climb out over the Atlantic Ocean. The pilot followed it to 200 miles over the ocean, the limit of Brazil's territorial waters. Another of the F-5Es had established radar contact with 10 to 13 objects near São José dos Campos. "The sky was clear," he later said, "but I didn't see anything," even though radar reported the objects to be a mere 20 miles distant in excellent visibility. At one point, ground radar informed him that the objects were closing on him just two or three miles behind: six on one side, seven on the other. He engaged in evasive maneuvers, and the objects disappeared.

Brazilian military jets remained in the air until 1 a.m. The objects had completely baffled them. They also outperformed them, moving with astonishing maneuverability at speeds between 160 and 990 mph. Brazilian President José Sarney learned of the chase late that night. Within days, the Brazilian military held a major press conference about the event, led by the Brazilian Minister of Aeronautics, Brigadier General Otávio Moreira Lima. It was the first time that a senior Air Force officer of any nation had come forward to admit the presence of UFOs, to say nothing of failed intercepted attempts. According to General Lima, President Sarney was "interested and curious" about the event. Lima said the objects saturated the Sao Paolo radar system and interfered with air traffic as far away as Rio de Janeiro, more than 200 miles to the east. The General stated the matter plainly:

> ... at least 20 objects were detected by Brazilian radars. They saturated the radars and interrupted traffic in the area. Each time that radar detected unidentified objects, fighters took off for intercept. Radar detects only solid metallic bodies and heavy (mass) clouds. There were no clouds nor conventional aircraft in the region. The sky was clear. Radar doesn't have optical illusions. We can only give technical explanations and we don't have them. It would be very difficult for us to talk about the hypothesis of an electronic war. It's very remote and it's not the case here in Brazil. It's fantastic. The signals on the radar were quite clear.

Major Ney Cerqueira, head of operations at the Brazilian Defense Center, who was deeply involved in the radar trackings of that night, said he had never seen anything like this case. All the pilots had something interesting to say. Kleber said the object he chased "was not a star. It couldn't have been another plane. It couldn't be anything now existing." Silva said that what he saw "wasn't like any of the classical flying objects seen in the movies. It wasn't in the form of a flying saucer or plate. Instead, what I saw were illuminated points."

News services around the world reported the event, although the case received only limited coverage in the United States. Chilean UFO reseacher

Antonio Huneeus aptly compared the Brazilian event, in its scope and defense impact, to the famous Washington D.C. case of 1952, with the major difference being in how the respective governments handled the matter publicly.

As to what exactly happened that night, a variety of explanations were offered, including a meteor shower, a reflection of the full Moon, ball lightning, radar malfunction, space debris, and spy planes. None of these seem plausible in light of the radar data and visual descriptions. A British space researcher named Geoffrey Perry noted that the Soviet space station Salyut-7 ejected several boxes of debris that night which reentered the Earth's atmosphere in central-western Brazil (reasonably close, but still more than a thousand miles away). The Brazilian press also theorized about the re-entry of NASA's Solarwind satellite. Both theories were discounted by Brigadier José Cavalcanti, from Brazil's Air Defense Command. "A metallic box with space debris can be detected by radar, but it will always fall in the same direction and at constant velocity. That was not the case of what was seen in Brazil, where the objects detected by radar had speeds that varied from very slow to extremely high."

The U.S. Defense Attaché office commented on the incident to the Defense Intelligence Agency. "While RO [Reporting Officer] does not believe in UFO's or all the hoopla that surrounds previous reporting, there is too much here to be ignored. Three visual sightings and positive radar contact from three different types of radar systems, leads one to believe that something arrived over Brazil the night of 19 May." [112]

UnFunded Opportunities

On July 11, 1986, a U.S. Air Force F-117 stealth fighter, the existence of which was still classified, crashed near Bakersfield, California. Rumors quickly spread of a secret stealth aircraft. The Air Force sealed off the crash site, extending a national security zone more than a mile out that was off-limits to civilian aircraft. One wonders whether a similar scenario could occur in the case of something even more classified than stealth technology. [113]

Meanwhile, an interesting correspondence was occurring between two prominent members of the aviation community. Ben Rich, head of Lockheed's "Skunkworks" Division, where several of the world's most famous and exotic aircraft were conceived and made, received a letter from John Andrews. Andrews was a long time friend of Rich's, and an illustrator for the Testor Corporation. On July 10, Andrews wrote:

The topic is UFOs. I 'believe' there are lots of UFOs. I am also tending to 'believe' they are of two categories:
A. Manmade UFOs.
B. Extraterrestrial UFOs.
I believe with certainty in manmade UFOs. I am tending to believe there are also extraterrestrial UFOs. Having the highest respect for you and Kelly [Johnson], I'd appreciate knowing if your belief covers category B as well as category A of the above? Purpose of question? Precision. Dr. [Robert] Sarbacher's response was without question a statement of his belief in category B. Do you also include category B, Ben?

Ben Rich's reply was succinct, and yet a tad enigmatic. "Yes," he wrote back to Andrews on July 21, "I'm a believer in both categories. I feel everything is possible. Many of our man made UFOs are Un Funded Opportunities. In both categories, there are a lot of kooks and charlatans – be cautious. Best regards, Ben Rich."

There are several key points here. First, it is noteworthy that the 1983 letter of Dr. Robert Sarbacher to UFO researcher William Steinman was well known to these two men. In that letter, Sarbacher had spoken explicitly of a UFO crash retrieval program within the U.S. national security and scientific community. He had also spoken of what he had heard about the aliens themselves. The letter did not receive a great deal of publicity; its existence was known to some UFO researchers, and now – with Rich and Andrews as exhibits A and B – to select individuals within the defense community.

Then there is the matter of what Rich actually said. "I'm a believer in both categories." A great deal of meaning can be contained within these words. By saying he believed in both, Rich was in fact saying he believed in the extraterrestrial presence on Earth. That much is clear. From the head of the world's most prestigious aviation division, such belief certainly carries a good deal of weight. After all, one can assume that Ben Rich, in the course of his career, had access to individuals of the highest intellectual caliber who in turn had access to some of the most sensitive secrets in the country. He himself was one such person, having managed the program to build the F-117 Stealth Fighter. By 1986, it would be safe to say that Ben Rich would have been in a position to know as much as anyone in the world on the matter of UFOs.

Whether or not he did is another matter. Thus, it is possible that by saying he "believed" in both categories, that he actually did not know, and was stating a personal position rather than offering certain knowledge. This is possible. However, it is also quite possible – likely, in fact – that Ben Rich would not have revealed everything he knew on this matter in a simple handwritten note, even to someone who was a personal friend, as John

Andrews was. Ben Rich was a CEO of a major defense corporation, a man who even under relaxed and friendly conditions would always remember who he was, and what he was. Such people chose their words carefully.

The most provocative part of Rich's reply is his remark about manmade UFOs being "Un Funded Opportunities." As to what this meant, two possibilities come to mind. One could be that the program to build UFOs was so secret, so "black," that all funding would be so deeply hidden as to be "non-existent" – hence the project would be "unfunded," so to speak. Such an explanation, however, does not easily explain the meaning of the word "opportunity." The other possibility is that man-made UFOs were derived from the active study of extraterrestrial UFOs, presumably in the form of crash retrievals or other "freebies." This would in fact give a more complete interpretation of the phrase "Un Funded Opportunities." Ben Rich left the matter ambiguous, though suggestive.

Meanwhile, it was in 1986 that the first reports emerged of strange sonic booms coming from near Los Angeles, going out to Groom Lake, Nevada. In other words, from the area known as Antelope Valley, home to many of America's leading aviation and aerospace companies: Lockheed, Northrop, and McDonnell-Douglas. Something new was being flown in the area, and nobody was sure what it was. Suspicion would soon settle on the alleged "Aurora," a hypersonic replacement to the venerable, but aging, SR-71 Blackbird, as America's leading high-speed, high-altitude, reconnaissance aircraft.[114]

Indeed, the line between "ours" and "theirs" seemed to be increasingly problematic to those people studying the matter of UFOs.

Politics and Scandal in late 1986

Little UFO activity was reported through the summer and fall of 1986, but the longstanding Cold War was showing signs of possible break-through. On October 11, Ronald Reagan and Mikhail Gorbachev met in Reykjavik, Iceland. Expectations were low going in, but Gorbachev surprised the Americans by offering comprehensive reductions in strategic arms, intermediate range missiles, and space weapons. Reagan did not have his prepared notes with him; he decided to "wing it." Secretary of State George Shultz called Gorbachev's opening position "fundamentally acceptable." The two sides continued the following morning, and agreed to a complete withdrawal of intermediate range missiles in Europe, as well as a 50 percent reduction in ballistic missiles (ICBM, SLBM) over five years. After lunch, they continued to surprise each other. Gorbachev suggested eliminating all strategic nuclear weapons within ten years. The response from Reagan was nothing short of astonishing: why not eliminate *all* nuclear weapons within ten years?

One problem remained in the way: Star Wars. Gorbachev called for SDI research to be limited to "the laboratory," as under the terms of the 1972 Anti Ballistic Missile (ABM) treaty. But here Reagan drew the line with a firm "no." It is difficult enough, said Gorbachev, to restrict arms on Earth; it will be impossible to restrict them in space. With this disagreement, the Reykjavik talks collapsed. A failure, but a near-great success. Reagan remarked that "the significance is that we got as close as we did." Standard histories of the talks note that key U.S. allies, such as the U.K. and West Germany, were greatly relieved by the failure of Reykjavik. To this, it must be added that enormous sectors of the western defense establishment and the international financial structure had been feeding off of it for generations.

The good will of Reykjavik was dampened by several revelations that came out of the Reagan White House during late 1986. In October, a plane flown by CIA operative Eugene Hasenfus crashed in Nicaragua. Documents recovered by the Sandinistas were soon linked to Marine Corps Lieutenant Colonel Oliver North and the White House.[115] This was part of a secret campaign of intimidation and secret war in Latin America, coordinated from Washington. Much of this was designed to win support for the contra war in Nicaragua, according to classified documents and interviews with U.S. and foreign officials. Toward the end of 1986, this campaign included an effort to force Panamanian General Manuel Noriega from power. The reason had nothing to do with Noriega's well known (within U.S. intelligence circles) participation in drug trafficking. Rather, it was his refusal to honor a personal request from U.S. National Security Advisor John Poindexter to increase training support for the Contras and assist with planning scenarios for the invasion of Nicaragua. Thus Noriega, a long-time CIA asset, was actually asked by Poindexter to resign. When he refused, the United States cut off aid to Panama, then leaked damaging classified documents about him to *The New York Times* and NBC News. Thus began the public chain of events that would culminate in "Operation Just Cause" in 1989.[116]

Meanwhile, the Iran-Contra scandal unfolded in November 1986. This was the biggest public scandal of the entire Reagan administration. Money from the illicit sale of weapons to Iran was being channeled to the Nicaraguan Contras. This was Reagan's first and most important publicity problem. It hurt his credibility around the world.

Amazing Encounter Over Alaska

On November 18, 1986, over the frozen Alaskan landscape, one of modern history's most important UFO events took place. This was the encounter by Japan Air Lines 1628, a Paris-Tokyo cargo flight filled with expensive French wine, with what the pilot later described as an immense object and two "space ships." The flight was in its middle leg, from Iceland to Anchorage, Alaska, having flown by the North Pole. In command was Captain Kenju Terauchi, a man with three decades of flying experience, accompanied by a copilot and a flight engineer. The weather was clear as the Boeing 747 flew at 35,000 feet over the Beaufort Sea to northern Alaska. At 5:11 p.m. local time, while on approach to Fort Yukon, Terauchi and his crew saw unexpected lights to their left and below. They gained the distinct impression that the lights were flying along with them. The fact that the lights were below their own altitude ruled out astronomical causes – an important point that would arise later when skeptics attempted to explain the sighting.[117]

Matters became more interesting a few minutes later. With great speed and suddenness, two objects – "spaceships," said Terauchi – maneuvered to the airplane's 11 o'clock position, one positioned above the other, both extremely close. The witnesses estimated the distance was not more than 1,000 feet, perhaps as little as 500 feet, nearly directly in front of them. They were rectangular or squarish and were so bright that Terauchi said the inside of the cockpit lit up and that he felt heat. Both objects had a dark stripe across their center that resembled black charcoal dotted with glowing orange embers. Terauchi estimated their size to be comparable to a DC-8 jet. In other words, fairly large. For three to five minutes, the two objects paced the jet, swaying slightly as they moved through the air, one positioned above the other. Then, abruptly, they rearranged their orientation to side-by-side.

Realizing that they were seeing something that was supposed to be impossible, the perturbed pilot and crew radioed Anchorage Air Route Traffic Control Center (AARTCC) at 5:19 p.m. The flight controller asked them to identify what they were seeing. They could not do this, but stated the objects had strobing lights that were yellow and white. The fact that none of the crew were fluent in English meant that some inaccuracies occurred in their descriptions to Anchorage. Later interviews indicated the actual colors were yellow, amber, and green. Communication was further hampered by the apparent radio interference caused by the objects: transmissions were garbled and weak during much of the UFO encounter.

Then, at 5:23 p.m. the objects very suddenly and quickly moved away. They appeared to have moved several miles to the left, toward a long, horizontal, pale light. To Terauchi, it looked as though the light connected to an immense object. The aircrew decided to use the on-board radar equipment to search for any nearby objects. "There it was on the screen," recalled Terauchi: a large, green, round object seven or eight miles away to their left. The crew informed AARTCC, although Anchorage had still not detected any radar anomalies. However, AARTCC did contact the nearby USAF Elmendorf Regional Operational Control Center (ROCC) to learn whether they had tracked anything.

At 5:25 p.m., before ROCC could even answer, AARTCC picked up an anomalous radar target. Although the position was wrong – five miles behind the JAL jet when in fact the object was to the left – at least something was being recorded. Bruce Maccabee, who later provided an in-depth analysis of this incident, concluded that the full radar data "indicated that the object was quite large and yet quite a weak reflector." In other words, it could have been able to reduce its radar cross section through some form of stealth technology. After all, the U.S. was already employing operational stealth aircraft at this time.

Moments later, the ROCC radar controller reported back to AARTCC that he was obtaining an occasional radar echo without a transponder signal. All commercial aircraft have transponders, which provide a specific signal to air traffic controllers. This is distinct from "primary radar," which traffic controllers also use to identify aerial objects. There were no military aircraft in the area, and the ROCC controller wondered if his tracking was erroneous. The AARTCC controller told him: "negative, it's not erroneous." At 5:26 p.m., both radar operators were tracking the unknown target eight miles ahead and to the left of the JAL flight.

A minute later, the object disappeared from all radar. But not visually. JAL 1628 was now approaching Fairbanks. At 5:30 p.m., there was enough ambient light from the Moon and possibly from Fairbanks below for Terauchi to see the object that had been pacing his airplane. Several miles off to his left, the horizontal pale white lights were still visible, but now he saw something else: "the silhouette of a gigantic spaceship." The object was of staggering size. Terauchi estimated its length as being equal to two aircraft carriers. Feeling an overwhelming need to get away from this object, the crew requested a change of course. The fifteen seconds during which they waited for permission seemed like an eternity. Finally, AARTCC instructed them to turn 40 degrees to the right. The JAL crew executed the turn, only to see the huge object still pacing them. They then received permission to descend to 31,000 feet and turn twelve degrees to the left. The unidentified object also descended and continued to pace the jetliner.

This was becoming too much. At 5:36 p.m., Anchorage air traffic instructed the JAL jet to make a full-circle, 360 degree turn. The crew gladly complied. While engaging in the turn, they lost sight of the object, and hoped they might succeed in escaping from it. Many miles to the south, ROCC radar picked up an unknown target following the plane. Once again, the object gave no transponder signal, only a primary return. As Terauchi completed his long circular turn, he looked to his left and backwards: the UFO was still there.

The JAL jet was running low on excess fuel and needed to get to Anchorage. Meanwhile, a United Airlines passenger jet had left Anchorage and was heading north toward Fairbanks at 29,000 feet. AARTCC asked the UA pilot to look for the JAL flight and any accompanying traffic. By 5:48 p.m., the two airliners were fast approaching. At this time, the UFO dropped back from the JAL jet, and was lost from the airplane's short range radar. By 5:50 p.m., the UA pilot saw the JAL airplane, but no UFO. When the planes passed each other a minute later, the JAL crew could no longer see their mysterious companion.

The final half hour of their flight was quiet, and JAL 1628 landed in Anchorage at 6:20 p.m. The crew was interviewed immediately by an FAA official who described them as "shook-up but professional." Two special agents also were there. One of them, Special Agent James Derry, wrote that he called a duty officer at NORAD, and learned that NORAD had tracked both JAL 1628 and the UFO on radar.

For a month afterward, the media was unaware of this case. As Christmas approached, one of the crew members appears to have leaked the story, and it broke worldwide on December 29. Terauchi had no hesitation telling anyone who would listen that the object most likely came from another world. The FAA confirmed the event and reopened its inquiry into the matter a few days later.

Contradictory statements emerged from the FAA. Spokesman Paul Steucke acknowledged that air traffic controllers tracked something pacing the JAL 007, that the encounter was a "mystery" and "a violation of air space." But there was also "nothing to investigate." The FAA records were being reconstructed, he said, and the alleged uncorrelated echoes could not be found. As for the Air Force, said Steucke, it no longer possessed its radar data but was attributing the apparent UFO to "clutter."

Steucke referred to the radar signal of the JAL and UFO as a "split image" caused by the FAA primary radar signal and JAL's transponder. Such things can happen, although hardly ever in the region of the JAL encounter. Normally, the transponder signal and the primary signal would be either directly adjacent or occupying the same spot. Steucke was in fact saying that the primary return reported by the AARTCC and ROCC controllers was a malfunction of the radar set, causing the two types of signals to separate and look as though they were distinct objects. Bruce Maccabee pointed out in his detailed analysis that if this were true, the extra echo would have come back with every sweep of the radar, which it did not. Steucke also did not mention that three AARTCC traffic controllers who were on duty explicitly denied this explanation. They told an Anchorage journalist that, while the radar signal from the UFO was not especially strong, it was not due to a split radar image. Everyone in the control room believed it was an actual object.

On January 22, long before the FAA inquiry was finished, the skeptic organization CSICOP issued a press release announcing that Philip Klass had solved the case. In apparent seriousness, Klass argued that the UFO sighting had been the planet Jupiter, and possibly Mars. He suggested that the crew was unaware of Jupiter's presence, even though it was very bright that evening. Klass had no access to the radar tracking data, and therefore could not know the precise locations and various directions of the plane. He ignored how the jetliner's onboard radar tracked an unknown object. He ignored statements by the other crew members which fully supported Terauchi, in particular about how the two objects had appeared in front of the plane. He failed to mention how Terauchi saw a "gigantic spacecraft" behind and to his left, in a direction nearly opposite the planets. Incredibly, he ignored Terauchi's widely publicized drawing of the object, which was as clear as could be. Klass's fast and sloppy explanation caused Maccabee to remark, "it appears that the CSICOP press release which was marked *For Immediate Release* should have been marked *For Premature Release*." But CSICOP won the public relations battle. The media quickly accepted the "explanation" and let the matter drop.

A year later, Klass revised his explanation, arguing that the JAL crew was confused by reflections of moonlight from the clouds and "turbulent ice crystals." These thin clouds also caused false radar echoes, argued Klass. This second attempt was a little better than the first embarrassment, although it remained highly speculative. It also failed to address the spectacular nature of the two objects that maneuvered in front of the jetliner: their brightness and maneuverability, the heat that Terauchi felt from them, and their description by the two other crew members (the co-pilot likened them to the lights of an oncoming aircraft).

On March 5, 1987, the FAA announced that it "was unable to confirm the event." It repeated Paul Steucke's January statement that the second radar target was a "split radar return" from the JAL jet. No attempt was made to explain the visual sighting – perhaps because CSICOP had already done so, after its own fashion.

The story died after this. Captain Terauchi was "grounded" for several years. It was primarily through the research of Richard Haines that Terauchi's reputation was restored with his employer and he was flying again. Considering such a severe penalty for reporting the event, it is no surprise that pilots so seldom come forward. One can only wonder how many other dramatic air encounters have taken place, but are never discussed outside the cockpit.

One interesting postscript to this case came in the person of FAA official John Callahan, Division Chief of the Accidents and Investigations Branch of the FAA in Washington, D.C. Many years later, Callahan revealed that the day after the event, FAA administrator, Admiral Donald D. Engen, convened a special briefing which included the FBI, CIA, a scientific study team from President Reagan, and others. Evidence in the form of video-taped radar tapes, air traffic voice communications, and paper reports were compiled and presented. At the conclusion of this meeting, the attending CIA members instructed everyone present that "the meeting never took place" and "this incident was never recorded." They confiscated all evidence that was presented, but did not realize there was more. "They never asked anyone if we had copies, so I never told them I did," said Callahan, who possessed videotape and audio evidence of the event. The CIA also advised the group that the media would not be informed of this event, as "it would scare the public." Years later, Callahan provided testimony of his involve-ment in this affair, including official memoranda and pilot transcripts, to Steven Greer, which were reprinted in Greer's book *Disclosure*.[118]

As an aside, it may be worth noting that one week after the JAL 007 encounter, a KGB "Blue Folder" UFO incident occurred at roughly the same latitude, although nearly 2,000 miles away in Eastern Siberia. As with most of the Soviet reports, details are lacking, but as the story goes, on the afternoon of November 25, 1986, civil and military personnel in Magadan

Airport discovered an unidentified radar target. Since there was another aircraft flying in the vicinity, air traffic control advised the pilot to be aware of a possible unknown object in his area. It turned out that "the plane and unknown object passed clear of each other," although no details were given. After this, however, "the object turned right [east] in the direction toward Shelekhov Bay." Soon it was traveling at 3,000 kph, or roughly 1,800 mph – that is, astonishingly fast. The object flew over water toward Kamchatka until it was lost from the radar screens. It is not clear whether the pilot ever obtained a visual of the UFO.[119]

The Young Internet

A final interesting development in 1986 hinted toward greater things to come. This was the growth of computer-based UFO information services such as Computer UFO Network (CUFON) and the bulletin board service known as Paranet. CUFON was originally managed by Michael Hart, but was taken over in 1986 by Dale Goudie. Operating out of Mercer Island, Washington, it functioned as a UFO bulletin board using a voice and data line connected to an IBM XT, an early personal computer for the consumer market. CUFON received most of its reports from Bob Gribble of the National UFO Reporting Center, which in turn received many reports from airports around the country. By late 1986, according to Goudie, CUFON had over 700 members and was receiving many calls per day. (MUFON members made up the largest segment). Most of these were "raw reports" with mundane explanations. Still, MUFON members, within the limits of their capabilities, did investigate a number of these sightings.[120]

Paranet started in 1986 as a facet of what was then the heart of the young Internet: the bulletin board system collectively known as Usenet. Managed by MUFON member James Speiser from 1986 to 1988, Paranet quickly developed into a thriving community where a full range of researchers, believers, skeptics, and cranks could "post" their articles. Michael Corbin became administrator in 1988 and ran it until the mid-1990s, when the World Wide Web supplanted Usenet as the dominant arena of the Internet. It eventually became evident that computerized services like Paranet and CUFON were more than just important new tools for researchers. They portended changes on an order of magnitude not seen since Gutenberg invented the printing press five centuries earlier. The Information Highway was arriving, and UFO researchers were learning how to drive along with everyone else. The biggest immediate impact was that it dramatically expanded the number (and types) of people who would be contributing to the field. As could be expected, this was a double-edged sword, since opinions are free and hence available to anyone with a mouth (or in this case fingers to type). However, there is no question that the young Internet, even in 1986, was expanding the world of ufology, transforming it from a small club to something much larger and, dare one say, populist.

Tracking Fastwalkers at Cheyenne Mountain

A final, fascinating, UFO event closed 1986, described by *New York Times* journalist Howard Blum.[121] This took place near the middle of December, at the U.S. Space Command's Surveillance Center inside Colorado's Cheyenne Mountain, where the thousands of satellites and miscellaneous space debris in Earth orbit are tracked. Commander Sheila Mondran was in charge when sensors detected something tripping the U.S. Naval Space Surveillance System – known as The Fence. This is a man-made energy field that reaches nearly 15,000 miles into space, and is able to determine the speed and size of any object in its range. The intrusion occurred in the skies above Lake Kickapoo, Texas.

Most such events are not a cause for concern, but this particular object fit no known category. Commander Mondran's team tracked its seemingly impossible maneuvers, including loops, backtracks, "crash dives," and astonishingly fast climbs. Mondran wondered whether the intruder could be an electronic intelligence (ELINT) or anti-satellite (ASAT) weapon. She discussed these possibilities with her technician, who was doubtful. According to Blum, when she asked his opinion, he replied, "just between you and me, ma'am," he replied, "it looks like we got someone joyriding up there."

Mondran sent a Flash Alert to CINC-NORAD. Such an alert was usually reserved for potentially dangerous situations, and always ended up on the desk of the President. But as suddenly as the object appeared, it then disappeared. Two searches were immediately ordered: one by the Space Detection and Tracking System, which was a worldwide network of radars, telescopes, cameras, and radios. Another was made by a computer linked system of sophisticated telescopes. Neither search found anything.

The Flash Alert was recalled the following day, but no answers were forthcoming. A summary of the incident was sent to the Joint Chiefs of Staff as well as President Reagan for his daily briefing. Essentially, an object had penetrated U.S. air space doing the impossible, then vanished. Blum reported that the UFO story caught President Reagan's attention. Without a trace of humor Reagan announced that he also had once seen a UFO while he was Governor of California. He recommended a follow-up investigation, but none is known to have occurred.

According to Blum, the NSA eventually favored the ASAT theory, although no one understood how the Soviets could have made an object move that way. The way it disappeared also caused some concern that the Soviets might possess stealth technology. Still, the obvious, unavoidable question was, "was this an actual UFO?"[122]

A So-Called UFO Working Group

Blum wrote that a report about the fastwalker ended up on the desk of a "Colonel Harold Phillips" in the DIA's Directorate for Management and Operations. Blum revealed that "Phillips" was also the DIA's "Associate Coordinator of Space Reconnaissance Activities." This was a powerful and sensitive position which helped determine missions for the U.S. spy satellites. Blum then described how Phillips organized an interdisciplinary "UFO Working Group" beginning in 1987. It was comprised of scientists and officers from throughout the defense and intelligence community, and worked deep within a secured "vault" within the Pentagon.[123]

Certain elements of Blum's narrative were correct. However, the name, time frame, and numerous other details were wrong. Later investigations by at least three researchers (Grant Cameron, Timothy Good, and the author) have corrected and added more detail to what actually occurred, although most of the group's activities still remain unknown to the public.

The identity of "Harold Phillips" is known to be Colonel John B. Alexander. Alexander was a former Green Beret Commander who participated in the Phoenix program during the Vietnam era, searched for Atlantis in the Bimini Islands, was an official of the Silva Mind Control organization, and a world expert in the field of non-lethal weapons. He had extensive background and knowledge of remote viewing as well as acoustic weapons which could embed subliminal messages or affect a person's physiology.[124]

In forming this group, Alexander sought to avoid undue attention, and certainly never called it anything as obvious as a "UFO Working Group." Instead, he selected the more suitably vague title of "Advanced Theoretical Physics Group." According to one group member who confidentially spoke to the author, the group met a total of four times: on May 21-22, 1985, August 6-7, 1985, April 24, 1986, and November 18, 1987. The first three meetings took place at the BDM McLean Secure Facility in Virginia, and the last at the Pentagon.[125] A memo leaked to Grant Cameron included information about the first meeting (according to which occurred from May 20 to 25, 1985), and included a partial list of attendees. Timothy Good later received a complete list of that meeting, which included Robert Wood (McDonnell Douglass), Ronald Blackburn (Air Force and formerly Defense Nuclear Agency), Milt Janzen, Don Keuble (Lockheed Aircraft), Harold Puthoff (head of SRI's remote viewing program, formerly employed by the NSA), Ed Speakman (Army Intelligence), Howell McConnell (NSA), and Bill Wilkinson (CIA), and Alexander.[126]

According to Good, the group's research effort appeared to be connected to a "major engineering project" under Admiral Bobby Ray Inman, former CIA Deputy Director, Director of Naval Intelligence, and Director of the NSA. This implies reverse engineering of alien hardware, although one member of the group told the author that such a statement was offered as a speculation, and that this possibility should be checked. "We had hard data on sightings," he said, "but no hard data on hardware or reverse engineering."

None of the group's members has publicly offered much information about its proceedings. Dr. Robert Wood, who attended two meetings, has perhaps been the most forthcoming. Wood said that although the meetings themselves were classified Top Secret, he heard "virtually nothing that was truly classified." He gave a presentation on UFO propulsion incorporating many ideas of the late NASA scientist Paul Hill.[127]

Other people known to the author to have had some sort of connection to this group were General Alexander Stubblebine, former commander of the Army Intelligence and Security Command (INSCOM) where he worked with Alexander, Jack Houck (a systems engineer at Boeing with an interest in paranormal phenomena), and remote viewer Ed Dames (who was said to have given a presentation on remote viewing alien bases on Earth with the suggestion that teams be sent to investigate them).

Blum also incorrectly described the group's purpose, which was not insipidly to explore whether the human race "was alone in the universe," or even if UFOs were extraterrestrial.[128] Its aim was more pragmatic. Alexander wanted to create a highly qualified study group that would obtain the best UFO evidence. He hoped that this in turn would enable him to locate and gain access to actual deep-black programs related to UFOs, or perhaps to provide consultation to such groups. In other words, he and his members held an implicit assumption that there was such a group, and they wanted in. The obvious question is, did Alexander succeed?

According to Alexander's public statements, the answer is no. Alexander said that he had reached very high levels within Pentagon (e.g. 4 star) and still found no evidence of any such program. "I've looked," he told listeners at a UFO conference, "and it's not there."[129]

The author, however, spoke to several group members who expressed skepticism and even outright denial about Alexander's position that there is "no evidence" of a black UFO program. One of them stated that he had key information about such an inside group. Although he would not or could not pass on any specific information, he implied strongly that there was an international or transnational structure to this group, something beyond the formal or full control of the U.S. President, or any other part of the official U.S. government.

At least two members of the Advanced Theoretical Physics Group belonged to another, somewhat overlapping group. This was a quiet collection of individuals with backgrounds in intelligence who shared an interest in UFOs and related topics. By the late 1980s, it would become known as "the Aviary."

The Aviary

The Aviary is one of the more romantic pieces of UFO lore, subject to much speculation. People have wondered whether it served as a secret UFO control group, or perhaps as a debunking or disinformation source. Others have seen it as a group of interested insiders who sought to navigate their way through the labyrinth of secrecy. Others still as simply a group of loosely associated people with a mutual interest in the topic.

The core of what became the Aviary appears to have been started by retired USAF Colonel Ernie Kellerstrauss, who had worked at the Foreign Technology Division (FTD) at Wright-Patterson AFB. In the fall of 1986, Kellerstrauss invited a number of individuals – Harold Puthoff, John B. Alexander, C. B. Scott Jones, Robert Collins, William Moore, and Jaime Shandera – to his home in Beavercreek, Ohio. Puthoff and Alexander, already discussed, were currently involved in the Advanced Theoretical Physics Group. Scott Jones was a Ph.D. and former Navy fighter pilot who was an aide to Senator Claiborne Pell (D-RI). Collins was an Air Force Captain who, like Kellerstrauss before him, was working at Wright-Patterson's FTD. Moore and Shandera, of course, were UFO researchers, although some people who knew Moore suspected him to be connected with the CIA or perhaps another intelligence organization.

In various permutations, this group met from time to time, generally discussing UFOs, the extraterrestrial presence on Earth, and Nevada's Area 51 (well before the area became public knowledge). Kellerstrauss, for one, had a great deal to say. He had known an Air Force officer named Robert Hippler who, said Kellerstrauss, had been in the "real Project Blue Book." Kellerstrauss knew of physiological studies that had been done on alien bodies during the 1960s. He also claimed that during the 1970s, the chief scientist at FTD, named Anthony Cacciopo, had a copy of a book which provided the complete covert UFO history from 1947 on. Kellerstrauss also discussed the presence of an alien base near Area 51, a bit northwest of Groom Lake. People who wandered into the area "never returned." The area was simply off limits, even to U.S. government personnel.[130]

It is not clear that such meetings amounted to anything more than the sharing of stories and theories about what was believed to be going on. Clearly, some of this information could be accurate. Bruce Maccabee, for example, researched the career of Robert Hippler, and determined that what Kellerstrauss said about Hippler could well have been true.[131] Other stories, such as the alleged alien base, were just that – stories – although one could argue that Kellerstrauss may have been in a better position than many to have gleaned something about it.

By the late 1980s, Moore and Shandera became concerned that their telephones were monitored, and so decided to assign a bird name to whomever they talked about. This could include any one at all (the President, for instance, was referred to as Eagle). Many of these people were associated with the group around Kellerstrauss, although this was hardly their primary connection. Some of them had professional and personal connections to each other, and most of them had a background in the world of science or intelligence. While they all shared a strong interest in the subject of UFOs and extraterrestrials, there was also a great deal of variance among them. Some of them had high level security clearances, others did not. Many of them disagreed on important issues.

By 1988 at the latest, Moore was referring to this collection of "birds" as the Aviary. Over time, the bird names have not been consistent, but the names appear to be as follows: Kellerstrauss was Hawk, Puthoff was Partridge, Jones was Hummingbird, Alexander was Chickadee, Collins was Condor. Other men had also become avians: Christopher (Kit) Green, a senior CIA officer with access to the Agency's UFO material – the so-called Weird Desk – was Blue Jay. Dale Graff, formerly of the Defense Intelligence Agency, was Owl, Air Force OSI Agent Richard Doty became the surrogate Falcon when the "real" Falcon was unavailable or dropped out.

Some of these people had substantial interest and some leverage within elite circles. One, known only as "Raven," appears to have been the most powerful of all, and within a few years would be connected to an alleged abortive disclosure of UFO reality. But the Aviary did not have any formal status among its "members." We can best understand it as a loose association of friends and associates, often with different assessments and attitudes concerning UFOs, given a name by Moore for reasons of convenience and security.

Summary

The middle of the 1980s were something of a holding pattern for ufology. No question, there were interesting events, both in research and sightings. Within the U.S. intelligence apparatus, circumstantial evidence points to the likelihood that some effort was made to cause confusion in the ranks, in particular regarding the case of researcher William Moore. However, Moore was riding high at this time, widely respected as one of ufology's top researchers and perhaps the best hope at ending the cover-up. Perhaps Moore himself believed this, as he often indicated. If so, it looks as though he was handed a false bill of goods, unless of course his involvement went deeper than this.

This holding pattern was now about to end quite dramatically. The year 1987 would prove to be the most important year in UFO research in decades, perhaps ever. The repercussions from these research developments would make a permanent impression on popular culture, as well.

Chapter 7

Ufology Explodes
1987-1988

[Object] dispersed 3-5 smaller flying objects that were zipping around rather quickly....
[They] had the ability to stop and hover in mid-flight.
— *U.S. Coast Guard report on a UFO over Lake Erie, 1988*

Question: Is this group like the Bilderbergs, Pugwash, or the Trilaterals?
Answer: (Silence for a long while). Something like that.
— *Retired defense scientist, Dr. Eric Walker, speaking about MJ-12.*

I know some. I know a fair amount.
— *George Herbert Walker Bush, answering a question on UFOs, 1988.*

A World About to Change

Throughout the 1970s and most of the 1980s, the world of UFO research evolved at a steady pace. Slowly but surely the idea of "scientific ufology" had taken hold among researchers and become a desired goal among the major UFO organizations not only in America, but around the world. Of course, budgets and means remained limited, but the goal was there. Within this environment, new issues like abductions, cattle mutilations, and crop circles had intruded, to say nothing of FOIA documents, black helicopters, and ever-increasing leaks from the black world. Dissension was the rule rather than the exception, but the debates took place within the relatively limited confines of UFO journals and conferences. The *MUFON UFO Journal*, for instance, had a circulation of less than 1,500 copies per month throughout most of the decade.

But things were about to change – computers were about to take over the world. The nascent information highway reached ufology before it reached most other fields. By early 1986, a bulletin board system (BBS) was dedicated to UFOs and related topics. ParaNet, founded by Jim Speiser, rapidly gained a following – and more importantly, participants – opening the field to a much larger public. At the same time, the MJ-12 and abduction controversies broke open into extensive public discussion.

Within a few short years, UFO research would be transformed.

Redefining Ufology

On February 16, 1987, Soviet President Mikhail Gorbachev made his own comments on a hypothetical alien threat. At a conference at the Grand Kremlin Palace in Moscow, he referred to Ronald Reagan's statement in Geneva, that if Earth faced an invasion by extraterrestrials, the U.S. and the Soviet Union would join forces. "I shall not dispute the hypothesis," said Gorbachev, "although I think it's early yet to worry about such an intrusion. It is much more important to think about the problems that have entered in our common home."[1]

Perhaps Gorbachev did not take an alien threat seriously; perhaps he did. The American general public did, at least according to a 1987 Gallup Poll. Forty-nine percent of respondents believed UFOs were extraterrestrial craft piloted by aliens, and nine percent claimed to have seen a UFO. One third denied the existence of UFOs. In general, these numbers were the same as those from a decade earlier.[2]

But in 1987, Ufology was about to undergo challenges so profound that collectively they amounted to a revolution. Within a few short years, attitudes of researchers and the general public alike would be transformed. Gone were the days of speculating whether UFOs were alien spacecraft here studying the Earth in preparation either to invade or help – a common theme from earlier years. Now a sense of darkness, urgency, and even fear became almost palpable. Claims centered on a long-term relationship between "us" and "them." A deal, so to speak. In this new scenario, the "visitors" were here for the long term, and elements of the U.S. government, perhaps a shadow government, were complicit. Researchers were beginning to believe that abductions were taking place on a scale never before contemplated. Some argued that, in return, technology was made available to human scientists working in the black world. Meanwhile, the great mass of humanity were mere pawns, "sold out" by their human masters and used by the aliens for their genetic material and who knew what else.

Abductions

February 1987 saw the near simultaneous publication of two of the most influential books on alien abduction that ever appeared: Whitley Strieber's *Communion* and Budd Hopkins' *Intruders*. Both superbly written, they handled the subject with a depth and immediacy that, to many students of the field, represented a leap forward in understanding the beings operating UFOs. Acceptance of alien abductions had developed slowly. During the 1950s and 1960s, most researchers flatly rejected claims that anyone had interacted with actual occupants of UFOs. It was as if the idea of alien spacecraft was strange enough, and the limits of belief had not yet grown to accommodate anything more. In time, this changed. Cases like the 1961 Hill abduction led researchers to admit that occasional interaction with (and abduction by) aliens did occur. A veritable explosion of alien abduction cases appeared during the 1970s. In 1979, the publication of *The Andreasson Affair* by Raymond Fowler introduced the idea of alien implants, and Budd Hopkins's *Missing Time* the following year argued the phenomenon was much more widespread than had even been suspected.

Now, with *Intruders* in 1987, Hopkins went further, describing the experiences of a family who encountered ongoing intervention by alien entities, entailing a sophisticated program of genetic experimentation involving sperm extraction and artificial insemination. To accomplish such a program, an incredible logistics operations involving the monitoring of abductees, in some cases since childhood, was called for.

Kathie Davis had written to Hopkins in 1983 after reading *Missing Time*. During one early evening in July 1983, she and her mother saw a light about two feet in diameter moving around the family pool house. Some days later they noticed a section of their backyard had turned brown, a circular area about eight feet in diameter. Hopkins spoke with Kathie and her family, and uncovered a pattern of strange events which had affected them for years. It appeared that Kathie, her mother, and two of her children were abducted at different points in their lives. Kathie and her mother had identical scars on their lower legs from apparent childhood abductions, and Hopkins believed that Kathie and her son Tommy had implants inserted near their brains, one through the nasal cavity and the other through the ear.

During hypnotic regression with Hopkins, Kathie revealed that her first pregnancy occurred in 1977, when she had a UFO sighting. Her doctor was curious when he later found her to be no longer pregnant. "Somebody took my baby," she told Hopkins. Hopkins described other accounts of abductees experiencing pregnancy while still virgins, then having the fetuses taken from them in later abductions. Several women remembered being shown infants aboard the alien craft and being made to feel that they were their offspring. Hopkins concluded that "abductions represent a genetically focused study of particular bloodlines," and that "the human species itself is the subject of a breeding experiment."[3]

Hopkins consistently emphasized the physical nature of the abduction phenomenon. He cited a "mass of evidence supporting the view that something is going on." Elements within reports, such as bodily marks or scars, were replicated from case to case to case. The marks, he said, were entirely consistent and were usually either a straight cut or scoop mark – a kind of depression in the skin. "These two patterns turn up over and over again." He showed the marks to physicians who replied that they looked artificial, perhaps suggesting surgery.[4] This was not some fantasy out of a deluded person's mind, but tangible evidence.

In general, UFO researchers were deeply impressed by Hopkins' work. Skeptics, however, saw him as a dangerous man: a brilliant and persuasive writer who happened to be wrong. Probably the most severe criticism leveled at him was that he was not a qualified hypnotherapist or medical professional and was actually doing harm to people who had suffered real trauma of some sort – not alien abductions.[5] Hopkins readily rebuffed such criticisms. He pointed out that in a number of the cases he investigated, the hypnotic regressions were performed by a licensed psychiatrist. In any case, his own ability to perform regression was never questioned by professionals who observed his work. He pointed out (in 1988) that two psychiatrists, four psychologists and 11 psychotherapists had come to *him* for hypnosis to help them recall the missing pieces of their own abduction experiences. He had inserted specific protocols so as not to elicit "favored" responses, and maintained that at all times his overriding concern was to help the person experiencing the trauma. It so happened that time and again the individual under regression would spontaneously recall the classic indicators of alien abduction. Moreover, he added, hypnosis was not responsible for all abduction claims: roughly a quarter of the cases he worked on involved conscious recall by the percipient of his or her experience.[6]

Yet, many skeptics failed to be convinced. Small body marks hardly impressed them. They doubted the existence of implants – none of which had been recovered, or else had vanished before analysis. And where were the reliable, independent observations of any abduction? Most likely, they hypothesized, there was some factor in the background of alleged abductees that caused them to go into something like an altered state of consciousness under hypnosis. Under such a state one could create an abduction story – and then sincerely believe it to be true. Presumably these would have been the result of some prior, non-alien related, traumatic experience. To such skeptics, the idea of the "fantasy prone personality" seemed best to explain the phenomenon.

The concept was fairly new in psychiatry. A small but significant percentage of the population – experts said about four percent – fit the fantasy prone profile. Such people typically made excellent hypnotic subjects. As children, they lived in make-believe worlds, replete with fairies and other airy creatures, but learned to become secretive about their fantasy life. As adults, they tended to spend a great deal of time fantasizing. They usually had vivid dreams, regarded themselves as psychic in some fashion, and were more likely than the average person to have an out-of-body experience or see apparitions. Yet, in every other respect, they were socially aware, normal, and healthy individuals.[7]

The problem with this hypothesis was that, in 1987, no work had been done to see whether abductions actually happened to such individuals. Hopkins for his part called the theory "plainly wrong." The vast majority of UFO abductees, he said, including many who had been psychologically tested, were not fantasy-prone individuals.[8]

There is another issue concerning the "fantasy-prone personality" idea. Its creators clearly adhered to a distinctively materialistic conception of reality. To such a mind, anyone who was inclined toward psychic interests, or who claimed to experience other dimensions of reality, or who claimed to see otherworldly beings, was someone who lived in a "fantasy." But what if the shoe, so to speak, were on the other foot? In other words, what if it *was* true that people who fit the "fantasy-prone" profile *were* more likely to have experiences with these other beings – but not because they were prone to fantasy? Instead, what if the reason was because their inherent sensitivity to other realms of existence made them more likely? What if the presumed extraterrestrials had psychic or telepathic capabilities that made them more interested in such people? If one substituted the phrase "fantasy-prone personality" with "psychically sensitive personality," the characteristics described in the type would still fit, but would give a very different coloration to the matter. After all, members of the U.S. military and intelligence community had been using remote viewers for quite some time, readily accepting that at least certain human beings possessed apparently powerful psychic gifts. This was a possibility, however, firmly outside the parameters of acceptable science and much of ufology in 1987.

Intruders made a major impact on UFO research and also sold well. *Communion*, however, became the number one best-selling paperback in the United States during its first three months of listing by the *New York Times*, and for millions of individuals became the first UFO-related book they ever read. It also boasted the most famous cover a UFO book ever had, a captivating portrait of an alien face by artist Ted Jacobs.

Whitley Strieber's account of his abduction experiences was personal, intense, and disturbing. On a night in December 1985, while resting in bed in his upstate New York cabin, he awoke to a strange whooshing sound which seemed to be coming from downstairs. His burglar alarm panel, situated near his bed, showed no disturbances. His bedroom door opened, and a small figure quickly approached him. Strieber made out two dark eyes, a rounded hat of some sort, and a square plate on its chest. He was paralyzed and floated naked out of the room. Outside in the woods, he drifted up to a room where small beings moved quickly all around him. He noticed four types of beings: a small robotlike creature, a group of short, stocky beings in dark blue overalls, a slender being about five feet tall with black slanted eyes, and several smaller beings with round black eyes.

One took out a hair-thin needle; telepathically, Strieber was told it would be inserted into his brain. When he began screaming, another being, whom he sensed was female, asked him telepathically, "what can we do to help you stop screaming?" He replied, "you could let me smell you." One of the beings put a hand against Strieber's face. It smelled like cardboard, and this helped give Strieber "an anchor in reality." An operation was performed on Strieber's head. His legs were separated and a long object was inserted up his rectum, which he thought was to take a sample. Although he felt no pain, he felt violated and furious. A painless incision was also made on his forefinger. That appeared to be the end of the procedure.

Strieber awoke the next morning not remembering his abduction, but feeling uneasy. All he could remember from that night was the image of a barn owl staring at him through the bedroom window. His right forefinger became infected and he felt rectal pain every time he sat. After he mentioned pain behind one ear, his wife noticed a tiny scab there. Then, one day, he suddenly recalled a smell, and the memories flooded back to him.

Strieber had heard of Budd Hopkins and contacted him. The two soon met. While talking, Strieber recalled another possibly odd encounter at the cabin from October 1985. At Hopkins' recommendation, Strieber hired Dr. Donald Klein of the New York State Psychiatric Institute to perform hypnotic regression. With Hopkins present, these sessions began in March 1986, and Strieber's memories poured forth. From the October encounter, Strieber remembered a short, hairless being with large slanted eyes standing over his bed. When the being touched his forehead with a silver tipped rod, Strieber saw a series of disturbing images of the world exploding and of his son dying. The being then raised the wand and caused a bang, waking everyone in the house. From the December encounter, he remembered telling the aliens they had no right to abduct him; they replied that "we do have a right," and "you are our chosen one." From further sessions, Strieber developed the belief that he had been abducted as a child.

Strieber continued to have strange experiences during 1986, at one point finding two small triangles inscribed on his forearm. He came to believe that the abduction experience had its "symbolic center in the number three and the triangular shape." The visitors often appeared in threes, they wore triangular emblems, and triangular marks often appeared on abductees.

Strieber was already an accomplished novelist before he wrote of his abduction experiences. As such, he was aware of the power of the human imagination. Although he believed his experiences were objectively "real," he could not state with certainty that the visitors existed independently of their observers.[9] Others wondered if Strieber the novelist was simply spinning a good yarn. Skeptics argued that the story was either an outright hoax, or "a classic, textbook description of a hypnopompic hallucination" (e.g. "waking dream") from a fantasy-prone personality.[10]

San Antonio journalist Ed Conroy was one of those initially skeptical of Strieber's story. Conroy interviewed Strieber and many others who knew him. To his surprise, Conroy himself began to have experiences in 1987 and 1988 similar to those reported by Strieber. These coincided with strange helicopter flybys over his office, noticed by several of his neighbors and even Strieber's own family on one occasion. Conroy observed that several people close to him also began to report nighttime experiences with entities, balls of light, and other strange phenomena. He began to believe that a "social element" accompanied the visitor experience – one person's experience being a catalyst for that of others – and that the abduction phenomenon had a direct link somehow with human consciousness.[11]

During the spring of 1987, Streiber and Hopkins were both busy responding to the media and writing articles for publication.[12] Meanwhile, others continued to perform abduction research. One was Thomas Bullard, a researcher with a Ph.D. and expertise in folklore. Bullard, more cautious than Hopkins or Strieber, noted the great similarities within hundreds of abduction cases over many years, from many countries, and by witnesses from all walks of life. While he believed no certain final answer was possible, three solutions came to mind. One, that abduction reports were essentially real experiences. Two, that they told of a purely subjective, mental experience, no less vivid than real events and believed by the witness. Or third, "abduction reports simply tell a story." That is, people learn what an abduction ought to be like from someone else's story, and then repeat it with a few modifications of their own. For Bullard, "a final verdict disappears miragelike whichever way we approach the evidence." One problem that plagued Bullard was, if abductions were real, why did they share so much in common with religion, mythology and folklore? The only solution: more research.[13]

Indeed, Bullard himself soon undertook a large scale comparative analysis of all known abduction narratives. He concluded there was a "sharp distinction between real and imaginary ones." In other words, those purporting to be real were consistent and coherent; not so with the known imaginary cases. At the same time, the first experimental test of the Fantasy-Prone Personality (FPP) thesis was conducted by Dr. Kenneth Ring, a psychologist at the University of Connecticut. He found no discernable psychological differences between individuals who reported having UFO close-encounters and a control group of non-UFO witnesses. In other words, there was no evidence that a so-called fantasy-prone personality contributed either to seeing a UFO or believing one had an abduction experience.[14]

Nevertheless, Ring saw abductions as something much stranger than strictly physical phenomena. He likened abductions to what he termed "imaginal" experiences. The word sounds pejorative, but Ring did not mean that the experiences did not occur. Rather, he hypothesized the existence of an "imaginal realm" as an intermediate place between mind and matter, or the source of "border phenomena" that "seem at once to partake of otherworldly and objective realities." Like stigmata – a physical effect that has been reliably witnessed with no discernable physical cause – many UFO and abduction encounters also expressed "the curious and disturbing blending of the seemingly objective with the bizarre and absurd." Those who had been labeled "fantasy-prone" were very likely accessing this reality, and Ring likened them more to visionaries than schizophrenics. As other folklorists have sometimes done, Ring argued that the imaginal realm is a self-existent world, accessible through altered states of consciousness. Real beings live there, with the ability to interact with the everyday material world "in ways that defy rational understanding." Ring suggested that researchers jettison their "outworn Cartesian habits of thought" and stop searching for aliens out in the galaxy. Not surprisingly, he came under widespread criticism from many abduction and UFO researchers, but simply replied that they must one day "deliteralize" him.[15] As to where exactly this imaginal space was located, presumably the answer would lie in other "dimensions" of existence, perhaps explainable by contemporary theories in physics.

Matters became stranger still within a few years with the publication (in 1990) of Raymond Fowler's *The Watchers*. Fowler had already written two books on the case of Betty Andreasson Luca, a landmark in UFO abduction investigations. As mentioned previously, this investigation introduced the idea of the "alien implant," and was also one of the earliest investigated cases of a life-long "repeater," that is someone with abduction experiences throughout his or her life. There seemed to be no question about the honesty of the witness, and the only way to dismiss her detailed descriptions of alien beings, examinations, and experiments would be as a possible confabulation. A close reading of her case, however, makes this a very difficult argument. A new twist in *The Watchers* were descriptions of being out of her body during many of these experiences. In addition to encountering the short, grey aliens that others had described, Betty had out-of-body experiences (OBE) during which she sometimes encountered entirely human-looking beings that were tall, blonde, blue eyed, and white robed – very much like the typical descriptions of "nordic" alien beings. They were apparently in charge of the other aliens. It appeared to Betty that the human race was being "watched" by these beings, who (as they told her) foresaw serious problems in the future regarding the survivability of the human species and had therefore been collecting an enormous repository of genetic material for the future.[16] Abductions were becoming strange indeed when they did not always appear to involve the physical body. Needless to say, this was a controversial position, but supported by Fowler's careful and even cautious investigation, the detail and consistency of the material uncovered, and the character of the witness herself, a conscientious and intelligent percipient.

Cracks in the Secret World

By 1987, it was reported that the Pentagon had a "black budget" which managed classified projects, the sum total of which was larger than the federal budget for Education, Transportation, Agriculture, or the Environment. Programs within the black budget were classified above Top Secret, and few, if any, federal investigators had the security clearances to audit them. In February, journalist Tim Weiner estimated its size at $35 billion, or eleven percent of the total Pentagon budget, and three times the total it was believed to have been in 1981. The Pentagon maintained that expenses were still overseen by members of the House and Senate Armed Services Committees. This may have been true in some technical, legalistic, sense. In practice, oversight did not appear to be rigorous.[17]

The black budget had existed for a long time. That it was finally being reported was a sign that cracks were appearing in the wall of secrecy that had dominated the Reagan White House. In April 1987, Knight-Ridder newspapers ran headline accounts of a secret meeting in early October 1980 between an emissary of Iran's Khomeini government and Richard V. Allen, who had been the chief foreign policy adviser of the Reagan-Bush Presidential Campaign. At this meeting, a deal was allegedly discussed to hold the American hostages until after the election, an act that would thereby ensure the defeat of incumbent Jimmy Carter. That Reagan's people were meeting with Iranian emissaries at that time would be not simply illegal, but politically explosive, a deliberate undermining of the elected U.S. government – aside from toying with the hostages whose lives were in jeopardy. The stonewalling and obfuscation by the White House ultimately saved the day from legal reprisals, but like the O.J. Simpson trial of the 1990s, it left the distinct impression that the guilty party got away with the crime. The available evidence suggests that the Reagan Administration shipped arms to Iran, both through Israel and directly, from 1981 until 1987, as payment for Iranian cooperation on that matter, and probably due to Iranian blackmail as well.[18]

Meanwhile, the U.S. Congress was conducting unprecedented investigations into the relationship between the CIA and drug traffickers. In April 1986, Senators John Kerry (D-MA) and Christopher Dodd (D-CT) proposed that hearings be conducted by the Senate Foreign Relations Committee regarding charges of Contra involvement in cocaine and marijuana trafficking. The Contras were the right-wing rebels in Nicaragua who opposed the Marxist Sandinista government. Sen. Richard G. Lugar (R-IN) chairman of the committee, agreed to conduct the hearings. Meanwhile, Kerry's staff began its own investigation, which took a year and involved interviews with many witnesses.

By 1987, the subcommittee had amassed a mountain of evidence indicating that Lt. Colonel Oliver North and other members of the Reagan administration had set up a private network involving the National Security Council (NSC) and the CIA to deliver military equipment to the Contras. Not only had none of this been authorized by Congress, but much of the funding came from drug trafficking. The testimony of DEA agents such as Celerino Castillo and Michael Levine made this clear enough. From 1985 to 1987, when Castillo ran anti-drug operations in El Salvador, he discovered that the Contras were transporting cocaine through El Salvador's Ilopango airport. Castillo tried to bust the operation, but discovered the traffickers were protected by the CIA. He came to realize "how hopelessly tangled DEA, the CIA, and every other U.S. entity in Central America had become with the criminals." Castillo was himself subjected to an internal investigation, and his career ended. Levine also worked in Central America and echoed these sentiments. "I watched the CIA protect drug traffickers throughout my career as a DEA agent," he said. "I have put thousands of Americans away for tens of thousands of years for conspiracy with less evidence than is available against Ollie North and CIA people." The subcommittee learned that money was even laundered through the U. S. State Department for Contra drug traffickers – in some cases after the traffickers had been indicted by federal law enforcement agencies on drug charges.[19]

The news media consistently buried the results of these investigations. A July 22, 1987 issue of the *Washington Post* actually ran a headline stating "Hill Panel Finds No Evidence Linking Contras to Drug Smuggling." In truth, the opposite conclusion had been reached. Committee member Charles Rangel (D-NY) informed the newspaper of this fact, but the *Post* refused to publish his letter. Not surprisingly, the combined House and Senate Iran-Contra hearings later in 1987 also ignored the drug issue. Instead, investigators granted immunity to Oliver North.[20]

Another problem was beginning to leak in 1987. This was the corruption and drug smuggling of Panamanian leader Manuel Noriega. Noriega had been on contract to the CIA since 1967, so insiders had long known he was rotten to the core.[21] The problem was that, by the mid-1980s, his brutality had become transparent, and his criminality impossible to hide. Despite becoming a liability, Noriega continued to retain U.S. government support throughout 1987, while spurning bribes to retire. When it became clear that he would not leave quietly, the White House began demonizing him in 1988 (as it would soon do to Saddam Hussein).[22]

The specific reasons for these leaks were varied, but generally speaking they were part of a simple backlash. By 1987, Ronald Reagan was in the second half of his final term as President. Insiders had long known about illegal operations that had been going on under the umbrella of his administration; there are always such open secrets in Washington, not to be publicly discussed. But in all U.S. presidencies, unspoken agreements seem to break down once the end is in sight. Preventing the leaks is impossible; the trick is in damage control, and this was accomplished reasonably well. *The Washington Post*, by the nature of its coverage at this time, clearly relished its role as Defender of Orthodoxy.

Leaking MJ-12

William Moore, Jaime Shandera, and Stanton Friedman had been holding the MJ-12 documents for more than two years. They had brought a limited number of other researchers into the secret, but Moore still hesitated about releasing the documents. Decades later, certain details still remain unclear, but it appears that Moore was receiving pressure from Richard Doty to release them. When he failed to do this, Doty took other measures.

The stories of British researchers Timothy Good and Jenny Randles become significant here. In late 1986 and early 1987, both were working on UFO conspiracy books, knowledge of which was fairly well known in the UFO field. During that period, they both received leaked information directly relevant to MJ-12.

Good received the MJ-12 documents in early 1987 – the same ones Moore and Shandera had received. How exactly this happened has long been a matter of speculation, as Good for many years has not revealed the exact source.[23] In July 1987, he told Jenny Randles that he felt the source "was probably the same" as the source that sent the file to Jamie Shandera.[24] In his 2006 book, *Need to Know*, he stated the source was "American."[25] In communication with the author, Good confirmed that the source, while not Richard Doty himself, was probably connected to Doty.[26] This should not surprise researchers who have looked into the matter, but until Good explicitly reveals his source, this is all conjecture.

More dramatic was an encounter by Jenny Randles during late 1986 over matters closely related to MJ-12. On October 28, 1986, she received a phone call from a British military man who refused to give his name or phone number. He said his commanding officer had given him Randles' phone number and suggested she might want what he had – about 600 pages of UFO-related reports which had come into his possession. One document appeared to be a report from 1948 which used the term 'befabs' to describe "beings from alien objects." Another file, from Wright-Patterson AFB in 1977, was titled "Elimination of Non-Military Sources."

Randles was suspicious yet intrigued. The two spoke again on the 30th and agreed to meet at a local pub. Randles got his consent for her to bring along a friend, a UFO researcher named Peter Hough. When the two researchers met their informant, they were surprised that he was in his late twenties. Nevertheless, this young man (Randles gave him the pseudonym, "John") was impressive. In detail, he told them how he had came to possess the files.

"John" said he had been in a branch of the Royal Army Corps until he left in February 1985. In 1983, his commanding officer spent time on assignment in the United States and had befriended a USAF officer at Wright-Patterson AFB. The American officer was a computer technician who accidentally tapped into UFO files. He copied many of the files, but was soon arrested for being in a secure area without permission. During interrogation, the American officer withheld the information that he still had copies of these files. Then, somehow, he told his British officer-friend where the files were, and asked him to get them out of the country. A few days later, while on remand, this American officer died in a car crash – the death certificate put down the cause as "intoxication." The British officer (John's commanding officer) returned to the U.K. with the files, and for a long time did nothing with them.

John noticed that occasionally his commanding officer would discuss UFOs with his men, picking out those in whom he saw a reaction and speaking with them in private. John had no idea why. In his own conversations with his commanding officer, John felt as though he was being tested. For two years, John was shown reports that had been submitted to the British Ministry of Defence, as well as a photo of a daylight disc that had come from the U.S. Air Force. In 1985, he left active duty to become a civilian.

A year later, in August 1986, John returned for a weekend reservist training camp. At that time, his commanding officer told him of the UFO files and gave him a key to where they were stored. Take them and read them, his commanding officer said, and if you have a good feeling after talking to Jenny Randles, you can give her the files. The files looked dusty and unimpressive, and since John knew little of UFOs, he merely flipped through them. However, the day before his meeting with Randles, he decided to take the time to study them more carefully. It was then that he appreciated their explosive content. He began to fear for his family, and was glad to get the documents off his hands.

Randles and Hough asked many questions, and seemed to be satisfied with the extensive answers John gave to them. "Never once did he strike us as evasive or dishonest," she later wrote. Neither researcher saw an obvious motive for a hoax. Still, they pointed out that they had to satisfy themselves this was not a set-up. Perhaps he was an "innocent messenger boy," unaware of the bogus nature of his material. John doubted this, and the researchers agreed the material might be genuine. But they made it clear that they did not want to look like fools. The meeting ended with an agreement for John to deliver the files the next time they met. For a long while afterward, Randles and Hough sat in the car, shaking their heads and saying, "my god – if he's telling the truth...."

A meeting was planned for eight days later. On the appointed day, Randles and Hough arrived and waited. Several hours went by, but John never appeared.

Some days later, John sent a letter to Randles. He claimed that two days after their meeting in the pub, "events took a dramatic turn." He had been invited to his home base "to assist in an internal investigation." He said this involved the use of force, and he was "urged" to remain on base for several days while the investigation was completed. He was interrogated about "sensitive" documents (whose nature was never discussed) and told these were "the creation of an educated prankster" to which "no credence could be attributed." He was finally released and told it was in his own interest that no mention be made of the documents. He apparently told this to Randles in order to "spread around enough information to insure that nothing can or will happen to me or my family without suspicions being aroused." He apologized for letting her down. She never heard from him again.

Randles never believed this was a simple prank in which, for instance, the hoaxer got cold feet at the last minute. She believed "John" had indeed been in the British miliary, just as he claimed, and that there were indeed documents as he described. Whether these documents were genuine or disinformation, this would indicate the British military was involved. If genuine, the implications are that the military was dealing with an extraterrestrial presence on Earth and was perpetrating a massive cover-up. If disinformation, the question arises: why create disinformation, unless the topic warranted it?

Randles acknowledged the possibility that John's story was true. Still, she also entertained the theory that the affair was "a plot to try to dupe me into promoting a dubious tale via my book." If so, it was aborted, and she left the account out of her next book, *The UFO Conspiracy*. It was only after the MJ-12 documents were made public that she told it.[27]

The MJ-12 Affair Breaks

As Good's research opus *Above Top Secret* was due to appear in Britain during the summer of 1987, it became clear to Moore that he was in danger of being "scooped" on the MJ-12 issue. Thus, in the spring of 1987, Moore began to talk. He mentioned that for the past six and a half years, he and a few close associates had "succeeded in establishing a cooperative relationship with a number of well-placed contacts within the American intelligence community." He provided a copy of one page of the MJ-12 documents. In this version, some text was blacked out in the typical FOIA style.[28] Shortly thereafter he wrote another article on Majestic 12. This time he included photocopies of all pages of documents. Now, however, certain areas that had been formerly blacked out were readable, although some blacked out segments continued to exist – unlike the completely clean copy printed shortly later by Good.[29] Why were there different versions of these documents? The answer turned out to be simple: Moore deliberately blacked out sections of the document in order to hold certain data back. In the event that the document was leaked elsewhere (as in fact it was), one could compare versions.[30] Moore also revealed another document at this time, known as the Cutler-Twining memo. This had been found in the U.S. National Archives through the combined efforts of Moore, Stanton Friedman, and Jaime Shandera. Dated July 14, 1954, it was a one-page memorandum from Robert Cutler, Special Assistant to President Eisenhower, and was directed to Air Force General Nathan Twining. Its subject line was "NCS/MJ-12 Special Studies Project," and referred to a briefing that was to take place on July 16. The memo did not identify MJ-12 or the reason for the briefing.

On June 11, 1987, Moore, Friedman, and Shandera held a press conference on the MJ-12 documents and the Cutler-Twining memo. Acknowledging that they were not in a position to endorse the authenticity of the documents, they nevertheless claimed the documents appeared to be genuine. Friedman, for instance, found that Eisenhower did attend a briefing in Washington on November 18, 1952 – the date listed on the "Eisenhower Briefing Document." Also, his research on Donald Menzel was a true eye-opener. Friedman had managed to obtain permission from Menzel's widow to visit his archives at Harvard University. He discovered that, unknown to anybody – including Menzel's widow – the astronomer lived a double life. The first was his public life as a world famous astronomer and UFO debunker. The second was as a leading cryptographer and elite member of the U.S. intelligence community. Menzel had high clearances and met regularly with the leadership of the NSA, CIA, and other intelligence organizations. It was not simply a case of Menzel working for the national security community, as so many scientists have done; Menzel was a leading light within that community. The MJ-12 documents had therefore provided Friedman with a fruitful lead. If they were a hoax, how could the authors have known about Menzel's secret life? Was it simply a lucky guess?[31]

With the documents now in the public realm, the debates began. Moore and Philip Klass appeared on a June 24 *Nightline* episode with Ted Koppel, then Moore spoke two days later at the MUFON symposium in Washington, D.C. One of the most prominent early points of contention were the claims about Menzel. Menzel's closest living friend was Dr. Ernest H. Taves, who happened to be a member of CSICOP. Taves strenuously denied that Menzel lived a double life or was involved in a UFO cover-up. He did, however, provide a strange defense for his old friend. "If an alien spaceship had crashed," Taves said,

> Donald would certainly have been one of the first to be called to participate in an investigation. He would have welcomed this with the greatest enthusiasm. If national security were involved – which some might have thought to be the case for several months or a year or so – Donald would have gone along with that. But as it became clear – as indeed it has, over the years – that if this incident had happened it had no bearing upon national security, he would have been unable to continue to participate in a misguided and unnecessary cover-up.

The flawed logic is not hard to see. Taves acknowledged that Menzel would have been an excellent choice for an MJ-12 group, but would have balked at the secrecy. How Taves concluded this is a mystery. The MJ-12 documents explicitly claimed that the reason for the secrecy was the crash of several alien UFOs. Rather than imply that such events were irrelevant to national security, Taves brushed them aside. His concept of national security was startlingly naive, apparently assuming that people in the classified world could reveal secrets without serious repercussions.[32]

The U.S. National Archives wasted no time in disclaiming the documents. On July 22, a spokesperson said that after extensive searches among its holdings for the USAF, the JCS, and the NSC records of the Truman and Eisenhower administrations, they found nothing to support the existence of an MJ-12 group. The lone exception was the Cutler-Twining memo, but the spokesperson offered a 10-point argument citing problems with the document. He concluded that simply because the National Archives maintains custody of a document, it could not "authenticate documents or the information contained in a document." One wonders if this argument had ever been offered for any other document that came from the U.S. National Archives. Briefly, the problems were: inquiries into MJ-12 with other agencies turned up empty, the memo was unsigned, lacked a top-secret registration number, carried an incorrect classification ("Top-Secret Restricted" on the first line, and "Security Information" on the second), had a different typeface from other Cutler memoranda, and lacked the characteristic eagle watermark that was said to be on all government onionskin paper.[33] A month later, Philip Klass essentially repeated these claims in an official press release by CSICOP.

Moore was unfazed. None of these arguments held up under careful examination, he said. In the first place, unsigned memoranda were common among government documents of that period, and besides, Cutler was out of the country at the time – he could not possibly have signed it. The memo covered only a minor administrative detail and would have been handled by Cutler's staff. The lack of a top-secret registration number meant nothing; this too was common from that era. Regarding the classification "Top Secret Restricted Security Information," Moore and Friedman both found that the caveat "Top Secret Security Information" was commonly used throughout the early 1950s. Also, the term "Top Secret Restricted Data" was in use for certain types of information connected with atomic energy. Objections on the document typeface were also misplaced, said Moore. Preliminary examination of the memo indicated that it was typed with an Emanuel Remington-Rand typewriter of proper vintage – commonly used by government offices. In any case, other Cutler memoranda from that era displayed several type styles. Finally, the absence of an eagle watermark on the onionskin paper was not unusual. Government offices at that time used many types of onionskin, some of which bore no watermark.[34]

Friedman added that when visiting the document review portion of the archives – which is where the Cutler-Twining memo was found – researchers were prohibited from bringing their own materials. The memo was not folded, so it would have been especially difficult to sneak in, and it was "obviously" an unsigned carbon on old paper. Also, the person working at the archives declared that it was certainly genuine.[35]

Adding impetus to the MJ-12 momentum was the release of Timothy Good's *Above Top Secret* during the summer, which contained clean copies of the documents. In general, the mainstream reviews of Good's book were dismissive, occasionally hysterical. Adrian Berry, science editor of the *London Spectator* wrote that it was "an evil book," practically primed to foment revolution and resurrect the guillotine. "Mr. Good's ideas are those of a maniac," Berry breathlessly exclaimed. "I have no reason to believe that Mr. Good advocates torture and murder. But he does not seem to realize that such things could all too easily happen if a frenzied mass movement were to take up his ideas."[36] Still, Good's book and the MJ-12 documents began quietly receiving attention within the U.S. national security community, as more than one military and intelligence source has told the author personally.

Even so, a week after the CSICOP press release, the *New York Times* restated Klass's argument as though it were unarguable scientific fact ("Report of U.F.O. Crash in '47 Called False by Science Panel.")[37] The "Science Panel" referred to CSICOP. Most of the major media outlets covered the story in a similar fashion, generally with an openly skeptical approach.

Such establishment denials frightened away many UFO researchers from the documents altogether. Others wondered whether the documents were a more sophisticated form of disinformation. Jenny Randles, thinking of her recent encounter with allegedly leaked documents, speculated that the recent FOIA gains prompted a counterattack of sorts. This would be to release false papers "making extreme claims of sufficient plausibility to UFO researchers ... but yet reporting things so bizarre (e.g. autopsies on dead aliens) that they have the effect of making many objective commentators question the valid material." Randles suspected that Moore's work on the Roswell case made him a target, and she found it "incredibly suspicious" that she and Good both received covert approaches offering documents.[38]

FOIA researcher Barry Greenwood gave one of the most prominent critiques of the MJ-12 documents. These were hoaxes, he said, most likely contrived by Richard Doty. No one knew where the documents came from – a significant problem by itself, compounded by the fact that no archive or library had found any other document mentioning MJ-12. Moore's longstanding association with Doty was also problematic. Greenwood cited a 1983 conversation between Doty and Peter Gersten in which it came out as a "virtual certainty" that Doty was Moore's source for much of his information. Doty had been the OSI agent on duty at Ellsworth AFB in 1977 when a report, later alleged to be a hoax, emerged about aliens having a gun battle with security guards. Suspiciously, Doty's later home base of Kirtland AFB happened to be mentioned several times in the various Moore-Shandera-Friedman papers.

Greenwood also questioned the content within the MJ-12 documents, most significantly the disparity between its extensive discussion of the Roswell crash, and the mere seven lines of text on an alleged 1950 crash in Texas. It seemed likely that this was simply because the forgers had only a limited amount of information about the less-well-known Texas crash.

He also argued that the Cutler-Twining memo was planted – by whom, he would not speculate. It was found in a virtually empty box containing a small number of non-UFO documents. How could it have escaped the notice of those who declassified it? If Moore and Shandera said they found it as early as 1985, why was their copy dated from January 1987? After all, researchers throughout 1985 and 1986 had wanted to find a way to verify the MJ-12 claims. To Greenwood, it appeared that someone planted the memo before 1987 and set it up to be "officially" discovered and officially released by archive personnel. Although Friedman claimed such a thing was virtually impossible to do, in fact it is easy, wrote Greenwood. He had been able to sign in at the desk, obtain a researcher's card and walk in without anyone so much as peaking at his folders. He had two folders filled with copies of government documents to help him in his research. During the time he was at the archives, Greenwood said, he had "ample opportunity" to have planted or stolen documents while the archivist was taking phone calls.

Greenwood's argument had a strong influence within ufology. Judging from the researchers he thanked in his postscript (Peter Gersten, Robert Todd, Robert Hastings, William Steinman, John Lear, David Jacobs, and others) it was clear that sides were being drawn regarding MJ-12.[39]

Several of Greenwood's arguments turned out to be flawed, however. Bruce Maccabee cleared up one issue regarding the Cutler-Twining Memo. The reason the memo was stamped from early 1987, explained Maccabee, was because he had gone to the archives himself to get his own copy. Moore had shown him the document in 1985, Maccabee said. When Maccabee decided to write an article regarding MJ-12, he decided that he needed to confirm the existence of the memo. Using Moore's instructions, he easily located the document and made his own copy. He furthermore had the date stamped on the front, instead of the back (Moore's copy was stamped on the back), and sent Moore a copy for use on his June 1987 press release. Maccabee believed the memo's physical features pointed to its authenticity. It was a blue carbon copy on white onionskin paper. Yellowing around the edges suggested that it sat flat in a pile of papers or at least was pressed into a file in such a way that the air could circulate freely around all four sides.

The paper was creased, indicating it had at one time been folded into thirds, as if for insertion into an envelope. "A comparison of this document," concluded Maccabee, "with other known Cutler memos suggests that it is genuine."[40]

By the end of 1987, not only had the MJ-12 question caused a schism among UFO researchers, but serious questions about Moore himself were being raised. Gersten made the explosive assertion that "William Moore, rather than being an innocent dupe, was and still is actively and intentionally engaged in a continuing program of disinformation involving fraudulent documents." Considering that Moore had been one of the most prominent UFO researchers throughout the 1980s, this was strong stuff.[41]

Much more damning was the research being done by Robert Hastings. Shortly before the June press conference, Hastings spoke with researcher Lee Graham, who had several dealings with Moore. Over the previous few years, Graham had come into possession of several documents that were relevant to MJ-12, including the "Project Snowbird" and "Project Aquarius" documents. Graham had told Hastings that his source for these documents worked for the government, either as an intelligence operative or information conduit. As a result of this, Graham had received a visit from two agents from the Defense Investigative Service (DIS). They wanted to know why Graham, who possessed a "Q" security clearance, possessed allegedly secret government documents that had not been properly classified.

Now, however, in 1987, Graham freely told Hastings that it had been Bill Moore who had given him the Snowbird and Aquarius documents. Hastings asked if this meant that Moore worked for the U.S. government. Graham replied that when Moore first approached him with the documents, he showed Graham a government ID card. It had Moore's picture on it, but an alias typed beneath it. Moore indicated he was working for the U.S. government in order to release sensitive UFO-related documents. An astounded and still skeptical Hastings asked Graham which agency Moore claimed to work for. Graham replied that Moore's ID badge was identical to the badges shown him by the DIS agents. Hastings asked, "You mean to tell me that Moore's badge looked like the DIS badges?" Graham said, "no, it was identical to them."

Graham said he had been introduced to Moore's "superior," whom Moore would only identify as "Richard." Graham wrote to the DIS about Moore's approach to him on May 8, 1986, yet, Moore appeared never to have been interrogated by any other government agency for impersonating a government agent – which after all is a crime. This would seem to imply that either Moore's visit to Graham was sanctioned by the U.S. intelligence community, or that he was an actual agent. And one is left to wonder whether "Richard" was Richard Doty.

None of this looked good for Moore, although one might argue it was a separate matter from the authenticity of the MJ-12 documents. But Hastings wondered about those, too. For one, Moore had a history of "retyping" documents. This was the case with the Project Aquarius document, the first known document to refer to MJ-12, and which was declared fake by AFOSI Headquarters. According to Richard Hall, Moore had privately admitted in 1983 that he had done a "cut and paste job" and then "retyped" the document. Why would any researcher do such a thing, wondered Hastings? Clearly, the retyped version, once discovered to have been tampered with (as would inevitably happen) would only raise doubts about the credibility of the information it contained. Moore never provided an original version of the document. How could anyone know if it were real?

Hastings did not formulate his results into a paper until 1989, but researchers were talking privately about Moore in this vein throughout the late 1980s. When Moore learned of these statements, he refuted them vehemently, but at times rather ineffectually. The Lee Graham incident had been a "joke." The government "ID" was a laminated MUFON card, Moore said. However, it is hard to believe that someone of Graham's background would not have noticed the difference between a government ID badge and a MUFON membership card.[42]

Ufology was heading for a showdown.

Dr. Eric Walker

During the late summer of 1987, another important development in the MJ-12 saga took place – albeit behind the scenes – when researcher William Steinman phoned Dr. Eric A. Walker. Several researchers had been involved in cultivating Walker. In 1983, Dr. Robert Sarbacher had told Stanton Friedman that he knew of at least one person who had attended meetings at Wright-Patterson AFB concerning recovered flying saucers, but could not remember the name. When Steinman spoke with Sarbacher in 1984, they realized the man was Eric Walker. Walker's most high profile public job had probably been as President of Penn State University, but he had a long history at the highest levels of national security planning. For five years he was Chair of the Institute for Defense Analysis (IDA), probably the most elite military think tank in the U.S. Previous to this, in 1950 and 1951, he was Executive Secretary of the Military's Research & Development Board. It was in this capacity that Walker was said to have attended meetings at Wright-Patterson concerning UFO crash retrievals.

Friedman phoned Walker and Steinman wrote to him. Both got the brush-off. Steinman's letter was actually sent back, with an added statement typed on the bottom: "STOP! DON'T TRY TO FIND ME...." Both researchers moved on to other matters.

The publication of the MJ-12 documents, however, added impetus to the investigation. Steinman decided to contact Walker again, this time by phone. On August 30th, 1987, the two men spoke. Steinman told Walker he was calling "in reference to the meetings that you attended at Wright-Patterson Air Force Base in/around 1949-1950, concerning the military recovery of Flying Saucers, and bodies of occupants."

Amazingly, Walker replied that he had: "Yes. I attended meetings concerning that subject matter." Why was Steinman so worked up over it, Walker wanted to know?

Incredulous, Steinman reminded Walker that they were, after all, "talking about the actual recovery of a flying saucer not built or constructed on this earth! And furthermore, we are talking about bodies of the occupants from the craft who were analyzed [to be] human-like beings not of this world!"

"So," replied Walker, "what's there to get all excited about? What's all the concern?"

Steinman had expected a challenging interview, but Walker's nonchalance was a surprise. He continued to ask questions: had Walker ever heard of the MJ-12 group or Project Majestic 12? Once again, Walker surprised the researcher with his frankness:

> Yes, I know of MJ-12. I have known of them for 40 years. I believe that you're chasing after and fighting with windmills. . . . You are delving into an area that you can do absolutely nothing about. So, why get involved with it or all concerned about it? Why don't you just leave it alone and drop it? Forget about it!

Steinman replied that he was not going to drop it, that the public had the right to the truth. He continued to press. Did Walker remember any details regarding UFO recovery operations and analysis? Walker said he was sure he had notes concerning the meetings at Wright-Patterson AFB. "I would have to dig them out and read them over in order to jog my memory," he said. Walker said he might contemplate cooperating further. "That's the best I can say for now," he concluded.[43]

Steinman wrote back to Walker the next day, asking whether he knew of Project Aquarius and reminding him to look for those notes. He also sent Walker a copy of the MJ-12 documents. Three weeks later, Walker replied, and a very odd letter it was. "Some things you have right," he wrote, "and some things you have very wrong." There was a "machine" recovered, "obviously a landing vehicle only," fully within the realm of current knowledge, and he believed it was still being stored near "Wright Field." No dead bodies were found at the site – only four normal looking males who were very much alive. Yet, the implication from the letter was that they were nonetheless alien:

> Unfortunately, they had no memory of anything in the past (probably by design), but they were highly intelligent. They learned the English language within a few hours and it was our decision not to make public spectacles of them, but allow them to be absorbed into American culture as soon as we were sure that they did not bring any contamination with them.

Each of the four, according to Walker, became highly successful in various fields of human endeavor: technology, sports, and finance. Walker could not remember what happened to the fourth individual. The letter was signed only by the initials, "E.A.W." [44]

Steinman puzzled over the letter. So did Grant Cameron and T. Scott Crain, two other researchers who were communicating with Steinman and looking into this matter. The letter was strange, to be sure. But it also contradicted statements in Sarbacher's 1983 letter to Steinman – Sarbacher had indicated the aliens were insect-like, not human. Frankly, it seemed implausible that the U.S. military would allow four human-looking aliens to merge seamlessly into human society. The three wondered if the letter was a joke, but decided against it. After all, Steinman could have chosen to publish the letter, which would surely cause embarrassment to Walker. But why write back at all? The researchers decided that Walker may have thought Sarbacher had revealed much more than he actually did.

Such was the state of affairs regarding Eric Walker circa 1987. The next several years would see further developments. T. Scott Crain, Jr. lived within ten miles of Walker's State College residence. For the next several years, he and Grant Cameron investigated as much of Walker's past as they could. Meanwhile, Steinman wrote again to Walker at his Florida residence in April 1988. Walker's letter of September 1987 had "bewildered" Steinman, but now he wanted to know about current members of MJ-12. "I understand," wrote Steinman, "that some of its present day members are: (1) Dr. Henry A. Kissinger, (2) Gnl. Lew Allen, (3) Dr. Edward Teller, (4) Bobby Inman, and (5) Vice Pres. George Bush." Steinman asked for information about these men, and asked Walker to "talk with the others to end this dangerous alliance that was set up with the other world beings (Project Aquarius)."

Walker gave another bizarre reply. Within a week of receipt, he mailed Steinman's handwritten note back to him – not from Florida but Penn State. Apparently, he considered the letter interesting enough to take with him to Pennsylvania. Over various words Steinman had written, Walker had written numbers from 1 to 26, in minuscule size and no recognizable pattern. At the top of Steinman's letter, Walker wrote "Must reply, did code (-1)." Neither Steinman, Cameron, nor Crain could make sense of the "Code Letter," until Cameron realized that Walker had once been Chairman of the Institute for Defense Analysis, an organization that had made and broken codes and ciphers for the NSA. But Walker's code itself remained an enigma.

Later in April 1988, Crain phoned Walker. As soon as Crain mentioned the U-word, Walker simply said, "that is a subject that I don't talk about." Crain tried to get Walker to budge, but to no avail. Walker did not deny anything, he simply offered no comment. Crain made several attempts during 1988; Walker gave him nothing. Steinman also called Walker again in November 1988. This time Walker acted as though he did not remember Steinman. No matter how much Steinman tried to jog his memory, Walker replied, "I don't know what you're talking about." Clearly, Walker had found a strategy that worked.[45]

That is, it worked on Steinman and Crain. But there was one other researcher who was able to engage Walker in extended conversation about this topic. This was Dr. Henry Azadehdel (also known as Dr. Henry Victorian), a British-Armenian physicist who had corresponded with Cameron and learned about Walker. He first wrote to Walker in December 1989, and the two established a cordial relationship. On January 26, 1990, Azadehdel telephoned him. Perhaps because the two could communicate as scientific colleagues, Walker opened up.

They first discussed a South African UFO case Azadehdel was investigating, which concerned alleged "insect-like" alien beings. Although Walker had previously written to Steinman that the aliens he knew about were perfectly human looking, Walker asked Azadehdel many questions about the specifics of these beings, appearing to accept Azadehdel's research and opinions with no problem. Some selected highlights of their conversation were as follows:

A: Doctor, have we ever captured anything at all? We must have.

W: Sure.

A: ... did we learn anything?

W: Yeah, I think so.

A: Is it determined from which star system they come from?

W: Ah, I do not think so.

A: Have we ever been able to make contact with them on the communication basis?

W: We promised not to tell.

A: Do they constitute any threat to the national security of any country?

W: Everybody decides that on his own.

A: Do you know whether there is any cooperation between them (EBEs) and us, as an advanced civilization?

W: I think so. There have been occasions, but then I can speak only for myself.

Azadehdel was understandably encouraged by this conversation, and phoned Walker a second time on March 8, 1990. More highlights:

A: Are the [MJ-12] documents authentic?

W: I don't think so.

A: Doctor, but is there any such group still alive?

W: (Silence). How good is your mathematics?

A: As good as it could be for a doctor in physics. But why?

W: Because only a very few are capable in handling this issue. Unless your mind ability is like Einstein's or likewise, I do not think how you can achieve anything.

A: Well, Doctor, for many years now I have been trying. But, are there government scientists?

W: Everybody mistakes about this issue. I gather by that you mean whether they work for the Defense establishments of the military.

A: Yes, Doctor, that is what I meant.

W: Well, that is where you are wrong. They are a handful of elite. When you are invited into that group, I would know.

A: Is this group like the Bilderbergs, Pugwash, or the Trilaterals?

W: (Silence for a long while). Something like that.

A: Are you a member of that group?

W: I cannot answer that. How good is your seventh sense? How much [do] you know about ESP?

A: I know to some degree about ESP and EVP. But, what has that got to do with it?

W: Unless you know about it, and know how to use it, you would not be taken in. Only a few know about it.

A: Doctor, are there any military people in that group?

W: No.

A: Have we used any derivative of the learnt technology in the military?

W: I cannot answer that question. You are trying to squeeze the answers out of me.

A: Are the members 10, 12, 14, are they all Americans?

W: I cannot give you the numbers, and no, not necessarily, they are not all Americans.

A: Doctor, have we master[ed] the knowledge, are we working together with the entities?

W: No, we have learnt so much, and we are not working with them, only contact.

A: Have we captured any saucers, any material from the discs to study?

W: The technology is far behind [author note: Walker apparently meant "beyond"] what is known in ordinary terms of physics that you take the measure and obtain measurements. You are pushing for answers, aren't you? .... As I said, it is far behind (sp) the known level of physics that is known. A very few have knowledge of it.

A final phone conversation between the two occurred on August 18, 1990. This time, Walker was more guarded. Increasingly, he stated that such matters were none of Azadehdel's business, and that he was not going to receive answers simply so that his personal curiosity could be satisfied. "It is not going to do any damn good except make you happy. Is it not true? Are we to change all the plans and regulations just to make you happy? If you say that you are looking for the truth, you will never get it anyway, so forget it."[46]

Walker spent his remaining years dodging questions from researchers. He died on February 17, 1995 of a heart ailment. The notebooks of his UFO meetings were presumably either at his home, possibly handed over to his children, or passed over to the Penn State University archives. Crain made several visits to these archives. Not only was there nothing related to UFOs, but there was also nothing concerning Walker's relationship to the Military's Research & Development Board, for which he served as Executive Secretary. According to Walker's son, Dr. Brian Walker, all of his father's official papers had been given to Penn State. Among the unofficial papers, of which he said he reviewed some 10,000 pages, he said he found no mention of UFO-related information.[47]

What can one make of the Eric Walker tale? Ultimately it may come down to how one chooses to value certain types of evidence. Walker's statements may or may not have been entirely truthful, but there is no question that – if the statements of Steinman and Azadehdel can be believed – he gave the impression of knowing a great deal about an ET presence on Earth. Certainly, his status and credentials were unassailable. The general appearance is that a member of the "inner circle," during his later years, decided to let his guard down with an occasional researcher or two. Whereas the Walker case cannot amount to "proof" of the existence of an MJ-12 type of group, it is suggestive and credible. Such is the inherent nature of off-the-record insider leaks.

Eric Walker's connection to UFOs and MJ-12 remained unknown to all but a few researchers in 1987. Still, his story makes it clear how the opening of one secret – whether fully genuine or as disinformation – could lead to other openings. Cracks were appearing, both in the secrecy and an increasingly fractured ufology.

1987: A Quiet Year of UFOs

While ufology was exploding throughout 1987, the year was strangely quiet regarding actual UFO activity. Of course everything is relative. As skeptics have long argued, even one *good* UFO case should be enough to prove the phenomenon.

Something strange happened in Britain's North Yorkshire area in March 1987. Near the town of Bishop Monkton, Jenny Randles investigated and obtained information from an anonymous military witness. At around 3 a.m., during a 24-hour British military exercise, several military witnesses reportedly saw a strange red light in sky. Within twenty minutes, the light completed three circuits around the immediate area. Two F-4 Phantom fighter jets then gave chase, resulting in the typical UFO cat-and-mouse scenario. "One moment it was in front of the pursuers," the witness told Randles, "the next it would move at speed behind them." After five minutes, the object accelerated away at incredible speed. The witness did not report the sighting through official channels.[48]

The Hudson Valley continued to generate a trickle of reports. On May 26, in the town of Newtown, Connecticut, over 100 people saw a slow, silent, low flying, and circular formation of lights. The object passed over route I-84, causing many cars to pull over and some to lose power. A state police officer was sent to investigate the event and photographed the object, which showed a nearly complete

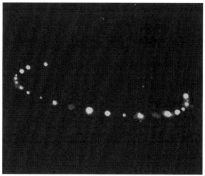

Police officer photo, May 26, 1987.

circle of multi-colored lights. Another witness named Randy Etting, who was an experienced commercial pilot, saw the object through binoculars. He called the state police, explaining that he had never seen anything like this before. The officer told him that he had merely seen ultralights in formation. Etting called this answer, "the prattling of idiots." Bruce Maccabee analyzed the photo. His findings indicated that the object was huge, perhaps over a thousand feet across, and that the lights showed a definite pattern.[49]

An interesting UFO sighting from Ghana on July 27 generated a U.S. Defense Information Report, and was also reported in the local news. Witnesses near the city of Accra and in the Volta region in southeastern Ghana reported a large and apparently silent object over southeastern Ghana and the Gulf of Guinea shortly before midnight. Some people reported the sound of explosions associated with the sighting. According to a U.S. Defense memo, a Ghana Air Force pilot privately said that he saw the object from the ground from near Accra. It traveled south and disappeared over the ocean. He initially wondered if the object was a falling meteorite. It then displayed a large, yellow light at its trailing end, similar to a rocket. Indeed, it was shaped very much like a missile or aircraft fuselage, except it was much larger – he estimated it to be two to three times larger than a Boeing 747. However, the object stopped falling and then began to climb. As it was gaining altitude over the ocean, he could make out details better in the clear evening sky. At this point, the single light disappeared, and eight smaller, bluish lights appeared. They were arranged in a circular formation around the end of the object, and seemed to be the object's source of propulsion. All the time, the witness never heard a sound from it. The U.S. Defense memo commented that the officer was a "qualified jet fighter pilot" who was "well known to the DAO [Defense Attaché Office] and others as a serious professional, not given to flights of fancy or to any desire to attract attention to himself." The memo added that he appeared to be embarrassed and mystified by his sighting and provided the details reluctantly, "mainly because the Air Force commander had asked the DAO to help identify the object."[50]

An interesting event is said to have occurred in the Soviet Union in early August 1987, repeated in a number of sources. Five servicemen from the Leningrad Military Region were sent to a unit in northern Karelia to guard an object which had recently been discovered to the north, near Viborg. They were ordered to prevent anyone getting near it. When someone disclosed to them that it was a UFO, they took a peek. The object resembled an American space shuttle and was said to be 46 feet long, 15 feet wide, and 8 feet high. It was seamless, greyish-tan in color, and smooth-looking, although its surface felt somewhat rough. The anonymous source for the story said the men experienced pain when they approached the object. A week after the object's arrival, a special commission of officers arrived to analyze it. They were unable to enter the object, and instead moved it to a hangar. The guards were sent back to their unit at this point, but the informant later learned from an officer that investigators were eventually able to enter part of it. Two men could barely fit inside, although there were two armchairs and what seemed like steering wheels and a control panel. It took one man 30 minutes to figure out how to put his hands on the "steering wheel." No one dared to sit in the chairs. The men tried to break off some shiny rods varying in length from 8 inches to 3 feet. Although they were wearing gloves, they burned their hands nonetheless. The object was gone by late September. Obviously, whether there is any truth, or even disinformation, to this story cannot be known without more investigation and documentation.[51]

In the United States, some activity was being reported in the eastern regions. According to Stan Gordon's research, a "a continuous wave of UFO activity" began in Pennsylvania during the summer of 1987, and which continued through the remainder of the decade. Hundreds of state residents were the source of many good-quality reports by MUFON and the Pennsylvania Association for the Study of the Unexplained (PASU). Many of these were close encounter cases.[52]

Other sightings were sporadically reported. On August 11, in Osbornville, New Jersey, a witness reported seeing a shiny, oval object that hovered, became brighter, and took off like a shot, leaving a white trail. It then stopped abruptly, maneuvered, flashed more lights, and shot straight up out of sight.[53] Another case was reported from September 1, in Bangor, Washington. An elliptical-shaped object with windows beamed a light down upon children at a playground. The children said they could see two humanoid-type creatures in the object.[54] Starting in September, a concentration of UFO sightings were reported in the Arkansas towns of Foreman and Ashdown. Over the next four months, the sheriff's office in Little River County took about 60 reports.[55]

On September 9, 1987, the interesting "Joe Le Taxi" landing case took place in France. This involved the sighting of "an intense light and sound phenomenon," followed by leaf damage to a tree and "functional disturbance of the photosynthetic system." A biochemical analysis was carried out by Professor Michel C. L. Bounias of the Biochemistry Laboratory at the INRA (National Institute of Research in Agronomy), University of Avignon.[56]

On October 5, in Southern California's Antelope Valley – a desert region close to Nevada and a major center of aerospace technology – a father and his two daughters (ages 14 and 11) saw a UFO. The Moon was full and the sky clear when, at 10:30 p.m., the older daughter pulled back the curtains of her bedroom. Through the window she saw "a perfectly round object encircled with lights, spinning, and moving slowly at low altitude past the edge of the roof." The younger daughter also saw it, and the girls became afraid. They called their father. He came over and saw the object, but was mystified by it. It looked large, and seemed to have a bulge on its topside as well as a kind of flange around the rim. The object passed from view beyond the rooftops of the apartments across the way. It passed through a narrow corridor between Edwards AFB air space and that controlled by

Palmdale air traffic control. The father reported the sighting to Edwards AFB and the Antelope Valley Sheriff's Department. No follow-up is known or recorded about the incident.[57]

In the middle of October, an interesting multiple witness sighting took place in the Hudson Valley. This was in Candlewood Lake in western Connecticut, a region with a history of UFO sightings during the 1980s. According to one witness, at around 6 p.m. he was driving home from work and saw what looked like a low-flying aircraft pass over trees to his left. He heard no sound and saw no crash, and so remained unconcerned. After making a turn, he noticed four cars stopped with no lights on, mostly on the side of the road. Then his car "just died." He had no electrical power at all. He got out and approached the other drivers, who were out of their cars, too. They said excitedly that a very large and bright aircraft flew over and seemed to have gone down over the hill in the west. The aircraft, they said, was very large, white in color, triangular in shape, and had amber colored lights. They added that it was also silent.

It was getting dark, and the witness saw a glow in the woods. Thinking there might have been a plane crash, he took his flashlight and went in alone, as no one wished to accompany him. He went about a quarter of a mile and came to a hill. The glow on the other side of the hill was getting brighter. As he reached the top, he saw a lighted object through the trees. He climbed down and came to a clearing. To his shock, he saw what looked like a dark triangle hovering in the trees. The object, he later emphasized, was not above the trees, but in them. "Like a ghost," he continued. "I mean an object that size should have broken tree branches and its engines should have been blowing the trees around, but there was nothing, just silence."

He moved closer and heard a noise coming from it. He then saw a figure wearing some kind of suit approaching the object. The witness hid behind a bush and watched "the man or whatever it was" get into the object and look in his direction. The witness heard thoughts in his head saying he should not come closer. He was "more than willing to obey." The figure raised his hand and vanished in a flash of red light. "The object then vanished like someone had just turned it off."

He ran back to the road and saw that only one motorist remained, and decided not to discuss his experience. He did, however, discuss the case with Philip Imbrogno.[58]

Toward the end of 1987, the Soviet Union recorded more interesting UFO reports. The largest display occurred in the Dalnegorsk and Primorye areas on the night of November 28. According to Soviet ufologist reports,

33 unknown objects flew at low altitude over the eastern coast of Primorye, near the Sea of Japan, between 9:10 pm and midnight. Many people saw the spectacle, assuming they were watching aircraft "crashing," although no one heard a sound. They described varied shapes: cylinders, cigars, globes. Inquiries made by Dvuzhilny showed there had been no flights of civil or military aircraft at that time, and that no carrier-rockets had been launched from Soviet cosmodromes. Moreover, continued Dvuzhilny, "the objects observed had nothing in common with the effects of rocket launching that are quite different. They were not like fireballs, ball lightning or plasmoids." Of the 33 UFOs, 13 flew over Dalnegorsk, the scene of a possible previous UFO crash. More than 100 witnesses were questioned by the Far Eastern Commission. The objects also reportedly caused a two minute disruption of electrical circuits, including televisions and computers. According to the Far Eastern Commission, 45 UFOs were registered in the Dalnagorsk region in 1987, with more in subsequent years.[59]

Sightings continued about 1,000 miles to the northeast, in Kamchatka with many sightings of ball-shaped UFOs near the Shiveluch Volcano. One officer correlated their appearance with the scheduled launching of combat vehicles, but others said these small "objects" did not appear in relation to any launching. For example, on December 16, 1987, an hour after a warhead had fallen to the ground, an orange ball was seen moving slowly and silently from north to south. Other sightings like this happened frequently and continued through much of 1988.[60]

Gulf Breeze

Since the mid-1980s, fewer UFOs had been reported worldwide, but 1987 ended with a very important development. Indeed, in terms of controversy, it nearly equaled the significance of the MJ-12 documents. This was the Gulf Breeze phenomenon.[61]

Gulf Breeze, Florida, lies at the Gulf of Mexico, at the very end of the Florida panhandle, just south of Pensacola. It is situated near many active U.S. Air and Naval bases, most notably the Pensacola Naval Air Station, Whiting Field Naval Air Station, Eglin AFB, and Hurlburt Field Air Force Special Operations Command. All of these bases are reachable within a half-hour's drive or less. Further east along the panhandle is Tyndall AFB, about 90 miles away. Roughly five miles west is the Pascagoula Naval Air Station and nearly 100 miles west is Keesler AFB.

On November 11, 1987, the first five photos of an unusual UFO were taken by Ed Walters, a local building contractor and member of the Gulf

Breeze City Planning Board. His wife, Frances, was president of the high school PTA. According to Walters, he was working late that afternoon when, at about 6 p.m., he noticed a light approaching his house from the west. He could barely see it through the branches of a pine tree in his front yard. He went to his front door to get a better view, and was astonished to see an object with the shape of a top, hovering just above the road and showing a glowing ring around its bottom. It had a row of dark squares which were separated with portals between them. His first thought was to call the police, but he realized the object could be gone by the time they arrived and he would have no proof of what he had seen. So he ran into his house and grabbed his Polaroid camera. He then stepped outside the front door and took several photos of the craft before deciding to get closer. As he paused in the street to take more photos, it moved almost directly over his head and hit him with a bright bluish beam, lifting him from the ground. Walters claimed to hear a voice say, "Don't worry, we will not harm you." Images entered his mind, "as if they were turning the pages of a book," said Walters. The next thing he remembered was falling face down onto the road, turning over and finding that the glowing UFO was gone.

The sighting was certainly dramatic, and the photos were formidable. The very first photograph Walters took, in fact, was interesting in that it showed the object clearly behind a tree. If it were a hoax, it was very, very good. However, what gave the sighting more power still were the claims by other witnesses to have seen the same UFO in the sky earlier during the same day. The first to see the object was Billie Zammit who, at about 2:30 a.m., took her dog outside and was

The first Gulf Breeze UFO photo taken by Ed Walters, November 11, 1987, cropped and lightened.

startled to see the object hovering over the canal in her backyard. A blue beam of light came down from the object and illuminated a spot on her dock. In her words, it was "about one mile high, 15 degrees to the northwest and there was a stream of light that came down into our canal." After watching this object for about five minutes she became so frightened that she grabbed the dog and ran into the house.[62] About six hours later, at 8:15 a.m., Jeff Thompson saw a similar object that moved slowly and hovered. Then, as two jets approached from the east, it zoomed upward with a flash of light. About nine hours later, and about half an hour before

Ed Walters' sighting, Charles and Doris Somerby saw the same object moving through the Gulf Breeze sky in a direction that would take it toward Walters' location. Charles was the former editor of the local newspaper, *The Gulf Breeze Sentinel*, and his stepson Duane Cook was the current editor.

The following week, on November 17, Walters took his photographs to the *Sentinel*. He wanted anonymity, however, so he told Duane that a person wishing to remain anonymous had given him the photos. Walters also related "Mr. X's" bizarre encounter with the craft. Soon after, he wrote a letter to the newspaper from Mr. X. With some misgivings, Duane planned to publish the photos. But then his father-in-law and mother visited the newspaper office and saw "Mr. X's" photos. They told Duane they had seen the same thing. All misgivings were removed and Duane published the photos and Mr. X's story. The story became big almost immediately. But for Walters, the journey was just beginning.

On November 20, he heard a hum and voices, as if communications were being made between individuals. Going outside, he noticed a small dot of light which was falling from the sky. It stopped and began to hover. He took a photo of it. On December 2, Walters received another visit. He was awakened at about 3:30 a.m. by the sound of his dog barking. He walked to his French doors and opened the blinds. There he saw a creature about four feet tall with large black eyes. He panicked and fell down from the shock. According to Walters, the being stared at him for a moment and then began to walk away. Walters followed it to the porch, but as soon as his body was no longer covered by the porch roof he was hit by a blue beam from above and immobilized. Meanwhile, the creature fled into the vacant field at the back of his house. The beam disappeared, and Walters could move again. He ran into the house, grabbed his camera, ran back outside and photographed the UFO shooting a blue beam into the field. "I believe that it was picking up the creature I had seen," wrote Walters. This was his eleventh photo.

More events followed on the morning of December 5th. A UFO hovered below the tree level near the high school behind Walters' house. Walters saw it from the fenced-in pool area behind his house. He heard a voice say "Do not resist. Stay where you are. You are in danger. We will not harm you… Zehaas." It then increased in height and hovered above the trees near the school. Walters photographed the object. According to Walters, the object moved toward him and he heard a voice say, "Step forward." Walters' angry response was "Come and get me." Then the object suddenly zipped upward and disappeared.

Before long, MUFON and CUFOS were looking into Ed Walters' story, as well as CSICOP and numerous independent investigators. MUFON considered the "Mr. X" sighting reports to be important, not because there were photos (which, as they knew, could in principle have been faked) but because of the reports by other witnesses who claimed to have seen the same object. Starting in November, MUFON investigator Donald Ware began to suspect that Walters, not the fictitious Mr. X, had taken the photographs. Late in November, he enlisted a friend of Walters' son to serve

Gulf Breeze photo #11, Dec. 2, 1987

as a "spy." The young man was very familiar with the Walters house, but never found anything unusual.

For the next several years, Gulf Breeze became the most electrifying and controversial UFO case, an ongoing event that drew more and more visitors, and Ed Walters was at the center of the storm. In time, MUFON officially supported Walters (MUFON Director Walter Andrus eventually called it "one of the most incredible cases in modern UFO history"), while CUFOS and CSICOP argued that he had hoaxed his photographs. By the end of 1987, however, all that lay in the future, as well as the fact that Gulf Breeze would soon become, like Roswell and the MJ-12 papers, one of Ufology's most polarizing issues.

The Lear Letters

That most interesting year of 1987 ended with yet one more controversy and portent of things to come. In December, two important letters by John Lear were published to the Internet's UFO forum known as Paranet. John Lear was the son of William Lear, who invented the Lear Jet and the 8-track tape. During the mid-1950s, the elder Lear claimed to have seen a UFO while flying in his aircraft. He had also made suggestive statements to the press that hinted of anti-gravity research in the defense community. By the late 1950s, however, the media had ceased reporting on such developments.

The younger Lear was also a man of significant accomplishment. Forty-five years old in 1987, John Lear was one of the world's top commercial pilots. According to a biographical statement at that time, he was a captain for a major charter airline, had flown 160 types of aircraft in over 50 countries, and held 17 speed records for the Lear Jet. He had flown missions worldwide for the CIA and other government agencies, and at the time was the only pilot to hold every airman certificate issued by the FAA.[63] He also inherited his father's interest in UFOs. By late 1987, John Lear was MUFON's State Director for Nevada.[64]

But it was Lear's public letters that gained him notoriety. For some time, he had been talking with Paul Bennewitz, and in two letters released on an Internet bulletin board in December 1987, he strongly reflected the themes Bennewitz had been dealing with.[65]

"The United States Government," wrote Lear, "has been in business with little grey extraterrestrials for about 20 years" and – "with the best of intentions" – has betrayed its citizens. Germany probably recovered a flying saucer in 1939, and the U.S. government has been examining flying saucers since at least 1946. UFOs were also recovered near Roswell, Aztec, and Laredo. The creatures operating this technology are vastly more advanced than us, and James Forrestal (incorrectly referred to as "General" by Lear) committed suicide over the "horrible truth."

There were several types of alien species, according to Lear, including three types of "Greys," various human-looking types, even inter-dimensional beings (oddly, he did not mention any reptilian types). Direct communication between at least one of these alien groups and the U.S. Government was initiated on April 30, 1964 at Holloman AFB in New Mexico. Then, between 1969 and 1971, MJ-12 made a deal with the aliens by which they would secretly receive alien technology. In return, however, they would ignore abductions of people and suppress information on cattle mutilations. The aliens said these abductions were simply a standard monitoring of "developing civilizations," and MJ-12 insisted that abductee names be submitted to themselves and the National Security Council. During 1972 and 1973, Lear wrote, the secret facility at Groom Lake, Nevada (still unknown to the general public in 1987), was closed so that a huge underground base could be built "for and with the help of the EBE's."

MJ-12 was pleased by its deal with the devil. But problems soon became all-too apparent. The alien need for body parts – both human and other – was much greater than they had let on. At least some of these aliens had a "genetic disorder" – possibly due to past wars or other mishaps – which had resulted in an atrophied digestive system. As a result, they used "an enzyme or hormonal secretion obtained from the tongues and throats of cows or humans." This secretion was mixed with other substances and absorbed through the skin, through which waste was also excreted. In other words, according to Lear, aliens consumed the enzymes and blood of cattle and humans, often apparently while the victims were still living.

Body parts were taken to underground laboratories, one of which was near Dulce, New Mexico, deep inside Archuleta Mesa. This was an enormous, jointly occupied (CIA-alien) facility where humans of all ages were kept in large test tube-like vats. The facility at Groom Lake was also apparently involved in this program. Incidentally, even though the Groom Lake facility was now equipped with alien technology, only the aliens were able to use it. Thus, by the late 1970s, the "deal" was not looking very advantageous, after all. Then, in 1979, "an altercation of sorts" occurred at the Dulce laboratory. Several people had discovered the gruesome truth about what was going on there, but were trapped inside. Delta Force was called in to try and free them, but 66 soldiers died in a futile effort.

After this, MJ-12 realized "that things were not going as planned." It became clear that the scope of the alien abduction program was massive – much more than a case of "simple monitoring." Aliens were inserting probes into human brains. They were making post-hypnotic suggestions about something important "that will occur in the next 2 to 5 years" (presumably between 1989 and 1992), at which time they would give certain instructions. They were creating a human-alien hybrid race. And many of the nation's missing children were actually being consumed by the aliens as food.

Not surprisingly, Lear continued, the prevailing mood among MJ-12 was close to panic by the early 1980s. All through the 1970s and early 1980s, they had promoted the "Good ET" concept to the public through such movies as "Close Encounters of the Third Kind" and "ET: The Extraterrestrial." They had even been planning to reveal the ET reality by the late 1980s. That plan now had to be scrapped. One faction wanted to alert the world to the horrible truth; the other argued that secrecy remained paramount, and that anti-ET weapons must be secretly developed under the guise of the Strategic Defense Initiative (SDI). According to Lear, MJ-12 member Edward Teller managed that project. Other MJ-12 members named by Lear included Henry Kissinger, Bobby Ray Inman, and "possibly Admiral [John] Poindexter."

Lear dropped other bombshells. He said that William Moore was being used as a conduit by MJ-12 to release information about the alien presence on Earth. Moore even received a videotape of an interview by two "well known newsmen" of a military officer associated with MJ-12 (Moore denied this). This officer gave information about the history of MJ-12, the recovery of flying saucers, the existence of a live alien (one of three living aliens, designated as EBE1, EBE2, and EBE3) being held in a facility at Los Alamos, New Mexico. This officer mentioned Harold Brown, Richard Helms, General Vernon Walters, and (the late Theodore) Von Karman as somehow connected to MJ-12. Most explosive of all was the officer's statement that the EBEs claimed to have "created" Christ. They even possessed a holographic recording of his crucifixion. Moore allegedly showed this interview video to about "five well-known persons" to judge their reactions. One of them was his friend, the well-known radio commentator Paul Harvey (who was apparently skeptical of at least some of this material).

Lear speculated that Moore might be an MJ-12 agent. As evidence, he offered the Lee Graham episode, as well as Moore's insistence that cattle mutilations were a "hoax" fostered by Linda Moulton Howe. Lear reasoned that if these events were to force a disclosure of the existence of aliens – and at the same time if these aliens were believed to be hostile – MJ-12 might decide to admit to aliens while concealing the more explosive information about mutilations and abductions. Thus, Moore might simply be toeing the party line.

What was actually going on, wondered Lear? After having engaged in probably hundreds of thousands of abductions and built countless underground bases, were the aliens ever planning to return home? Were they planning something big for the future? The most likely scenario, he thought, was that "the invasion is essentially complete and everything is over but the screaming." Forget the mass landings and ray guns, said Lear. A highly advanced civilization could probably complete its program before anyone knew what happened.

Lear's letters immediately made waves. His background and credibility were hard to question. He seemed sincere to those who met with him. Still, could he be plying disinformation? After all, his claims were far beyond mainstream UFO research, and even beyond the cutting edge established by Budd Hopkins and Whitley Strieber. Aliens eating humans sounded like a bad science fiction plotline, not anything resembling responsible ufology.

People wanted answers from Lear. In May 1988, MUFON Director of Investigations Dan Wright posed a series of open questions to Lear, nearly all of which concerned Lear's sources. Lear answered that most of his information came from confidential sources within the intelligence community, while a lesser portion came from open sources and his own "informed speculation."[66]

Deciding what to think about John Lear has never been easy for many UFO researchers. Was he genuinely reporting inside information, as he claimed, or spreading disinformation to undermine the credibility of the field? This author has spoken confidentially to several individuals with reasonably good connections to Lear. All have indicated that he was indeed in a good position to have gained potentially "inside" information; several commented on his erudition and broad-ranging intelligence; many were skeptical or even frankly incredulous at his claims. The discrepancy is not easy to resolve.

1987: The Year in Review

In every respect, 1987 marked a watershed in the history of UFOs. The abduction phenomenon moved to the forefront not simply of UFO research, but became a topic of national discussion. The idea of a "government conspiracy" also became a major issue. The release of the MJ-12 documents had much to do with this, as did Timothy Good's *Above Top Secret*. Later in the year, Philip Imbrogno's research on the Hudson Valley cases was also published, adding fuel to the fire.[67] Many researchers were surprised by the generally positive mainstream coverage they received, particularly on television. As the year progressed, more and more of the attention became critical, often zealously so, as in the over-the-top review of *Above Top Secret* in the August 1 edition of the *London Spectator* ("an evil book.")[68]

Such strong reactions could be expected, considering the deep implications of all this new research. By its very nature, the abduction phenomenon raised troubling questions: who were these abductors and what was their agenda? The study of UFOs was no longer a safe, theoretical, intellectual endeavor, but the confrontation with a truly *alien* intelligence that seemed cold and manipulative. It was also a far cry from the idea of friendly "space brothers." In its own way, the MJ-12 topic also brought an unsettling sense of danger. What if the fundamental claims about MJ-12 were true? What if there was a secret agency dedicated to maintaining control and secrecy over the UFO topic? Disclosing its existence could threaten the foundations of political stability, to say nothing of exposing secrets that could be very dark indeed. Hence the importance of the statements by John Lear, which built directly upon the foundations laid by the MJ-12 controversy and opened Pandora's box.

Lear's letters heralded another new factor in UFO research. This was the world-changing nature of the Internet. Undoubtedly, the existence of Internet newsgroups like Paranet enabled his statements to attract immediate and widespread attention. This would have been vastly more difficult in earlier years. The Internet, even at this early stage, was showing very robust capabilities in easing communication among researchers throughout the United States, and indeed anyone in the world able to get "on line." It would help to transform a great deal of UFO research in the next few years, just as it would change so much else in the world.

Finally, the sightings of something unusual over Gulf Breeze, Florida, proved to be an energizing factor that brought many people to ufology. It also contributed to a deep rift among researchers that would last for quite some time.

Thus, 1987 marked the year that UFO research exploded. It was an exciting year for those who lived through it, and anticipation was high that the following year would bring new developments and revelations. Indeed, according to Jerome Clark, rumors persisted at this time that the orchestrators of the cover-up were "deeply concerned about the direction of UFO events" and feared that the cover-up might soon be over. This might force them to "come clean."[69] Such rumors had existed for years, of course. The coming year would see this one only grow stronger.

The Knowles Family Encounter

With the exception of Gulf Breeze and a few other developments, 1988 was not especially notable for UFO sightings. Even so, several of these were memorable, interesting, and occasionally well-documented.

One of the strangest cases occurred early in the year along the south coast of Western Australia. A family was driving east across the continent, along the desolate Eyre Highway. Faye Knowles was accompanied by her sons Patrick (24), Sean (21), and Wayne (18), as well as their two dogs. It was 4 a.m. on January 21, and the sky was still dark. Sean was driving, and the family had just passed the tiny town of Madura on the way to Mundrabilla.[70]

A bright light appeared ahead, low over the road. As the family approached, it looked like "a slightly angular egg in an egg-cup shape." It swayed back and forth and was nearly blinding. Sean approached very close to it and swerved to miss it. In the process, he almost hit a station wagon coming at him in the other direction. After this near-miss, the egg-like object began to follow the station wagon. Fascinated by this unknown object, Sean made a U-turn to pursue it, and for a short while followed the station wagon and the bright light. However, he soon developed second thoughts, as it looked like the object had changed course and was coming toward him. Now positively frightened, he turned around again and tried to speed away from the UFO.

The family was in a panic, and Sean was frantically driving at close to 100 mph when they all heard a loud thud on the roof of their car; a weight or force was pressing down on them. Worse still, the family felt their car being lifted off the road, or at least this is what they all later insisted. Faye Knowles bravely rolled down the rear window and reached for the roof. She felt something very warm, soft, and rubbery that covered her hand in a blackish dust. "It felt like a warm sponge," she said. Patrick, in the front passenger seat, rolled down his window and became covered in dust. A smell like dead bodies filled the car. This was followed by a high-pitched sound which agitated the dogs.

The family became disoriented. Their voices felt slower and lower in pitch. They thought they were going to die. Faye said she felt something "going into our heads," and Patrick felt that his "brain was being sucked out." According to the family, the car was in the air this whole time (how high or how long is not known). But now they hit the road, bursting the rear right tire. Sean screeched to a halt and the family ran out, hiding for 15 minutes by some bushes before changing the tire and driving to the nearest town.

During the Knowles family encounter with this UFO, a truck driver named Graham Henley – who was ahead of the Knowles' on the road – saw an intensely bright light in his rear view mirror for five minutes, although he did not see any car headlights beneath it. He said the light looked like a "big fried egg hung upside down," rather similar to the description offered by Sean Knowles. Shortly after Henley pulled into Mundrabilla, the Knowles family arrived in a state of panic and disorientation. They described their experience to him; he inspected the damaged tire, saw the dents, and smelled something burnt. Accounts differ as to whether he saw the fine black ash inside the car: some say he did; others indicate he saw only normal road dust.[71] Henley then went with another trucker to inspect the scene of the incident. They found fresh skid marks and footprints.

Ten hours after the incident, the family spoke to police in Ceduna, who noted their emotional distress and the dents in the roof. Samples were collected for forensic analysis. Meanwhile, police soon learned that the same or a similar object was witnessed 30 minutes later and 50 miles away from the Knowles encounter by some tuna fishermen in the Great Australian Bight. These men claimed that a UFO buzzed their boat, and that the crew suffered the same kind of voice distortion reported by the Knowles family. The police investigator was certain the fishermen could not have known about the other incident. The Royal Australian Air Force stated that it had no aircraft in the region at the time.

The police forensic analysis apparently was never conducted, but about half of the material was later returned to Australian ufologists Keith Basterfield and Ray Brooke, who gave it to an independent laboratory for testing. The test revealed ordinary materials: sodium chloride, sodium, aluminum, magnesium, sulphur, silicon, potassium, chlorine, clay particles and calcium.

Meanwhile, the affair quickly became a media sensation. The family was offered a fee by Australian Channel 7 television in return for exclusive rights. Not only did this make it difficult for independent researchers to gain access to the family, but the family soon became disillusioned by the circus atmosphere and ended all interviews. Channel 7 arranged for additional samples to be collected from the car. These were tested at the Australian Mineral Development Laboratories (AMDEL), which found a similar composition to the independent analysis. AMDEL's conclusion: this was dust from a tire blow-out. The smell, smoke, and vibrations from the incident were attributed to running on a blown tire. The lab also concluded that the roof dents were not recent.

A third set of samples were taken from the car some 700 miles from Mundrabilla, by the Victoria UFO Society (VUFORS). Materials were sent to two different laboratories, again with commonplace results: brake dust, ordinary dust, dog hairs, fibers and common elements such as carbon, oxygen, aluminum, silicon and calcium. However, one analysis, by Dr. Richard Haines in the United States, concluded that the interior and exterior dust were different and that there was a "possible trace of astatine, which is a radioactive chemical that can only be produced synthetically." Astatine has a very short half-life, and its presence was inferred only when the particles were under extreme magnification, as they exhibited signs of potential radiation. What makes this of possible importance is that Faye Knowles' hand became red and swollen in the days after the event, a sign of possible radiation exposure (and something that had occurred in 1980 to Betty Cash after her encounter with a diamond-shaped UFO near the town of Huffman, Texas).

Skeptics offered several possible explanations for the encounter. The family had been on the road for 24 hours and could easily have been overtired. In such a state the first hint of a rising sun could have combined with atmospheric conditions or some other optical illusion to startle them. One physicist said the culprit was a rare carbonaceous meteorite. Others blamed a rare type of electrical storm.

There are good reasons to be cautious about the Mundrabilla encounter. The laboratory tests offered nothing conclusive. Of course, unless the dust were from the Moon, one wonders what conclusions could be reached. Still, the potential of radiation cannot be discounted. The possibilities seem to be either a gross misidentification of some unexpected but natural phenomena by overtired and panicky people, or else something solid, intelligent, and perhaps radioactive was attacking cars – and boats – in Southern Australia. If the latter, one has to wonder about the black dust, which according to the Knowles family smelled like dead bodies. A gruesome scenario comes to mind, easily leading the casual or serious observer fervently to hope the truth lies in the depths of an overtired, overactive, imagination.[72]

The U.S. Coast Guard Encounters a UFO

Six weeks after the Knowles family encounter in Australia, another dramatic UFO event occurred. This one was in the United States, and was much better documented. On the evening of March 4, 1988 near Eastland, Ohio, not far from the Pennsylvania border, Sheila Baker and her children were driving home along the shore of Lake Erie. At 6:30 p.m., their attention was drawn to a large, bright object apparently hovering over the lake. It seemed almost like a blimp. Bright lights appeared at each end of it, and the whole thing was rocking end to end like a seesaw. The brighter of the two lights was strobing. Once home, she persuaded her husband, Henry, to accompany her and the children to the beach.

There, standing on the shore of Lake Erie, they all saw the object. It was gun-metal grey and positively enormous – Henry later said it was "larger than a football held at arm's length." It made no sound that they could hear. Somehow, however, it caused the lake ice to rumble and crack, perhaps by application of heat. The object then began to circle slowly over part of the lake, coming nearly overhead at just 1/4 mile altitude.

Feeling nervous, they drove back and watched the object from their home. From there, they saw it descend; red and blue blinking lights were along its bottom edge. More interesting, however, were five or six bright yellow triangular lights that detached from its side. These lights hovered around the main object, then darted and zig-zagged in the night sky at high speeds. Henry believed these objects were smaller than a one-seat Cessna and "crossed 50 mile stretches low over the ice in the snap of a finger." They approached the shore, made right-angle turns, and shot straight up. Several passes were toward the nearby Perry Nuclear Plant. One neighbor of the Bakers also saw this display, and tried (unsuccessfully) to photograph the object.

In response to several phone calls, two members of the Coast Guard, Seaman James Powers and Petty Officer John Knaub, drove to the beach. As they arrived, the triangular objects approached them, prompting them to turn off their vehicle's headlights. The men continued to watch the triangles fly over the lake, one of which accelerated straight at them, then veered east, zoomed straight up, and came down beside the parent object. The Bakers were back at the beach now, and listened to the Coast Guard personnel communicate by two-way radio with their base in Detroit. What they overheard was:

> . . . be advised the object appears to be landing on the lake .... There are other objects moving around it. Be advised these smaller objects are going at high rates of speed. There are no engine noises and they are very, very low. Be advised these are not planets.

At the same time, 15 miles to the southeast, not far from the Perry Nuclear Plant, Cindy Hale was walking her dog. She saw a triangular light hovering above her, and her dog began to whine. The triangle flashed a sequence of multicolored lights, and she responded by flicking her cigarette lighter. This went on for 30 minutes, until the triangle accelerated and left without a sound.

Another local resident, Tim Keck, was watching the stars through his telescope when he saw a bright triangular object. Luckily, he had his camera with him – a cheap 110 Instamatic he had received as a Burger King promotion, but it worked. He took a picture of the object before it silently moved beyond the horizon, catching about half of it before it moved fully out of the frame. Because of the nature of the camera, part of the object appeared beyond the formal edge of the negative's frame.

Tim Keck's photograph of a triangular UFO, 1988

Meanwhile, back at the lake, the large ship was nearly directly on the ice. Henry Baker continued to listen to Powers and Knaub tell their base, "you should be advised that the object is now shining lights all over the lake and it's turning different colors." The ice made cracking noises so loud that Powers and Knaub had to yell in order to be heard. Suddenly the triangles were back, returning one by one into the large object. The ice boomed louder and louder, then all the lights went off, the ice stopped making noise, and everything became "dead silent." After another 30 minutes, the object could not be seen. The witnesses could only assume it had gone below the surface.

On the morning of the 5th, unusually huge pieces of broken ice were seen where the object had been. That day, a Coast Guard representative told the Bakers that they had been instructed by the Army and NASA (whom Sheila had also phoned) *not* to investigate the matter further, nor to take their ice cutter out to the lake to examine the ice. The matter was "out of their league and out of their hands." They said all information was being forwarded to Wright-Patterson AFB and a facility in Detroit. For its part, Wright-Patterson refused to confirm or deny any interest in the matter.

The Coast Guard created an Incident Report on March 5, 1988, describing the event in concise detail. The report stated that a large object had landed a quarter mile east of the nuclear power plant, and that it had

> ... dispersed 3-5 smaller flying objects that were zipping around rather quickly. These objects had red, green, white, and yellow lights on them that strobed intermittently. They also had the ability to stop and hover in mid-flight.[73]

During the night of March 5, Sheila Baker saw what she thought was the same UFO, hovering over the lake, only at a higher altitude than the night before. The Coast Guard sent some men out who arrived too late and saw nothing. The Coast Guard then contacted the Lost Nation Airport in Willoughby, Ohio. The control tower operator told them that "the two bright lights" were Venus and Jupiter, which were in near-alignment. The flashing lights were "gases in the atmosphere." Never mind that Baker did not mention two bright lights, but a large object. The Coast Guard promptly wrote a follow-up report on the original encounter, laying the whole matter to rest.[74] The entire series of events was then debunked in the *Cleveland Plain Dealer* and other newspapers.[75]

Whatever the cause of the March 5 sighting, to attribute the events of March 4 to Venus and Jupiter goes well beyond the boundaries of credibility. MUFON, to its credit, continued to investigate the sighting, even placing a classified ad in the newspaper looking for witnesses. The tactic worked; others did come forward, including Cindy Hale, Tim Keck, and others. All of these people described UFO activity from that night between 10 and 10:30 p.m., and all described triangles. Bruce Maccabee analyzed Keck's photograph, determining that it was a legitimate image of an unexplained object. Years later, Shiela and Henry Baker remained adamant about what they saw.[76]

Amazingly, according to Hudson Valley-based UFO researcher Philip Imbrogno, a number of triangular objects were seen by multiple witnesses near the Indian Point nuclear facility in New York State on March 4, 1988 – that is, the same night as the sightings in Ohio. Not much in the way of followup occurred, however, and little else is known of the incident.[77]

Due to the caliber of the witnesses, the official documentary evidence, the photographic evidence, and the intrinsic nature of the event itself, the Lake Erie UFO incident must be considered one of the most compelling UFO events in modern history. All evidence points to the conclusion that an intelligently operated and enormous object came down over the Lake Erie ice; that this object released several bright triangles that flew beyond the ability of any known aircraft; that these triangles were interested in the nearby nuclear facility; that they interacted with the witnesses who observed them; that the Coast Guard officials were convinced the event was something important; that the Coast Guard itself was prevented from pursuing this incident by higher agencies; and that the matter was successfully disabled by the national security apparatus and the media.

There was one other interesting triangle sighting during the spring of 1988. This took place on the other side of the Atlantic Ocean, in Stafford, Britain, on the evening of May 16. A couple out on a stroll saw two triangular shapes hovering over trees. The objects were "lit up, but somehow they didn't seem like solid objects." Very suddenly, they disappeared and then reappeared, then finally disappeared for good. The objects were "absolutely silent." Another witness saw the object through binoculars, accompanied by two neighbors. She saw it move slowly and silently across the sky, looking exactly as described by the couple. She commented on an array of lights that were orange, red, and blue. Jenny Randles, speaking for the British UFO Research Association (BUFORA) told the press that the sighting was probably the American stealth fighter – not yet officially revealed but widely assumed to exist

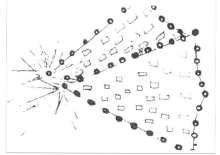

Witness drawing of the two triangles over Stafford, UK, May 16, 1988.

– or possibly a remotely piloted vehicle.[78]

It is interesting how the stealth fighter and bomber have so frequently been used to explain UFO sightings. In this instance, the connection is specious. While both aircraft are quieter and can fly at slower speeds than previous generations of aircraft, they cannot simply drift across the sky or hover. Nor are they silent. On top of this would be the illogic of flying a stealth fighter at low altitudes over populated British towns when the aircraft's very existence remained classified. Nor do they light up like Christmas trees. The theory of a remotely piloted vehicle holds more promise, although it would be a matter of great significance that an RPV would be the solution to the tenacious mystery of the triangles.

Gulf Breeze: 1988

The sightings in Gulf Breeze, Florida, became a major event in UFO history not because Ed Walters took many photographs of unidentified objects starting in 1987, nor because other people claimed to have seen the same objects. The Gulf Breeze sightings became a major event because the sightings simply would not cease. Throughout 1988 and beyond, this region near Pensacola became the major hotspot of UFO activity in the United States.

Still, during 1988 it was the photographs of Ed Walters that amazed
people the most and garnered most
of the attention. Walter had sightings and experiences through 1988,
continuing to take photographs that
were astounding for their clarity and
dramatic import. For example, during the evening of January 12, 1988,
he took what is possibly his most
famous photo – a brightly lit object
hovering just above a road.

The Gulf Breeze "Road Shot" of Jan. 12,
1988, cropped and light enhanced.

The MUFON investigation began in November but it wasn't until early January, 1988, that Walters was willing to admit that he had been "Mr. X".[*] Local investigators Donald Ware and Charles Flanagan interviewed Walters at length, learning for the first time of his many sightings and photos that had not been reported in the newspaper. They interviewed the

---

[*] He made this admission to the MUFON investigators only; he did not allow his name to be used in public until 1990, as described below.

Walters family, feeling that Ed and his wife Frances were truthful. Budd Hopkins visited in February, gaining the same impression. Hopkins then asked Bruce Maccabee to review the photographic evidence. Maccabee was skeptical, but arrived on February 19. After spending several days interviewing Walters and performing photo experiments with Walters's camera, he was still undecided.[79]

Meanwhile, Ed Walters passed two polygraph tests given by a skeptical polygraphist, Harvey McLaughlin, on February 18 and 23, 1988. On the 26th, he took ten photographs of a UFO with a wax-sealed stereo camera provided by Thomas Deuley and San Antonio MUFON. Walters also sketched this object, which was cigar-shaped with many lights. Walter Andrus flew to Pensacola and arranged a press conference for March 4. There, with television cameras documenting the process, Andrus cut away the camera's wax seal, removed the film canister, and handed it to the manager of a local photo service for developing. All ten exposures contained four images of the object, since each of the four lenses in the camera had recorded an image. All images were given to local newspapers and television, as well as to Deuley and Maccabee for analysis.[80]

Throughout March and April, a major sighting flap occurred in Gulf Breeze, independent of Ed Walters. Many of these cases were investigated by MUFON. On March 2, one woman saw a twenty-foot long, dark oval object slowly pass through a wooded area adjoining her property. She ran outside and saw evenly spaced, round yellow-white lights. During the five minutes the lights were in view, she was amazed that they avoided the trees as they continued in a straight line through the woods.[81] During the early evening of March 11, a minister and a babysitter observed a silent rotating disc hover nearby, then move off beyond a treeline. It gave off a bluish light from "windows" on the lower half.[82] On the 14th, two women, while driving, followed a "disc with portholes" for three minutes. It gave off orange light and had a ring of light underneath. At one point, it moved directly in front of their car. They tried unsuccessfully to photograph it.[83] On March 17th, and 20th, Ed Walters took more UFO photos with his stereo camera, still telling the world that the anonymous "Mr. X" had taken the pictures. On April 28, a retired military aircraft technician saw a circular object traveling above the treetops as he was driving. When he turned onto a road toward his house, he saw that it had a bright orange light at the bottom, emitted a blue beam of light across the highway, and another beam downward. He stopped and watched it for ten seconds or so. It was quite close to him: about 150 feet away and 100 feet above ground.

His car window was open but he heard no noise. He drove quickly the rest of the distance to his house and went inside to get his wife. However, by the time they went outside it was gone. Ten to fifteen minutes later he saw three small aircraft circle the area.[84] This sighting occurred less than a mile from the location of Ed Walters' "road shot" described above.

There is another interesting case from that spring, although it was not reported or investigated until the following year. At around 9 p.m., a woman while driving saw a very large, dark "arrowhead" or boomerang-shaped object moving above nearby treetops. It was slow enough that a jogger could have kept up with it. She estimated it to be more than 150 feet wide, and more than 100 feet long. Around its entire perimeter were floodlight-sized white lights. She slowed down her car, and noticed other drivers doing the same. The object passed slowly over her car. Through her open sunroof, she noticed that the underside comprised sections and panels rather than a continuously smooth surface. She drove on, apparently passed it again, and continued to see it in her rearview mirror for a short while. The sighting lasted for five minutes.[85]

Gulf Breeze - Criticisms

The Gulf Breeze sightings were spectacular. Like those in the Hudson Valley previously, they were poised to break out into a major media event. A documentary had already been produced, and the sightings were on the ascendant. But criticisms surfaced early. In the spring of 1988, Robert D. Boyd and Ray Stanford argued that the Ed Walters photographs were "most probably" a hoax. Stanford was a long-time UFO investigator and photographic analyst. Studying the photos from Walters' first sighting, he argued that the cloud images in the sky proved that they were not taken on November 11, as Walters had claimed. However, a MUFON investigation showed that Stanford's analysis was incorrect: Stanford had mixed up sighting directions. Therefore Stanford withdrew his analysis.

Boyd was a member of both CUFOS and MUFON, and had been asked by Andrus to help investigate. He prepared a report and then co-authored a paper with CUFOS Director Mark Rodeghier. "Ufologists have better things to do with their valuable time and resources," the two wrote, "than spend endless hours listening to tales of UFO visitations from Mr. X." The fact that Walters passed two polygraphs was irrelevant – "sociopathic personalities" could be lying and still pass such tests, they wrote.[86] (Walters' polygraphist, who claimed to have done several thousand such tests, later expressed his opinion that Ed was *not* a sociopath capable of faking the test.)[87]

Jerome Clark of CUFOS also added what many people were thinking: that the photographs simply did not pass the smell test. The Gulf Breeze UFO, as photographed by Walters, was unlike any other UFO photograph. Clark thought the images looked like small models. The fact that "Mr. X" had photographed this object so many times, or that he claimed to be in some kind of telepathic communication with the beings inside, certainly did not help.[88]

The position of CUFOS caused a rift with MUFON's leadership. Andrus thought some of the criticisms bordered on slander. Boyd's report was "biased" and "in direct contradiction to good investigative practices, procedures, and policies," Andrus wrote. When Boyd pointed out that Ed Walters' wife had not even signed any formal statement supporting her husband, Frances Walters replied with a 27-page rebuttal to each of the Boyd's accusations.[89]

These early Gulf Breeze criticisms focused primarily on the photographs by Ed Walters. Although this left out the already large number of other witnesses from consideration, it is true that Walters was always in the thick of it. Starting Tuesday, April 26, 1988, Walters began a nightly "skywatch" at Shoreline Park. He wanted to find out if he could get a good stereo photo with a special "self-referencing" stereo camera he had built according to the design proposed by Bruce Maccabee. He and Frances went out during three nights. They saw nothing. On Friday, Frances had to leave with their son to attend a four-day high school "band trip." She implored Ed to stay at home during the nights that she was gone, but he rejected her request. He saw nothing Friday night so he went out again Saturday night. He set up the camera on the shore at about 11:30 p.m. and waited. This time he did have a sighting during which he succeeded in taking stereo photos using two Polaroid 600 LMS Sun cameras, mounted 2 feet apart and supported by a heavy tripod. It was 1 a.m. on May 1, and Walters was in his pickup truck when he heard the familiar hum in his head. He immediately manned his cameras. At 1:10 a.m., he saw a lighted object in the southeast sky toward the Bob Sikes Bridge. He took excellent simultaneous photos with the right and left cameras, each image clearly showing an object with a dim horizontal glowing line, and an intense glow coming from beneath. Walters also noticed a smaller lighted object closer to him. This startled him and he flinched and squeezed the right hand camera shutter button, taking one more photo with the right camera. Immediately, he said, he was hit by a white light and passed out. He awoke lying face down in the sand twenty feet away from his cameras. Feeling dizzy, he walked back to his cameras and noticed that the time was now 2:25 a.m. There was a black substance under his fingernails and a bad odor emanating from his right hand. Suddenly he thought of his daughter at home alone. He immediately picked up the camera and drove home where he sat outside her bedroom door until dawn.

The next morning at home, he noticed a red mark on his forehead between his eyes, red marks on his temples, and a bump at the back of his head. The marks remained visible for days and MUFON investigator Charles Flanagan photographed them. During the following weeks, Maccabee analyzed the UFO images. The excellent parallax data, which included images of lights on the Bob Sikes bridge that provided a reference for calculations, enabled him to deduce that the bright light was about 500 feet away and 14 feet in diameter. The smaller object was 134 feet away and about 3 feet long. Although a hoax was remotely possible, Maccabee concluded, it would have required exceptional photographic sophistication, well beyond the capabilities of Walters.

The investigators of the case wrote in the *MUFON UFO Journal* that "the overwhelming evidence is in. Gulf Breeze is indeed one of the most incredible cases in modern UFO history...."[90] Maccabee was also won over. He cited many reasons: the evidence of the stereo photographs; Walters twice passing a polygraph test; the inability of local investigators to find any proof of hoax; an unexplained circle of dead grass behind the Walters home; Frances' testimony; the many UFO reports (including some with photographs) by others in Gulf Breeze; Walters' "obvious distress" when describing to Maccabee his May 1 sighting and missing time experience just 12 hours after it happened; Maccabee's failure to find any reason in Walters' background to create a UFO hoax; Walters' continual cooperation in carrying out the many requests for information and his willingness to perform experiments that could have provided conclusive proof of a hoax.

Walters also had gone through several psychological tests and eight hours of hypnotic regression by Dr. Dan C. Overlade, a clinical psychologist who had been the President of the Florida Psychological Association. This appeared to uncover numerous abduction experiences, including from May 1. Overlade felt that Ed was a "classic abductee." Like the polygraph tester, Harvey McLaughlin, Overlade believed that Walters was sincere, entirely normal and not a sociopath.[91]

There matters stood until late June 1988. Then, at the MUFON Symposium in Lincoln, Nebraska, key members of CUFOS (including

Jerome Clark, Donald Schmitt, and George Eberhard) listened to detailed analyses of the Gulf Breeze photographs by Maccabee and Andrus. Maccabee, who took about three hours to present his complete report, did not go so far as to pronounce the Walters photographs to be genuine. Instead, he argued that they could not be easily written off as a hoax. Referring to the many other sightings in the area, he reasoned it was illogical to declare Walters' sightings a hoax while accepting all or any of the similar reports as true. This was especially so regarding sightings in which the witnesses claimed to have seen the same thing that Walters photographed.[92] The CUFOS members also met with investigator Donald Ware, who presented evidence of about 65 "non-Walters" sightings by Gulf Breeze residents. These objects seemed very much like those in Walters' photographs. The CUFOS contingent was persuaded that their skeptical position was premature. Clark publicly changed his mind. "Gulf Breeze proponents," he wrote, "clearly have the lead in the debate." Doubters, he said, first had to explain where Maccabee went wrong and what all those other witnesses were seeing.[93]

But doubters remained. Researchers Richard Hall and Willy Smith admitted the difficulties of a hoax, yet remained agnostic, perhaps skeptical. In the following months they argued that claims had outstripped the evidence, and no one other than Maccabee had done any photo analysis. The claim that there were a large number of supporting cases was "totally unfounded." they said. Worse still, Ed and Frances were in the process of publishing a book, which threw doubt over their motivations, and they were even receiving help from Ware, Hopkins, and Maccabee. This lack of detachment was not scientific, argued Hall and Smith – outside investigation was necessary. They were especially suspicious of Ed Walters, and continued to suspect he was hoaxing, using his knowledge of taking double exposures with his Polaroid camera.[94]

Pennsylvania Wave of 1988

There may well have been other areas of heavy UFO activity during 1988, but given the nature of UFO sightings in general, in which witnesses frequently never file reports, such matters are inherently difficult to judge. The Commonwealth of Pennsylvania was fortunate, however, that it had a dedicated researcher in Stan Gordon, who year after year methodically accepted and investigated reports of UFOs and other anomalous phenomena (including Bigfoot sightings). Other regions surely had fine investigators out there; Gordon just always seemed to have more dedication than most. He was not only an active member of MUFON and contributor to its journal, but created and ran an independent organization called the Pennsylvania Association for the Study of the Unexplaned (PASU). Starting in the latter half of 1987, Gordon recorded a dramatic upswing in reports of UFOs among Pennsylvania residents, mostly in the state's western half, which continued throughout 1988. Dozens of these remained baffling after an investigation.

A case from February 10, 1988 occurred in rural southwestern Pennsylvania, not far from Johnstown. That evening, several independent witnesses saw a 60-foot long object with several rows of lights. One said it looked like "a small cruise ship in the sky." The object passed over cars and trees at an altitude between 50 and 100 feet over the ground, giving off a slight humming sound and projecting several bright beams of light toward the ground.

Several bizarre cases were recorded in July in the vicinity of the Homer City Power Plant. For several weeks, residents reported slow dropping fireballs and strange sounds. On the night of July 17, several people saw a pair of objects with red and green flashing lights make two criss-cross passes near the facility. One object later dropped from the sky and made two passes about 200 feet off the ground. It was about the size of a large car, circular in shape, and had four lighted legs protruding from the bottom. A hissing noise was heard as the object passed close by.

In the town of Ebensburg, another small town in central-western Pennsylvania, during a sunny afternoon on September 2, a man sitting by a pond at home saw a strange object come out of the sky from the north. It moved toward him and hovered just 50 feet away from him, less than 30 feet off the ground. It was spherical and about 15 to 20 feet in diameter. The upper section was red, and the underside orange-red. A glass-like amber colored window divided the sections, and lights flashed inside it. He said it hovered silently for two minutes, giving off a kind of mist before it departed back toward the north. After it left, the tall grass below was swirled in a counter clockwise fashion.

PASU's last important case of 1988 took place in eastern Pennsylvania on December 4, in Dauphin County. A law enforcement officer driving to work at 5:25 a.m. noticed a brilliant glow in the sky ahead of him. It was so bright that he could hardly see, and he swerved to a stop. About 150 feet in the air was a 75-foot long, highly polished silver object shaped like an elongated oval. It gave a humming sound and bathed the car in intense light. It moved left and right, shot straight up in the sky and stopped. Then it departed out of sight. Afterwards, the officer felt ill, suffered from a sunburn-like effect on his face, severe eye irritation, headache, and neck pain. The paint on his car also appeared to be dulled, and an unusual powder-like substance was found on the car's exterior.[95]

Presidents Talking UFOs

During his campaign to become President, George Bush was unexpectedly cornered into making a statement regarding UFOs. On March 7, 1988, at a political rally in Rogers, Arkansas, Bush was about to meet with reporters when a man named Charles Huffer approached him. Carrying his tape recorder, Huffer asked Bush if, once elected President, he would "tell the truth about UFOs." "Yeah," replied Bush – quickly adding, "if we can find it, what it is. We are really interested." "You'll have it, you'll have it," said Huffer. "It's in there. Declassify it and tell us, ok?" "Okay, alright, yes," Bush said as he entered the building to meet with the press.

When Bush re-emerged some time later, Huffer was still there. Tape recorder running, he said, "going to hold you to that promise." "Alright," replied Bush. "Okay," said Huffer, "you're going to get it," meaning the UFO information. Bush cleverly replied, "why don't you send me some information about it?" he asked. "Naw," said Huffer. "You're a CIA man. You know all that stuff." "I know some," replied Bush. "I know a fair amount."

This was a very interesting revelation. The current Vice President and former CIA Director openly stating he knew "a fair amount" about UFOs. The problem was that Huffer was just a private citizen, not a journalist, and so the story never took off. True, UFO researchers quickly learned that there had been some kind of confirmation made by the Vice President, but the details were unclear. Some versions had him admitting to being a member of MJ-12, which he had not done. Huffer had come close to a surprise breakthrough on the UFO cover-up. The lack of follow-up by American journalists, however, ensured that the story died by the time Bush became President.[96]

Two months later, on May 4, President Ronald Reagan made yet another reference to an alien invasion. Significantly, he made it when asked what he considered to be the most important need in international relations. "I've often wondered," he said, "if all of us in the world discovered that we were threatened by ... a power from outer space, from another planet. Wouldn't we all of a sudden find that we didn't have any differences between us at all, we were all human beings, citizens of the world, and wouldn't we come together to fight that particular threat?"[97]

In early June 1988, Reagan met with Gorbachev in Moscow. Still, no progress had been made on the Strategic Defense Initiative. The Soviets wanted SDI gone, and Reagan would not budge. At one point during their talks, Gorbachev asked Reagan directly, "what is SDI for? What missiles is it supposed to bring down if we eliminate all nuclear weapons?" Reagan's reply: "it will be there just in case."[98]

The End of APRO

Coral Lorenzen, founder and dominant force behind the Aerial Phenomena Research Group (APRO), died on April 12, 1988. Her husband James had died in 1986. The Lorenzens had never cultivated anyone to succeed them in the management of their far-flung organization. With her death, the remaining board members decided to dissolve the group. It was a sad ending to such a noteworthy enterprise, one which had played such a critical role in the history of UFO research.

The greatest tragedy, however, concerned APRO's files. This consisted of 18 filing cabinets filled with files, letters, photographs, fragments, and artifacts. Among its contents were the famous 1957 Ubatuba, Brazil UFO fragment and the gloves worn by Steven Michalich during his physical encounter with a UFO at Canada's Falcon Lake in 1967. It has been estimated that 15,000 UFO sighting reports were contained within the filing cabinets, many of which existed nowhere else. Jim and Coral Lorenzen had wanted their files to remain together and freely available to all researchers. Tragically, neither Lorenzen left instructions on this matter in a will.

The APRO files could easily have gone to CUFOS, which had a reasonably good relationship with the Lorenzens (unlike Walt Andrus of MUFON, whom Coral Lorenzen despised). Indeed, according to Mark Rodeghier, CUFOS was attempting to purchase the archive, when someone convinced Larry Lorenzen, Coral and Jim's son, that the files should not go to CUFOS. Larry, who had no interest in UFOs, advised the APRO board not to deal with CUFOS. He also said he wanted the archive to stay in Arizona. Rodeghier believed that "whoever spoke to Larry Lorenzen did so for malicious reasons."[99]

Enter two individuals named Tina Choate and Brian Myers, the former of whom is said to have come from the wealthy and well-connected Choate family in Massachusetts.[100] In 1985, Myers and Choate had created a Phoenix-based UFO research group, and Choate then persuaded J. Allen

Hynek to move to Arizona with promises of money and support. Hynek, however, quickly became disillusioned with Choate and Myers, and died the following year.

With their dubious Arizona-based organization now named the "International Center for UFO Research" (ICUFOR), Choate and Myers convinced the APRO Board that they were the most logical recipients of the files. The board members knew only that Hynek had worked with the two, not that he had quickly soured on them. Clearly, they were able to talk a good game. They were willing to take the priceless files off the APRO board's hands. Thus, a year after Coral Lorenzen's death, the board agreed and gave the files to Choate and Myers – free of charge![101] Years later, former APRO board member Robert Dean called the two "a couple of scam artists," adding that their acquisition of the files was "one of the darkest points of my life."[102]

Immediately upon taking control of the files, Choate and Myers barred anyone else from reviewing them. Although ICUFOR had a small office for a while, most of the archive was apparently kept in their garage, alternately said to be in Scottsdale, Tucson, or perhaps Sedona.[103]

But what were the pair trying to do? Several sources have described them as a contactee-oriented couple.[104] Eventually, it became clear that they had no interest in actual UFO research, and some observers assumed they simply acted out of greed and were planning to sell the archive for the right price. Robert Dean was one who believed this. But after the blunt refusal of every purchase offer, Dean later speculated that "one of the agencies" was involved.[105]

It is unavoidable to speculate otherwise, even lacking proof. Two unknown people sweep APRO's board off its feet, obtaining the irreplaceable APRO archives for free, and permanently close them off to everyone, forever, and answer no questions about the matter, to anyone.

Strangeness in the Antelope Valley

Gulf Breeze was not the only region in the U.S. experiencing a wave of strange aerial sightings in 1988. Another was Southern California's Antelope Valley, a large, arid region east of Los Angeles. For many years, the area had been a key military and aerospace center. Edwards AFB, where a great deal of flight testing occurs, is there. USAF Plant 42 in northeast Palmdale is also there, home to – among other aerospace concerns – Lockheed-Martin, Boeing, Northrop-Grumman, and BAE Systems. Among the many aviation/aerospace projects designed or produced in the Antelope

Valley were the space shuttle, the B-2 stealth bomber, and the F-117 stealth fighter. For many years the region was sparsely populated, but a real estate boom in the 1980s led to a dramatic growth in the local population.[106]

During the summer and fall of 1988, residents reported various odd-shaped objects. On July 16, a woman living in Lancaster allegedly saw two dark objects "shaped like ice cream cones" descend silently near her yard at around dusk. They looked smaller than private planes and seemed perforated, somewhat like a fishing net. After descending, they ascended and were lost to sight.[107] Another odd sighting took place in Lancaster during the late morning of August 3, when a woman saw an object come in from the northwest, hover briefly over the Sierra Highway, and vanish in a matter of seconds. "It wasn't a dirigible, it wasn't a plane and it wasn't a helicopter," she told the local media. "It was shiny ... slow. It hovered. All of a sudden, it just evaporated. It disappeared. Became invisible. It was so unusual, it stuck out like a sore thumb."[108]

Boomerang-shaped craft, similar to those reported across the country in the Hudson Valley, were also being reported in the region. A multiple-witness sighting of two such craft occurred shortly after 8:30 p.m. on October 26, 1988. These craft were very large (estimated span of 600 feet) and traveling at a mere 30 mph. Stranger still, about 15 to 20 smaller disc-shaped objects followed the two large boomerangs. The last one of the discs flashed a light that alternated between yellow and red. Later in the evening, about 150 miles to the northwest, residents of Fresno saw two similar or identical boomerangs.[109]

Many of these UFO investigations were done by William Hamilton. Among the stranger cases was an apparent abduction event that summer concerning two individuals and a subterranean base. The two, named Ray and Nancy, worked at the Northrop B-2 assembly facility in Palmdale, and had taken a midnight trip to the Tehachapi Mountains. Near 1 a.m., they were watching the stars when they noticed one of them moving. They directed a flashlight at it, then saw a basketball-sized orb hovering nearby. When they woke up next morning at sunrise, the last thing they could remember was approaching the orb. Four hours of time were missing. They knew Hamilton, who introduced them to a local hypnotist, who then regressed Ray (Nancy refused, fearful of what she might learn). Ray remembered the two of them being abducted and taken underground. He said there was an area near the Tehachapi Mountains called "the Kern River Project." This, he said, was a large underground base – indeed, a city – with huge hangers, laboratories, and tunnels connecting to everywhere. Aliens were in there, too, said Ray, performing humans dissections with government knowledge. With great distress, he recalled grey aliens strapping Nancy to a table, but the two also believed they had contact with a benevolent race of aliens who had observed their capture.

Some months later, Ray and Nancy told Hamilton that they no longer wanted to take part in any investigation. According to Hamilton, they were afraid of being monitored and announced their intention to go to Bible classes. They wanted "refuge from this enormous evil that had encroached upon their lives."[110]

The reference to the "Kern River Project" is certainly odd. This was the name of the first interstate pipeline built in California, which began transporting natural gas in early 1992. It took seven years to plan and build.[111] By early 1988, construction was well underway in the area. Why would Hamilton's witness use this name in conjunction with an alien-military underground facility? Was the couple having fun at Hamilton's expense? Judging from Hamilton's assessment, this seems unlikely. Perhaps a delusion was involved, although much of it would have been jointly shared – a "folie a deux." Considering that both individuals had responsible jobs in the defense industry, this would be surprising. Or, was a covert operation using a public one for cover?

Enter Bill Cooper

UFO researchers had long been used to strange stories, but by now stories were becoming *really* strange. During the summer of 1988, Jim Speiser's Paranet bulletin board service received a post by a man claiming to have had a UFO sighting while serving as a U.S. Navy sailor onboard a submarine, the USS Tiru, in 1966. The poster added that, based on his own insider knowledge, he could verify "50 percent" of John Lear's 1987 paper (this would later be changed to "150 percent"). That poster's name was Milton William Cooper.[112]

A few days after posting his submarine story, Cooper claimed on Paranet that he had been fired from a high paying job because of his previous communication, as well as because he spoke with Stanton Friedman. Following this, he posted several files dealing with UFO information he claimed to have seen while in the Navy. In an August 1988 posting, Cooper claimed he had held a Top Secret SI Clearance, and said that after leaving the Navy he had remained involved in intelligence work until 1980. At this time, Cooper fully supported not only John Lear, but William Moore and Jaime Shandera regarding their MJ-12 research.[113]

On October 4, 1988, Cooper and Lear spoke by phone for the first time. On October 8, Cooper received a FedEx package from Lear. In addition to sending his own writings to Cooper, Lear's package included several other historically important items.

One of these was the "O. H. Krill" document. This had been written shortly after John Lear's hypothesis was published in December 1987 by an Air Force non-commissioned officer named John Grace. Grace had composed his thoughts on the extraterrestrial situation, very much in line with those of Lear. Not wanting to use his own name, as he was still on USAF active duty, Grace asked Lear for any ideas on a pseudonym. Lear came up with "Krill," an inside joke referring to an entity ("Crlll") allegedly channelled by a woman in Robert Emmenger's film, *UFOs: It Has Begun*. According to Lear, Grace added the initials O. H. "out of thin air." Thus, the O.H. Krill document was born. It also seems likely that Lear sent Cooper another document written by Grace (under the pseudonym Valdamar Valerian) entitled *The Matrix*. This had been privately published in September 1988 with a limited print run of 100 copies, and was essentially a much-expanded version of the O.H. Krill document.[114]

Among the Krill document's many conclusions were that the U.S. government had a longstanding working relationship with aliens with the goal of perfecting gravitational propulsion, beam weaponry, and mind control. Advances in these and other areas vastly exceeded anything the public knew about, and the space program was a public relations cover for more serious space operations. Live aliens had been "hostage" to the U.S. government, alien autopsies had been conducted, and abductions, murder, and mutilation had all occurred in connection with the UFO situation. People were being killed to hide the truth. The CIA and the NSA were so deeply involved that exposure would threaten their very existence. The aliens, according to Krill/Grace, had intervened in human genetic development and religion, had bases on the Earth and Moon, and actively controlled elements of human society. But this was not a simple situation of extraterrestrial beings; humans inhabited a multi-dimensional world visited by a large number of hostile and friendly entities from other dimensions. The Krill document predicted an overt alien presence "within five to ten years" (e.g. by 1993 to 1998).

Lear also sent Cooper a version of the Zapruder film depicting the assassination of John F. Kennedy. Lear himself had received it from an investigative journalist named Lars Hansson. Hansson knew two men who believed that Kennedy's true assassin had been his limousine driver, Secret

Service Agent William Greer. Although skeptical, Hansson helped the two enhance the film (already a fourth or fifth generation copy) and to their shock they saw what looked like Greer shooting a pistol at the moment of the fatal shot. Hansson needed financing to make a movie; he knew that Lear had an interest in conspiracies, and assumed he was heir to the Lear family fortune. Hansson cleaned up the tape, added titles and narration, and mailed it to Lear. It was titled, "The Truth Betrayed, Dallas Revisited." Lear sent a copy along to Cooper.[115]

Another document Lear sent to Cooper was his personal transcription of statements by a former Green Beret captain named William English. These were regarding an alleged Project Grudge/Blue Book Report #13. The USAF had released many Blue Book reports, culminating in Report #14.[116] Report #13 had never been published, however, and many researchers assumed it never existed. But in 1977, English was working at an RAF listening post as an information analyst. His job was to evaluate intelligence reports and judge each one's probability of being true. He claimed that in June of that year, he was asked to analyze the 624-page Grudge Report #13.

The report showed many UFO photographs from around the world, contained unsettling discussions of lopsided military encounters with UFOs, alien abductions, even more unsettling claims about missing children, and gruesome photographs of human mutilations by aliens. There was also a great deal on the retrieval of crashed UFOs, including photos of discs and alien autopsies. The creatures depicted were very short, had dark bluish-grey skin, a slightly enlarged "rounded cranium," almond-shaped eyes, slits where a nose would be, holes where ears would be, an extremely small mouth, and no visible genitalia. Their arms were proportionately longer than a normal human arm, with the wrist coming to within 2 to 3 inches of the knee. There was no identifiable hand, but simply three digits (no thumb) extending from the wrist. Some photos showed internal organs, but no apparent stomach or digestive track. An analysis in the report theorized that nourishment was taken in through mouth but that the waste products were excreted through skin. The report concluded that the photos depicted a genuine UFO crash and alien body. Startlingly, at least one signatory to the report was J. Allen Hynek. Hynek apparently had not viewed the bodies personally, but had studied the photographs and autopsy reports.

English's personal story was equally spectacular, and he told it over the next few years with great detail, consistency, and passion. Unfortunately, it also lacked proof of any sort, and sounded like the plot of a Hollywood movie. According to English, after he read the Grudge Report in June 1977, he was abruptly terminated from his position and deported to the U.S. Presumably he was not meant to read it. He began experiencing brushes with death, including fires to his home and black limousines attempting to run him off the highway. He joined APRO and got to know the Lorenzens and William Moore. Moore interviewed English extensively – there was no Grudge Report #13, Moore told him. English also spoke privately with Allen Hynek about the report, which Hynek initially denied existed. However, after English heatedly confronted him about what he knew, Hynek admitted to it, but added that he would never admit it publicly. English asked Hynek "why me?" (e.g., why it was he who had to analyze the document and lose everything). Hynek replied, "Somebody had to do it."[117]

Indeed, English also telephoned Linda Moulton Howe in March 1980. He explained his story to her and said the Grudge Report #13 was real. Howe did not know what to believe at the time. Since this was not long before the broadcast of *A Strange Harvest*, there was not enough time to research English's claims, and so the matter was not included in her documentary. Howe did, however, publish the account in her 1989 book, *An Alien Harvest*.[118]

Events culminated for English in 1982 when he met with his former supervisors from Britain, who had also been forced out of their jobs. One of them had heard there was an alien craft somewhere along the edge of the White Sands Missile Test Range. Because it was too large to transport, it was simply buried there. "Being the fools that we were," English wrote, "we decided to check it out." They purchased a van, stocked it with provisions and electronics, and drove off. Late in the evening, they reached their destination and brought out the metal detectors. They had been there for 90 minutes, slowly poring over the area. English was walking in front; behind him were his two companions in the van, driving with the headlights on. English heard the sound of an incoming rocket and instinctively hit the dirt. The rocket hit the van and killed his companions. For several days, he traveled alone at night, avoiding helicopters and search parties. Eventually, he reached the home of Wendelle Stevens in Tucson, then decided it was "time to disappear." He trekked to San Diego, Los Angeles, and eventually his mother's farm in Virginia. For several years he worked at radio and television stations as an announcer and cameraman.

English stayed out of circulation until July 1988, when John Lear went searching for him and contacted his father. English did nothing until

September. He got back in touch with Wendelle Stevens (who had assumed he was dead), and then contacted Lear, who flew to Virginia to meet with him. Privately, he told Lear that he maintained inside contacts and believed the U.S. Government definitely supported a project dealing with UFOs and captured aliens. According to his information, he said one alien being was still alive in captivity. Lear transcribed English's statement and now sent this along to Cooper.

Yet another bit of data Lear sent to Cooper was a paper on a Project "Excalibur." This came from Lear's new friend Bob Lazar in September, 1988. Lazar had claimed to have written the paper while working at Los Alamos, and said the project was about an "earth-penetrating, nuclear-tipped missile designed to destroy underground facilities."[119]

Cooper spent the morning and afternoon going through it all. By his own admission, the experience left him "numb." The information Lear had sent him, he said, "confirmed everything I personally knew and had seen first hand."[120] It was not long before Cooper would create a series of breathtaking lies about this information, and in so doing turn himself into a legend, of sorts.

UFO Cover-Up? Live!

Outer space and aliens were popular entertainment during the 1970s and 1980s. UFOs, on the other hand, were usually ignored in the major media, seldom taken seriously, and *never* considered in connection with conspiracy. That would be for the next generation to deal with – and the first such attempt at this was *UFO Cover-Up? Live!*, a two hour documentary which aired throughout North America on October 14, 1988.

Produced by Michael B. Seligman and hosted by Mike Farrell (of TV's "*M*A*S*H**"), the show highlighted interesting recent cases, such as the Cash-Landrum incident of 1980 and the Hudson Valley sightings. William Moore, Jamie Shandera, and Stanton Friedman were interviewed regarding Roswell and the MJ-12 documents. Alien abductions were featured, hypnotic regressions were videotaped, and Budd Hopkins was pitted against a skeptical medical doctor. Rather more off the beaten path was the alleged Holloman AFB film, said to have depicted the landing of an alien craft. Film maker Robert Emenegger said that he was shown Air Force footage of three flying saucers, one of which landed. Three human-sized aliens came out; they had grey complexions, large noses, tight fitting jump suits, and communication devices on their heads.

Much of the above was already controversial within 1980s ufology, but the show also delved into murky waters where even dedicated UFO researchers were cautious, if not skeptical. Two men described as "Falcon" and "Condor" presented alleged inside information about the longstanding relationship between the U.S. government and extraterrestrials. Although their faces were darkened and their voices electronically altered, they were later identified respectively as Richard Doty and Robert Collins, both recently retired from the Air Force.

The two made a number of statements on controversial topics long familiar to UFO researchers. Regarding UFO crash retrievals, they said there had not merely been the one crash of a UFO at Roswell, but several. MJ-12, they said, was a policy-making group based at the Naval Observatory in Washington, D.C. With Presidential approval, MJ-12 handled all ET-related matters, entrusting field responsibility and policy implementation to the U.S. Navy.

Much of what they said accorded with the recent statements of John Lear. There had been three successive alien "guests" of the U.S. government, they said, the third of which was still alive in U.S. custody. There was also an exchange program of sorts, in which one or more humans were living with the aliens. The U.S. agreed to conceal the aliens as long as the aliens did not interfere in human society and agreed to operate from a base within the United States. This base was in Nevada, in a place called "Area 51" or "Dreamland." (This was the first time Area 51 was ever mentioned on television). Within their designated area, the ETs had complete control, although human scientists were very much involved in studying and testing alien technology. Indeed, according to Falcon, the Cash-Landrum sighting had actually been an alien craft piloted by the military that had developed flight problems.

But it was the show's discussion of the aliens that really turned heads. These were described as less than four feet tall, with large eyes, almost no nose, and insect-like in appearance – rather different from Emenegger's aliens. Their brains were highly complex and their IQs were believed to exceed 200. They had four fingers with no thumb, and their feet were web-like. They normally lived between 350 and 400 Earth years.

There was a book known as "The Bible," containing a history of relations with the extraterrestrials from the Truman era through the present, as well as technological and biological data about the aliens (including autopsy data), and even information of their social and political structure. A "Yellow Book" was written by the second alien guest. It discussed their origin (the Zeta Reticuli star group), culture, and interactions with humans. There was also a crystal which could display images of the alien home planet or of Earth's distant past.

The aliens had a religion of sorts, in which they posited the universe itself as a supreme being. They were said to enjoy all types of music, and were most fond of ancient Tibetan music. They liked eating vegetables, but their favorite snack was strawberry ice cream.[121]

Years after the show aired and was all-but-forgotten, people remembered the remark about strawberry ice cream. But herein lies the failure of the documentary, in which so much had been possible and nothing accomplished. The show's chief writer, Barry Taff, expressed disgust at how the hard work and good intentions of the show's researchers were wasted by producer Seligman. When the original treatment and teleplay were presented, Seligman allegedly told Taff that the subject matter was too serious: he wanted "copy, schlock, camp... not screenwriting." Attempts to persuade Seligman to use FOIA documents were to no avail.[122] It also appears there were other forces and motives at work. In Bill Moore's own words, "some of the stuff on the show was real, and some was disinformation." Unfortunately, he never expanded on this statement, or revealed which was which.[123]

With a few exceptions (Walt Andrus called it "outstanding"[124]), most ufologists were unimpressed, even appalled. Bill English was furious. For years, Moore had been claiming that English was lying about Grudge Report #13. Now English watched in disbelief as Moore's "two song birds" parroted everything that he had been saying all along. "If I'm a liar," said English, "what does this make him?"[125]

Most interesting was the absence of commentary by the mainstream media or political community. Major claims had been made on national television which, if even *one* of them were true, should have caused a political firestorm. But researchers scoured the broadcast and print media in vain for any word on the show. The resultant vacuum prompted one long-time UFO afficionado, bookseller Robert Girard, to wonder whether the program was a test of a "conditioning program" designed to deaden the public with mindless entertainment As he put it,

> ... time was – until very recently – that some spokesperson would have to step in and save the day when the masses showed signs of paying too much attention to a flurry of UFO activity. But the last 12 months have seen a steady barrage of leaks of highly sensitive UFO information (or disinformation – actually, it no longer matters which), and a series of books which just a few years ago would have been soundly suppressed in the 'interests of national security.'[126]

This was true. A program like *UFO Cover-Up? Live!* would have been unthinkable in earlier decades, precisely because the public reaction would have been explosive. Girard had discovered a profound truth: that a deft combination of disinformation, entertainment, spin, and public apathy were more effective at concealing truths than old-fashioned, heavy-handed censorship.

Into the Dark Side

FOIA and Leonard Stringfield had begun the politicization of ufology during the late 1970s, making it clear that a major cover-up was under way. By 1987, the MJ-12 controversy had taken center stage in this process. Now, just a year later, ufology had become the Lear and Cooper Show or, as many were now putting the matter, "the dark side" had taken over ufology.

Cooper's actual credentials have long been debated. His 1975 honorable discharge from the U.S. Navy showed an E-6 paygrade and the rank of Quartermaster First Class. There is some evidence, although not conclusive, to show Cooper did have a connection to UFOs at that time. Researcher Linda Moulton Howe spoke to a close friend of Cooper's from the early 1970s, named Robert Swan. Swan had even been the best man at Cooper's wedding in 1972. In 1989, he told Howe that he and Cooper used to discuss UFOs frequently. Swan was not in the military, and there were things Cooper simply could not discuss. But Cooper did tell Swan that "every space flight was accompanied by UFOs." Swan also said that the night before Cooper's wedding, he was shown "some documents which I believe to be classified information. It was about an alien base on the back side of the Moon," as well as other unspecified matters. Years later, Swan still believed the documents were legitimate and true. "Unfortunately," he continued, "all I can remember is space shots and the bases on the Moon.... Discussions of the assassination of JFK came up but I cannot remember where they led. I have given that evening a great deal of thought ... this is all I can come up with." He added that Cooper had given him copies of certain documents that night as a kind of insurance, but they had disappeared.[127]

It appears, then, that Cooper had a longstanding interest in UFOs. The fact that Swan could not remember anything relevant pertaining to the Kennedy assassination, however, is intriguing. One would think that anyone would remember the claim that Kennedy's driver was the killer – unless one argues that Cooper would have deliberately held such information back. The few matters Swan did recall are interesting, but they are different from the themes Cooper was working in the late 1980s. Some time later, John Lear stated that, while he doubted much of Cooper's story, he still believed that Cooper had learned a few things about UFOs while in the Navy.[128]

Whatever Cooper knew during his years of military service is unlikely to be proven. What is beyond question, however, is that by 1988 he had a hair-trigger temper, a penchant for drink that only made him meaner, and an evident ability to believe fanatically anything he said. Such qualifications would soon enable William Cooper to become the most famous person in UFO research, especially amazing since he was never a researcher.

The combined effect of Lear's FedEx package and *UFO Cover-Up? Live!* affected Cooper deeply. Back in August 1988, he had spoken with great gravity on "Top Secret Magic-Restricted Data," and claimed that the MJ-12 documents produced by Moore were "photographic copies of genuine documents which were procured at great risk." Now, on October 15, 1988, just a week after receiving Lear's materials (and one day after the airing of *UFO Cover-UP? Live!*), Cooper announced to Paranet that any document using the term "Magic" (sic) was a fraud, and that he could prove "beyond a shadow of a doubt ... that most of the information released by William Moore, et al.... are obvious and deliberate forgeries." His public explanation for the turnaround was that he had been testing researchers all along.

Cooper also began to make other suspiciously timely claims. He, too, had read Grudge Report #13 during the early 1970s, while in the U.S. Navy's Intelligence section, CINCPAC. He, too, had known about Kennedy's limo driver, William Greer, from another report he had read at that time. Kennedy, Cooper would soon tell the world, was about to say the wrong things about UFOs and had to be silenced.* Cooper soon went further. He would soon tell the world that he had also read the Krill Report, again while he was in "Naval Intelligence" during the early 1970s! When, in the spring of 1989, John Lear asked Cooper incredulously how he could make such a claim – when the Krill Report had obviously been written in early 1988 and for which Lear himself had contributed the title – Cooper called Lear a liar and CIA disinformation agent. And that would be that.

Thus, by late October 1988, Paranet administrator Jim Speiser was seeing his brainchild being dragged into the mud. Another disturbing development convinced him that Cooper was a menace who had to be stopped. Speiser had met a young man named Jeff Felix who claimed to

---

* Not bothering to explain why any intelligence agency would put in written form how and why they would have assassinated the President.

have been an NSA cryptology technician. Felix claimed that while "fooling around" on the NSA computer, he had stumbled across the Majestic and Aquarius files. Speiser spoke to several people with intelligence backgrounds and returned to Felix with follow-up questions to test whether he was legitimate. According to Speiser, Felix failed the test. Felix did mention, however, something called "Project X-calabur" (sic). When Speiser asked Cooper during a phone call if he had heard about this project, Cooper said he had, but that it was very top secret and knew nothing else about it. Later that same day, Cooper called Speiser back and said that "Project Excalibur" was a project by MJ-12 to extract technology from extraterrestrials. At this point, Speiser became deeply suspicious of Cooper.

On top of this, it must be remembered that Lear had sent Cooper information on a Project Excalibur, courtesy of Bob Lazar. Lazar's version was not about extraterrestrials, but about missiles that would destroy underground facilities. Lazar later heard Cooper talking about this project, claiming to have known about it in the early 1970s, which would have been an impossibility.

As a result, on October 26, 1988, Speiser ejected Cooper and Lear from the Paranet BBS.[129] At the time, it was a significant move, as there were few places on the nascent Internet for in-depth UFO-related discussion. But even at this early stage, there was one other place: the CompuServe network.

On December 18, 1988, Cooper made another statement about MJ-12 and alien life forms. He claimed to have seen two key reports while serving as a quartermaster with an intelligence briefing team for U.S. Admiral Bernard A. Clarey, Commander in Chief of the Pacific Fleet. These were the Project Grudge/Blue Book Report # 13 and the "Majesty Briefing." His description of the Grudge Report # 13 was very close to that of William English, while the "Majesty Briefing" contained information on the alien presence on Earth. Cooper released names and summaries of various secret projects and terms, including Aquarius, Pounce, Pluto, Redlight, Snowbird, Luna, Gabriel, Excalibur, ALF, and others. Redlight was to test fly recovered alien craft, Snowbird was a cover for Redlight. Gabriel was a project to develop a low frequency pulsed sound generator, believed to be effective against alien craft. Luna was a code name for an alien underground base in New Mexico, and Excalibur was to develop a ground penetrating weapon system to destroy underground alien bases (not, as he had recently told Speiser, to extract technology from extraterrestrials). Cooper mentioned an alien base on the far side of the Moon, which had been seen by

Apollo astronauts. He also mentioned the "National Reconnaissance Organization" – the existence of the National Reconnaissance Office (NRO) was still classified in 1988, although it had been exposed in the *New York Times* in 1985.[130] ALF was an abbreviation for "alien life form" – ironically, Cooper neglected to mention that "ALF" was a sitcom television show that ran from 1986 to 1990, dealing with an "alien life form" secretly living with an Earth family. Whether this was a joke on his part, or someone else's part, or whether the television show producers were provided with inside knowledge is anybody's guess.* Cooper discussed alien "guests" held in exchange for humans who had become "guests" of the aliens. He also said there was an alien craft at a hangar in Edwards AFB in California, heavily guarded by "non-Edwards personnel, NRO-Delta forces."

On January 10, 1989, Cooper revised his statement. This time, instead of giving the title "Majesty Briefing" for one of the reports, he said the actual title was "Majority Briefing." The reason he gave a different title this time was that he was testing "the reactions of people, especially the government, to the wrong names in the first version." From Cooper's perspective, in which he argued his life was in danger and enemies were everywhere, this could be seen as a clever tactic. Naturally, detractors could point out that he had a history of making mistakes in his pronouncements, then needing to perform the requisite clean-up.

One thing is certain, by the time 1989 had arrived, the field of UFO research had been turned upside down. What had recently been dominated by an enclosed group of researchers was now a wide-open field where a flurry of newcomers, most of them not true researchers but claiming deep inside knowledge, were trumping – or appearing to trump – the old guard who had relied on the conventional methods of cautious argumentation and fact checking through use of open sources. There is no question that the advent of computerized bulletin boards were a critical development in this process. "Scientific ufology" this certainly was not. The real question, however, was whether it was getting closer to the truth.

If so, Cooper could not claim any credit. There is no evidence that he had anything to contribute, except stories stolen from other people – primarily via Lear – which he claimed as his own. It is easy to conclude that Cooper was a liar, plain and simple. This could well have been so, except that in the opinion of several people who knew him, he seemed very

---

*
In the 1990 series finale, ALF was captured by the U.S. military and taken to a secret base.

sincere. It has been suggested that Cooper was not so much a manipulative deceiver as someone who was naive and easily manipulated. Getting to the bottom of William Cooper, however, is a difficult undertaking. All that can be said for certain is that he entered the UFO field, latched on to stories that were then circulating, and promptly laid waste.

Revealing Stealth Secrets

The F-117A Night Hawk stealth fighter, built by Lockheed, had been secretly operational since 1983. Through the 1980s, there were a few instances in which sightings of the aircraft had to be covered up by the authorities. But by 1988, the Air Force wanted to expand its operations for the F-117A, including daytime flights. It would be impossible to keep the secret much longer.[131] Then there was the problem of the new stealth bomber: the Northrop B-2 Advanced Technology Bomber, of which the USAF was expecting to develop a fleet of 132. Some sort of admission became as obvious as it was inevitable.[132]

Thus, on November 10, 1988, the U.S. Air Force made a virtue of necessity and revealed the existence of the F-117A. Less than two weeks later, on November 22, it also displayed the B-2 – surely one of the most distinctive aircraft in aviation history.[133] Acknowledging these two aircraft to the world was good public relations: little hard data was actually given, and the Soviets already knew in general terms that Americans had developed stealth technology.[134] Both major powers had developed an impressive system of global signals intelligence; very little was being hidden from each other.[135]

But there remained important secrets. Although the Pentagon gave some general information about the B-2's outward design and stealth capabilities, it was silent about much else. Indeed, two decades later, the U.S. Air Force has still never revealed any image of the B-2 with its access panels removed that show the engine placement. However, in the early 1990s, black-world scientists disclosed to *Aviation Week and Space Technology* that the B-2 electrostatically charged its leading edge wing with a high positive charge, while a strongly negative charge was given to the exhaust gasses.[136] What this meant was that the B-2 could in fact have an electrogravitic propulsion system.*

Electrogravitics had been pioneered by American scientist Thomas

---

* The claim has naturally been controversial and disputed ever since. It has not been proven that the wings of the B-2 are charged and, if so, whether this would be for purposes relating to electrogravitics, or to create a boundary layer control that reduces aerodynamic drag.

Townsend Brown. Following on concepts derived from Nicola Tesla, Brown's research from the 1920s onward led him to conclude that an electric field could polarize an object, and that this in turn could counteract or alter the effects of gravity. Brown maintained that this effect was different from well-known electrostatic effects, and that electrogravitics could be used as a means of propulsion for aircraft and spacecraft. During 1956 and 1957, enthusiastic talk of electrogravitics made it into the mainstream press, then disappeared. The reason for the sudden disappearance has been disputed. Conventional opinion holds that the research hit a dead end and nothing worthwhile came of it. It surely did not help that Brown was intensely interested in UFOs – he was the original founder of NICAP in late 1956. The connection to UFOs is one reason why mainstream scientists avoided electrogravitics for so long. There are scientific objections, however, to electrogravitics as a form of propulsion. A 2005 paper on the Levi-Civita effect (which shows distortion of the spacetime metric by electric and magnetic fields) shows that, at least in terms of present general relativity theory, the field strengths generated by high-voltage electrogravitic experiments have been too weak for practical use.[137]

Still, others have argued that electrogravitic research went "black" during the 1950s.[138] Regarding the B-2, the idea is that the high electrical charge of the aircraft would, in theory, create a kind "gravity well" in front and a "gravity hill" behind. Once this was established, one could shut off the engine and ride a gravitational wave. Considering the awesome cost of each B-2 (more than $1 billion each in the beginning, and more than $2 billion each by the end), perhaps some of that cost went in this direction. Such was the speculation in *AWST*.

The *AWST* article prompted Dr. Paul LaViolette, an expert in electrogravitics, to expand on the matter. In 1993, he proposed that the B-2 was essentially a realization of Townsend Brown's patented electrogravitic aircraft. An electrogravitic drive would enable the B-2 to cut its fuel consumption possibly to zero under high speed flight conditions. It would essentially be able to create "an artificial gravity field." A caveat was that the system could only be used under dry flying conditions.[139]

The concept met with skepticism or outright dismissal within the mainstream. Yet, as late as 2000, the respected aviation writer, Bill Gunston, studied the specifications of the B-2 and concluded that it was vastly underpowered – unless there was a way to reduce its mass or increase its lift beyond conventional aerodynamic means. "I have numerous documents, all published openly in the United States," wrote Gunston,

> ... which purport to explain how the B-2 is even stranger – far, far stranger – than it appears.... They deal with such topics as electric-field propulsion, and electrogravitics (or anti-gravity), the transient alteration of not only thrust but also a body's weight. Sci-Fi has nothing on this stuff.[140]

Indeed, the B-2's official thrust/weight ratio is 0.205, obviously a far cry from fighter aircraft, some of which have a ratio in excess of 1.0 (enabling vertical ascent). But even for a bomber, it is very low, possibly the lowest for any major bomber aircraft in the world. By comparison, the B-52 Stratofortress and B-1B Lancer have more typical ratios of 0.31 and 0.37, respectively.[141] Still, the claim that the B-2 is underpowered has not gone unchallenged. As the aircraft is "a pure flying wing," its thrust/weight ratio can be deceptive. Unlike traditional aircraft with a fuselage and stabilizers to create drag, all of the B-2's surface creates lift. For cruise purposes, at least, some analysts believe the B-2 to be adequately powered.[142] Nevertheless, it seems strange that an aircraft which costs from $737 million to over $2 billion each (depending on how many costs one wishes to factor in), has such a mediocre official flight performance.[143]

Nick Cook, a senior aviation editor at *Jane's Defense*, also examined claims about the B-2. He asked a Northrop-Grumman spokesman whether the B-2 charged its surface electrostatically. "Absolutely not," was the answer, as such a system "would fry the onboard electronics." However, a physics consultant of Cook's called the spokesman "either an idiot or a liar." Cook then learned that "Northrop won the contract based on its use of electrostatics to make it ultra-stealthy." Although he personally doubted the B-2 employed any anti-gravity, Cook learned that electrostatics "improved [the B-2's] aerodynamic efficiency and reduced its drag."[144]

One matter regarding such claims comes immediately to mind: if it is true that the B-2 used electrostatics, or some form of electrogravitics, and furthermore that such a system could generate substantial savings in fuel, the implications for commercial aviation would be extraordinary. There is little question that there would be many angry individuals and groups in the "white world" over the hoarding of such classified knowledge for so long. Considering the astounding amount of fuel expended by commercial airliners every day, such anger could be very difficult to assuage.

As an aside it is worth noting that during the late 1980s, there were many rumors in the aerospace community of a stealthy reconnaissance aircraft capable of Mach 6 – the fabled *Aurora*. Even the *New York Times* in February 1988 had reported insider Pentagon allegations that the Air Force was working on an aircraft of this type. Subsequent attempts to follow-up, however, ran into a dead-end.[145] Well into the 1990s, Ben Rich at Lockheed's Skunkworks Division denied the existence of the Aurora, but never offered a plausible explanation for what Lockheed had been up to since the last F-117A had been built in 1990. In the opinion of aviation experts, neither the YF-22 prototype nor F-22A Raptor could account for the tremendous activity going on at Skunkworks.[146] Actually, there never appears to have been a flying vehicle called *Aurora*, although there seem to have been hypersonic craft that fit the general description. In all likelihood, the aircraft mistakenly known as Aurora has gone under one or more of the following codenames: Blackstar, Copper Coast, Copper Canyon, Brilliant Buzzard, and Centennial. According to aviation researcher Michael Schratt, it is a virtual certainty that America had been building trans-atmospheric vehicles (TAV), despite the absence of official acknowledgment.[147]

Deniability on such matters, to say nothing of UFOs, would be impossible without the active cooperation from the major players in the news media. Lest one entertain the notion that the major media outlets functioned as a true "watch dog" for the general public, consider the words of *Washington Post* publisher Katherine Graham in 1988. That year, Graham told a CIA gathering:

> ... there are some things the general public does not need to know and shouldn't. I believe democracy flourishes when the government can take legitimate steps to keep its secrets and when the press can decide whether to print what it knows."[148]

When the publisher of one of the nation's leading journals of record makes a statement like this, it is easy to understand why the rank and file of American journalism is generally unwilling to challenge national security strictures. It is also easy to fear for the health of a democratic society.

The Norton/Lockheed ARV

Even more sensitive than the specifications of the B-2 or probable trans-atmospheric vehicles was the astounding event of November 12, 1988. On that day, Norton AFB in California held an open house and air show. According to the detailed statement of one individual, a hangar at Lockheed's Palmdale facility the same day contained what appeared to be three fully functioning flying saucers. Within classified circles, this type of craft is known as the "Alien Reproduction Vehicle" (ARV), as well as the Flux Liner.[149]

Aviation illustrator Mark McCandlish received this account directly from a close friend, aviation designer Brad Sorensen. McCandlish has twice held secret security clearances, and has done extensive conceptual art for leading aerospace industry defense contractors. The two had planned to attend the airshow together, but McCandlish had other last-minute obligations. Sorensen attended the airshow at Norton that day, accompanied by a friend. This was no ordinary friend, but a very important gentleman. According to Sorensen, he had been prominent within the Department of Defense – although Sorensen never revealed his identity, the person had been either a former Secretary or Undersecretary. While they were at Norton, Sorensen's friend said "follow me." They walked to the other end of the airfield, away from the crowds, and arrived at an enormous hangar – nicknamed "The Big Hangar" at the base. This was surrounded by a cordon and military police armed with M-16 rifles. Sorensen's companion requested that one of the guards go inside and bring out an acquaintance of his, who was in charge of the show. The two men recognized one-another, and when the man in charge inquired about Sorensen's presence, Sorensen's companion said that Sorenson was his "aide."

At this point the story becomes somewhat confusing. Sorensen originally told McCandlish and others that the exhibit of exotic craft took place within the Big Hangar. In later tellings he added a twist: that in fact the demonstration did not occur at Norton. Rather, the group was escorted aboard an Air Force passenger jet and flown 50 miles northwest to Palmdale. They arrived at the Lockheed Skunkworks facility at the west end of the complex, and it was here that the entire exhibit was held. It appears Sorensen was originally trying to withhold certain pieces of the story.

They entered the Lockheed hangar, and it was obvious that the exhibit was for politicians and military officials who were cleared for high-security information. As McCandlish and aviation researcher Michael Schratt later put it, "the expressed purpose of the exhibit was to garner additional support for classified 'black,' or SAR 'special access required' programs."[150] Evidently, Sorensen's powerful friend was surprised by the magnitude of what was inside. He told Sorensen:

> There are a lot of things in here that I didn't expect they were going to have on display – stuff you probably shouldn't be seeing. So, don't talk to anybody, don't ask any questions, just keep your mouth shut, smile and nod, but don't say anything – just enjoy the show. We're going to get out of here as soon as we can.

The pair were shown several fascinating aircraft, each of which had a plaque highlighting their various specifications. Among these were the Lockheed-Rockwell losing competitor to the Northrop B-2. There were also two advanced hovercraft, which later went to the commercial market. Finally, there was a flattened football, diamond-shaped aircraft, known as the Pulser or "Flaming Pumpkinseed." This last craft was an unmanned vehicle which could launch a 1/10th megaton warhead within less than a tenth of a second. According to Schratt, 18 of these extremely fast and stealthy craft were built during the Reagan Administration. Its exterior also featured the same heat ablative thermal resistant tiles that were used on the space shuttle, strongly indicative of a trans-atmospheric capability and mission.[151] But it turns out this was only the warm-up.

A large black curtain divided the hangar into two areas. Behind the curtain was a large, darkened area. The men turned on the lights and saw an astonishing sight. In McCandlish's words, they saw "three flying saucers floating off the floor – no cables suspended them from the ceiling holding them up, no landing gear underneath – just floating, hovering above the floor."

The three objects were all of different size: 24 feet, 60 feet, and 130 feet in diameter. One of them had some panels removed, and Sorensen saw large oxygen tanks inside. He meticulously noted that the tanks were between 16 and 18 inches in diameter and about 6 feet long. An interesting feature of the craft was a small articulated robotic arm. Evidently, this could be extended, perhaps for releasing satellites or collecting samples.[152]

Nearby, a general (number of stars unclear) was speaking at a lectern to a group of people. He referred to the vehicles as "Alien Reproduction Vehicles," also as the Flux Liner (because they used high voltage electricity). He mentioned several fascinating features of the ARV. One was that it could perform at "light speed or better." Another was that it ran on energy obtained through the vacuum – presumably this is the zero point energy field, better described scientifically as the "quantum zero point fluctuations of the vacuum." It had extraordinary acceleration and maneuverability, able to move from a ground-level hovering position to 80,000 feet within 2.5 seconds.* It was also apparently stated that the ARV had by this time already performed a general reconnaissance of all planets of the solar system in a search for life, and that no life was found. Sorensen noted that the ARV looked "ancient" and as though it had been used extensively. A video exhibit nearby showed the smallest of the three vehicles hovering over a dry lake bed. It made three quick, hopping motions, then accelerated straight up and out of sight within seconds. It was unclear whether the vehicle was silent, or whether the tape simply lacked sound.

---

* McCandlish stated that in subsequent years, he has had multiple sightings of exactly this type of astonishing acceleration. Correspondence with the author.

Sorensen observed as carefully as he could. Eventually, he told McCandlish what he had seen. Not all was revealed right away; the process took several months. Sorensen never sought publicity about this, and over the years spoke only to a very select few investigators – not always in the most forthcoming manner. He never confirmed the identity of his distinguished benefactor.

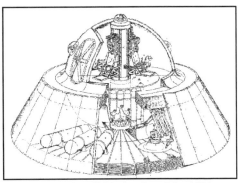

Mark McCandlish's drawing of the ARV

In 1992, McCandlish met a man named Kent Sellen who had been a crew chief at Edwards AFB years before. In 1973, Sellen unintentionally went into an area where he saw a craft exactly matching the description of Sorensen's ARV. At that point, he was thrown to the ground at gunpoint, blindfolded, taken into custody and interrogated about his presence there and what he thought he had seen. Sellen even provided McCandlish with details and data about the object that had been unknown to Sorensen.[153]

It would appear, then, that this was a fully operational American-made spaceship – not merely a liquid propelled space shuttle. The statement about deriving energy from the vacuum is suggestive, naturally, of zero point energy. This is intriguing because the seminal work in ZPE by Dr. Hal Puthoff was in its earliest stages.[154] If true, it would mean that "black world" science had achieved a substantial, revolutionary breakthrough on this matter well ahead of "white world" science. This issue has been debated over the years: can major scientific breakthroughs be made outside the open, public world of science, where a much larger exchange of ideas and talent would theoretically exist? Many scientists think not. However, with an enormous supply of money, and the ability to create a massive classified scientific infrastructure, is it really impossible? Consider how for decades the Cold War itself inhibited the exchange of scientific ideas among so many intellectual disciplines. It can truly be said that, to a large extent, Soviet-bloc and western societies represented two fundamentally separate infrastructures that co-existed and competed for generations. Could not a classified infrastructure, with sufficient money – perhaps unfettered by legal, environmental, or ethical restrictions – become a rival to, or even master of, the official infrastructure?

In early 1995, a video was leaked to the television show *Hard Copy* that showed a very unusual object zipping around the airspace of what was later confirmed to be Nellis Test Site. It had been captured in flight by radar-controlled tracking cameras. Two range operators could be heard discussing the object, mystified at what they were seeing. "I don't know what the hell that is," one of them said, "that's a helo [helicopter], isn't it?" "What is that?" "I have no idea!" "It's weird looking!" and so on.

In addition to showing the image itself, the video displayed the time, radar return signal, continuous range, bearing, and height readings of the object. This made it possible for analysts to conduct a detailed study. At certain points in the video, the object looked as though it could change shape, although this cannot be certain. At times, it looked like a smaller version of the ARV, roughly 15 feet across and 10 feet high. Within just a few minutes, it moved as slowly as 30 mph and as fast as 700 mph. It made a right angle turn at approximately 140 mph.[155]

The Nellis UFO can be reasonably conjectured to be in some sort of relationship to the Norton/Lockheed ARV. It may be the same type of craft, or perhaps a later generation. Its basic shape looked the same, and its flight characteristics were comparable to those attributed to the ARV.

A final comment on the ARV. Its very name, "Alien Reproduction Vehicle," obviously implies that it was built by reverse engineering an *actual* alien craft. How such a craft was obtained – whether via the Roswell crash, other crashes, or some other means – was not indicated by Sorensen. It does, however, lend support to the idea of UFO crash retrieval, which had been developed during the previous decade by Stringfield, Friedman, and others.

Sightings in the World, 1988

Outside of the United States, there were few especially dramatic UFO sightings during 1988. A few interesting instances of triangular craft were observed in Britain, most notably in September 1988, when many people in Essex saw a large black object that appeared triangular. It was said to be silent, very low in the sky, and had red, green, and yellow lights.[156] More unusual aerial activity was reported the following month, in Kent and Sussex. These included police and civilian witnesses, all giving similar descriptions, typically of an oval-shaped object with four bright white lights and a red light in the center, flying low, and giving off a deep hum. Two witnesses said the object suddenly climbed vertically into the evening sky.[157]

The Soviet Union also had a few UFO events, the most notable occurring in September. That month, two bright, fiery spheres were said to have been observed over the nuclear reactor at the Kiev Research Institute. They gave off bright red rays, and were described as almost identical to the UFOs claimed to have been over Chernobyl in 1986.[158] On the 17th of September, two separate cars near Vladivostok had close encounters with a UFO. One driver lost control of his car. Another report, undated, from the *Krasnoye Znamia* (Red Banner) newspaper, discussed an entire section of Vladivostok being illuminated between 2 and 4 a.m. by an unknown beam of light.[159]

Summary

Two short years changed UFO research dramatically. The MJ-12 revelations had split the field and opened up many new research leads. Even considering the argument that the documents could have been planted in some way by the intelligence community, they had led to such individuals as Dr. Eric Walker. There appeared to be fire as well as smoke.

The documents were problematic for several reasons, including lack of known provenance as well as alleged intrinsic features. One could look at the documents in two ways. They could feasibly be variations of a legitimate document, one of presumably several versions, some of which may have been destroyed, others still existing. It is not hard to imagine that factions could develop among those with a "need to know," that the decision-making procedure even on something as important as the UFO cover-up is not monolithic, and that as a result certain documents with a genuine pedigree could be leaked.

They also certainly could be fakes. If so, there is only one scenario that seems feasible. This would be an intelligence community operation, as evidenced by the April 9, 1983 meeting between Richard Doty and Linda Moulton Howe. That encounter proves beyond any reasonable doubt that some version of the MJ-12 documents was being disseminated by Air Force intelligence. If Moore was later involved in creating or faking the documents, all evidence points to his doing so in a helper-type role. Of course, if the documents were fakes, the most logical purpose would be to disable the genuine threat that was then being posed to UFO secrecy. By the 1980s, there were two such threats: the newly released FOIA documents and the growing number of UFO crash retrieval stories. Neither had been significant prior to the late 1970s. By the early 1980s, their ultimate impact was still an unknown factor. Disinformation in the form of false documents and stories could well have been the most effective counterstrike.

Either way then, as authentic or fakes, the MJ-12 documents point to the importance of the UFO topic to the U.S. intelligence community.

But the MJ-12 leaks were only part of the story of these pivotal years. Although these were not the most dense years of UFO sightings, several cases provided strong evidence that somebody's technology was flying about – technology that appeared to be far beyond anything that was supposed to exist. It seems unlikely that all of these sightings were "ours," but surely some could have been, especially when reviewing certain leaks emanating from the world of secrecy, most specifically the so-called ARV. It is of course unknown how much truth is inherent in such leaks, but it is undeniable that they were increasing. It makes perfect sense that if UFO crash retrievals had ever taken place, programs would be created to exploit them. By the 1980s, it is possible that breakthroughs could have been made. If, however, the ARV did represent a breakthrough in propulsion, and if it occurred by way of using the "vacuum," then it did so in a way that contemporary "white world" scientists still do not understand.

Behind all the change of 1987 and 1988 was the revolutionary presence of personal computers and the young Internet. Although it was nothing like the World Wide Web of later years, the bulletin board system was radical enough to enable a dramatic expansion of communication among researchers and other interested parties. Like all major changes, the results were positive and negative. More communication meant more fresh ideas; it also meant a greater frequency of irresponsible and disruptive people becoming involved. For better and for worse, the playing field had opened up.

Chapter 8

Into Dreamland and Beyond
1989-1990

. . . almost as if it were fashioned out of wax and then slightly melted.
— *Bob Lazar, describing an alleged flying saucer at Groom Lake, Nevada, 1989.*

We are being manipulated by a joint human/alien power structure which will result in a one-world government and the partial enslavement of the human race.
— *William Milton Cooper, 1989.*

The whole story of Government/ alien involvement, treaties with aliens, underground bases, a plot to take over the planet . . . . was all cooked up by the counter-intelligence people for the purpose of discrediting [Paul] Bennewitz.
— *William Moore, 1993.*

The UFO hovered above the ground and then flew with a speed exceeding that of modern jet fighters by two or three times. . . . At the present time, terrestrial machines could hardly have such capabilities.
— *General Igor Maltsev, Chief of Soviet Air Defense Forces, on UFO over Moscow, 1990.*

The Air Force has arrived at the conclusion that a certain number of anomalous phenomena have been produced within Belgian airspace.
— *Major-General Wilfried De Brouwer, Deputy Chief, Royal Belgian Air Force, 1990.*

The Bush White House

On January 20, 1989, George Bush became the 41st U.S. President. He generally continued Reagan's policies while tweaking a few areas. Relations with the Soviets underwent a full review – Bush and his key advisors* (wrongly) concluded that Gorbachev's reforms were "cosmetic." Although they understood that the Brezhnev era was long gone, they noted that the Soviets were still giving weapons to the hated Sandinistas, and in any case a military coup seemed like an ever-present possibility. The future still looked unpredictable.

Attitudes toward the Strategic Defense Initiative also changed. Bush never expressed the zeal for this program that Reagan had shown. His public statements stressed that the technology was too expensive and too exotic; he wondered whether it was diverting funds from more practical, conventional needs.[1] Conventional analyses of Star Wars have called it a "brilliant failure" – the first time that space was considered seriously as a

---

* Secretary of State James Baker, National Security Advisor Brent Scowcroft, and Secretary of Defense Richard Cheney.

theater of war, and a program that led to antisatellite (ASAT) systems, "the inevitable next step of warfare."[2] Such an understanding of SDI leaves out the many rumors of a covert side, one that was related to UFOs. Whether a shift away from SDI led into more deeply secret space programs is another possibility. The demonstration of the ARV had taken place immediately after George Bush's election victory. It therefore looked as though the *real* space program was going to continue just fine, no matter what happened to the very public SDI. A study of available data from the DSP satellites, for instance, makes it clear that fastwalkers were being tracked on a regular basis, with information going to Air Force Intelligence and the NRO, at the very least. A covert component to the SDI program would appear to be a "no brainer." It must be considered that the de-emphasis of SDI was nothing other than a means to provide cover for a deep black space program: a proposition that cannot be proven but which nonetheless has merit.

Certainly the Bush administration continued the Reagan policy carte blanche for activities by CIA and other intelligence agencies – much of which were hidden behind shell companies existing on paper only. If one needed to supply (for example) the Islamic fundamentalist Mujahideen rebels in Afghanistan with stinger missiles, then one had to find money that was not bound by Congressional (or other legal) restrictions. Thus, the notorious spike in heroin production in Afghanistan after 1979 was a carefully designed project of the CIA, controlled by CIA assets. Money from the sale of drugs and weapons was recycled through CIA shell companies and banking institutions around the world into "covert money."

Such shenanigans were becoming increasingly understood by critics by the late 1980s, as demonstrated by the scandal involving the Bank of Commerce and Credit International (BCCI). Founded in London by a Pakistani financier, the bank engaged in a massive money laundering operations. In 1988, BCCI was implicated in drug trafficking and was called "the CIA's money-laundering facility." It was also available for the National Security Council when the NSC needed a conduit for Contra money or other covert measures. BCCI not only financed arms deals that governments wanted to keep secret, but the bank shipped goods in its own ships, insured them with its own insurance agency, and provided its own manpower and security. Drugs were a major part of its revenues. Among clients of BCCI were Manuel Noriega, Ferdinand Marcos, and Saddam Hussein. Not only this, but one of the inside sources of the murdered journalist Danny Casolaro told him that the bank financed large private business deals between George Bush and Manuel Noriega, as well as between Bush and Saddam Hussein. These were not government deals, but private business deals. By 1991, BCCI was shut down, with $10 billion missing. The Justice Department vigorously impeded an investigation of its activities. But BCCI was only one bank; there were many others ready to service the needs of the world's power players.[3]

Then there was the UFO connection. Throughout the Reagan and Bush years, rumors spread through the UFO community that George Bush was a member of MJ-12. It appears that this rumor spread in part due to the brief exchange between candidate Bush and Charles Huffer in 1988, although MJ-12 was never part of their conversation. When UFO researcher Grant Cameron contacted the Bush Library, he was informed that there was only one UFO document in the entire Presidential collection. This prompted Cameron to ask rhetorically whether UFOs disappeared during the Bush years, or was all relevant data simply deflected to other agencies such as the Air Force, NASA, or black-budget programs set-up to deal with the information.[4]

Another UFO story concerns an attempt by the new National Security Advisor, General Brent Scowcroft, to be "read into" the secret UFO program. He wanted to see the Project Manager, who happened to be known as "Raven" within the Aviary. According to Robert Collins, who told the story, Scowcroft "asked like a child: may I see something please?"[5] The identity of Raven is not publicly known. The two main candidates are Jack Verona, a senior Pentagon scientist and former head of the DIA's Scientific and Technical Intelligence Directorate; and Richard Helms, Director of the CIA under Presidents Johnson and Nixon. Additional speculation has centered on Henry Kissinger.[6]

Paranoia and Its Discontents

While the U.S. intelligence community continued to operate without meaningful oversight, the rift between the ufologically paranoid and the conservative grew ever wider. Jerome Clark dismissed the wild claims of the "new school of unhinged types" who believed extraterrestrials were here to serve men ala "some cosmic McDonald's." While "even democratic" governments had secrets, scandals such as Watergate and Iran-Contra showed that conspirators were usually caught. Lest one marvel at such naivete, Clark conceded that rules were different regarding UFOs. Here, the watchdogs were not merely sleeping on-the-job; they were not even on-the-job. Even so, he argued that it remained highly speculative as to just what the government did and did not know about such topics as Roswell or UFOs in general. Rushing into conspiracy theorizing, he maintained, did not help scientific ufology.[7]

Claims and counter-claims of conspiracy, however, ruled the day. Early in 1989, William Moore stated that he was not "a forger, a hoaxer, a fabricator or counterfeiter; nor, to the best of my knowledge, have I ever participated in any illegal or un-American activity in connection with my more than eight-year involvement with the MJ-12 controversy."[8] As time would soon prove, this was not exactly true, unless one considers the witting unhinging of a friend (Paul Bennewitz) in the cause of disinformation to be proudly American.

Leonard Stringfield continued to research and uncover new leads regarding UFO crash retrievals. In early 1989, he issued a new Status Report which discussed possible recent cases, as well as alleged intimidation and cover-up by military agencies.[9]

Abduction issues also remained highly charged, including debates on whether or not cross-species hybridization would ever be possible (no according to Michael Swords; yes according to David Jacobs).[10] In another argument, Hopkins and Jacobs took sides against Jacques Vallee, who questioned the utility of hypnosis in abduction research and accused ufology's two best-known abduction researchers of lacking proper training and credentials to perform hypnotic regression. "Regression," wrote Vallee, "should never be conducted by individuals who hold strong personal beliefs about the nature of the experience they are investigating, and who are searching for confirmation of their specific interpretation of the phenomenon."[11]

Another interesting development was the growing suspicion of some UFO researchers about Dr. Carl Sagan. Sagan, one of the world's most famous astronomers, had once been host to the enormously successful television show, "Cosmos." Over his career, he frequently expressed his belief that the universe was teeming with life. His public statements on UFOs were a different matter. Based on minimal evidence of research or effort, Sagan dismissed the extraterrestrial hypothesis, arguing that such beliefs amounted to little more than wish fulfillment.[12] In late 1988, Sagan stated that "every flying saucer 'sighting' when given a genuinely tough scientific scrutiny has been judged either a mistake or a fraud."[13]

In one of history's intriguing coincidences, Stanton Friedman and Sagan had been classmates at the University of Chicago. In early 1989, Friedman wrote an open letter to Sagan (his third) expressing his sadness at having to correct "false and misleading" statements on UFOs. Contrary to Sagan's claim,

> . . . every large scale scientific study of flying saucers has produced a significant number of cases which not only cannot be identified, but which clearly indicate that some so called flying saucers are manufactured objects behaving in ways that we Earthlings cannot yet duplicate with our manufactured objects.

Friedman suggested that Sagan had taken over from Donald Menzel the role of "UFO disinformation specialist."[14]

The Eastern Empire Cracks

1989 marked Mikhail Gorbachev's fourth year as leader of the USSR. His promotion of *perestroika* ("restructuring") and *glasnost* ("openness") electrified the people under Soviet rule, even as the Bush administration remain unimpressed, perhaps nonplused. What had started as an attempt to bring competitiveness to the economy of the Soviet Union was already beginning to spiral out of control. Once "openness" had become a part of official policy, it became increasingly difficult to hide the full extent of past government criminality and misdeeds. It was well known that Stalin's rule had brought misery, famine, and terror to the nation, but such things had never been openly discussed. What would happen when they were? Would the very legitimacy of the Communist Party itself be challenged? Moreover, how would the many non-Russian subject nationalities respond to the chance to express themselves more openly?

The answer to this question was already known. Major riots had occurred in Azerbaijan back in 1987, brought about by a Muslim populace that had never been happy under Soviet rule. Other nationalities were now about to follow. In January 1989, the Hungarian parliament allowed freedom of association and assembly. It was the first Eastern bloc country to do this. In March, the USSR held its first largely free elections in seventy-five years. Several key party chiefs failed to get elected, although the popular Mayor of Moscow, Boris Yeltsin, was swept back into power. Riots in Soviet Georgia took place in April; these were brutally suppressed with the resulting deaths of twenty protesters. In May, Hungarian border guards cut down the barbed wire fence that marked the Austrian boundary. It was the first chink in the Iron Curtain; thousands would soon flee to the West.

Events were moving faster than anyone had expected. When U.S. Secretary of State James Baker met with Soviet Foreign Minister Eduard Shevardnadze in May, he was met with the announcement that the Soviets were unilaterally withdrawing 500 nuclear warheads from Eastern Europe.

He had nothing to offer from Washington. However, on May 12, President Bush, speaking to the graduating class at Texas A&M University, stated that the United States was ready to welcome the Soviet Union "back into the world order."[15] In mid-May, Gorbachev met with Deng Xiaoping in China to normalize relations. It was the first visit by a Soviet head of state to China in thirty years and signaled the beginning of troop withdrawals at the Sino-Soviet border.

Meanwhile riots in Beijing were getting worse. China, after all, had slowly been liberalizing under Deng's leadership, and the Chinese people were heartened by what they were learning about the Soviet example. They too wanted greater freedom of expression. The result was the disgraceful massacre of Chinese protesters in Beijing's Tiananmen Square on June 3, 1989. CNN carried live coverage of the deaths of hundreds of Chinese citizens at the hands of their military. It became clear that China's leadership was bent on purely economic reforms while retaining political orthodoxy. Ironically, this showed Eastern Europeans that they could succeed with large demonstrations, knowing their governments could not engage in the same crackdowns. In June, Poland's communist leadership allowed open elections, and the opposition party, Solidarity, won 99 of the 100 seats in the Senate, as well as a majority in the lower house.

Several strange events occurred within the Soviet Union during this time. Most prominent of these was the failure of the Phobos 2 Soviet probe to Mars. Phobos 1 and 2 were launched by the Soviet Union in July 1988 to study Mars and its moonlets Phobos and Deimos. Each probe was a complicated set of devices with three television cameras, a spectrometer, guidance system, and video recording system. Although the probes were Soviet, there was substantial international support, with much cooperation coming from the U.S., France, and Switzerland. Data was transmitted to the European Mission Center and NASA.

Phobos 1 experienced a software error that led to its shutdown on September 2, 1988. Phobos 2 also had several problems on the way to Mars: by late 1988, many of its instruments were "running hot," it had lost two of its three television channels, and was using a backup transmitter. Still, the probe made it into Mars orbit on January 29, 1989. It then undertook an orbit that brought it in synchronicity with the moonlet Phobos, just a few hundred meters away. One of its main missions was to emit a laser ray at the surface of Phobos in order to cause a small explosion; it was then supposed to gather data from the evaporated substances.

Problems developed when Phobos 2 aligned itself with its namesake. In mid-March, the probe took video images of the Martian surface. While appearing on Soviet television, two oddities were evident. First, near the Martian equator was a network of straight lines with geometric relationships; some lines were short, others long, some were thin, others were wide enough to look like rectangular shapes. The pattern covered an area of some six hundred square kilometers (more than two hundred and thirty square miles). During the same broadcast, an unusual oblong shadow became apparent on the Martian surface. It was clearly a shadow: surface features of the planet could be seen in the lighter portions at the ends. It was very different from the shadow that would have been cast either by the probe itself or the moonlet Phobos.

Then, on March 25, 1989, the probe took an infrared photograph of what appeared to be a large and long cylindrical object very close to the moonlet Phobos. If this "Phobos Mystery Object" (PMO) was at the same distance as Phobos itself, it would have been roughly two kilometers wide and 20 kilometers (roughly 15 miles) long. Its surface brightness was the same as that of the moonlet. Its sides were parallel and both the ends were rounded; the

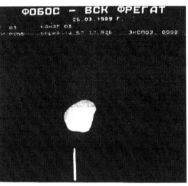

The final photograph taken by the Phobos 2 probe.

end towards Phobos narrowed slightly; the other end seemed to have a slight protrusion.

This was the last image captured by the probe. On March 27, Phobos 2 failed to re-establish communications with Earth: it was commanded to reposition itself for an imaging session, but did not do so. Instead, it had gone into a spin. On the next day, the Soviet mission control center announced that they had lost communication with the spacecraft.

The images are puzzling. The "shadow" image does not conform to any known object; indeed, the only object it bears a superficial resemblance to is the equally strange PMO. Alexander Dunayev, Chairman of the Soviet Glavkosmos space organization, discussed the failure of Phobos 2 on March 29, mentioning that an odd-shaped object was seen between the spacecraft and Mars. He speculated this was either debris or an autonomous propulsion sub-system that was jettisoned after the spacecraft was propelled into Mars orbit. Not everyone seemed convinced. Other Soviet experts went on the record to mention the PMO as anomalous. Roald Kremnev, of the Babokin Space Testing Center, stated on April 14, 1989 that the most discussed aspect of the Phobos 2 mission was the gigantic object registered just days before the accident. Two years later, Colonel Dr. Marina Popovich, a Russian cosmonaut and pilot, publicly revealed the PMO image, arguing that the object was anomalous. More conventional explanations followed: the object was said to be a "trailed moonlet" traveling at a faster speed than the probe or Phobos itself. As the exposure time of the photograph was eight seconds, the elongation could have been caused by the object's motion.[16] This seems reasonable, except that it does not explain the irregularities of the PMO, including its apparent narrowing at one end, its protrusion at the other, and the many small bumps that are evident along its shaft.

Are the anomalies related to each other? Did something "out there" cause the failure of the mission? Whatever the cause, none of these oddities are mentioned in official accounts of the Phobos 2 mission. Instead, mission failure is usually attributed to a malfunction of the on-board computer; this resulted in faulty positioning of the solar cells, ultimately leading to a drained battery.[17]

The failure of the Phobos 2 mission was the most intriguing Soviet UFO event of early 1989, but the cracking of the Iron Curtain enabled many other stories to reach the west. A large, low-flying cylindrical UFO was reported in the Transcaucasus region by "thousands" of witnesses on February 13. It had spotlights in front and back, porthole-like openings along the sides, and traveled at the leisurely speed of about 65 mph. As it flew over the city of Nalchik, it drifted down to an altitude of 150 feet, then flew off.[18]

Another large object was seen hovering at an altitude of 1,000 feet over the city of Cherepovets on April 24.[19] Two months later, in the central Russian Vologda region on June 6, school children near the village of Konantsevo saw a luminous dot in the sky. It became larger, turned into a shining sphere, landed in meadow, and moved to a nearby river. The children watched it from a quarter-mile away. It seemed to split and "something resembling a headless person in dark garb" appeared. The creature and sphere became invisible; three more spheres were later said to have landed in the same meadow.[20] All very strange, all questioned by a skeptical western media. Yet, matters would become even stranger in the Soviet Union as the year progressed.

Fyffe, Alabama

Elsewhere in the world, most of the interesting UFO activity was occurring in Florida's Gulf Breeze and Nevada's Area 51. However, one sighting from early 1989 stands out among the rest. This occurred in the area around a small town in northeastern Alabama named Fyffe, a stone's throw from the Tennessee and Georgia state lines. On the night of February 10, the DeKalb County Sheriff's office received over 50 telephone calls from citizens over a 25 mile radius regarding "a silent thing streaking through the dark." The first report came in at 8:42 p.m. when a woman in the town of Grove Oak told the Fyffe police department that she had watched the object for over an hour with a pair of binoculars. The aircraft was curved, she said, with the side upright, like a "banana." There was a red light on each end and a white light in between them, she told the police. The top of the curve was outlined in green light. When the craft turned, the green lights splayed outward "like fireworks" in a circular shape. Police Chief Junior Garmany and assistant chief Fred Works drove to the site. The two officers saw the object immediately. It was at an altitude of roughly 1,000 to 1,500 feet, and completely silent. "We got out of the car and we turned off the engine and the radio," said Garmany. "When we started towards it, it began moving away." The officers drove after the object, following it for about twelve miles when it suddenly reversed direction and silently flew over them. "We figured it was going about three or four hundred miles an hour," said Garmany. Initially, it looked like an airplane, but the shape was difficult to describe. It appeared diamond-shaped, but rounded on the edges, with flashing green, white, and red lights along the sides. Three white lights were along the bottom, "like landing lights." Works said the white lights underneath appeared to shine upward, illuminating the bottom of the craft. It did not appear to be especially thick from top to bottom, and had no windows, lettering, or wings. "I'm not saying it was a flying saucer," said Works. "But what really got me was the lack of sound."

After the object left, it was seen by a state trooper and by police officers in the towns of Crossville, Geraldine, and Collinsville. On one occasion, police officers reportedly saw three of the aircraft at one time. Several citizens were deeply upset by what they saw. A county official said that one terrified resident was "about to have a heart attack, and his wife was screaming." Maxwell AFB had no explanations, and a weather service official ruled out weather balloons.

A few nights later, on the evening of February 15, 1989, Fyffe police officer Sgt. Dennison Scott, along with two other officers, investigated a citizen's report of a strange object in the sky. Scott said the hovering object could be seen from anywhere in the city, flashing multi-colored lights for more than an hour, until it moved away to the northwest toward Huntsville. A report was sent to the Alabama Department of Public Safety. Officials at nearby Fort Rucker, Fort Benning, Maxwell AFB, and the FAA could not identify the object. Junior Garmany and Fred Works believed they saw the UFO again on February 17, and other sightings were reported in subsequent days and weeks.

The sightings near Fyffe received extensive news coverage. Many people in the region began to stay out at night to try to spot UFOs, sometimes with success, often without. As the word spread, thousands of outsiders came. For a while, Fyffe rivaled Gulf Breeze and Area 51 as a UFO hotspot where tourists vastly outnumbered the locals. Next came the jokes, directly against Fyffe police officers or against the town in general. A case in point was the March 7 issue of the British tabloid the *Daily Star*, which described the late pianist Liberace descending over Fyffe from a giant banana in the sky, playing old showtunes. Garmany later stated, "if I had known the kind of ridicule we were going to get, I'd have kept my mouth shut. And I'd have shot Fred if he'd opened his."

Sightings in Fyffe continued in March, while thousands continued to descend upon the town (including representatives of MUFON, as well as unconfirmed reports of FBI and Air Force investigators). There were weeks in which sightings occurred every night, often multiple witness affairs. While national and international media phoned the Fyffe police department looking for a story, citizens continued calling in their UFO reports. The four-man police force was kept busy. Some of the sightings called in were determined to be stars, classic misidentifications of bright celestial objects like Venus. Others were suspected by law enforcement and MUFON representatives to be aircraft. But on Sunday night, March 12, several witnesses saw an extremely large object with red and green flashing lights on the side, and two white lights on the bottom, hovering about five miles away. While one witness went to get binoculars, the object simply vanished before the eyes of the remaining witness. At the same time, another man was directly under the object, which he said was the size of a football field. In addition to noticing the same lighting configuration described by the more distant witnesses, he noticed a metallic blue color to the craft, which he said would probably not have been visible against the night sky without the huge lights. He went inside the house to get a camera; the object was gone when he returned.

There did turn out to be a series of interesting photographs taken in March by a photographer and journalist team of the local *Weekly Post* newspaper. Using time lapse photography, they captured the bright UFO at some distance low in the sky as it was ascending, just before it vanished. The photograph shows no features of the craft at all, simply its movement, which does not correspond to that of any aircraft.

One other factor regarding Fyffe is that before and after the UFO wave, the area had been the scene of many animal mutilations, mostly of cattle. This phenomenon lasted well into the 1990s and was subject to serious concern by Chief of Police Garmany and the Mayor, Boyd Graben. Just like the many cases of mutilations that had occurred elsewhere, the dead animals in Fyffe showed signs of "precise surgical cutting." No one was ever caught in the act, and no agency ever took responsibility for the actions.[21]

Ultimately, these events in northeastern Alabama remain unexplained. As with similar developments elsewhere, either answer to the "ours" versus "theirs" issue leads to unsettling implications.[22]

The Bob Lazar Story

In the spring of 1989, journalist George Knapp of KLAS-TV in Las Vegas began airing a series of interviews he conducted with a scientist who claimed to have spent a brief period at a secure area inside the Groom Lake facility called S4. This was just south of the then-barely-known but already legendary "Area 51." The scientist, known by the pseudonym "Dennis," was shown only in silhouette. The military, he said, had nine extraterrestrial flying discs and was trying to "back engineer" the technology. He had broken his security oath, and now had gone public in order to protect his life. By the end of 1989, "Dennis" was revealed to be one Robert Lazar. Over many interviews with Knapp and subsequent investigators, he told an astonishing story.

During the early 1980s, Lazar said, he earned Masters degrees from MIT and Cal Tech in physics and electronics technology and also worked as a physicist at Los Alamos National Laboratory (LANL). During this time, he had occasion to meet the famous physicist Edward Teller. The two had a cordial conversation, as Lazar had just been mentioned in the local news for having installed a jet engine on his car.* By 1988, however, Lazar was out of physics – a bored 29 year-old proprietor of a small photographic processing business. He wanted a career opportunity and began sending out resumes, including Teller as one of the recipients. On November 29, 1988, Teller called him and gave him the name of someone in Las Vegas. Lazar phoned this person (later losing the name and number), and some time later received a phone call from EG&G, a company dealing in high technology and with contracts in the Nevada test site. Lazar interviewed with them on December 1, but was informed that he was overqualified for the position in question. A day or two later, however, EG&G contacted him regarding a position in propulsion – in "an outer area" – connected to the U.S. Navy. He interviewed again on Monday, December 5, 1988. This seemed like a part-time position, at least for a while, which would allow him to continue his duties as a photolab processor. The next day, December 6, Lazar reported to the EG&G building at McCarran Airport. There, he met with a security officer named Dennis Mariani. Mariani escorted him on his flight to Area 51 at Groom Lake, where Lazar signed a secrecy agreement that required intensive monitoring of his activities. He and Mariani boarded a bus with blacked out windows and rode for a half hour down a dirt and gravel road. They arrived at a base near Papoose dry lake bed, otherwise known as S4. Armed guards were everywhere. Lazar's ID was prepared, he was given a physical and was tested for allergic reactions to unknown substances.

The precise activities and chronology of Lazar's few reported visits to S4 are not entirely clear. He claimed to have gone out to S4 on six or seven occasions between December 1988 and April 1989. The first two visits were apparently filled with "briefings," where he sat alone in a room and read documents. Most of this was to become acquainted with his project, named "Galileo," which dealt with gravity and propulsion. He also read about a second project, named "Looking Glass," which was concerned with the physics of seeing back in time. There was also some hands-on bench work to learn the operation of an "anti-matter reactor."

Lazar said he was at S4 twice before he saw a disc. The first time he saw it was essentially a "look but don't touch" visit. He walked into a hangar. There, resting on three legs, was an absolutely classic-looking flying saucer.

---

*
Knapp confirmed that Lazar was employed in 1982 by the firm Kirk Meyer, Inc., a subcontractor at LANL. He also located a June 27, 1982 edition of the *Los Alamos Monitor* which referred to Lazar as "a physicist at the Los Alamos Meson Physics facility" and described his achievement of installing a jet engine on his Honda Civic hatchback. Teller, it was determined, was in Los Alamos for a lecture at that time.

It bore a striking resemblance to the "perfect" UFOs allegedly photographed by Billy Meier. Lazar had an ominous feeling, "almost ... that you shouldn't be there." The object was roughly 35-40 feet in diameter and 15 feet tall. It had a single color of grey pewter. Believing it was manmade, he thought, "well, this explains all the UFO stories."

Following this visit, he read more briefings which explicitly described the craft as extraterrestrial. During his stay at S-4, according to Lazar, he saw a total of 9 flying saucers, each distinctive in design and size. His assignment, however, concerned just the one craft: the perfect one he had nicknamed, "the sport model."[23]

Lazar returned for a second time to examine the craft, followed by security personnel. He walked around the craft. It had no sharp corners, "almost as if it were fashioned out of wax and then slightly melted." It had three levels; he was cleared for the lower two. He crawled underneath on the sub-floor. There were three gravity amplifiers. Their function was to amplify and focus the "Gravity A" wave, which in turn came from the "total annihilation" reactor, situated in the center level of the craft. Lazar then entered the center level. Other than containing the reactor, this level was fairly empty. A few items had apparently been removed or sawed off at the base. There was a possible control panel, and a space where another panel might have been. There were extremely small chairs – much too small for human-sized pilots. There were no obvious sleeping quarters, but Lazar did notice possible "evidence of writing." Rather amazingly, part of the skin of the craft could become transparent, and one could see outside as if it were a window. Even without seeing the top level, Lazar was now convinced he was dealing with extraterrestrial technology.

According to Lazar, the fuel for this craft was the super-heavy Element 115, which was housed in the reactor. There, it underwent bombardment and spontaneous fission, producing anti-matter particles that were converted to electricity with 100 percent efficiency. While this appeared to contradict the first law of thermodynamics, Lazar said there was no detectable loss of energy in the process. This tremendous power then operated the amplifier, distorted the surrounding gravitational field, and caused the craft to become invisible. More importantly, it allowed the vehicle to shorten the distance to a charted destination. In effect, the craft could bend space and time. Speed of light limitations were irrelevant. The problem with Element 115 was that it could not be manufactured on Earth. Nevertheless, Lazar said, there were roughly 500 pounds of it available (courtesy of the aliens). It was also remarkably stable, he said, and just 223 grams of it would fuel a craft for a very long time.[24]*

On one occasion, said Lazar, he was brought outside to see a demonstration of a craft. Several other people were there, including one person next to Lazar who was in radio contact with it. The disc "lifted off the ground, slid over to the left, then back to the right, and set back down."[25]

Lazar's conviction that these craft were extraterrestrial was reinforced by additional reports he read. He always emphasized that what he read was "simply words on paper," and could have been disinformation. But by his own estimate, he read more than 100 documents. These dealt not only with Element 115, the discs, and other technical matters, but the aliens themselves.

The documents said the aliens traveled about 30 light years to Earth from the Zeta Reticuli 1 & 2 star system. Popularly known as "greys," the Reticulans were greyish in color, 3 to 4 feet tall, and weighed 25 to 50 pounds. Their heads and eyes were large, their nose, mouth, and ears were practically non-existent, and they had no hair. Lazar even saw photographs of alien bodies, including details that would surface again in 1995 with the infamous "Alien Autopsy video" of Ray Santilli. According to Lazar, the alien "carcass" was cut up and had what appeared to be very dark blood. It also "seemed to [have] one large organ in the body as opposed to identifiable heart and lungs and that sort of thing."[26]

The Reticulans referred to humans as "containers" (whether of genetic material, souls, or something else), and claimed to have genetically "externally corrected" human evolution up to 65 times over the last 10,000 years. The documents mentioned a great deal about recombinant DNA methods and viral weaponry, and there was speculation that viruses were used to redirect human evolution – since viruses are the only known organism that can attach to humans and impart a new genetic code. The Reticulans also claimed to have given humanity its religion "to prevent the 'containers' from destroying themselves."** Disconcertingly, they were able to exert a form of mind control on people, most effective when the subject was relaxed, preferably asleep. Stimulated states of consciousness made mind control difficult.

The documents also mentioned an exchange of information and hardware between the U.S. government and the Reticulans until 1979,

---

*
   Since there are about 454 grams in one pound, this would be enough for just over 1,000 discs.

**
   Questionable (suspicious?) logic, considering the prominent role played by religion in the history of human warfare.

when a conflict occurred – very much like the scenario offered in 1987 by John Lear. The aliens left at that time, but were expected to return in the future. This was when, according to the documents, the U.S. government began its back-engineering program. Then, in May 1987, some scientists took an antimatter reactor to an underground Nevada test facility. Unfortunately, their experiment required them to cut the reactor open, and they were killed. Lazar was a replacement for one of those scientists.

All in all, an exciting adventure for an unemployed physicist who had just turned 30. Hardly any conversation ever took place among Lazar's estimated 22 co-workers. Still, he once asked someone how the UFO secret could be kept for so long. The answer: it was "the easiest thing to keep secret," precisely because it was so unusual.

But Lazar had a cavalier attitude about secrets. He soon told Gene Huff and John Lear about S4 and the discs. On March 21, Lazar asked Lear if he wanted to see one of their test flights. Sure, replied Lear, but how can we do that? Lazar said he knew a spot where they could see it from public land every Wednesday night. Thus, on the evening of Wednesday, March 22, Lazar took his wife, Huff, and Lear to the Groom Lake road. Before long, they saw a bright light rise above the mountains between them and S4. Through Lear's Celestron telescope, they saw what looked like a saucer-shaped object. A week later on March 29, Lazar, Huff, and Lear repeated the trip, taking Lear's Celestron telescope and video equipment. At around 8:30, they saw a disc – the videotape shows a bright light apparently maneuvering. When the camera zoomed in close to the object, it seemed to be spinning. The three men watched it descend behind a mountain.[27]

The group did this once more on Wednesday, April 5, 1989. This time they were chased off Bureau of Land Management land. According to Huff, "a Lincoln county cop ... pulled us over and hassled us. He took our I.D.s and radioed our identities into the security base station."

This ended Lazar's career at S4. His security clearance was revoked, and his superiors tried to convince him to go out to the Nevada Test Site for a "final debriefing." He refused, believing that he might never be allowed to leave again. Concerned for his safety, Lazar decided to go public. In May 1989, Lear introduced him to journalist George Knapp. Knapp was surely the best option for Lazar, possessing strong investigative skills and an open mind. Knapp also possessed a good knowledge of activities at the Nevada test site. His interviews with Lazar ("Dennis") were a sensation, helping him earn a UPI individual achievement award.

Lazar's story raised more questions then it answered. Verifying his background proved to be an ordeal.[28] Knapp checked Lazar's credentials, but found no records of his schooling – no trace of Lazar's alleged attendance at either MIT or Cal Tech ever turned up. Knapp also received denials from Los Alamos National Laboratory that Lazar had ever worked there – although he did find Lazar's name in a LANL telephone book from the early 1980s, as well as several Los Alamos persons who remembered Lazar. He then found a Los Alamos newspaper article of June 27, 1982 that featured Lazar, and even found speeding tickets of Lazar's indicating he lived in Los Alamos. This was enough evidence to persuade Knapp that Lazar had worked at Los Alamos in some capacity, apparently as a physicist.

The Bob Lazar story percolated throughout 1989, publicized by degrees through the investigations of George Knapp. On November 10, 1989, Knapp began airing a series of stories about Area 51, using Lazar as his principal source, and at this time revealed his true name. Lazar repeated his basic statement: the secret technology being tested at the S4 sector of the Nevada Test Site was of alien origin, that he had worked at Los Alamos National Laboratories in 1982 and 1983, possessed a degree from MIT, and so on. Now that Lazar had gone "official," other investigators had the opportunity to verify his claims.

Stanton Friedman quickly found problems with them. Like Knapp before him, Friedman tried to obtain records of Lazar's time at MIT; and like Knapp was unable to do so. None appeared to exist. Lazar also told Friedman he had also attended Pierce College and Cal State, but Friedman could only verify that Lazar took electronics courses at Pierce College, without obtaining a degree. Lazar claimed that his academic records were missing because the government was trying to turn him into a "non-person."

There were other problems with Lazar's story. It was learned that earlier in his life, Lazar was known by a different name, which made it difficult to follow his personal history. His polygraph test was inconclusive. His memory of large blocks of time was also fuzzy – Lazar suspected his employers used mind control techniques to block his memories. To overcome this, he met with Layne Keck, a licensed hypnotherapist. Keck found the results of his sessions with Lazar puzzling, and suggested that mind-altering chemicals may have been used to confuse Lazar's memory.[29]

For the next several years, questions about Lazar dominated ufology. In addition to the problem of his academic credentials, many researchers expressed deep skepticism over a number of other issues. Among these was the alleged stability of Element 115. Another was Lazar's apparent ability to traipse into an incredibly secure "dream job" with no pedigree or prior credentials. Another still was his ability – once within this secure environment – to obtain such rapid access to information concerning aliens, their background, and their technology. Finally, researchers wondered why any person who obtained such a security clearance would so quickly and carelessly reveal it all to the world. Many experts in the field of UFOs, aviation, and Area 51 (such as Tom Mahood, Stanton Friedman, Glen Campbell, John Alexander, and others) spent a great deal of time investigating Lazar's claims, generally concluding they were fraudulent.

Edward Teller was on one occasion confronted about Bob Lazar. After the Lazar story broke, Teller was asked by a television reporter if he had helped Lazar gain employment, and if he knew what was going on at Area 51. Teller's reply:

> Look, I don't know Bob Lazar. All this sounds fine. I probably met him. I might have said to somebody I met him and I liked him, after I met him, and if I liked him. But I don't remember him . . . I mean you are trying to force questions on me that I simply won't answer.[30]

Still, Lazar has retained supporters over the many years. Knapp, while acknowledging the problems with Lazar's account, continues to maintain a cautious acceptance of its core – in no small part because he subsequently obtained corroboration from some two dozen other Groom Lake insiders regarding key parts of Lazar's scenario. Another person who voiced strong support for Lazar was DSP satellite expert Ron Regehr, who knew Lazar throughout most of the 1980s and told the author that Lazar was "one hundred percent" authentic. Huff, too, has continued to be a strong advocate for Bob Lazar.

Lazar never seemed to care what UFO researchers thought of him. Despite the incredible nature of his story, his manner of presentation was always low-key and scientific in tone. In the many interviews and talks he gave during the 1990s, he was as consistent as he was laconic, never seeking to speculate, guess, or expand on what he claimed to have directly experienced. He even acknowledged he may have been manipulated, or even subject to mind control, while he was at S4.

Along these lines, one may engage in the following speculation. If the alleged zero-point breakthroughs of the Lockheed ARV (as described by Brad Sorensen in 1988) were true, one might consider allowing Lazar into S4 specifically so that he might leak incorrect data. If flying saucers were thought to require Element 115 – jokingly referred to as "unobtanium" – then private attempts to replicate the technology would be doomed to failure. It would imply a dead end to prospective researchers seeking the next propulsion breakthrough. Could it be that Lazar was quickly "sized up" and deemed to be a useful conduit for the release of such disinformation? Such speculation cannot be proven within the hall of mirrors that is the U.S. national security establishment. It could be that Lazar was a fraud, plain and simple; or that he was telling the truth as he knew it; or that he was manipulated in some way for purposes unknown.

Whatever the ultimate truth behind Lazar's story, it was the dam breaker. After Lazar, throughout most of the 1990s, Area 51 drew interested people to its perimeter, armed with cameras and video equipment. The most secret place in the world suddenly became the star attraction of conspiracy hunters everywhere. Not all the attendees were interested in UFOs; presumably guards were on the lookout for "tourists" with especially sophisticated equipment engaged in espionage of the more traditional sort. Still, if one assumes that crash retrievals of UFOs had taken place, and accepts the possibility that some of the retrieved technology had been taken to "Area 51" (or, more accurately, S4), then it is easy to understand the concern that might be elicited from behind closed doors.

Cooper on the Secret Government and MJ-12

Meanwhile, William Cooper crystalized his newly found ideas into a paper that quickly became an underground "classic." This was "The Secret Government: The Origin, Purpose, and Identity of MJ-12."[31] Quite simply, Cooper let it all hang out, incorporating many elements of the UFO reality into the broader realm of one-world-government conspiracy theories. He presented a nearly overwhelming amount of facts, many of which were entirely true, others unverifiable, and others provably false.

His claims included: at least 16 downed alien craft, 65 bodies, and one live alien retrieved between 1947 and 1952; at least 10 more UFO crash retrievals during the Eisenhower years.* Such a situation forced the creation of a "secret government," dominated by the CIA and Air Force during the early years. Insiders who objected to the new system, such as former Secretary of Defense James Forrestal, were eliminated. Cooper described Forrestal (very generously and none too accurately) as "a very idealistic and religious man who believed that the public should be told." Further measures were taken during the 1950s to manage the UFO/alien problem. The National Security Agency was founded in deep secrecy in 1952,

---

* Needless to say, these claims remain unverifiable and well beyond the speculations of most UFO researchers.

primarily for the purpose of "alien communications." The true MJ-12 group was born, said Cooper, during the early 1950s, when President Eisenhower brought Nelson Rockefeller into the picture. Similarly, the Bilderbergers were founded in 1954, at least partly in order to enable the international elites to manage the UFO/alien situation. Other secret societies had connections to the secrecy, including the Jason Society, Skull and Bones, the Council on Foreign Relations, and the Trilateral Commission.

Speaking of the aliens, there were several types, said Cooper, including those that looked totally human; others with large noses. One group met with President Eisenhower and signed a treaty with the U.S. According to Cooper, the first Alien Ambassador was named His "Omnipotent Highness Krll" – pronounced Krill – although the Americans secretly called him "Original Hostage Krll." This of course was lifted directly from John Grace and John Lear. Cooper also described an early version of what years later became known as the Serpo story, involving an exchange of human and alien "guests." The alien flag was known as the "Trilateral Insignia," and was on their craft and uniforms.

Much of the money to hide relevant programs was controlled by the Military Office of the White House. Cooper accurately discussed this office, using as his source a 1980 expose entitled *Breaking Cover*.[32] The author, Bill Gulley, described the layers upon layers of secrecy connected with that office and (in language nearly lifted nearly verbatim by Cooper) described how money "was channeled through a circuitous route the cleverest spy, or accountant, would have trouble following." Gulley did not state there was a UFO connection to the many underground facilities funded by the Office, but Cooper did.

There was much more in Cooper's 12,000 word paper. His main thesis was that "...we are being manipulated by a joint human/alien power structure which will result in a one-world government and the partial enslavement of the human race."

Cooper was generally dismissed and shunned by UFO researchers, which was not surprising considering the unfounded nature of some of his claims, to say nothing of the instances in which he was known to fabricate his data. It must be said, however, that much of Cooper's research in his paper was solid enough, and all-too-ignored by mainstream researchers, whether within ufology or beyond. Writing about the influence of the Bilderbergers, the Council on Foreign Relations, the Trilateral Commission, or Skull and Bones was simply *not done* in 1989. Whether Cooper got everything right is another matter, but bringing widespread attention to the powerful influence exerted by these entirely non-elected groups was long overdue. His work was surely derivative from other, more careful researchers, but Cooper put together an outline that seemed plausible to many researchers seeking to understand the true structure of power in the world. The problem was that this scenario was irretrievably soiled by his own obvious mental instability and repeated instances of plagiarism.

But there was one thing Cooper was not: a right-wing, "fascist" conspiracy theorist, which is how he was frequently characterized.[33] Cooper's political orientation was in fact opposite that of true fascism, which (as classically demonstrated by Mussolini, Hitler, and Franco) demanded intimate collaboration between corporate and government loci of power, and the subsequent stifling of all opposition. It was exactly this development that Cooper opposed, something that he argued was being created not merely within the United States, but on a global basis. Before long, it would have a name: The New World Order.

Bill Moore's Confession

By 1989, suspicion about William Moore was widespread among UFO researchers. In June, Robert Hastings published a damning article about Moore in the *MUFON UFO Journal*. Hastings lined up an impressive series of main points. It was not simply, he said, that the MJ-12 papers remained an orphan child, with no governmental agency claiming them. The Project Aquarius message was known to have been faked (as in altered) by Moore. Moore had also acknowledged that Richard Doty – with whom he was known to collaborate – forged the Ellsworth AFB document. Doty's typewriter at Kirtland AFB was also implicated in the Weitzel case from 1980, an incident that did have a core UFO sighting which was greatly altered by Doty. Doty had given data to Linda Moulton Howe in April 1983 that was similar to but contradicted data in the Eisenhower briefing memo.[*] Moore, by his own account, faked a government ID card and passed himself off as an intelligence operative to at least one person for two years. Hastings' argument was simple: how could anyone believe Moore and Doty were truthful regarding the MJ-12 documents?[34]

Matters blew up at the MUFON International UFO Symposium, held from June 30 to July 2, 1989 at the Aladdin Hotel and Casino in Las Vegas. The theme, appropriately, was "The UFO Cover-Up: A Govern-

---

[*] Of course, this could argue against Moore – or anyone – having faked *both* documents. otherwise, wouldn't they likely agree with each other?

ment Conspiracy?" Before the symposium even began, several MUFON members had resigned from the organization, upset that John Lear had been asked to chair the conference.[35]

The real news was over William Moore's presentation. Before a packed house, Moore – going well beyond his allotted time – "confessed" his connection to the U.S. intelligence community. "In early September 1980," he told a stunned audience, "I was approached by a well-placed individual within the intelligence community who claimed to be directly connected to a high-level government project dealing with UFOs." He later code-named this person "Falcon," whom he stressed was not Richard Doty, who instead served as the liaison between Moore and Falcon. As Moore was then on the Board of Directors at APRO, he was expected to provide information on that organization's activities, and also those of Paul Bennewitz. In return, Moore was promised inside information relating to UFOs and the cover-up.

Bennewitz, of course, had been filming and photographing unknown objects over Kirtland AFB and Manzano Weapons Storage Area. He was also monitoring what he believed to be low frequency EM signals whereby aliens communicated with surgical implants placed in human abductees. He had written a computer program to translate these signals. Moore suggested the signals were not extraterrestrial, but related to something else of importance, perhaps SDI or something related, and therefore attracted the attention of the AFOSI. Bennewitz had to be defused with disinformation, and Moore collaborated with Doty "largely [as] a freelancer providing information on Paul's current thinking and activities." He had visited Bennewitz several times, gave him deliberately misleading information, such as the Aquarius document, and reported back to his superiors.

Amid growing numbers of shouts, accusations, and walk-outs from the audience, Moore said this disinformation campaign succeeded beyond their expectations. But it went beyond Bennewitz. Moore had withheld information from certain researchers, and had also reported on their actions to his intelligence contacts. He had withheld and blacked out certain parts of UFO-related government documents. He said that AFOSI's disinformation had succeeded against Linda Moulton Howe in 1983. It was not until 1984, said Moore, that he realized the documents he received from AFOSI were false, at which point he withdrew from participation (although he would receive MJ-12 negatives at the end of that year).

The false scenario portrayed by Doty and AFOSI, perpetrated against Bennewitz and the UFO research community, "contained the notion that two groups of aliens are present on the planet, one benign, and one, the 'greys', not so benign." The greys were responsible for cattle mutilations, human abductions, and implants in human abductees. According to this false scenario, the greys also made and then broke a secret treaty with the U.S. government, maintained a secret underground base under Mount Archuleta near Dulce, and supplied the U.S. government with defective space hardware and weapons. All of this preceded the scenario described by Lear and Cooper by five years or more. All, said Moore, originated as disinformation directed at Paul Bennewitz, who ended up in a psychiatric hospital in large part as a result of this campaign. Moore promised all would be revealed in due time, answered no questions, and left the stage through a back door.[36]

By the time Moore walked off the stage, his reputation as a credible UFO researcher was in ruins. Moore later argued that he provided a service to ufology in "coming out" as he did, that he could have continued to keep matters hidden. But this was not really true. If nothing else, Hastings was already causing problems for him, and other researchers were surely ready to follow up.

Many rejected everything Moore had said and done as tainted. Others saw shades of grey, recognizing that, as Moore later said, "you don't learn how to swim unless you get into the water.... When you do get involved, there are rules. And they're not your rules. You either play by them, or they very quickly find somebody else who will."[37]

In a 1993 interview with his friend, Gregory Bishop, Moore elaborated his position.

> The whole story of Government/ alien involvement, treaties with aliens, underground bases, a plot to take over the planet, implants, two different races of aliens, one hostile and one friendly, etc. was all cooked up by the counter-intelligence people for the purpose of discrediting Bennewitz. He bought it, and a lot of other people in the UFO community bought it, and they continue to buy it today. All of that stuff was cooked up as part of the operation against Bennewitz. Bennewitz was meeting with everybody who was anybody and telling that story to anyone who would listen. John Lear, and ultimately through him to Bill Cooper, Bill English, Wendelle Stevens...they all revolved around that information. It was the kind of paranoia that they wanted to hear.... Then I get up and tell them, "Folks, you've been had. And here's how I know. It isn't that I've heard it, I was part of it. I was there. I watched it happen. I knew who was doing it, and I was privy to it.[38]

Not that this campaign discredited the gravity of the UFO phenomenon, continued Moore. On the contrary, it indicated that powerful interests took it seriously, and continue to do so.

> There is something to the subject that is so important that they're devoting all this time and effort to it. They wouldn't devote it to stories about Hitler being alive in Antarctica.

It says there's something there: What? .... Whatever the secret is, it's such a high magnitude of importance and would have such an impact on the mundane day-to-day circumstances of our society that anyone who gets close enough to see what it is says, "Oh my God. We can never tell anyone this. Because if we do, it will bring down the whole fabric of our society." That to me automatically suggests certain things.[39]

An interesting statement. Over the years, there has been a tendency among researchers to support Moore's statement that the disinformation from AFOSI was to divert Bennewitz not from ET related data, but more conventional fare. Yet this 1993 interview four years later could well be seen to imply that an ET connection was in fact the case.

Meanwhile, the bad feelings within MUFON over John Lear's participation had prompted Walter Andrus to remove him from the symposium. This was an especially strong snub, considering that the proceedings were taking place in Lear's home territory of Las Vegas. Lear quickly organized his own "alternate" symposium for Sunday morning. In addition to himself, he brought in William Cooper, Don Ecker, and William English, each with dedicated followers. Many who attended were less than impressed, however, feeling that little evidence supported some of the assertions, especially those emanating from Cooper. Not surprisingly, Cooper again claimed that Kennedy's driver had shot him in November 1963, that a group of 80 dissident scientists opposed to the alien/US government diplomatic treaty were massacred in a single day, and other equally sensational – and unsupported – claims.[40]

UFOs Mundane and Extraordinary

As summer arrived in 1989, more sightings of strange craft occurred in California's Antelope Valley. During late May and into June, a security guard at Air Force Plant 42 reported several highly unusual objects. Late one sunny morning, while a B-1B was performing "touch and goes" on the landing strip, "Archie" observed a silvery object high in the sky, moving slowly from north to south. The following week, the same object reappeared, this time coming from the west. It stopped low in the sky, maintained its position, then moved south across the base. On his radio, Archie asked the FAA control if something had fallen off the B-1; the answer was negative. The silver speck disappeared; then, from the same spot, three round balls appeared out of nowhere, moved south, changed color, then disappeared. This prompted another call to the control tower. "I don't know what the hell is happening around here," he told them, "but I just saw three balls fly across the base." The control tower replied, "we believe you." Soon, a large white helicopter with Air Force markings flew in from the north and orbited in the vicinity for ten minutes, then left. The story was researched and reported by William Hamilton. The fact that a helicopter was sent to investigate would seem to indicate that the silver balls were unknown to the base operators. Were they secret technology of some other portion of the national security infrastructure? Were they part of a "Majestic" group, beyond the reach of ordinary military and legal control? Were they alien? The answer is unknown.[41]

Frame from Japanese video, July 1989.

As the 1980s neared its end, greater numbers of UFO videos were being taken. One was taken on July 6, 1989 in the central Japan city of Hakui, along the west coast facing North Korea. During a clear sunny day, an observer used a Sony video recorder to capture over a minute of video of the object as it descended rapidly toward the Earth. It then changed directions and rose at a steep angle so rapidly that it disappeared from several frames. It was not an airplane, balloon, kite, or model airplane. The object initially appeared as a bright spot against the blue sky, but when the photographer, Yasuhiko Hamazaki, zoomed in, a Saturn-shaped object with a ring encircling it in the horizontal plane became plainly visible. The video was shown on Japanese and American television. Dr. Richard Haines and Dr. Bruce Maccabee independently analyzed it, finding the object to be a genuine unknown.[42]

Of course, mundane objects are often mistaken for UFOs. One was captured on video the following month in Spain along the southeastern coast in the town of Estepona, not far from Gibraltar. At around 9 p.m. on August 10, Dr. William Heijster, a Dutch military psychologist who worked at the Ministry of Defense in The Hague, was driving with his family when they all saw an object hovering over a mountain. Heijster stopped the car, retrieved his camcorder, and videotaped the object off and on for the next hour. He thought it appeared to be rotating rapidly, but the video did not show this. However, the video did show an apparent change in its shape from conical to circular. After an hour, the object split into two parts, which separated and then faded away. This part was not captured on video, however. Bruce Maccabee performed an initial analysis, but the case was plausibly explained by Spanish researcher Vicente-Juan Ballester Olmos, who learned that a series of atmospheric balloons launched from Sicily corresponded precisely in time, location, and appearance to the objects videotaped by Dr. Heijster.[43]

In Britain, triangles were being seen. That summer in Essex, a witness saw odd hovering lights, then watched them through binoculars. "It certainly was no an aircraft," he told investigators. "All I could see was a triangular shape and it was fairly big." This was one of many sightings investigated by the MoD.[44] But there was one sighting of a triangle that summer which was unquestionably of a manmade craft. This occurred in August, 60 miles off the Norfolk coast at a North Sea gas rig. The witness was a former Royal Observer Corps member named Chris Gibson, one of the world's leading experts in aircraft identification. Gibson in fact was writing an aircraft recognition manual at the time, and actively competed in international recognition tournaments where a long distance image of an aircraft would be flashed on a screen for a fraction of a second. While working at the rig, Gibson observed a matte-black aircraft refueling from a KC-135, accompanied by two F-111s. The aircraft was slightly bigger than an F-111, and was "a perfect triangle," with a 30 degree angle at the nose. The formation was heading towards the UK coast. "I am trained in instant recognition," Gibson said. "But this triangle had me stopped dead.... I was totally out of ideas. Here was an aircraft, flying overhead, not too high and not particularly fast. A recognition gift and I was clueless. This was a new experience."[45]

The sighting was not made public until 1992. When it was, General Walter Hogle, chief of USAF Public Affairs, suggested that the aircraft might have been an RAF Vulcan bomber – an aircraft not only incapable of refueling from a KC-135, but which is almost as large as the tanker. Gibson replied, "A Vulcan? I think I learned that one when I was three years old." The Air Force finally acknowledged the sighting "will probably remain unchallenged, simply because there is not enough information available to even hazard a guess."[46]

Not surprisingly, several aviation experts have offered guesses as to what Gibson saw. Bill Sweetman pointed out that the craft corresponded "almost exactly in shape and size" to hypersonic reconnaissance aircraft studied in the 1970s and 1980s by McDonnell Douglas and the USAF. Sweetman knew of no other aircraft, other than a highly supersonic vehicle, or a test aircraft for such a vehicle, that had ever been built or studied with such a planform.[47] Other speculation has suggested the craft may have either been a prototype of the canceled U.S. Navy A-12 Avenger II, several of which are reported to have flown, or perhaps the TR-3A Black Manta, allegedly built by Northrop.[48] The A-12, built by McDonnell Douglas and General

Dynamics to be an all-weather, carrier-based stealth bomber, was canceled in 1991 due to high costs. Officially, only mockups were ever built. The Black Manta, widely believed to be a subsonic stealth spyplane, has always been denied by the Air Force even to exist. The real problem is that both of these are of the wrong shape to match what Gibson so precisely described, with the angles of their respective noses being far wider than 30 degrees.

One thing that can be taken away from the experience is the virtual certainty that the U.S.-U.K. military establishment was flying a perfectly triangular aircraft, the existence of which has been denied to the present day.

The (Non) UFO Shootdown Over Long Island

During the night of September 28, 1989, UFO activity was recorded over Long Island and Connecticut, roughly speaking within a 35 mile north-south stretch. For many years, the claim has been made that a UFO was shot down that night by an American "Star Wars" weapon over Moriches Bay along the south shore of Long Island.*

At the center of the controversy was John Ford. During the mid-1980s, Ford developed an overriding interest in UFOs – some called it an obsession – after learning about the nearby Hudson Valley sightings. In 1985, he co-founded the Long Island UFO Network (LIUFON), whose activities were described in Ford's *Long Island UFO Newsletter*. Ford soon claimed to have developed inside sources describing the extraterrestrial presence, how U.S. satellites monitored ET activity, and other aspects of the cover-up. In the ten years he actively investigated UFOs, Ford also claimed to have learned about three UFO crash retrievals on Long Island. Ford was not just an investigator, he saw himself as someone who would single handedly bring down UFO secrecy. Soon, he was engaged in street activism to end UFO secrecy. He made countless telephone calls to fellow researchers as well as designated enemies. John Ford was nothing if not intense. But the real question is whether or not he was reliable. Certain indications point to a negative conclusion.

Ford claimed that a UFO was shot down and retrieved at Moriches Bay in Long Island on the night of September 28, 1989.[49] It turns out that UFOs were reported that night from the southern coast of Long Island up

---

* Nearby is Brookhaven National Laboratory, established in 1947 by the Atomic Energy Commission. Brookhaven, of course, has its own legends associated with time travel and the infamous Philadelphia Experiment.

to Connecticut. The problem is that Ford's accounts show gross inaccuracies and exaggerations where cross-checking is possible, throwing doubt over the rest of his account.

At around 5:30 p.m., residents of Moriches Bay noticed strange lights hovering over the bay. Ford said this was a large triangle which interfered with TV reception of some households. Something was still there after 7 p.m., and by 8 p.m., a few miles north near the town of Calverton, a woman and her son saw six bright amber lights above a field. According to Ford, they discerned a huge triangular craft silhouetted against the night sky, which the mother assumed was an experimental aircraft from the nearby test facility.

At 8:10 p.m., UFOs were seen across the Long Island Sound in Connecticut. Ford claimed that he learned from Philip Imbrogno that there had been a major UFO sighting at the "Hartford International Airport" in Connecticut. There, said Ford, employees saw an immense object hovering over an unused portion of the airfield. They described it as boomerang-shaped with six bright amber lights. As they watched in disbelief, a blue beam of light came down from the object, on which five beings glided down to the ground. Some of the airport workers reportedly chased the creatures, but the beam lifted them back to safety. According to Ford, one of these witnesses later spoke with Imbrogno on the condition of anonymity, saying that he and his co-workers had been warned by the FAA to keep silent about the affair.

Imbrogno did investigate a UFO sighting over an airport in Hartford, although not the Hartford International Airport (which does not exist). It concerned unidentified lights that were seen by employees: no clearly identifiable object, no beams, no aliens, no enforced silence. When asked about Ford's claims, Imbrogno had no explanation, except to say that they were untrue. Imbrogno did add, however, that Ford frequently presented him with UFO videos and other evidence. Unfortunately, detached observers almost never saw the "UFOs" that Ford was convinced had been captured on film or otherwise documented.[50]

Ford claimed that UFO activity continued over Moriches Bay well into the night, some of which was videotaped by a local resident. The culmination was said to be an encounter between a large number of military and police helicopters and a triangular UFO, which (Ford said he later learned from an inside source), was shot down with a "Star Wars" type weapon that penetrated the UFO's plasma field. There may be truth in here, or not. Presently, it is impossible to know. There is, however, one suggestive fact that might cause one to wonder: Moriches Bay was where TWA flight 800 mysteriously crashed in August 1996. Federal authorities attributed the probable cause of that crash to an explosion of the center wing fuel tank, most likely as a result of faulty wiring. However, nearly 40 witnesses reported seeing a streak of light or bright object ascend vertically and hit the aircraft.[51] What was this streak of light? Could it have been related to technology from nearby Brookhaven National Laboratory, which Ford was convinced was part of the UFO cover-up and was developing ET-related weaponry?

Ford's story ended tragically not so much because of UFOs as because he became a nuisance, maybe a threat, to a powerful man. This was John Powell, the head of the Suffolk County Republican Party, whom Ford accused of covering up information on UFO crash retrievals and engaging in an array of criminal activities. Whether Powell had any knowledge of UFOs is not known, but within a few years he pleaded no contest to charges of extortion and racketeering. Ford was clearly on to something about the man, but picked the wrong fight. Ford told friends his car was vandalized, and a physical attack occurred against LIUFO member Joe Mazzachelli in which he was warned by the assailants to "stay out of our business." Then, on June 12, 1996, Ford and Mazzachelli were arrested in a sting operation involving phone taps and a wired paid informant. In a conversation filled with laughter and garbled statements, the informant said they should kill Powell and two other local politicians by tainting the toothpaste of the victims with radium. Police immediately broke in to arrest Ford and Mazzachili. It is not hard to imagine a man as corrupt as Powell making arrangements to have this nuisance gotten rid of. [52]

The scenario seems improbable, even absurd. The idea of breaking into Powell's secure residence, locating toothpaste solely for Powell's use, and somehow getting enough radium inside the tube – all without being caught – is clearly an impossible plan. In any case, such radium poisoning would hardly be fatal within an efficient period of time, possibly not for many years. Some openly wondered whether the radium found in Ford's house had been planted, although Philip Imbrogno told the author that Ford did collect radium from old watches, albeit in amounts that were insignificant.

Among people who knew him from LIUFON, Ford had his defenders and detractors. Elaine Douglass, who would continue on in UFO research, said that those who knew Ford never doubted his innocence, and that none believed him capable of the act of which he was accused.[53] A different view of Ford was expressed by LIUFON's former Director of Investigations,

John Stout, who claimed that Ford was a fanatic who regularly and conveniently found crashed saucers near his house. Stout claimed the 1989 Moriches Bay incident was another instance of Ford seeking to prove a preconceived fantasy. In reality, said Stout, that event was a mistaken identification of "a mast light on a boat traveling at night."[54]

Whatever Ford's personality, he appears to have been railroaded. He had no criminal record, but was jailed and denied bail for well over a year. A psychological team hired by the DA's office concluded that, even though Ford understood his legal predicament very well, he was not competent to stand trial. It seems that Ford was sunk by his conspiracy beliefs. Of particular comment, in the opinion of Robert H. Berger, director of Forensic Psychiatry at Bellevue Hospital Center, was Ford's belief that "the criminal case against him [was] in reality an intelligence operation being run by the CIA together with the Israeli intelligence agency Mossad." Despite this medical pronouncement, the prosecution refused to drop charges. John Ford was sent to a mental institution after his conviction. He has never been released.[55]

The Strange Soviet Summer of 1989

1989 was a year of high strangeness, and events in the Soviet Union were strangest of all. Perhaps it was merely coincidence that the world's oldest communist society was spiraling out of control, or perhaps the intelligence behind the phenomenon took extra interest in that country. Or, perhaps the greater number of reports were simply due to the new openness that permeated Soviet life. What is undeniable is that the UFO phenomenon became major news in the Soviet Union, and Soviet UFOs became news around the world.

In July, while the once-conquered nations of Lithuania, Latvia, and Estonia were declaring their sovereignty as independent nations, the USSR was seized by a wave of UFO sightings and encounters without known precedent. Quite a few abduction cases were reported in the sober journal, *Socialist Industry* on July 9. One especially striking case occurred on July 4 – one reason is because it was a failed attempt. At twilight, two women were walking with a six year old girl by the shore of the Dnieper River in a park near Kiev, when they saw a "boat" with three beings aboard. According to the witnesses, the three had absolutely identical faces: extremely pale, long blond hair, large eyes, and collarless silver shirts which looked like nightgowns. Not surprisingly (considering the circumstances) they informed the women they were from another planet. "Every day," they told the astonished women, "we take one person from Earth to our world. We will take you. Our ship is nearby, we will show it to you." They all walked together, during which time the women experienced odd physical sensations and begged to be let go. They saw a ship behind some trees, and the small girl became frightened. The beings relented. "We will find others," they said. They entered the craft by a ladder which then retracted, the door silently closed, and the craft departed without a sound. It soon appeared as a small star. Alexander F. Pugachev, with a Ph.D. in Physics and Mathematics, investigated the case and believed it to be genuine, although in general Soviet academicians ignored this and the many other cases reported that summer.[56]

Quite a few military encounters occurred during the year. Although no exact date appears to be available, it appears that sometime during 1989 an advanced Soviet interceptor was lost, flown by an experienced pilot, while a UFO sighting was being reported. This was in a statement from Moscow PVO (National Air Defense Forces) district commander Anatoly Kornukov in a 1993 press conference. Kornukov was among the most senior Soviet generals, and had been the man who gave the order in 1983 to shoot down the KAL-007 flight.[57]

Then there are the KGB "Blue Folder" reports which came to light as the nation was disintegrating in 1991. One of these includes a radio transcript describing UFOs near the Black Sea coast in Krasnodar Krai on July 26, 1989. At 2:40 p.m., the Sochi Airport controller, R. H. Stepanian, received information from a crew flying from Simferopol that they had seen UFOs at a distance of 30-50 kilometers (20-30 miles). According to the pilots, first one, then two "strange objects" paced them to their left. One was almost exactly square, while the other was elongated in the shape of a rhombus. At the time of the radio transmission, the two objects were swiftly moving away and beginning to separate. Apparently two other flights reported multiple UFOs to the airport traffic control center.[58]

Another KGB case, complete with first-hand testimony from soldiers, described a July 28-29, 1989 incident near Kaspustin Yar, the rocket launch and development site in the southeastern Soviet Union.[*] The file is undoubtedly incomplete, but provides enough information to indicate something fascinating happened. Near midnight, a disc shaped object flew silently toward the rocket weapons depot, flashing an intensely bright light from its underside. It then hovered above the weapons site at a height of 20

---

[*] It had been at Kaspustin Yar where, in 1947, the Soviets launched their own captured German V-2 rockets.

meters. It was roughly 13 to 17 feet in diameter, and its hull was illuminated with a dim green, phosphorus-like, color. A bright beam appeared from beneath it, and the object circled two or three times. It moved toward a railway station, still flashing its lights, then returned to the weapons depot at a height of 60 to 70 meters. According to the available documents, orders were made to scramble a fighter jet to intercept the object, "but it was not able to see it in detail, because the UFO did not let the aircraft come near it, evading it. Atmospheric conditions were suitable for visual observations."[59] The object remained visible in the vicinity for more than an hour. At around 1:30 a.m., it flew towards the town of Akhtubinsk and disappeared.

Testimony from seven Soviet soldiers and officers strongly corroborate each other. Three individuals, from their vantage point, stated that the object performed incredible acrobatic maneuvers, and at one point approached them very rapidly. It then divided itself into three shining points and took the shape of a triangle. "No aircraft could fly in this manner," said one witness, a Corporal Levin. Another witness, Lieutenant Klimenko, stated that the object "accelerated abruptly and also stopped abruptly, all the while doing large jumps up or down."

Before this object left, another appeared, and then another still, at low altitudes of 300 to 400 meters. The last of these gave flashes of red light at constant intervals, then lights of all colors. Witnesses made it out as cigar-shaped. It flew to the first UFO, and the two disappeared beyond the horizon. The available records do not make it explicitly clear, but it seems that a second jet intercept took place at this time, although this might have been the same attempt as previously mentioned. Unfortunately, no information on the scramble mission or radar data was ever made available.[60]

The similarity of this case with countless American cases is evident. This does not appear to be a misidentification of weather phenomenon; the witnesses all described a maneuvering craft that outperformed intercepting jets. Explaining this as secret "black" technology raises interesting questions: would it be the same group that presumably was responsible for similar air space violations over American or European bases? The available evidence indicates that the Soviets did not know the origin of these UFOs, just as it shows the Americans were equally in the dark regarding *their* UFOs.

If anything, things became stranger as the year progressed, just as the political situation continued to radicalize. On September 10, 1989, the nation of Hungary announced that its border to the West would be available to East Germans. This was an unprecedented decision, and effectively made the Berlin Wall obsolete, although it lasted for two more months. Within days of this announcement, thousands of East Germans left their country. Through it all, the U.S. remained cautious, even aloof to the point where Senator majority leader George Mitchell accused President Bush of being "almost nostalgic about the Cold War."[61] By the end of September, U.S. Secretary of State James Baker met in Washington with Soviet Foreign Minister Eduard Shevardnadze. The Soviets gave up their former opposition to Star Wars, agreed to dismantle a giant phased array early warning radar installation at Krasnoyasrk, Siberia (without asking for any corresponding American actions in Greenland or Britain), and made other major concessions – all in the hopes of kick-starting arms reduction talks. Finally, the Bush team realized that the Soviets were "for real" with their reforms. Still, Baker rejected all Soviet proposals. This was a hard defeat for Gorbachev, who needed something to appease his hardliners.[62]

The Soviet collapse continued apace. In October, Hungary officially abandoned Leninism and declared itself to be a free republic. On October 6, 1989, Gorbachev was in Berlin for the 40th anniversary of the German Democratic Republic, telling the Germans to get started on their reforms, listening to chants of "Gorby save us," and being glared at by East German leader Erich Honecker. The day after Gorbachev's departure, 70,000 protesters marched in Leipzig. Honecker had actually given the order to open fire, but local party leaders refused. Instead, Honecker was ousted and replaced by Egon Krenz, in what was the final gasp of the East German regime.

Throughout the remainder of the year, landing cases and abduction cases proliferated within the Soviet Union. Between August and November, according to a Soviet UFO researcher at the Academy of Sciences, there were thirty recorded UFO landings in the single Ukrainian region of Nicolayev near the Black Sea. These landings were analyzed in the field and laboratory by teams of scientists.[63] Several of these were truly spectacular and fantastic, such as a September 16 case in which a young woman waiting for a tram was lifted 160 feet in the air; the crowd below her screamed, and she was eventually returned to the ground.[64] On the same day, about 300 miles north in Chernobyl, an amber colored, elliptical object was once again reportedly seen when another radioactive leak occurred at Reactor 4.[65]

As incredible as they were, these and all the other Soviet cases were overshadowed by the events in Voronezh, a city of nearly a million people a few hundred miles to the east of the Ukrainian sightings, within Russia

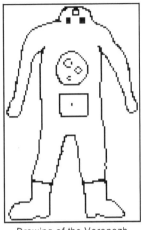

Drawing of the Voronezh creature by a child witness.

proper. For two and a half weeks, between September 21 and October 7, a heavy UFO concentration took place, including four landings and three different kinds of entities being reported. These cases were sensational, and it is almost certain that if they are true, then significant distortions have occurred in the telling. Several boys were said to have seen a landed sphere on the evening of September 21, with two humanoid beings and a robot-like entity emerging from it.[66] On the 24th, an engineer saw a maneuvering object that resembled an airship.[67]

It was the event of September 27, however, that raised eyebrows around the world. It was covered by the Soviet news agency, *Tass*, and as such carried something of a stamp of approval. Still, despite the advent of glasnost, the story was incredible enough that many researchers doubted its veracity. Sorting through the sensationalism to find the facts has been a challenge ever since.

As reported in *Tass*, during the early evening, a large number of school children were playing in the park, supervised by about forty adults. At 6:30 p.m., people noticed a pink or red light in the sky. This became a dark red sphere which circled forty feet above the ground and soon flew away. A few minutes later, it returned and hovered over the park. While still in the air, a hatch opened up and an enormous being appeared – ten feet tall. It wore silver-looking coveralls and bronze colored boots. It also appeared to have three eyes, or at least two eyes plus something else that looked like an eye. The being observed the terrain and then closed the hatch. The sphere came lower, brushed against a tree, and landed. It appeared to be forty-five feet in diameter. The tall being re-emerged, accompanied by a robot of some sort. The being said something unintelligible, and a luminous rectangle, about four feet long, appeared on the ground. It said something else, and the rectangle disappeared. It then adjusted something on the robot's chest, causing it to walk in a mechanical way. One of the boys cried out in fear and the alien looked at him. When it did so, the boy became "frozen," unable to move. People began to shout, and the sphere and beings vanished on the spot. That was not the end of it, however. Within five minutes, the sphere and the being reappeared. This time, the being carried a tube about four feet long and pointed it at a teenage boy. In front of the astonished crowd, the boy disappeared, the alien entered the sphere and flew off, and the boy reappeared at the same time.

The case was initially investigated by Genrikh Silanov, head of the Voronezh Committee for the Study of Anomalous Phenomena. He and his group were speaking with witnesses by early October. Silanov stated that although the Soviet media took creative license with his report, an extraordinary event seems to have happened, supported by extensive corroboration among many high caliber witnesses, including members of the local militia, a police lieutenant, a senior economist, a chief engineer, and other professionals. Something appeared to have either come down very low or landed. Many witnesses spoke of an unnaturally strong fear in the presence of the object. What exactly this event was may well remain shrouded in conjecture and folklore for many years.[68]

Tass reported the Voronezh story on October 9, 1989; within days it was worldwide. While a few UFO researchers were willing to believe something important happened, few if any took the story at face value. While the opinions among researchers ranged from caution to outright skepticism, the western media started with skepticism – then moved on to ridicule. Many believed the case to be a hoax.[69] One of the strange additions to the story was that Soviet television displayed an insignia, allegedly worn by the alien, that was none other than the discredited UMMO symbol. This had been a near-certain hoax case that was prominent in Spain and France during the 1960s and 1970s, involving alleged communications with extraterrestrials. Jacques Vallee, who had traveled to the Soviet Union to investigate Voronezh, and also had investigated the UMMO affair, considered it a spurious addition, "the result of unfortunate contamination induced by overenthusiastic believers."[70] Still, he was appalled by the Western media's portrayal of the case as emanating from children in a park with nothing better to do than make up fantasies.[71]

Meanwhile, the strangeness continued. An incident in the city of Kirov took place on October 5, with reportedly more than one hundred objects seen in the sky.[72] A dangerous close encounter case reportedly occurred on October 11 near the town of Nalchik, in the Caucasus region. A sixteen year old young woman saw a "net" falling from the sky, apparently around her, in the center of which was a bright point. She tried to push it away, but received a shock. She screamed (her voice sounded distorted) and her family rushed out of the house. A flying disc was hovering less than fifty feet away, but soon vanished. The girl was left paralyzed for a while, the tips of her fingers burned and enlarged, and she was hospitalized. Investigators described her as intelligent and rational.[73]

On October 7, *Pravda* reported that the Soviet Union had just opened an official center for the study of UFOs, located near Moscow. Physicists, geologists, astronomers, and psychologists were to teach courses on the various characteristics of UFOs that had been reported and were to be given the equipment necessary to investigate.[74]

On October 12, just after announcing the Voronezh story, *Pravda* reported that a group of scientists visited a field in Perm Oblast to investigate claims that a UFO had landed in the area and left behind a circular impression measuring 62 meters in diameter.[75] It was soon suggested that mass hysteria was playing a role in the Soviet UFO reports, and the Soviet media was blamed for fanning the flames. Skeptical Soviet scientists, for instance, believed that recent fragments supposedly from an extraterrestrial craft (such as the Dalnegorsk case) were actually from failed rocket launches. Other sightings, they argued, probably resulted from the inability of people to recognize ball lightning.[76]

Maybe so, but there were people within the Soviet Union taking this seriously. A conference later in October in Petrozavodsk included about 100 Soviet scientists representing various branches of science and technology. Their main topic of discussion was the multitude of claims of recent UFO sightings in the USSR. According to the magazine *Soviet Culture*, "more questions about UFOs were raised at this conference than answered."[77]

Also, mass sightings continued. The October 21 edition of *Socialist Industry* reported that hundreds of residents had reported a UFO in Omsk, many of whom reported the story directly to the newspaper's office in that city. It included a report by a Major V. Loginov, who said that it was a shining sphere about one and a half times the apparent size of the Moon. Radar failed to detect it as it passed over.

Four projectors – some parallel and some at angles to the Earth – were casting very bright beams. The object was in the field of vision for about 5 minutes ... hovering ... over the civil airport before descending a little. Then the projectors were turned off and a whirling plume trail instantaneously appeared around this shining sphere.... Pilots were able to observe it visually, but they could not detect it on their radar screens....Radar signals could not be reflected from it. This object was immediately reported up the chain-of-command, and our colleagues in the Altay Kray, in the area toward which the object flew, reported back to us within 5 minutes that they had it under visual observation. That means that it had covered a distance of approximately 600 kilometers at a speed of about 7,000 kilometers per hour. It is entirely possible that the estimates of speed were incorrect, but this appears to have been an object of unusual design that had complete radar-stealth capability combined with exceptional maneuverability.[78]

A KGB "Blue Folder" report described a case from the same day, more than 2,500 miles away in the eastern region of Magadan. Near the village of Burkhala, several local residents watched a flying object silently approach an electric power transmission line, then sharply change course and climb. Higher in the air, it reduced speed, enabling the witnesses to see it more clearly. About seven to nine lights were seen shining along the edge of the object. One of the witnesses, who had formerly worked at the Baikonur space center, estimated the object's speed at close to 1,000 kph (600 mph). He knew of no aircraft that could have executed such a maneuver.[79]

Strange sightings went on into November and December. By then, Voronezh had become a pilgrimage by correspondents seeking sensational news for their newspapers, regardless of the nature of the evidence of the actual event.[80]

The monumental news of late 1989, of course, was the opening of the Berlin Wall on November 9 – a date of longstanding significance to Germans.* The Wall had been a fixture of German and international politics since 1961; now, with breathtaking speed, it was gone. Indeed, it can easily be argued that with the fall of "die Mauer" marked the real end of the Cold War itself. Yet, Gorbachev had not intended this result when he had begun his reforms. Like Stalin many years before, he now privately worried about the likely reunion of the Germanies. But events were spinning out of control. Before the end of the year, bloodless revolution would sweep through Bulgaria and Czechoslovakia; and a bloody one would strike Romania with lightning speed. All this can be seen as the unintended consequences of liberalization within a repressive regime.

With the fall of the Berlin Wall, there appear to have been a few quiet conversations and reassessments as to whether or not a UFO cover-up was necessary any longer (more on this later). After all, with the "evil empire" on the verge of crumbling, what need would there be for secrecy? From whom were the secrets being kept, if not America's longtime enemy, the Soviet Union?

Actually, the collapse of Soviet power itself is instructive by way of answering this question. Consider the parallels of Soviet and UFO secrecy. Gorbachev inherited a Soviet regime that had existed for seven decades, during which it had systematically falsified its history, repressed nationalities, murdered millions, and committed countless other crimes. Within the United States of 1989, (and surely other nations), the UFO secret had been

---

*
The abdication of the Kaiser in 1918 which established the Weimar Republic, and the infamous Kristallnacht of 1938.

going for at least four decades. It, too, required a systematic falsification of history and undoubtedly the creation of a substantial secret infrastructure equal to the task of managing the problem. Such an infrastructure would by definition be illegal within any reasonable understanding of what constitutes an "open" society – or at least there would be many people expressing that opinion. A disclosure of the UFO reality would unquestionably lead to revelations threatening the established order. Initially, as with Gorbachev's reforms, the process might begin slowly, but uncomfortable questions would inevitably arise: What is the extent of the black infrastructure that deals with this issue? How much money has been diverted? Has revolutionary technology been hidden from the general population? Why did the mainstream media and academic institutions ignore this for so long? What, if any, international cooperation and secrecy has existed on this matter? Who are the beings that are here? Do they abduct people? Has the military abducted people? Have alien beings influenced our society in any way? If so, have they recorded our history – and if so, what revelations would a review of that history unveil? Would such claims even be believed?

All by way of starting the conversation. Undoubtedly, much more would open up, bringing revelations that could well result in a tidal wave.

The Belgian Triangles

By 1989, sightings of triangular UFOs had been going on for some time. Indeed, the first major flap occurred fourteen years earlier in North Carolina, and sporadic sightings even earlier than that. The Hudson Valley sightings of the early 1980s made the triangle phenomenon into something that serious researchers could no longer ignore. Sightings of triangles and boomerangs over California's Antelope Valley (amid other strange aerial objects in that region) also became an important element of UFO research during the late 1980s. These were still going on there at the end of 1989 – a case in point was a November 18 occurrence, when a large, black, boomerang glided over downtown Lancaster during the early evening. Low intensity lights, similar to stars, outlined its frame. The witness, Robert Puskas, estimated its size at between 800 feet and 900 feet in span. Off its left tip he saw a silvery metallic disc, about 30-40 feet in diameter, reflecting the street lights.[81]

Placing an exclamation point on the triangle phenomenon were the extended, mass sightings over the nation of Belgium in 1989 and 1990. From late autumn through the spring, triangular UFOs were frequently seen traversing Belgian skies. Sightings had taken place through November

1989, but the first major event took place at the end of the month, on November 29, in the city of Eupen, very close to the German border.

Just before 5:30 p.m., two on-duty Belgian police officers saw a large triangular craft descend close to their position at a low altitude. It had a bright light at each corner, and a large reddish-orange pulsating light in the center. They were sure this was a large structured craft, perhaps as long as 200 feet. It glided over the terrain, stopping and starting with ease, and was nearly completely silent except for a faint hum. As it hovered over a field close to them, it gave off a brilliantly intense light, much brighter than a standard searchlight. This illuminated their patrol car. When the object began to move again, they decided to follow it. They watched it move toward the Gileppe Dam, whereupon it descended and hovered directly over the water for 45 minutes. While this was going on, a second triangle rose from a nearby ravine – a perfectly silent, brightly lit, enormous object with a lit dome on top, less than 300 feet away from the awestruck policemen. It departed toward the town of Henri-Chapelle.

There were other witnesses to triangular craft that night. The Belgian UFO research organization, SOBEPS, collected nearly 120 reports from November 29. One of the objects moved southwest about 13 miles and hovered over the city of Spa for 30 minutes before disappearing. In the nearby town of Lontzen, a family saw the object, which frightened the children. The mother called the police in various places, including Aix-la-Chapelle. She later told a serious investigator that the police laughed at her derisively.[82]

Sightings continued at a high pace throughout December. On the evening of December 1, several witnesses described a four-cornered, lozenge-shaped object over Eupen, more than 100 feet long. Large and intensely bright white lights flashed on and off regularly, while in the center was an orange light. On December 5 or 12 (the witnesses, trying to recall the event, could not be sure), a married couple was driving in the town of Aix-la-Chapelle at 9:50 p.m., when they saw a flying object cut across the road directly in front of them. It had very bright lights, and emitted beams downward. It also had an orange light on the underside. The witnesses initially wondered if it was simply an exceptionally low-flying aircraft, but its maneuvers and lighting arrangements did not support this theory. While home near Aix-la-Chapelle at 11:15 p.m., they saw the exact same object flying low above their street. It was extremely large and made no sound.[83]

A landing case reportedly occurred on December 12, 1989, at 2:15 a.m., at the town of Jupille, about 35 miles southwest of Eupen, by an enormous oval object which seemed jammed between several trees. It had small lights, changing back and forth from red to blue, around its circumference. The witness could make out a logo of sorts on the object, which were several ellipses crossing themselves. Several times the object rose slightly, settled back to the ground and gave off a different sound each time it did so. It moved toward a neighbor's meadow, shining down three beams of light. For a while the witness lost sight of the object, but then saw a bright, well-defined, shaft of light shoot out into the sky. The witness reported this incident to the police and military, which soon investigated and found a gigantic circular trace in the meadow. At the center, the grass had been expertly shorn as if by a lawn mower, but grass clippings were nowhere to be found, and the grass within the circle had turned yellow. The witness later reported to local UFO investigators that the military expressed little interest in his testimony, "as if they knew what it was all about."[84] Sightings like these continued throughout the remainder of the year and throughout most of 1990.

From the beginning, attempts were made to explain these sightings away. UFO researcher Auguste Meessen discovered one of the early attempts by a Flemish journalist who had written an article under the impressive sounding headline "Explanation from Washington." It suggested that all the "hysteria" was caused by secret flights of the F-117A. When Meessen contacted the journalist, he learned that the writer had simply read an article on the F-117A. No research had gone into the sightings themselves. Thus started the baseless but tenacious rumor that the Belgian triangle was actually the stealth fighter. One definite effect of such reporting was to dampen the public's willingness to report what they saw, even though most estimates put the witness total at around 3,000 for 1989 and 1990.[85]

Abduction in Lower Manhattan

1989 was truly an extraordinary year of UFOs. As the Belgian flap was in its early phase, a spectacular event occurred on the other side of the Atlantic. This was the Linda Cortile (pseudonym for Linda Napolitano)[*] abduction case of November 30, in which she was taken out of the twelfth floor window of her lower Manhattan apartment by a beam of light, accompanied by alien beings, and taken into a UFO. More than a dozen independent observers appear to have seen this, many of whom were directly interviewed by Budd Hopkins, and three by this author. One of the

---

[*] Although "Linda Cortile" has been known for some time to be Linda Napolitano, I am electing to use the pseudonym, as it is this name which has become identified with the case.

witnesses to the event was a major political figure, whose identity Hopkins has never revealed but is widely understood to have been then-Secretary General of the United Nations, Javier Perez de Cuellar. Indeed, as shall be seen, de Cuellar was in all likelihood not just a witness, but himself an abductee that early morning. Two other witnesses were security men who were with de Cuellar, another was a woman who happened to be driving across the Brooklyn Bridge while the abduction was occurring. Years later, two other witnesses, truck drivers for the *New York Post*, came forward and added yet more supporting testimony. All of these people saw a UFO hovering above the apartment building, a bluish white beam of light shining down from its underside, and watched Linda, together with three aliens, floating high above the street.

Long before the event, Linda had held a belief that she had experienced alien abductions, and had been meeting with Budd Hopkins for that reason. By 1989, however, she assumed her abductions were a thing of the past. On the morning following her experience, she phoned Hopkins in a very agitated state. She woke up feeling that she had been dropped into her bed, and had tried to wake her husband. He was so unresponsive that she thought he was dead. Her children seemed the same way. She thought, "they've killed my family." She even retrieved a hand mirror and placed it under the nose of one of her sons to check. Only then did she experience the relief that her family was alive, after all. Soon after, they all woke up in a groggy state.

Three days later, Linda met Hopkins for a hypnotic regression session. During this, she recalled three or four small figures approach her bed, move her into the living room, and take her outside through a closed window into a bluish-white beam of light. Floating vertically, twelve stories above the ground, she ascended into a large object hovering above the building, and was subjected to a "fairly typical" physical examination. It appeared that when she was returned to her bed, her family was still "switched off," which is why they appeared dead.

In early February 1991, more than a year after the event, Hopkins received a typewritten letter, signed by the names "Richard" and "Dan." They said they were police officers who had seen a woman being lifted out of the window of a large building between 3 a.m. and 3:30 a.m. in late November 1989. They described the bright light, the object, and three "ugly but smaller humanlike creatures" accompanying her. They said they wrote to Hopkins out of a feeling of guilt and worry over what happened to the woman. Since they knew where she lived, they also soon contacted her. It was an emotional meeting, and the two were amazed that they actually had gotten to meet her. In time, Richard and Dan informed Hopkins that they were not actually police officers, nor were they alone in their car that morning of the abduction. They were, in fact, security agents escorting an important political figure to a downtown heliport.

Hopkins also learned that Linda had received correspondence from a man who claimed to have witnessed the abduction. His car had stalled two blocks away, he said, and he and the two men with him had seen the whole event at around 3:30 a.m. In other words, this was the important political figure being protected by Richard and Dan.

This man was United Nations Secretary General Javier Perez de Cuellar. It turned out that Perez de Cuellar was in New York City, traveling from a heliport with his two secret service agents. After further investigation, Hopkins determined that Perez de Cuellar was not simply a witness, but had been abducted as well. This fact was confirmed by Linda's son, who identified de Cuellar from twenty photos of men shown to him by Hopkins. This, said Linda's son, was the man who was with him and comforted him during the abduction. Hopkins contacted Perez de Cuellar about the incident, and met with him face-to-face on one occasion. Significantly, de Cuellar did not deny his involvement, but Hopkins declined to name him in his book.[*]

Another witness (pseudonym: "Janet Kimble") came forward in the fall of 1991 and described the abduction as it appeared from her vantage point on the Brooklyn Bridge. In a manilla envelope, she sent a letter and drawings to Hopkins, describing what she had seen. She had been returning from a retirement party, and was more than halfway across the Brooklyn Bridge on her way to Manhattan when, just before 3 a.m., her headlights dimmed and then went out. Through her rearview mirror she saw other cars in the same situation. She saw what she thought was a building on fire in Manhattan. "The whole sky lit up. Mr. Hopkins, words can't express what I saw that morning up on the Brooklyn Bridge...." Her drawings were of the bright lights and the object she saw; the second showed four figures ("children," she wrote) being lifted in the air. "While I watched," she added, "I could hear the screams of the people parked in their cars behind me." The third drawing described the craft rising above the building and departing at a fast speed.

"I have often wondered what happened to these poor children," she

---

[*] In 1996, de Cuellar, under pressure from the media and then a private citizen, denied the incident.

concluded. "It felt good sharing this with you, but I don't think I will ever share this with anyone again." She left her phone number, and Hopkins phoned her. He investigated her claims, which showed no sign of deception, and they met for an extended face-to-face interview. "She answered every question I asked with complete openness, accuracy, and appropriate emotion," Hopkins later wrote. He even drove over the Brooklyn Bridge at 3 a.m. to see what he could see. Indeed, Linda's building was clearly visible. It was just as "Janet Kimble" described.

There were other witnesses to the event that Hopkins interviewed, and a great deal of miscellaneous investigation. Eventually, he put the story together in a 1996 book, *Witnessed*. After the story gained notoriety, other witnesses continued to come forward. One of these, a driver for the *New York Post* newspaper (whose headquarters are in the neighborhood where the event took place), recalled the event years later, after seeing a documentary about it on television. Under the pseudonym Yancy Spence, he described his experience of having seen the abduction at 3:15 a.m. while he was driving over the Manhattan Bridge. Moreover, he learned that other *Post* employees on the job also saw it. Spence and another *New York Post* employee later met with Budd Hopkins. The author also interviewed both of these individuals, as well as a third *New York Post* employee, all of whom provided consistent testimony. One of these individuals recalled not simply being a witness, but also being abducted as well. Indeed, they also provided clear witness evidence to the (highly unusual) presence of a line of stretch limousines outside the *Post* newspaper office at that late hour, and description of what strongly appeared to have been Javier Perez de Cuellar.[86]

The likelihood that this case involved one of the world's most prominent leaders is of undoubted importance. But what might it mean? Steven Greer – who did not believe this was an alien abduction but rather a "covert kidnapping" – said that "a first hand witness" (a friend of de Cuellar and himself a head of state) personally related the details of this abduction to him. Greer said de Cuellar was trying to promote a disclosure of the extraterrestrial reality and "was made to disappear, as it were, in a faked or hoaxed abduction attempt." Once on board, de Cuellar was told to "cease and desist from any further attempt to bring this information out." The group behind the abduction was opposed to any disclosure plans, and would terrorize anyone foolish enough to think that the end of the Cold War might augur truly radical change. Greer added that his source and de Cuellar both believed the event to be an actual alien abduction – even though Greer implied that he knew better. It is for reasons like this that many researchers have considered Greer's longstanding opposition to the claims of alien abduction as nothing less than dogma, blindness in the face of an overwhelming mass of data. This author heard Greer on one occasion state categorically that all cases of alleged alien abduction were in reality military abductions. As of this point, the identity of the captors can only be conjecture, although it must be acknowledged that all of the abductees maintained their captors were alien.

Greer added another interesting claim: that the event had so panicked the Bush White House, its own UFO disclosure plans were immediately called off. Although evidence for this is lacking, UFO researcher Grant Cameron raised several points that support the idea. Was there a plan to release the UFO secret following the end of the Cold War, wondered Cameron, and was the abduction an attempt by some group – whether human or alien – to stop it?

Cameron noted that on the day following the abduction, President George Bush left Washington for Malta to meet with Gorbachev and announce the virtual end of the Cold War. Also, just hours before the abduction, Canadian Prime Minister Brian Mulroney had briefed Bush at the White House regarding his recent meeting with Gorbachev. There were also rumors that Mulroney traveled to New York City following his visit with Bush, and was part of the de Cuellar motorcade. Finally, according to "Richard" (one of de Cuellar's two secret service agents), the motorcade was heading for the heliport at Governors Island – a secure complex managed by the U.S. Coast Guard. The year before, it had been the site of a summit that included President Reagan, President-elect Bush, and Soviet leader Gorbachev.

Thus, the timing and location of the abduction, as well as the high-level person(s) connected to it, suggest geopolitical significance. As Cameron put it, this event occurred on a night that the U.N. Secretary General and other world leaders "were in New York, in effect, to oversee the end of the cold war."[87] Still, without more information, the most one could say is that there are several possible agendas to the events in lower Manhattan.

Panama: Dress Rehearsal for a New World Order

The collapse of Soviet power changed everything. For generations, whenever either superpower contemplated a major action, it had to consider the likely response of the other. Now, the United States was unexpectedly liberated from that concern. This would be most obviously expressed during the 1991 Gulf War, but an important dress rehearsal took place at the end of 1989, in Panama. The invasion of Panama was an event of global importance. Although it lacked direct connections to the UFO phenomenon, it was a key moment in the development of the American "National Security State" and as such demands a brief analysis.

By the time he became President, George Bush had turned on his old friend, Panamanian "strong man" Manuel Noriega. The public change started at the end of the Reagan years, when Vice President George Bush and New York Senator Alfonse D'Amato demonized Noriega as a drug-dealing dictator who brutalized his own people. All of which was true, but Noriega had done these things for many years as a key asset of the CIA since the 1950s – on contract with the Agency since 1967. He was trained at the infamous School of the Americas at Fort Gulick (Panama) and Fort Benning (Georgia), and trained in psyops at Fort Bragg, North Carolina. For years he had acted as a back channel to the communist government of Fidel Castro in Cuba, and was described by an Air Force colonel as "the best source of information the United States had in Latin America."[88]

Noriega's real problem was that he had become a wild card who knew too much. He had acquired a list of telephones throughout Latin America that were tapped by the NSA. Worse, he had collected incriminating evidence of the CIA's involvement in the Iran-Contra affair – including the smuggling of cocaine into the U.S. He was suspected of supplying intelligence not only to the U.S. and its allies, but to Cuba as well. Then there was the matter of the Panama Canal. Built by U.S. money and manpower in the early 20th century, ownership of the canal was due to revert to Panama in 1990. As long as a loyal regime was in power during this transition, the situation might be tolerable to U.S. policymakers. In later years, Noriega insisted that U.S. hostility developed from his refusal to support the right-wing Nicaraguan Contras. "Made" and protected by the U.S. intelligence community in order to run Panama, Noriega's loyalty was no longer assured. He had to be removed.

In April 1989, on the eve of the Panamanian Presidential election, the U.S. secretly supplied Noriega's political opponents with $10 million. The

---

* American news media has falsely claimed that Noriega's CIA connection did not come to light until "well after the invasion" (Anderson, Curt, "His US sentence served, Noriega fights extradition," AP 1/7/09), but this author recalls reading German publications in December 1989 that described Noriega's longstanding relationship with the CIA.

amount seems small by American standards, but in a poor nation with a population of just over 2 million people, it was a staggering sum. Noriega canceled the balloting, violence broke out, and the U.S. sent in 2,000 troops. The CIA was given $3 million to arrange a *coup d'état*. Meanwhile, General Colin Powell, Defense Secretary Dick Cheney, and Undersecretary of Defense Paul Wolfowitz planned Noriega's demise. Troops and weapons were secretly moved into the region. A U.S. Delta Force team staged phony "attacks" on U.S. soldiers; these were reported in the media as attacks by "terrorists" against American positions. American troops set up roadblocks in civilian neighborhoods, conducted offensive maneuvers outside U.S. jurisdiction, and challenged Panamanian Defense Force (PDF) troops – all in an effort to provoke Noriega into doing something foolish.

Laws and customs that might have inhibited U.S. actions were brushed aside. One such law prohibited the White House from ordering the assassination of foreign leaders. The obvious loophole was to plan an operation in which Noriega would probably be killed, without explicitly ordering his death.[89] Assistant Attorney General William P. Barr did his part to facilitate a legal revolution, when he argued that U.S. law enforcement officers were, in fact, allowed to arrest foreign leaders inside their own country and deliver them to U.S. courts for prosecution. U.S. law was also re-interpreted to allow American soldiers to conduct covert operations targeting foreign politicians, effectively a license to kidnap.[90]

On December 16, 1989, a group of U.S. Marines that specialized in provocations were fired on in front of PDF headquarters. An Intelligence Officer was killed, and a Navy officer and his wife were detained and beaten. President Bush now had his pretext for "Operation Just Cause." Officially, it involved 26,000 U.S. troops, and was America's largest military action since Vietnam. Soon, B-1 bombers, Apache attack helicopters, and F-117A stealth fighters engaged in a massive attack on Panama City. The initial midnight bombardment killed between 3,000 and 4,000 civilians – the exact number was never revealed, as more than a dozen mass graves were quickly dug in secrecy. Witnesses also testified that they saw many captured PDF soldiers bound and summarily executed by U.S. troops.

The United Nations and the Organization of American States both condemned the invasion, and declared the civilian deaths to be a war crime. Little of this received comment in the U.S. media. Instead, Americans were treated to the drama of how to remove "Pineapple Head" (as Noriega was dubbed) from the safety of the Vatican Embassy.

The Pentagon tested many of its new weapons, all with great success. Stealth fighters, for example, representing only two percent of the attack aircraft in the theater of war, destroyed over forty percent of the strategic targets.[91] Also tested were a variety of other secret weapons such as poison darts fired from the air and laser weapons that sliced through automobiles and "melted" human bodies.[92]

The war obliterated the PDF to such an extent that in 1991, Guillermo Endara, Panama's new leader, proposed abolishing the Panamanian army. The U.S. Congress soon passed a law calling for a renegotiating of the Panama Treaties, as Panama clearly could not defend itself or the canal. The U.S. therefore maintained control. Incidentally, not only did the new Panamanian regime fail to "restore democracy" (one of the stated goals of President Bush), but narcotics trafficking noticeably increased, possibly doubling.[93]

The invasion of Panama offered a glimpse not only into American *realpolitik*, but also of the contempt held by America's leadership for its professed ideals, and the extent of America's secret and illegal international activities. It therefore highlighted most starkly the desperate need by its leaders to suppress truth at all cost – a fact of significance in the matter of UFOs. America remained a democracy in name and republic in form, but these terms were losing all meaning. The reality was that America had become an oligarchy using the forms of the old republic for its own ends. Perhaps it had always been so, as some have argued. Perhaps the difference was that now, without the Soviet counterweight, America was losing her inhibitions. "Victory" in the Cold War had brought with it the fatal poison of *hubris*.

Going to Area 51

With the coming of 1990, as the world was in the process of transformation, the revelations of Bob Lazar were already turning the Groom Lake facility into the Promised Land for UFO devotees. Lazar had said that the best place to see these objects was called "the Mailbox," at the 29½ mile marker on the road closest to Area 51. Wednesdays were the best night to go. In January 1990, video captured a very unusual light phenomenon moving like a kite in the wind, except the distances covered and speed were vastly greater. By way of comparison, the video also captured a standard aircraft which showed conventional flight characteristics.[94]

On February 21, Norio Hayakawa, a television journalist, took a crew to see the test flight of an object from Groom Lake. Shortly after sundown, the group saw an orange-yellow light appear above the hills. They had a second sighting later that evening when an object went to the right, descended, performed a back turn, and a 5,000 foot sudden descent, more or less instantly. "I have never seen anything like that in my life, ever, said Hayakawa. "It is definitely a test flight of a highly unusual object."[95]

A week later, on February 28, a man named Gary Schultz went to the Mailbox accompanied by his wife, Pearl. At 7:30 p.m. he leaped out of his lawn chair when the first craft came out. Every 45 minutes, a new object arrived – six in all. According to Schultz, two or three of the craft were "amazing" bright, pulsing, ellipsoid objects. He took photos, one of which clearly captured an object shaped rather like a bell.[96]

More dark rumors and claims continued to percolate. In early 1990, on the popular Billy Goodman KVEG radio talk show in Las Vegas, an anonymous caller with the pseudonym of "Yellow Fruit" claimed to be a security officer at the Nevada Test Site. He said that Area 51 contained underground bases and tunnels concealing activities relating to aliens. William Hamilton met with this informant at Rachel's Bar and Grill, located fairly close to the Test Site. There, he gave Hamilton an account of an impending conflict between the "benevolent ones" and another group of small aliens – the EBEs. He told Hamilton that "Yellow Fruit" was the designation for the first level of security at Area 51. The second level, much harsher, was called Seaspray. These classifications did indeed exist. Groups named Yellow Fruit, Seaspray, Delta Force, Quick Reaction Team, Task Force 160, Intelligence Support Activity, and Special Operations Division were creations of the Pentagon, fully functional by 1981 with no Congressional oversight. They staged secret missions throughout Central America, the Middle East, Southeast Asia, Europe, complete with front companies and proprietaries. Perhaps they were doing work at Area 51, as well.[97]

The Wackenhut private security firm worked closely within this structure, providing perimeter security for the Nevada Test Site. To UFO hunters combing that perimeter, the "Wackenhut SS" became a familiar sight. Toting machine guns, wearing military camouflage but no insignias, and driving unmarked 4x4 vehicles, they became notorious for their harassment of citizens who got too close, even while they were on public land and well within their legal rights. This cat-and-mouse game between UFO watchers and security personnel would continue for several more years, until the Air Force took all the useful bordering lands through a Congressional grant.

Gulf Breeze Revisited

Throughout 1988, 1989, and into the 1990s, Gulf Breeze continued to be the scene of UFO sightings, as much of a Mecca for UFO watchers as Area 51. Whatever one thought of Ed Walters, it was obvious that something very interesting was going on there. By early 1989, more than 135 of Gulf Breeze's 6,000 residents had reported seeing strange craft hovering in the skies during the previous year and a half.[98]

Sightings were a common occurrence throughout 1990. A particularly interesting one occurred on the night of February 8, 1989, when a Gulf Breeze man woke to the sounds of a restless dog outside. He saw a small object descending low over a nearby lot. It appeared to be two connected discs, one on top of the other, not more than three feet in diameter. A white light was on top, many other lights blinked in shades of red, orange, and green. The witness clearly had strong nerves: he decided to bring the object into his house. As he approached it, however, it disappeared in a flash of light. The entire event lasted for about 12 minutes; it was investigated by MUFON's Charles Flanagan.[99] Later that spring in nearby Crestview, Florida, another stout-hearted witness observed a humming, hovering disc with a brilliant white light on its underside. This man aimed his rifle at the object, but a light beam engulfed him, and he misfired his rifle. The object then sped away.[100]

For its part, nearby Eglin AFB claimed that it had no record of UFO sightings or radar trackings. The base director of public affairs vehemently denied that Air Force planes had pursued unknowns, and denied that Eglin personnel were studying the Gulf Breeze incidents. He did hint that some of the sightings might inadvertently have been caused by base activities: "we normally operate in the daylight hours, but some systems need testing at night." A similar statement was made by the Pensacola Naval Air Station, which emphasized that it had very little after-dark activity. Residents, however, did notice two large vans with NASA logos parked at various locations throughout Florida's panhandle during the late 1980s. A NASA spokesperson said they were not there to monitor UFOs.[101]

Perhaps not, but more than once the U.S. military appeared to be observing them. On January 8, 1990, half a dozen Gulf Breeze residents saw a dark object, either round or elliptical, moving across the sky with a red light. Several witnesses photographed it, then noticed military helicopters apparently following. The following day, witnesses checked with the air traffic control tower at the Pensacola Naval Air Station, and were told that "unusual activity over Gulf Breeze requir[ed] the deployment of search and rescue helicopters." When asked what they were searching for, traffic control said, "given the nature of things that are going on over Gulf Breeze, take your best guess."[102]

Interesting cases continued throughout the spring of 1990. A woman feeding her infant on March 7 noticed a beam of white light about three feet in diameter descend to the ground beyond her window. She felt a slight vibration, and two seconds later it was gone. The following morning her husband found a circle of burned grass eleven feet in diameter near the window. Several people detected a strong "perfume" odor from the scorched area. The case was investigated by MUFON.[103]

Another Gulf Breeze case occurred on April 5, 1990, also investigated by MUFON. A motorist driving near the shore at 8:15 p.m. saw what looked like a jet fighter about to crash. Meanwhile, two military jets approached from the north, and the original object immediately shot laterally south-ward, halting one to two miles away. The man got out of his car to watch. The object appeared to be a white disc, with red and green lights spaced evenly around the side, and an unlit dome at the top. Slowly, it began to rise. He got to a telephone and called a friend (who contacted MUFON investigators) and also the Sheriff's office. Two deputies were soon on the scene, and for the next two hours the three witnesses watched a bright light continue to ascend slowly and at variance with the stars.[104]

Five days later, a couple driving north on the Bay Bridge saw an object that looked like a long isosceles triangle with a centered red light on the bottom and pairs of white lights at the three apexes. In other words, an object with a passing resemblance to the Belgian triangles. As they neared the end of the bridge, the object moved toward the west of their position. They pulled over and watched it hover, then move off over the bay and out of sight.[105]

A mini-wave was occurring in Gulf Breeze. On the evening of April 11, several residents watched a red light move toward the southwest and then out into the Gulf of Mexico before winking out. Some witnesses thought they saw clusters of balloons associated with the light, while others disagreed. On the following night, two witnesses saw a bright red light hovering over Little Sabine Island. It stayed there for several minutes, then blinked out. On the 13th, the same witnesses saw another light to the west of Gulf Breeze. It hovered for a few minutes and disappeared. The witnesses were experienced in the use of flares, and were convinced that this was not the explanation. During the same evening, at least five other witnesses saw a red light to the north of Gulf Breeze. The light hovered for a few minutes, then shot up when an aircraft approached. After the airplane passed the location, the red light reappeared for a while, then shot straight up again and vanished.

On the 14th, at least seven people reported a red light to the north of Gulf Breeze. It approached from the east at a very high speed and came to a dead stop. It hovered, moved back and forth several times, then ascended out of sight. A second group of people saw another red light north of Gulf Breeze hover for a few minutes and then disappear. Yet a third red light was seen by witnesses at the south end of the Bay Bridge. It approached from the south-southeast, passed nearly overhead, and then moved toward the northeast over the East Bay where it promptly blinked out. MUFON Florida State Section Director Rex Salisbury believed that at least three red lights were in the area at about the same time. More red lights were seen in Gulf Breeze on April 17 and then on the 18th a red light was seen moving at a speed between 35 and 45 mph, according to Bruce Maccabee's triangulation based on visual and photographic data, although the wind speed was only 6 mph and was almost across the path of the light.

Analyzing the spring sightings, Salisbury conceded that pranksters might have been responsible for some of the events, but also believed that the multiple sightings in different locations at the same time and moving in different directions would have posed tough problems for a hoaxer, to say nothing of the very high speed achieved in the case of one of the objects.[106]

Hoaxing was certainly the idea that Philip Klass believed to explain events at Gulf Breeze. On April 28, 1990, an advertisement was placed in the *Pensacola News Journal* stating: "Warning: Hoax 'UFO' balloons being flown near Gulf Breeze by unknown persons are an ILLEGAL HAZARD to civil and military aircraft, and thus to persons on the ground." The ad requested anyone with information on the parties responsible for "this illegal and potentially dangerous activity" to call a phone number listed in the ad. When two UFO investigators independently called the number, they reached Klass. He was attempting to build a case that provided a prosaic explanation for the Gulf Breeze sightings.[107]

Dirty Tricks: The Gulf Breeze "Model"

Despite the proliferation of Gulf Breeze witnesses of UFOs, Ed Walters continued to be the lightning rod of media interest. In January 1990, his book on Gulf Breeze received a positive commentary from *Kirkus Reviews*.[108] However, any positive media coverage he garnered was damaged by a June 10, 1990 article by Craig Myers in the *Pensacola News Journal* announcing that a UFO model had been found in the attic of his former residence.[109]

The model caused many to question Ed Walters' credibility, but it quickly raised a problem of another sort. The key was that it was made from foam plates and a strip of Walters' blueprint paper. Incriminating, indeed, except for one thing: the paper was from architectural plans Walters developed in September 1989 for a home he was planning to build. When the project fell through, he threw the plans in the trash. By this time, however, Walters no longer lived in his old residence – he had moved in December 1988. Thus, Walters could not possibly have built the model while living in his prior residence. He had developed the plans after moving out of his old house. The paper used for the Gulf Breeze model, therefore, had to have made the journey from Walters' new home to his old home, and then been placed in the attic. There is no other possibility.

Since it defies all reason that Walters would have planted the model himself in his old home, the only sensible scenario is that someone picked his trash (something of which he had long been complaining), built the model, and planted it in the still vacant house, presumably to discredit him.

The discovery of the model itself is curious. The house remained vacant until October 1989, when the new owner Robert Menzer moved in. Upon moving out, Walters had removed his ice-maker refrigerator, leaving a shut-off valve at the end of the water supply line. In March 1990, when Menzer connected his ice-maker refrigerator, there was no water in the line. Assuming there was another valve somewhere along the line, Menzer followed it into the attic above the garage (a search which Menzer later duplicated for Gulf Breeze investigator, Bob Reid). There, the new homeowner found a crimp in the copper pipe that appeared to have been made with a pair of pliers. The UFO model was found carefully tucked beneath the insulation, next to the crimped pipe. This location was significant because, although the house was locked, access to the garage was fairly simple. In fact, there was even a built-in ladder leading up to the area where the model was hidden. Most convenient, indeed.[110] On June 4, Menzer was interviewed by Craig Myers of the *Pensacola News Journal.* Myers asked Menzer three questions: have you seen any

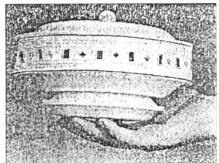

The Gulf Breeze model, as presented for the newspapers.

UFOs (No), have you seen any UFO photos lying around (No), and have you found "any models of UFOs, anything like that?" Apparently a very lucky question, as Menzer then produced the model.

The model convinced some that Walters had hoaxed the photos. Gulf Breeze Mayor Ed Gray announced that Walters had engaged in a grand public deception in the quest for financial reward, but was undone by a "careless error."[111] Others were not impressed by the spectacle. Shirley McConnell, who had seen a UFO with her husband in 1988, told the newspapers that what they had seen "was not a little model. What we saw looked exactly like Ed Walters' photograph. There were definite differences in the model and what we saw." Another man, Adam Dye, had seen a UFO over Gulf Breeze in November 1987, shortly before Ed Walters' first sighting. "Seeing is believing," Dye said, "and I was not looking at a model." Certainly, an examination of the model photographs shows distinct differences from the object in the photographs.[112]

Craig Myers published a second damaging story a few days later. This concerned Tommy Smith, a former Gulf Breeze resident who claimed Walters had hoaxed the photos.[113] A telephone interview with the young man had been arranged with Mayor Ed Gray, police chief Jerry Brown, television reporter Mark Curtis, and Myers. Smith stated that Walters photographed two UFO models, that his family was in on the hoax, and that he had tried to enlist Tommy's help.

As with the Gulf Breeze model, questions quickly arose regarding these claims. Smith claimed that he was not present during hoaxing of any of the published photos, but stated that Walters told him how some of the photos had been created, such as the blue beams in two of the photos (peeling the back of the film and exposing it to light, an explanation rejected by several analysts and manufacturers). Most of Walters' hoaxed shots, said Smith, were done by using a double exposure method with the Polaroid camera. This included the much publicized photo #19, also known as the "Road Shot," although Smith could give no specifics on how the shot was done.* He added that a circle of dead grass found in a school soccer field behind the Walters home, allegedly caused by a UFO, had actually been made by

---

* Incidentally, other than Bruce Maccabee, who concluded the "Road Shot" photo was genuine, two other respected photo analysts, William Hyzer and Jeff Sainio, studied it. Hyzer, who did not have access to the original photos, concluded that the Road Shot was a double exposure. Sainio originally set out to prove the photos were fake. Instead, he encountered evidence that Walters could not have generated his photographs with his equipment and the double exposure technique. By the early 1990s, Sainio rejected the debunkers and Tommy Smith. See Hufford, Art, "Ed Walters, The Model, and Tommy Smith," *MUFON UFO Journal*, 1/93.

Walters turning a trampoline upside down and jumping on it for several hours. This claim seems farfetched at best, considering that grass did not grow within that circle for 18 months subsequent to the event.

Generally speaking, it seems odd that Walters would have brought Smith into an inner circle for an alleged hoax, as Smith was not a close friend to anyone in the family. Complicating the picture was another young man named Hank Boland, whom Smith claimed had taken part in the hoax. Boland, however, fully supported Walters and denied involvement in any such activity. Needless to say, Walters' wife and son also denied participating in any hoax.[114]

The controversy prompted MUFON to reopen its case on Ed Walters. In July, Walt Andrus selected Rex and Carol Salisbury to investigate Tommy Smith's claims and determine whether the model had been used in Ed Walters' photographs. Later that summer, Rex Salisbury released a provisional conclusion to the local press, stating his belief that a hoax had indeed occurred. Yet Andrus continued to wait for Salisbury's final report. After repeated requests, Andrus asked MUFON investigator Gary Watson to assume the investigation. Watson presented his conclusion, "Ed Walters is telling the truth," at the 1991 MUFON symposium. This left Andrus open to the charge that he replaced the Salisburys because he did not like their conclusion (which he finally received from them in 1992).[115]

The confluence of evidence against Ed Walters generated more heat than light, as well as widespread suspicions that the evidence against him was essentially fraudulent. Added to this was a demonstrably false picture from early 1990, created by a New York City photographer, of a Gulf Breeze-type craft that was supposed to be flying near the Chrysler Building in New York City.[116] Willy Smith, although knowing it was a fake, promoted the picture as if it were real in his attempt (unsuccessfully) to lure Ed Walters into the trap of using the fake photo as proof that his were real. It certainly could appear to disinterested parties that machinations were afoot to discredit Ed Walters.

Sightings by Gulf Breeze residents, including Ed Walters, continued into the 1990s. Between November 1990 and July 1992 a group of people who carried out a nightly skywatch recorded nearly 200 sightings, including red lights, rings of light and other shapes. Researcher Bruce Maccabee was witness to a strange ring of lights in September 1991.[117]

The Soviet UFO of March 21, 1990

The Soviet Union continued to spiral into oblivion. In January 1990,

Mikhail Gorbachev was in Lithuania, which the previous month had voted for independence from Moscow. Gorbachev tried to compromise while somehow preserving the Soviet Union. Meanwhile, far to the south, the Soviet Republic of Azerbaijan was beset by rioting and civil war between Muslims and Christians. In early February, the East German government proposed a reunited and neutral Germany. Gorbachev grudgingly accepted this, although Soviet hardliners were displeased. Then, on February 5, Gorbachev proposed that the U.S.S.R. become a multiparty democratic state. In March, Lithuania formalized its declaration of independence (which Gorbachev said was "illegitimate"), Estonia voted for independence, and Hungary held its first free elections since 1945. Preserving the U.S.S.R. had become a losing battle.

Meanwhile, UFOs continued to make the news. On February 22, *Rabochaya Tribuna* published a report by Soviet militiamen in the Siberian city of Krasnoyarsk who claimed that two disc shaped UFOs had followed their patrol cars, one of which landed on a nearby hill and "harassed them" with rays of colored lights before flying away.[118] Another news item described fast and silent objects near Moscow on March 12 that could stop suddenly and dart in different directions. Many residents spent their night on the rooftops to watch.[119]

The greatest Soviet UFO sighting of the year took place on March 21, 1990, east of Moscow. That night, between 8 p.m. and midnight, unknown objects were seen over a wide area encompassing Pereslavl, Zalessky, Novoselye, Zagorsk, Yakovlevo, Ploshevo, Dubki, Kablukovo, Fryazino, and Kirzhatch. Radar stations and aircraft were placed on alert. Residents phoned authorities, describing flashes of white light that followed one another after two or three seconds. All had difficulty in describing the appearance of the objects. In one area, an object was said to hover low, illuminating the ground below. Members of a watch post in Zalessky stated they saw an object with red lights approach from the west at 9:19 p.m. at a speed "much greater than that of any plane." Fifteen minutes later, this object had "disappeared" but was followed by a similar object with white lights, which would occasionally be lost from view.

Two Soviet interceptors were dispatched that night. One of them was scrambled at 9:38 p.m., flown by pilot Colonel A. A. Semyonchenko. At the time, the unknown was above Pereslavl-Zalessky at an altitude of 2,000 meters. At 10:05 p.m., Semyonchenko saw the target's two white flashing lights, ahead and slightly to the right. He tracked it on aircraft radar, distinguishing it from nearby commercial traffic. By radio, he ordered the target to identify itself; instead it only changed its speed and altitude. Semyonchenko then turned steeply and noticed something like the aurora borealis in the north and northwest. He re-approached the UFO, passing above it just 500 to 600 meters away. He saw the two flashing white lights, and briefly saw the silhouette of the object against the background of the city. "It was difficult to determine its nature or classification," he stated, "due to the limited lighting." He was then ordered to return to the airfield.

The personnel in Zalessky observed this encounter. When Semyon-chenko approached the UFO, they noticed that it would disappear. They also saw the unknown object make a turn and approach the jet "at a very high speed." The object then disappeared, only to reappear behind and above Semyonchenko's jet. It played cat-and-mouse games like this for a while longer, before it finally disappeared and Semyonchenko was ordered to return.

A number of Soviet military witnesses got a better view of the object than did Semyonchenko. Captain V. Birin said "the object looked like a flying saucer with two very bright lights along the edges." Judging by its shining lights, he estimated its diameter at between 100 and 200 meters, or between 300 and 600 feet, certainly rather large. He described a less intense light, "which looked like a porthole," between the two bright lights. He noticed a relationship between the speed of the object and the speed of the flashing lights: "the more often they flashed, the faster the speed of the UFO, and vice versa. While hovering, the object extinguished its lights almost completely." At 10:30 p.m. he saw the object depart toward Moscow. He enclosed a drawing of the craft for his superiors.

Captain V. Ivchenko said he "clearly saw two lights flashing with a definite periodicity." The UFO, he said, carried out an "S-turn" flight. Captain N. Filatov said the object's light sources appeared to merge and divide; its brightness was far greater than for signal lights of ordinary aircraft. He also described its movements as an "S-turn, horizontally and vertically." Other witnesses saw the red identification lights of two aircraft accompanying the main UFO.

Deputy Minister of Defense Ivan Tretyak spoke about the matter. While he refused to acknowledge the UFO or speculate what it was, he said the pilots refrained from attacking it because it might have possessed a formidable capacity for retaliation. The key statement about the event came from General Igor Maltsev, Chief of the Soviet Air Defense Forces. Maltsev acknowledged that several radar stations had tracked an unknown object, over 100 visual observations were made by military personnel, and two photographs of the UFO were taken. Based on all the data, he said the UFO was a disc approximately 100 to 200 meters in diameter, able to perform an 'S-turn' flight horizontally and vertically, as well as hover and then fly "with a speed exceeding that of the modern jet fighter by 2 or 3 times." All the while, it had been silent when doing these things. Maltsev commented that these objects were "completely devoid of inertia." Whoever was operating them, "they had somehow 'come to terms' with gravity." Although he refused to speculate on the identity of the object, he said that "at the present time, terrestrial machines could hardly have any such capabilities."[120]

The event was soon reported in full detail in the Soviet newspapers and translated by the CIA's Foreign Broadcast Information Service (FBIS), and detailed accounts were soon published in the *MUFON UFO Journal* and the *International UFO Reporter*. The CIA's reaction appears to have been noncommittal, although copies of its Foreign Press Report were sent to the Joint Chiefs of Staff, the FBI, Navy, and elsewhere.[121]

The Night of the Belgian Triangles

For the previous six months or so, much of Europe had experienced a wave of UFO sightings. In terms of sheer drama, the climax occurred over Belgium and northern Germany on the night of March 30-31, 1990. At 10:50 p.m., the NATO radar station at Glons received a telephone call from a policeman in the city of Wavre who reported three unusual lights forming an equilateral triangle. Fifteen minutes later, a police patrol confirmed the observation and soon reported a new set of lights. Meanwhile, the radar screens at Glons detected an unknown target moving at the slow speed of 40 kph. For the next two and a half hours, other police officers and civilians observed strange maneuvers of up to three sets of triangular lights in the outskirts of Brussels. The lights were substantially larger in appearance than stars, often accelerated, and sometimes glowed red. Some witnesses claimed that the lights were attached to the underside of a huge triangular craft, readily visible when it hovered at low altitudes. Its variation in speed was remarkable, from slower than an automobile to faster than a jet.

NATO radar stations at Glons and Semmerzake tracked these unexplained blips. At 11:56 p.m., the NATO Air Defense Sector Commander authorized the scrambling of two F-16s, which were airborne just after midnight. The two aircraft quickly achieved radar lock-ons to their targets. However, an odd thing occurred: each time they got close, the radar lock was broken and the object took evasive action. Ground witnesses also reported that the object's lights dimmed completely when the F-16s arrived.

The object being pursued employed exceptional evasion tactics. During the first radar lock-on, according to the report issued by the Royal Belgian Air Force, the UFO's speed immediately changed from 150 knots to 970 knots and dropped its altitude from 9,000 to 5,000 feet. It quickly returned to 11,000 feet, then dropped again to close to ground level. The pilots then lost radar contact with it. In fact, the UFO had dropped its altitude by nearly one mile in a mere second, a simply astonishing maneuver. This event was tracked on Air Force radar while amazed ground witnesses saw it. Another radar lock-on was obtained, but then broken by what the report called "a jamming signal on the screen." The object also exploited inherent weaknesses in radar tracking capability. When it dipped to an altitude of 200 meters from the ground, all five radar screens (three ground-base and two airborne) lost track of it. In addition, since the radars filtered out slow moving or stationary targets (on the assumption that they were not jets), the pilots could not close on the object whenever it slowed down or stopped. The pilots were never actually able to see the objects. After 75 minutes of futility, the intercept chase was called off.

On the ground, military and police continued to observe "four white luminous spots forming a square" until around 1:30 a.m., when the four lights dimmed and seemed to depart in four different directions. The weather conditions on that night were very clear, allowing ground witnesses to observe the objects in detail, as well as the pursuit by the F-16s. A final estimate placed the number of witnesses in Belgium and northern Germany at well over 2,000. On the next morning, newspapers reported the F-16s "came home with an empty bag."[122]

The Belgian Air Force Talks

This was not true, however. On May 19, 1990, following an analysis of its data, the Belgium Air Force Headquarters announced that five different military radars (two on the F-16s and three radar stations) had detected unidentified echoes at the same moment and in the same place as indicated by witnesses on the ground. Moreover, the data all confirmed that the objects had moved at incredible speeds. The "Report Concerning the Observation of UFOs During the Night of March 30 to 31, 1990," authored by Belgian Air Force Major P. Lambrechts of the Air Force General Staff in Brussels, included a full chronology of the events, as well as many enclosures with eyewitness descriptions from several police officers and other data.

Belgian Air Force analysts had examined and rejected many alternative hypotheses for the UFOs, said Lambrechts, including "optical illusions, confusion with planets or other meteorological phenomena ... weather balloons ... meteorological inversions ... holographic projections." More significantly, "the speeds measured at the moment of the change of altitudes, exclude the hypothesis that the UFOs observed could be confused with aircraft." This even included the new stealth aircraft such as the B-2 or F-117, as well as remotely piloted vehicles, ultra light aircraft, Airborne Warning and Control System (AWACS), or anything else known to fly. There were many puzzling features of the unknown objects, said Lambrechts. For example, why was no shock wave created by the UFOs, even though several times it surpassed the sound barrier? In Lambrechts words, "here, no explanation can be given."[123]

Another Belgian Air Force figure who spoke about the events was Major-General Wilfried de Brouwer, Deputy Chief of the Royal Belgian Air Force. His statements were blunt. The dramatic changes of velocity and altitude taken by the object, he said, including a 2,000 meter drop within the space of one second, involved a fantastic acceleration equivalent to 40 g-forces, or five times what a human pilot can withstand. Moreover, the F-16 had no chance of keeping up with the speed of the UFO when it approached ground level, due to the greater air density. "There was a logic behind the motions of the object," he said. De Brouwer later added that "the day will come undoubtedly, when the phenomenon will be observed with techno-logical means of detection and collection that won't leave a single doubt about its origin.... But it exists, it is real, and that in itself is an important conclusion."[124]

Sightings of triangular craft continued in Belgium through April and afterward. Sometime in very early April, a young man took a photograph of the alleged triangle above the city of Petit-Rechain. The image is of among the most spectacular UFOs ever captured. With light enhancement, it shows a perfectly triangular aircraft with rounded edges, white lights at the corners, and a red light in the center. The object appears to be moving, and a pulse of some sort is visible behind the object. The Belgian Air Force Academy analyzed the image, found no evidence of a hoax, and said the picture appeared to be authentic.

Belgian UFO: Opinions

Many mainstream sources were quick to throw cold water on all this silly UFO news. The *Financial Times* of London focused on "the UFO-obsessed Belgian media," how some sightings "resemble a lamp-post more closely than a UFO," and how "surprising" it was that the Belgian military should take UFOs seriously. In the traditional manner of British establishment press, analysis of an extraordinary event was replaced by glib sarcasm: Belgium may not have found its UFO, "but it has found a nice new use for its air force now that its services are needed less and less by earthlings."[125]

Many explanations centered on the stealth fighter and bomber. The triangular shape of the UFO did seem to be a rough match with these newly unveiled aircraft, but in fact their performance was no different than most other subsonic military aircraft; what made them special was their extremely low radar cross section. A memo from the U.S. Defense Intelligence Agency* also stated that the Americans privately confirmed to the Belgians that "no USAF stealth aircraft were operating in the Ardennes area during the periods in question."[126] Of course, the wording of that memo was legalistically careful: "no USAF stealth aircraft" could still leave open other possibilities. A few years later, Nick Pope, who was employed at the British Ministry of Defence's "UFO Desk," also learned from his contacts in the Belgian government that the answer did not appear to be American aircraft. "They had no idea what the object was," wrote Pope, "and would dearly love to find out."[127]

The Belgian UFO research organization SOBEPS obtained access to the Belgian Air Force reports and radar data, as well as 25 different videotapes made during the sightings. Possessing a respected team of scientists, including Leon Brenig, a nonlinear dynamics theorist at the Free University in Brussels, and Professor August Meessen, a physicist from the Catholic University at Louvain, the organization was well positioned to perform an independent analysis of the events of March 30-31. Several of SOBEPS senior officers and investigators were among the many witnesses to the object. SOBEPS members considered the conventional culprits: ultralights, military aircraft, astronomical mistakes, holograms, lasers, and temperature inversions. Their conclusion: "none of these hypotheses make any sense." The radar tape, analyzed by Professor Meesen, was considered to be hard evidence of an extraordinary craft with nonterrestrial performance characteristics.[128]

---

* It was distributed to the White House, CIA, State Department, Defense Department, USAF Headquarters in Europe, NATO, and the Commander in Chief of U.S. Naval forces in Europe.

Dr. Jean-Pierre Petit, who was an aeronautical engineer, a cosmologist specializing in plasma physics, and a Director of France's National Center for Scientific Research (CNRS), also studied the data. In an interview, he argued that the Belgian Triangle was not manmade:

> Given the speed of those machines, more than 1,800 kilometers per hour, they could not have been weather balloons. Given the trajectory, it could not have been a meteorite or any satellite in the re-entry phase of space flight. Given the meteorological conditions, it could not have been either natural phenomena or false radar echoes. Given the accelerations that were measured – 40 Gs – this could not have been an airplane. Let's recall that one of the machines accelerated in one second from 280 ktph to 1,030 kph.... There is at this moment no man made machine that is capable of performing at mach 1.5 close to the ground because of heating due to the high air density.... To manufacture such a machine would require that the engine develop an amount of power equivalent to that of a large nuclear power generating plant. And if there is anything not amenable to miniaturization, it is a nuclear power plant. Conclusion: the machines seen in Belgium are not of terrestrial origin.[129]

Petit added that the data derived from the recent military reports provided scientists with hard data that could enable a true re-evaluation of the seriousness of the UFO phenomenon. He was right about the data, although the re-evaluation did not occur.

Not all investigators believed an extraordinary event had occurred. Wim Van Utrecht disagreed with the Belgian Air Force and maintained that the radar observations were not in good agreement with the recorded visual sightings. His main argument, however, concerned the photograph taken in early April, which he suspected was a hoax. The photographer had kept the image slide in a drawer for months, said Utrecht, despite the event being major news all that time. He believed that statements given by the photographer contradicted certain claims of his girlfriend, who was with him at the time. Moreover, the exact day of the purported photograph was unknown, and the image contained no background information to allow verification of the object's actual size and distance. Utrecht also claimed to have duplicated the picture himself.[130]

No matter what the answer to the Belgian mystery – to say nothing of the great Soviet sighting of March 21 – it is obvious that the F-117A or B-2 were not it. Yet, the triangles of 1990 did have similarities with the objects reported in the previous decade in the Hudson Valley of New York and Connecticut, to say nothing of the triangular UFOs seen in Fyffe, Alabama, the Antelope Valley, and elsewhere. Ruling out conventional aviation technology as the explanation for the sightings of 1990, could an even deeper, blacker, technology be responsible – one made not by extraterrestrials but human beings?

One vocal proponent of this position was Tony Gonsalves, a researcher from East Providence, Rhode Island, who been a jet mechanic and plane captain for the U.S. Navy. He argued that the boomerangs of the Hudson Valley and the Belgian Triangles were "American made UFOs," most probably a modified covert version of the B-2 stealth bomber. Gonsalves believed this craft had been fully operational since the early 1980s, and that the official B-2 bomber unveiled in 1988 was a decoy. This does not mean extraterrestrial technology was irrelevant. Gonsalves suggested the American made UFO could well incorporate alien technology obtained from UFO crashes.

There is much to be said for this, whether or not one credits such stories about reverse engineering alien craft in Nevada's S4, or accounts of the Alien Reproduction Vehicle. Assuming the evidence is sufficient of a UFO crash retrieval on even a single occasion, one must assume that all efforts would have been made covertly to understand and – to whatever extent possible – replicate the technology. How far could secret efforts have gotten by 1980? 1990? A few months after the Belgian sightings, the aerospace publication, *Aviation Week & Space Technology,* nearly let the proverbial cat out of the bag. Its October 1, 1990 edition focused heavily on unconventional technologies and aircraft that were rumored to be under development and possibly operational, including a "large, triangular wing-shaped aircraft" being tested out of the Nellis Air Force range in Nevada and the Tehachapi Mountains in California. It mentioned several sightings of "triangular-shaped aircraft," and quoted Air Force sources who stated that diamond and triangular-shaped vehicles were "the trend now." It also mentioned unconfirmed reports that some of these aircraft were designed to fly at Mach 10 or higher.

But 1990 is receding farther and farther into the past. As of this writing, there remains no hard evidence that the U.S. military has used anything like the triangle that was seen over Belgium, nor anything like the Hudson Valley boomerang. When we consider that a triangular craft definitely flew in 1990 – and has not been seen in any military campaigns since – if it is of terrestrial manufacture, then its use must be secret. Since 1990, expensive and protracted wars have been fought in Afghanistan and Iraq, during which such aircraft would surely have been very useful. Why would such incredible weapons be held back when they could well have ended two wars that hemorrhaged the U.S. economy to the point of catastrophe?

One reason might be that they were designed to deal with the extraterrestrial presence on Earth, a scenario that might be so overwhelming that all other considerations would become seen as irrelevant. If it were decided that the extraterrestrial presence had to be kept secret at all costs for as long as possible, then the need for a secret infrastructure becomes self evident. One would have to secure massive funding to build and maintain a covert air force and space program, cultivate research and development programs that would feed off of the mainstream world but not contribute conspicuously to it, and control the key points of the media and political process at an international level.

Another likelihood to consider is that the control of the UFO cover-up moved further away from official offices such as the U.S. Presidency. Consider the firm control held over the Presidencies of Gerald Ford, Jimmy Carter, Ronald Reagan, and George Bush by such internationally based groups such as the Trilateral Commission, the Bilderbergers, and the Council on Foreign Relations (the last of which is formally an American group but entirely globalist in outlook). The subjugation of the Presidency to such groups has hardly been discussed within academic circles, either because those circles are themselves under the sway of such groups or (among the lower levels of academia and media) for fear of being labeled a "conspiracy nut." Yet the world has become a global village almost without any formal acknowledgment of the fact, and it can truly be said that the 1980s and 1990s witnessed the death of the nation state in several key respects. With private, international power showing such prominent sway over the major directions of the domestic and foreign policies of nearly all nations, how hard is it to conceive that practical control over UFO technology and related secrets also migrated to levels higher than the U.S. Presidency?

In reviewing the Belgian Triangle sightings, a final question might be: why 1989-1990, and why Belgium? Several possibilities present themselves. First, Belgium was and remains the headquarters of NATO, containing many bases and nuclear facilities. It is also one of the leading economic centers of the European Union, which was ready to be born in 1992. At a time when the Berlin Wall had come down and the Soviet Union was on the verge of collapse, perhaps the UFO activity was related to the sudden transformation in the world geopolitical structure.

All of which still begs the question: whether the Belgian Triangles were extraterrestrial or human in origin, what was the technology that enabled them to perform as they did? Can this technology be used by the rest of human civilization? If it were to become available, what results might we expect?

Soviet UFOs – Again

UFOs continued to be reported throughout April in the Soviet Union. Many of these made the newspapers and were duly collected by the CIA. Among the highlights were reports of multiple UFOs hovering over power lines along the Tallinn Highway in Estonia on April 5.[131] On April 10, a triangular UFO was seen for ten minutes over the Siberian city of Abakan.[132] On the 15th of April, *Rabochaya Tribuna* published a report from Major V. Stroynetsky who said that he and several hundred other witnesses had repeatedly seen low-flying triangular UFOs over the Yaroslavl Highway near Moscow. These objects flew at great speeds, made sudden stops, and suddenly accelerated dramatically. Information came to the newspaper's office that Air Defense forces near Moscow had tracked one of these objects on radar.[133]

Perhaps not surprisingly, on April 16, Moscow television announced the establishment of a new Soviet organization for the study of UFOs,* and mentioned that the Soviet Union's Ufological Commission was receiving reports every day of Soviet UFO sightings, as well as 10-15 daily from around the world.[134]

On April 26, 1990, Mikhail Gorbachev was visiting the Uralmash plant in Sverdlovsk when he was asked, "does the USSR government study UFOs?" It is the first documented instance in which the Soviet leader was asked about this topic. His answer was as nondescript as they come: "I know that there are scientific organizations which study this problem."[135] This, of course, was already known to be true. Gorbachev avoided discussing anything else of substance on the matter on that occasion, but is reported to have made a more direct statement on May 4, 1990. A Riga newspaper contained a full page article stating that during a recent meeting with Ural workers, Mikhail Gorbachev said "the UFO phenomenon is real and we should approach it seriously and study it."[136]

Ufological history was made, of sorts, on May 21, 1990, when a joint Soviet and Chinese endeavor to study UFOs was initiated in the town of Dalnegorsk; essentially, agreements were made to exchange video and photographic materials on new sightings. Dalnegorsk, in the eastern Soviet Union, was the scene of significant UFO activity during the late 1980s. It was also close to China, where similar incidents had been reported.[137] A Chinese UFO report from March 28, 1990 was collected in U.S. Defense files. An unknown, silent, object had been seen about 25 miles north of

---

* The All Union Inter-Industrial Ufological Scientific Coordination Center of the USSR Academy of Sciences.

Chongqing at 11:20 p.m. local time. It was about 65 feet long, with orange and pale green lights, and flew silently toward the northeast at the very low altitude of about 150 feet. Large blocks of text were blacked out of the U.S. memo.[138]

American Technology Ascendant

By the end of the Cold War, American military technology had hit overdrive. Stealth, of course, was a major development that rendered much, if not most, of the Soviet air defense system obsolete. But by 1990, other developments added great momentum toward making America the sole true superpower in the world.

A hint of something extraordinary took place early in 1990, when the SR-71 (Blackbird) reconnaissance aircraft – officially speaking, the world's fastest aircraft – was retired from service with no stated replacement. It was said that advances in satellite technology meant that the Blackbird would no longer be necessary.[139] The odd thing was that there was no word of dissension within the military over this. Aviation writer Bill Sweetman pointed out that "never in its history had the Air Force ... walked away from a manned mission, however mundane, without a fight." The alleged annual savings of $300 million was insignificant. Analysts pointed out that satellites, while useful, simply could not perform the types of missions for which the Blackbird was perfect.[140] A suspicion within the aviation and aerospace community was that there was a secret replacement for the Blackbird, something better. That several have since been recalled to active duty in subsequent years could mean that the Bush administration made a genuine mistake, or it could mean that the Blackbird's reactivation was necessary to provide cover for its replacement.[141]

It was at this time that *Aviation Week and Space Technology* first broke the news that the alleged hypersonic aircraft, "Aurora," was inadvertently released in the 1985 U.S. budget. This was as an allocation of $455 million for black aircraft *production* for fiscal year 1987. In other words, for building aircraft, not simply R&D. By 1990, people in the vicinity of Edwards AFB in California were hearing extremely loud aircraft seemingly "ripping" the sky. Observers saw and heard a distinctive aircraft flying over the Mojave desert at high altitude and speed, leaving contrails described as "doughnuts on a rope."[142] Was this the Blackbird's replacement? A trans-atmospheric vehicle?

Meanwhile, satellite capabilities continued to improve. Although the great public demonstration of new space technology was the deployment of the Hubble Space Telescope on April 25, 1990, a more significant space deployment had occurred just a few weeks before. On March 1, the space shuttle Atlantis launched the first "stealth satellite" for the National Reconnaissance Office (NRO), called "Misty." Little is known about it, except it reportedly had visual and radar stealth characteristics, making it difficult to detect (and thus predict when it would fly overhead).[143] Incidentally, the very existence of the NRO was not publicly acknowledged for several more years, despite the fact it had existed since 1961. Journalist James Bamford had exposed the NRO in a 1985 *New York Times* article, but the agency remained a classified secret until 1992. Officially, the NRO's function is to build and monitor spy satellites. However, considering its extreme secrecy even among America's officially acknowledged intelligence agencies, the NRO could well have taken on other missions, such as those related to UFOs. Indeed, its capabilities make it ideally suited for this.

Interesting weapons were also being developed, including those with significant space applications. The Shiva Star, connected to the SDI program, could fire a 'plasma bullet,' described as a doughnut shaped ring of ionized gas, at 10,000 kilometers per second. Capable of tremendous energy, its stated purpose was to destroy incoming nuclear warheads, although once again the UFO connection would seem to be a logical possibility.[144]

It is also known that anti-gravity was being studied, although no breakthroughs seemed to be in the offing. In 1990, the NATO Advisory Group for Aerospace Research and Development (AGARD) published a study regarding gyroscopes which concluded that they could in theory counteract gravity. Unfortunately, any anti-gravity force produced by known gyroscopic machines was too weak to be practical. The defense group BAE Systems was also conducting trials on anti-gravity in 1990, one of which appeared to indicate success (although the results could not be repeated). Later that year, the Air Force published an "Electric Propulsion Study" as part of its efforts to learn whether any theory existed that might permit the engineering of an anti-gravity device.[145]

Such studies and activities of 1990 show very great strides in America's military capabilities. Yet they also show serious limits, if we are to look to these for explanations of the UFO phenomenon. Consider the latest and greatest aviation developments of 1990. One of these was the X-31A, an "enhanced fighter maneuverability" demonstrator, designed to prove technologies that would allow close-in aerial combat beyond normal flying parameters. The aircraft could execute a fast minimum-radius, 180-degree "J-turn" turn, well beyond the aerodynamic limits of other conventional aircraft. Of course, it looked nothing like a triangle, and could not match the performance of the Belgian triangles.[146] Meanwhile, Grumman was in the process of rolling out the F-14D "Super" Tomcat. It had improved radar, an airborne jamming system, Infrared Search and Track (IRST), and much more. Still, as capable as the fighter was, Secretary of Defense, Dick Cheney called it "1960s technology," and was pushing hard for an Advanced Tactical Fighter (ATF) variant.[147]

The ATF was a term for what the USAF considered to be an "air superiority" replacement for its excellent but increasingly outdated F-15 Eagle. The idea was to incorporate emerging technologies, such as advanced alloys and composite material, advanced fly-by-wire flight control systems, higher power propulsion systems, and stealth technology. By 1990, there were two such aircraft in competition for the contract. The losing bid was the Northrop/McDonnell Douglas YF-23A "Black Widow" prototype, while the

The F-22 Raptor; designed in the 1980s and 1990s; in service in 2005.

Lockheed YF-22A won the bid in 1991. This became the F-22 Raptor, considered by many to be the most outstanding fighter jet ever built. Yet the Raptor would require many years before it even saw service. Indeed, it did not formally enter USAF service until December 2005. In 1990, neither of these prototype aircraft were even close to being ready for mass production.[148]

Such is an incomplete but general picture of the state-of-the-art American military technology circa 1990. Certainly very impressive, and well beyond the capabilities of any other nation, including the Soviet Union. Yet, it is also clear that the above weapons and technologies were not equal to the objects seen for decades – objects known as UFOs. Even the F-22 Raptor of the 21th century cannot duplicate the maneuvers of the Belgian triangle or hundreds of other UFOs that have been tracked by the militaries of the world.

Yet something was obviously going on at deeply classified levels. In May 1990, George Knapp, who had recently broken the Bob Lazar story, interviewed journalist and investigator James Goodall for Las Vegas' KLAS-TV. With Knapp, Goodall told his story of having talked with an engineer at Lockheed Aircraft's Advanced Systems Division (better known as the Skunkworks) which tested machines at Area 51. When Goodall asked about UFOs, the engineer replied "Absolutely, positively without a doubt, they exist." Goodall also spoke with a master sergeant with three tours of duty at Groom Lake who told him "the United States government and the military has things that are out there – you can't describe them as airplanes – that are literally out of this world. And he says they are alien to anything that you've ever seen." Goodall pressed for more detail, but his source replied he had said too much already. KLAS-TV also interviewed Ben Rich, who said the technology at Area 51 was "just good American ingenuity." Of course, Rich had not long before written privately to John Andrews about his belief in both manmade and extraterrestrial flying saucers.[149]

Crop Circle Explosion

Crop circles, a fascinating mystery in their own right, are sometimes seen as connected to the UFO phenomenon, sometimes not. There are valid reasons for both positions, but the main reason to think "yes" is quite simple. Both phenomena have certain difficult cases that do not seem explainable by natural or manmade reasons. In the case of some crop circles, the size, complexity, and precision, especially when taking into account the suddenness with which they appear, beg for a credible explanation. Many individuals have taken credit for creating crop circles, but none have been caught "in the act," unless to provide a public demonstration.

Crop circles have reportedly been around for centuries in Britain, which is where they still most frequently appear. For a long time, however, they were a peripheral phenomenon, not appearing in large numbers until the 1970s. Then, each summer, a certain number of mysterious circular patterns began to appear in the fields of southwestern England. In 1985, there were 17 reported circles, and 17 again the following summer. A major upswing occurred in 1987, with 75 reported circles. 1988 was higher still, with 110, and there were 305 formations reported during the summer of 1989. In 1990, the crop circle phenomenon truly exploded with more than 1,000 reported circles that summer.

The patterns had become much more complex, too. The circles of the late 1970s and through most of the 1980s were just that: circles, usually appearing alone, within which the stalks were usually laid down in a spiral pattern. From the beginning, a fair portion of media coverage assumed that pranksters had secretly created patterns by means of rope and planks of wood. The problem with this explanation is that most English farms at that time did not have the hallmark tractor lines that in later years famously crossed the fields in parallel lines every 60 feet or so. With the tractor lines, a hoaxer could walk along such paths so as not to leave an obvious footpath. Without the tractor lines, this is difficult, as the stalks of wheat are typically brittle and easily break. Yet such traces were not in evidence with these early circles.

An early scientific explanation was offered by physicist Dr. Terence Meaden, who argued that the spiral patterns in crop circles were the result of atmospheric phenomena. Meaden suggested that wind currents were manipulated by surrounding hills to create whirling air currents and ionized plasmas, very much like a dust devil or tornado, which created the patterns.* His main hypothesis was that a previously unknown type of "plasma vortex" created the circles. The idea of plasma may have merit, as several investigators believe that some kind of light energy is a factor in creating the circles.[150] Meaden, however, presented his theory in terms of purely natural causation. This was easier to defend as long as the circles remained relatively simple.

The problem was that they did not. In 1988, the first "quintuplet" formation occurred, in which a large circle was surrounded by four smaller circles at a significant distance, each smaller circle aligned to one of the cardinal points. The formation was remarkable for its precision. In 1989, the famous "swastika" formation occurred, not really a swastika so much as a circle divided into four quadrants, within which the stalks were laid down exactly according to one of the four magnetic compass points. Even more remarkable, the stalks at the center were rotated and counter-rotated in three distinct movements. At the boundary edge, a thin band was rotated clockwise with stalks weaving over and under the stalks in the quadrants. It was extremely complex, and a fatal blow to Meaden's weather-based theory. If it was a hoax, it was one of unprecedented complexity, which would have to have been done in the middle of the night, silently, and perfectly. Given the circumstances, many felt that a hoax was therefore out of the question.

Of course, other naturalistic explanations were out there: magnetic anomalies, seismic events, sound waves, electromagnetic radiation, or cosmic radiation. No one suggested that any one of these was adequate to explain the total phenomenon. Explanations of the more mystical type were

---

* This author had the opportunity to see a dust devil first-hand while in the American southwest in 2006. Suffice to say that in his opinion, no dust devil on Earth has the capability of creating an actual crop circle.

also prevalent. A sizable number of crop circle students began to wonder if there was a link with the many ancient stone sites across the English countryside.

1990 brought crop circles to a new level altogether in terms of both quantity and complexity, and media coverage became major. Of the many extraordinary patterns created that year, one truly stood out as exceptional. This was an 80 meter (260 foot) long pictogram in the small Wiltshire town of Alton Barnes, and which became a national sensation after its discovery on July 11. Thousands of people made pilgrimages to see and experience it. Once again, as with all previous formations, it appeared overnight, without a hint as to who created it, or (just as interesting) *how* it was done. But a UFO connection was made explicitly that month, when Steven Alexander filmed a shiny, metallic object by the pictogram, clearly looking as though it were under intelligent control.[151]

That summer, a year before the "confession" of Doug Bower and Dave Chorley, a 59-year-old man named Fred Day told the media he had been creating crop circles since he was a boy. The British press, already preparing to label the circles as hoaxes, jumped on this as an explanation for many of the formations. Hoaxing was becoming more high profile and increasingly muddied the waters.[152]

However, experienced circle students (known as cereologists) such as Colin Andrews, Pat Delgado, and others pointed out that circles created by pranksters typically lacked a precision that "genuine" formations typically had. Even by 1990, several additional distinguishing features were apparent. Within genuine circles, stalks were bent but not broken, essentially undamaged – hoaxed circles always showed residual damage from trampling, and usually a good deal of mud. Increasingly, the genuine formations showed incredible refinement, including sharp edges and multiple layers in different directions. Some formations were made very lightly, with the stalks pressed down only a little, and with no sign of footprints or other disturbances, making a hoax explanation exceedingly difficult. Some formations had very narrow rings surrounding the circles, sometimes just a few inches wide and impossible to see at ground level without walking through and damaging the crop – again, with no signs of this having happened. Also, in general, the scope and precision of the large pictograms were becoming truly awesome, presenting substantial challenges for any covert Leonardo Da Vincis wandering through the fields of southwestern England. Matters were more complicated still, if one considered the testimony of some people who claimed to see the creation of the circles. They typically said it looked as through an invisible force was pressing down the crop.[153]

By 1990, crop circles were being reported worldwide, although England was always the "place to be" for any serious cereologist. Perhaps copy cat hoaxers explained some of this, but the real difficulty was in explaining how some of these formations were created at all.[154]

Summary

The most striking feature of the UFO history in 1989 and 1990 is its volatility. The UFO research community was beset by controversy, betrayals, and admitted penetration by the intelligence community. Paranoia among researchers continued to rise. Area 51 went from being completely unknown to being a household term. The UFOs over Gulf Breeze continued to amaze. An alien abduction case appears to have taken place before multiple witnesses in lower Manhattan. Crop circles came into their own as a truly mystifying phenomenon, possibly related to UFOs. Extraordinary UFOs were seen over Belgium, culminating in the failed interception by two F-16s of one or more triangular objects which were tracked on multiple radars and observed by ground witnesses. Residents of the Soviet Union witnessed a wave of UFOs as their nation entered its final phase of existence. The United States wasted no time in becoming the world's only hegemonic power, manipulating its media, flexing its muscles, and invading the nation of Panama. The technology at the disposal of the U.S. military was clearly superior to that fielded by any other nation in the world. Yet, American weapons, despite their excellence, were clearly not at the level of any of the well-documented UFOs.

There was, however, reason to believe that a secret program existed to create manmade UFOs. The money was there, properly covert and laundered. The technology was there, via crash retrievals of prior UFOs. The time by now had been fairly substantial: more than four decades in which to study and replicate. The secrecy was there, via an enormous black budget combined with dominant control over the press, Congress, and other governments. And the motive – in the form of real, actual UFOs below the waters, in the skies, and beyond Earth's atmosphere – was certainly strong enough.

The real question is whether, by 1990, matters had progressed sufficiently to where a secret program operated by the Majestic group (or whatever name it may have taken) had made a "breakthrough" enabling it to fly some of the UFOs being reported, objects such as those seen over

Gulf Breeze, Fyffe, Moscow, or Belgium. Objects displaying capabilities clearly beyond that of any aircraft of 1990, or for that matter of the 21st century. If any of those UFOs were "ours," we must ask seriously what the mission of such craft would be. Their total absence in all theaters of war suggests the answer. These manmade UFOs – if manmade they be – were designed for missions explicitly related to "true" UFOs. That is to say, for dealing with the problem of aliens. Logically, since many UFOs are tracked in the upper atmosphere, Earth's orbit, and beyond, we can assume that any manmade UFO program would also deal with matters that are "off-world."

Surely the situation would be complex no matter how one looked at it, but in 1990, matters became more complicated still. With the end of the Cold War looming, one of the foundational reasons for secrecy was undermined. The question facing thoughtful members of the Bush administration was, do we attempt to end UFO secrecy? If so . . . how?

Chapter 9

False Dawn
1990-1991

Out of these troubled times . . . a new world order can emerge.
— *President George H. W. Bush, September 11, 1990.*

Among black programs, further distinction is made for "waived" programs, considered to be so sensitive that they are exempt from standard reporting requirements to the Congress.
— *1997 U.S. Senate Report on the black budget.*

The [UFO] program was transmogrified and became private, just as many, many other projects become private.
— *Senior U.S. intelligence source, speaking confidentially to the author.*

The natural progress of things is for liberty to yield and government to gain ground.
— *Thomas Jefferson*

The Structure of UFO Secrecy

At this stage, let us describe a probable "big picture" scenario of the UFO and secrecy situation circa 1990.

Since the Second World War and (especially) its immediate aftermath, there had been a decidedly confrontational attitude between the militaries of the world and at least some of these UFOs. In particular, the U.S. military had a nearly continuous relationship with these unknown objects, a relationship consisting of attempted interceptions, most or perhaps all ending in failure. Responsible members of the national security establishment had taken the matter of UFOs very seriously.

A few key military memos, mostly obtained through the Freedom of Information Act, make these facts obvious. The 1947 secret memo from USAF General Nathan Twining described these objects as "real, not visionary or fictitious ... circular or elliptical in shape, flat on bottom and domed on top." He added that they were silent and demonstrated outstanding maneuverability.

Subsequent documents provided yet more information. A 1949 FBI memo referred to UFOs as "Top Secret;" a 1950 document from the Hanford Nuclear Facility described violations of its airspace by circular objects; a 1952 memo to the Director of the CIA stated that sightings of UFOs over U.S. defense installations "are of such nature that they are not attributable to natural phenomena or known types of aerial vehicles."

Other reports and memoranda describe a host of sightings, radar trackings, aerial encounters, attempted interceptions, and even a few UFO landings, such as one which occurred in 1966 at Minot AFB in North Dakota. In 1967, nuclear missiles at Malmstrom AFB inexplicably went offline while a glowing red UFO hovered above. Documents from the 1970s and 1980s continued to emphasize the gravity of the UFO situation. The 1975 events across the northern U.S. and into Canada demonstrated that unknown objects flew unmolested over military bases and easily evaded interception attempts. The 1976 Iranian jet fighter incident, described in U.S. DIA documents, underscored this many times, as did the 1981 memo by USAF Colonel Charles Halt and DIA documents on the 1990 Belgian UFO.

Other countries experienced much the same thing. By 1990, it was obvious that the Soviet Union and China had their own tumultuous histories with these strange craft, as did European, South American, Middle Eastern, and African nations. Australia had a long and dense history of encounters, and the remote land of New Zealand had several extraordinary events. This was, in fact, a global phenomenon affecting nearly every nation on Earth.

And yet, these dramatic encounters worldwide were being withheld from public view or discussion. There was trouble in paradise, but it was being hidden. We can create a reasonable scenario of how this was possible, as long as we remember the facts along the way.

Let us assume President Truman was informed at some point during the 1940s not only that intelligent alien beings were here on Earth, but that – however improbable it might seem – one or more of their craft had come down and had been recovered by the military. At that time, the U.S. was unwilling to share its newly acquired atomic technology with the rest of the world, a significant public issue during the late 1940s. It would seem obvious that the President would similarly decide to withhold knowledge of technology that was even more exotic, more revolutionary, more powerful. Perhaps just as important, the President would need to know just what he was dealing with. Were these other beings friendly? Hostile? How much panic was likely? Would major industrial or financial interests be threatened? For all these reasons, secrecy would seem to be the safest option, at least for the immediate term.

The most logical action would be to gather a team of top individuals, each with a particular specialty, to decide on plans for the short and long term. The very existence of such a group would have to be deeply secret, even from Congress, and certainly from the American people. For once the rest of the world learned of America's possession of such awesome technology, it would only be a matter of time before such technology would be shared. Meanwhile, all the myriad other implications of such an overwhelming disclosure would also have to be studied. Not only is this a logical scenario, but the testimonies from Eric Walker, Ph. D., Robert Sarbacher, Ph. D., and other insiders support it.

Secrecy could well have had public-spirited reasons behind it, but secrecy has a way of maintaining its own *raison d'etre*. For secrecy breeds not only power, but private gain, and it surely appears that much of the UFO secret went private. Consider a piece of alien hardware in the possession of the U.S. Army. The Army wants such technology studied carefully and ultimately replicated to the greatest extent possible. Who gets the job of studying it? There are many brilliant minds employed by the U.S. defense establishment, but when something needs to be *built*, private contractors are the answer: General Electric, Lockheed, Boeing, McDonnell Douglas, SAIC, E-Systems, Hughes, Raytheon, Bell Laboratories, Bechtel, and other companies who could incorporate exotic technologies into new weapons and applications.

Thus, at some point, a form of joint custody over alien technology would take place – the "military-industrial complex" that President Dwight Eisenhower warned about on January 17, 1961, in his final address as President. Inevitably, the lawyers would work out the details, which would most probably entail some level of "ownership" passing to the corporations. Indeed, why not? All through the 20th century, the U.S. government had been dominated by the leaders of industry and finance. The President's senior advisors were all members of the Council on Foreign Relations, the powerful political organization specifically by and for those leaders. Moving matters "private" also helped with secrecy, as private interests would be much more impervious to public requests for information.

Still, the research would be expensive, and the money would need to be hidden. One way to provide covert funding was through classified federal spending; i.e. the "black budget." This evolved over the years into a system of Special Access Programs (SAP); from these grew "unacknowledged" and "waived" SAPs, which officially do not exist – except that they do. Better known as deep black programs, a 1997 U.S. Senate report described them in this way:

> Among black programs, further distinction is made for "waived" programs, considered to be so sensitive that they are exempt from standard reporting requirements to the Congress. The chairperson, ranking member, and, on occasion, other members and staff of relevant Congressional committees are notified only orally of the existence of these programs.[1]

The Senate report noted that persons involved in unacknowledged SAPs were ordered to deny that their program existed, even to superior officers. Saying "no comment" was not good enough. Physical security for the program typically included "elaborate and expensive cover, concealment, deception, and operational security plans." Such a summary offers a glimpse of the incredibly compartmented, labyrinthian, and Byzantine system of Pentagon spending and secrecy.

One well-placed source, with upper level connections to the CIA, told this author that early in the 1980s, if not before, "the [UFO] program was transmogrified and became private, just as many, many other projects become private." Another source, equally well placed, told this author that enormous sums have been spent on a deep black program to study extraterrestrial technology, providing the interesting fact that security for the program was seven to eight times more expensive than the science. The source held a strong opinion that private contractors had taken the lead role in the secrecy structure. Two other insiders known to the author also arrived at this judgment.

Such was also the conclusion of Bill Sweetman in what was possibly a unique study on Special Access Programs.[2] Sweetman estimated there were approximately 150 SAPs within the Pentagon at the close of 1999, many of which were unacknowledged. They often had completely independent systems of classification, with total control exercised by the program manager. Most interesting, Sweetman concluded, was that most of SAPs were dominated not by Defense personnel, but by private contractors. He said he had no idea how these programs were funded.

In this vein, the story of Vice Admiral Thomas R. Wilson is relevant. During the late 1990s, Wilson was Chief of Intelligence of the Joint Chiefs of Staff, a position known as J-2. In 1997, Dr. Steven Greer, leading a UFO "disclosure" initiative, was able to obtain an audience with Wilson – he was able to do so because accompanying him was Apollo 14 astronaut, Dr. Edgar Mitchell. They had expressed their concern about the "rogue" nature of certain Special Access Programs connected to the study of alien technology; that is to say their concern that these programs were dominated not by government personnel, but by private contractors, possibly as runaway programs beyond formal government control. According to claims later made by Greer, as well as personal investigation by the author, Wilson did look into the claims of these two men. After two months of investigating, he found that the claims were true. When he was finally able to get a meeting with a representative of the SAP (not the program manager but its attorney), Admiral Wilson was informed in no uncertain terms that he lacked a need to know. Not only this, but the only reason he was granted a meeting at all was to find out how he learned of the program.

In attempting to validate this story, the author communicated with Dr. Mitchell, the office of Dr. Greer, and a third source well connected to this matter. All three sources confirmed the above sequence of events. The author also contacted Mr. Wilson himself, who (understandably) attempted to deny everything after initially stating that his memory was "foggy." He eventually recalled the meeting after the author made it clear that he had multiple confirmations about it. Yes, conceded Wilson, they had a meeting, only because he was curious why a man of Dr. Mitchell's stature would be interested in such a matter. However, Wilson maintained that everything else described by Greer was "poppycock." He then abruptly ended the phone call.

It would be unfair to have expected Admiral Wilson to say otherwise. To support Greer's claim would not only have jeopardized his security clearances, but would have constituted a near-revolutionary act. It would have been an admission of the highest order, an acknowledgment that the U.S. government had been hijacked by private corporate interests regarding the possession of extraterrestrial technology.

Nevertheless, the cumulative information the author has received on this matter convinces him that it is true.

It is likely that a great deal of missing money has gone into this program. In 1994, a law was passed requiring the federal government to account for its money in a business-like way. After this, several reports described the loss of not billions but *trillions* of dollars.[3] The most perplexing of these claims came from Secretary of Defense Donald Rumsfeld on July 16, 2001, when he spoke to the House Appropriations Committee regarding the Pentagon's Fiscal Year 2002 budget.

. . . the financial systems of the department are so snarled up that we can't account for some $2.6 trillion in transactions that exist, if that's believable.[4]

The amount of $2.6 trillion seems incomprehensible, especially when considered in relation to the Pentagon, which at the time of Rumsfeld's statement had an annual budget of roughly one-eighth that amount. Lest one believe this was a simple mistake, members of Congress discussed the amount, and the Pentagon's accounting office later amended it to $2.3 trillion. The number was clearly offered as legitimate.

Secretary Rumsfeld could make such a statement because it was part of the fiscal mess he inherited from the Clinton administration, so it was not a political liability to him. Still, the number is so far beyond anything that makes sense: how is it possible to lose track of seven or eight times one's annual budget? How long had this problem been developing?

For a very long time, it appears. Considering the obvious importance of the UFO phenomenon, the need for a secret infrastructure to deal with it, the leaks pertaining to secret facilities and reverse engineered objects, a detached analyst can assume that some of this lost money went to deep black programs connected to UFOs. Moreover, through a combination of leaks, logic, and observation, we can gain a reasonable idea of what "the program" is all about.

In the first place, it has been about trying to make a flying saucer. Testimony regarding the recovery of crashed UFOs, statements from Brad Sorensen and the controversial Bob Lazar regarding the existence of a back-engineering program, the insider who told James Goodall that "we have things out there that are literally out of this world," and the many eyewitness accounts of UFOs over Groom Lake and Antelope Valley all support this hypothesis.

"The program" also appears to be about studying alien bodies and conducting related biotech research. Less information exists on this, but at least one of Leonard Stringfield's sources described it. Such a program would be obvious if any alien bodies were ever recovered.

Yet another feature of the program seems to involve activities in space, whether this be covertly in Earth orbit or even the Moon and beyond. There is good evidence of anomalous activity being observed and recorded in space. Ron Regehr's collection of DSP satellite data makes it clear that "fastwalkers" are tracked with regularity. If these anomalies are genuine, they are by themselves sufficient motivation to develop a secret space program. It would be necessary to interact with that phenomenon in some way, whether through observation, communication, or hostilities. For this reason, there is every likelihood that the SDI program initiated during the Reagan years had a covert component related to

UFOs.[5]

We may then ask, who has been in charge? To what extent has the office of the President been involved in the UFO cover-up? Such a question leads us to examine the evolving structure of global power. During the 1950s, American sociologist C. Wright Mills described a "power elite" in the United States comprised of corporate, military, and government elements. It was a radical analysis at the time. Over the decades, however, it has become clear that corporations – or more accurately, transnational corporations – attained a dominant role in this relationship.

By the late 1980s, they were poised to begin a global transformation which future historians will undoubtedly recognize as the death of the nation state. The birth of the Internet, coinciding with the impending end of the Cold War, opened new opportunities for corporate visionaries, primarily in the way of access to cheap labor. The goal became to create an international legal structure to facilitate this process. For many years, the U.S. Presidency had been beholden to transnational-oriented entities such as the Trilateral Commission, the Council on Foreign Relations, and the Bilderbergers. Now, at the Cold War's end, the members of these groups, on behalf of the corporations they owned, set about on an agenda.

One facet of this was the promotion of the North American Free Trade Agreement (NAFTA). Their leading spokesman, President George H. W. Bush, predicted the creation of new American jobs created by "free trade." The actual result was the dismantling of the U.S. manufacturing infrastructure. Lest one attribute the promotion of NAFTA as simply an honest mistake, consider the judgment of Catherine Austin Fitts, who served on the Bush cabinet at the time as Assistant Secretary of the Department of Housing and Urban Development (HUD). In a private conversation, Ms. Fitts told the author that "it was an explicit corporate-political policy of the Bush administration circa 1990 to export the U.S. economy to China." Her clear implication was that the goal was to dismantle and export the U.S. manufacturing infrastructure to places where the labor was so cheap as to be practically free.

It seems incomprehensible that an American President would willfully undertake a nationally suicidal strategy, unless one understands that he does not represent the interests of "the people" so much as multinational corporations. Such entities have no national loyalties, but are driven by need to grow sales, reduce costs, increase profits, and promote shareholder value.

Other enforcers of the new world order were the International Monetary Fund (IMF), World Trade Organization (WTO), and World Bank, the last of which was described as a "tool for takeover" by its one-time Chief Economist, Joseph Stiglitz. Throughout the 1990s, it implemented a basic "four-step plan" for debter nations, ostensibly to correct archaic economic policies and promote globalization, but which were, in reality, designed to result in their complete ownership by international finance. The WTO did much of the same work, consistently promoting privatization of natural resources (such as water), and deeming environmental, health, and food safety laws of nations to be barriers to trade.

In a situation where the elected office of the U.S. Presidency had become fairly hijacked by such interests, it may very well be that UFO secrecy also gravitated to groups beyond the U.S. governmental structure. They would continue to use the U.S. military to manage the problem. To the extent that the various Presidents have been involved in this issue, their actions have furthered the aims and desires of their controllers.

Furthermore, it is not even clear that all U.S. Presidents are briefed on this subject. It is well known that Presidents are not briefed on most black budget programs until they absolutely need to know about them. A second, perhaps less interesting reason, is that there is simply not enough time to brief them on all such operations. One of the author's sources said that he had "professional knowledge" that Presidents Reagan and Bush (senior) were briefed on the matter of UFOs and extraterrestrials, and that he believed that President Carter had been briefed. He was less certain about President Clinton, and felt confident that President George W. Bush was not briefed.

Thus, by 1990, it looked as though at least some UFOs were operated by entities not of our human civilization; confrontations had taken place with various national militaries; the secrecy on this was maintained through extreme compartmentation and control of the world's major media sources, siphoning off enormous sums of public money for the purpose of replicating alien technology and developing a secret space program. Furthermore, the entire process undermined the formal political system in favor of powerful private entities, a process that accelerated from the mid-1980s onward.

The world was going through a silent revolution. Just who exactly was in charge was not a matter of public discussion, but they were creating a new global structure of power. To all appearances, this structure included control over the UFO secret.

Invasion of Kuwait

On August 2, 1990, Iraqi leader Saddam Hussein invaded Kuwait, precipitating Operations Desert Shield and Desert Storm, and ushering in what President Bush would call "the New World Order." The invasion is a study in the duplicity of geopolitics and the mass media.

After the invasion, Saddam was quickly portrayed by President Bush and the rest of the western establishment as the new Hitler. Forgotten in the din were some uncomfortable facts. Until recently, Saddam had been on good terms with Kuwait, which had loaned Iraq $40 billion during the bloody Iraq-Iran war of the 1980s. The war was ruinous for both sides, enriching international arms dealers and leaving Saddam's regime hard pressed to repay. Kuwait would not pardon the debt, so Saddam sought to raise the price of oil through production cuts. Not only did OPEC block this, but Kuwait increased its production, further driving down the price of oil and worsening Iraq's situation. Kuwait's actions cost Iraq some $14 billion annually. Such "economic warfare" (in the opinion of Saddam) was aggravated by accusations that Kuwait was using advanced drilling techniques to extract oil from Iraq's share of the Rumaila Field, a technique popularly called "slant-drilling." All Iraqis remembered that oil-rich Kuwait had not long ago been part of their country, broken off by Britain when Iraq was powerless to stop it.

Throughout the Iran-Iraq war, which lasted from 1980 until 1988, U.S. policy had been openly pro-Iraq (although quietly supporting Iran as well via the Iran-Contra initiative). George Bush had intervened many times on behalf of Saddam Hussein with financial aid and access to high-tech equipment critical for nuclear and chemical weapons. Even after that war ended, Bush's support for the dictator continued.[6] It seems George Bush represented interests trying to take control of Iraq's oil supply, which was then under Iraqi state control. For example, in June 1989, a delegation representing Kissinger Associates Ltd., Bankers Trust, Mobil, Occidental Petroleum, and others met with Saddam in Baghdad. This group was heavily connected to David Rockefeller (with whom Saddam had also met several times during this period). Before supporting any infrastructure improvements, they insisted Iraq's national debt be paid and the oil industry be privatized, at least in part.[7] Saddam refused to sell off his country's cash cow. He began to realize that he would not get what he wanted from the Rockefeller clique.

George Bush continued to court Saddam, however, approving another $1 billion in new aid in late 1989 – critically important, as international bankers had cut off nearly all loans to Iraq. Bush's decision was opposed by the Federal Reserve, the Treasury Department, and the Commerce Department on the grounds that Iraq was not creditworthy and was developing plans for weapons of mass destruction.[8] As late as April 1990, the National Security Council overruled such concerns.[9] Throughout July, as Iraq's diplomatic crisis with Kuwait reached its climax, the Bush administration continued to try to finance Saddam. By July 15, Iraqi troops were massed at the Kuwaiti border; the U.S. said nothing.

Finally, on July 25, Saddam sought advice from the U.S. on his intentions to reclaim Kuwait. He met with the U.S. Ambassador to Iraq, April Glaspie, who told him:

> I have direct instructions from President Bush to improve our relations with Iraq. We have considerable sympathy for your quest for higher oil prices, the immediate cause of your confrontation with Kuwait... I have received an instruction to ask you, in the spirit of friendship not confrontation, regarding your intentions: Why are your troops massed so very close to Kuwait's borders?

Saddam stated that while he was ready to negotiate his border dispute with Kuwait, his design was to "keep the whole of Iraq in the shape we wish it to be." This was a bold statement, especially in the language of diplomacy. After all, why would the "shape" of Iraq be on the agenda when the dispute was over oil and monetary reparations? Saddam obviously meant to change Iraq's shape so that it would once again include Kuwait. When Saddam asked for the U.S. opinion, Glaspie replied:

> We have no opinion on your Arab-Arab conflicts, like your dispute with Kuwait. Secretary [James] Baker has directed me to emphasize the instruction, first given to Iraq in the 1960s, that the Kuwaiti issue is not associated with America.

April Glaspie then left for her summer vacation, and then an extended public silence. It would not be until long after the Gulf War ended that the world learned of her conversation with Saddam.[10]

Over the next few days, Bush said nothing about the Gulf situation, although the CIA managed to warn the Kuwaiti ruling family, which fled the country with its most valuable possessions. After Iraqi troops invaded on August 2, Bush mobilized a U.N. force and declared Saddam to be the next Hitler. Saddam suddenly found himself in an untenable position. Kuwait had to be liberated, its ruling family restored.[11]

The allegation that the U.S. gave a "green light" to Saddam Hussein has received little mainstream support. Instead, the standard argument is that Bush grossly misunderstood Saddam's intentions. An examination of the facts, however, shows how pathetic this claim is. The international situation was clear in late July. Thousands of Iraqi troops were massed at the Kuwaiti border amid a major diplomatic crisis. A simple statement supporting Kuwait's sovereignty would have sufficed to defuse it; instead, the U.S. explicitly turned away. It is not a stretch to interpret this as tacit permission from Saddam's longtime supporter, George H. W. Bush, to allow the Iraqi dictator to seize what he felt was rightfully his. Whether or not Saddam was truly "suckered" into invading Kuwait, his action was a godsend to the American military establishment and the financial establishment that supported it. He provided them with a perfect replacement enemy, now that the Soviet Union had ceased to be viable in that role. The money could keep pouring in.

Within the U.S., matters became surreal. The man who had invaded the sovereign nation of Panama just one year before now told the world that "America stands where it always has, against aggression, against those who would use force to replace the rule of law." The media and educated classes largely supported such Orwellianspeak. Talk of a "new world order" followed. On August 23, National Security Advisor Brent Scowcroft, a protégé of Henry Kissinger, said they were "creating the beginning of a new world order out of the collapse of the U.S.-Soviet antagonisms."[12] On September 11, 1990, President Bush told the nation: "Out of these troubled times ... a new world order can emerge."

First with Panama, now with Iraq, a key feature of this new world order was becoming obvious: that the U.S. would invade and spin as it saw fit in order to remake the world on behalf of the international private interests that it represented. In other words, to engage in the age-old game of imperialism and theft.

Greifswald Lights

In the early days of August 1990, many witnesses by the Baltic Sea, near the cities of Rostock, Greifswald, and the isles of Ruegen and Usedom, reported seeing what appeared to be groups of luminous spheres. They displayed unusual behavior contrary to airplanes, balloons, luminous ammunition and atmospherical phenomena. They accelerated very rapidly and abruptly. One witness, Gerald Schwab, told a German newspaper that the lights "stood there for three minutes before they accelerated rapidly forward."[13]

Then, on August 24 at 8:35 p.m., just six weeks before Germany's reunification, many hundreds – perhaps thousands – of witnesses saw a formation of seven luminous objects over the Baltic Sea. The objects hovered for nearly 30 minutes near Peenemunde (the former Nazi V-2 construction site) and the nuclear power plant at Griefswald. Five people, including nuclear physicist Dr. Ludmilla Ivanova, videotaped the event, enabling researchers to triangulate the lights and reconstruct their position. The combination of eyewitness reports, supported by video and photographic evidence, makes this a particularly strong UFO case.

A German UFO organization, MUFON-CES, obtained six videos and 11 photographs from different individuals, and also interviewed more than a dozen witnesses. The team concluded that the phenomena was in fact two groups of luminous spheres which hovered nearly motionless for about 30 minutes over the Pomeranian Sea. The brighter and closer group formed a circle of six luminous spheres. The second group formed the shape of a 'Y.' One group of witnesses observed that the objects in the Y-formation performed individual movements; some of them moved back and forth between the two groups of lights. They were able to move extremely fast, estimated by one witness as "supersonic velocity," and were able to come to a dead stop upon reaching the formation. One witness was heard to say on video, "I don't believe in UFOs and such nonsense, but I have never seen anything like this in my whole life."

Some skeptics argued the lights were signal flares fired by the Russian or Polish Navy, although the lights were clearly over German seas. Any military maneuver so shortly before the German reunification would have been considered an aggression and caused major diplomatic protests. The Russian and Polish navies both denied any maneuver at the time in question. Actually, the Soviets by this time had closed all nearby military installations and were no longer active in the area.

No scientific explanation has been determined for the lights.[14]

Soviet UFO Acknowledgment

The Soviet Union continued to be the scene of many UFO reports, a portion of which were misidentifications of ordinary objects, such as balloons or Kosmos space launches.[15] Late on September 2, for instance, residents of the northern city of Murmansk saw a large illuminated ball above the sea. It was very high up, gave off no electronic signals, and moved slowly toward the shore. Soviet Air Defense thought it resembled a large airship. The area was too densely populated to fire a missile at it.

By the early morning hours, it was well over the peninsula, and the order was finally given to destroy it. It turned out to be an enormous weather balloon.[16] For such reasons, it is not surprising that some establishment Soviet scientists were annoyed by the proliferation of UFO reports. Vladimir Migulin, a member of the USSR Academy of Sciences and UFO skeptic, told the media he was "extremely irritated" with the deluge of UFO reports in his country, pointing out that some foreign journals such as the *Skeptical Inquirer* were discussing the "paranormal babble" in the Soviet Union.[17]

Other stories were dramatic but questionable, such as an event reported from September 13, 1990. A radar unit in the Volga-Ural military region tracked an approaching object that apparently caused the equipment to malfunction and go blank. Coming outside, the operators saw a flying black triangle giving off three bright rays. It landed nearby and gave off more bursts of energy. They watched it for more than an hour, and two sentries allegedly disappeared then reappeared without realizing they had been gone. The case was investigated by a military reporter who was told by the regional chief that nothing of the sort had occurred.[18]

A much more solid Soviet UFO case took place on September 27, 1990, in Earth's orbit. Cosmonauts Gennady Manakov and Gennady Strekalov were aboard the *Mir* space station. While Strekalov was looking down at Newfoundland through a clear atmosphere, he saw a glittering, iridescent, perfect sphere appear before his eyes. He called Manakov, and together they studied the object. Strekalov said "it shone like the balls that hang on trees at Christmas, greenish in color and all shimmering. It was impossible to take your eyes off it." The two agreed that it could not have been a natural phenomenon: it appeared to be 20 to 30 kilometers above the Earth, was enormous, and had "an absolutely even shape." They watched it for ten seconds, when it disappeared as suddenly as it had appeared. Unfortunately, they did not get to a camera quickly enough to capture an image. Choosing their words carefully, they told Mission Control that they had observed "a kind of unusual phenomenon." Later, they confessed to having no idea what it was. "Perhaps an enormous, experimental sphere or something else ..."[19]

A Soviet military encounter with two UFOs reportedly took place on October 8, 1990. Unfortunately, the article in *Rabochaya Tribuna* did not give a location, only details about how the object was tracked on ground radar screens, apparently blocked airborne radar, but then was seen visually by the intercepting pilot. "Suddenly," he reported, "something made me turn my head. To the rear and to the right I saw two cigar-shaped objects of considerable dimension. The length of the first one was approximately 2 kilometers and the second about 400 meters." He saw these clearly, he said, against the background of a clear sky. They were too distant to make out details or structural features, and when he began to close on them, both targets disappeared from his field of vision – although ground radar continued to track them for some time.[20]

If Soviet UFO skeptics found all of these UFO reports distasteful and embarrassing, the Soviet Deputy Minister of Defense, Ivan Tretyak, found himself more than willing to discuss the matter. Tretyak's credentials were most impressive; he was Commander in Chief of the Air Defense Forces, General of the Army, and the boss of General Igor Maltsev, who had investigated the March 21, 1990 UFO encounter near Moscow. On November 9, Tretyak spoke with *Literaturnaya Gazeta*, a large weekly newspaper with a national circulation.

Tretyak confirmed that fighter-interceptors had encountered UFOs in Soviet air space. The "unidentified flying machine" of March 21 was photographed by interceptor pilots and gave off optical and thermal signals, although it had some "stealth-like" capacity that blocked airborne radar. It was definitely not an airplane, Tretyak said. Still, it was premature to say that UFOs were violations of Soviet sovereignty. Most of them, he said, were explainable as natural phenomena, rocket launches, satellites, or other conventional events. Admittedly, some pilot reports showed UFOs to be of artificial origin, but their real nature remained unknown.

Tretyak understandably hedged his statement about UFOs. He openly stated that some were "real," and at one point seemed to consider an extraterrestrial explanation. Elsewhere, however, he denied believing in extraterrestrials. "I believe something else," he said. "That modern science and technology are capable of creating such spacecraft that could appear above us. . . . You have to believe in man's ingenuity." If so, then he gave a very curious answer as to why no order was given to shoot down the object of March 21. "It would be foolhardy," he said, "to launch an unprovoked attack against an object that may possess formidable capacities for retaliation."[21]

In other words, one of the top defense officials of the Soviet Union admitted that unknown objects with (apparently) vast superiority to Soviet aircraft had violated his nation's air space and paralyzed its military. Did Tretyak believe these were American craft? Something else? Only during the final days of glasnost could such statements be made. The Soviet Union was a very different place in 1990 than it had been at any other time, or would be in the future. While the country continued to break apart, openness enabled more and more information to reach the outside. In the parlance of the day, a "window of opportunity" was being exploited.

Dreamland becomes Leakland

Since the late 1980s, residents of the Antelope Valley in California, as well as the UFO-watchers gathering outside Area 51, had been observing strange aircraft. In the Antelope Valley especially, people were seeing large, quiet, triangular objects that maneuvered extremely well. Although the Air Force would neither confirm nor deny such reports, by the fall of 1990 they were being covered by the Associated Press and *Aviation Week and Space Technology*. The speculation was that the triangles represented secret advanced-technology warplanes.[22]

The real bombshell came with the October 1, 1990 issue of *AWST*. Of particular interest was an article by senior engineering editor William Scott, entitled "Multiple Sightings of Secret Aircraft Hint at New Propulsion, Airframe Designs." Scott, a former flight test engineer and graduate of the U.S. Air Force Test Pilot School, analyzed 45 daylight and nighttime sightings of strange craft over the southwestern desert. Some of these described objects moving as slowly as 20 mph, then accelerating to supersonic speeds. Scott concluded that there were "at least two – but probably more – types of vehicles" beyond the F-117A and B-2. One was a "triangular-shaped, quiet aircraft seen with a flight of F-117A stealth fighters several times since the summer of 1989." Another was a "high speed aircraft characterized by a very deep rumbling roar ..." A third was a high altitude, high speed aircraft, typically observed as a bright, pulsating light, moving much faster than other aircraft, giving no engine noise or sonic boom. Scott believed the second and third aircraft might be the same.[23]

He also wrote of "exotic" propulsion systems being used in new aircraft, and came very close to stating that these might be anti-gravity units. When UFO researcher William Hamilton spoke privately to him about this, he said that Scott stated his opinion that anti-gravity was indeed being used.[24]

While establishment voices like *AWST* were just beginning to discuss such matters, other researchers and journalists were going further. By the early 1990s, for example, journalist George Knapp had spoken with perhaps twenty Area 51 insiders who corroborated various parts of Bob Lazar's claims. None were willing to talk publicly, however, and many were later pressured into silence. One source, who claimed to have seen a disc under a tarp at Groom Lake, agreed to do a limited interview as long as his face was blackened out. On the morning of the scheduled interview, he saw a car parked in front of his house; inside were two men, one of whom was speaking into a radio. They followed him to work, and then home. That was enough to frighten him into canceling. Another of Knapp's sources worked for a defense contractor. She told him that she had attended discussions between her employer and the military regarding extraterrestrial "wreckage" from Roswell that had been taken to Area 51. On the day of her interview, she was visited by her former employer who reminded her that she was still under oath. "We know you do a lot of traveling," she was told. "We'd hate for an accident to happen to you or to your family." She, too, backed out. Yet another informant, a man who prepared tax returns for people at Area 51, phoned Knapp at the TV station to arrange an interview. The following day, he was visited by men claiming to be from the secret service and pressured into silence. There were gaps, to be sure, but a picture was definitely forming of acquired alien technology and human efforts to replicate it.[25]

Journalist Norio Hayakawa, of Nippon TV, similarly looked into deep black projects. One source told him of a new type of craft, called the "Pumpkin Seed," being tested at the Papoose Lake Facility, a few miles south of Groom Lake. This was quite possibly one of the objects seen by Brad Sorensen at the "secret-famous" November 1988 exhibition, mentioned earlier. It was a diamond-shaped craft using pulse detonation propulsion, which can operate from subsonic up to hypersonic speeds. Hayakawa suspected there were deep black programs even beyond this, possibly involving anti-matter. He began leading groups of "Area 51 watchers" who were often harassed while taking legal photos and video.

Beyond those investigators working for media companies, many independent researchers undertook their own investigations, developing their own sources or just shooting their own video. By 1990 and 1991, Area 51 was positively leaking out of Nevada.

Linda Moulton Howe was one of these researchers. While working as Supervising Producer and Original Concept Creator for the Paramount

Studios and FOX-TV special, *UFO Report: Sightings*, she heard from a retired U.S. military officer who told her enigmatically, "the alien technology is so advanced and the beings are so strange that no one would believe it. Keeping the public and media away from what's really happening isn't difficult. It's a story that no one wants to tell, that no one knows how to tell. The truth is stranger than fiction.[26]

Wendelle Stevens, a retired Air Force lieutenant colonel, was another researcher delving into Area 51. He interviewed Derek Hennesy, who claimed to have been an S4 security guard and described at least four underground levels there – only two of which military personnel could enter. Security measures included biometrics such as retina scans and hand prints. Alien bodies and flying discs were kept there, although technicians had not learned how to operate the crafts. Levels three and four were off-limits, but Hennesy heard that live "EBEs" were there, completely identical to each other in appearance, as if cloned. Stevens had heard similar rumors elsewhere, and believed Hennesy was truthful.[27]

Another source of leaked claims came from Bill Uhouse, a military mechanical design engineer. Uhouse had previously worked on aircraft simulator projects, then was asked to join a simulation project involving flying discs. He said that no human could fly one of "theirs," but scientific data was provided by the greys. According to Uhouse, "we took their avionics and transferred them to our science and technology, and used the avionics we know." His description of discs was similar to Bob Lazar's. Unlike Lazar, however, Uhouse said he was introduced to greys that were associated with the project, perhaps up to ten times.[28]

In addition to the stories were the video cameras – still primitive by the standards of later years, but common enough by now. Whatever was flying out of Area 51 appeared to be reaching Las Vegas, as evidenced by the video of a cylindrical grey object maneuvering over the city, captured by Roger Beard on Christmas Eve, 1990. Others were videotaping equally strange objects, such as a highly maneuverable "ball" flying low over Las Vegas, or two metallic-looking hat-like objects zipping around the Vegas skies.[29]

Sean David Morton began going to Area 51 and recorded several interesting objects. Early in 1991, he and a friend taped a glowing disc-shaped object which came to within a few hundred yards. It glowed so brilliantly that the men thought it might explode. Several times, it shot straight up, then descended with a falling leaf motion. They returned with burned faces and mild radiation poisoning. Morton later took more video showing glowing objects with extraordinary acceleration and maneuverability. Alleged insiders soon contacted him, including someone who claimed to have transported large, disc-like and bell-shaped objects which he considered to be alien. He spoke of numerous underground levels, had seen living aliens, alien bodies in tanks (suspended in liquid), and even several humanoid aliens allegedly from the Pleiades.[30]

Similar snooping was going on in the Antelope Valley. Bill Hamilton had been looking into this area for some years by now, but now so were others. It had become obvious that the sites operated by the Northrop, McDonnell Douglas, and Lockheed corporations had substantial underground facilities. There were also rumors of covert military activity associated with these installations, even alien activity, abductions, and missing time episodes.

The Northrop facility was nicknamed "The Anthill," and located near the Tehachapi Mountains, 25 miles northwest of Lancaster, California. It was said to have as many as 42 levels, with tunnels linking it to other facilities, and was believed to be involved in electronic or electromagnetic research. The McDonnell Douglas facility was located northeast of Llano, and the Lockheed installation a few miles north of Helendale. Each had large radar or microwave dishes and strange looking pylons to which various objects could be attached, perhaps to send out electromagnetic radiation. These pylons rose up from underground out of diamond-shaped openings in the middle of long paved surfaces that resembled aircraft runways, but which were not used by aircraft.

Strange objects were seen near these installations, including glowing spheres and discs, boomerangs, and triangles, some of which were very large. One of Hamilton's witnesses, a pilot whose flight plan took him over the Tehachapi Mountains, saw four white rectangular objects hovering over the Northrop facility. Another person, who claimed to be a paint contractor who worked on underground tunnels beneath the Anthill, told Hamilton and Linda Moulton Howe that the tunnels had round openings below, force fields instead of doors, and lights for identification and entry. His job was to spray a "self-illuminating surface on the walls and ceilings." He said he took an elevator from the ground level down for several minutes before the door opened into a tunnel complex where they worked. Most fantastic, he described tiny globes hovering in the tunnels that followed him and his crew around. He thought these were sensors in use by the Air Force. The first time one of the glowing, levitating, orbs came into the space where he was working, it startled him. No one had briefed him about such a thing – and he sprayed it with his spray gun. Whatever it was fell to the floor with a "plop" sound, and he could see a solid spherical shape beneath the paint. Within seconds, black-garbed security people with guns ran into the space. The contractor was warned never to interact with the orbs in any way, but no one explained to him what they were. On one occasion, he observed a flying saucer emerge from inside the Northrop perimeter fence, and then fly off. Clearly, some of these technologies seemed incredible in 1990 – but could they simply have been ahead of the rest of the world by a few decades? Most extraordinary of all, the contractor claimed that on another occasion, he was spraying near a crack in a wall that he knew was a sliding door. Suddenly, the door opened. A few feet away on the other side was "a 7-foot-tall, mint green, non-human in a white lab coat talking with a short, Oriental-looking man." Soon after that, the contractor lost his clearance and job.[31]

The Gulf War

From August 1990, events in the Persian Gulf and Washington led inexorably to war. Operation "Desert Shield," designed ostensibly to protect Saudi Arabia from an Iraqi attack that was neither planned nor feasible, quickly went into action. Soon, hundreds of thousands of coalition soldiers were in the Middle East. The Gulf War was a world-changing event, but three aspects will suffice here: technological considerations, propaganda vs. reality, and interesting UFO stories.

Operation Desert Shield became Operation Desert Storm on January 17, 1991. This was a "war" in the loose sense that two armies opposed each other. But it was the most lopsided in modern history, greater than Hitler's blitzkriegs or even the U.S. invasion of Panama. The sheer quantity of firepower brought into the Gulf by (primarily) U.S. and British forces was beyond anything previously undertaken. The Iraqi forces were completely unequipped for this. Within 24 hours, their command and control system was destroyed, the nation's electrical production was shut down, and its surface-to-air missile sites and antiaircraft batteries were nearly crippled. As in Panama, stealth aircraft played a dominant role, constituting less than 3 percent of all fighter and attack aircraft, but attacking 31 percent of the targets on the first day of fighting. This effectiveness depended on America's dominance of space, in particular its Global Positioning System. As military historians George and Meredith Friedman pointed out, had the Iraqis been able to destroy the GPS satellite system, most of the allied advantage would have dissipated. "For the first time in history, the center of gravity of a military operation was located outside the earth's atmosphere."[32]

Another element of the coalition's success was precision-guided munitions (or "smart bombs") and Tomahawk cruise missiles. They were effective and also made great propaganda, considering that more than 90 percent of all ordinance dropped against the Iraqis were the old-fashioned "dumb bombs." The result was tremendous carnage. The official U.S. totals for Iraqi civilians killed was 2,278 (with 5,965 reported wounded).[33] This number is wildly off from other estimates, some of which exceed 100,000.[34] Years after the fact, the statistic remains so politically charged that one wonders how the truth can ever be reached.

Whatever the actual total, there can be no question that the American public was shielded from seeing the destruction, thanks to vastly improved media control by the military. A Pentagon document entitled "Annex Foxtrot" described the new policy.[35] Journalists were forbidden from visiting front lines or interviewing soldiers without prior military approval. Once approval was given, they had to be accompanied by officers and subjected to censorship. As a result, most of the information about the war came from military briefings. Ostensibly, this was to prevent sensitive information from being revealed to Iraq. Considering how Iraq was overmatched in every way, the deeper motivation seems clear enough: control of public opinion.[36]

Astonishingly, not a single photographic record of actual combat ever managed to be made by journalists. The sole western journalist who disobeyed U.S. military orders to leave Bagdad prior to the assault was Peter Arnett of CNN, a former Pulitzer Prize winner. Arnett's reports on civilian damage were sharply criticized by the military and the Bush White House. On January 25, 1991, the White House claimed that he was a tool for Iraqi disinformation; CNN even received a letter from 34 members of Congress accusing Arnett of "unpatriotic journalism."[37]

Kuwait was officially liberated on February 27, 1991; Iraq surrendered the following day. The rapid and total military victory by the coalition forces, and the minimal casualties they suffered, made a dramatic impression of American global hegemony.

Yet a few mysterious encounters by American pilots, very reminiscent of the World War II foo fighters, may raise some questions as to whether any other "group" was operating over the desert skies. There are very few publicly revealed UFO stories associated with the Gulf War, but the combination of the war's brevity and the unprecedented control over information make this easy to understand.

UFO researcher Joel Carpenter of the UFO research organization "Project 1947" found an interesting reference to this subject in a government collection of Gulf War military encounters. According to the study, several American F-111 "Aardvark" pilots reported being intercepted by Iraqi aircraft that approached them, illuminated them with searchlights, but never fired on them. The mysterious flyer was nicknamed "Baghdad Billy," and the subject of a homespun ballad penned by an American pilot.[38] The document even stated that an F-111 crashed on one occasion when its pilot attempted to escape from one encounter – far more serious than the foo fighter incidents, of which there are no known cases of aircraft being lost.[39] Perhaps the Iraqi air defenses were not shut down as completely as had been thought, although this seems odd in the context of the coalition's total air superiority.

There is another interesting Gulf War UFO story known to the author, obtained during a personal interview with a U.S. army captain who served in the war. During Operation Desert Shield, this individual was stationed in the Iraqi desert with his unit, "with nothing but sand for hundreds of miles in any direction." On one occasion, he was informed by a superior command that his unit was not to fire on any objects that might appear within a particular, rather restricted, sector of the sky. "Sure enough," said the captain, "a few nights later, we saw something." In the sky were several bright objects maneuvering in an extraordinary fashion. "We could not have shot them down if we had tried," he said. When asked what he and his soldiers thought they saw, he initially offered no opinion. When asked whether they wondered if these were UFOs, he said, "absolutely. Of course!" The story is intriguing. It would seem to mean that the UFOs seen by the American soldiers were "made in America," unless one were to argue that the U.S. military had advance notice of alien operations, whether via open communication or other intelligence gathering techniques. Or, the U.S. military-industrial complex was collaborating with one or more alien intelligences.

The Gulf War was a watershed in modern history, marking the true turning point from the old to the new. America had exhibited unmatched dominance not just in the field of battle but in control over information. Moreover, in the greatest military action since the end of World War Two, the Soviet Union had been little more than an afterthought. Although it would continue to exist until the year's end, the final nail in the Cold War's coffin had been driven. The New World Order had arrived.

Aerial Encounters in 1991

Throughout late 1990 into 1991, the U.S. had three ongoing UFO hotspots: Gulf Breeze, Area 51, and the Antelope Valley. Elsewhere in the world, most of the interesting UFO reports were coming from Europe, particularly Great Britain. During the last few months of 1990, there were dozens of reports of strange aerial objects in Britain and Europe.[40] An interesting case occurred over the North Sea on November 5, during a Boeing 737 British Airways flight from Rome to London's Gatwick Airport. The pilot and copilot noticed a large silver disc-shaped object. They brought two crew members into the cockpit to observe it with them before it went out of sight. Ground radar found nothing unusual. The same night, in the same area, a patrol of RAF Tornados over the North Sea was overtaken at high speed by what the pilots could only describe as a large aircraft of some sort. It appeared to come so close that they took violent evasive action.[41]

There were several more commercial aviation encounters during the spring of 1991, each over a different continent. On the evening of March 6, 1991, a glowing turquoise cigar-shaped object crossed the path of an airliner over Kingston, Ontario, Canada.[42] On March 18, over Kunshan, China, the pilot of an airliner saw a ring-shaped object, two rectangular objects moving back and forth, and a red blaze of light coming from the ring.[43]

On April 19, an event took place in the Soviet Union that, although not an aerial encounter, was still startling. In the Kazak city of Alma-Ata, two militiamen on patrol noticed a kind of fire at the top of Kok-Tyube mountain. They watched flames go up and down, and then saw an array of red beams of light. They drove to within 200 meters of a hovering UFO. At that point, they said, "a few rays swept across the car and it stopped dead." The object then dimmed its lights and disappeared. The men made it back to the police station, but could not recall how they did so. Radio tapes concerning the UFO were recorded. According to a newspaper account, there were "impartial witnesses" to the event, the account of which was collected by the CIA.[44]

A near-tragic aerial collision with a UFO occurred on the evening of

April 21, 1991, when an Italian airliner was on final approach to Heathrow Airport. Just off the coast of Romney, Kent, the pilot saw a grey object cross his path less than 100 feet away. Although he could not get a clear image of its shape, describing it as either round or missile-like, the event was confirmed by radar. The airliner had nearly been blown out of the sky. Nick Pope, soon after he took the job of investing UFO reports for the British Ministry of Defence, investigated the matter. He learned that the army denied firing any missiles, nor could it have fired missiles to that height. The British CAA concluded that "extensive enquiries have failed to provide any indication of what the sighting may have been." Nick Redfern noted that the description of the UFO was consistent with a pilotless drone of the type used for defense practice. Either the Ministry of Defence admitted that a UFO nearly caused a midair disaster, or it was using UFOs as a smokescreen to hide its mistakes. One must agree with Redfern's assessment: either way, the case deserved further investigation. Unfortunately, it was never solved.[45]

Through the spring of 1991, Britain was scene to unexplained sightings. On May 22, a husband and wife in Nottingham saw an array of lights in an "elongated triangle." This same object was seen 15 minutes later by another man in the area. He said it was about 1,000 feet high and gave off a low humming noise.[46] Through the next month there was heavy UFO activity reported in Nottingham, including many triangular sightings. People often described two separate triangular objects flying in close formation, each with very bright lights that were much larger than those of any known aircraft. Throughout, the Ministry of Defence was silent about it.[47]

The most compelling UFO case of 1991, however, occurred not in Europe or the U.S., but in Paraguay. This was a radar-visual case which was reported by the pilots of two airplanes. It involved an object hovering over a runway, electronic failures, astonishing departure speeds, and an official investigation. Fortunately, it was investigated thoroughly by MUFON's representative to Paraguay, Jorge Alfonso Ramirez, who interviewed many of the principal witnesses and obtained an official report from Paraguay's Ministry of Defense.

On June 8, Cesar Escobar, pilot of a Cessna Model 210, took off from a farm near the city of Concepcion at about 6 p.m. Shortly after being airborne, an interesting conversation came over his radio between the traffic control operator at Silvio Petirossi Airport and a Lineas Aereas Paraguayas (LAP) airliner. This was LAP Flight 702, enroute from

Asunción to Miami. The pilot of the LAP advised the control tower that another aircraft was traveling toward him. The tower then asked him if he could see the object. "I have it just in front of me," came the nervous reply. Airport radar was able to confirm this object's presence – something surely was there. The Paraguayan controllers asked their counterparts in Bolivia if they knew anything about the unknown traffic: the answer came back negative. The object then flew straight toward the LAP airliner and passed over it at an incredible speed, an event that Escobar heard being described as it happened on the radio.

Just a few minutes later, Escobar saw a UFO. A strong, bluish-white light to his right attracted his attention. "It all happened so fast," he said "that I couldn't understand what was going on.... I began to be concerned when my two passengers asked me what that object was and why it was flying so close to us." Airport radar control radioed him to ask if he had traffic on his right. Yes, he replied, he certainly did. For the next 25 minutes, the UFO accompanied his aircraft. Its light was so intense that he could not distinguish any other features. At times the object closed on his position, causing his instruments to go wild (and frightening him considerably). To Escobar, the object seemed to be under intelligent control, causing him to believe that its operator was toying with him. "I've never been so afraid in all my life," he said. "I didn't believe these things existed."

The object stayed with him until he descended toward Asunción at 7:22 p.m. Radar control informed the tower duty operator, Anibal Gavigan, that Escobar's plane was preparing to land, accompanied by a strange object. Gavigan immediately saw it: a luminous object flying next to Escobar's plane. After Escobar landed, Gavigan ordered the field's lights to be shut off, then on again, in order to have a better idea of the object's position. While the lights were out, he and other witnesses saw the object hovering motionless over the field about 600 meters away, a sighting confirmed by radar. Gavigan watched the object for five minutes, sometimes through binoculars. It was completely still, with a strong reddish light. Then something spectacular happened. The object shot a bright ray to the western horizon. Although it lasted for just a fraction of a second, during that brief moment, it was "a perfect yellow line going as far as you could see to the west." After this, the object left instantly at an astonishing speed. Gavigan told Ramirez, "the speed of that object was incredible. I was shocked. I've never seen such a thing in my life."

The radar operators also tracked the object's departure, which was too fast to measure. The radar made one revolution every five seconds with a range of 150 nautical miles, and the object disappeared from the screen during one revolution. Thus, that would have to be at least 26 miles per second, which translates to over 1,500 miles per minute, to the unbelievable speed of more than 90,000 mph.

Jorge Ramirez had some difficulty reaching LAP representatives, who told him that the flight reports had been destroyed according to company rules. After two months, he was finally granted an interview with a copilot on the LAP Flight 702, Colonel Angel David Farina. Farina told him that he and several members of the crew saw the object. He confirmed the flight altitude as reported in the records and said the observation lasted for about thirty minutes while they flew past the Paraguayan city of Filadelfia. He confirmed Escobar's account of what had been heard over the radio, and added that the object had a strong reddish light and an oval shape. "It was very, very close, no doubt."[48]

UFOs Over Mexico

During the afternoon of July 11, 1991, a solar eclipse occurred over the world's largest city, Mexico City. This was no ordinary eclipse. Before it occurred, some Mexicans were talking about an ancient Mayan prophecy known as the "Dresden Codex." Despite a gulf of 1,200 years, the prophecy was believed to have predicted that the 1991 eclipse would usher in major earth changes and greater cosmic awareness, specifically from encounters with the "Masters of the Stars." With such a cultural buildup, thousands of Mexicans were ready for the event and watching the skies. Many of them had camcorders. They were not to be disappointed; indeed, they saw much more than they ever expected.

For more than half an hour, several bright objects were seen hovering over the region. Video was recorded as far south as the cities of Puebla and Oaxaca, the latter of which was more than 200 miles away. Skeptics claimed that this was the planet Venus, visible during the period when the sun was blocked. But the full eclipse lasted just under seven minutes, and this object was seen for more than a half hour before, during, and after the event.

Afterwards, Mexican television journalist Jaime Maussan, host of the television show "60 Minutos," received a videotape of the UFO. It showed an object hovering in the sky, looking not like a star at all, but rather like a silver disc. Intrigued, he asked his viewers to share any unusual sightings they may have had during the eclipse. Fifteen video-tapes soon arrived, each one taken by a witness from a different location within the broad region of the sighting. Maussan enlisted the technical help of his television station's video experts for digital enhancement and enlargement work. The quantity and quality of these videos, combined with the analyses performed on them, made them especially important and compelling. They showed solid, metallic-looking objects that re-flected light. Maussan's team checked into possibilities such as balloons, helicopters, or other conventional aerial phenomena, but came up empty.

The objects were not astronomical objects. They moved as if by intelligent control across the sky while other heavenly bodies remained stationary by comparison. Digital enhancements of the images revealed a "hockey puck" shape, not anything resembling a star or planet. The clincher was that many of the objects moved in front of passing clouds.

This mass sighting signaled the beginning of a UFO wave over Mexico that lasted throughout the 1990s. Just why this began on the date of the eclipse, and just why it seemed to be connected with a Mayan prophecy, can only be a matter of conjecture. Once the Venus argument became untenable, skeptics argued that the UFO (or UFOs) were simply "anom-alous" objects – which indeed they were – and shrugged off the connec-tion to the Dresden Codex. But two things are clear. First, the objects recorded on so many videos were unlike anything that was supposed to be in the air. Second, a major series of UFO sightings followed in their wake.[49]

The Military Abduction Question

As if alleged abduction by aliens were not controversial enough, by the dawn of the 1990s a new twist in this phenomenon was being experi-enced and researched. This was the alleged abduction of people by completely human, military groups who sought to extract as much information about the alien agenda and related matters as possible. The pioneer researcher of these "military abductions" (MILABs) was Karla Turner, an Oklahoma resident who had earned a Ph.D. in literature and taught at Texas University.

In 1988, while Karla and her husband were in counseling to learn why they were feeling physical symptoms of stress, she read two books about alien abduction: *Missing Time* and *Communion*. She soon recalled having seen an odd light in the sky as a girl, and began to dream about UFOs.

Having learned hypnotic relaxation techniques from her therapist, she regressed her husband, whereupon he remembered several childhood encounters with grey aliens.

Several nights after that regression, Karla awoke to sounds of clicks and bumps in the house, followed by disembodied voices in her bedroom. She later remembered a nightmare from childhood in which an insect-like being held her hand and told her it was her mother. Soon she and her husband underwent regression by an Oklahoma UFO researcher. Her own regressions produced accounts of repeated abductions since childhood, and evidence that her whole family was involved. After one session, Karla, her husband, and a third person saw a lighted disc-shaped craft hovering over them. Two weeks later she again heard voices in the night and loud knocking sounds. She woke to find small punctures on her inner wrist and three white circles on her abdomen. Through the remainder of 1988 and into 1989, more body marks appeared on Karla, including a solid red triangle on her arm, puncture wounds, scratches, and bruises. Poltergeist phenomena also occurred. The Turners began to notice a white car parked near their house, and unmarked helicopters seemed to follow them. They began to suspect the U.S. military was monitoring them. The account of all this appeared in her 1992 book, *Into The Fringe*.[50]

Turner continued to investigate. She was disturbed to learn that at least ten people close to her seemed to have a pattern of alien intrusions and disturbances. Soon she was meeting with more abductees and published another book in 1994, called *Taken*. It included the accounts provided by eight women, none of whom knew each other, all of whom consciously recalled a large portion of their experiences without the aid of hypnosis.[51]

Many details were widely shared, such as UFO sightings, missing time, "virtual reality" scenarios, telepathic communication, and human-alien collaboration. They described a variety of alien types: greys, insectoids, reptoids, humanoids, blue humanoids, and dwarves. Several of the women described not only hybrid nursery rooms (something described in earlier abduction literature), but also "cloning rooms," in which living but inert humans – as many as 20 identical specimens –

Dr. Karla Turner

were suspended in liquid-filled cylinders. There were accounts of aliens apparently taking human souls and placing them into a box. One alien group appeared to harvest "negative emotional energy." Not all experiences were harmful or exploitative; some women claimed to have had miraculous healings by aliens. Still, Turner suggested that this did not make aliens humanity's benefactors. If they cared for humans, she suggested, it could well be the way a farmer cares for his cattle.

Four of the eight women featured in *Taken* described being abducted by human military personnel. Some of these recollections were quite clear, and they described being taken not to an alien craft, but a very human, military-looking facility, often underground. Human and alien workers were sometimes described as being there. The abductees remembered being questioned by military types who asked such questions as "what do you know about the alien agenda? What have they told you? What implants did you receive? What procedures have they carried out on you?" A number of medical problems developed, apparently related to the abductions: sudden-developing cancer, depression, post-traumatic stress disorder, sexual dysfunction, suicide, and more.

The phenomenon of military abductions caused Turner to argue that "a revolution has taken place," and that a hidden power structure unknown to most people had "appropriated the UFO phenomenon." Ordinary politics had nothing to do with this cover-up. Although she did not use the term "shadow government," this was what Turner meant. One thing that perplexed her was why – if there was indeed human-alien collaboration – military groups would need to interrogate abductees about alien intentions. She did not have an answer to this. Of course, if one hypothesizes the existence of multiple alien groups, the problem might make more sense. One or more of the human groups could have allied itself in some way with one or more of the various alien groups. There could be a web of complex and covert relationships.[52]

In 1991, MILAB research was in its infancy. Throughout the 1990s, people such as Kathy Jordan, Leah Haley, and Melinda Leslie described their own experiences. Soon after Karla Turner died of cancer in early 1996, another researcher, Helmut Lammer, followed up on the growing body of MILAB testimony. He also focused on the probable technologies involved in these experiences.

Like Turner before him, Lammer found that a typical MILAB experience was distinct from traditional accounts of alien abduction. Instead of feeling paralyzed, MILAB subjects were usually tied to an examination table or a gynecological chair, given a strong drink that contained drugs, and interrogated about their alien encounters. Doctors or scientists in white lab coats examined or removed alien implants, sometimes performed gynecological examinations, and sometimes placed their own implants into the individual. Lammer noted the growing numbers of accounts of human-alien collaboration, humans in clear tanks, and bizarre genetic experimentation.[53]

The question of mind and memory control becomes evident. It is one thing for technologically advanced aliens to be able to wipe a person's memory (at least mostly), but was this within the realm of human capability? Lammer's answer was yes. As far back as the 1960s, Professor J. Anthony Deutsch of New York University showed that an excess of the chemical acetylcholine in the brain can interfere with memory. He found that this excess could be artificially produced through either drugs or radio waves – the latter process being called Electronic Dissolution of Memory (EDOM). Memory creation could be inhibited or distorted for as long as the radio signal continued, and time-orientation was destroyed. Lammer argued that EDOM appeared to be the method of choice used against MILAB abductees, leaving the victim with no memory of what had transpired. At least, this was the case most of the time. Mind control technologies remain imperfect, people are not all the same, and memories can occasionally be retrieved.[54]

Another technology of interest to Lammer was the creation of what Turner described as Virtual Reality Scenarios (VRS). Many MILAB victims described vivid images being flashed inside their minds. Here, too, argued Lammer, human technology was up to the task. Specifically, the implanting of an intracerebral device might enable its operators to send images and even memories into the brain of abductees. As far back as the 1960s, important work was done along these lines by Dr. Jose Delgado, Dr. Joseph Sharp, and Dr. Allen Frey. The last two pioneered the transmission of spoken words directly into the audio cortex via pulsed microwaves, known as the Frey effect. Such was all within the open literature on the subject: what might have been accomplished secretly in the black world, especially during the funding bonanza of the 1980s? Of course, if images and memories could be somehow implanted into a person, could this mean that some of the information coming from MILAB abductees were cover stories induced by the hypno-programming of military psychiatrists?

The technology of implants themselves had been solved by 1990.

Already by then, millions of animals worldwide had been implanted with small transponders, passive radio frequency identification tags, the smallest of which was the size of an uncooked grain of rice. A similar biochip for humans had been designed and developed by Dr. Daniel Man, who in 1989 received a patent for a homing device that could be implanted in humans – its stated purpose was to find missing children. He advised that the best location for his implant might be behind the ear. Coincidentally or not, several MILAB subjects claimed to have had implants placed behind their ears.[55]

The theory of military abductions found very few supporters. Skeptics argued that such wild stories were nothing more than fantasies and fabrications.[56] Traditional abduction researchers tended to ignore the claims, which represented a small fraction of their research and were difficult for them to assimilate. Mind control researchers found the MILAB phenomenon perfectly credible, except that most of them (not believing in UFOs) concluded that the entire "alien abduction" phenomenon was staged by the intelligence community as a cover for its illegal experiments.[57]

Certainly, all possibilities, including the last, had to be considered, but there were problems with neat solutions. Why did MILAB reports surface so late in the game? After all, mind control technology was surely better in the 1980s than during the 1960s – one would think there would have been more MILAB reports during earlier years, before the technology had been perfected. Another problem was that the mind control literature contained many cases of victims with no connection to UFOs or alien abductions. And why should the military be interested in gynecological examinations of female abductees? Lammer and Turner, unfazed by the skeptics, both argued that the most logical scenario was that military abduction developed in response to a genuine alien abduction phenomenon.

Thus, by the early 1990s, a variant twist to the UFO phenomenon must be considered. A deep-black program could well have existed, operating beyond the boundaries of the open legal system, possibly beyond the boundaries of the standard military system, working for unknown superiors, which used extraordinary means and technology to take humans for testing and interrogation. If we also consider the possibility of covert breakthroughs in propulsion technology, and the "off the grid" nature of the deep-black world itself, we come to the possibility that we are dealing with, in effect, a "breakaway civilization." One with loose connections at various points to the open civilization of humanity, but with great independence, secrecy, and a monopoly of certain key scientific secrets. The history of the Cold War showed that separate infrastructures could, to some extent, evolve. Western politics, economy, science, and culture developed along paths that were very different from those in the Soviet Union or China. Important breakthroughs occurred in secrecy – stealth being a prominent example. Granted, the level of separation implied for a breakaway civilization would be vastly greater than any Cold War examples. In principle, however, such a development is possible, and responsible research must consider the strength of supporting evidence and clues.

The Abortive Disclosure

What follows is only alleged, not proven. It was introduced in Robert Collins' and Richard Doty's book *Exempt from Disclosure* in 2004, but received additional confirmation by someone closely connected to the events in question, and who was interviewed by the author. Until others openly come forward, this will remain a matter of uncertainty and debate. Even with this caveat in place, however, there is reason to believe it may have happened.

According to the account presented by Collins and Doty, the person known as "Raven" (in the terminology of the Aviary) entered the UFO disclosure picture in 1991. This person's public identity remains unknown, but he is said to have had long-time experience with Los Alamos National Laboratory and MJ-12, and apparently believed that the time had come to consider the end of UFO secrecy. During the summer of 1991, Raven set up a meeting in which key members of the Bush administration were briefed on the UFO reality. Although Bush himself was not thoroughly briefed on this occasion, it is said he was told that there was a movement to determine whether disclosure was feasible, and that he gave his permission to explore the possibility of moving ahead.

Attempts were then made to gain support from agency heads for UFO disclosure. One meeting took place in a vault room at Kirtland AFB, allegedly attended by Raven, Senator Claiborne Pell (D-RI), and others.[58] Representatives of the President wanted to ensure that the information was revealed with the proper spin so as to minimize government bashing. They also wanted television programming that portrayed the "Ebens" as non-hostile explorers, and emphasizing that any military aircraft lost during encounters with them had not been due to hostile action on their part. The Aviary's proposal "was received very well" and taken back to Washington.

A great deal apparently hinged on the confirmation hearings of Robert Gates for the position of CIA Director. Senator Pell reportedly said, "if Gates does not get in, there is no way in hell this thing is going forward." Meanwhile, the briefing of agencies continued, with several conducting their own research regarding the likely impact of UFO disclosure and relevant costs. Some favored the idea; many more opposed it. NASA was said to favor disclosure on the assumption that it would liberate money from Congress for future space projects. Over at the Department of Defense, Secretary Dick Cheney was said to be strongly opposed, feeling that the administration had "nothing to gain" and would need to respond to a massive influx of FOIA requests. The Justice Department also was opposed, recommending that the President keep the matter strictly covert. The Auditor General's office worried that the government might face enormous lawsuits from angry citizens. The most vivid image presented was that of outgoing CIA chief, William Webster. When he was briefed, he reportedly went into a rage. He kicked a chair and yelled, "you can't do this to me! I've had Senators and other high level people sit in that chair and I've told them there is nothing to this!"

The confirmation hearings of Robert Gates were delayed through July 1991. As August progressed, proponents were concerned that the briefing process was taking longer than expected. Even so, a meeting was scheduled to present the entire matter to President Bush at his retreat in Kennebunkport, Maine on Wednesday, August 23, 1991. In addition to Bush, it was supposed to include some fifteen leading government officials. Raven thought perhaps the meeting might succeed, that there was a chance a consensus could be achieved which would enable Bush to "green light" some form of disclosure. Schedule conflicts, however, forced the meeting to be pushed back for the following weekend, presumably the 26th or 27th.

But the meeting never happened. The Soviet military coup of August 19-21, 1991 caused the disclosure plans to be aborted – specifically by whom is not known.[59]

The story is impossible to verify for now, but perhaps in time it can be. The author spoke to a senior official who, while not directly involved in the events recounted above, knew the main individuals concerned and was aware at the time that such an attempt was being made. He added further that such discussions tend to occur "every five years or so."

There are two interesting side notes regarding Senator Claiborne Pell. First, his longtime friend and aide, C. B. Scott Jones, indicated that Pell – despite public protestations to the contrary – did have a strong interest in UFO/ET phenomena. However, he was already politically exposed by his known interest in psychic phenomena. Therefore, not wanting to give his critics and future opponents any more ammunition to use against him, Pell accepted Jones's suggestion that he refer to his UFO interest "as being in consciousness research." Indeed, as a member of Pell's staff, Jones visited China and the Soviet Union to study "consciousness research." What he learned apparently drew interest from some elite circles. According to Jones, one of Pell's very close friends, Hans-Adam, Prince of Liechtenstein, had a very strong interest in all matters relating to UFOs. Whenever the Prince visited the United States, Pell's standing order was for Jones to tell the Prince everything he had learned in his international travels about UFOs.

While this is surely interesting, it does not answer the question as to whether or not Pell was briefed on UFOs, or whether there was an attempt at disclosure in 1991. In the end, Jones felt that Pell "very well may have" received a formal briefing on UFOs. However, he had no information on any disclosure effort from 1991.[60]

A second intriguing "UFO-connection" to Claiborne Pell is that he attended the 1987 MUFON International Symposium, which took place at American University in Washington, D.C. During a break period, some of the attendees approached him and asked why he was there. One of the attendees was Peter Robbins, who reported that "Pell responded with a smile that he was also interested in the subject – in his capacity as a private citizen, of course." This might make Pell the only American Senator ever to have attended a public conference dedicated to UFOs.[61]

It should not be surprising that the end of the Cold War would prompt fresh discussions on the viability of a long-term UFO cover-up. The Cold War had, after all, been a leading reason for the establishment of UFO secrecy, and for half a century remained an important factor in the equation. Over the years, however, UFO secrecy dug in like a tenacious plant, developing a vast root system that went far beyond its original domain. It turned out to be far more entrenched than the Cold War itself.

The Soviet Coup and Aftermath

All through 1991, morale among Soviet leaders was as low as it could be. The year opened with riots in Lithuania and Latvia, culminating in "Bloody Sunday" in Vilnius on January 21, when 14 Lithuanians were killed by Soviet troops. American dominance in the Gulf War further demoralized Soviet leaders. On July 1, 1991, the Warsaw Pact formally disbanded. From the vantage point of the Communist Party, Perestroika was reaching a very unhappy conclusion.

The result was a coup against Gorbachev by old guard Communist, Army, and KGB leadership from August 19 to 21, 1991. An "Emergency Committee" announced that Gorbachev was too ill to rule and placed him under house arrest. However, the coup never gained popular support and its leaders soon lost heart. In Moscow, many people refused to obey orders from the new group, and Moscow Mayor Boris Yeltsin rallied support for Gorbachev. A dramatic scene followed in which Yeltsin and his supporters were surrounded by troops and tanks. In the midst of this, Estonia and Latvia declared their independence, while Lithuania reaffirmed its declaration from 1990. On the 22nd, Yeltsin sent a plane for Gorbachev while several plotters committed suicide. Gorbachev quickly learned that the Communist leadership had been behind the attempt.

Events then moved like lightning. Within two weeks of the failed coup, Gorbachev resigned as leader of the Soviet Communist Party and disbanded the Central Committee, the Soviet Communist Party dissolved itself, the Baltic States achieved recognition from the U.S. and Soviet governments, and the Soviet republic of Georgia severed its ties to the Soviet Union.

Gorbachev also moved quickly to dissolve the KGB, completing his task by November 1991.[62] In the process, many coveted files found their way abroad, particularly to the CIA. This included the KGB's UFO files, the infamous "Blue Folder," which were released in October upon request of the famous cosmonaut Pavel Popovitch. The files were quite a bonanza, repeatedly confirming the reality of UFOs in the air and on the ground, seen by Soviet military personnel and registered on their radar screens. In time, western journalists had the opportunity to examine the files. One was ABC correspondent David Ensor, who studied them for several months during 1995. Ensor interviewed dozens of Russian military personnel, government officials, and scientists, and learned of some 40 major incidents – one of which prompted fears of starting an accidental nuclear war. Although the files were clearly not complete, they provided something of a counterpart to the cache of American files that had been previously released through FOIA. In both cases, the files were released as a result of political crisis. In the case of America, the dual crisis of Vietnam and Watergate led to a resurgence of Congressional authority and a strengthening of FOIA. In the case of the Soviet Union, it was the breakup of the nation itself.[63]

Faking Crop Circles

The crop circles continued to amaze. Some 600 new circles, ever more complex, appeared in 30 countries around the world during the summer of 1991, from farms in southwestern England to wet rice paddies in Japan. The most astounding formation was discovered on August 12, 1991, in a wheat field near Ickelton, about ten miles south of Cambridge, England. At 124 feet in diameter, its size was substantial enough. Its design, however, was extraordinary. This was a "Mandelbrot set," a design that had first been generated on a computer and was named after Benoit Mandelbrot. Mandelbrot, a mathematician of genius, had developed the field of fractal geometry, used to study chaos theory and its applications to patterns of growth in the natural world. Natural objects that approximate fractals to a degree include clouds, mountain ranges, lightning bolts, coastlines, snowflakes, and seashells. The Mandelbrot crop circle was brilliantly done, laid to perfection. Like all the other formations, no one saw it being created, and it appeared overnight. Once people realized what they were seeing, the general reaction was one of astonishment. Whoever was behind these circles was taking them to an entirely new level.[64]

This and other impressive formations received tremendous press worldwide. Then came the deflating news from two pensioners in their sixties named Doug Bower and Dave Chorley. On September 9, 1991, they told the British press that they had hoaxed some 250 circles in the region. They began, they said, in 1978 and were disappointed that it took two years for the world to notice their work. Their method was to use planks to flatten the crops in conjunction with ropes attached to a central pole, although they said their formations had become increasingly elaborate over the years. Indeed, some of Bower's and Chorley's recent work was good enough to have fooled circle expert Pat Delgado into pronouncing one of their creations to be "genuine" – that no human could have been responsible for it. Just a month later, another crop circle analyst was fooled. This was Terence Meaden, who promoted the vortex theory of crop circles. After pronouncing one particular circle to be genuine – on British television no less – a group called the Wessex Sceptics claimed it as their own creation. It became evident that some hoaxed circles were quite good. If an expert could be fooled by even some of these, how could one be sure if any were truly anomalous? The upshot of all this was a flurry of press coverage proclaiming that the crop circle mystery had been solved. There was no mystery, after all, just some pranksters and copycats.

Nothing is as simple as it seems, however. Soon after their confession, Bower and Chorley gave a demonstration of their work. Their noticeably slipshod circle failed to impress. They could provide no evidence of their handiwork other than their own anecdotal testimony and a few diagrams. Not only this, but cereologists had long been pointing out that, although some hoaxed circles were well done, many were easy to identify. It was the circles of extreme precision and complexity that had not been explained, they said. Thus, despite the media saturation claiming to have "solved" the mystery, many observers continued to believe that hoaxers could not have created all of the thousands of circles showing up in southern England, to say nothing of other regions of the world.[65]

As the 1990s continued, cereologists arranged for scientific studies that detected measurable chemical and biological effects within the plant stalks of "genuine" crop circles. For instance, soil and plant studies conducted by biophysicist W. C. Levengood from 1991 to 1993 showed a number of distinguishing characteristics of affected plants, including "cell pit" changes to the stalks, evidence of rapid heating to the nodes of stalks (identical to that created by microwave radiation), dramatic changes in seed growth, bent and cracked growth nodes, and ion transport in bract tissue. Levengood argued that rapid and intense energy had produced cell changes in the affected plants. These effects were not significantly found in samples from known hoaxed circles. Whatever was creating true crop circles, concluded Levengood, was "affecting the fundamental biophysics and biochemistry of the plants."[66]

Studies by Levengood and others did not sway the scientific or media establishments. Although many of them appeared to have been conducted competently, they were private endeavors with no institutional backing. As such, they carried little weight within the scientific community. In the realm of public opinion, they were handicapped by the long durations required to undertake a proper study: by the time an analysis was complete, the circle was long gone and attention was focused on other matters. As far as the mainstream media was concerned, the Doug and Dave episode made crop circles safe and prosaic. No matter how questionable some of their claims were, a safety rail now existed for all doubters. Of course, the *London Times, New York Times, 60 Minutes* and other august investigative media did not tempt fate by examining the matter on their own. When the story did come up, the wrong questions were being asked. It was not so much the *who* that mattered as the *how*. Lost in the general discussion was how the most complex and perfect formations were created overnight without detection or any sign of human activity.

UFOs in Space: STS-48

For years, anomalous events had been noted during many American and Soviet space missions. The most famous of these took place on September 15, 1991, during the NASA Space Shuttle *Discovery* mission known as STS-48. NASA's cable channel provided live broadcasts of the shuttle flights, and Donald Ratch of Dundalk, Maryland, recorded it on the downlink provided by a local community college. His video recorded a truly bizarre-looking event. The shuttle was 355 miles above the Earth, its camera trained on the planet's outline, when a bright object entered the frame from the top right, seemingly from deeper space. It moved steadily toward Earth's atmosphere. Within seconds, a flash appeared from the lower left portion of the screen and the object performed an about-face. As this occurred, another object shot out from the lower left portion of the frame, looking every bit like a projectile of some sort, and seemed to just miss hitting the original object. For a few seconds more, the camera continued to track the original object moving off into space. Adding to the mystery, the camera ceased broadcasting about 65 seconds after the encounter.[67]

Common sense gave an obvious interpretation: this was an altercation in space, the firing of an unknown weapon at an unknown object. The question is whether or not common sense was correct in this instance.

Ratch sent the video to his congresswoman, Helen Bentley. He also contacted Vincent DiPietro, a NASA engineer at the Goddard Space Flight Center, who in turn contacted his congresswoman, Beverly Byron. Byron sent a copy of the tape to George E. Brown, Jr., Chair of the Congressional Committee on Science, Space, and Technology. Brown and staff were told by NASA that the objects were probably urine ice particles released from the shuttle. They believed the apparent change of the original object's direction was most likely due to the firing of one of the shuttle's attitude adjustor rockets, known as the Reaction Control System (RCS). They suggested the bright flash at the lower left portion of the screen was in fact the firing of the RCS. Martin P. Kress, an assistant administrator for legislative affairs at NASA, concurred with this theory, and James Oberg wrote an analysis arguing this position. NASA computer records later indicated that the shuttle's RCS jet did fire at the time in question, although critic Lan Fleming argued that NASA's time stamps on the video were "phony."[68]

Dr. Jack Kasher, a professor of physics and astronomy at the University of Nebraska, disagreed with NASA's ice particle theory. "To the best of my knowledge," he said, "the individuals who suspected ice particles merely watched the videotape and did no further scientific analysis." Kasher, who was a NASA consultant and also a member of MUFON, performed a detailed analysis of the STS-48 tapes. He argued that there were at least a dozen or more distinct events, each different from one another and not commonly seen on other shuttle tapes. When he requested more technical information to assist in his analysis, NASA refused. Kasher interpreted this refusal to mean that the subject had national security implications.[69] Regarding the anomalous objects themselves, he concluded that they behaved oddly for any type of particle, whether ice or otherwise. Assuming their change of direction was caused by the firing of a shuttle rocket, their directional paths should have traced back to a single source. They did not. Moreover, one of the particles appeared to remain motionless for almost half a second, a great oddity considering that any acceleration in space should have been continuous. Equally odd were streaks of light that appeared to pass through the space vacated by both objects. Kasher demonstrated five proofs that discounted the ice particle theory. "It's hard not to think that the objects were some kind of spaceship at a considerable distance from the shuttle, and although it's only speculation, the streaks of light look like missiles fired in their direction." Depending on the exact distance from the shuttle – assuming a distance between one mile and 1,710 miles – the velocity of the second object would have been between 250 mph to 430,000 mph. "There is just no way," he stated. "The evidence strongly indicates they can't be ice particles."[70]

Jeff Challender, who spent many years prior to his untimely death in 2007 collecting and studying anomalous data from space missions,

pointed out that the distant object diverted 135 degrees and sped out
into space. Challender rebuked NASA's claim that the relative motion of
this object was caused by the RCS jet firing. "The RCS jets," he wrote,

> . . . are mounted on the extreme nose and tail of the Shuttles. They fire vertically, and
> in the vacuum of space, the exhaust plume expands upward in a teardrop shape. The
> aft thrusters are some 20 to 25 feet away from the camera, and even further away
> [from] the debris field. Objects nearer than the controversial one are barely affected.
> The RCS gas plume could not have greatly influenced our anomalous object at the
> distance it MUST be from the jet plume. Therefore, I conclude that the object must
> be independently propelled.[71]

Some analysts could not explain the speed of the projectile that was
fired. Challender pointed out that it could not be a laser or particle
beam, both of which move at the speed of light. The streaks had to be
something other than energy weapons, yet he knew no missile technology capable of moving at the velocities observed in the video.[72] Actually,
however, some of the weapons developed under SDI did fire projectiles
that could reach speeds within the range of Kasher's estimates. The
"Kinetic Energy Weapon," for instance, developed under SDI during the
1980s, could fire a tiny projectile at a velocity of over 15,000 mph.
Undoubtedly other more deeply classified weapons could well have done
the same.[73]

A few other individuals claim to have had evidence that the objects in
the STS-48 video were truly anomalous. Harry Jordan, a former radar
operator on the USS Roosevelt, said he was listening on a ham radio
during the time of the flight and heard the astronauts saying they had a
"UFO" – which they then described as "the alien spacecraft" – under
observation. "It just stunned me," he said. Jordan stated that afterward
he received visits and surveillance from "guys in suits" whose vehicle was
registered at an air force base. He was also visited by an Air Force intelligence officer who wanted to see his ham radio equipment.[74] Sam
Sherman, a movie producer who had previously done work for NASA,
claimed to have digital video copies of the NASA master tapes of the
STS-48 event. He took them to a sophisticated video studio for analysis
and stated that when he asked the technician to enlarge one of the
objects to the limits of the system's resolution, it took on a disc shape
with a dome protrusion.[75]

One other intriguing dimension may have been part of this event. It is
possible that the Space Shuttle *Discovery* was accompanied by another
American-made craft during its STS-48 mission. According to former
NASA space craft operator (ScO) Clark McClelland, it was almost

certainly in September 1991 that two NASA astronauts told him to watch the passage of the shuttle very carefully, as "the next space shuttle" would be following some distance behind. Sure enough, that night McClelland saw the space shuttle flying overhead in a clear night sky. Soon thereafter he saw the "new" craft in orbit, trailing the shuttle. It came overhead and, to his great surprise, abruptly turned to the left and completely disappeared. A few weeks later, one of the astronauts gave him a sly grin as if to say, "I told you, Clark." McClelland did not speculate whether the trailing object was an alien craft, but was "almost certain" the astronaut would not have disclosed an object if it were anything other than an advanced technological development by the United States. He later decided that he had either seen the craft called Aurora or the X-43A, NASA's hypersonic, unmanned, experimental vehicle – although the latter was not supposed to have flown until the 21st century.[76]

Whatever the truth of the STS-48 event, it is interesting that soon after the controversy arose, NASA decided to delay all broadcasts of its missions. Henceforth none would broadcast live. The most reasonable conclusion is that someone at NASA became responsible for analyzing images prior to broadcast. Presumably, too, the NASA hierarchy felt that censorship might be necessary from time to time.[77]

Creating the New World Order

As the Cold War ended, a new world was forming. On December 8, 1991, three core states of the Soviet Union – Russia, Ukraine, and Belarus – signed a pact ending the Soviet Union's existence and creating the Commonwealth of Independent States (CIS). Most tellingly, they informed George Bush about it first, then Gorbachev. Although Gorbachev denied that they had the authority to do this, the Russian parliament ratified it anyway. Within days, so did nearly all the other Soviet republics. The Soviet military also signed on, supporting Yeltsin and the CIS. Gorbachev had no choice. He announced that all Soviet central structures would cease at the year's end. In fact, the end came a week early, on Christmas Day. At the Kremlin, the Red flag was lowered for the last time, and Gorbachev resigned from his non-existent office. Many people had played their part to end the Cold War, including Presidents Reagan and Bush, but Gorbachev had been the one indispensable man.

The collapse of the Soviet Union left the United States as the world's sole superpower. Invincible on the battlefield, overwhelming economically, it was poised to lead the world into a true "American Century." President Bush spoke several times of a peace dividend, the savings gained from dramatically reduced military spending. The world was coming to be a "kinder and gentler" place. The night had been long and dark, but now came the dawn.

It was a false dawn. America's decline was swifter than anyone could have guessed. By the early 21st century, a new geopolitical power structure had arisen, a multi-polar world in which Russia had regained much of its old status, and China had risen to the rank of a major power. More significant was the clear assertion of transnational organizations and international financial groups which wore away the old concept of national sovereignty. Added to this were systematic policies, running across Presidential administrations, that eroded American manufacturing strength. Finally came the ruinous foreign policy decisions to engage in wars during the 21st century that simply could not be paid for. Within a mere two decades of its victory in the Cold War, the United States found itself in the midst of a financial crisis and with its international stature vastly diminished. But that is a story for another book.

Summary

Ufologically speaking, the years 1990 and 1991 brought more strange cases of unknown objects in the skies and orbit of the Earth. Some of the events, such as the UFOs that appeared over Mexico, were as brazen as they were inexplicable. Others, such as the Greifswald lights or the various aerial encounters of the period, continued the long history of impossible, yet all-too-real technologies demonstrating that some group – whoever or whatever it might be – had surpassed the level of our open, officially constituted, human civilization. The STS-48 encounter provided unsettling evidence that a secret war could well have been underway, whether between humans and aliens, or even between groups of aliens seeking influence over the beautiful blue marble of our solar system.

UFO research entered new, equally disturbing, areas. The idea that aliens were abducting people was bad enough, but if it were true that elements of the military were also doing this, it would mean that a grave breach in the rights of citizens had occurred. And yet, the claims were beginning to build, slowly at first but there all the same. Meanwhile, the investigation of Area 51 broadened and deepened. Although the U.S.

government continued to deny its existence, it was obvious to anyone with an ounce of reason that the place was real. The claims of Bob Lazar were far from the only reason to consider that truly alien technology was housed there. Faced with government stonewalling, researchers simply gathered what evidence they could, none of which received official confirmation. Nonetheless, they gathered a great deal by the end of 1991.

That the U.S. government refused to discuss UFOs openly with the public was nothing new. From the point of view of those groups holding any secrets of value, there always seemed to be more to lose than to gain by revealing what they knew. Yet the end of the Cold War may well have prompted a fresh discussion on all this. Opportunities to start over do not come often. The collapse of Soviet power presented just such an opportunity, practically offered on a silver platter. Among a few, scattered people within earshot of President Bush, the inevitable philosophical questions must have arisen. How long should UFO secrecy last? Is this the time to end it? Can humanity truly move into a new and better era, brightened by the light of truth?

In the end, it was not philosophy but pragmatism that ruled the day. The brief attempt to discuss the end of UFO secrecy, an attempt that appears to have been undertaken during the summer of 1991, died because it was too big for the American government.

Which begs the question of who was actually "in charge" of the UFO secret? Clearly, the President of the United States, to the extent he could know about the topic, would have to have dealt with it in the most secretive fashion possible. Considering the exceedingly public nature of the American Presidency, this seems next-to-impossible. Perhaps the President retained some measure of formal authority over the matter, but in practice the operational aspects of the UFO secret had to have devolved elsewhere, undoubtedly someplace very "black." By the end of the Cold War, the structure of UFO secrecy had moved far beyond any laws authorized by Congress, the federal judiciary, known Presidential directives, or anything in the Constitution itself. In other words, UFO secrecy had become an agent that undermined the U.S. government. That this was never discussed in the open made the change so much more ominous. By the Cold War's end, it looked as though the center of gravity regarding UFO secrecy had shifted away from the *official* toward the *unofficial*. Perhaps it had always been so. Private power brokers like the Bilderbergers had exercised dominant king making ability for many years, and U.S. domestic and foreign policies had long reflected the interests of financial elites. Yet it is conceivable that control over "the secret" became increasingly international and private as the years went by. Such is the tone of the few credible leaks on the matter, and this would conform with the general trend of global politics and power during the late 20th century. In other words, it is conceivable that by the end of the Cold War, the UFO problem had gone beyond the control of the U.S. President.

Only a full and open review of the history can allow us to know whether such a turn of events is true, or was inevitable. If the UFO reality, however, portended something dangerous, or something that threatened the social fabric, it is not hard to see how a covert arm of the government would be seen as a necessity. If secrecy were truly of paramount importance, such an arm could in time become separate from its creator – perhaps even independent, like colonies breaking away from their mother country.

It was not only the human power structure that had secrets. The intelligences behind the UFOs themselves clearly were not interested in announcing themselves. Divining an alien agenda from the mass of UFO reports has not proven to be particularly fruitful, but reports through the early 1990s made at least two things clear: that secrecy was important to the UFO operators, and they were actively engaged about their own business. Indeed, it would appear that the Earth did not have visitors so much as long-term residents, presumably with a substantial infrastructure. By the end of the Cold War, the available evidence pointed not so much to the existence of aliens arriving from outer space (although elsewhere in the universe remains a reasonable point of origin) as to an alien civilization living here on Earth, whether permanently or with some long-term goal.

Conclusion

It is curious to note the old sea-margins of human thought. Each subsiding century reveals some new mystery; we build where monsters used to hide themselves.
— *Henry Wadsworth Longfellow*

The most important scientific revolutions all include, as their only common feature, the dethronement of human arrogance from one pedestal after another of previous convictions about our centrality in the cosmos.
— *Stephen Jay Gould*

The evidence is conclusive: an intelligent UFO phenomenon beyond the control of our civilization existed during the period under review of this study. Documented military encounters alone ran into the hundreds, many of which have been included here. Hundreds more "fastwalkers" were recorded by the Defense Support Program (DSP) satellite system, including an exact match with the famous Tehran incident of 1976. Regardless of the actual source of the UFOs themselves, it is undeniable that they triggered a significant response by military agencies around the world. This fact alone warrants the most meticulous scrutiny by responsible researchers.

The military dimension was only one side of it, however. Vastly greater numbers of ordinary people had experiences for which their concept of reality had not prepared them. In the face of such overwhelming shocks, comfortable certainties quickly broke down. Whether it was a car passenger screaming in terror, a person haunted by nightmares from an apparent abduction, a disillusioned citizen who learned that her government was indifferent to her unexplained encounter, or simply the lasting shock to a witness from something that was supposed to be impossible, the UFO phenomenon forced people to pick up the pieces of their shattered worldviews.

Unfortunately, they were usually constrained to do so privately. No matter how dramatic their experience or disturbing the aftermath, disbelief and ridicule accompanied anyone indiscreet enough to talk about their experience in public, often with negative professional repercussions. So it was that ordinary people who had undergone the most incredible and sometimes traumatic event of their lives were left to cope in the most unsatisfactory, atomized, way possible.

That the major institutions of society have not fought for the truth on this matter seems at first baffling. However, if one considers the awesome nature of the phenomenon itself, the transformative power inherent in the knowledge of something so vastly different, and the probable disruption to established institutions that would occur in the event of its disclosure, perhaps it is not so surprising, after all. On the contrary, it is easy to see how exceptional measures would be deemed necessary to deal with it. In a relatively open, republican system of government, it posed a serious problem. A way had to be found to keep the system alive while creating another, increasingly separate, system that would be empowered to deal with the extraordinary intrusion of "others" into our world. This would be especially so if human authorities determined the "others" were manipulating global geopolitics for their own non-human agendas, a possibility that any responsible government would need to investigate.

In such a circumstance, only one of two things can happen. The President, or some other legally constituted authority, would make a statement informing the world of the reality of UFOs and "aliens." The world would then go through its obligatory baptism by fire. Various governments would need to explain not only the *whys* of UFO secrecy, but the *hows*. This would undoubtedly get into matters of the construction and funding of the black budget, and very likely would lead into areas in which citizens might wish to engage in legal actions of all sorts. The implications for the petroleum, steel, and electronics industries could well be catastrophic, assuming that better versions of each are inherent in the UFO matrix of reality. No doubt many other major industries would be similarly affected. Thus, the short-term repercussions would be a problem of the greatest magnitude.

The other scenario would be an ever-deepening code of silence. If it were decided that the post-disclosure ride would be too rough, the outcome too uncertain, then absolute secrecy would have to be maintained. But how? In a world in which free inquiry ostensibly reigns, where thousands of major universities, newspapers, and news media outlets compete to inform the general public, could long-term secrecy be possible? The answer is that it could be, if the right relationships were established with leading academic and media sources. Key figures within those industries would serve as the sheep dogs, charged with keeping the rest of the herd together. Meanwhile, with virtually limitless black budgets and little meaningful oversight, the secret surrounding UFOs could go deeper and deeper, developing into a strict policy of denial on all ET-related matters in the interest of national security. Lies could even become operational priorities, while truth becomes a threat.

It looks as though the UFO secret involved more than mere knowledge of the presence of aliens of some sort. During the 1970s and 1980s, researchers made a strong case that alien artifacts were recovered and studied by the U.S. military. Conceding that such exotic technology would be vastly ahead of anything developed by human civilization, how long would it take before some clever team of humans scientists developed major new insights that might transform existing technologies, or even create new fields of study altogether? It is not evident that all black world developments would eventually become public. On the contrary, it is entirely feasible that some breakthroughs would in turn lead to other breakthroughs, and so on in the manner very typical of science, in which successes build upon each other with ever greater speed and effectiveness.

Thus, there exists the possibility of what I have come to call a "breakaway civilization." This would entail a situation in which black world science and technology has reached a sufficient level beyond the "official" world, in which its foundational areas of knowledge are so different (understanding of non-terrestrial intelligences, spacetime, dimensionality, etc.), that it can fairly be called a separate civilization. Throughout human history, multiple civilizations often existed simultaneously, possessing disparate levels of technology and operating on vastly different assumptions of the world. There is no inherent reason to doubt that something like this can happen again – or has already happened.

Indeed, the 1988 demonstration of the "Alien Reproduction Vehicle" (ARV) points to the existence of such a major breakthrough. Supporting this even further is the complete absence, even two decades later, of anything like the ARV in the arsenal of the U.S. military. The object was reportedly described as having gone into space on many occasions, and even to have explored the solar system. The person who carefully observed it and described it to friends noted that it looked as though it had been in service for a long time. This would indicate that the mission of the ARV had nothing at all to do with U.S. military mandates, at least not in any conventional geopolitical sense. Just as clearly, its mission would logically have something to do with the presence of non-human intelligences. It would be, in effect, humanity's homemade "UFO" designed to deal with extraterrestrials. In such a situation, the ARV would never be deployed to wars among Earth's nations. Its off-world mission would be too important to compromise by sending it off to fight in Bosnia, Afghanistan, Iraq, or elsewhere.

In all likelihood, secrecy relating to UFOs was a logical course of action initially that became an addiction the longer it continued. The longer it was maintained, the harder it was to reveal, and the greater the gap between official and black-world societies. One might therefore think that this secrecy, which continues to this day, is bound to last indefinitely.

Such a conclusion would be logical and perhaps even seem to be inevitable. Yet it would be wrong. Under normal circumstances, it is true that perpetual secrecy would be the desired outcome by elites in relation to UFOs. By the end of the Cold War, such circumstances still applied, despite the confusion created by the collapse of the Soviet Union. This is because even then, although the world's infrastructure showed signs of strain, it remained in place. Energy remained sufficient to meet humanity's growing needs, adequate supplies of fresh water were declining but still available for much of the world, ecosystem degradation was severe but not yet at a universally widespread point of crisis. Well into the 21st century, however, it is now evident that the path on which humanity has been traveling cannot continue much longer.

Consider something as basic as human population. In 1900, it was still less than two billion people. It took sixty more years to reach the total of three billion. Then, within the next thirty years, two billion more had been added, so that by 1990 more than five billion people were living on planet Earth. Now, less than twenty years later, the world is fast approaching a total of seven billion. All these people need more than simply a place to live. They need resources, and here is the problem. Without new sources of energy, ways of obtaining more fresh water, and a halt to the rapid degradation of the global ecosystem, a crisis of unprecedented dimensions threatens the human race. Already it has become a breeding ground for political and financial crisis, a sad fact of life in the early 21st century.

Humanity's situation, then, is most surely not business as usual. If it continues to worsen, the matter of unexplained advanced technologies being operated by unknown agencies could well become a final, unavoidable avenue to explore as a way of getting out. It would not come without a heavy price, and it is for this reason that those 'in the know' will surely wait until the eleventh hour, when no other options are available, before they move ahead with anything like a "disclosure." It may well be that revelations on this matter will not come from official pronouncements anyway, but perhaps from a major, public event that, for some reason or another, cannot any longer be denied. The world was not at that place by 1991, but it may well be there soon.

Still, the path toward understanding the UFO phenomenon – and its associated cover-up – took major strides during the period under review. I subtitled this book, "The Cover-up Exposed" because it was during the 1970s and 1980s that the UFO cover-up was shown to have existed beyond any reasonable doubt. Prior to the age of FOIA, government denials about UFOs could not as easily be refuted. Undoubtedly, good research had been done in the 1950s and 1960s that demonstrated the UFO reality and the likelihood of a cover-up. But it was only after thousands of pages of government documents were released under the Freedom of Information Act that researchers could prove with an overwhelming avalanche of data that military and intelligence agencies had taken the matter with extreme consideration and care. UFOs were proven to be serious business, regardless of their ultimate origin.

The cover-up was exposed still further by the growing number of leaks that began to occur during the late 1970s. Some were more persuasive than others, but all pointed to the existence of UFO crash retrievals and the existence of a back-engineering program. By 1980, it looked as though luck might favor those researchers seeking to end the cover-up. Although this did not occur, it is still true that many aspects of UFO secrecy were attacked and revealed during the 1970s and 1980s. Despite the arguments, controversies, and even disinformation that pervaded the field at times, progress was made.

As the world transformed, so did ufology. The advent of the Internet immediately and profoundly changed the nature of research into this subject. Many researchers were not happy with these changes, but the wide-open nature of the information highway brought many new opportunities to share data and ideas. It also made implementing the cover-up more problematic, at least until better control over it could be achieved by political and corporate elites. This is a struggle that continues to the present day, the final outcome of which has yet to be determined.

Perhaps the most important development of the period under review is how ufology turned its attention to the aliens themselves. It was one thing to study specific UFO sightings in an attempt to find patterns and understand the technologies involved. But what happened during the 1970s was the beginning of the first focused attempt by the human race to understand the beings behind the phenomenon, while making proper exception of course for those black-world people and groups who had (probably) already been trying to do this secretly. It was the moment in which the object of study – that is, humanity – attempted to turn the situation around and understand just who or what was studying it. The moment was a significant one not simply in the history of ufology, but of human consciousness. Such efforts were only the beginning, of course, and years later much still needs to be done.

Understanding the intelligences behind the UFO phenomenon remains the great challenge of the subject. Developing the necessary insight will require a change not simply to our social, economic, and political world, but to our consciousness itself. Whoever and whatever these beings are, they appear to exist and act in ways that most humans are not prepared or able to match. In a world in which billions go hungry, and billions more spend their waking hours in repetitive jobs, mindlessly surfing the Internet, playing video games, or watching the television, it is safe to say that most people are not ready to deal with the existence of an alien race that may be of exceptional intelligence, and may well be telepathic – if numerous claims of abductees and experiencers are to be believed. Nor of an alien race that surely has an agenda of some sort.

But 'not being ready' has never yet prevented something from happening. The pace of history will force change to arrive soon enough. People will not be ready and the shock will be great, but the opportunities will be vast. People, being people, will learn to cope and thrive. All the efforts of those keeping this matter secret will be in vain, for the end of secrecy will come as a terrible swift sword. Destiny will not be denied.

Bibliography

The following list includes all books and major journals that were used in researching this book. It does not include specific government documents, archival repositories, newspapers, various journals, or most web-based material, all of which will be found in the Endnotes.

Adams, Thomas R. *The Choppers . . . and the Choppers: Mystery Helicopters and Animal Mutilations.* (Project Sigma, 1978).

Aerial Phenomena Research Organization (APRO), *The APRO Bulletin,* 1958-1985.

Allen, Gary. *The Rockefeller File.* ('76 Press, 1976).

Alexander, John B. *Future War: Non-Lethal Weapons in Twenty-First-Century Warfare.* (St. Martin's Press, 1999).

Andrews, Colin & Delgado, Pat. *Circular Evidence: A Detailed Investigation of the Flattened Swirled Crops Phenomenon.* (Bloomsbury UK, 1989).

Baker, Robert A., and Nickell, Joe. *Missing Pieces: How to Investigate Ghosts, UFOs, Psychics, and Other Mysteries.* (Prometheus, 1992).

Bamford, James. *Body of Secrets: Anatomy of the Ultra-Secret National Security Agency.* (Anchor Books, 2002).

Berliner, Don with Marie Galbraith and Antonio Huneeus. *UFO Briefing Document: The Best Available Evidence.* (UFO Research Coalition, 1995). Also published by (Dell, 2000)

Berlitz, Charles, and Moore, William. *The Roswell Incident.* (Grosset & Dunlop, 1980).

Bishop, Gregory. *Project Beta: An Adventure in the Disinformation Age.* (Paraview Pocket Books, 2005).

Blum, Howard. *Out There: The Government's Secret Quest for Extraterrestrials.* (Pocket Books, 1990).

Bowen, Charles, Editor. *Encounter Cases from Flying Saucer Review.* (Signet Books, 1977).

Boyne, Walter J. *Beyond the Wild Blue: A History of the U.S. Air Force, 1947-1997.* (St. Martin's Press, 1997).

Boyne, Walter J. and Lopez, Donald S. Editors. *Vertical Flight: The Age of the Helicopter.* (Smithsonian Institution Press, 1984).

Bruni, Georgina. Forward by Nick Pope. *You Can't Tell the People: The Definitive Account of the Rendlesham Forest UFO Mystery.* (Sidgwick & Jackson, Ltd., 2000).

Brzezinski, Zbigniew. *Between Two Ages: America's Role in the Technetronic Era.* (The Viking Press, 1970).

Buckley, Kevin. *Panama: The Whole Story.* (Simon & Schuster, 1991).

Butler, Brenda; Street, Dot and Randles, Jenny. *Sky Crash: A Cosmic Conspiracy.* (Grafton, 1986).

Burnham, David. Forward by Walter Cronkite. *The Rise of the Computer State.* (Random House, 1983).

Cameron, Grant. "Records of the Clinton OSTP Related to UFOs and

Extraterrestrial Intelligence" (Internet, 2001).

Cameron, Grant. *The Presidents UFO Web Site: A Tale of Extraterrestrial Politics in the White House.* http://presidentialufo.com

Cameron, Grant & Crain, T. Scott, Jr. *UFOs, MJ-12 and the Government. A Report on Government Involvement in UFO Crash Retrievals.* (Privately published, 1991).

Center for UFO Studies (CUFOS), *International UFO Reporter (IUR),* 1976-Present.

Chernow, Ron. *The House of Morgan: An American Banking Dynasty and the Rise of Modern Finance.* (Grove Press, 2001). Check!

Clark, Jerome. *The UFO Book. Encyclopedia of the Extraterrestrial.* (Visible Ink Press, 1998).

Coleman, Loren, & Clark, Jerome. *The Unidentified, Creatures of the Outer Edge.* (Warner Books, 1975).

Collins, Robert & Doty, Richard. *Exempt from Disclosure: The Disturbing Case About the UFO Coverup.* (Peregrine Communications, 2005).

Committee for Skeptical Inquiry (CSI), *The Skeptical Inquirer,* 1976-Present.

Conroy, Ed. *Report on Communion.* (William Morrow, 1989).

Cook, Nick. *The Hunt for Zero Point: Inside the Classified World of Antigravity Technology.* (Broadway Books, 2002).

Davidson, Leon. *Flying Saucers: an Analysis of the Air Force Project Blue Book Special Report No. 14.* (Blue-Book Publishers, 1976).

De Brouwer, W. Preface, *Vague d'OVNI sur la Belgique - Un Dossier Exceptionnel.* (Brussels: SOBEPS, 1991).

Dolan, Richard M. *UFOs and the National Security State: An Unclassified History, 1941-1973.* (Keyhole Publishing Company, 2000). Republished as *UFOs and the National Security State: Chronology of a Cover-up, 1941-1973.* (Hampton Roads Publishing, 2002)

Dong, Paul and Stevens, Wendelle C. *UFOs over Modern China: A Survey of the Phenomenon, Translated from Chinese by the Foreign Language Bureau of Peking.* (UFO Photo Archives, 1983).

Emerson, Steven. *Secret Warriors: Inside the Covert Military Operations of the Reagan Era.* (G.P. Putnam's Sons, 1988).

Estulin, Daniel. *The True Story of the Bilderberg Group.* (TrineDay, LLC, 2007).

Fawcett, Lawrence and Greenwood, Barry. *Clear Intent: The Government Coverup of the UFO Experience.* (Prentice-Hall, Inc., 1984).

Filer, George A. *Filer's Files, MUFON Skywatch Investigations.*

Fowler, Raymond E.. *The Andreasson Affair: The documented investigation of a woman's abduction aboard a UFO* (Prentice-Hall, Inc., 1979).

Fowler, Raymond E. *The Allagash Abductions.* (Wild Flower Press, 1993).

Fowler, Raymond, E. *The Watchers: The Secret Design Behind UFO Abduction.* (Bantam Books, 1990).

Freedman, Lawrence and Karsh, Efraim. *The Gulf Conflict: Diplomacy and*

War in the New World Order, 1990-1991. (Princeton, 1993).

Friedman, George and Meredith. *The Future of War: Power, Technology, and American World Dominance in the Twenty-First Century.* (St. Martin's Griffin, 1998).

Friedman, Stanton T. and Berliner, Don. *Crash at Corona.* (Paragon House, 1992).

FSR Publications, Ltd., (Kent, UK), *Flying Saucer Review*, 1955-Present.

Good, Timothy. *Above Top Secret: The Worldwide UFO Coverup.* (William Morrow and Company, 1987).

Good, Timothy. *Need to Know: UFOs, The Military and Intelligence.* (Sidgwick & Jackson, 2006).

Greer, Stephen M. M.D. *Disclosure: Military and Government Witnesses Reveal the Greatest Secrets in Modern History.* (Prepublication Rush Edition, Carden Jennings Publishing Co., 2001).

Gulley, Bill with Reese, Mary Ellen. *Breaking Cover.* (Simon and Schuster, 1980).

Haines, Richard F. Ph. D. *CE-5: Close Encounters of the Fifth Kind, 242 Case Files Exposing Alien Contact.* (Sourcebooks, Inc., 1999).

Hall, Richard H., ed., *The UFO Evidence.* (National Investigations Committee on Aerial Phenomena, 1964).

Hall, Richard, H. *The UFO Evidence, Volume II.* (The Scarecrow Press, Inc., 2000).

Hall, Richard. *Uninvited Guests: A Documented History of UFO Sightings, Alien Encounters & Coverups.* (Aurora Press, 1988).

Hamilton, William F., III. *Alien Magic: UFO Crashes, Abductions, Underground Bases.* (The New Millennium Edition, 1996, 2005).

Hamilton, William F., III. *Cosmic Top Secret: New Evidence,* Inner Light - Global Communications, 2002).

Hannaford, Peter. *The Reagans: A Political Portrait.* (Coward-McCann, 1983).

Hansen, Terry. *The Missing Times: News Media Complicity in the UFO Cover-up.* (Xlibris Corporation, 2000).

Harr, John and Johnson, Peter. *The Rockefeller Conscience; An American Family in Public and in Private.* (Scribner, 1991).

Haselhoff, Eltojo H., Ph.D. *The Deepening Complexity of Crop Circles: Scientific Research & Urban Legends.* (Frog, Ltd, 2001).

Hausdorf, Hartwig. *The Chinese Roswell: UFO Encounters in the Far East from Ancient Times to the Present.* Translated from the German by Evamarie Matheay and Waltraut Smith. (New Paradigm Books, 1998).

Herman, Edward S. and Brodhead, Frank. *Demonstration Elections: US-Staged Elections in the Dominican Republic, Vietnam and El Salvador.* (South End Press, 1984).

Hesemann, Michael. *Secrets of the Black World* (video), 1995

Hill, Paul R. *Unconventional Flying Objects: A Scientific Analysis.* (Hampton Roads Publishing Company, Inc., 1995).

Hopkins, Budd. *Intruders.* (Ballantine Books, 1987).

Hopkins, Budd. *Missing Time: A Documented Study of UFO Abductions,* with an Afterward by Aphrodite Clamar, Ph.D. (Richard Marek Publishers, 1981).

Hopkins, Budd. *Witnessed: The True Story of the Brooklyn Bridge UFO Abductions.* (Pocket Books, 1996).

Hougan, Jim. *Secret Agenda: Watergate, Deep throat, and the CIA.* (Random House, 1984).

Howe, Linda Moulton. *An Alien Harvest: Further Evidence Linking Animal Mutilations and Human Abductions to Alien Life Forms.* (Pioneer Printing, 1989).

Howe, Linda Moulton. *Glimpses of Other Realities, Volume One: Facts and Eyewitnesses.* (LMH Productions, 1994).

Howe, Linda Moulton. *Glimpses of Other Realities, Volume Two: High Strangeness.* (LMH Productions, 1998).

Howe, Linda Moulton. *A Strange Harvest,* video. (1980)

Hunt, Linda. *Secret Agenda: The United States Government, Nazi Scientists, and Project Paperclip.* (St. Martin's Press, 1991).

Imbrogno, Philip J., Pratt, Bob, and Hynek, Dr. J. Allen. *Night Siege: The Hudson Valley UFO Sightings.* Second Edition Expanded & Revised. (Llewellyn Publications, 1998).

Isaacs, Jeremy and Downing, Taylor. *Cold War: An Illustrated History, 1945-1991, companion to the CNN TV Series.* (Jeremy Isaacs Productions and Turner Original Productions, 1998).

Keith, Jim. *Black Helicopters Over America.* (IllumiNet Press, 1994).

Keith, Jim. *Mind Control, World Control: the Encyclopedia of Mind Control.* (Adventures Unlimited Press, 1995).

Klass, Philip J. *UFOs Explained.* (Random House, 1974).

Klass, Philip J. *UFOs: The Public Deceived.* (Prometheus Books, 1983).

Koster, R.M. and Sanchez, Guillermo. *In the Time of the Tyrants: Panama, 1968-1990.* (Norton, 1990).

Lammer, Dr. Helmut & Lammer, Marion. *MILABS: Military Mind Control and Alien Abductions.* (IllumiNet Press, 1999).

Leonard, George. *Somebody Else is on the Moon.* (Pocket Books, 1977).

Lobster, The Journal of Parapolitics. (Robin Ramsey, Editor. 1983-2001).

Loftus, Elizabeth, *Memory.* (Addison-Wesley, 1980).

Lorenzen, Jim and Coral. *Abducted! Confrontations with Beings from Outer Space.* (Berkeley Medallion Books, 1977).

Maccabee, Bruce. *Hawk Tales* (Bruce Maccabee, 2005)

Maccabee, Bruce S., Ph.D. *The Gulf Breeze Sightings: The Untold Story.* (Unpublished, 1994).

Maccabee, Bruce. *UFO FBI Connection: The Secret History of the Government's Cover-Up.* (Llewellyn Publications, 2000).

Marrs, Jim. *Rule by Secrecy: The Hidden History That Connects the Trilateral Commission.* (Harper Collins Publishers, 2000).

Mayer, Jane & McManus, Doyle. *Landslide: The Unmaking of the President, 1984-1988.* (Houghton Mifflin, 1988).

Mutual UFO Network. *MUFON UFO Journal* (formerly *Skylook*), 1967-Present.

National Investigations Committee on Aerial Phenomena (NICAP), *The UFO Investigator,* 1957-1980.

Norman, Paul A.; Auchettl, John W. *The Knowles Family Encounter: A study of the UFO phenomenon over the Nullarbor Plain.* (Victorian UFO Research Society, 1990).

Noyes, Ralph, Ed., (photographs by Busty Taylor). *The Crop Circle Enigma: Grounding the Phenomenon in Science, Culture and Metaphysics.* (Gateway Books, 1990).

Pope, Nick. *Open Skies, Closed Minds. For the First Time, a Government UFO Expert Speaks Out.* (Pocket Books, 1997).

Randle, Kevin D. *The Randle Report: UFOs in the '90s.* (M. Evans and Company, Inc., 1997).

Randles, Jenny. *The UFO Conspiracy: The First Forty Years.* (Javelin Books, 1988).

Randles, Jenny. *UFO: Crash Landing? Friend or Foe? The True Story of the Rendlesham Forest Close Encounter.* (Blandford Book, 1998).

Redfern, Nicholas. *A Covert Agenda, The British Government's UFO Top Secrets Exposed.* (Simon & Schuster, 1997).

Regehr, Ronald S. *How to Build a $125 Million UFO Detector.* (Self Published by Ronald S. Regehr, 1998).

Richelson, Jeffrey T. *The Wizards of Langley: Inside the CIA's Directorate of Science and Technology.* (Westview Press, 2001).

Rockefeller, David. *Memoirs.* (Random House, 2002).

Rush, George. *Confessions of an Ex-Secret Service Agent, the Marty Venker Story.* (Donald I. Fine, Inc. 1988).

Sagan, Carl. *The Demon-Haunted World: Science as a Candle in the Dark.* (Ballantine Books, 1996).

Sauder, Richard. Ph.D. *Underground Bases and Tunnels. What is the Government Trying to Hide?* (Adventures Unlimited Press, 1995).

Schnable, Jim. *Remote Viewers: The Secret History of America's Psychic Spies.* (Dell, 1997).

Second Look, Washington, D.C., 1978-1980.

Sheaffer, Robert. *The UFO Verdict: Examining the Evidence.* (Prometheus Books, 1986).

Silva, Freddy. *Secrets in the Fields: The Science and Mysticism of Crop Circles.* (Hampton Roads Publishing Co., 2002).

Society for Scientific Exploration, *Journal of Scientific Exploration (JSE),* 1987-Present

Spencer, John. *The UFO Encyclopedia.* (Avon Books, 1991).

Springmeier, Fritz. *Be Ye as Wise as Serpents.* (Pre-Publication edition, 1991).

Stonehill, Paul (consultant, Philip Mantle). *The Soviet UFO Files: Paranormal Encounters Behind the Iron Curtain.* (CLB International/Quadrillion Publishing, Inc., International, 1998).

Stonor Saunders, Francis. *The Cultural Cold War: The CIA and the World of Arts and Letters.* (New Press, 2001).

Strieber, Whitley. *Communion: A True Story.* (William Morrow, 1987).

Stringfield, Leonard H. *Situation Red: The UFO Siege!* (Doubleday, 1977).

Stringfield, Leonard. *UFO Crash Retrievals: Amassing the Evidence.* (Published privately, 1982).

Sullivan, George. *Modern Combat Helicopters. Military Aircraft Series.* (Facts on File, Inc., 1993).

Swann, Ingo. *Penetration: The Question of Extraterrestrial and Human Telepathy.* (Ingo Swann Books, 1998).

Sweetman, Bill. *Aurora: The Pentagon's Secret Hypersonic Spyplane.* (Motorbooks International, 1993).

Sweetman, Bill. *Northrop B-2 Stealth Bomber.* (Motorbooks International, 1992).

Sweetman, Bill. *Stealth Aircraft: Secrets of Future Airpower.* (Motorbooks International, 1986).

Tarpley, Webster G. and Chaitkin, Anton. *George Bush: The Unauthorized Biography.* (Progressive Press, 2004).

Taylor, Michael J.H. and John W.R. *Jane's Pocket Book of Helicopters.* (Collier, 1981).

Thomas, Gordon. *Gideon's Spies: The Secret History of the Mossad.* (St. Martin's Griffin, 2000).

Thomas, Gordon. *Journey Into Madness: The True Story of Secret CIA Mind Control and Medical Abuse.* (Bantam Books, 1989).

Thomas, Kenn and Keith, Jim. *The Octopus: Secret Government and the Death of Danny Casolaro.* (Revised Edition, Feral House, 2004).

Trainor, Joseph. *UFO RoundUp.* (Weekly UFO news, 1995-2005).

Turner, Karla. *Inside the Alien-Human Abduction Agenda, lecture recorded in 11/94.* (Published by Alienresistance.org , 1994).

Turner, Karla. *Into the Fringe: A True Story of Alien Abduction.* (Berkeley Books, 1992).

Turner, Karla. *Taken: Inside the Human-Alien Abduction Agenda.* (Kelt Works, 1994).

UFO Magazine, Los Angeles, CA, 1986-Present.

UFO Universe, New York, NY, 1975-1994.

Vallee, Jacques. *Messengers of Deception - UFO Contacts and Cults.* (And/Or Press, 1979).

Vallee, Jacques. *The Invisible College: What a Group of Scientists Has Discovered About UFO Influences on the Human Race.* (E. P. Dutton & Co., Inc., 1975).

Vallee, Jacques. *UFO Chronicles in the Soviet Union: A Cosmic Samizdat.* (Ballantine Books, 1992).

Vesco, Renato. *Intercettateli Senza Sparare,* U. Mursia & Co., Milan, Italy, 1968. English translation Intercept – But Don't Shoot. (Grove Press, Inc., 1971). Republished as *Intercept UFO: The True Story of the Flying Saucers.* (Pinnacle Books, Inc., 1974).

Vesco, Renato & Childress, David Hatcher. *Man-Made UFOs 1944-1994: 50 Years of Suppression.* (Adventures Unlimited Press, 1994).

Walters, Ed and Frances. *The Gulf Breeze Sightings, The Most Astounding Multiple Sightings of UFOs in U.S. History.* (William Morrow, 1990).

Walters, Ed and Frances. *Abductions in Gulf Breeze.* (Avon, 1994).

Walters, Ed and Maccabee, Bruce. *UFOS Are Real: Here's the Proof.* (Avon, 1997).

Walton, Travis. *Fire in the Sky: The Walton Experience.* (Marlowe and Company, 1996).

Warren, Larry and Robbins, Peter. *Left At East Gate: A First-Hand Account of the Bentwaters-Woodbridge UFO Incident, its Cover-Up, and Investigation.* (Marlowe & Company, 1997).

Webb, Gary. *Dark Alliance: The CIA, the Contras, and the Crack Cocaine Explosion.* (Seven Stories Press, 1999).

Weiner, Tim. *Blank Check: The Pentagon's Black Budget.* (Warner Books, 1990).

Wright, Susan. *UFO Headquarters: Investigations on Current Extraterrestrial Activity.* (St. Martin's Press, 1998)

Endnotes

Chapter 1 - Global Strangeness, 1973-1975

1. Chalker, Bill, "The North West Cape Incident: UFOs and Nuclear Alert in Australia," *International UFO Reporter*, Jan-Feb, 1986; Good, Timothy, *Above Top Secret*, p. 174-175.
2. Jacques Vallee, *The Invisible College: What a Group of Scientists Has Discovered About UFO Influences on the Human Race.* Jacques Vallee. (E. P. Dutton & Co., Inc., 1975), p. 40.
3. Fawcett & Greenwood, *Clear Intent*, p. 207; "NICAP: The Bitter Truth," by Richard Hall, *MUFON UFO Journal*, 3/80.
4. "News 'n' Views," *MUFON UFO Journal*, 7/86.
5. Stringfield, Leonard H. *Situation Red: The UFO Siege!*, Doubleday, 1977.
6. Larsen, Sherman J., "Documentation: Evidence of Government Concern," Sherman J. Larsen and Bill Laub, Co-Investigators. *1971 Midwest UFO Conference*, June 12, 1971, St. Louis, Missouri, Holiday Inn - North.
7. "Hynek: UFO Movement Basically Amateurs," Coral Lorenzen, *APRO Bulletin*, Vol. 33, No. 2, Jan. 1986
8. "Five Arguments Against the Extraterrestrial Origin of Unidentified Flying Objects," Jacques F. Vallee. *Journal of Scientific Exploration*, V. 4, N. 1, 1990.
9. Clark, Jerome. *The UFO Book. Encyclopedia of the Extraterrestrial* (Visible Ink Press, 1998), p. 437.
10. Hall, Richard, Editor. *The UFO Evidence, Volume II*, (Scarecrow Press, 2001), p. 312.
11. Redfern, Nicholas. *A Covert Agenda, The British Government's UFO Top Secrets Exposed.* (Simon & Schuster, 1997), p. 116.
12. Redfern, Nicholas, *Covert Agenda*, p. 118-124; "How Alien's My Valley?", *Daily Mirror* of London, 10/22/99.
13. Hansen, Terry. *The Missing Times: News Media Complicity in the UFO Cover-up.* (Xlibris Corporation, 2000), p. 187-188; Good, Timothy, *Above Top Secret*, p. 129; Bowen, Charles, Editor. *Encounter Cases from Flying Saucer Review.* (Signet Books, 1977), p. vii-xi; Vallee, *Invisible College*, p. 56; Berliner, Don with Marie Galbraith and Antonio Huneeus. *UFO Briefing Document: The Best Available Evidence* (UFO Research Coalition, 1995), p. 174.
14. Hall, Richard, *The UFO Evidence, Vol. 2*, p. 493.
15. "Italian Photo Unexplained," *APRO Bulletin*, v24, n3, 9/75.
16. "Formation Seen by Air Crews," *APRO Bulletin*, V.22, No. 5, March-April 1974; Hall, Richard, *The UFO Evidence, Vol. 2*, p. 17, 121.
17. Hall, Richard, *The UFO Evidence, Vol. 2*, p. 18, 121, 243.
18. Spencer, John, *The UFO Encyclopedia*, p. 16-17, 55.
19. The Spanish UFO accounts that follow are contained in "Department of Defense Intelligence Information Report," in Six Pages. United States Defense Attache Office, Madrid, Spain, 1974.
20. Redfern, Nicholas, *A Covert Agenda*, p. 126.
21. Vike, Brian, HBCC UFO Research. http://www.hbccufo.org/modules.php? name=News&file=print&sid=1507.
22. Benítez, J.J., *La Gaceta del Norte*, Bilbao, Spain, June 27, 1976; Benítez, J. J., "Release of Further Official Spanish Documents on UFOs," trans. by Gordon Creighton, *Flying Saucer Review*, 3-4/79.
23. Johnson, Donald A., "Do Nuclear Facilities Attract UFOs?," *International UFO Reporter*, Summer 2002.
24. Hall, Richard, *The UFO Evidence, Vol. 2*, p. 18, 415.
25. Good, Timothy, *Above Top Secret*, p. 430-431; Spencer, John, *UFO Encyclopedia*, p. 222.
26. Spencer, John, *UFO Encyclopedia*, p. 38-39; Hall, Richard, *The UFO Evidence, Vol. 2*, p. 276-278.
27. Hill, Harry, "The Bizarre Ancient Astronauts of Tibet," *UFO Update* Issue #5, Winter 1980; Trainor, Joseph, *UFO Round Up*, V2, N23, June 8, 1997.
28. "Recent Sightings Reported in New Mexico," *NICAP UFO Investigator*, July 1974.
29. Howe, Linda Moulton, "Glowing Disc Encounter with Military in Albuquerque, NM," www.earthfiles.com, November 29, 2007.
30. "Car Disabled by UFO?," *APRO Bulletin*, V. 22. No. 6, May-June 1974; Hall, Richard, *The UFO Evidence, Vol. 2*, p. 18, 202, 218-219, 275-276.
31. Hall, Richard, *The UFO Evidence, Vol. 2*, p. 18, 121.
32. Good, Timothy, *Above Top Secret*, p. 200.
33. Good, Timothy, *Above Top Secret*, p. 201, Spencer, John, *The UFO Encyclopedia*, p. 53.
34. Hall, Richard, *The UFO Evidence, Vol. 2*, p. 175.
35. Howe, Linda Moulton, *An Alien Harvest*, p. 14; "Mysterious Cattle Mutilations," *APRO Bulletin*, v23, n4, Jan.-Feb. 1975.
36. "Another Mysterious Circle," *APRO Bulletin*, v23, n4, Jan.-Feb. 1975; Hall, Richard, *The UFO Evidence, Vol. 2*, p. 18, 48-49; Clark, Jerome, *The UFO Book*, p. 336-338.
37. Regehr, Ronald S. "How to Build a $125 Million UFO Detector," (Self Published by Ronald S. Regehr, 1998), p. 23.

38. Long, Greg, "Strangeness at Yakima," *International UFO Reporter*, July/August 1994.
39. DoD Intelligence Information Report. Subject: Balls of Fire II. Date of Report, 8 Jan 75, Report Number 6 873 0004 75. Originator: USDAO Islamabad, Pakistan.
40. Good, Timothy, *Above Top Secret*, p. 318.
41. Rush, George, *Confessions of an Ex-Secret Service Agent, the Marty Venker Story*, Donald I. Fine, 1988.
42. Cameron, Grant, Presidential UFO Website, http://www.presidentialufo.com/nixon1.htm
43. Mayer, Jane & McManus, Doyle, *Landslide: The Unmaking of the President, 1984-1988*, Houghton Mifflin, 1988, p. 34, 402; Christy, Mark, "Reagan In UFO Fright," *Daily Star*, London, 10/1/88; "Reagan: I Saw UFO," *New Truth*, Dunedin, New Zealand, 10/17/88; *Filer's Files*, 4/25/00; Cameron, Grant, http://presidentialufo.com; http://stealthskater.com
44. Mayer, Jane & McManus, Doyle, *Landslide: The Unmaking of the President, 1984-1988*, p. 34.
45. "Reagan: I Saw UFO," *New Truth*, Dunedin, New Zealand, 10/17/88.
46. Former friend of Ronald Reagan, private conversation with Richard Dolan; Cameron, Grant, http://presidentialufo.com
47. "A conversation with Peter Dale Scott," *Lobster Magazine*, February 1985, Issue #7; Hougan, Jim, *Secret Agenda: Watergate, Deep throat, and the CIA*, Random House, 1984.
48. Fawcett, Lawrence & Greenwood, Barry. *Clear Intent: The Government Cover-up of the UFO Experience*, Prentice-Hall, Inc., 1984, p. 5.
49. Greenwood, Barry, "UFOs: Government Involvement, Secrecy, and Documents" http://www.project1947.com/bg/ufogov.htm
50. McMasters, Paul, "FOIA, It's Always There," *Quill*, 10/96; and also http://www.spj.org/foia_history.asp
51. Fawcett, Lawrence & Greenwood, Barry, *Clear Intent*, p. 181.
52. FBI Office Memorandum, "Protection of Vital Installations," January 31, 1949.
53. Rockefeller, David, *Memoirs* (Random House, 2002), p. 405.
54. Allen, Gary, *The Rockefeller File*, ('76 Press, 1976), p. 6.
55. Estulin, Daniel, "The Bilderberg Club: a Secret Society of the Richest and Most Influential People Conspiring to Achieve a World Government," *Michael*, June-July-August 2006; *http://www.michaeljournal.org/bilder.htm*
56. Springmeier, Fritz, *Be Ye as Wise as Serpents*, Pre-Publication edition, 1991
57. Estulin, Daniel, *The True Story of the Bilderberg Group* (TrineDay, LLC, 2007), p. 22.
58. Rivera, David, *Final Warning: A History of the New World Order: Illuminism and the Master Plan for World Domination*, 1994, at The Modern History Project, *http://www.modernhistoryproject.org/*
59. Cameron, Grant, "Disclosure Pattern, 1972-1975," in http://www.presidentialufo.com/disclosure_72-75.htm; Bishop, Gregory, *Project Beta*, p. 200-202; Howe, Linda Moulton, *Alien Harvest*.
60. "Soldiers reported UFO in Spain," *Sky Look*, April 1975.
61. *Sky Look*, 2/75; Creighton, Gordon, "UFO Lands on Spanish Air Force Target Range," *Flying Saucer Review*, 3/79; Hall, Richard, *The UFO Evidence, Volume 2*, p. 18, 77, 87; Spencer, John, *The UFO Encyclopedia*, p. 34.
62. Lobet, Lieut-Colonel, "Another Close Contact on Reunion, Pt. 1" (trans. by Gordon Creighton), *Flying Saucer Review*, 3-4/79; Lobet, Lieut-Colonel, "Another Close Contact on Reunion, Pt. 2" (trans. by Gordon Creighton), *Flying Saucer Review*, 5-6/79; Lagarde, F., "Thoughts on the Reunion Landing" (trans. by Gordon Creighton), *Flying Saucer Review*, 5-6/79; Hall, Richard, *The UFO Evidence, Volume 2*, p. 18-19, 382, 490; Spencer, John, *The UFO Encyclopedia*, p. 276.
63. Hall, Richard, *The UFO Evidence, Volume 2*, p. 19, 203, 219-221.
64. Haines, Richard F., Ph. D. *CE-5: Close Encounters of the Fifth Kind, 242 Case Files Exposing Alien Contact.* (Sourcebooks, Inc., 1999), p. 109.
65. Hall, Richard, *The UFO Evidence, Volume 2*, p. 19, 45-46, 175.
66. U.S. Department of State Telegram; 07 March 1975; From: Embassy Algiers; To: SecState Wash DC; Subject: "Unidentified Flying Objects Over Algeria."
67. Connelly, Dwight, "Landing reported in N. Carolina," *Skylook*, May 1975; Hall, Richard, *The UFO Evidence, Volume 2*, p. 19, 347-348.
68. "UFOs Escort Mexican Aircraft," *APRO Bulletin*, v24, n2, 8/75; Phillips, Ted, "Several Possible Traces Reported in 1975," *Skylook*, 12/75; Gribble, Bob, "Looking Back," *MUFON UFO Journal*, 5/90; Hall, Richard, *The UFO Evidence Volume 2*, p. 19, 133-134, 461-462; Hall, Richard, *Uninvited Guests*, p. 36, 280-281.
69. *Skylook*, February 1976, Hall, Richard, *The UFO Evidence, Volume 2*, p. 19, 461-462, 490.
70. Clark, Jerome, "Carlos De Los Santos and the Men in Black," *Flying Saucer Review*, v. 24, no. 4, 1/79.
71. Redfern, Nicholas, *A Covert Agenda*, p. 128-129.
72. Anonymous to Maj. Colman VonKevickzy, 3 November 1976. NATO Headquarters, Bruxelles, Belgium; Haines, Richard F., Ph. D. *CE-5: Close Encounters of the Fifth Kind*, p. 225-226

73. "California Pilot Encounters UFO," *Skylook*, 2/76

74. Matthews, Tim, letter to *Filer's Files*, 6/13/98; "The Aereon Hypothesis," National Institute for Discovery Science, *http://www.nidsci.org/news/il_aereon.php*; and Easton, James, "Triangular Craft ½" February 2, 1995 on Skunk-Works-Digest Mailing List *http://www.netwrx1.com/skunk-works/v05.n196*; Wright, Susan, *UFO Headquarters*, p. 134-145, 140; and Dolan, Richard M., "What Are The Triangles?" *http://keyholepublishing.com*.

75. Sweetman, Bill. *Northrop B-2 Stealth Bomber*, (Motorbooks International, 1992), p. 18; Sweetman, Bill, *Stealth Aircraft: Secrets of Future Airpower*, (Motorbooks International, 1986), p. 28.

76. Sweetman, Bill. *Northrop B-2 Stealth Bomber*, p. 11; Sweetman, Bill, *Stealth Aircraft: Secrets of Future Airpower*, p. 28-30, 59; Wright, Susan, *UFO Headquarters*, p. 133.

77. Sweetman, Bill. *Stealth Aircraft: Secrets of Future Airpower*, p. 63-64; Sweetman, Bill. *Northrop B-2 Stealth Bomber*, p. 15; Cook, Nick, *The Hunt for Zero Point*, p. 116; Boyne, Walter J., *Beyond the Wild Blue: A History of the United States Air Force, 1947-1997*, p. 405.

78. Sweetman, Bill. *Northrop B-2 Stealth Bomber*, p. 14-15, 38; Sweetman, Bill, *Stealth Aircraft: Secrets of Future Airpower*, p. 20.

79. Boyne, Walter J., *Beyond the Wild Blue*, p. 403-404.

80. Boyne, Walter J., *Beyond the Wild Blue*, p. 196.

81. Milton, Richard, "The Royal Institution is Not Amused," http://www.alternativescience.com/eric-laithwaite.htm, see also Cook, Nick, *The Hunt for Zero Point*, p. 83.

82. Rumsfeld, Donald H., U.S. Secretary of Defense, "DOD Acquisition and Logistics Excellence Week Kickoff – Bureaucracy to Battlefield," Remarks delivered at The Pentagon, Monday, September 10, 2001, *http://www.defenselink.mil/speeches/2001/s20010910-secdef.html*.

83. "The War On Waste," CBS News, Jan. 29, 2002; *http://www.cbsnews.com/stories/2002/01/29/eveningnews/main325985.shtml*

84. Hunt, Linda, *Secret Agenda: The United States Government, Nazi Scientists, and Project Paperclip*. St. Martin's Press, 1991.

85. Vesco, Renato, *Intercettateli Senza Sparare*, U. Mursia & Co., Milan, Italy, 1968. English translation *Intercept – But Don't Shoot*, Grove Press, Inc., 1971. Republished as *Intercept UFO: The True Story of the Flying Saucers*, Pinnacle Books, Inc., 1974.

86. Vesco, Renato, *Intercept UFO*, p. 295.

87. Vesco, Renato & Childress, David Hatcher, *Man-Made UFOs 1944-1994: 50 Years of Suppression*, Adventures Unlimited Press, 1994.

88. Cook, Nick, *The Hunt for Zero Point: Inside the Classified World of Antigravity Technology*, Broadway Books, 2002., p. 209.

89. Cook, Nick, *The Hunt for Zero Point*, p. 46, 53.

90. Cook, Nick, *The Hunt for Zero Point*, p. 205-220.

91. Cook, Nick, *The Hunt for Zero Point*, p. 182-184; 229-234.

92. "Director's Message," *Skylook*, June 1975.

93. Druffel, Ann, "CIA Declassified Robertson Panel Report," *Skylook*, 5/75.

94. Wright, Susan, *UFO Headquarters*, p. 66-67; Zechel, W. Todd, "Report on Air Force and CIA UFO Research Programs," *MUFON UFO Journal*, 9/76.

95. Goldwater, Barry, Letter to Shlomo Arnon, March 28, 1975, See CUFON: Verified Documents Directory; http://www.cufon.org/cufon/foia_005.htm

96. Smith, W. B., Canadian Department of Transport Memo, November 21, 1950.

97. Clark, Jerome & Coleman, Loren, *The Unidentified: Notes Toward Solving the UFO Mystery*, Warner Paperback Library, 1975; Clark, Jerome, *The UFO Book*, p. 497-498.

98. Hall, Richard, "Recapping and Commenting," *Skylook*, 9/75.

99. Klass, Philip J., *UFOs Explained*, Random House, 1974; Friedman, Stanton T., "Klass Book Unscientific," *Skylook*, 9/75.

100. McKay, Henry H., "UFO, Humanoid Reported in Ontario," *Skylook*, 10/75.

101. "Fort Smith UFO Meeting Expanding," *Skylook*, 8/75.

102. *Skylook*, 12/75

103. Thomas, Gordon, *Journey Into Madness, The True Story of Secret CIA Mind Control and Medical Abuse* (Bantam, 1989), p. 276.

104. Schnabel, Jim, *Remote Viewers: The Secret History of America's Psychic Spies* (Dell, 1997), p. 97.

105. Swann, Ingo, *Penetration: The Question of Extraterrestrial and Human Telepathy* (Ingo Swann Books, 1998), p 19-23. The specific factors are: the existence of a hydrogen mantle; storms and wind (of the dimensions and unexpected intensities Swann described); something like a tornado (confirmed as strong rotating cyclones); high infrared reading; temperature inversion; cloud color and configuration; dominant orange color; water/ice crystals in atmosphere; crystal bands reflecting radio probes; magnetic and electromagnetic auroras, e.g. rainbows; a planetary ring inside the atmosphere (and it is indeed inside the crystallized atmospheric layers); liquid composition (hydrogen in liquid form). The single non-confirmed remote viewing was of mountains and a solid core.

106. Schnabel, Jim, *Remote Viewers: The Secret History of America's Psychic Spies*, p. 113.

107. Schnabel, Jim, *Remote Viewers: The Secret History of America's Psychic Spies*, p. 148-151
108. Frost, Cassandra, "Remote Viewing Underground Bases," *Soul Travel Magazine*, 2005. See http://www.soultravel.nu/2005/1127-UFO-Bases/index.shtml. See also Schnabel, Jim, *Remote Viewers*, p. 118.
109. Frost, Cassandra, "Remote Viewing Underground Bases," *Soul Travel Magazine*, 2005. See http://-www.soultravel.nu/2005/1127-UFO-Bases/index.shtml
110. Swann, Ingo, *Penetration*, p. 23-61.
111. Schnabel, Jim, *Remote Viewers*, p. 213.
112. "Church Committee," Wikipedia entry. http://en.wikipedia.org/wiki/Church_Committee
113. Burnham, David, *The Rise of the Computer State*. Foreword by Walter Cronkite. (New York: Random House, 1983), pp. 124, 130, 206.
114. Bamford, James, *Body of Secrets*, p. 435-441.
115. *Filer's Files*, 4/30/98
116. Central Intelligence Agency, Domestic Collection Division Foreign Intelligence Report. Subject: international Congress of Space Medicine. January 29, 1976.
117. "Canadian Photo Case," *APRO Bulletin*, v24, n4, 10/75.
118. Phillips, Ted, "Several Possible Traces Reported in 1975," *Skylook*, 12/75.
119. Hall, Richard, "Southern Africa Reports Several UFO Sightings," *Skylook*, 10/75.
120. Hall, Richard, *The UFO Evidence, Volume II*, p. 19, 493-494.
121. Hall, Richard, *Uninvited Guests*, p. 40-41, 281-282.

Chapter 2 - Intruder Alert, 1975-1976

1. Linda Moulton Howe reported that since the 1960s, mutilation cases have been documented in the following countries: Canada, United States, Mexico, Central America, South America, Australia, the Canary Islands off the coast of Africa, parts of Europe and Japan. See Howe, Linda Moulton, *Glimpses of Other Realities, Volume One*, p. 95. See also Greenwood and Fawcett, *Clear Intent*, p. 99-100; Howe, Linda Moulton, *Strange Harvest*, p. 107; Vallee, Jacques, *Messengers of Deception*, p. 164, 168; Pope, Nick, *Open Skies, Closed Minds For the First Time, a Government UFO Expert Speaks Out* (Dell, 1998), p. 127.
2. Howe, Linda Moulton, *Glimpses of Other Realities, Volume One*, page 100; Howe, *Strange Harvest*, p. 17, 412; also, Howe, Linda Moulton, private correspondence with the author, June 2009.
3. Vallee, Jacques, *Messengers of Deception*, p. 164; Adams, Tom, *Mysterious Helicopters*, 1993, cited in Howe, Linda Moulton, *Glimpses of Other Realities, Volume One*, p. 149.
4. Howe, Linda Moulton, *Alien Harvest*, p. 18; Howe, Linda Moulton, *Glimpses of Other Realities, Volume One*, p. 96.
5. Adams, Thomas R., *The Choppers . . . and the Choppers: Mystery Helicopters and Animal Mutilations* (Project Sigma, Paris, TX, 1978), p. 6-21; Keith, Jim, *Black Helicopters Over America* (IllumiNet Press, Lilburn, Ga., 1994), pages 20-27.
6. Vallee, Jacques, *Messengers of Deception*, p. 168; Howe, Linda Moulton, *Strange Harvest*, p. 21-22.
7. Adams, *Mysterious Helicopters*, 1993, cited in Howe, Linda Moulton, *Glimpses of Other Realities, Volume One*, p. 149.
8. Vallee, Jacques, *Messengers of Deception*, p. 164.
9. Vallee, Jacques, *Messengers of Deception*, p. 174.
10. Interview with Gabriel Valdez, conducted by the author, June 23, 2006.
11. Adams, Tom, *Mysterious Helicopters*, 1993, cited in Howe, Linda Moulton, *Glimpses of Other Realities, Volume One*, p. 149-150.
12. "New Abduction Cases," *APRO Bulletin*, v24, n3, 9/75; Lorenzen, L.J., "The Moody Case," *APRO Bulletin*, v24, n12, 6/76; Lorenzen, L.J., "The Moody Case: Conclusion," *APRO Bulletin*, v25, n1, 7/76; Lorenzen, Coral and Jim, *Abducted! Confrontations with Beings from Outer Space* (Berkeley Medallion Books, 1977), p. 38-51.
13. "Woman Records Abduction, Examination," *Skylook*, 3/76; Lorenzen, Coral & Jim, *Abducted! Confrontations with Beings from Outer Space*, p. 52-69.
14. Fawcett, Lawrence & Greenwood, Barry, *Clear Intent*, p. 111.
15. Howe, Linda Moulton, *Alien Harvest*, p. 22.
16. Vallee, Jacques, *Messengers of Deception*, p. 172.
17. Howe, Linda Moulton, *Alien Harvest*, p. 13.
18. Druffel, Ann, "California Report: The Mystery Helicopters," *Skylook*, 2/76.
19. Gribble, Bob, "Looking Back," *MUFON UFO Journal*, 8/90.
20. Hansen, Terry, *The Missing Times*, p. 16-17, 25.
21. Fawcett, Lawrence & Greenwood, Barry, *Clear Intent*, p. 34-37.
22. Fawcett, Lawrence & Greenwood, Barry, *Clear Intent*, p. 34, 100-102.
23. Fawcett, Lawrence & Greenwood, Barry, *Clear Intent*, p. 101.

24. Fawcett, Lawrence & Greenwood, Barry, *Clear Intent*, p. 32-37.
25. Fawcett, Lawrence & Greenwood, Barry, *Clear Intent*, p. 33-34, 36;Hansen, Terry, *The Missing Times*, p. 25-30; and Wolverton, Keith, *Mystery Stalks the Prairie*, p. 64-65.
26. Ridge, Francis, "The Night NORAD Went on Top Alert," *MUFON UFO Journal*, 2/84.
27. Memo, U.S. National Military Command Center, Defense Message Center, October 29, 1975; Fawcett, Lawrence & Greenwood, Barry, *Clear Intent*, p. 16-26.
28. Fawcett, Lawrence & Greenwood, Barry, *Clear Intent*, p. 21-22.
29. Fawcett, Lawrence & Greenwood, Barry, *Clear Intent*, p. 21-22.
30. Fawcett, Lawrence & Greenwood, Barry, *Clear Intent*, p. 24.
31. Hansen, Terry, *The Missing Times*, p. 42
32. Fawcett, Lawrence & Greenwood, Barry, *Clear Intent*, p. 16-18; Hall, Richard, *UFO Evidence, Volume 2*, p. 20, 88-89
33. Fawcett, Lawrence & Greenwood, Barry, *Clear Intent*, p. 24-25.
34. Lorenzen, Coral and Jim, *Abducted! Confrontations with Beings from Outer Space*, Berkley Medallion Books, 1977, p. 70-79; Fawcett, Lawrence & Greenwood, Barry, *Clear Intent*, p. 25-26.
35. Fawcett, Lawrence and Greenwood, Barry, *Clear Intent*, p. 41-46.
36. Persinos, John, "Quiet Technology: The Silent Treatment" *Aviation Today*, April 2002.
37. *Jane's Pocket Book of Helicopters*, p. 139; see also http://www.boeing.com/companyoffices/history/mdc/ah-64.htm and http://www.helis.com/70s/h_h64.php
38. Fawcett, Lawrence & Greenwood, Barry, *Clear Intent*, p. 102; Phillips, Ted, "Several Possible Traces Reported in 1975," *Skylook*, 12/75.
39. Files from the Office of the Assistant Secretary of Defense, Fawcett, Lawrence & Greenwood, Barry, *Clear Intent*, p. 48-50.
40. Fawcett, Lawrence & Greenwood, Barry, *Clear Intent*, p. 51-52.
41. Fawcett, Lawrence & Greenwood, Barry, *Clear Intent*, p. 30-36.
42. "24 NORAD Region Senior Director Log, November 1975," Berliner, Don, *UFO Briefing Document*, p. 90; Fawcett, Lawrence & Greenwood, Barry, *Clear Intent*, p. 48; Hansen, Terry, *The Missing Times*, p. 26.
43. CINSAC Offutt AFB message, "Subject: Defense Against Helicopter Assault," November 10, 1975.
44. Fawcett, Lawrence & Greenwood, Barry, *Clear Intent*, p. 34-35.
45. Official U.S. Air Force Report, NORAD, November 11, 1975. See also Fawcett, Lawrence & Greenwood, Barry, *Clear Intent*, p. 47-51; Good, Timothy, *Above Top Secret*, p. 202-203; Hall, Richard, *The UFO Evidence, Volume 2*, p. 20, 92-94.
46. Gribble, Bob, "Looking Back," *MUFON UFO Journal*, 11/90; Pratt, Bob, "Verdict on UFO Cover-Up: Guilty," *MUFON UFO Journal*, 10/83.
47. Gribble, Bob, "Looking Back," *MUFON UFO Journal*, 11/90; Pratt, Bob, "Verdict on UFO Cover-Up: Guilty," *MUFON UFO Journal*, 10/83.
48. Fawcett, Lawrence & Greenwood, Barry, *Clear Intent*, p. 50-51; Wright, Susan, *UFO Headquarters*, p. 72.
49. Fawcett, Lawrence & Greenwood, Barry, *Clear Intent*, p. 22-46.
50. Fawcett, Lawrence & Greenwood, Barry, *Clear Intent*, p. 37; Hansen, Terry, *The Missing Times*, p. 26, 35.
51. Fawcett, Lawrence & Greenwood, Barry, *Clear Intent*, p. 36, 103; Hansen, Terry, *The Missing Times*, p. 26
52. NMCC memorandum. Subject: Requests for Temperature Inversion Analysis, November 13, 1975; see also *Clear Intent*, p. 6-7.
53. Fawcett, Lawrence & Greenwood, Barry, *Clear Intent*, p. 31.
54. Sigismond, Richard, "Lonely Road, Black Night," *International UFO Reporter*, 5-6/84.
55. Letter to Brian Vike, Director HBCC UFO Research; http://groups.yahoo.com/group/HBCC_UFO_Newsletter/; see also *Filer's Files*, 7/21/04.
56. Letter to Brian Vike, Director HBCC UFO Research; http://groups.yahoo.com/group/HBCC_UFO_Newsletter/
57. Letter to Brian Vike, Director HBCC UFO Research; http://www.hbccufo.com
58. The literature on this case is vast. On the Internet, the reader is directed to the balanced description in Wikipedia, at http://en.wikipedia.org/wiki/Travis_Walton. In addition, Jerome Clark's account in *The UFO Book*, p. 627-653, is possibly the best sympathetic description of the case. The primary skeptical accounts are Philip J. Klass, "The Travis Walton Abduction," *The MUFON UFO Journal*, July and August 1976; Philip J. Klass, *UFOs: The Public Deceived* (Prometheus Books, 1983); and "The Klass Files" in *The Skeptics UFO Newsletter*, available at http://www.csicop.org/klassfiles/SUN-50.html. Robert Schaeffer's *The UFO Verdict: Examining the Evidence* (Prometheus Books, 1986, p. 19-20) also offers a brief description of the Walton case from the skeptical viewpoint. Travis Walton tells his own story in *Fire in the Sky: The Walton Experience* (Marlowe and Company, 1996). See also "The Travis Walton Case," *APRO Bulletin*, v24, n5, 11/75; and "The Walton-Klass Controversy," *APRO Bulletin*, v25, n1, 7/76.

59. Price, Goeff, "The Travis Walton UFO Abduction Case," http://www.cohenufo.org/Geoff%20Price% 20Rprt%20on%20Walton%20Case.htm
60. "Alleged Arizona Conduction Case Study," *Skylook*, 12/75.
61. Clark, Jerome, *The UFO Book*, p. 649.
62. See also "Travis Walton case continues: APRO, NICAP, GSW Reports Disagree," *Skylook*, 2/76; "NICAP Report Erred in Walton Case," *Skylook*, 3/76; "Waltons Pass Polygraph Exam," *Skylook*, 3/76; "Walton Explains Controversies," Skylook, 4/76.
63. Hall, Richard, "Recapping and Commenting," *Skylook*, 4/76.
64. "The Edge of Reality," *Skylook*, 4/76; Editor's Column, *Skylook*, 4/76.
65. "MUFON Deputy Director resigns: Schuessler says UFO info unavailable," *Skylook*, 2/76; Editor's Column, *Skylook*, 3/76.
66. Editor's Column, *Skylook*, 5/76
67. Dornbos, Nancy (ed.), *Proceedings of the 1976 CUFOS Conference*, Center for UFO Studies, 1976; "Hynek's Conference Set for April 30-May 1," *Skylook*, 2/76; "In Others Words," *MUFON UFO Journal,* 1/77.
68. Hynek, J. Allen, "Estimate of the Situtation," *International UFO Reporter*, 11/76.
69. Zechel, W. Todd, "Report on Air Force and CIA UFO research programs," *MUFON UFO Journal*, 9/76; February 20, 1976 NSA letter to Robert Todd; Fawcett and Greenwood, *Clear Intent*, p. 46, 181; Good, Timothy, *Above Top Secret*, p. 416.
70. Zechel, W. Todd, "Report on Air Force and CIA UFO research programs," *MUFON UFO Journal*, 9/76.
71. Stringfield, Leonard, "The Stringfield Report," *Skylook*, 3/76.
72. Dononvan, Roberta & Wolverton, Keith, *Mystery Stalks the Prarie*, T.H.A.R. Institute, Raynesford, Montana, 1976.
73. Weiner, Tim, *Blank Check: The Pentagon's Black Budget*, Grand Central Publishing, 1990.
74. Cameron, Grant, http://presidentialufo.com
75. Cameron, Grant, http://presidentialufo.com; Berliner, Don, *UFO Briefing Document*, p. 161; "The Carter Sighting," *APRO Bulletin*, v25, n5, 11/76.
76. "From the Editor," *MUFON UFO Journal*, 10/76; Hall, Richard, *The UFO Evidence, Vol. 2*, p. 20.
77. NMCC Memorandum for the Record. Subject: Report of UFO - Cannon AFB NM. Reference: AFOC Phonecon 21055 EST Jan 76.
78. "Clovis, NM, sightings,' *Skylook*, 2/76; Stanford, Ray, "Clovis, NM, 'UFO' was unfocused Saturn," *Skylook*, 5/76.
79. Vike, Brian, Director HBCC UFO Research, http://www.hbccufo.org.
80. Fawcett, Lawrence & Greenwood, Barry, *Clear Intent*, p. 52; NMCC Memorandum for the Record, Subject: Unidentified Flying Object Sighting, 31 January 1976.
81. CIA Directorate of Operations, Domestic Collection Division Foreign Intelligence Information Report. Subject: International Congress of Space Medicine, 29 January 1976.
82. CIA Domestic Collections Division 14 April 1976. Cite: DCD / XXXX To: Priority Administration Attention: XXX Subject: Case XXX UFO Research.
83. Fawcett, Lawrence & Greenwood, Barry, *Clear Intent*, p. 145. Good put this date at 7-14-76, cf. Good, Timothy, *Above Top Secret*, p. 360-361.
84. Good, Timothy, *Above Top Secret*, p. 360.
85. Leonard, George, *Somebody Else is on the Moon* (Pocket Books, 1977); Swann, Ingo, *Penetration*, p. 62-70; http://www.abovetopsecret.com/forum/thread198430/pg1
86. Saccheri, Vito, "The NASA Moon Photos: My Story of Dealing with NASA in the 1970's, Literary Freeware Foundation http://www.sacred-texts.com/ufo/moon.htm; "Witness Says NASA Photos Show Structures on Moon," *CNI*, June 26, 1995. There was some confusion over where the transmission were switched to, as Saccheri had originally understood Czarnick to mean they were sent directly to CIA headquarters in Langley, Virginia (which is what was originally published in CNI News. A correction was issued and is available at *http://www.anomalies.net/archive/ cni-news/ CNI.0339.html*
87. NMCC Memorandum for the Record. Subject: Reports of Unidentified Flying Objects (UFOs). 30 July 1976.
88. New Mexico State Police report, December 15, 1976, cited in Redfern, Nicholas, *Covert Agenda*, p. 288-289.
89. Fowler, Raymond E. *The Allagash Abductions*, Tigard, Oregon, Wild Flower Press, 1993; Raymond E. Fowler, "The Allagash Abductions," *MUFON UFO Journal*, 4/93; Booth, Billy, "1976 - The Allagash Abductions", in http://ufos.about.com/od/aliensalienabduction/p/allagash.htm
90. Bourdais, Gildas, "Summary of Some Cases Noted in the Cometa Report," *MUFON UFO Journal*, 9/99.
91. Hall, Richard, *UFO Evidence, Volume 2*, p. 122.
92. *Mayoria*, 3/17/76, Buenos Aires, translated by Jane Thomas, submitted to the *MUFON UFO Journal* by Richard Hall. "UFO's Tracked on Radar and Venezuelan Airport," *MUFON UFO Journal*, 1/77.

93. See, for instance, "Canary Islands UFOs in the 70s: Space Experts Confirm They Were Missiles," at http://www.anomalia.org/canen.htm

94. "Deposition No. B-07 of the Captain of Corvette in the Spanish Air Force file," English translation by Gordon Creighton, *Flying Saucer Review*, Vol. 23, No. 3, 1977; *National Enquirer*, September 28, 1976; Gribble, Bob, "Looking Back," *MUFON UFO Journal*, 6/91; Berliner, Donald, *UFO Briefing Document*, p. 91-93; 178-179; Good, Timothy, *Above Top Secret*, p. 153-154; Haines, Richard F., Ph. D. *CE-5: Close Encounters of the Fifth Kind*, p. 112-113.

95. Benétez, J.J., *La Gaceta del Norte*, Bilbao, Spain, June 27, 1976; Good, Timothy, *Above Top Secret*, p. 152.

96. Verkaik, Robert, "UK's Ministry Of Defense UFO Files Released," *The Independent* (UK), January 22, 2005.

97. Fawcett, Lawrence & Greenwood, Barry, *Clear Intent*, p. 80-81.

98. This case has been widely discussed. See CUFON: Verified Documents Directory; http://www.cufon.org/; Berliner, Don, *UFO Briefing Document*, p. 98-104; Clark, Jerome, *The UFO Encyclopedia*, Vol. 3, p. 267-269; Clark, Jerome, *The UFO Book*, p. 309-313, Good, Timothy, *Above Top Secret*, p. 318-321; Randles, Jenny, *The UFO Conspiracy*, p. 72-75; Hall, Richard, *The UFO Evidence, V2*, p. 20, 94-95; Redfern, Nicholas, *A Covert Agenda*, p. 280-282; Haines, Richard F., Ph. D. *CE-5: Close Encounters of the Fifth Kind*, p. 175, 228-232; Shields, Captain Henry S., HQ USAFE/INOMP, "Now You See It, Now You Don't," Declassified from NSA files, 4 Dec 1981; "UFO-Jets in Chase Over Tehran," *APRO Bulletin*, v25, n3, 9/76; as well as innumerable additional sources on the World Wide Web.

99. Petrozian, transcript of interview with Hosain Perouzi, 12/22/76, filed with the Fund for UFO Research; cited in Berliner, Don, *UFO Briefing Document*, p. 100.

100. Greenwood, Barry & Fawcett, Lawrence, *Clear Intent*, p. 83-85.

101. Pratt, Bob, *UFO Danger Zone, Terror and Death in Brazil – Where Next?* Foreword by Jacques Vallee (Horus House Press,1996), p. 144.

102. http://vista.streamguys.com/strieber/102205.wma; *Filer's Files*, 11/2/05.

103. Defense Information Report Evaluation, DIA, October 12, 1976.

104. Regehr, Ronald S., *How to Build a $125 Million UFO Detector*, Ronald S. Regehr Research/Investigations, 1998, p. 83; Stacy, Dennis & Hughe, Patrick, "Cosmic Conspiracy: Six Decades of Government UFO Cover-Ups, Part Five," *Omni*, 8/94; *Filer's Files*, 4/9/98.

105. Azhazha, Vladimir G., "Are We Alone in the Universe?" *MUFON UFO Journal*, 7/78.

106. Fawcett, Lawrence & Greenwood, Barry, *Clear Intent*, p. 86-89; Clark, Jerome, *The UFO Encyclopedia, Vol. 3*, p. 328-330; Clark, Jerome, *The UFO Book*, p. 404-406.

107. Hall, Richard, *The UFO Evidence, Vol. 2*, p. 20, 134.

Chapter 3 - Great Expectations, 1977-1978

1. Shoup, Laurence H., "Jimmy Carter and the Trilateralists: Presidential Roots," excerpted from *Trilateralism*, edited Holly Sklar, South End Press, 1980. See also http://www.thirdworldtraveler.com/Trilateralism/JimmyCarter_Trilat.html

2. Harr & Johnson, *The Rockefeller Conscience; An American Family in Public and in Private*, 1991, p. 217.

3. Marrs, Jim, *Rule by Secrecy*, p. 53

4. Allen, Gary, *The Rockefeller File* ('76 Press, 1976), p. 28.

5. Banyan, Will, "Trilateralism and the Legacy of David Rockefeller," © 2002, 2003, Extracted from *Nexus Magazine*, Volume 11, Number 1 (December-January 2004), http://www.nexusmagazine.com/articles/rockefeller.5.html.

6. Brzezinski, Zbigniew, *Between Two Ages: America's Role in the Technetronic Era*, (The Viking Press, 1970), p. 293, 295-297, 308.

7. Banyan, Will, "Trilateralism and the Legacy of David Rockefeller," © 2002, 2003, Extracted from *Nexus Magazine*, Volume 11, Number 1 (December-January 2004), http://www.nexusmagazine.com/articles/rockefeller.5.html.

8. Shoup, Laurence H., "Jimmy Carter and the Trilateralists: Presidential Roots," from *Trilateralism*, edited by Holly Sklar, South End Press, 1980.

9. Banyan, Will, "Trilateralism and the Legacy of David Rockefeller," © 2002, 2003, Extracted from *Nexus Magazine*, Volume 11, Number 1 (December-January 2004), http://www.nexusmagazine.com/articles/rockefeller.5.html.

10. Helgerson, John, L., *CIA Briefings of Presidential Candidates*, "Chapter Five: In-Depth Discussions with Carter," Center for the Study of Intelligence, 1996. *https://www.cia.gov/library/center-for-the-study-of-intelligence/csi-publications/books-and-monographs/cia-briefings-of-presidential-candidates/cia-8.htm*

11. Sheehan, Daniel, statement at X-Conference "Clinton-Carter Panel," September 2007, Gaithersburg, MD; see also Cameron, Grant, "President Carter, Daniel Sheehan, and Donald Menzel: The Congressional Research Service UFO Studies for President Jimmy Carter," at Presidential UFO, *http://www.presidentialufo.com/marcia_smith_story.htm*.

12. Stanton Friedman, email correspondence with the author, August 23, 2006; Cameron, Grant, http://presidentialufo.com

13. Susan Wright, *UFO Headquarters*, p. 67.

14. Cannon, Martin, "Mind Control and the American Government," *Lobster* June 1993, #23.

15. Cameron, Grant, http://presidentialufo.com. Interestingly, Press recorded geophysical events, not only on the Earth's surface, but also on the Moon and other planets. He also sat on the board at Rockefeller University. See "Dr. Frank Press" entry in *Society of Exploration Geophysicists Virtual Geoscience Center* at http://www.mssu.edu/SEG-VM/bio_dr__frank_press.html.

16. Sturrock, Peter A., *Report on a Survey of the Membership of the American Astronomical Society Concerning the UFO Problem*, Stanford University, Institute for Plasma Research, 1977; *MUFON UFO Journal*, February 1977.

17. Bryant, Larry, *UFO Politics at the White House: Citizens Rally 'round Jimmy Carter's Promise,* (The Invisible College Press, LLC, 2001), Cameron, Grant, http://presidentialufo.com

18. Cameron, Grant, http://presidentialufo.com

19. Cameron, Grant, http://presidentialufo.com

20. Maccabee, Bruce S., "UFO Related Information from the FBI File, Part One," *MUFON UFO Journal*, 10/77.

21. "Joint Army-Navy-Air Force Publication 146(E)" (JANAP 146E) (CIRVIS/MERINT), May 17, 1977, as released on February 28, 1994 by the Assistant to the Secretary of Defense. See CUFON: Verified Documents Directory, *http://www.cufon.org/cufon/janp1462.htm*

22. "International Ufology Conference to be held in Acapulco,: *MUFON UFO Journal*, 11/76; Hauck, William, "The Acapulco Conference," *MUFON UFO Journal*, 4/77.

23. "Directors Message," *MUFON UFO Journal*, 4/78.

24. For two fairly detailed descriptions of the following account, see Grant Cameron's *Presidential UFO Website* at http://presidentialufo.com; and *Filer's Files*, 6/25/00. For a sample of Tibetan writing, see *http://www.ancientscripts.com/tibetan.html*.

25. Alfred Webre, correspondence with the author; see also Greer, Steven, *Disclosure*, p. 441-443.

26. Cameron, Grant, http://presidentialufo.com

27. The document "Executive Correspondence: Project Aquarius" is available on the web at http://www.think-aboutit.com/ufo/project_aquarius.htm

28. Shirley MacLaine, telephone interview with Richard Dolan; Cameron, Grant, http://presidentialufo.com

29. Cameron, Grant, http://presidentialufo.com

30. OASD FOIA files; Good, Timothy, *Above Top Secret*, p. 368-369; Cameron, Grant, http://presidentialufo.com.

31. Cameron, Grant, http://presidentialufo.com

32. Hall, Richard, *The UFO Evidence, Volume 2*, p. 82-83.

32. Stringfield, Leonard, "Retrievals of the Third Kind, Part 2," *MUFON UFO Journal*, 8/87; Redfern, Nicholas, *A Covert Agenda*, p. 262.

33. Stringfield, Leonard, "Retrievals of the Third Kind, Part 2," *MUFON UFO Journal*, 8/78.

34. Stringfield, Leonard, "Retrievals of the Third Kind," *MUFON UFO Journal*, 7/78.

35. Cameron, Grant, http://presidentialufo.com

36. Good, Timothy, *Above Top Secret*, p. 369; Cameron, Grant, http://presidentialufo.com

37. Greer, Steven, *Disclosure*, p. 441-446.

38. Alfred Webre, communication with the author.

39. Peter Schwarz, communication with the author.

40. 1997 conversation by Gairy with journalist W.E. Gutnam, cited in Cameron, Grant, http://presidentialufo.com

41. *MUFON UFO Journal*, 11/77.

42. Cameron, Grant, http://presidentialufo.com

43. Cameron, Grant, http://presidentialufo.com

44. Berliner, Donald, *UFO Briefing Document*, p. 224-225; Stringfield, Leonard H. "My Advisory Role for Grenada's UFO Mission at the United Nations," *The MUFON UFO Journal,* 11/77.

45. Andrus, Walt, "NASA Assigned UFO Responsibility," *MUFON UFO Journal*, 10/77.

46. OASD files, Fawcett and Greenwood, *Clear Intent*, p. 193.

47. Andrus, Walt, "NASA Assigned UFO Responsibility, *MUFON UFO Journal*, 10/77.

48. Fawcett and Greenwood, *Clear Intent*, p. 23-24.

49. Hansen, Terry, *The Missing Times*, p. 232-239.

50. Fawcett and Greenwood, *Clear Intent*, p. 5-6; Hansen, Terry, *The Missing Times*, p. 33.

51. Hall, Richard, "Recapping and Commenting," *MUFON UFO Journal* 9/77.

52. "British government investigates UFOs, but ..." *MUFON UFO Journal*, 10/83.
53. Good, Timothy, *Above Top Secret*, p. 135-136; Spencer, John, *The UFO Encyclopedia*, p. 126; Hall, Richard, *The UFO Evidence, Volume 2*, p. 21.
54. Spencer, John, *The UFO Encyclopedia*, p. 180.
55. Good, Timothy, *Above Top Secret*, p. 430.
56. *El Tiempo*, Bogota, Colombia, Feb. 18, 1977; Haines, Richard F., Ph.D. *CE-5: Close Encounters of the Fifth Kind*, p. 115-116; Hall, Richard, *UFO Evidence, Volume 2*, p. 21, 135.
57. "UFO Followed Italian Jet," *London Daily Telegraph*, 1/10/80; "Italian Government Report," *MUFON UFO Journal*, 4/80.
58. Bourdais, Gildas, "Summary of Some Cases Noted in the COMETA Report," *MUFON UFO Journal*, 9/99; www.ufocasebook.com/cometa2.html
59. *International UFO Reporter*, 2/78; Hall, Richard, *Uninvited Guests*, p. 207.
60. Smith, Dr. Willy, "Unknown Intruder over Portugal," *International UFO Reporter*, 11-12/85; Good, Timothy, *Above Top Secret*, p. 154-156, 564.
61. Good, Timothy, *Above Top Secret*, p. 144.
62. Rowles, Jerry, Lt. Col. USAF Ret. "The Mystery of Aviano," *MUFON UFO Journal*, 2/96.
63. Derr, John S., "Quake light?" *MUFON UFO Journal*, 4/96.
64. Rowles, Gerald E. "Update on Aviano," *MUFON UFO Journal*, 11/98.
65. "Boulmer Reports of UFO Sightings Were Hushed Up," *Northumberland News Today*, 28 January 2005, http://www.northumberlandtoday.co.uk/
66. Dong, Paul & Stevens, Wendelle C., *UFOs over Modern China: A Survey of the Phenomenon*, Translated from Chinese by the Foreign Language Bureau of Peking, (UFO Photo Archives, Tucson, AZ, 1983), p. 93-94.
67. Dong, Paul, & Stevens, Wendelle, *UFOs over Modern China*, p. 117-118.
68. Dong, Paul & Stevens, Wendelle, *UFOs over Modern China*, p. 96; *China Report, Science and Technology* (CIA FOIA files).
69. Pratt, Bob & Luce, Cynthia, "Former Brazilian Intelligence Officer Relates Experiences," *MUFON UFO Journal*, 4/99; *Filer's Files*, 6/1/05; http://www.ufo.com.br/secrecy.php; see also "Colares UFO flap" from *Wikipedia, the free encyclopedia*.
70. Swann, Ingo, *Penetration*, p. 85-100.
71. "Italian Government Report," *MUFON UFO Journal* 4/80.
72. Redfern, Nicholas, *A Covert Agenda*, p. 131-133.
73. Good, Timothy, *Above Top Secret*, p. 115-116.
74. Redfern, Nicholas, *A Covert Agenda*, p. 133.
75. Hall, Richard, *UFO Evidence, Volume 2*, p. 21, 244; Gribble, Bob, "Pilot sightings and Radar Trackings, *MUFON UFO Journal*, 3/83.
76. Stonehill, Paul & Mantle, Philip, *The Soviet UFO Files*, p. 84-85; Pope, Nick. *Open Skies, Closed Minds. For the First Time, a Government UFO Expert Speaks Out* (Dell, 1998), p. 181.
77. Yu. V. Platov, B.A. Sokolov. "History of UFO State Research in the USSR." translated from *Vestnik Rossiiskoi Akademii Nauk*, V. 70, No. 6. 2000, pp. 507-515.
78. Vallee, Jacques. *UFO Chronicles in the Soviet Union: A Cosmic Samizdat* (Ballantine Books, 1992), p. 29
79. "Italian Government Report," *MUFON UFO Journal*, 4/80.
80. Good, Timothy, *Above Top Secret*, p. 146.
81. Gribble, Bob, "Pilot Sightings and Radar Trackings," *MUFON UFO Journal*, 3/83.
82. Gribble, Bob, "Pilot Sightings and Radar Trackings," *MUFON UFO Journal*, 3/83.
83. Gribble, Bob, "Pilot Sightings and Radar Trackings," *MUFON UFO Journal*, 3/83.
84. Gribble, Bob, "Pilot Sightings and Radar Trackings," *MUFON UFO Journal*, 3/83.
85. Andrus, Walter, ed. "Radar-Visual Case Involving Police Helicopter," *MUFON UFO Journal*, 12/77.
86. Hall, Richard, "Veteran Pilot Sites Daylight Disk," *MUFON UFO Journal*, 1/78; Hall, Richard, *The UFO Evidence*, Volume 2, p. 22, 136-138.
87. Stacy, Dennis, "The 1970s: Todd Zechel and the Freedom of Information Act. Project Open Book: Cosmic Conspiracy," *OMNI*, Vol. 16, No. 10, 8/94.
88. Fawcett, Lawrence & Greenwood, Barry, *Clear Intent*, p. 194.
89. Fawcett, Lawrence and Greenwood, Barry, *Clear Intent*, p. 6-7, 147.
90. Fawcett, Lawrence & Greenwood, Barry, *Clear Intent*, p. 7; Bruce Maccabee, *UFO FBI Connection: The Secret History of the Government's Cover-Up*, Llewellyn Publications, 2000.
91. Hall, Richard, "Lawsuit Filed Against CIA," *MUFON UFO Journal*, 5/78.
92. Zechel, W. Todd, "CAUS to File FOIA Lawsuit against the Air Force," *MUFON UFO Journal*, 8/78; Fawcett, Lawrence & Greenwood, Barry, *Clear Intent*, p. 192-193.
93. Fawcett, Lawrence & Greenwood, Barry, *Clear Intent*, p. 181.
94. Fawcett, Lawrence & Greenwood, Barry, *Clear Intent*, p. 198.

95. Berlitz, Charles & Moore, William, *The Roswell Incident*. Grosset & Dunlop, 1980; Friedman, Stanton T. & Berliner, Don, *Crash at Corona*, Paragon House, 1992; Stringfield, Leonard, "Retrievals of the Third Kind, Part Two," *MUFON UFO Journal*, 8/78.

96. Stringfield, Leonard, "Retrievals of the Third Kind, Part Two," *MUFON UFO Journal*, 8/78.

97. Stringfield, Leonard, "Crash Retrievals of the Third Kind, Part Two," *MUFON UFO Journal*, 8/78,

98. Greenawald, Walt, "The Nominal UFO Researcher," *MUFON UFO Journal*, 4/78.

99. Virgil Staff, "UFO Crash/Retrievals: A Critique of Greenwell's Critique," *MUFON UFO Journal*, 4/81.

100. Andrus, Walt, "The 1978 MUFON UFO Symposium," *MUFON UFO Journal*, 7/78; Stringfield, Leonard, "Retrievals of the Third Kind," *MUFON UFO Journal*, 7/78; Crain, T. Scott, Jr., "An MJ-12 Informant," *MUFON UFO Journal*, 1/90.

101. Hall, Richard, *Uninvited Guests*, p. 75-76.

102. "Canadian Gallup Poll," *Toronto Star*, March 22, 1978; Hall, Richard, *Uninvited Guests*, p. 221; Vallee, Jacques, *Messengers of Deception*, p. 228.

103. O'Toole, Thomas, "Astronaut Cooper Believes UFO Sightings No Joke," New *Orleans Times-Picayune*, 4/9/78.

104. Presidential Executive Order # 12065: "Classification and Declassification of National Security Information and Material." See "Appropriate Criteria for Classification of Historical Records: Balancing the Public's Right to Know with the Protection of Sensitive Information." http://www.denix.osd.mil/denix/Public/ES-Programs/Conservation/Legacy/Classify/paper1.html; "The Declassification Backlog of Historic Records: A Problem For Both the Department of Defense and All Those Who Seek a Better Understanding of the Cold War." United States Department of Defense Legacy Resource Management Program. Prepared in Cooperation with the Organization of American Historians December, 1994; Cameron, Grant, Presidential UFO, http://presidentialufo.com.

105. Good, Timothy, *Above Top Secret*, p. 327-328; Anonymous, "The Fund for CIA Research?"; Cameron, Grant, http://presidentialufo.com

106. Good, Timothy, *Above Top Secret*, p. 277; 379-380; Berliner, Don, *UFO Briefing Document*, p. 158-159, 225-227; *Filer's Files*, 3/21/01; Cameron, Grant, http://presidentialufo.com; "BBC On This Day," http://news.bbc.co.uk/onthisday/hi/dates/stories/march/13/newsid_2804000/2804259.stm

107. Fawcett and Greenwood, *Clear Intent*, p. 54-56.

108. Stringfield, Leonard & Hall, Richard, "Dix-McGuire Update," *MUFON UFO Journal*, 6/87; Hall, Richard, *The UFO Evidence, Volume 2*, p. 22, 97-98; Clark, Jerome, *The UFO Encyclopedia*, Vol. 3, p. 207-210.

109. Filer Interview in Greer, *Disclosure*, p. 284-288; "George Filer Interview," UFO Experiences, http://ufoexperiences.blogspot.com/2006_09_01_ufoexperiences_archive.html

110. "Fort Dix/McGuire AFB Investigation: Abstract," National Institute for Discovery Science, http://www.nidsci.org/news/mcguire_abstract.php

111. *Filer's Files*, 5/27/00.

112. Hall, Richard, *UFO Evidence, Volume 2*, p. 22, 348.

113. Gribble, Bob, "Pilot Sightings and Radar Trackings," *MUFON UFO Journal*, 3/83.

114. Fawcett, Lawrence & Greenwood, Barry, *Clear Intent*, p. 194-195.

115. U.S. Department of Defense Memo, JCS Message Center 051933Z Apr 78, "Booms, Bangs and Balls of Fire"; Fawcett, Lawrence & Greenwood, Barry, *Clear Intent*, p. 96-98; "Bell Island," from *Wikipedia, the free encyclopedia*, http://en.wikipedia.org/wiki/Bell_Island

116. "Flying Object Baffles Computer with Maneuvers in Florida Sky," *International Herald Tribune*, 5/18/78; Sheaffer, Robert, "Did a UFO Penetrate Restricted Airspace?" *Second Look*, 4/79; Klass, Philip J., "Klass on Radar," *Second Look*, 5/79; Hendry, Allen, "Hendry Responds to Sheaffer and Klass," *Second Look*, 10/79; Pratt, Bob, "Verdict on UFO Cover-Up: Guilty," *MUFON UFO Journal*, 10/83; Clark, Jerome, *The UFO Book*, p. 423-425; Hall, Richard, *The UFO Evidence, Volume II*, p. 22, 53.

117. Haines, Richard F., Ph. D. *CE-5: Close Encounters of the Fifth Kind*, p. 124-125; *International UFO Reporter* 3, No. 7 (July) 4-5.

118. Fawcett, Lawrence and Greenwood, Barry, *Clear Intent*, p. 74-75.

119. Gribble, Bob, "Pilot Sightings and Radar Trackings," *MUFON UFO Journal*, 8/83.

120. Nick Pope, for instance, suggested that the Spielberg movie was primarily responsible for the wave. See Pope, Nick, *Open Skies, Closed Minds*, p. 47-48. See also Hall, Richard, "From the Editor," *MUFON UFO Journal*, 4/78, and Hall, Richard, *The UFO Evidence, Volume II*, p. 22, 348-352, 491-492.

121. Rosales, Albert, "1978 Humanoid Reports," http://www.ufoinfo.com/humanoid/humanoid1978.shtml

122. Spencer, John, *The UFO Encyclopedia*, p. 13.

123. See also "UFO crash in Bolivia witnessed by thousands of people," at http://www.ufoevidence.org/cases/case635.htm

124. Fawcett, Lawrence & Greenwood, Barry, *Clear Intent*, p. 201-205.

125. Huneeus, J. Antonio, "A Chilean overview," *MUFON UFO Journal*, 6/86; Huneeus, J. Antonio, "A Historical Survey of UFO Cases in Chile," *MUFON 1987 International UFO Symposium Proceedings* (MUFON, 1987).

126. "Select Triangular UFO Cases (Bob Pratt files)," http://www.cohenufo.org/BPrattSelectTriCases.html

127. *OVNIvision Chile*, 12/26/02; *UFO Round Up*, V. 8, N. 2, 1/8/03; *Filer's Files*, 9/17/03.

128. Good, Timothy, *Above Top Secret*, p. 145-146.

129. GEPAN Report to the Scientific Committee (June, 1978, Vol 1, Chapter 4); "French Government UFO Study," *MUFON UFO Journal*, 9/78.

130. Pope, Nick. *Open Skies, Closed Minds*, Appendix 1; Redfern, Nicholas, *Covert Agenda*, p. 134.

131. Good, Timothy, *Above Top Secret*, p. 116-118; Spencer, John, *The UFO Encyclopedia*, p. 89.

132. Spencer, John, *The UFO Encyclopedia*, p. 122.

133. Fawcett, Lawrence & Greenwood, Barry, *Clear Intent*, p. 92-93

134. Good, Timothy, *Above Top Secret*, p. 146-147; Spencer, p. 96-97.

135. *Daily Mirror*, London, August 18, 1978; Good, Timothy, *Above Top Secret*, p. 72.

136. *Middlesex Chronicle*, September 15, 1978, cited in Good, Timothy, *Above Top Secret*, p. 72.

137. Toselli, Paolo & Russo, Edoardo, "Three Landings in Italy," *Flying Saucer Review*, 3/79; Pinotti, Roberto, "Landings, E.M. Effects and Entities at Torrita Di Siena," *Flying Saucer Review*, 11/79; Verga, Maurizio, "Another CEIII Report from Italy," *Flying Saucer Review*, 11/79; Hall, Richard, "The Italian UFO Wave of 1978," *MUFON UFO Journal*, 11/80; Hall, Richard, *Uninvited Guests*, p. 297; Hall, Richard, *UFO Evidence, Volume 2*, p. 23, 495-496.

138. Hall, Richard, *Uninvited Guests*, p. 299-300.

139. U.S. Defense Intelligence Agency file: DoD JCS message center 230800Z Jul 78. "UFO spotted over North of Teheran Iran," from Iranian newspaper source, July 19, 1978; Good, Timothy, *Above Top Secret*, p. 322; Fawcett, Lawrence & Greenwood, Barry, *Clear Intent*, p. 89.

140. Wilson, Jim, "Six Unexplainable Encounters: These UFO Sightings Continue to Defy Science and the Skeptics," *Popular Mechanics*, July 1998.

141. U.S. Defense Intelligence Agency file: DoD JCS message center 230800Z Jul 78; Good, Timothy, *Above Top Secret*, p. 321-322; Fawcett, Lawrence & Greenwood, Barry, *Clear Intent*, p. 89.

142. Wilson, Jim, "Six Unexplainable Encounters: These UFO Sightings Continue to Defy Science and the Skeptics," *Popular Mechanics*, July 1998.

143. U.S. Department of State Telegram, January 29, 1979, "'UFO' Sightings Cause Security Concern in Kuwait," From American Embassy Kuwait To Secretary of State, Washington, DC.; *Kuwait Times*, Nov. 16, 18, 1978; *Arab Times*, Nov. 23, 25, 1978; "UFOs in Arab Nations," *MUFON UFO Journal*, Jan-Feb, 1979; "UFOs Over Kuwait, *The APRO Bulletin*, January 1979; Fawcett, Lawrence & Greenwood, Barry, *Clear Intent*, p. 90-91.

144. Rubtsov, Vladimir V., "Soviet Ufology," *Fate Magazine*, December 2005.

145. Platov, Yu. V. & Sokolov, B.A., "History of UFO State Research in the USSR." translated from *Vestnik Rossiiskoi Akademii Nauk*, V. 70, No. 6. 2000, pp. 507-515.

146. Rubtsov, Vladimir V., "Soviet Ufology," *Fate Magazine*, December 2005.

147. Stonehill, Paul & Mantle, Philip, *Soviet UFO Files*, p. 43, 52.

148. Rybalko, Pyotyr N., "Bureaucratized Pseudoscience," Letter to the Editor, *RIAP Bulletin*, 2000, Vol. 6, No. 2-3, pp. 11-12.

149. Vallee, Jacques, *UFO Chronicles of the Soviet Union*, p. 27-29.

150. Spencer, John, *The UFO Encyclopedia*, p. 200-201; http://www.users.globalnet.co.uk/~hex/ufo/text/pages001-025/page06.html

151. Stonehill, Paul & Mantle, Phillip, *The Soviet UFO Files*, p. 73, 76.

152. Dong, Paul, *UFOs Over China*, 119-120; CIA FOIA files, China Report, Science and Technology; Good, Timothy, *Above Top Secret*, p. 213-214.

153. Dong, Paul, "Chinese UFO Research," *MUFON UFO Journal*, 1/81; Hausdorff, Hartwig, *The Chinese Roswell*, p. 149

154. Richard Haines, who studied the Valentich tapes in detail, pointed out that Valentich's strong Australian accent caused aviation officials to misinterpret his transmission to Melbourne to be, "It seems like it's stationary." Haines concluded that this interpretation was mistaken, and that Valentich in fact had said, "It seems like it's chasing me." See Haines, Richard F., Ph.D., *Melbourne Episode: Case Study of a Missing Pilot* (LDA Press, 1987), in particular the technical analysis in Chapter 8.

155. "Pilot disappears after reporting UFO," *MUFON UFO Journal*, 8/78; Chalker, W. C., "The Missing Cessna and the UFO," *Flying Saucer Review*, 3/79.

156. Haines, Richard F. & Norman, Paul. "Valentich Disappearance: New Evidence and a New Conclusion." *Journal of Scientific Exploration*, Spring 2000, Vol. 14 No. 1. p. 19-33.

157. Spencer, John, *The UFO Encyclopedia*, p. 201; Pope, Nick, *Open Skies, Closed Minds*, p. 214-215

158. Good treatments of the Valentich case can be found in Good, Timothy, *Above Top Secret*, p. 175-182; Fawcett, Lawrence & Greenwood, Barry, *Clear Intent*, p. 93-96; Hall, Richard, *The UFO Evidence, Volume II*, p. 23, 138-140.

159. The website "The Aerospace Corporation" has a summary of recovered reentry debris http://www.reentrynews.com/recovered.html which states: "In April 1972 four titanium pressure spheres (diameter 0.38 m, mass 13.6 kg each) were found in an area near Ashburton, New Zealand. A fifth sphere was found six years later near Eiffelton, New Zealand. Probably from Soviet Cosmos 482, launched 31 March 1972, part of which reentered 2 April 1972." Thus, there is only mention of one of the spheres from 1978. Moreover, the U.S. DoD estimate was that at least one of the objects was determined to have fallen recently.

160. Basterfield, Keith, "New Zealand Radar-Visual and Film Cases," *MUFON UFO Journal*, 11-12/78; Maccabee, Bruce, "New Zealand Film Report: II," *MUFON UFO Journal*, 6/79; Bowen, Charles, "Spanners in the Works," *Flying Saucer Review*, v24, n5, 3/79; "Round-Up Item: N.Z. Pilot Rejects Official Explanation," *Flying Saucer Review*, v24, n5, 3/79; Chalker, W. C., "A Re-Viewing of the Great Nocturnal Light," *Flying Saucer Review*, v26, n1, 6/80; Berry, Kevin R., "The Kaikura Controversy," *Flying Saucer Review*, v26, n2, 8/80; Fogerty, Quentin, "The N.Z. Film: A Reply to the Debunkers," *Flying Saucer Review*, v26, n2, 8/80; *UFO Round Up*, 10/12/98; http://ufos.about.com/od/visualproofphotosvideo/a/kaikoura.htm; Clark, Jerome, *The UFO Book*, p. 415-418; Hall, Richard, *The UFO Evidence, Volume II*, p. 23, 244, 352.

Chapter 4 - The Empire Strikes Back, 1979-1980

1. Hall, Richard, *Uninvited Guests*, p. 38-39, 302-303; Hall, Richard, *The UFO Evidence, Volume II*, p. 24, 257; Sweetman, Bill, *Stealth*, p. 71.

2. CIA FOIA files, China Report, Science and Technology

3. Hall, Richard, *The UFO Evidence, Volume II*, p. 24; Hall, Richard, *Uninvited Guests*, p. 303-304.

4. Hall, Richard, *Uninvited Guests*, p. 39, 304-305.

5. Zechel, W. Todd, "NI-CIA-AP or NICAP?" *MUFON UFO Journal*, 1-2/79.

6. Vallee, Jacques, *Messengers of Deception*, (And/Or Press, 1979), Vallee, Jacques, *UFO Chronicles of the Soviet Union*, p. 126; White, Vincent, "Messengers of Deception: A Review," *APRO Bulletin*, v27, n.12, 6/79.

7. Marchetti, Victor, "How the CIA Views the UFO Phenomenon," *Second Look*, 5/79.

8. Grant Cameron provides a good discussion of this issue in *http://presidentialufo.com*

9. House of Lords, "Debate on Unidentified Flying Objects," *Hansard* (Lords), vol. 397, no. 23, January 18, 1979; Clark, David, "UFOs in the House of Lords," *Fortean Times* #201 (2005) http://www.uk-ufo.org/condign/secfillords1.htm; Good, Timothy, *Above Top Secret*, p. 73-75; Pope, Nick, *Open Skies, Closed Minds*, p. 46-47, 63; Berliner, Don, *UFO Briefing Document*, p. 172-173.

10. Good, Timothy, *Above Top Secret*, p. 101.

11. Good, Timothy, *Above Top Secret*, p. 72-73.

12. FBI Document, 16 February 1979, cited in Redfern, Nicholas, *A Covert Agenda*, p. 113.

13. Howe, Linda Moulton, correspondence with the author, June 1, 2009.

14. Hall, Richard, *UFO Evidence, Volume 2*, p. 24, 226.

15. Blann, Tommy Roy, "UFO Connection in Dulce and Taos, New Mexico?" *MUFON UFO Journal*, 8/79; "Directors Message," *MUFON UFO Journal*, 5/79; Bishop, Gregory, *Project Beta*, p. 11-13..

16. "Director's Message," *MUFON UFO Journal*, 5/79; Deuley, Thomas, "Mutilations Hearing in New Mexico, *MUFON UFO Journal*, 7/79; Howe, Linda Moulton, *Glimpses of Other Realities, Vol. 1*, p. 102.

17. Howe, Linda Moulton, correspondence with the author, June 1, 2009.

18. "Argentine Oil Field Landing: Physical Evidence and Animal Reactions. No author citation. *MUFON UFO Journal*, 9/79; Hall, Richard, *The UFO Evidence, Volume II*, p. 24, 265, 431.

19. Clark, Jerome, *The UFO Book*, p. 356-363.

20. Good, Timothy, *Above Top Secret*, p. 214; Spencer, *The UFO Encyclopedia*, p. 131.

21. Dong, Paul, "China UFO research," *MUFON UFO Journal*, 1/81.

22. Greenwood, Barry J., "Project Moon Dust," *MUFON UFO Journal*, 9/86.

23. Bryant, Larry W. "UFO Secrecy Update," *MUFON UFO Journal*, 10/79.

24. Bryant, Larry W., "UFO Secrecy Update," *MUFON UFO Journal*, 10/79.

25. Bryant, Larry W., "UFO Secrecy Update: The UFO Paper Chase," *MUFON UFO Journal*, 2/80.

26. Bryant, Larry W., "UFO Secrecy Update," *MUFON UFO Journal*, 11/79.

27. Bamford, James, *Body of Secrets*, p. 382-385.

28. Caravelle makes emergency landing at Valencia after encountering UFO(s)," *United Press International*, 11/12/79; Benitez, J. J., "Jetliner 'Intercepted' by UFO Near Valencia, (trans. by Gordon Creighton), *Flying Saucer Review*, 9-10/79; "Spanish Airliner Case," *MUFON UFO Journal*, 12/79; Good, Timothy, *Above Top Secret*, p. 156-157; Spencer, John, *The UFO Encyclopedia*, p. 292-293.

29. Velasco, J. J., "Action of Electromagnetic Fields In The Microwave Range On Vegetation," presented at a meeting of the Society for Scientific Exploration in Glasgow, Scotland, August 1994.

30. Stonehill, Paul, & Mantle, Philip, *Soviet UFO Files*, p. 51.
31. Dong, Paul & Stevens, Wendelle, *UFOs Over China*, p. 140-141.
32. Stonehill, Paul, & Mantle, Philip, *Soviet UFO Files*, p. 77.
33. Hall, Richard, "Book Review," *MUFON UFO Journal*, 3/80
34. Farish, Lucius, "In Others' Words," by *MUFON UFO Journal*, 4/80; on Gene Pope and the CIA, see Hansen, Terry, *The Missing Times*, p. 233-239, 246; Charles Berlitz had spent 26 years as a U.S. Army Intelligence Officer; see "Charles Berlitz, 90, Author on the Paranormal," *New York Times* Obituary, 12/31/03; regarding Moore's capabilities in Russian, see Bishop, Gregory, *Project Beta*, p. 70.
35. Gribble, Bob, "Looking Back," *MUFON UFO Journal*, 3/90
36. Clark, Jerome, *The UFO Book*, p. 413.
37. Stringfield, Leonard, "Status Report on Alleged Alien Cadaver Photos," *MUFON UFO Journal*, 12/80.
38. Stringfield, Leonard, "Status Report on Alleged Alien Cadaver Photos," *MUFON UFO Journal*, 12/80,
39. Stacy, Dennis, "UFO Waters Still Run Deep," *MUFON UFO Journal*, 7-8/84.
40. Hall, Richard, *The UFO Evidence, Volume II*, p. 25.
41. *Daily Herald*, Biloxi-Gulfport, Mississippi, 5/14/80; Hall, Richard, *Uninvited Guests*, p. 307-308.
42. Hall, Richard, *The UFO Evidence, Volume 2*, p. 164-165.
43. Hall, Richard, *The UFO Evidence, Volume 2*, p. 226.
44. Blum, Howard, *Out There*, p. 232-234; Clark, Jerome, *The UFO Book*, p. 147; Bishop, Greg, *Project Beta*, p. 15-28.
45. Richard Sauder, Ph.D. has written about this at great length. See *Underground Bases and Tunnels: What is the Government Trying to Hide?* (Adventures Unlimited press, 1995), p. 25-28 and elsewhere.
46. Bishop, Gregory, *Project Beta*, p. 105-107.
47. Hooper, Terry, "UFO Interceptions Attempted," *Flying Saucer Review*, v26, n4, 11/80; Gribble, Bob, "Looking Back," *MUFON UFO Journal*, 5/90.
48. Department of Defense Joint Chiefs of Staff Message Center, June 3, 1980. Title: UFO Sighted in Peru. Antonio Huneeus related the details of his interview with the Peruvian base commander to the author in April 2008.
49. Redfern, Nicholas, *A Covert Agenda*, p. 162.
50. Stonehill, Paul, & Mantle, Philip, *Soviet UFO Files*, p. 59.
51. U.S. Department of State Telegram, July 8, 1980, "Investigation of Unusual 'Light Phenomenon' Seen in Kuwait's Skies."
52. Howe, Linda Moulton, *A Strange Harvest* (video), 1980, 52 min.; Howe, Linda Moulton, *An Alien Harvest: Further Evidence Linking Animal Mutilations and Human Abductions to Alien Life Forms*, Pioneer Printing, Cheyenne, Wyoming, 1989; Howe, Linda Moulton, "Two Scientists Describe An Extraterrestrial Biological Entity Called *J-Rod*," October 5, 2002, *http://www.earthfiles.com/*.
53. Interviews by the author with several Dulce residents in July 2006.
54. Bishop, Gregory, *Project Beta*, p. 31-32.
55. Stringfield, Leonard, "Status Report on Alleged Alien Cadaver Photos," *MUFON UFO Journal*, 12/80; Stringfield, Leonard, "The Puzzling Case of the Cadaver Photos," *MUFON UFO Journal*, 9/81.
56. Bishop, Gregory, *Project Beta*, page 54-57, 64-66; Good, Timothy, *Above Top Secret*, p. 405-408.
57. Maccabee, Bruce, "UFO Landing Near Kirtland Air Force Base: Welcome to the Cosmic Watergate," http://brumac.8k.com/kirtland1.html
58. Klass, Philip J., Letter to Dr. A. G. McNamara, Herzberg Institute of Astrophysics, National Research Council, Ottawa, Canada, 8/15/80. Interim Box, Records Group 77, Accession 1990-1991/073, Canadian National Archives, Ottawa.
59. Dolan, Richard M., "New Philip Klass Letter Found," 10/18/05, *http://keyholepublishing.com*
60. "Directors Message," *MUFON UFO Journal*, 10/83.
61. Morgan, Robert, "Triangular UFO: Preliminary Report," *MUFON UFO Journal*, 1/81.
62. Levine, Gary, "Report Roundup," *MUFON UFO Journal*, 10/84.
63. Hall, Richard, *Uninvited Guests*, p. 310-311; Hall, Richard, *The UFO Evidence, Volume 2*, p. 25.
64. Blum, Howard, *Out There*, p. 224-227; Bishop, Gregory, *Project Beta*, p. 59-63; "Disinformation: From Euros to UFOs," *Lobster* 40 Winter 2000/2001.
65. Stringfield, Leonard, "Status Report on Alleged Alien Cadaver Photos," *MUFON UFO Journal*, 12/80.
66. Paul Bennewitz, private notes in the possession of the author.
67. Bishop, Gregory, *Project Beta*, p. 34-35, 135-137.
68. Bishop, Gregory, *Project Beta*, p. 41-44.
69. "Disinformation from Euros to UFOs," *Lobster Magazine* 40; Bishop, Gregory, *Project Beta*, p. 43.
70. Doty, Richard, Interview on *Coast to Coast* with Art Bell, February 27, 2005.
71. Doty, Richard, correspondence with the author, August 2, 2007.

72. Sauder, Richard, conversation with the author, July 18, 2009.
73. Regehr, Ron, interview with the author, March 25, 2009.
74. Regehr, Ron, interview with the author, March 25, 2009.
75. See discussion in Bishop, Gregory, *Project Beta*. For more information about the Starfire Optical Range, see the Kirtland Air Force Base website, *http://www.kirtland.af.mil/afrl_de/* and the "Starfire" page at Globalsecurity.org, *http://www.globalsecurity.org/space/systems/starfire.htm*
76. Howe, Linda Moulton, correspondence with the author, June 1, 2009.
77. Clark, Jerome, *The UFO Book*, p. 147-153; Bishop, Gregory, *Project Beta*, p. 120, 124-129.
78. Bishop, Gregory, *Project Beta*, p. 71-73.
79. Dong, Paul, and Stevens, Wendelle, *UFOs Over Modern China*, p. 190.
80. Good, Timothy, *Above Top Secret*, p. 215-216.
81. "Chinese Panel to Study UFOs," *Washington Post*, 11/14/80; *MUFON UFO Journal*, 12/80.
82. Redfern, Nicholas, *A Covert Agenda*, p. 136.
83. Benitez, Juan, J. "Anniversary Aerial Encounters," *Flying Saucer Review*, v26, n6, 3/81.
84. There has been extensive investigation of this case. The major books are: Butler, Brenda; Street, Dot; and Randles, Jenny, *Sky Crash: A Cosmic Conspiracy*, Grafton, 1986; Pope, Nick, *Open Skies, Closed Minds*, Pocket Books, 1997; Redfern, Nicholas, *A Covert Agenda: The British Government's UFO Top Secrets Exposed*, Simon & Schuster, 1997; Warren, Larry and Robbins, Peter, *Left At East Gate: A First-Hand Account of the Rendlesham Forest UFO Incident, Its Cover-up, and Investigation*, Marlowe & Company, 1997; Randles, Jenny, *UFO: Crash Landing? Friend or Foe? The True Story of the Rendlesham Forest Close Encounter*, Blandford Book, 1998; and Bruni, Georgina, *You Can't Tell the People: The Definitive Account of the Rendlesham Forest UFO Mystery*, Sidgwick & Jackson, Ltd, 2000. Among the many helpful websites, two are especially noteworthy: "The Rendlesham Forest Incident" at *http://ufoevidence.org*; "The Rendlesham Forest Incident" at *http://-rendlesham-incident.co.uk/rendlesham.php*. Primary documents associated with the case include Halt, Lt. Col. Charles I., USAF, Memorandum to Ministry of Defence, "SUBJECT: Unexplained Lights," January 13,1981; and British Ministry of Defence files on the Rendlesham Incident at *http://www.mod.uk/DefenceInternet/FreedomOfInformation/PublicationScheme/SearchPublicationScheme/UnidentifiedFlyingObjectsufoRendleshamForestIncident1980.htm*
85. A very good synopsis of this encounter, indeed of the entire Rendlesham Incident, is at "The Rendlesham Forest Incident" at http://rendlesham-incident.co.uk/rendlesham.php, which draws much useful information from the Sci Fi Channel's "UFO Invasion at Rendlesham," 2004.
86. "The Bentwaters Rendlesham Forest Incident - Cosmic Conspiracies," in *http://www.ufoevidence.org/documents/doc659.htm*; Huneeus, Antonio, "The Testimony of John Burroughs," *Fate*, 9/93.
87. Easton, James, "The Rendlesham Forest Incidents 1/3," August 30, 1997 at *http://www.hyper.net/ufo/vs/m30-034.html*
88. Easton, James, "The Rendlesham Forest Incidents 2/3," August 30, 1997, The UFO UpDates Archive, *http://www.hyper.net/ufo/vs/m30-035.html*
89. "The Rendlesham Forest Incident" at *http://rendlesham-incident.co.uk/rendlesham.php*
90. Halt's audio tape transcript available at "The Bentwaters Rendlesham Forest Incident," *http://www.ufos-aliens.co.uk/cosmicrend.html*.
91. "The Rendlesham Forest Incident" at *http://rendlesham-incident.co.uk/rendlesham.php*
92. "The Rendlesham Forest Incident" at *http://rendlesham-incident.co.uk/rendlesham.php*
93. Warren, Larry and Robbins, Peter, *Left At East Gate*, p. 413; also Peter Robbins, personal communication with the author, April 16, 2009.
94. For Larry Warren's full story, see Warren, Larry and Robbins, Peter, *Left At East Gate: A First-Hand Account of the Bentwaters-Woodbridge UFO Incident, Its Cover-Up, and Investigation*. Marlowe & Company, 1997.
95. This last information was relayed by Warren to Linda Moulton Howe during a 3-hour recorded interview in 1986. Howe, Linda Moulton, correspondence with the author, June 12, 2009.
96. Pope, Nick, "Rendlesham - The Unresolved Mystery," *http://www.ufoevidence.org/documents/doc641.htm*
97. Warren, Larry and Robbins, Peter, *Left at East Gate*, p. 121; also, Robbins, Peter, communication with the author.
98. Ian Ridpath's analysis on Rendlesham is at *http://www.ianridpath.com/ufo/rendlesham.htm*.
99. See "Kevin Conde" at *Wikipedia, the free encyclopedia*, http://en.wikipedia.org/wiki/Kevin_Conde; and "Rendlesham - UFO Hoax," *BBC Inside Out*, Monday June 30, 2003.
100. Schuessler, John, "Cash-Landrum Case, Investigation of Helicopter Activity," *MUFON UFO Journal*, 9/83; Baker, Dave, "MUFON's Schuessler Looks to the Future," *MUFON UFO Journal*, 1/00; Fawcett, Lawrence & Greenwood, Barry, *Clear Intent*, p. 106-108; Hall, Richard, *UFO Evidence, Volume 2*, p. 26, 226-229; Stancill, Nancy, "Women Seek Damages in UFO Sighting," *Houston Chronicle*, 1/21/84.
101. Bishop, Gregory, *Project Beta*, p. 171; interview with John Schuessler by the author, 3/10/07.

102. Adams, Tom, *Mysterious Helicopters*, cited in Linda Howe, *Glimpses of Other Realities, Volume One*, p. 153-154

Chapter 5 - Cloak and Dagger, 1981-1983

1. Velasco, Jean-Jacques, "Report on the Analysis of Anomalous Physical Traces: the Trans En Provence 1981 UFO case," *Journal of Scientific Exploration*, Vol. 4, Number 1, 1990; Vallee, Jacques, "Return to Trans-en-Provence," by Jacques F. Vallee, *Journal of Scientific Exploration*, Vol. 4, Number 1, 1990; Berliner, Don, *UFO Briefing Document*, p. 112-120.
2. "Reagan Steps Up Attack on Carter's Foreign Policy," *New York Times*, 2/8/80.
3. Allen, Gary, *The Rockefeller File*, 1976.
4. *W Magazine*, 9/26/80.
5. Marrs, Jim, *Rule by Secrecy*, p. 32.
6. McGowan, David, "All the President's Men: Nazis, the Attempted Assassin, and the Serial Killer," in *You Are Being Lied To: The Disinformation Guide to Media Distortion, Historical Whitewashes, and Cultural Myths*, Russ Kick, ed. The Disinformation Company Ltd., 2001, p. 98; see also Marrs, Jim, *Rule by Secrecy*, p. 32.
7. Keith, Jim, *Mind Control, World Control: the Encyclopedia of Mind Control*, Adventures Unlimited Press, 1995, p. 180, 190.
8. Tarpley, Webster G. & Chaitkin, Anton. *George Bush: The Unauthorized Biography*, Chapter 18: "Iran Contra."
9. Goslin, Tony, Ed., "Conferences Before 1991," *Bilderberg Conferences Reference Page*, at http://www.bilderberg.org/bilder.htm
10. Boyne, Walter J, *A History of the United States Air Force*, p. 250, 253-254.
11. To begin, see Bernstein, Carl, "The CIA and the Media," *Rolling Stone*, 10/20/77; and Stonor Saunders, Francis, *The Cultural Cold War: The CIA and the World of Arts and Letters* (New Press, 2001).
12. Thomas, Kenn and Keith, Jim. *The Octopus: Secret Government and the Death of Danny Casolaro*, p. 94-95. See also "Savings and Loan Crisis," *Wikipedia, the free encyclopedia*, http://en.wikipedia.org/wiki/Savings_and_Loan_crisis#_note-0
13. Reagan's 1974 UFO sighting has already been described. An earlier sighting was said to have occurred during Reagan's Hollywood years, presumably the 1950s or 1960s. As the story goes, Ron and Nancy showed up a half hour late for a dinner party with some friends. They arrived very upset and said they had seen a UFO coming down from the coast. According to one version of the story, as told to the author by an anonymous friend of former President Reagan, they said the craft had in fact landed on the road ahead of them. Of course, Reagan's several explicit references to aliens during his Presidency is well known. See also Grant Cameron, presidentialufo.com.
14. Zechel, W. Todd, "NI-CIA-AP OR NICAP?" *MUFON UFO Journal*, 1-2/79.
15. Andrus, Walt, "Directors Message," *MUFON UFO Journal*, 3/81.
16. "MUFON Featured on Nationwide Broadcast," *MUFON UFO Journal*, 3/81.
17. Andrus, Walt, "Directors Message," *MUFON UFO Journal*, 4/81.
18. Andrus, Walt, "Directors Message," *MUFON UFO Journal*, 2/81.
19. Bishop, Gregory, *Project Beta*, p. 158-159.
20. Bishop, Gregory, *Project Beta*, p. 138.
21. Redfern, Nicholas, *A Covert Agenda*, p. 162.
22. "Soviet Cosmonaut Saw UFOs in Space," http://english.pravda.ru/science/19/94/378/13760_astronaut.html *Pravda*, August 16, 2004; Berliner, Don, *UFO Briefing Document*, p. 187-188; "Russian Cosmonaut sees UFO while in orbit aboard Salyut-6 Space Station," http://www.ufoevidence.org/cases/case396.htm.
23. Stonehill, Paul, & Mantle, Philip, *Soviet UFO Files*, p. 66-67; Paul Stonehill, email correspondence with the author, March 26, 2007.
24. Greer, Steven, M.D., *Disclosure*, p. 238-245.
25. Fawcett, Lawrence and Greenwood, Barry, *Clear Intent*, p. 188; Good, Timothy, *Above Top Secret*, p. 417-419.
26. Andrus, Walt, "Director's Message," MUFON UFO Journal, 1/81.
27. Bryant, Larry, *MUFON UFO Journal*, July, 1981.
28. *MUFON UFO Journal*, 4/81.
29. Bishop, Gregory, *Project Beta*, p. 120-123; "Pursuit of Project Aquarius," Computer UFO Network, http://www.cufon.org/cufon/Aquarius/aquarius.htm.
30. Stacy, Dennis, "UFOs: the Hidden Evidence," *MUFON UFO Journal*, 9/81.
31. Hall, Richard, "Center for UFO Studies Conference," *MUFON UFO Journal*, 10/81.
32. Lorenzen, Jim and Coral, *Abducted: Confrontations with Beings from Outer Space*, Berkeley, New York, 1977.

33. Fowler, Raymond E. *The Andreasson Affair*, Prentice-Hall, New York, 1979. Fowler's other titles on the Andreasson saga include: *The Andreasson Affair Phase Two, The Watchers, The Watchers II*, and *The Andreasson Legacy*.
34. Hopkins, Budd. *Missing Time: A Documented Study of UFO Abductions*, with an Afterward by Aphrodite Clamar, Ph.D., Richard Marek Publishers, New York, 1981.
35. Letters, *MUFON UFO Journal*, 3/81.
36. Evans, Hilary, "Signpost to a Parallel Universe?" *Flying Saucer Review*, 5-6/79; Evans, Hilary, "Abducted by an Archetype," *MUFON UFO Journal*, 4/81.
37. Loftus, Elizabeth, *Memory*, Addison-Wesley, 1980.
38. Good, Timothy, *Above Top Secret*, p. 217.
39. Spencer, John, *The UFO Encyclopedia*, p. 140-141
40. Hall, Richard, *UFO Evidence, Volume 2*, p. 26-27.
41. Hall, Richard, *UFO Evidence, Volume 2*, p. 27; Hall, Richard, *Uninvited Guests*, p. 314.
42. Hall, Richard, UFO Evidence, Volume II, p. 27, 166, 229-231.
43. Spencer, John, *The UFO Encyclopedia*, p. 182.
44. Good, Timothy, *Above Top Secret*, p. 98-101.
45. Hall, Richard, *UFO Evidence, Volume 2*, p. 26.
46. Redfern, Nicholas, *A Covert Agenda*, p. 157-158.
47. Haines, Richard F., "Analysis of a UFO Photograph," *Journal of Scientific Exploration*, (Vol. 1, No.2); http://www.scientificexploration.org/jse/abstracts/v1n2a3.html.
48. Stonehill, Paul, & Mantle, Philip, *Soviet UFO Files*, p. 48-49.
49. Evans, Hilary, "Northern Lights," *MUFON UFO Journal*, 7/83; Stacy, Dennis, "Hessdalen: An Introduction," *MUFON UFO Journal*, 1/88; Havik, Leif, "Project Hessdalen," *MUFON UFO Journal*, 1/88; Hall, Richard, *UFO Evidence, Volume 2*, p. 27; Haines, Richard, p. 310-312.
50. *Cameron, Grant, http://presidentialufo.com*
51. Goldwater, Barry, "Letter to Lee Graham," October 19, 1981.
52. Fawcett, Lawrence & Greenwood, Barry, *Clear Intent*, p. 11-12.
53. Fawcett, Lawrence & Greenwood, Barry, *Clear Intent*, p. 188.
54. Gordon, Stan, "Pennsylvania Low-Level UFO Sightings," *MUFON UFO Journal*, 6/82, and "UFO-Bigfoot Update," *MUFON UFO Journal*, 7/82.
55. Schuessler, John, "Policemen Encounter Diamond Shaped UFO," *MUFON UFO Journal*, 4/83.
56. "Subject: Finland/USSR/Lights in the Sky," *U.S. Defense Informational Report*, 25 March 1982.
57. Stacy, Dennis, "Hessdalen: An Introduction," *MUFON UFO Journal*, 1/88.
58. Good, Timothy, *Above Top Secret*, p. 242.
59. British CAA report, in Redfern, Nicholas, *A Covert Agenda*, p. 162.
60. Dong, Paul, "UFOs Over China," *MUFON UFO Journal*, 2/84.
61. British CAA report, in Redfern, Nicholas, *A Covert Agenda*, p. 162.
62. Chalker, Bill, "UFOs and the RAAF: The Inside Story, Parts One and Two," *MUFON UFO Journal*, 9/82 and 10/82.
63. Bishop, Gregory, *Project Beta*, p. 209.
64. Liljegren, Anders, "Designing False Reports: Another Recent Example," *MUFON UFO Journal*, 3/83.
65. Fawcett, Lawrence & Greenwood, Barry, *Clear Intent*, p. xvi, 188-190.
66. Executive Order 12356 http://www.epic.org/open_gov/eo_12356.html; Wright, Susan, *UFO Headquarters*, p. 68; Stacy, Dennis, "The 1970s: Todd Zechel and the Freedom of Information Act," *OMNI* v. 16, n. 10, 8/94.
67. Cox, Billy, "UFOs won't be in the Platform, but..." *Florida Today*, 8/17/88; Moore, William L. "President Reagan on Aliens," *Focus Magazine*, 11/1/87; Cameron, Grant, *http://presidentialufo.com*; Howe, Linda Moulton, correspondence with the author, June 1, 2009.
68. Cameron, Grant, *http://presidentialufo.com*
69. Bishop, Gregory, correspondence with the author, 8/13/07; Bishop, Gregory, *Project Beta*, p. 95-96.
70. Sarbacher, Dr. Robert I., Letter to Mr. William Steinman, 11/29/83.
71. Crain, T. Scott, Jr., "An MJ-12 Informant," *MUFON UFO Journal*, 1/90.
72. Stringfield, Leonard, *UFO Crash Retrievals: Amassing the Evidence*, published privately, 1982.
73. Andrus, Walt, "Directors Message," *MUFON UFO Journal*, 7/82.
74. *MUFON UFO Journal*, 6/82.
75. Hansen, Terry, *The Missing Times*, p. 182.
76. Andrus, Walter, "Nova: Directors Open Letter," and J. Allen Hynek, "Nova: Guest Editorial," *MUFON UFO Journal*, 9/82; Hansen, Terry, *Missing Times*, p. 256-257.
77. See, for example, Herman, Edward S. & Chomsky, Noam, *Manufacturing Consent: the Political Economy of the Mass Media* (Pantheon Books, 1988); and Chomsky, Noam, *Necessary Illusions: Thought Control in Democratic Societies* (South End Press, 1999).
78. Good, Timothy, *Above Top Secret*, p. 247.
79. Bamford, James, *Body of Secrets*, p. 400-401.

80. Indeed, one can argue that a private takeover of the U.S. federal government occurred in the nineteenth century. In 1895, for instance, when a great financial panic gripped the U.S. and the Federal Treasury was nearly out of gold, President Grover Cleveland allowed financier J.P. Morgan to create a private American and European syndicate to supply the U.S. Treasury with $65 million in gold, floating a bond issue that restored the treasury surplus. The maneuver gave Morgan and his London allies control over the U.S. public debt, not especially popular with Democratic Presidential candidate William Jennings Bryant. But Morgan and Wall Street gave heavily to Republican candidate William McKinley, who was elected in 1896 and reelected in 1900 on a gold standard platform. See Chernow, Ron. *The House of Morgan: An American Banking Dynasty and the Rise of Modern Finance*, 2001.

81. Brandt, Daniel and Badrich, Steve, "Pipe Dreams: The CIA, Drugs, and the Media," *Lobster* 33, Summer 1997; Herman, Edward S. and Brodhead, Frank, *Demonstration Elections: US-Staged Elections in the Dominican Republic, Vietnam and El Salvador*, South End Press, Boston 1984.

82. Keith, Jim, and Thomas, Kenn, *The Octopus*, p. 137.

83. ibid, p. 5-6,

84. ibid, p. 23-24.

85. ibid, p. 57.

86. ibid, p. 25.

87. ibid, p. 179.

88. Thomas, Gordon, *Gideon's Spies: The Secret History of the Mossad*, St. Martin's Griffin (2000).

89. "Sighting off Coast in Brazil," *MUFON UFO Journal*, 9/84; Letters, *MUFON UFO Journal*, 5/85

90. Stonehill, Paul, & Mantle, Philip, *Soviet UFO Files*, p. 81.

91. Velasco, Jean-Jacques, "Action of Electromagnetic Fields In the Microwave Range On Vegetation," paper presented at a meeting of the Society for Scientific Exploration in Glasgow, Scotland, August 1994; Sturrock, Peter, Physical Evidence Related to UFO Reports: Injuries to Vegetation http://www.ufoevidence.org/documents/doc490.htm; Bourdais, Gildas, "Summary of Some Cases Noted in the Cometa Report," *MUFON UFO Journal*, 9/99.

92. Hall, Richard, *The UFO Evidence, Volume II*, p. 27-28; 108-109.

93. Imbrogno, Philip, *Night Siege*, p. 6-9.

94. Issacs, Jeremy & Downing, Taylor, *Cold War: An Illustrated History, 1945-1991. Companion to the CNN TV Series* (Little, Brown and Company, 1998), p. 342

95. Boyne, Walter J., *Beyond the Wild Blue*, p. 407.

96. Issacs, Jeremy & Downing, Taylor, *Cold War*, p. 343-344.

97. Regehr, Ronald S., "How to Build a $125 Million UFO Detector," p. 83-87.

98. Regehr, Ronald S., *How to Build a $125 Million UFO Detector*, p. 27-28, 84.

99. See Cameron, Grant, http://presidentialufo.com.

100. Lovekin, Stephen, interview with Peter Janney, September 20, 2005. Audio file in the possession of the author.

101. A detailed analysis of the large number of apparently anomalous space objects caught on video had been on the website of the late Jeff Challender, Project P.R.O.V.E. (*http://projectprove.com*). Challender died in October 2007, and the website domain expired on July 6, 2009. Complete website mirror is in the possession of the author.

102. Bruce Maccabee, correspondence with the author, December 11, 2008.

103. An excellent detailed analysis of the video includes Carlotto, Mark J., Digital Video Analysis of Anomalous Space Objects, *Journal of Scientific Exploration*, Vol. 9, No. 1, pp 45-63, 1995, available at http://www.nicap.org/sts48.htm; the most prominent skeptical argument on STS-48 is Oberg, James, "Proof of the Prosaic Nature of the STS-48 Zig-Zag Video." This and many other articles relating to the shuttle mission can be found at *STS-48 Space Shuttle Video* http://www.ufoevidence.org/topics/sts%2d48.htm.

104. Regehr, Ronald, *How to Build a $125 Million UFO Detector*.

105. Hansen, Terry, *The Missing Times*, p. 90; Whatley, Frederick W., "Reagan, National Security, and the First Amendment: Plugging Leaks by Shutting Off the Main, https://www.cato.org/pub_display.php?pub_id=903&full=1

106. Smith, Gary, "Operation Just Cause: How to Stage a Regime Change," *The-Edge*, 10/18/02; http://www.earthisland.org/

107. Schnabel, Jim, *Remote Viewers: The Secret History of America's Psychic Spies*, p. 287.

108. Webb, Gary, *Dark Alliance: The CIA, the Contras, and the Crack Cocaine Explosion*, Seven Stories Press, 1999.

109. Keith, Jim & Thomas, Kenn, *The Octopus*, p. 175.

110. Keith, Jim & Thomas, Kenn, *The Octopus*, p. 86; see also "National Endowment for Democracy" in *Wikipedia, the free encyclopedia*.

111. Sauder, Richard, *Underground Bases and Tunnels*, p. 66.

112. Imbrogno, Philip, *Night Siege*, p. 9-14.

113. Imbrogno, Philip, *Night Siege*, p. 18-25.

114. Imbrogno, Philip, *Night Siege*, p. 27-28, 61.
115. Clark, Chris, "Boomerang!" *International UFO Reporter*, May-June 1984.
116. Imbrogno, Philip, *Night Siege*, p. 29-59
117. Imbrogno, Philip, *Night Siege*, p. 15-18.
118. Imbrogno, Philip, *Night Siege*, p. 74-76.
119. Imbrogno, Philip, *Night Siege*, p. 179-185.
120. Howe, Linda Moulton, *An Alien Harvest: Further Evidence Linking Animal Mutilations and Human Abductions to Alien Life Forms* (Pioneer Printing, Cheyenne, Wyoming, 1989), p. 135-136; Clark, Jerome, "Ufological Tall Tales," September 1991; http://home.pacbell.net/joerit/docs2/misc/ jclark.htm; Greenwood, Barry, "MJ-12 Magic Act," *MUFON UFO Journal*, 12/87; Hastings, Robert, "The MJ-12 Affair: Facts, Questions, Comments," *MUFON UFO Journal*, 6/89.
121. Howe, Linda Moulton, *An Alien Harvest*, p. 133-134.
122. Howe, Linda Moulton, *An Alien Harvest*, p. 143-155.
123. Howe, Linda Moulton, *An Alien Harvest*, p. 155-156.
124. Howe, Linda Moulton, *An Alien Harvest*, p. 156. For other commentary on the Howe-Doty saga, see: Howe, Linda Moulton, *Glimpses of Other Realities*, V. 1, p. 99;
125. Howe, Linda Moulton, *An Alien Harvest*, p. 156; 252-254.
126. Doty, Richard C., letter to Larry W. Bryant, March 5, 1988, reprinted in Howe, Linda Moulton, *An Alien Agenda*, p. 255-256.
127. Doty, Richard C., correspondence with the author, 1 February 2008.
128. Ramsey, Robin, "View from the Bridge," *Lobster* 35, Summer 98; Cannon, Martin, "Read, but don't copy," alt.alien.visitors. January 20, 2001.
129. Howe, Linda Moulton, correspondence with the author, 2 February 2008.
130. Bishop, Gregory, *Project Beta*, p. 202-207.
131. Alleged leaked Top Secret CIA/MJ document, DCDR5. MA-Q3. REF: Memo 5-7A, reproduced in Collins, Robert & Doty, Richard, *Exempt from Disclosure*, p. 156.
132. Alleged leaked CIA/MJ document, DCDR2, NSA/MJ12 Executive Briefing (Memo), June 24, 1982, reproduced in Collins, Robert & Doty, Richard, *Exempt from Disclosure*, p. 157.
133. Alleged leaked CIA/MJ document. DCDR-3/55. MJ12. REF: TA Memo 3-20, reproduced in Collins Robert & Doty, Richard, *Exempt from Disclosure*, p. 158.
134. Collins, Robert & Doty, Richard, *Exempt from Disclosure*, p. 133-135.
135. Collins, Robert & Doty, Richard, *Exempt from Disclosure*, p. 153-155. In a series of email conversations, Mr. Doty would not acknowledge the above story, and disavowed his connection to the book.
136. Hall, Richard, "From the Editor," *MUFON UFO Journal*, 4/83.
137. Stacy, Dennis, "1983 MUFON UFO Symposium: UFOs - A Scientific Challenge," *MUFON UFO Journal*, 7/83.
138. Havrik, Leif, "Project Hessdalen," *MUFON UFO Journal*, 1/88; Stacy, Dennis, "Hessdalen: An Introduction," *MUFON UFO Journal*, 1/88.
139. Hall, Richard, "From the Editor," *MUFON UFO Journal*, 7/83; *National Enquirer*, 14 June 1983.
140. Andrus, Walter, "Director's Message," *MUFON UFO Journal*, 7/83.
141. Andrus, Walter, "Financing the North American UFO Federation," *MUFON UFO Journal*, 9/83.
142. Good, Timothy, *Above Top Secret*, p. 140, 247-248.
143. Andrus, Walter, "Director's Message," *MUFON UFO Journal*, 11/83
144. Good, Timothy, *Above Top Secret*, p. 104-105.
145. Good, Timothy, *Above Top Secret*, p. 243.
146. Stonehill, Paul, & Mantle, Philip, *Soviet UFO Files*, p. 86-87.
147. Imbrogno, Philip, *Night Siege*, p. 96
148. Haines, Richard, *CE-5*, p. 132-133.
149. Levine, Gary, "Report Roundup," *MUFON UFO Journal*, 10/84
150. Gordon, Stan, "Pennsylvania Flap Is Biggest Since 1973," *MUFON UFO Journal*, 10/83; Wylie, Nancy, "UFO Sightings Head List of Unexplained Pa. Phenomena," *Bedford Gazette*, 1/25/84.
151. Issacs, Jeremy & Downing, Taylor, *Cold War*, p. 346-348; "Korean Air Lines Flight 007," *Wikipedia*, http://en.wikipedia.org/wiki/KAL_007.
152. Issacs, Jeremy & Downing, Taylor, *Cold War*, p. 345; "Invasion of Grenada," *Wikipedia the free encyclopedia*; Boyne, Walter, *History of the U.S. Air Force*, p. 285
153. Issacs, Jeremy & Downing, Taylor, *Cold War*, p. 349-350
154. "UFO Lifts Car up on its Side," *MUFON UFO Journal*, 11/83.
155. "Recent Sightings in North Carolina," *MUFON UFO Journal*, 4/84.
156. Imbrogno, Philip, *Night Siege*, p. 2-4
157. "Recent Sightings in North Carolina," *MUFON UFO Journal*, 4/84.
158. Gresh, Bryan, "Soviet UFO Secrets," *MUFON UFO Journal*, 10/93
159. *News of the World*, October 23, 1983; Redfern, Nicholas, *A Covert Agenda*, p. 160-161.
160. Dong, Paul, "UFOs Over China," *MUFON UFO Journal*, 2/84.

161. Farish, Lucius, "In Others Words," *MUFON UFO Journal*, 10/83.
162. Randles, Jenny, "Rendelsham Forest Update," *MUFON UFO Journal*, 4/85.
163. Randles, Jenny, "Rendelsham Forest Update," *MUFON UFO Journal*, 4/84.
164. Sarbacher, Dr. Robert, correspondence to William Steinman, November 29, 1983.
165. *MUFON UFO Journal*, January 1990.
166. Crain, T. Scott, Jr., "The Book on MJ-12," *MUFON UFO Journal*, 4/91.

Chapter 6 - Calm Before the Storm, 1984-1986

1. Hall, Richard, *The UFO Evidence, Volume 2*, p. 28.
2. Schuessler, John, "Estimate of the Situation 1984: The (Sad?) State of Ufology," *MUFON UFO Journal*, 1/84.
3. Hynek, J. Allen, "Two Great Mysteries of Ufology," *International UFO Reporter*, Jan.-Feb., 1984.
4. Hynek, J. Allen, "A Cosmic Watergate?" *International UFO Reporter*, Jan.Feb, 1984.
5. Hynek, J. Allen, "The UFO Phenomenon," *International UFO Reporter*, 7-8/84; "AAAS Meeting to include UFO Phenomenon Talks," *International UFO Reporter*, 1-1/84; "AAAS Preview," *International UFO Reporter*, 3-4/84.
6. "Abductees are 'Normal' People, no author citation, *International UFO Reporter*, 7-8/84.
7. Pratt, Bob, "Verdict on UFO Cover-Up: Guilty," *MUFON UFO Journal*, 10/83; Bletchman, Robert, "Clear Intent Book Review," *MUFON UFO Journal*, 3/84; "Director's Message," *MUFON UFO Journal*, 4/84; "Director's Message," *MUFON UFO Journal*, 7-8/84.
8. Wanderer, Robert, "News 'N' Views," *MUFON UFO Journal*, 11/85.
9. Eberhart, George M., "Clear Intent Reviewed," *International UFO Reporter*, 7/8 1984.
10. Andrus, Walter, "Director's Message," *MUFON UFO Journal*, 9/84; "Directors Message," *MUFON UFO Journal*, 11/84; Stacy, Dennis, "News 'n' Notes," *MUFON UFO Journal*, 10/84.
11. Andrus, Walter, "The Big Picture," *MUFON UFO Journal*, 4/84. As an aside, this closing of ranks would not last long. After Dennis Stacy became Editor of the Journal later in 1984, the *MUFON UFO Journal* slowly began to include more and more skeptical contributors well into the 1990s.
12. On Pope, the *Enquirer*, and the CIA, see Terry Hansen's analysis, *The Missing Times*, passim.
13. *London Observer*, 4 March 1984; Spencer, p. 184; "British Government Releases UFO Files," *MUFON UFO Journal*, 5-6/84; Good, Timothy, *Above Top Secret*, p. 112-113; Pope, Nick. *Open Skies, Closed Minds*, Appendix 1.
14. Chalker, Bill, "The North West Cape Incident: UFOs and Nuclear Alert in Australia," *International UFO Reporter*, 1-2/86.
15. Wright, Susan, *UFO Headquarters*, p. 77.
16. Stonehill, Paul & Mantle, Philip, *Soviet UFO Files*, p. 53.
17. Redfern, Nicholas, *A Covert Agenda*, p. 193, 203, 210.
18. Strand, Erling, Msc.EE., "Project Hessdalen 1984 - Final Technical Report," at http://www.hessdalen.org/reports/hpreport84.shtml#conclusion
19. Havik, Leif, "Project Hessdalen," *MUFON UFO Journal*, 1/88.
20. Project Hessdalen website, http://www.hessdalen.org/pictures/H-a12.shtml
21. Project Hessdalen website, http://www.hessdalen.org/pictures/description.shtml
22. Coyne, Shirley, "Twelve See UFOs in Michigan," *MUFON UFO Journal*, 4/84.
23. Gordon, Stan,"Diamond-Shaped UFO in Pennsylvania," *MUFON UFO Journal*, 4/84.
24. Peace, Mitchell E., "Local Woman, Daughter Report 'Close Encounter,'" *Claxton Enterprise*, 3/29/84.
25. Gribble, Bob, "UFO Hotline Reports," *MUFON UFO Journal*, 5-6/84.
26. Gribble, Bob, "UFO Hotline Reports," *MUFON UFO Journal*, 4/84.
27. From: US Embassy in Bridgetown, Barbados. To: Sec State and DIA. Subject: Incident Report: Unidentified Objects Observed on Radar Screen at Grantley Adams International Airport. Date April 13, 1984. See CUFON: Verified Documents Directory; State Department UFO Documents; http://www.cufon.org
28. Gribble, Bob, "UFO Hotline Reports," *MUFON UFO Journal*, 4/84.
29. Imbrogno, Philip, *Night Siege*, p. 71-73.
30. Imbrogno, Philip, *Night Siege*, p. 78-83.
31. Imbrogno, Philip, *Night Siege*, p. 83-87.
32. Imbrogno, Philip, *Night Siege*, p. 150-151.
33. Imbrogno, Philip J., "Westchester Boomerang: March 24, 1983," *International UFO Reporter*, 9-10/84.
34. Imbrogno, Philip, *Night Siege*, p. 90-93.
35. Imbrogno, Philip, *Night Siege*, p. 162-164.
36. Imbrogno, Philip, *Night Siege*, p. 96-97.
37. Levine, Gary,"Report Roundup," *MUFON UFO Journal*, 10/84.
38. "ET Circling the Area? UFO sightings over Wanaque Reservoir," *Today* (Wayne, NJ), 7/4/84.

39. Imbrogno, Philip, *Night Siege*, p. 100-101.
40. Imbrogno, Philip, *Night Siege*, p. 97.
41. Imbrogno, Philip, *Night Siege*, p. 98.
42. Guarino, Trink, "'We're not alone,' says UFO center of light-sightings," *Danbury News-Times*, 7/14/84; Winslow, Olivia, "Area police get reports of UFOs," *Danbury News-Times*, 7/20/84; Imbrogno, Philip, *Night Siege*, p. 103-121
43. Imbrogno, Philip, *Night Siege*, p. 117-124.
44. Imbrogno, Philip, *Night Siege*, p. 159-168.
45. Imbrogno, Philip, communication with the author, January 22, 2009; also, "Phil Imbrogno Releases New Indian Point 1984 UFO Sighting Information," Dec. 16, 2008, http://greennuclearbutterfly.blogspot.com/2008/12/phil-imbrogno-releases-new-indian-point.html
46. Imbrogno, Philip, *Night Siege*, p. 125-128.
47. Imbrogno, Philip, *Night Siege*, p. 132-135.
48. Bryant, Larry W., "UFO Town Hall Meeting: A Case Study," *MUFON UFO Journal*, 10/84; Imbrogno, Philip, *Night Siege*, p. 135-147.
49. Higbie, Janet, "NY Cop May Have Solved Mystery of Lights in Sky," *Danbury News-Times*, 7/26/84; Schmalz, Jeffrey, "Strange Lights Brighten the Night Skies Upstate," *New York Times*, 8/25/84; Hansen, Terry, *Missing Times*, p. 215-217.
50. Imbrogno, Philip, *Night Siege*, p. 155-157.
51. NICAP's fine collection of UFO reports, *The UFO Evidence*, published in 1964, listed nine probable shapes of UFOs based on witness testimony. Most of these were disc-variants or spherical, one was cylindrical, one triangular. See Hall, Richard H., ed., *The UFO Evidence*, (National Investigations Committee on Aerial Phenomena, 1964), p. 144.
52. Anonymous author, "Hypothesis: The Illinois Flying Triangle is a Department of Defense, Not an ET Craft," submitted to the National Institute for Discovery Science, July 2002.
53. Stonehill, Paul & Mantle, Philip, *The Soviet UFO Files*, p. 91.
54. Ilyin, Vadim K.,"KGB's 'Blue Folder' Reveals Shootings, Landings in USSR," http://www.mufon.com/znews_kgb.html; Dremin, Alexander, "Soviet Army Fought UFOs," Jan. 23, 2004, http://english.pravda.ru/science/19/94/378/11873_UFO.html
55. Stonehill, Paul, & Mantle, Philip, *The Soviet UFO Files*, p. 88-89; Vallee, Jacques, *UFO Chronicles of the Soviet Union*, p. 128-129.
56. Haines, Richard F., "CE2 in the Eastern Urals," *International UFO Reporter*, 11-12/92.
57. Berry, Adrian, "Soviet UFO Reports 'Illegal Arms Tests,'" *Daily Telegraph*, London, 5/31/84.
58. Jackson, Robert. "KGB takes to the flying saucers!" *Northern Echo*, Darlington, England, 3/15/84.
59. Imbrogno, Philip, *Night Siege*, p. 169.
60. Garelik, Glenn, The Great Hudson Valley UFO Mystery, *Discover*, 11/84; Hansen, Terry, *The Missing Times*, p. 263-265; Farish, Lucius, "In Others' Words," *MUFON UFO Journal*, 12/84; Rogin, Gilbert L., "Our man in Kazakhstan - 'Discover' writer Glenn Garelik," *Discover*, June 1987, http://findarticles.com/p/articles/mi_m1511/is_n6_v8/ai_6167767; Garelik, Glenn, "The Spies Who Stayed Out in the Cold," *New York Times*, 11/27/94.
61. Hansen, Terry, *The Missing Times*, p. 83-84.
62. Andrus, Walter, "Directors Message," *MUFON UFO Journal*, 10/85.
63. Wright, Susan, *UFO Headquarters*, p. 95.
64. Bamford, James, *Body of Secrets*, p. 389-390.
65. "Buffs Baffled By UFO," *Chicago Sun-Times*, 20 Jan. 2000; http://www.suntimes.com:80/output/news/ufo19.html
66. Sweetman, Bill, *Stealth*, p. 89; Sweetman, Bill. *Aurora:*, p. 15.
67. Bamford, James, *Body of Secrets*, p. 393.
68. Boyne, Walter, *History of the U.S. Air Force*, p. 409.
69. Estulin, Daniel, "The Bilderberg Club: a Secret Society of the Richest and Most Influential People Conspiring to Achieve a World Government," *Michael*, June-July-August 2006, at *http://www.michaeljournal.org/bilder.htm*; Goslin, Tony, Ed., "Conferences Before 1991," *Bilderberg Conferences Reference Page*, at *http://www.bilderberg.org/bilder.htm*
70. See the HAARP home page at http://www.haarp.alaska.edu/
71. Kao, A., *Literature Survey of Underground Construction Methods for Application to Hardened Facilities*, Southwest Research Institute, San Antonio Texas, April 1985. http://handle.dtic.mil/100.2/ADA155212; Sauder, Richard, *Underground Bases and Tunnels*, p. 10, 13, 100.
72. Sauder, Richard, conversations with the author, March 22, 2008 and July 16, 2009.
73. *Filer's Files*, 7/8/01.
74. James Goodall interview in Hesemann, Michael, *UFOs and Area 51: Secrets of the Black World*, Video, 1994.
75. Howe, Linda Moulton, *Glimpses of Other Realities, Volume Two*, p. 128-143.
76. Andrus, Walter, "Director's Message," *MUFON UFO Journal*, 2/85.
77. Clark, Jerome, "A Ufology for the 1980s," *International UFO Reporter*, 3-4/85.

78. "The Hudson Valley Sightings: A Reply to Dick Ruhl and APRO," Imbrogno, Philip J., Clark, Jerome, "A Ufology for the 1980s," *International UFO Reporter*, 1-2/85; Editorial, *International UFO Reporter*, 3-4/85; "Editorial, Letter to the Editor from the Editor in Chief," *International UFO Reporter*, 7-8/85.

79. Jacobs, David, "Crashed Discs: No," *International UFO Reporter*, 7-8/85, Hall, Richard, "Crashed Discs: Maybe," *International UFO Reporter*, 7-8/85.

80. Randles, Jenny, "Land Without Freedom," *MUFON UFO Journal*, 11/86.

81. *APRO Bulletin*, Vol. 33, No. 1. 7/85.

82. Andrus, Walter, "Director's Message," *MUFON UFO Journal*, 10/85, 11/85, and 3/86.

83. Svahn, Clas, "Unique UFO Archive Hidden in Warehouse," *http://www.ufo.se/english/articles/apro.html* and *http://www.ufoevidence.org/documents/doc1145.htm*

84. Ilyin, Vadim K., KGB's 'Blue Folder' Reveals Shootings, Landings in USSR," http://www.mufon.com/znews_kgb.html; Dremin, Alexander, "Soviet Army Fought UFOs," *Pravda*, January 23, 2004; http://english.pravda.ru/science/19/94/378/11873_UFO.html

85. Ilyin, Vadim K., KGB's 'Blue Folder' Reveals Shootings, Landings in USSR," http://www.mufon.com/znews_kgb.html; Stonehill, Paul, & Mantle, Philip, *Soviet UFO Files*, p. 76.

86. Stonehill, Paul, & Mantle, Philip, *Soviet UFO Files*, p. 95.

87. Stonehill, Paul, & Mantle, Philip, *Soviet UFO Files*, p. 77-78.

88. Imbrogno, Philip, *Night Siege*, p. 189-192.

89. *People's Daily*, July 28 and August 9, 1985; "UFO Caused Peking Duck," *Toronto Sunday Sun*, 8/11/85; "China Air Crew Sees Huge UFO," *Japan Times*, Tokyo, 7/30/85; Good, Timothy, *Above Top Secret*, p. 218-219.

90. *Filer's Files*, 3/16/05.

91. "Zimbabwe Jet Planes Fail to Catch UFO," *Mainichi Daily News*, Tokyo, 8/4/85; Thorne, David, letter to Timothy Good, 10/24/85; Hind, Cynthia, "African Report," *MUFON UFO Journal*, 11/85; Good, Timothy, *Above Top Secret*, p. 433-434; Spencer, p. 91; Berliner, Donald, *Best Evidence*, p. 180-181; *The London Times*, 8/3/85; Oberg's remark is found at http://members.tripod.com/ancientknightsc/id168.htm.

92. "UFO Fired On, Iranian Report Says," *UPI* (*Arkansas Gazette*, Little Rock, AR), 8/7/85.

93. Huneeus, Antonio, "A Chilean Overview," *MUFON UFO Journal*, 6/86.

94. Hall, Richard, *UFO Evidence, Volume 2*, p. 28-29.

95. Imbrogno, Phillip & Pratt, Robert, *Night Siege*, p. 193-194

96. *International Herald Tribune* and *Daily Telegraph*, 12/5/85; Cameron, Grant, http://presidentialufo.com; Berliner, Donald, *The Best UFO Evidence*, p. 161.

97. White House transcript of "Remarks of the President to Fallston High School Students and Faculty," December 4, 1985; Cameron, Grant, http://presidentialufo.com

98. Hall, Richard, *The UFO Evidence, Volume 2*, p. 29.

99. Gordon, Stan, "Pennsylvania Wave," *MUFON UFO Journal*, 12/86.

100. Imbrogno, Philip, *Night Siege*, p. 5-6, 194.

101. Hall, Richard, *The UFO Evidence, Volume 2*, p. 29.

102. Imbrogno, Philip, *Night Siege*, p. 197-198.

103. Gordon, Stan, "Pennsylvania Wave," *MUFON UFO Journal*, 12/86.

104. Imbrogno, Philip, *Night Siege*, p. 198-199.

105. McClelland, Clark, personal communication with the author; *Filer's Files*, 10/5/05.

106. Huneeus, Antonio, *Foreign News Tribune*, New York, NY, June 14, 1990; http://ufoarea.bravepages.com/crashes_1986_siberia.html; Stonehill, Paul & Mantle, Philip, *The Soviet UFO Files*, p. 92-95; Vallee, Jacques, *Soviet UFOs*, p. 103, 128.

107. Stonehill, Paul & Mantle, Philip, *The Soviet UFO Files*, p. 68-69; *UFO Round Up*, V. 9, n49, 12/8/04; *Pravda*, September 16, 2002; "UFO Prevents Blast at Chernobyl Nuclear Plant," at http://www.ufoevidence.org/documents/doc1005.htm

108. Webb, Walter N., "Allen Hynek As I knew Him," *International UFO Reporter*, 1-2/93.

109. Hastings, Robert, "The MJ-12 Affair: Facts, Questions, Comments," *MUFON UFO Journal*, 6/89; Greenwood, Barry, "MJ-12 Magic Act," *MUFON UFO Journal*, 12/87.

110. Goudie, Dale and Lambright, Christian, "The Ice Documents Press Conference," June 25, 1987; Letter from National Security Agency to The Honorable John Glenn, 27 January 1987; see CUFON: Verified Documents Directory; http://www.cufon.org.

111. Hopkins, Budd, "Abduction Reflections," *MUFON UFO Journal*, 4/86; Strieber, Whitley, "My Experiences with the Visitors," *MUFON UFO Journal*, 12/86.

112. Department of Defense JCS Message Center, Subject: B6/BAF Has a Close Encounter of the First Kind. Date: 20 May 86. Subject: Numerous Unidentified Objects Were Cited in the Skies over Brazil. But BAF Fighters Were Unable to Intercept Them; Berliner, Don, *The UFO Briefing Document*, p. 121-127; Huneeus, J. Antonio, "UFO Alert in Brazil," *MUFON UFO Journal*, 11/86; Andrus, Walt, "UFOs Over Brazil," *MUFON UFO Journal*, 9/86; Smith, Dr. Willy, "The Brazilian Incident," *International UFO Reporter*, 7-8/86; Smith, Dr. Willy, "More on Brazilian OVNIs," *MUFON UFO*

Journal, 9/86.

113. *New York Times*, July 15, 1986; *MUFON UFO Journal*, 8/86.

114. Sweetman, Bill. *Aurora*, p. 12-13.

115. *Lobster*, Issue 14, 11/87.

116. Chardy, Alfonsos, "Threats Abetted Contras," *The Philadelphia Inquirer*, 5/10/87; Willson, S. Brian, "The Case of Panama: U.S. Continues its Bully Ways as International Outlaw. Analysis of the Dec. 20, 1989 U.S. Invasion in Historical Context." December 1989 (updated 1991) http://www.brianwillson.com/awolpanama.html.

117. On this matter, see Bruce Maccabee's analysis, "The Fantastic Flight Of JAL 1628," *International UFO Reporter*, March/April 1987, also available at http://brumac.8k.com/JAL1628/JL1628.html and http://ufoevidence.org/documents/doc1316.htm

118. Federal Aviation Administration (FAA), "Chronological Summary of the Alleged Aircraft Sightings by Japan Airlines Flight 1628," January 6, 1987; Andrus, Walter H., "Strange Alaskan Encounter," *MUFON UFO Journal*, February 1987; Maccabee, Bruce, "The Fantastic Flight of JAL 1628," *International UFO Reporter*, March-April 1987; "Extraterrestrial Object Involved in Japan Air Lines Pilot's UFO Sighting, According to Leading UFO Investigator," Committee for the Scientific Investigation of Claims of the Paranormal, January 22, 1987; "FAA Releases Documents on Reported UFO Sighting Last November," by Paul Steucke, Office of Public Affairs, Alaskan Region, Federal Aviation Administration (FAA), U.S. Department of Transport, March 5, 1987; Klass, Philip J., "FAA Data Sheds New Light on JAL Pilot's UFO Report," *The Skeptical Inquirer*, Summer, 1987; Greer, Steven, *Disclosure*, p. 79-93; *Filer's Files*, 6/19/02. For more resources, see "JAL Flight 1628 Over Alaska," in http://ufoevidence.org/topics/jalalaska.htm

119. Ilyin, Vadim K. "KGB's 'Blue Folder' Reveals Shootings, Landings in USSR," http://www.mufon.com/znews_kgb.html

120. Andrus, Walter, Director's Message, *MUFON UFO Journal*, 2/86, 7/86, and 11/86. The collection of Paranet files can be accessed at http://www.paranetinfo.com/ufofiles.html

121. Blum, Howard, *Out There: The Government's Secret Quest for Extraterrestrials*, (Pocket Books, 1990)

122. Blum, Howard, *Out There*, p. 25-32.

123. Blum, Howard, *Out There*, p. 25-32.

124. Alexander, John B., *Future War: Non-Lethal Weapons in Twenty-First-Century Warfare*, St. Martin's Press, 1999. See also "John B. Alexander," from *Wikipedia, the Free Encyclopedia*

125. The author obtained information about the Advanced Theoretical Physics Group from several of its members, including John Alexander (who has also spoken publicly about the group at various conferences).

126. Good, Timothy, *Need To Know: UFOs, the Military, and Intelligence*, Sidgwick & Jackson, 2006 (corrected and amended by Mr. Good, April, 2007), p. 340-341.

127. Wood, Dr. Robert R., interview with the author, November 2008. See also Hill, Paul R., *Unconventional Flying Objects: A Scientific Analysis*, Hampton Roads Publishing Company, Inc., 1995.

128. Blum, Howard, *Out There*, p. 44-45, 49.

129. Alexander, John, *X-Conference*, Gaithersburg, MD, April 2008; also private interview with the author, November 2008.

130. Collins, Robert & Doty, Richard, *Exempt from Disclosure*, p. 8, 86; Maccabee, Bruce, *Hawk Tales*

131. Maccabee, Bruce, *Hawk Tales* (Bruce Maccabee, 2005) http://brumac.8k.com/HAWKTALES/.

Chapter 7 - Ufology Explodes, 1987-1988

1. *Soviet Life Supplement*, May 1987; Berliner, Don, *UFO Briefing Document*, p. 179-180.

2. Hall, Richard, *Uninvited Guests*, p. 221.

3. Hopkins, Budd, *Intruders*, Ballantine Books, 1987.

4. Clark, Jerome, "A Conversation with Budd Hopkins," *International UFO Reporter*, November/December 1988.

5. Wanderer, Robert, "Abductions and Credibility," *MUFON UFO Journal*, 7/87.

6. Clark, Jerome, "A Conversation with Budd Hopkins," *International UFO Reporter*, 11-12/88.

7. Basterfield, Keith and Bartholomew, Robert E. "Abductions: A Fantasy Prone Personality Hypothesis," *International UFO Reporter*, May-June 1988.

8. Hopkins, Budd. "Letter," *International UFO Reporter*, 5-6/88

9. Strieber, Whitley, *Communion: A True Story*, William Morrow, 1987.

10. Baker, Robert A., and Joe Nickell. *Missing Pieces: How to Investigate Ghosts, UFOs, Psychics, and Other Mysteries*. Prometheus, 1992, p. 227.

11. Conroy, Ed, *Report on Communion*, William Morrow, 1989.

12. Strieber, Whitley, "On the Road (With Visitors)," *International UFO Reporter*, January-February 1987; Hopkins, Budd, "Contact Fantasies and Abduction Realities," *International UFO Reporter*, 1-2/87.

13. Bullard, Thomas E., "Abductions in Life and Lore," *International UFO Reporter*, 7-8/87.

14. Bullard Thomas E., "Hypnosis and UFO Abductions: a Troubled Relationship," *Journal of UFO Studies 1*, 1989; Ring, Kenneth, and Rosing, Christopher J., "The Omega Project: A Psychological Survey of Persons Reporting Abductions and Other UFO Encounters," *Journal of UFO Studies 2*, 1990; Clark, Jerome, *The UFO Book*, p. 502-503.

15. Ring, Kenneth, Ph.D., "Toward an Imaginal Interpretation of 'UFO Abductions,'" *MUFON UFO Journal*, 5/89.

16. Fowler, Raymond, E. *The Watchers: The Secret Design Behind UFO Abduction*, Bantam Books, 1990.

17. Weiner, Tim. "Fastest-growing Sector of Budget Kept in Dark," *Charlotte Observer*, North Carolina, February 22, 1987; Sweetman, Bill. *B-2*, p. 25-26.

18. *Miami Herald* and *San Jose Mercury News*, April 12, 1987; Hannaford, Peter, *The Reagans: A Political Portrait*, p. 285; Sick, Gary, *All Fall Down*, p. 422.

19. U.S. Senate, "Selections from the Senate Committee Report on Drugs, Law Enforcement and Foreign Policy, chaired by Senator John F. Kerry," at http://www.pinknoiz.com/covert/contracoke.html

20. Brandt, Daniel and Badrich, Steve. "Pipe Dreams: The CIA, Drugs, and the Media," *Lobster* 33, Summer 1997.

21. Blum, William. *The CIA, Contras, Gangs, and Crack*, 1996.

22. Smith, Gar, "Operation Just Cause: How to Stage a Regime Change," *The-Edge* October 18, 2002; Koster, R.M. and Sanchez, Guillermo, *In the Time of the Tyrants: Panama, 1968-1990*. Norton, 1990.

23. In *Above Top Secret*, Good said that the documents were "made available" to him "unofficially early in 1987 prior to release in the United States." Good, Timothy, *Above Top Secret*, p. 544.

24. Randles, Jenny, "A Cover-up in England," *International UFO Reporter*, 9-10/87.

25. Good, Timothy, *Need to Know: UFOs, The Military and Intelligence*, (Sidgwick & Jackson, 2006), p. 127.

26. Good, Timothy, conversation with the author, Denver, Colorado, July 2007, and correspondence August 22, 2008.

27. Randles, Jenny, "A Cover-up in England," *International UFO Reporter*, 9-10/87.

28. Moore, William L. "Research Update," *MUFON UFO Journal*, 6/87.

29. Moore, William, "Majestic 12," *MUFON UFO Journal*, 7/87.

30. Friedman, Stanton, correspondence with the author, July 30, 2008.

31. Stacy, Dennis, "18th International Symposium," *MUFON UFO Journal*, 8/87; Greenwood, Barry, "MJ-12 Magic Act," *MUFON UFO Journal*, 12/87.

32. Andrus, Walter, "Menzel Mystery," *MUFON UFO Journal*, 9/87.

33. U.S. National Archives website, http://www.archives.gov/foia/ufos.html

34. Clark, Jerome, "MJ Jury Still Out," *MUFON UFO Journal*, 11/87.

35. Friedman, Stanton, "MJ-12: The Evidence So Far," *International UFO Reporter*, Sep-Oct., 1987.

36. Berry, Adrian. "Book Review of *Above Top Secret*." *London Spectator*, August 1, 1987.

37. "Report of U.F.O. Crash in '47 Called False by Science Panel," *The New York Times*, Wednesday, August 26, 1987.

38. Randles, Jenny, "A Cover-up in England," *International UFO Reporter*, 9-10/87.

39. Greenwood, Barry, "The MJ-12 Fiasco," *Just Cause*, 9/87; Greenwood, Barry, MJ-12 Magic Act, *MUFON UFO Journal*, 12/87.

40. Maccabee, Bruce, "Cutler Correction," *MUFON UFO Journal*, 7/88.

41. Gersten, Peter, Letters, *MUFON UFO Journal*, 2/88.

42. Hastings, Robert, "The MJ-12 Affair: Facts, Questions, Comments," *MUFON UFO Journal*, 6/89.

43. Cameron, Grant & Crain, T. Scott, Jr. *UFOs, MJ-12 and the Government. A Report on Government Involvement in UFO Crash Retrievals*, (Privately published, 1991), p. 7-11.

44. Cameron, Grant & Crain, T. Scott, Jr. *UFOs, MJ-12 and the Government. A Report on Government Involvement in UFO Crash Retrievals*, (Privately published, 1991), p. 15.

45. Cameron, Grant & Crain, T. Scott, Jr. *UFOs, MJ-12 and the Government. A Report on Government Involvement in UFO Crash Retrievals*, (Privately published, 1991), p. 16-22.

46. Cameron, Grant & Crain, T. Scott, Jr. *UFOs, MJ-12 and the Government. A Report on Government Involvement in UFO Crash Retrievals*, (Privately published, 1991), p. 27-35.

47. Crain, T. Scott, Jr., "An MJ-12 Informant," *MUFON UFO Journal*, 1/90; Crain, T. Scott, Jr., "UFO Notes Missing," *MUFON UFO Journal*, 5/96.

48. Redfern, Nicholas, *A Covert Agenda*, p. 163-164.

49. Imbrogno, Philip, *Night Siege*, p. 200-201; http://ufos.about.com/od/visualproofphotosvideo/ig/Best-UFO-Photographs/1987connecticut-jpg.htm

50. U.S. Defense Department Information Report, August 20, 1987. From JCS; To AIG; Subject Unidentified Flying Object; Item Number 00427453.

51. Stonehill, Paul and Mantle, Philip, *Soviet UFO Files*, p. 96-97; Ilyn, Vadim K., "KGB's 'Blue Folder' Reveals Shootings, Landings in USSR," http://www.mufon.com/znews_kgb.html; Dremin, Alexander "Soviet Army fought UFOs," January 23, 2004, http://english.pravda.ru/science/19/94/378/11873_UFO.html; *Filer's Files*, 1/28/04.

52. Gordon, Stan, "Pennsylvania Law Officer Reports CE2 Incident," *MUFON UFO Journal*, 5/89.

53. Hall, Richard, *The UFO Evidence*, Vol. 2, p. 30, 411.

54. Hall, Richard, *The UFO Evidence*, Vol. 2, p. 30, 492.

55. Hall, Richard, *The UFO Evidence, Vol. 2*, p. 30.

56. Valasco, J-J., "Action of Electromagnetic Fields in the Microwave Range on Vegetation," paper presented at a meeting of the Society for Scientific Exploration in Glasgow, Scotland, August 1994; Berliner, Don, UFO Briefing Document, p. 118; Sturrock, Peter, "Physical Evidence Related to UFO Reports (Sturrock Panel): Injuries to Vegetation," http://www.ufoevidence.org/documents/doc490.htm

57. Hamilton, William, F. III, *Cosmic Top Secret: America's Secret UFO Program*, William F. Hamilton III (Inner Light Publications, 1991)., p. 61.

58. Imbrogno, Philip, *Night Siege*, p. 201-203.

59. Huneeus, J. Antonio, "Great Soviet UFO Flap of 1989 Centers on Dalnegorsk Crash," *Foreign News Tribune*, New York, NY, 6/14/90; Stonehill, Paul and Mantle, Philip, *The Soviet UFO Files*, p. 94.

60. Stonehill, Paul and Mantle, Philip, *The Soviet UFO Files*, p. 78.

61. Walters, Ed and Frances, *The Gulf Breeze Sightings, The Most Astounding Multiple Sightings of UFOs in U.S. History*, William Morrow, 1990; Booth, B.J., "The Gulf Breeze, Florida, UFOs," http://www.ufocasebook.com/gulfbreeze.html and http://ufos.about.com/od/visualproofphotosvideo/p/gulfbreeze.htm; Maccabee, Bruce, "The Scale Remains Unbalanced," *MUFON UFO Journal*, 4/89; Ware, Donald M., "The Gulf Breeze, Florida UFO Encounters," privately published, February 1, 1989.

62. Maccabee, Bruce S., Ph.D., *The Gulf Breeze Sightings: The Untold Story*, (unpublished, 1994).

63. A Brief Biography of John Lear, February 13, 1988," Internet posting, see http://www.skepticfiles.org/mys3/learbiou.htm

64. Andrus, Walter, "Director's Message," *MUFON UFO Journal*, 12/87.

65. Lear, John. Letter, December 13, 1987, http://www.geocities.com/Area51/shadowlands/6583/maji010.html; and statement released on Paranet, December 29, 1987 http://www.ufomind.com/area51/people/lear/original.html.

66. Letter, Dan Wright, MUFON Deputy Director of Investigations, to John Lear, MUFON State Director for Nevada, May 4, 1988, http://www.skepticfiles.org/ufo1/leardanw.htm.

67. Hynek, Dr. J. Allen; Imbrogno, Philip J.; Pratt, Bob. *Night Siege: The Hudson Valley UFO Sightings*. Ballentine Books, 1987.

68. Berry, Adrian. "Book Review of *Above Top Secret*," by Timothy Good. *London Spectator*, August 1, 1987.

69. Clark, Jerome, "The Year That Was, Part One," *International UFO Reporter*, Sept-Oct 1987.

70. One account places the time at 1:35 a.m., although most put the time at around 4 a.m. See Cosnette, Dave, "Cosmic Australia," http://www.ufos-aliens.co.uk/cosmicaustralia.htm

71. UFO Research Queensland, "The Knowles Family" http://www.uforq.asn.au/casefiles/knowles.html. Siani, "UFOs on the Nullarbor Plain," http://strangedayz.co.uk/2007/09/ufos-on-nullarbor-plain-part-2.html

72. See UFO Research Queensland, "The Knowles Family" http://www.uforq.asn.au/casefiles/knowles.html. Norman Paul A.; Auchettl, John W. *The Knowles Family Encounter: A study of the UFO phenomenon over the Nullarbor Plain*, Victorian UFO Research Society, 1990. Andrus, Walter, "The Mundrabilla Incident," *MUFON UFO Journal*, 3/88; Tsitas, Evelyn, "Riddle of the alien 'dust,'" *Australasian Post*, Melbourne, 11/26/88; Incident at Mundrabilla, Australia (no author attibution) http://www.subversiveelement.com/ufoMundrabilla.html; Cosnette, Dave "Cosmic Australia," 2006, http://www.ufos-aliens.co.uk/cosmicaustralia.htm.

73. United States Coast Guard Incident Report: Unidentified Flying Objects, 5 Mar 88.

74. U.S. Coast Guard, "Incident Report: Unidentified Flying Objects," 6 Mar 88.

75. "Cozying of Jupiter, Venus light up sky," *Cleveland Plain Dealer* 3/7/88; "Sky-gazers mistake planets for UFOs," *Lake County News-Herald*, 3/7/88.

76. Dell'Aquila, Richard, "Ohio Flap," *MUFON UFO Journal*, 1/89. U.S. Coast Guard "Incident Report: Unidentified Flying Objects," 3/5/88; Evans, Christopher, "Space Case: The Night the Coast Guard Got Buzzed," *The Cleveland Plain Dealer*, 7/12/92. Maccabee, Bruce, correspondence with the author, 9/28/08.

77. Imbrogno, Philip, correspondence with the author, September 27, 2008.

78. Heafield, Barry, "I stood under it for 15 minutes," *Stafford (UK) Newsletter*, 7/1/88.

79. Maccabee, Bruce, "The Scale Remains Unbalanced," *MUFON UFO Journal*, 4/89.

80. Andrus, Walter, "Director's Message," *MUFON UFO Journal*, 4/88.

81. Wright, Dan, "Current Case Log," *MUFON UFO Journal*, 5/90.

82. Wright, Dan, "Case Submittals: A Two-Year Time Exposure," *MUFON UFO Journal*, 5/89.

83. Wright, Dan, "Case Submittals: A Two-Year Time Exposure," *MUFON UFO Journal*, 5/89.

84. Wright, Dan, "Case Submittals: A Two-Year Time Exposure," *MUFON UFO Journal*, 5/89.

85. Wright, Dan, "Current Case Log, *MUFON UFO Journal*, 4/90.

86. Rhodighier, Mark and Boyd, R "Gulf Breeze, Florida: The Other Side of the Coin," *Center for UFO Studies (CUFOS), Special Bulletin*, 4/88

87. Maccabee, Bruce,"The Scale Remains Unbalanced," *MUFON UFO Journal*, 4/89.

88. Clark, Jerome, "Ill Breeze," *International UFO Reporter*, 3-4/88.

89. Ware, Donald M.; Flannigan, Charles; Andrus, Walter, "The Gulf Breeze, Florida photographic and CE-3 Case, Part Three," *MUFON UFO Journal*, 6/88; Ware, Donald M.; Flanigan, Charles; Andrus, Walter, "The Gulf Breeze, Florida photographic and CE-3 Case, Part Four," *MUFON UFO Journal*, 7/88

90. Ware, Donald; Flannigan, Charles; and Andrus, Walter, "The Gulf Breeze, Florida Photographic and CE III Case - Part V," *MUFON UFO Journal*, 8/88; Ware, Donald; Flannigan, Charles; and Andrus, Walter, "The Gulf Breeze, Florida Photographic and CE III Case - Part III," *MUFON UFO Journal*, 6/88.

91. Maccabee, Bruce,"The Scale Remains Unbalanced," *MUFON UFO Journal*, 4/89.

92. Maccabee, Bruce S., Ph.D, *The Gulf Breeze Sightings: The Untold Story* (unpublished, 1994)

93. Clark, Jerome, "Breeze from the Gulf," *International UFO Reporter*, 5-6/88. Ware, Donald M.; Flannigan, Charles D.; Andrus, Walter H.;"The Gulf Breeze Florida Photographic and CEIII Case, Part IV," *MUFON UFO Journal*, 7/88.

94. Hall, Richard & Smith, Willy, "Balancing The Scale: Unanswered Questions About Gulf Breeze, *MUFON UFO Journal*, 12/88.

95. Gordon, Stan, "Number of UFO Reports In State Unprecedented in '88," *Latrobe Bulletin*, 1/9/89.

96. Cameron, Grant, *Presidential UFO*, http://presidentialufo.com

97. Cameron, Grant, *Presidential UFO*, http://presidentialufo.com

98. Isaacs, Jeremy and Downing, Taylor. *Cold War: An Illustrated History, 1945-1991*, p. 371.

99. Svahn, Clas, "Unique UFO Archive Hidden in Warehouse (APRO Archives and Files)" at UFO Evidence, http://www.ufoevidence.org/documents/doc1145.htm

100. I have not found confirmation of this, but according to Peter Gersten, who knew the two, "apparently someone has money because neither one is ever employed." Peter Gersten, correspondence with the author, April 26, 2008.

101. One claim, that Choate and Myers payed $6,000 dollars for the files, is incorrect. Robert Dean lent the two $6,000 when they claimed to be in need of cash. He never got the money back, although he briefly enlisted the support of his friend, the attorney Peter Gersten, who remained in touch with the two. Robert Dean, interview with the author, April 25, 2008.

102. Dean, Robert, interview with the author, April 25, 2008.

103. As of this book's publication, the files remain out of circulation. Gregory Bishop indicated the files were in Tucson. See *Project Beta*, p. 91-92.

104. Clark, Jerome, *The UFO Encyclopedia, Volume Two*, p. 14; Moseley, James, *Saucer Smear*, V. 50., N. 3, July 5, 2003.

105. Dean, Robert, interview with the author, April 25, 2008.

106. "Antelope Valley," from *Wikipedia, The Free Encyclopedia*

107. Hamilton, William F., *Cosmic Top Secret*, p. 61.

108. Valaitis, Robin, "Van Driver Reports Sighting UFO in Sky Over Lancaster," *Antelope Valley Press*, Palmdale, CA, 8/4/88.

109. Hamilton, William F. III, "Flying Wings and Deep Desert Secrets," *MUFON UFO Journal*, 11/90; Hamilton, William F., III, *Cosmic Top Secret*, p. 61.

110. Hamilton, William F. *Cosmic Top Secret*, p. 41-42.

111. Clarke, Robyn D.; Gite, Lloyd; "A Piping Hot Career: Head of Transco Energy Co.," *Black Enterprise*, June 1999, http://www.allbusiness.com/specialty-businesses/minority-owned-businesses/266684-1.html

112. Cooper, William, Paranet posting (undated) http://www.sacred-texts.com/ufo/usstiru.htm

113. For an outstanding chronology and analysis of Cooper's foray into the world of UFO research, see Ecker, Don, "Dark Days Revisited: Chaos in the UFO Underground," *UFO Magazine*, 2-3/02.

114. Krill, O.H. (a.k.a. John Grace), "A Situation Report on Our Acquisition of Advanced Technology and Interaction with Alien Cultures," January 1988. Valerian, Valdamar (a.k.a. John Grace), *The Matrix: Understanding Aspects of Covert Interaction with Alien Culture, Technology and Planetary Power Structures*, Arcturus Book Services, 1988.

115. Ecker, Don, "Dark Days Revisited: Chaos in the UFO Underground," *UFO Magazine*, 2-3/02

116. Davidson, Leon, *Flying Saucers: an Analysis of the Air Force Project Blue Book Special Report No. 14* Blue-Book Publishers, 1976

117. English, William S., "Update/Situation Report for 1988," Published to ParaNet, available at http://www.book-of-thoth.com/archives-article-3985.html and http://www.textfiles.com/ufo/chapt1asc.ufo

118. Howe, Linda Moulton, *An Alien Harvest*, p. 59-61.
119. "William Cooper Exhibit," http://www.geocities.com/CapitolHill/Embassy/1154/ WilliamCooperExhibit.html; "William Cooper Exposed!" Encounters Forum File, http:// archive.anomalies.net/index.php?dir=cooper/&file=coop1.htm; and Ecker, Don, "Dark Days Revisited: Chaos in the UFO Underground," *UFO Magazine*, 2-3/02.
120. Cooper, William, posting on Paranet 1988 (undated), http://www.skepticfiles.org/ufo1/toalldoc.htm
121. *UFO Cover-Up? Live!* Air date 14 October 1988; excerpts reprinted in ParaNet Information Service, 1991.
122. Taff, Barry E., "UFO Cover-Up? Live!: The Untold Story," republished in Paranet, 1991.
123. Bishop, Gregory, *Project Beta*, p. 212.
124. Andrus, Walter, "Director's Message," *MUFON UFO Journal*, 11/88.
125. English, William S., "Update/Situation Report for 1988," Published to ParaNet, available at http:// www.book-of-thoth.com/archives-article-3985.html and http://www.textfiles.com/ufo/chapt1asc.ufo
126. Girard, Robert C., "This is a Test," *MUFON UFO Journal*, 3/89.
127. Swan, Robert J. Letter to Linda Moulton Howe, April 5, 1989, in: Howe, Linda Moulton, *An Alien Harvest: Further Evidence Linking Animal Mutilations and Human Abductions to Alien Life Forms*, Pioneer Printing, 1989, p. 299.
128. Lear, John, "A Public Briefing," Las Vegas, May 14,1990, http://www.thelivingmoon.com/ 47john_lear/02files/A_Public_Briefing_John_Lear_May_14_1990_Las_Vegas.html.
129. Speiser, Jim, "Lear and Cooper: an Explanation (But Not an Apology), Paranet posting, 10/26/88. Ecker, Don, "Dark Days Revisited: Chaos in the UFO Underground," *UFO Magazine*, February/March 2002
130. Bamford, James. "America's Supersecret Eyes In Space." *The New York Times*, January 13, 1985.
131. Cook, Nick, *The Hunt for Zero Point*, p. 120.
132. Sweetman, Bill, *B-2*, p. 27.
133. Sweetman, Bill, *B-2*, p. 27-28; Boyne, Walter J., *Beyond the Wild Blue*, p. 260, 410.
134. Schratt, Michael, correspondence with the author, September 28, 2008.
135. Indeed, by this time, the American led program commonly known as Echelon was fairly mature. This was a global electronics intelligence sweet that grew out of the 1946 UKUSA Communications Intelligence Agreement, and included the U.S., Britain, Canada, Australia, and New Zealand. Electronic communications globally were swept up, exchanged, and analyzed. See Bamford, James, *Body of Secrets*, p. 394.
136. "Black world engineers, scientists, encourage using highly classified technology for civil applications," *Aviation Week & Space Technology*, March 1992 [no author attribution].
137. H. E. Puthoff, C. Maccone and E. W. Davis, "Levi-Civita effect in the polarizable Vacuum (PV) representation of general relativity," *Gen. Rel. and Grav.* 37, 483-489 (2005).
138. Two sources on Thomas Townsend Brown and electrogravitics are: Valone, Thomas, Ph.D., *Electrogravitics II: Validating Reports on a New Propulsion Methodology*, Integrity Research Institute, 2004 [http://www.integrityresearchinstitute.org]; and Schatzin, Paul, *Defying Gravity: The Parallel Universe of T. Townend Brown* (forthcoming), http://www.ttbrown.com
139. LaViolette, Paul A. Ph.D., "The U.S. Antigravity Squadron," 1993; http:// www.americanantigravity.com/laviolette-b2-bomber.shtml
140. Gunston, Bill, "Military Power," *Air International*, January 2000.
141. Thrust/weight numbers obtained from entries for "B-1 Lancer," "B-52 Flying Fortress," and "B-2 Spirit" in *Wikipedia, the free encyclopedia*.
142. An interesting discussin on this issue can be found at the website abovetopsecret.com. See "B2 - Photo of electro-gravitic field kicking in," at *http://www.abovetopsecret.com/forum/thread18541/pg1*
143. The cost of each air vehicle averaged $737 million per plane in 1997. Total procurement costs averaged $929 million per plane, which includes spare parts, equipment, retrofitting, and software support. The total program cost, including development, engineering and testing, averaged $2.1 billion per aircraft (in 1997 dollars). see "B-2 Bomber: Cost and Operational Issues" U.S. General Accounting Office, (Letter Report, 08/14/97, GAO/NSIAD-97-181) at *http://www.fas.org/man/gao/ nsiad97181.htm*
144. Cook, Nick, *The Hunt for Zero Point*, p. 124, 133-134, 137.
145. Sweetman, Bill. *Aurora: The Pentagon's Secret Hypersonic Spyplane*, p. 13.
146. Cook, Nick, *The Hunt for Zero Point*, p. 144.
147. The author thanks aviation researcher Michael Schratt for clarification on this issue.
148. Hansen, Terry, *The Missing Times*, p. 83.
149. For a detailed account of this event, see Greer, Steven M., M.D. "Testimony of Mr. Mark McCandlish, US Air Force December 2000," in *Disclosure*, p. 497-510.
150. McCandlish, Mark & Schratt, Michael, "The Super –STOL," http://www.markmccandlish.com/
151. Interview with Michael Schratt, in Howe, Linda Moulton, "Do Black Budget Trillions Support A Secret American Space Program?" 2007. http://thestrongdelusion.com/

152. McCandlish, Mark, Statement at Disclosure Press Conference, National Press Club, Washington, DC, May 9, 2001.
153. McCandlish, Mark, correspondence with the author, October 2, 2008.
154. See Puthoff, H. E., "Ground State of Hydrogen as a Zero-Point-Fluctuation-Determined State," *Physics Review*, D 35, 3266, 1987. Puthoff, H. E., "Zero-Point Fluctuations of the Vacuum as the Source of Atomic Stability and the Gravitational Interaction," *Proceedings of the British Society for the Philosophy of Science International Conference*, 1988. Puthoff, H. E., "On the Source of Vacuum Electromagnetic Zero-Point Energy," *Physics Review*, A 40, 4857, 1989.
155. Powell, Martin J., "'Where's it Come From?': A Study of the 1994 Nellis UFO Video Footage," *http://homepage.ntlworld.com/mjpowell/Nellis/Part1/Part1.htm*. Rudiak, David, "The Nellis Range UFO Video," *http://roswellproof.homestead.com/nellis_discussion.html*
156. Redfern, Nicholas, *A Covert Agenda*, p. 181.
157. Redfern, Nicholas, *A Covert Agenda*, p. 166.
158. Stonehill, Paul and Mantle, Phillip. *The Soviet UFO Files*, p. 57
159. Huneeus, Antonio, *Foreign News Tribune*, New York, NY, 6/14/90.

Chapter 8 - To Dreamland and Beyond, 1989-1990

1. Peterson, Bill, "Bush Acts to Reassure Conservatives on SDI; Nominee `Surprised' Commitment Is Doubted," *The Washington Post, 8/31/88*; Buckley, William F., Jr., "What's Going On? – George Bush on Strategic Defense Initiative," *National Review*, 9/30/88.
2. Friedman, George, and Friedman, Meredith, *Future of War*, p. 354-355.
3. McCoy, Alfred, "Drug Fallout: The CIA's Forty Year Complicity in the Narcotics Trade," *The Progressive*, August 1, 1997; Thomas, Kenn and Keith, Jim, *The Octopus: Secret Government and the Death of Danny Casolaro*. Revised Edition, Feral House, 2004, p. 95-96.
4. Cameron, Grant, http://presidentialufo.com
5. Collins, Robert & Doty, Richard, *Exempt from Disclosure*, p. 106.
6. See *http://www.abovetopsecret.com/forum/thread60571/pg1*. The author can add two pieces of information on this matter. First, one private inquiry with an Aviary member received the reply that , although he did not believe Helms was "Raven," he was sure that Verona was not. Second, according to Linda Moulton Howe in a private communication with the author, one source that crossed her path said that Raven "definitely" was Richard Helms.
7. Clark, Jerome, "Paranoia," *International UFO Reporter*, January/February 1989.
8. Moore, William L. MJ-12: An Open Letter," *MUFON UFO Journal*, 1/89.
9. Stringfield, Leonard, "Crash/Retrievals: Status Report V," *MUFON UFO Journal*, 1/89 and 2/89.
10. Jacobs, David, Ph.D., "Hybrid Thoughts," *MUFON UFO Journal*, 2/89.
11. Hopkins, Budd; Jacobs, David; Vallee, Jacques, "Letters to the Editor," *MUFON UFO Journal*, 2/89.
12. Sagan, Carl, *The Demon-Haunted World: Science as a Candle in the Dark*. Ballantine Books, 1996.
13. *Toronto Star*, 10/16/88.
14. Friedman, Stanton T., "An Open Letter to Dr. Carl Sagan," *MUFON UFO Journal*, 5/89.
15. Bush, George H. W., "Commencement Address at Texas A&M University (May 12, 1989)," at http://millercenter.org/scripps/archive/speeches/detail/3421
16. Anonymous; "Mystery Object Encountered by Russian Phobos Spacecraft," *Meta Research Bulletin*, 1:1, March 15, 1992; http://ufologie.net/htm/phob12.htm
17. Selivanov. A.S. and Gektin. U.M., "The Mysterious End of Phobos 2," *Planetary Report* Jan-Feb 1993, http://ufologie.net/htm/phobrep.htm; a good overview of this case appears in Stonehill, Paul & Mantle, Philip, *The Soviet UFO Files*, p. 70-73.
18. Vallee, Jacques, *UFO Chronicles of the Soviet Union*, p. 32-33.
19. Vallee, Jacques, *UFO Chronicles of the Soviet Union*, p. 11.
20. Vallee, Jacques, *UFO Chronicles of the Soviet Union*, p. 11-12.
21. Howe, Linda Moulton, *An Alien Harvest*, p. 40, 86-87, 94-102; Fyffe Police Department Press Conference, Wednesday, April 7, 1993, at *http://www.ob1.com/fyfecow.html*.
22. Roberts, Elton, "Friday Night UFO Remains a Mystery," Fort Payne (AL) *Times Journal*, 2/14/89. Stockman, Susan, "They're Back: UFOs Sighted in Dekalb," *Weekly Post*, Rainsville, AL, 2/16/89. Alabama UFO baffles police, Fort Payne (AL) *Times Journal*, 2/18-19, 1989. "Woman in UFO Incident Seeks Data on State Sightings," *The Associated Press*, 2/18/89. "Policemen Not Laughing at UFO Jokes," *The Associated Press*, 2/23/89. "Sand Mountain UFO Sighting Reports Grow," *The Associated Press*, 3/3/89. UFOs draw 4,000 to town in Alabama, *The Associated Press*, 3/5/89. Stockman, Susan, "3,500 people descend on Fyffe to see no-show UFO," *Weekly Post*, Rainsville, AL, 3/9/89. "Some say UFO is as big as a football field," *Weekly Post*, Rainsville, AL, 3/16/89.
23. Hesemann, Michael, *Secrets of the Black World*, video, 1993.

24. The Billy Goodman Happening Radio Show, Guest: Bob Lazar, November 21, 1989, http://www.ufomind.com/area51/people/lazar/goodman_nov21.html; Aggen, Erich A. Jr., "Black Holes and Robert Lazar," *MUFON UFO Journal*, 6/90. See also Lazar, Robert & Huff, Gene, *The Lazar Tape*, Tri Dot Productions, 1991.

25. Billy Goodman Happening Radio Show, Guest: Robert Lazar, December 20, 1989.

26. George Knapp, producer/host; Robert Lazar, guest. *On the Record*, KLAS-TV, December 9, 1989.

27. Hesemann, Michael, *Secrets of the Black World*, video.

28. Two good starting points regarding Lazar's credentials are Tom Mahood, "The Robert Lazar Timeline: As Assembled from Public Records and Statements," Version 1.10, October 1995, Originally released July, 1994; and a detailed rebuttal (untitled) by Gene Huff, posted to *alt.conspiracy.area51* on March 12, 1995. A good overview on the Lazar story is contained in Susan Wright's *UFO Headquarters*, p. 167-179.

29. Cameron, Grant R., Crain, T. Scott, and Rutkowski, Chris. "In the Land of Dreams," *International UFO Reporter*, Sept/Oct 1990.

30. Lazar, Robert & Huff, Gene, *The Lazar Tape*, Tri Dot Productions, 1991; Cameron, Grant, "Presidential UFO" at http://presidentialufo.com

31. Cooper, Milton William. "The Secret Government: The Origin, Identity, and Purpose of MJ-12," published on the Internet May 23, 1989, and republished countless times since on the world wide web.

32. Gulley, Bill with Reese, Mary Ellen, *Breaking Cover*, New York, Simon and Schuster, 1980.

33. Clark, Jerome, "Flying Saucer Fascism," *International UFO Reporter*, July/August 1989.

34. Hastings, Robert, "The MJ-12 Affair: Facts, Questions, Comments," *MUFON UFO Journal*, 6/89.

35. Schuessler, John F., "Unidentified Flying Objects: A Futurist Perspective," *MUFON UFO Journal*, 10/89.

36. Bishop, Gregory, *Project Beta*, p. 220-224; Clark, Jerome, *The UFO Book*, p. 163-164; Stacy, Dennis, "MUFON Las Vegas Symposium," *MUFON UFO Journal*, 8/89.

37. "Interview with Bill Moore," Gregory Bishop, 1993, www.excludedmiddle.com

38. "Interview with Bill Moore," Gregory Bishop, 1993, www.excludedmiddle.com

39. "Interview with Bill Moore," Gregory Bishop, 1993, www.excludedmiddle.com

40. Stacy, Dennis, "MUFON Las Vegas Symposium," *MUFON UFO Journal*, 8/89.

41. Hamilton, William F., III,"Flying Wings and Deep Desert Secrets," *MUFON UFO Journal*, 11/90; Hamilton, William F., III, *Cosmic Top Secret*, p. 61-62.

42. "UFO seen over Kanazawa," *Japan Times*, 9/23/89; "UFO Videotaped Over Kanazawa," *Mainichi Daily News*, 9/26/89; Haines, Richard F., "Japanese Video," *MUFON UFO Journal*, 3/90; Maccabee, Bruce, "Recent UFO Videotapes," *MUFON UFO Journal*, 5/90; Maccabee, Bruce, "A Rare Photo Coincidence," *International UFO Reporter*, 5-6/90.

43. Maccabee, Bruce, "Recent Videotapes," *MUFON UFO Journal*, 5/90; Hall, Richard, *UFO Evidence, Volume 2*, p. 31; Ballester Olmos, Vicente Juan, "Casos OVNI provocados por globos estratosfericos," http://stratocat.com.ar/ovnis/es890810.htm

44. Redfern, Nicholas, *A Covert Agenda*, p. 183.

45. Wright, Susan, *UFO Headquarters*, p. 137.

46. Sweetman, Bill. *Aurora: The Pentagon's Secret Hypersonic Spyplane*, p. 88-89.

47. Sweetman, Bill. *Aurora: The Pentagon's Secret Hypersonic Spyplane*, p. 64.

48. See "The Aurora Aircraft Page," http://aurorapage.tripod.com/

49. For John Ford's description of the Moriches Bay case, see Ford, John, "UFO Captured at Moriches Bay?," *East Ender*, Long Island, 2/9/90. Also, see "The Mysterious UFO Crash And Retrieval (?) At Moriches Bay, Long Island," *http://alienview.net/fordnew.htm*

50. Philip Imbrogno, interview with the author, January 13, 2009.

51. "TWA Flight 800," from Wikipedia, the free encyclopedia.

52. "UFO Researcher Accused of Plot Against Politicians," *Reuters*, 6/13/96.

53. Douglass, Elaine, "The Ordeal of John Ford," *MUFON UFO Journal*, 11/96.

54. Stout, John (signed "Harry Hepcat"), "Long Island's Ordeal," *MUFON UFO Journal*, 1/97.

55. *UFO Round Up*, V. 2, n45, 11/23/96; "Radiation Suspect is Delusional," *Newsday* 11/14/97. For more background on John Ford, see "The John Ford Affair: From The Unopened Files of UFO Magazine, at *http://www.alienview.net/fordstor2.html*; and Lawhon, Loy, "John Ford," at *http://www.alienview.net/fordstor2.html*

56. Vallee, Jacques, *UFO Chronicles of the Soviet Union*, p. 12, 37-39.

57. "Moscow Air Defense to Be Downsized, Receive Su-27s." April 10, 1993; FBIS-SOV-93-069, CIA: FBIS Concatenated Daily Reports, 1993.

58. Ilyn, Vadim K."KGB's 'Blue Folder' Reveals Shootings, Landings in USSR," http://www.mufon.com/znews_kgb.html; Stonehill, Paul and Mantle, Philip, *Soviet UFO Files*, p. 74-76.

59. KGB file entitled "Communications on Observation of Anomalous Event in the District of Kaspustin Yar (July 28, 989); English translation by Dimitri Ossipov; cited in Berliner, Don, *UFO Briefing Document*, 1995, p. 134.

60. "Classification: Secret – from the KGB Files," *AURA-Z*, No. 1, Moscow, 1993; Stonehill, Paul & Mantle, Philip, *Soviet UFO Files*, p. 79; Berliner, Don, *UFO Briefing Document*, p. 133-138; Bourdais, Gildas, "Summary of Some Cases Noted in the COMETA Report," *MUFON UFO Journal*, 9/99.

61. Friedman, Thomas L., "Senate Leader Asserts U.S. Fails To Encourage Change in East Bloc," *New York Times*, September 19, 1989.

62. Issacs, Jeremy & Downing, Taylor, *Cold War*, p. 385-386.

63. Vallee, Jacques, *UFO Chronicles of the Soviet Union*, p. 165.

64. Vallee, Jacques, *UFO Chronicles of the Soviet Union*, p. 36.

65. Stonehill, Paul and Mantle, Philip, *Soviet UFO Files*, p. 68-69.

66. Vallee, Jacques, *UFO Chronicles of the Soviet Union*, p. 44.

67. Hall, Richard, *UFO Evidence, Volume 2*, p. 31, 492.

68. "Aliens Visit Voronezh," *Moscow News (Tass)*, Oct. 11, 1989; Vallee, Jacques, *UFO Chronicles of the Soviet Union*, p. 40-61; Stonehill, Paul & Mantle, Philip, *Soviet UFO Files*, p. 98-99.

69. "Soviets' close encounter leaves experts skeptical," *Republican*, Waterbury, CT, 10/10/89; Jacobson, David, "Space aliens look foreign to skeptics," *Hartford Courant*, 10/11/89; "A thought provoking conversation with alien beings described," Reuters, 10/13/89; Mott, Patrick, "Galactic Glasnost," *Los Angeles Times*, 10/26/89; Mitchell, Alison, "Bizarre tales: glasnost or psychosis?" *Newsday*, 10/29/89; Shiflett, Dave, "Invasion of the Mind-Snatchers, *Wall Street Journal*, 10/30/89.

70. Vallee, Jacques, *UFO Chronicles of the Soviet Union*, p. 40-61.

71. Vallee, Jacques, *UFO Chronicles of the Soviet Union*, p. 45-46.

72. Vallee, Jacques, *UFO Chronicles of the Soviet Union*, p. 32.

73. Vallee, Jacques, *UFO Chronicles of the Soviet Union*, p. 36-37.

74. CIA FOIA files, FBIS Foreign Press Notice, 10/7/89.

75. CIA FOIA files, FBIS Foreign press notice, Oct. 12, 1989.

76. CIA FOIA files, FBIS Foreign press notice, Oct. 13, 1989

77. CIA FOIA files, FBIS Foreign Press Notice, 10/28/89.

78. CIA FOIA files, FBIS Foreign Press Notice, October 21, 1989.

79. Ilyin, Vadim K., "KGB's 'Blue Folder' Reveals Shootings, Landings in USSR," http://www.mufon.com/znews_kgb.html

80. CIA FOIA files, FBIS Foreign Press Notice, 11/1/89.

81. Hamilton, William F. III; "Flying Wings and Deep Desert Secrets," *MUFON UFO Journal*, 11/90; Hamilton, William F. III, *Cosmic Top Secret*, p. 62.

82. Berliner, Don, *UFO Briefing Document*, p. 139-144; Pratt, Bob, "The Belgium UFO Flap," *MUFON UFO Journal*, 7/90; Greer, Stephen M., MD, "UFOs over Belgium," *MUFON UFO Journal*, 5/92; Meesen, Auguste, "The Belgian Sightings," *International UFO Reporter*, 5-6/91.

83. Meesen, Auguste, "The Belgian Sightings," *International UFO Reporter*, 5-6/91.

84. Vidal, Patrick and Rozencwajg, "The Belgian Wave," *International UFO Reporter*, 7-8/91.

85. Meesen, Auguste, "The Belgian Sightings," *International UFO Reporter*, May/June 1991.

86. "An Open Letter from Budd Hopkins, *MUFON UFO Journal*, 6/92; Hopkins, Budd, "The Linda Cortile Abduction Case," *MUFON UFO Journal*, 9/92; Hopkins, Budd, The Linda Cortile Abduction Case, Part II, *MUFON UFO Journal*, 12/92; Cortile, Linda, "A Light at the End of the Tunnel," *MUFON UFO Journal*, 6/93; Hopkins, Budd, *Witnessed: The True Story of the Brooklyn Bridge UFO Abductions* (Pocket Books, 1996); Spence, Yancy (pseud.), "The Day Manhattan Stood Still: A True Eye-Witness Account of the South Street Abductions," *UFO Magazine*, Oct-Nov 2002, and *http://-www.ufocasebook.com/daze.html*

87. Cameron, Grant, http://presidentialufo.com

88. Anderson, Curt, "His US sentence served, Noriega fights extradition," AP 1/7/09

89. See Buckley, Kevin, *Panama: The Whole Story* (Simon & Schuster, 1991).

90. Smith, Gar, "Operation Just Cause: How to Stage a Regime Change," *The Edge* October 18, 2002, *http://www.earthisland.org*. See also Willson, S. Brian, "Analysis of the Dec. 20, 1989 U.S. Invasion in Historical Context." December 1989 (updated 1991) http://www.brianwillson.com/awolpanama.html

91. http://lowobservable.virtualave.net/Nighthawk.htm

92. Smith, Gar, "Operation Just Cause: How to Stage a Regime Change," *The Edge*, October 18, 2002, *http://www.earthisland.org/*

93. Smith, Gar, "Operation Just Cause: How to Stage a Regime Change," *The Edge*, October 18, 2002, *http://www.earthisland.org/*

94. Hesemann, Michael, *Secrets of the Black World.*, video.

95. Hesemann, Michael, *Secrets of the Black World*, video.

96. Hesemann, Michael, *Secrets of the Black World*, video,

97. Cameron, Grant R.; Crain, T. Scott; Rutkowski, Chris, "In the Land of Dreams," *International UFO Reporter*, Sept/Oct 1990; See also Emerson, Steven. *Secret Warriors: Inside the Covert Military Operations of the Reagan Era*. New York: G.P. Putnam's Sons, 1988.

98. Maccabee, Bruce, "The Scale Remains Unbalanced," *MUFON UFO Journal*, 4/89; "Look Up in the Sky," *News*, Parkersburg, WV, 1/30/89.
99. Wright, Dan, "Current Case Log, *MUFON UFO Journal*, 2/90.
100. Hall, Richard, *The UFO Evidence, Volume II*, p. 31.
101. Tucker, Jennifer, "Eglin Base Has No Record of UFOs," *Tribune-Times*, Tampa, FL, 1/29/89.
102. Huneeus, Antonio, "Florida Symposium Airs Controversial UFO Case," *MUFON UFO Journal*, 8/90.
103. Wright, Dan, "Current Case Log," *MUFON UFO Journal*, 5/90.
104. Wright, Dan, "Current Case Log," *MUFON UFO Journal*, 5/90.
105. Wright, Dan, "Current Case Log," *MUFON UFO Journal*, 8/90.
106. Salisbury, Rex, "Red Lights in the sky! Hoax or Real?" *MUFON UFO Journal*, 6/90.
107. Salisbury, Rex, "Red Lights in the sky! Hoax or Real?" *MUFON UFO Journal*, 6/90.
108. *Kirkus Reviews*, 1/15/90; *MUFON UFO Journal*, 2/90.
109. Myers, Craig, "Gulf Breeze Model Found," *Pensacola News Journal*, 6/10/90; "Model of UFO found in Gulf Breeze attic," *Daily News*, Fort Walton Beach, FL, 6/11/90.
110. Bob Reid, correspondence with the author, July 14, 2009.
111. Gray, Ed, "Ed Walters perpetrating UFO hoax," Gulf Breeze *Sentinel*, 6/14/90.
112. Lynn, Adam, "UFO model confirms disbelief of some, others say it doesn't resemble photos," *Pensacola News Journal*, 6/11/90; "UFO model appears to be fake!" *Gulf Breeze Sentinel*, 6/14/90; Hufford, Art, "Ed Walters, The Model, and Tommy Smith," *MUFON UFO Journal*, 1/93.
113. Myers, Craig, "Witness says he saw UFO photos faked," *Pensacola News Journal*, 6/17/90; "Smith says he saw pictures faked," *Gulf Breeze Sentinel*, 6/21/90.
114. Huneeus, Antonio, "Florida Symposium Airs Controversial UFO Case," *MUFON UFO Journal*, 8/90.
115. Myers, Craig, "Experts to reopen Gulf Breeze UFO probe," Gulf Breeze *Sentinel*, 6/14/90; Hufford, Art, "Ed Walters, The Model, and Tommy Smith," *MUFON UFO Journal*, 1/93; Andrus, Walter, "Conclusion by MUFON on the Reopening of the Walters Case," *MUFON UFO Journal*, 1/93.
116. Huneeus, Antonio, "Florida Symposium Airs Controversial UFO Case," *MUFON UFO Journal*, 8/90; Wright, Dan, Gulf Breeze Update, *MUFON UFO Journal*, 2/91.
117. Reports on these further sightings and other sightings by Ed Walters are contained in the books *Abductions in Gulf Breeze* (Ed and Frances Walters, Avon, 1994) and *UFOS Are Real: Here's the Proof* (Ed Walters and Bruce Maccabee, Avon, 1997).
118. CIA Foreign Press Report: Concatenated PROD Reports, 1988-1994; Headline: USSR: UFO Sightings No. 2 – General Maltsev Comments. Report Number: FB PN 90-123.
119. CIA document collection. Subject: UFOs reported near Moscow, April 15, 1990.
120. "UFOs on Air Defense Radars," *Rabochaya Tribuna*, Moscow, 4/19/90; English translation by the U.S. Foreign Broadcast Information Service (FBIS).
121. CIA Foreign Press Report: Concatenated PROD Reports, 1988-1994; Headline: USSR: UFO Sightings No. 2 – General Maltsev Comments. Report Number: FB PN 90-123; See also "Soviet Air Defenses Baffled by Huge UFOs," *MUFON UFO Journal*, 6/90; Musinsky, V. D.,"Through the Secrecy Barrier," *International UFO Reporter*, 7-8/90; Ilyin, Vadim K., "KGB's 'Blue Folder' Reveals Shootings, Landings in USSR," http://www.mufon.com/znews_kgb.html; Vallee, Jacques, *UFO Chronicles of the Soviet Union*, p. 139; Berliner, Don, *UFO Briefing Document*, p. 138; Stonehill, Paul and Mantle, Philip, *The Soviet UFO Files*, p. 50-51.
122. For good summaries of the Belgian triangle case, see Pratt, Bob, "The Belgium UFO Flap," *MUFON UFO Journal*, 7/90; "Remarkable military encounter in Belgium," *International UFO Reporter*, July/August 1990; de Brosses, Marie-Therese, "F-16 Radar Tracks UFO" translated by Robert Durant, *MUFON UFO Journal*, 8/90; Huneeus, Antonio, "Breaking down the wall of UFO silence," *UFO Universe*, June/July 1991; Greer, Steven M., M.D., "UFOs Over Belgium," *MUFON UFO Journal*, 5/92; Berliner, Don, *UFO Briefing Document*, p. 139-144.
123. Lambrechts, Major P., "Report Concerning the Observation of UFOs During the Night of March 30-31, 1990," preliminary report dated May 31, 1990.
124. De Brouwer, W., Preface, *Vague d'OVNI sur la Belgique - Un Dossier Exceptionnel*, Brussels: SOBEPS, 1991.
125. "Flying triangle has Belgians going round in circles," *Financial Times*, London, 4/18/90.
126. Memo, "SUBJ; IIR6 807 0136 90 Belgium and the UFO Issue," Joint Chiefs of Staff, Washington, DC, 1990; see also Marhic, Reynaud, "Ovnis belges: nouvelle rumeur," *Phénomèna* no. 13, Jan/Feb 1993, SOS OVNI, Aix-en-Provence, France, cited in Berliner, Don, *UFO Briefing Document*, p. 144.
127. Pope, Nick, *Open Skies, Closed Minds*, p. 148-150
128. Pratt, Bob, "The Belgium UFO Flap," *MUFON UFO Journal*, 7/90.
129. *Paris Match*, 8/9/90; de Brosses, Marie-Therese, "An Interview with Professor Jean-Pierre Petit," *MUFON UFO Journal*, 1/91.
130. Utrecht, Wim Van "Letter to the Editor," *MUFON UFO Journal*, 8/92.
131. CIA Foreign Press Report: Concatenated PROD Reports, 1988-1994; Headline: USSR: UFO Sightings No. 2 – General Maltsev Comments. Report Number: FB PN 90-123.
132. Stonehill, Paul and Mantle, Philip, *The Soviet UFO Files*, p. 110.

133. CIA Foreign Press Report: Concatenated PROD Reports, 1988-1994; Headline: USSR: UFO Sightings No. 2 – General Maltsev Comments. Report Number: FB PN 90-123.

134. CIA documents; Subject: State Center for Study of UFOs Established. Date undated.

135. *Pravda*, April 27, 1990; Berliner, Don, *UFO Briefing Document*, p. 180.

136. Murkhortov, Pavel, "Only from Official Sources" *Sovetskaya Molodezh*, 5/4/90; CIA Foreign Press Note FB PN 91-014; Cameron, Grant, *http://presidentialufo.com*; *Filer's Files*, 6/9/04.

137. CIA document. Subject: USSR, PRC Scientists in Joint Study of UFOs, Date 21 May 1990. Moscow Domestic Service in Russian 2100 GMT 21 May 90.

138. US DIA memo dated June 28, 1990. Subject IIR [blacked out] Defense Science, Technology and Industry Report, 1-15 April, 1990.

139. Boyne, Walter, *Beyond the Wild Blue*, p. 413.

140. Sweetman, Bill. *Aurora: The Pentagon's Secret Hypersonic Spyplane*, p. 4.

141. Pope, Nick, *Open Skies, Closed Minds*, p. 196.

142. The Aurora Aircraft Page; *http://aurorapage.tripod.com/*; Sweetman, Bill. *Aurora: The Pentagon's Secret Hypersonic Spyplane*, p. 13

143. Richelson, Jeffrey T., *The Wizards of Langley: Inside the CIA's Directorate of Science and Technology*, 2001; Priest, Dana, "New Spy Satellite Debated on Hill," *Washington Post*, 12/11/04; Jehl, Douglas, "New Spy Plan Said to Involve Satellite System," *New York Times*, 12/12/04; Misty (classified project), From *Wikipedia*, the free encyclopedia.

144. Cook, Nick, *The Hunt for Zero Point*, p. 14, 96; "Shiva Star," from *Wikipedia*, the free encyclopedia.

145. Cook, Nick, *The Hunt for Zero Point*, p. 83-84.

146. Boyne, *Beyond the Wild Blue*, p. 413; see also http://www.dfrc.nasa.gov/PAO/PAIS/HTML/FS-009-DFRC.html

147. Boyne, Walter, *Beyond the Wild Blue*, p. 413 Saul, Stephanie. "Cheney Aims Barrage at F-14D," *Newsday*, 8/24/89.

148. Boyne, Walter, *Beyond the Wild Blue*, p. 414; F-22 Raptor, from *Wikipedia, the free encyclopedia*.

149. Cameron, Grant R. Crain, T. Scott, and Rutkowski, Chris, "In the land of dreams," *International UFO Reporter*, 9-10/90.

150. Hussey, Brian, "Theories on the Formation of Crop Circles," at *http://ufoevidence.org*.

151. Howe, Linda Moulton, *Glimpses of Other Realities, Volume One*, page 11; Pope, Nick, *Open Skies, Closed Minds* p. 122.

152. Pope, Nick, *Open Skies, Closed Minds* p. 113.

153. Migliore, Vince, Crop Circles: The Mystical View, *MUFON UFO Journal*, 6/91.

154. Good overviews of the crop circle phenomenon include: Andrews, Colin & Delgado, Pat. *Circular Evidence: A Detailed Investigation of the Flattened Swirled Crops Phenomenon*, 1989; Noyes, Ralph, Ed., (photographs by Busty Taylor), *The Crop Circle Enigma: Grounding the Phenomenon in Science*, Culture and Metaphysics, Gateway Books, 1990; Haselhoff, Eltojo H., Ph.D. *The Deepening Complexity of Crop Circles: Scientific Research & Urban Legends*, Frog, Ltd, 2001; Silva, Freddy, *Secrets in the Fields: The Science and Mysticism of Crop Circles*, Hampton Roads Publishing Co., 2002.

Chapter 9 - False Dawn, 1990-1991

1. 1997, U.S. Senate Document 105-2, "Report of the Commission on Protecting and Reducing Government Secrecy," see also Joel van der Reijden, "USAPs: Unacknowledged Special Access Programs," 9/10/05 at http://www.bibliotecapleyades.net/sociopolitica/sociopol_USAP.htm

2. Sweetman, Bill, "In Search of the Pentagon's Billion Dollar Hidden Budgets: How the U.S. Keeps its R&D Spending Under Wraps." *Jane's International Defence Review*, January 5, 2000.

3. "$3,400,000,000,000 Of Taxpayers' Money Is Missing," *Washington Times*, 4/1/99; "Why Is $59 Billion Missing From HUD?" *Insight Magazine*, 11/6/00; "The Cabinet: Inside HUD's Financial Fiasco," *Insight Magazine*, 6/25/01; "Rumsfeld Inherits Financial Mess," *Insight Magazine*, 9/3/01; "Wasted Riches," *Insight Magazine*, 9/28/01; "The War on Waste: Defense Department Cannot Account For 25% Of Funds – $2.3 Trillion," *CBS News*, 1/29/02; "Government Fails Fiscal Fitness Test," *Insight Magazine*, 4/29/02; "Military waste under fire $1 trillion missing – Bush plan targets Pentagon accounting," *San Francisco Chronicle*, 5/18/03; "Pentagon Fights For (Its) Freedom," *CBS*, 5/19/03; "So much for the peace dividend: Pentagon is winning the battle for a $400bn budget," *The Guardian*, 5/22/03; "Congressman Dennis Kucinich mentions the missing trillions," National Public Radio Morning Edition, 6/28/03; "NASA costs can't be verified, GAO report says," *USA Today*, 4/6/04.

4. Rumsfeld, Donald, Testimony before the House Appropriations Committee: Fiscal Year 2002 Defense Budget Request. July 16, 2001.

5. Another reason is that it was the brainchild of Edward Teller, a man whose name has intersected with UFOs more than once.

6. Frantz, Douglas and Waas, Murray, "U.S. Loans Indirectly Financed Iraq Military," *Los Angeles Times*, February 25, 1992.
7. Iraq was about more than oil. John Perkins, author of *Confessions of an Economic Hit Man*, pointed out it was also about water. The Tigris and Euphrates were the most important sources of water in the arid Middle East. The importance of controlling water had become obvious to certain groups which "looked toward privatizing water systems in Africa, Latin America, and the Middle East." see Perkins, John, *Confessions of an Economic Hit Man*, Berrett-Koehler Publishers, Inc., 2004, p. 183-184.
8. Friedman, Alan, "U.S. backed Dollars 1bn Iraqi loan prior to invasion of Kuwait," *Financial Times* (London), 5/3/91; Frantz, Douglas and Waas, Murray, "Bush Secret Effort Helped Iraq Build Its War Machine," *Los Angeles Times*, February 23, 1992.
9. Frantz, Douglas and Waas, Murray, "Bush Secret Effort Helped Iraq Build Its War Machine," *Los Angeles Times*, February 23, 1992.
10. Tarpley, Webster G. and Chaitkin, Anton, *George Bush; The Unauthorized Biography*, Executive Intelligence Review, Washington D.C., 1992.
11. Marrs, Jim, "An Overview Of The War On Terrorism," 2001.
12. "Bush's Talk of a 'New World Order': Foreign Policy Tool or Mere Slogan?, *Washington Post*, 5/26/91
13. *Bild*, 8/31/90.
14. Ludwiger, Illobrand von, *Best UFO Cases, Europe*, National Institute for Discovery Sciences, 1998, p. 70-79; *http://www.ufoevidence.org/photographs/photohome.asp*; Ludwiger, Illobrand von, "The Greifswald Lights: Example for a Class B UFO Report," *http://www.mufon-ces.org/text/english/greifswald.htm*
15. CIA Foreign Press Note FB PN 91-014.
16. FBIS Concantenated Daily Reports, 1990, "Subject: Airship-Like UFO Sighted Over Murmansk. 4 September 90," 06 Sep 90, FBIS-SOV-90-173.
17. CIA Foreign Press Note FB PN 91-014.
18. Stonehill, Paul, & Mantle, Philip, *Soviet UFO Files*, p. 50.
19. *Rabochaya Tribuna*, 10/16/90; CIA Foreign Press Note FB PN 91-014; *The Secret NASA Transmissions. The Smoking Gun, Pt. 2*; *Filer's Files*, 7/30/02; Hesemann, Michael, "UFOs and the MIR space station," *http://www.ufoevidence.org/documents/doc438.htm*
20. *Rabochaya Tribuna*, 10/20/90; CIA Foreign Press Note FB PN 91-014.
21. FBIS Foreign Press Notes: FB PN 89-292, 22 Nov 90, "USSR: Media Reports Multitude of UFO Sightings" and FB PN 90-123, 22 May 90, "USSR: UFO sightings No. 2, General Maltsev Comments;" FBIS Concatenated Daily Reports, 1991, 15 jan 91, FBIS-SOV-91-015.
22. Hamilton, William F. *Cosmic Top Secret*, p. 62.
23. Scott, William, "Multiple Sightings of Secret Aircraft Hint at New Propulsion, Airframe Designs," *Aviation Week and Space Technology*, October 1, 1990; see also Cook, Nick, *The Hunt for Zero Point*, p. 125-126; and Hamilton, William F., *Cosmic Top Secret*, p. 35
24. Hamilton, William F. III, "Flying Wings and Deep Desert Secrets," *MUFON UFO Journal*, 11/90.
25. Hesemann, Michael, *Secrets of the Black World*, video.
26. Howe, Linda Moulton, *Glimpses of Other Realities, Volume Two*, p. 1.
27. Hesemann, Michael, *Secrets of the Black World.*, video.
28. Hesemann, Michael, *Secrets of the Black World.*, video.
29. Hesemann, Michael, *Secrets of the Black World*, video.
30. Hesemann, Michael, *Secrets of the Black World*, video.
31. Hamilton, William F. *Cosmic Top Secret*, p. 42, 60-62; Howe, Linda Moulton, correspondence with the author, June 13, 2009; Sauder, Richard, *Underground Bases and Tunnels*, p. 67-68.
32. Friedman George and Meredith, *Future of War*, p. 302-303; Boyne, Walter, *Beyond the Wild Blue*, p. 302.
33. Freedman, Lawrence and Karsh, Efraim, *The Gulf Conflict: Diplomacy and War in the New World Order, 1990-1991* (Princeton, 1993), 324-29.
34. Cormick, Craig, "Gulf War still causing civilian deaths," *Green Left Online*, 12 June 1991, http://www.greenleft.org.au/1991/16/1161
35. "Annex Foxtrot," From *Wikipedia, the free encyclopedia*.
36. Hansen, Terry, *The Missing Times*, p. 86, 116-118.
37. "Peter Arnett," From *Wikipedia, the free encyclopedia*
38. The TACC log reports a ballad about "Baghdad Billy" that runs as follows:
    I'm an F-111 Jock, and I'm here to tell
    of Baghdad Billy, and his jet from hell.
    We were well protected, with F-15 Eagles in tight,
    but that didn't stop the man with the light.
    RJ, AWACS, they didn't see
    as Baghdad Billy snuck up on me.

Then I found a spotlight shining at my six
and my whoozoo [weapons systems officer] said, whooly s***.
I popped off some chaff and I popped a flare,
but that Iraqi bandit, he didn't care.
I had tracers on my left, and tracers on my right
with a load of bombs, I had to run from the fight.
I rolled my 'Vark over and took her down
into the darkness and finally lost the clown.
When I landed back at Taif and gave this rap,
CENTAF said I was full of crap.
I'm here to tell you, the God's honest truth
that Iraqi bandit, he ain't no spoof.
You don't have to worry, there is no way
you'll see Baghdad Billy if you fly in the day.
But listen to me son, for I am right
watch out for Baghdad Billy if you fly in the night!

39. *Gulf War Air Power Survey, Vol. II: Operations / Effects and Effectiveness, Part 1,* (Washington, D.C., Government Printing Office, 1993), p. 194; see *Filer's Files*, 2/20/98.
40. Redfern, Nicholas, *A Covert Agenda*, p. 168.
41. Redfern, Nicholas, *A Covert Agenda*, p. 169; Pope, Nick. *Open Skies, Closed Minds*, p. 198.
42. Hall, Richard, *The UFO Evidence, Volume II*, p. 33, 127.
43. Hall, Richard, *The UFO Evidence, Volume II*, p. 127.
44. CIA documents from the newspaper *Vechernya Alma-Ata,* 19 April 1991, Subj: Alma-Ata Patrolmen Report UFO Sighting.
45. Redfern, Nicholas, *A Covert Agenda*, p. 170-172; Pope, Nick, *Open Skies, Closed Minds*, p. 218; Hall, Richard, *The UFO Evidence, Volume II*, p. 33.
46. Redfern, Nicholas, *A Covert Agenda*, p. 184.
47. Redfern, Nicholas, *A Covert Agenda*, p. 184.
48. Ramirez, Jorge Alfonso, "UFO Intercepts Aircraft Over Paraguay," *MUFON UFO Journal*, 2/94.
49. "Messengers of Destiny" a film by Lee Elders & Brit Elders, Genesis III, 1992; see also *Filer's Files*, 6/9/04.
50. Turner, Karla, *Into the Fringe: A True Story of Alien Abduction*, Berkley Books, 1992.
51. Turner, Karla, *Taken: Inside the Human-Alien Abduction Agenda*, Kelt Works, 1994.
52. Turner, Karla, "Inside the Alien-Human Abduction Agenda," private lecture, unspecified location, 11/94.
53. Lammer, Dr. Helmut & Lammer, Marion. *MILABS: Military Mind Control and Alien Abductions*. IllumiNet Press, 1999.
54. Lammer, Dr. Helmut & Lammer, Marion. *MILABS: Military Mind Control and Alien Abductions*, p. 89. See also Martin, Harry V. And Caul, David, "Mind Control," copyright, *Napa Sentinel*, 1991, http://www.bariumblues.com/monkey_experiencing_electrode_st.htm.
55. Lammer, Helmut, Ph. D. "Preliminary Findings of Project MILAB: Evidence for Military Kidnappings of Alleged UFO Abductees," *MUFON UFO Journal*, 12/96.
56. Alexander, Victoria, "MILAB Misdemeanor?" *MUFON UFO Journal*, 2/97.
57. Cannon, Martin, "The Controllers: A New Hypothesis of Alien Abduction," *MUFON UFO Journal*, 10/90.
58. Part of this apparently included a visit to the "ET Communication Center," located inside the Manzano Weapons Storage Area in Plant 3, although it was said Pell did not go to this. Of course, Project Sigma was said to be located at Kirtland. If it is (or was) involved in communications with extraterrestrials, it would clearly be relevant in this instance.
59. Collins, Robert & Doty, Richard, *Exempt from Disclosure*, p. 103-108.
60. C. B. Scott Jones, correspondence with the author, April 30, 2009.
61. Robbins, Peter, "Politics, Religion and Human Nature: Practical Problems and Roadblocks On the Path to Disclosure," *Proceedings of the 40th Annual International MUFON Symposium* Denver, CO, August 6-9, 2009.
62. Its services were divided into two separate organizations; the Federal Security Service (FSB) for internal security and the Foreign Intelligence Service (SVR) for foreign intelligence gathering.
63. Ilyin, Vadim K., "KGB's 'Blue Folder' Reveals Shootings, Landings in USSR," http://www.mufon.com/znews_kgb.html; Stonehill, Paul, & Mantle, Philip, *Soviet UFO Files*, p. 74-81.
64. Gaskell, John, "Cornfield phantom has farmers foxed," Sunday Telegraph, London, 8/25/91; Baynes, L. L. "Why it was a Mandelbrot" (letter), Sunday Telegraph, London, 9/1/91; Pope Nick, *Open Skies, Closed Minds*, p. 114; Howe, Linda Moulton, *Glimpses of Other Realities*, Vol. 1, p. 6.

65. "A load of crop!" *Daily Star*, London, 9/10/91; "Round in circles?" *Weekly News*, Leeds, 9/12/91; Eisler, Dale, "We're going full circle with theories," *Star-Phoenix*, Saskatoon, Saskatchewan, 9/15/91; Kasher, John, "Crop Circle Mystery Not Fully Solved," *World Herald*, Omaha, NE, 9/28/91; Randles, Jenny, "Round and round in the circle game," *International UFO Reporter*, 11-12/91; Stacy, Dennis, The UFO Press, *MUFON UFO Journal*, 5/94; Pope Nick, *Open Skies, Closed Minds*, p. 115-116.

66. Howe, Linda Moulton, *Glimpses of Other Realities*, Vol. 1, pp. 43-52.

67. A very good overview of this event is "STS-48 Space Shuttle Video" at *http://www.ufoevidence.org/topics/sts-48.htm*

68. Oberg, James, "NASA STS-48 'UFO' Video," June 28, 1992 at http://www.debunker.com/texts/sts48_ufo.html; Fleming, Lan, "Proof That Time Stamps on the STS-48 Video Released by NASA Are Phony," 2003, http://www.vgl.org/webfiles/STS-48/LOS.htm; see also Wright, Susan, *UFO Headquarters*, p. 149-150.

69. Sherman, Sam, Letter, *Filer's Files*, 12/31/99.

70. Stacy, Dennis, The 1994 MUFON UFO Symposium, *MUFON UFO Journal*, 8/94.

71. Challender, Jeff, Letter to *Filer's Files*, 4/10/00. Challender's analysis of STS-48 and other space missions, formerly available at http://projectprove.com, are in the author's possession.

72. Challender, Jeff, Letter to *Filer's Files*, 4/10/00.

73. Pahl, David, *Space Warfare And Strategic Defense*, Bison Books (1987) and "Strategic Defense Initiative," from *Wikipedia, the free encyclopedia*.

74. Greer, Steven, *Disclosure*, p. 201.

75. Sherman, Sam, Letter to *Filer's Files*, 2/25/99.

76. McClelland, Clark, letter to *Filer's Files*, 6/4/01; See "X-43 Hyper-X Program" at *http://www.globalsecurity.org/space/systems/x-43.htm*

77. Randle, Kevin, *The Randle Report: UFOs in the '90s*, M. Evans & Co., 1997, p. 82-90.

Index

About the Author

Richard Dolan has researched UFOs and related phenomena since the early 1990s. Prior to this, he had been a Rhodes Scholar finalist, earned a Bachelor's and Master's degree in History, and received a Certificate in Political Theory at Oxford University.

In 2000, he published *UFOs and the National Security State: An Unclassified History, Volume One: 1941-1973* (republished two years later as *UFOs and the National Security State: Chronology of a Cover-up, 1941-1973*). That 500-page history provided detail not only about the major UFO cases of the early Cold War era, but the attitudes and policies toward UFOs by the military and intelligence community, as well as the fascinating development of the citizen movements to end UFO secrecy.

Richard has written many articles and spoken at conferences around the world on these and related themes. He has also done a great deal of television work, having appeared on many documentaries for the History Channel, Sci Fi Channel, BBC, and elsewhere. In 2006 he was host to a six-episode series for the Sci Fi Channel, called *SciFi Investigates*.

With the completion of Volume Two of his historical study, Richard is writing a third volume which will take the history of the UFO reality and cover-up to the present day.

Visit his website at *http://keyholepublishing.com*.

17622136R00369

Printed in Poland
by Amazon Fulfillment
Poland Sp. z o.o., Wrocław